Debian GNU/Linux® Bible

Debian GNU/Linux®
Bible

Steve Hunger

Hungry Minds™

Hungry Minds, Inc.

Indianapolis, IN ✦ Cleveland, OH ✦ New York, NY

Debian GNU/Linux® Bible

Published by
Hungry Minds, Inc.
909 Third Avenue
New York, NY 10022
www.hungryminds.com

Library of Congress Catalog Card No.: 2001089113

ISBN: 0-7645-4710-0

Printed in the United States of America

10 9 8 7 6 5 4 3 2 1

1B/SW/QU/QR/IN

Distributed in the United States by Hungry Minds, Inc.

Distributed by CDG Books Canada Inc. for Canada; by Transworld Publishers Limited in the United Kingdom; by IDG Norge Books for Norway; by IDG Sweden Books for Sweden; by IDG Books Australia Publishing Corporation Pty. Ltd. for Australia and New Zealand; by TransQuest Publishers Pte Ltd. for Singapore, Malaysia, Thailand, Indonesia, and Hong Kong; by Gotop Information Inc. for Taiwan; by ICG Muse, Inc. for Japan; by Intersoft for South Africa; by Eyrolles for France; by International Thomson Publishing for Germany, Austria, and Switzerland; by Distribuidora Cuspide for Argentina; by LR International for Brazil; by Galileo Libros for Chile; by Ediciones ZETA S.C.R. Ltda. for Peru; by WS Computer Publishing Corporation, Inc., for the Philippines; by Contemporanea de Ediciones for Venezuela; by Express Computer Distributors for the Caribbean and West Indies; by Micronesia Media Distributor, Inc. for Micronesia; by Chips Computadoras S.A. de C.V. for Mexico; by Editorial Norma de Panama S.A. for Panama; by American Bookshops for Finland.

For general information on Hungry Minds' products and services please contact our Customer Care department within the U.S. at 800-762-2974, outside the U.S. at 317-572-3993 or fax 317-572-4002.

For sales inquiries and reseller information, including discounts, premium and bulk quantity sales, and foreign-language translations, please contact our Customer Care department at 800-434-3422, fax 317-572-4002 or write to Hungry Minds, Inc., Attn: Customer Care Department, 10475 Crosspoint Boulevard, Indianapolis, IN 46256.

For information on licensing foreign or domestic rights, please contact our Sub-Rights Customer Care department at 212-884-5000.

For information on using Hungry Minds' products and services in the classroom or for ordering examination copies, please contact our Educational Sales department at 800-434-2086 or fax 317-572-4005.

For press review copies, author interviews, or other publicity information, please contact our Public Relations department at 650-653-7000 or fax 650-653-7500.

For authorization to photocopy items for corporate, personal, or educational use, please contact Copyright Clearance Center, 222 Rosewood Drive, Danvers, MA 01923, or fax 978-750-4470.

is a trademark of Hungry Minds, Inc.

About the Author

Steve Hunger has spent the last 10 years in the computer industry, the last four supporting and integrating multiple platforms for a Fortune 500 Company. Having been introduced to UNIX while attending Purdue University, he quickly latched onto Linux as the primary platform for his startup Web hosting and development business in 1996. He continues operating his Web business, consulting with local businesses, and freelance writing. When not conquering the world with Linux, he has co-written and contributed to several books for Macmillan USA and Brady Games, including work on the line of Mandrake Linux products. His latest work has been for AOL Press called *Powering Up the Internet*.

In his spare time he enjoys relaxing with his wife, riding bicycles, and tinkering with an R/C model that is evolving into something that looks amazing like a plane. He is also on the Board of Directors for the Central Indiana Linux Users Group (www.cinlug.org). Steve can be reached at steve@rhinoworld.com.

Credits

Acquisitions Editor
Terri Varveris

Project Editor
Gus A. Miklos

Technical Editor
Steve Schafer

Copy Editors
Victoria Lee O'Malley
Luann Rouff

Project Coordinator
Dale White

Graphics and Production Specialists
Amy Adrian
Sean Decker
Gabriele McCann
Kendra Span

Quality Control Technicians
David Faust
Susan Moritz
Marianne Santy
Charles Spencer

Permissions Editor
Laura Moss

Media Development Specialist
Travis Silvers

Media Development Coordinator
Marisa Pearman

Proofreading and Indexing
York Production Services, Inc.

This book is dedicated to my beloved wife, Sandy. Without her love, support, and encouragement to carry me on days I needed it, this book would not have been possible. And to my father, who also saw me through this book.

Foreword

In January 1993, while browsing USENET news one evening after work, I ran across a thread with a subject line that read, simply, "LINUX." I'm not sure what it was about the word "LINUX" that made me hit Enter, but I did, and within a few minutes, it was clear to me that I had to have it.

Unfortunately, that's about where I hit a brick wall. I had just enough information about Linux to whet my appetite, but there was precious little more of it to be found. Over the course of the next few weeks, I hunted down and pieced together the rest of what I needed to know: where to find it, how to download it, how to install it, and what I could do with it once I had installed it.

It was a tedious process, because only scraps of information were available, and those scraps were scattered about all over the place — a bit on a USENET group here, a bit more on an FTP site there. And even when found and pieced together, the scraps did not form a complete picture — I had to fill in large gaps for myself. All in all, it was a tremendous learning experience, but it was also a tremendously frustrating and time-consuming experience, and if presented with the same obstacles today, I likely would not have had the time or the inclination to overcome them.

Fortunately, becoming a Linux user is much easier today than it was in 1993. The software itself has come a long way, and a wide range of books on the subject are available, from installation and use to programming to administration and management. These days, the local bookstore has all the information you need to get started and become productive as a Linux user.

One subject that has not been covered as extensively as others, a subject near and dear to my heart, is Debian, a project I founded not long after discovering Linux. Debian has much to offer the Linux user — a huge selection of software, an open development process that leads to rapid bug fixes and improvements, an unparalleled software management facility that allows software to be installed easily and systems to be upgraded non-disruptively, and much more — but it has long remained a daunting prospect to piece together the information you need to get there.

And, so, I am extremely pleased to see books such as my friend Steve Hunger's *Debian GNU/Linux Bible*. *Debian GNU/Linux Bible* contains all the information you need to know to get the most out of Debian, from installing it to using its powerful package management system to install software and upgrade your system to setting up a Web server and other advanced topics. With *Debian GNU/Linux Bible* by your side, you will be well prepared to join the large and growing group of users that call Debian home. I hope this book serves you well.

Ian Murdock
Founder of Debian and Co-founder of Progeny Linux Systems, Inc.

Preface

As Linux becomes more and more popular, resources to learn and use Linux become more important. These resources help to guide, direct, and inform an individual to make the best use of the tools available, just as a stack of boards, nails, and a hammer don't make a house — it takes the skilled craftsmanship of a carpenter to turn the parts into a whole house. *Debian GNU/Linux Bible* gives you the skilled guidance to help you turn the individual parts into a system.

Whom This Book Is For

This book covers the many aspects of the Debian GNU/Linux system, from the initial install of this reputable operating system to the more advanced functions like Web servers or file servers. You do not need to have any special programming experience to use this book. You may just want to learn how to use Debian as a workstation environment.

This book does assume some level of general computer knowledge, even though not specifically related to Linux or UNIX. Many people get introduced to Linux after becoming familiar with another operating system. You may be someone who wants to learn something new, someone who wants to know what all the buzz is about Linux, or someone who just likes the idea that the software and upgrades are free.

Whatever the reason you are reading this book, I'm sure that you will find assistance in the pages of this book. You will find everything from installation to administration to server setup. This book will give you the boost needed to set up a home or office network and to maintain that network of computers.

How This Book Is Organized

This book is organized in a progression of skill as well as function. The beginning of the book starts out with an overview of Linux. It then progresses to the concepts needed for average use. Then, it concludes with the concepts needed for more intense use.

For those who are fairly new to Linux, this book will help them get their feet wet. Some of the basic concepts, commands and tools are explained in the beginning chapters of this book. As you become more experienced with Linux and specifically

Debian GNU/Linux, you move into the intermediate areas of the book, namely the middle sections. Lastly, the experienced administrator who will from time to time need instruction on specific services can find this information in "Part III: Administering Linux."

Now that you have an idea of the overall layout of the book, let's look over the book chapter by chapter. The following will describe the contents of the book in slightly more detail.

Part I: Getting Started

Part I provides the basic introduction to Debian GNU/Linux. The chapters in this part start with background on Linux in general and the beginnings of the Debian distribution; walk you through the important steps on getting Debian GNU/Linux installed on your system; cover the essential base set of commands used to navigate through the newly installed system; cover the differences between desktop managers, desktop environments, and window managers; explain the requirements and configuration of setting up a network and describe tools used to test, diagnose, and evaluate the network once installed; and help you connect your system to the Internet and explain some of the applications you'll need for such things as e-mail, news, and Web browsing.

Part II: Working with Debian

Chapters in Part II explain how to install additional applications on the system, cover the features and functions of the popular Office-like application suites available to Linux, describe the intermediate commands found on the system (useful to those interested in going on to the next step), provide examples of applications that appeal to the senses — sight and sound alike, and list the multitude of games available for Linux (no computer user is complete with out at least trying some of the games).

Part III: Administering Linux

The chapters in Part II cover the concerns that administrators face when managing one system or many, deal with the programming environment found with Linux (including the most common environments, like Perl, Tk/Tcl, and C), explain the most amazing environment that makes Linux so powerful and how to mix the environment with the programming of scripts, detail the core part of the Linux system — the kernel, and explain how to modify and create new versions of the kernel specifically designed for your needs.

Part IV: Maintenance and Upgrade

Chapters in this part direct you on keeping the system updated and current to prevent problems from creeping in, describe some of the hardware and how to make changes to the system to accommodate additions, and explain why backups are important.

Part V: Linux Server

In Part V, chapters detail how to lock down the security of a Linux system to prevent intrusion; cover how Debian can be used as the first line of defense to protect a home or office network; show you how to publish Web pages on the network or Internet; explain how to set up a server to allow the transfer of files from any number of clients using the File Transfer Protocol; provide information on setting up a central Network Information Server to manage a medium-sized to large network or account; describe how to create a central point from which to share, store, and archive files in one place; and list the servers used to handle electronic mail, one of the most-used forms of communication among most medium-sized to large companies.

Appendixes

The book concludes with three appendixes.

+ Appendix A, "What's On the CD-ROM," provides you with information on the contents of the CD-ROM that accompanies this book.

+ Appendix B, "Linux Commands," covers many of the commands found in the common areas on the Linux filesystem.

+ Appendix C, "Debian Packages," presents a list of commonly used Debian packages with a short description of each.

System Requirements

Nearly all software has some level of requirements when referring to hardware that it is run on. Debian GNU/Linux is no different. Even though Debian is available for different platforms, the one used in this book is the i386-based platform. This includes processors ranging from the Intel series (386, 486, Pentium class, and other variations), AMD, and any of the other "Intel clone" processors. Other processor platforms will operate similarly, so this book can still operate as a reference even though they may not be specifically referred to.

Beyond the core processor, the other components will be supported to varying levels. For each of those, I will redirect you back to the manufacturers or to one of the many Web site where the information about using hardware with Linux is available. One such site is `www.linuxdoc.com`.

At the minimum, your systems should include at least a i486 class processor with 8MB of RAM, a 500MB hard disk and either a bootable floppy drive with CD-ROM drive or a bootable CD-ROM drive. However, this distribution of Debian GNU/Linux will work on systems with less. If you intend on using the i486 class processor as a workstation, I recommend a higher standard for better response.

Conventions

There are several conventions used within this book that will help you to get more out of it. The first is the use of special fonts or font styles to emphasize a special kind of text; the second is the use of icons to emphasize special information.

+ There are some situations when I'll ask you to type something. This information always appears in bold type like this: Type **Hello World**.

+ Code normally appears on separate lines from the rest of the text. However, there are some special situations when small amounts of code appear right in the paragraph for explanation purposes. This code will appear in a monospaced font like this: `Some Special Code`. URLs for Web sites are also presented in monospaced font like this: `http://www.microsoft.com`.

+ Definitions are always handy to have. I use italics to differentiate definitions from the rest of the text like this: A *CPU* is the central processing unit for your machine.

+ In some code examples, I won't have an exact value to provide so I'll give you an idea of what you should type by using italics and monospaced font like this: Provide a `Machine Name` value for the `Name` field.

The following icons identify useful and important asides from the main text.

Note   Notes help you to understand some principle or provide amplifying information. In many cases, a Note is used to emphasize a piece of critical information that you need.

Caution   Any time that you see a Caution, make sure that you take special care to read it. This information is vital. I always uses the Caution to designate information that will help you to avoid damage to your application, data, machine, or self. Never skip the Cautions in a chapter and always follow their advice.

All of us like to know special bits of information that will make our job easier, more fun, or faster to perform. Tips help you to get the job done faster and more safely. In many cases, the information found in a Tip is drawn from experience, rather than from experimentation or from the documentation.

There are times when information in another area of the book will help you to better understand the current discussion. I always include the Cross-Reference icon to indicate additional material that you might need.

Acknowledgments

I would first like to thank the Debian development community. Without their hard work, high standards, and volunteer efforts, this Linux distribution would not have the reputation it does today. So these thanks goes out to the hundreds of those volunteers.

I would also like to thanks the two contributors to this book, John Goerzen and Shawn Voss. John wrote the chapter on the available programming environments in Debian. Shawn wrote the chapter on the shell environments and shell scripts.

I would also like to thank everyone who has worked to produce this book—specifically, Terri Varveris for her efforts in planning, scheduling, and the other details involved with getting a book like this to the shelves and Gus Miklos for all his work making sure that what I wrote down could actually be read and understood by others. I'd also like to thank Steve Schafer for his efforts editing the technical aspects of the book content. And a thanks go out to all the other involved at differing levels on this book.

Thanks to all those who has had to listen to me get on my soap box about Linux over the years—especially my wife for her patience while I spent the hours chained to the computer working on some project or other.

Contents at a Glance

Contents

Part I: Getting Started   1

Part II: Working with Debian   131

Part V: Linux Server   395

Getting Started

Introduction to Linux

Welcome to the *Debian GNU/Linux Bible* where you can find hints, tips, and helpful instructions on most areas of this robust operating system. As you begin to learn more about this distribution of the Linux operating system, I'm sure you will find that you have made an excellent choice. Debian GNU/Linux is one of the best-kept secrets from the general public.

Note   In case you were wondering, *GNU* stands for *GNU's Not UNIX*, which still doesn't answer the question of the definition of GNU. That's the best I can come up with.

This chapter covers the background of Linux, what makes it special, and how Debian compares to other operating systems. You will discover the true meaning behind free software and why it is so important to Debian.

Before you begin to read about the origins of this great operating system, I open with a definition of the operating system. This helps to define how you look at the accomplishments described later.

Understanding the Role of the Operating System

The operating system controls the interaction between hardware and the software applications. The *hardware* consists of the processor, hard drives, video cards, sound cards, and more. Each processor has built into it a language that only it understands, plus each manufacturer creates a different language for its processor. For instance, an Intel x86 processor uses a different internal language than, say, a Motorola 68000 processor. Therefore, any software must be *complied* (converted into the processor language) or customized for the *processor* (often referred to as the *computer platform*). Some of the platforms include:

✦ x86 (Intel [386, 486, Pentium, Pentium II, Pentium III, Celeron], AMD [K6-2, Athlon, or others equivalent to the Intel line])

✦ Alpha (Was DEC, Now Compaq)

✦ Power PC, also known as PPC (Motorola/IBM Power PC)

✦ M68k (Motorola 68000 series)

✦ Sparc (Sun Microsystems's SPARCstation)

The core component to the operating system is called the *kernel* in UNIX and UNIX-like operating systems. The kernel communicates with the basic computer hardware like the microprocessor, memory, and device controllers. All interaction between the hardware and any programs must be negotiated through the kernel. The kernel takes care of translating the requests into the form the particular device speaks. This includes everything from drawing a picture to saving a file to a floppy to printing a document. In addition to the kernel, the user interface, device drivers, file system, and system services complete the whole operating system and make it functional for someone to use.

✦ The user interface makes it possible for the individual to interact with the computer to issue commands, launch programs, and generally control the computer. This usually starts as a command-line interface and later becomes some kind of graphical interface. One example of the interface is the shell which allows commands to be typed in and the output gets displayed to the screen in text form. Chapters 4 and 14 cover the graphical interface and shell interface respectively.

✦ The device drivers allow the kernel to talk to the various devices, such as hard drives and modems, which are connected to the computer. Each hardware device speaks its own language, and the operating system must be capable of interacting with it. In order for a specific piece of hardware to be used, like the mouse, hard drive or sound card, the corresponding driver must be installed for it to get used. See Chapter 17 for more information about hardware or Chapter 15 for the kernel details.

✦ The information for the operating system — such as programs, data, and such — gets stored to a disk. The filesystem sets the method that the information gets stored. Different operating systems use different methods of storing their data. For instance Windows 3.1 uses File Allocation Tables (FAT) fir its filesystem. Newer versions of Windows like 95 and 98 use a more advanced version called FAT32. And Windows NT uses NTFS for its filesystem. Not all of these filesystems are compatible with all operating systems, even among the Windows family. Windows NT can read FAT and NTFS, but not FAT32. Like wise, Windows 95 and 98 can read FAT and FAT32, but not NTFS. Linux uses EXT2, but can read FAT and FAT32 using the VFAT driver. You can learn more about this scattered through the book.

✦ When the computer starts up, some functions, features, or services start to manage the system. For instance, when Linux first starts, it loads the filesystems, network interfaces, and any background services known as *daemons*. When the filesystem loads, it assigns what drives get used. The network interface gets initialized and configured to communicate on the network.

Note   A daemon is a program that runs in the background without anyone being aware of it until it is needed. (This is referred to as services in the Windows NT world.) For instance, a Web server (Chapter 21) runs in the background because it was designed to work with out human intervention.

Now that you have a better understanding of what an operating system is, you can move on to see what Linux is all about.

History of GNU/Linux

Free operating systems are not a new concept in the computer world,. (The academic versions of UNIX, Slackware, and FreeBSD come to mind.) Then a student of the University of Helsinki, Linus Torvalds announced in 1991 that he had created a very experimental operating system core called a kernel, based on a clone of UNIX called Minux. This new operating system kernel later became known as Linux. Torvolds chose this UNIX variant because of the well-respected stability, design and functionality of the UNIX operating system developed by Bell Laboratories.

This new operating system kernel was refined for maximum performance on the Intel 386 microprocessor, which made this new Linux kernel platform specific. This generated criticism from some corners of the UNIX software world. Traditionally, UNIX was independent of platform, meaning that you could use the softeware with different computer processors without much trouble. This didn't stop Torvalds from continuing to develop his kernel. His efforts eventually led him to the free software community where programmers got behind his efforts and contributed to the new kernel.

However, long before Torvalds started work on his Linux kernel, Richard M. Stallman left his job at the MIT Artificial Intelligence Lab to develop a UNIX-like operating system. He formed the Free Software Foundation and developed the GNU General Public License (GPL). Stallman began working on various software programs for his GNU operating system project. (By the way, GNU is pronounced with a hard G, *ga-nu*) By 1991, he had most of the software pieces of the GNU operating system complete with the exception of the kernel. In 1990, he started working on the kernel and named it *HURD (Hird of UNIX-Replacing Daemons)*. Hird stands for Hurd of Interfaces Representing Depth. According to an interview with Stallman, people interested in the GNU project began to put Torvald's Linux kernel with Stallman's GNU operating system to form the GNU/Linux operating system.

Note   The HURD project is a rewrite of the UNIX kernel. The difference between this kernel and others is that it has an object-oriented structure that enables you to change, add, or remove components without major rewrites of the entire kernel. Currently, HURD only works with the Intel i386 and the last official release was back in 1997. However, it remains an active project. Had the Linux kernel been available in 1990, Stallman says they would not have started their own.

Note In truth, from its adoption as an operating system, the rightful name of Linux is really GNU/Linux. Linux is really only the kernel (the core component) and GNU contains the supporting applications around the kernel that make it functional. These supporting applications include the user interface and all other applications (editors, Most refer to GNU/Linux as simply Linux, which you may even see in this book from time to time for the sake of brevity. Please understand I mean no disrespect to the developers.

Linux versus Other Operating Systems

When Bill Gates, founder of Microsoft, made his deal with IBM to include his disk operating system (DOS) with IBM personal computers, his goal was to put a computer in every home. Today many homes do have personal computers (PCs), and most use some type of Microsoft operating system. Until recently, a Microsoft operating system was your only preinstalled choice when purchasing a new personal computer. Now, many name brand PC manufacturers — such as Dell, Compaq, and others — offer other operating systems. Table 1-1 shows a list of many of the operating systems.

Table 1-1
Popular PC operating systems and platforms

Operating System	Platform
Linux (Debian)	Intel x86, PowerPC, M68k, Alpha, Sparc, ARM
Windows 95/98	Intel x86
Windows NT/2000	Intel x86, PPC
MacOS	PPC
Be OS	Intel x86
OS/2 Warp	Intel x86, Alpha
Solaris	Sparc, Intel x86

As you can see from Table 1-1, no other operating system can be used with nearly as many platforms as Linux can. Plans are in the works by Linux developers to include others, such as sparc64, MIPS, and PS-RISK. Development teams of programmers from all around the world are credited for this outstanding growth.

Even though the Windows 95/98 operating system gained vast popularity due to its professed user friendliness, GNU/Linux has made steady improvements to reach the same level of user friendliness. In 1999, the growth rate seen by Linux exceeded the growth of Windows NT. Despite the strong marketing power, available resources, and influence of the big boys, the cheap (by price only) operating system called Linux is taking the world by storm.

Table 1-2 lists some significant differences between Linux and the other operating systems:

Table 1-2 **Benefits of Linux**	
Benefit	*Description*
Costs nothing	Linux is the only operating system that costs nothing. All others listed have some purchasing fee ranging from just under $100 to several hundred dollars. For a business with several servers and workstations, this can add up fast.
Downloadable	With a fast Internet connection, you can have your operating system available in a short period of time. No need to order it, have it shipped, or visit a local computer dealer to get the copies you need.
Freely distributed	Make as many copies of Debian GNU/Linux as you want or need. There is no copyright with GPL software except that the source code must be included. Other operating systems require a purchased license for each installation.
Built by volunteers	Other operating systems are company creations in which all the work is either contracted or programmed in-house. Volunteers make up the primary programming body of Linux. Some companies contribute to the cause for the benefit of the whole. This volunteer principle contributes to its overall stability.
Source code available	When you buy an operating system off the shelf, you only get the compiled version ready to run straight out of the box. If there is a problem or a minor change you want to make, you have no chance to make it because of no available source code. Linux encourages individual adjustments, modifications, and fixes because the source is always available. As a result of the available source code, fixes to problems can take place literally overnight.
Reliable	Though this may not be unique to Linux, it is important nonetheless. Linux is very stable as are some of the other operating systems. I have known Linux servers to run without needing to be restarted for months at a time (and then only for hardware maintenance). In contrast, some Windows NT servers need to be restarted every day to ensure their reliability.
Flexible	With the vast numbers of programs available for Linux, its uses can range from a single task as a monitor, to uses as a workstation for calculating advanced mathematical formulas or graphics. You can use Linux as an Internet router, firewall, proxy, Web server, or mail server that is as powerful as any on the open market.

The Word on Free Software and Open Source

The Free Software Foundation believes, of course, that software should be free. This includes the source code for the executable programs. When they say free, they mean it.

The foundation, which developed the GNU General Public License (GPL), promotes sharing of free software (including the source code). The purpose of this is to allow the programming community to make changes to the code. According to the GPL, no software that claims this license can be distributed without the source code. When source code is included, the programming community can respond to defects, bugs, and cracks faster. A fix for a commercial operating system can take up to six months to be released, compared to a few days in the Linux world.

Just because software is free and the source gets included doesn't mean that it's a free-for-all on the program. Once a developer releases GPL software, any licensing changes made to that software must be made with the consent of the author. However, you can freely distribute, modify, and use it. Although most software released with Debian uses the GPL and is free, some software discussed in this book and found elsewhere is not free as it is sold commercially. However, most software for Linux is free.

The Open Source community differs slightly from the Free Software movement, although both desire to see freely available software. The Open Source movement is less concerned with whether anyone makes a profit along the way, but more concerned with the distribution of free software. Eric Raymond cofounded the Open Source Software Group out of a concern that businesses weren't getting the word. As a result of his efforts, some companies have adopted the Open Source philosophy. One such company, Cygnus Solutions, produced the GNUPro Developers Kit as an Open Source product. Red Hat acquired this product, which is now called GNUPro ETS.

Having corporations involved in the development and promotion of Linux helps everyone. Companies bring training, certification, and support to an otherwise hobby operating system. Without this kind of support, many people (and companies) stay away from a product to avoid its potential failure of an unknown future. As more companies get behind a system — for better or worse — it gains more credibility in the minds of businesses. Therefore, having companies involved in the development of Linux is a good thing.

What's So Special about GNU/Linux?

Stallman's dream of having an operating system free from commercial purse strings came true with the completion of the kernel by Torvalds. As the community of programmers grew, so did the draw to GNU/Linux. The metamorphosis of the operating system grew to gain the attention of the world.

More and more people started joining the Linux movement by adopting GNU/Linux as their operating system of choice. Many migrated to it looking for a stable environment from which to create programs, while others sought something that wouldn't crash when performing simple daily tasks like word processing. Both groups of users were pleasantly surprised with GNU/Linux.

With the popularity of GNU/Linux increasing, some programmers created special distributions of the operating systems by adding in their own special programs as enhancements. You can easily obtain some of these systems, while others encourage the purchase of their packages. Still others include software at a price, which dilutes the openness of the source. Table 1-3 lists some of the more popular Linux distributions. All can be purchased from store (except Debian) or downloaded from a site like www.linuxiso.org where all you have to do is burn the distribution image to a CD for you own copy.

Table 1-3 Linux distributions and Web sites	
Distribution	**Web Site**
Debian GNU/Linux	www.debian.org
Red Hat	www.redhat.com
SuSE	www.suse.org
Caldera OpenLinux	www.caldera.com
Slackware Linux	www.slackware.com
Linux-Mandrake	www.mandrake.com
Corel Linux	linux.corel.com
Storm Linux	www.stormix.com
Turbo Linux	www.turbolinux.com

Some of these distributions listed in Table 1-3 were created from other distributions. For instance, Linux-Mandrake uses a Red Hat base while Corel and Storm Linux both originated with Debian. Surprised? Even though some of the distribution originated from other distributions (like Linux-Mandrake originated from Red Hat), each one adds something a little different to the mix — a graphical installer, special configuration tools, or even hardware detection software.

Understanding the Debian Distribution

One of the oldest distributions of Linux, Debian GNU/Linux has an awesome reputation. At the heart of this distribution is a faithful community of programmers, all dedicated to advancing free software. This is the purest in the sense of non-commercial and most stable flavor of Linux because all base components are community created, community supported, and no-strings-attached free. There are over 500 developers working together from around the world to put out the latest version. Debian is the oldest distribution that does not have corporate strings attached. However, because this distribution is volunteer driven, the releases tend to be slow. This slowness could be considered a drawback, but in my opinion, it's worth the wait.

Tip   If you are interested in getting connected to the Debian community, check out one of the many mailing lists at www.debian.org/MailingLists/subscribe. If you are interested in becoming a Debian Developer, subscribe to one of the developer lists and become known. Official Developers must be invited so don't expect to become one overnight.

Note   To date of the known Linux installations, Debian makes up 21 percent compared to Red Hat at 29 percent (as reported by the Linux Counter at counter.li.org). This is remarkable because no marketing teams, corporate strategies, or distribution channels promote the Debian distribution.

How did Debian get its start? In 1993, Ian Murdock attempted to create a distribution that combined the Linux kernel with GNU. In the process, the concept of packages developed. A package is a collection of all the compiled components needed to make a program work. Each package includes information about install location, configuration and any other packages it need to use. These packages were organized to allow others to contribute to the distribution. Table 1-4 shows the timeline for this distribution.

Table 1-4		
Time Chart for Debian		
Release Date	*Name*	*Contributors*
Nov 1995	First Release	60
Jun 1996	Buzz	60
Dec 1996	Rox	120
Jul 1997	Bo	200
Jul 1998	Hamm	400+
Mar 1999	Slink	450+
Aug 2000 (approximate)	Potato	500+

In 1996, Ian stepped down as the Debian leader and started up *Progeny Linux Systems,* an Open Source company that to offer a product called *Linux NOW* to organizations with large numbers of computers. This company's goal is to take a network of computers and make it function as if it were one computer. Progeny chooses to use the Debian GNU/Linux distribution instead of creating its own highly customized flavor. It also plans on adding to Debian the same easy-to-use features that the commercial distributions enjoy. Progeny Linux Systems is completely behind the Debian distribution and wants to see it become as competitive as the commercial versions.

With over 4,000 packages available and six complete ports to different platforms, Debian is by far the largest distribution. Debian GNU/Linux is not only the largest distribution, but it is also the most tightly guarded in terms of being freely distributed. No software that contains licensing variants other than the terms found in the Debian Free Software Guidelines — which plainly states the core values of its development model — are allowed. The Debian developers work hard to achieve zero down time from installations, configurations, and upgrades and Debian is the only distribution that comes close. Debian's package-management system seamlessly performs complete, in-place upgrades without the need for system restarts.

Even though this chapter mentions some important names associated with Debian, the real heart and soul behind Debian is the community. These men and women spend their free time working on the code with an understanding that the software is shared freely around the world. The future of Debian rests on the shoulders of these people. Are you ready to become one?

Summary

Debian GNU/Linux is one of the best-kept secrets, found mostly among developer communities, hobbyists, and academia. Though Debian isn't destined for the fast-track commercial distribution, there is a strong movement just the same to make Debian a viable alternative to compete with those other distributions.

The future of Debian is bright. Expect it to include distributions for more platforms as time passes. Debian doesn't have a corporation marketing it, but that doesn't mean that there is nothing worthwhile about it. Actually, because a corporation is not pushing it along, it is one of the strongest, most stable Linux distributions available.

✦   ✦   ✦

Installing Debian

Installing the Debian GNU/Linux operating system on a
computer is no different than installing any other operating
system by following straightforward guidelines. This chapter
covers those guidelines and, if followed, will get Debian
GNU/Linux installed on your system (barring any unforeseen
troubles like hardware incompatibility).

Experienced Linux users can use this chapter as a reference
for things to watch for during the installation process. Those
who are less familiar with Linux or installing operating systems
can follow along step by step to accomplish the installation.

Also covered in this chapter are the different ways to install
applications on a Debian system. With over 4,000 applications
to choose from, most can be installed using the Debian package-management system. However, some applications aren't
available in the format used by the Debian package-management system; for these you will learn other installation
methods.

Although many of the applications covered here are available
on the book's CD, others are accessible from one of many
archives found on the Internet. This chapter also describes
how to access those archives.

Preparing Your System

Before beginning the installation process, you need to prepare
your system. Namely, you need to take inventory of your
machine's hardware. At certain points during the installation,
you are asked questions about the hardware, such as monitor
refresh rate, network card used, and such. Clearly, opening
the machine to find that information is very inconvenient, to
say the least. Therefore, proper preparation will save you the
headaches later.

If you purchased your computer as a commercial system, you might be able to go to the company's Web site for a specification sheet on all its components. This should include the specifications for your monitor, such as maximum resolution and horizontal and vertical refresh rates.

Tip To avoid trouble during the installation process, check out the manufacturer's Web site on any questionable system components, even on a commercial system. More and more sites are including helpful information about using Linux with their products. You can also find out if the manufacturer even supports Linux. If so, you can get any special drivers needed before you install.

If you have saved the original paperwork provided with the system, the specification sheets will contain all the information you need.

If you are a Windows user and want to have a dual boot system or want to remove Windows and use Linux only, be sure to record the information about your system first.

Tip Every distribution supports slightly different hardware, but for the vast majority of hardware, you can find the correct drivers. However, some proprietary hardware is not supported. You can find a fairly comprehensive list of compatible hardware at `www.linuxdoc.org/HOWTO/Hardware-HOWTO.html`.

You can easily access many of the needed specifications for the Windows Device Manager in the following way:

1. Right-click the My Computer icon on the desktop. Then select Properties from the menu that appears.

2. Click the Device Manager tab in the dialog box that appears. From here you can see all the devices installed on your system.

3. If you have a printer connected to your system, press the Print button at the bottom of the dialog box. (If you don't have a printer, print to a file or jot down the essential information, including network card, video card, and all related information, such as interrupts for any older ISA cards.)

4. The next dialog box lets you specify how much information prints out — Summary or All. The summary provides all the information that you will most likely need. The All option includes the Windows drivers used in addition to the Summary listing.

Note As more people use Linux, more drivers are being developed for the various hardware that people use. Hardware that would not work five years ago is now supported by the manufacturer. It is to the manufacturer's advantage to support its products with Linux drivers and to include instructions for its use.

For those of you who choose to build a dual boot system, you will need to prepare the hard drive by creating enough space below the 1,024 sector point on the disk. (This is at approximately the 10GB point on the disk.) This is the limitation for the Linux *boot loader*. The boot loader is the program that manages which operating system gets started at boot time. Regardless of whether you use the Linux boot loader or some other boot loader, this limitation determines where to install Debian.

You will also need space on the hard drive to install the operating system. Make a note of the amount of memory your video card has when the system boots up.

Note If you currently use Windows and would like to continue using Windows after installing Debian, you need to create a partition large enough to install this Linux operating system. Included on the CD is a tool called *FIPS*, short for *First Nondestructive Interactive Partitioning System*. It is found in the \tools directory in a compressed archived format. You can use WinZip or Gzip (included also) to extract the contents of fips20.zip. Read the documentation on how to use FIPS.

Basic Debian Installation

Because every computer and situation is a little different, your results may be slightly different from what you find here. These instruction were written to be as generic as possible; however, at some points you will find notes indicating deviations, such as between networks and standalone systems.

Cross-Reference For information about the CD's contents, see Appendix A.

More tools, applications, and utilities are available than what you will find on the CD accompanying this book; however, what you have is enough to get the base system set up and running. See the section "Using the Debian Package Management System" for details on accessing any packages not found on the CD.

Caution Before beginning the installation process, make sure that you save all pertinent data on your system. Even if you are sure that you don't need anything currently on the hard drive, it is always a good idea to make a backup before proceeding. The chances are slim that you will have a problem, but it is always better to be safe than sorry.

One final instruction before continuing: You can navigate the menus with the arrow keys or the Tab key. You can select options with multiple choices using the spacebar. Now you are ready to begin the installation of Debian GNU/Linux on your system.

Booting off the CD

The book's CD is bootable for those systems with the BIOS that allow you to boot from CD drives. If for some reason you are unable to boot from the CD, you can create boot floppies to get the installation started. You will need two DOS pre-formatted floppy disks. From DOS or Windows, go to the \dists\potato\main\ disks-i386\2.2.20.0.1-2000-12-03\dosutils directory on the CD and execute the rawrite.exe program. When asked for the source file, enter ..\images-1.44\rescue.bin. For the destination, enter A:. Repeat again, replacing root.bin for the filename of rescue.bin for the second floppy.

If you are lucky enough to have access to a Linux distribution, you can use the Direct Dump (dd if /path/file of /dev/fd0) command to make the disks as well. Make sure that the floppies are DOS formatted first in either case.

Once you have the disks made, you can boot your system using the rescue disk first, then the root disk when asked. The down side of using the floppy disks is that you could end up with the compact kernel found on the floppies. The compact kernel doesn't have all the functionality of the full kernel, which means that you may have trouble getting all your hardware to work without having to tweak the kernel. This is why I suggest using the CD to boot from at the start.

After the system is booted, you will see a prompt warning you that if you continue, you may lose data already on your hard drive. Pressing Enter initiates the loading of the installation process. At this time, you are actually running a scaled-down version of Linux for the installation.

The first screen that appears welcomes you to the Debian install, indicates that this is Debian GNU/Linux 2.2, and gives credit to all the programmers and companies who have contributed to this distribution. Press Enter to continue.

The main menu

The main menu in Figure 2-1 shows the different steps along the way. Using the arrow keys, you can navigate this menu if you ever need to select a menu option other than the one automatically selected. The first option in the menu is choosing a keyboard configuration. Press Enter to accept the menu default.

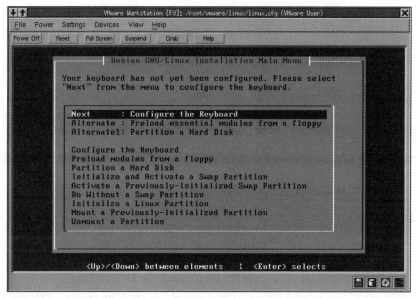

Figure 2-1: From the main installation menu, you have access to any step in the first install stage.

Configuring the keyboard

Here you can chose from a number of keyboards. For most American PCs, you will use the default qwerty/us option. Once you have selected the keyboard you wish to configure, press Enter to return to the main menu.

Partitioning a hard disk

This is the time to create the partitions you need to install Debian. You need to create a swap partition as well as a Linux partition. First create the Linux partition starting at the beginning of the free space. You only need one Linux partition for the complete installation. This partition should start somewhere before the 1,024 sector so that it will be bootable. Leave room on the system to create a swap partition. You should have at least a 64MB swap partition, but I recommend a 128MB partition, or twice the RAM size of your system.

From the main menu, press Enter to begin the process of partitioning the hard drive. You will be asked to select the drive to partition. If you have only one drive, the choice is simple. If you have more than one drive, then pick the one that you want to install Debian on. After you select the drive, an informational dialog will appear. This screen tells you what the limitations are of the bootloader — LILO on older systems. After you have read this screen, press Continue to proceed.

The `cfdisk` utility then starts, which offers you the ability to make changes to the drive partitions. This tool identifies any partitions currently created, and any unused space. The up and down arrows select the partitions on the drive. The left and right arrows navigate the menu options at the bottom. Scroll through the menu options until New is selected. Press Enter to create a new Linux partition (be sure to leave enough room for the swap partition). Now create the swap partition in the same manner, except you need to specify the type as `swap`. When all the partitions are created, use the Write menu option to commit them to the disk. Finally, use the Quit menu option to return to the installation.

 Note The step of partitioning the hard drive is skipped if Linux and swap partitions already exist.

Initializing and activating a swap partition

After the drive is partitioned for the install, it needs to be *initialized,* which means that it is formatted for use. Select the desired swap partition (normally only one) and press Enter. The next dialog box asks you whether you want to skip the bad blocks check. The default, Yes, skips the check. You should perform this check on older drives that you have had for more than a couple of years; however, it takes some time, depending on the size of the partition and the speed of the computer. Lastly, you are asked if you are sure that you want to initialize the partition. Remember that data on the partition will be lost.

Initializing a Linux partition

Time now to initialize the Linux partition. This formats and sets up the main partition on the hard drive where you will install Debian. Select the partition on which you wish to install Debian. If you only have one partition created for Linux, you should only see one partition. Press Enter to accept the partition.

Next you will see a dialog box in Figure 2-2 asking if you want to maintain Pre 2.2 Linux Kernel Compatibility. (The kernel is the heart of the operating system.) This means that you intend to use older kernels on this hard drive. This is a newer formatting method for the Linux partition that allows for added functionality with the newer kernel. The default is Yes, but I recommend choosing No unless you know for sure that you intend to compile and run older kernels.

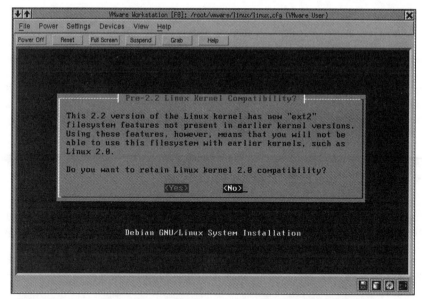

Figure 2-2: The new ext2 kernel allows you to use the new filesystem.

You will now see another dialog box concerning the bad block check. Again, this can be a time-consuming process depending on the size of the hard drive and the speed of the computer. By default, Yes skips the check.

A final dialog box asks you whether you are sure you want to do this. If you are using a pre-existing Linux partition to load Debian on, all data will be lost from it. However, if you just created the partition, there is nothing to lose. Proceed with the file system creation.

The next dialog box asks if you want to mount the root of the file system on this partition. You must have one partition with the root file system mounted or you will not be able to build a Linux system. Root is the foundation for the entire directory structure that Linux uses. Therefore, you want confirm with Yes.

Initializing the operating system kernel and modules

Now that the disk is prepared, the fun begins as the kernel and the needed modules are installed on the new system. Press Enter to accept the highlighted menu option to start this process of installing the kernel and modules.

You must first select an installation medium from the dialog box. Your choices are CD-ROM, /dev/fd0 (the first floppy drive), /dev/fd1 (the second floppy drive), hard drive, or mounted. Use the floppy drive if you do not have a CD-ROM. Normally, you will choose the CD-ROM, as the rest of this installation process assumes.

Cross-Reference   See Chapter 15 for more details about the kernel and the modules used with it.

You now need to select the CD drive. For systems with multiple CD drives, choose the one that contains the installation disk. The next dialog box asks you to insert the installation disk. After going through both dialog boxes, you need to enter the Debian archive path (/dist/stable). You can get there a couple of ways, but the easiest is by pressing Enter twice—once for the path shown, and again for the default stable archive.

Configuring device driver modules

After the core kernel gets loaded on your system, you need to configure the modules to go with the kernel. A *module* is nothing more than a driver that enables the kernel to interact with a particular component. Some modules must be provided after the installation because they come from the manufacturer. Debian comes with many modules from which to choose. Here is where the inventory of your system comes in handy. Press Enter on the highlighted Configure Device Driver Module menu option to begin the module selection.

You are then asked if you have a driver disk to add modules for any special hardware devices. The modules on the disk must be on the standard modules tree. This is not a required step and can be skipped. In fact, this step can be skipped for most systems.

The Select Category dialog box shows several categories. See Table 2-1 for a brief description of each category. The most important ones to look through are fs, misc, and net. In the fs category, you can select all the other file systems that you want the kernel to access, such as a Windows FAT32 partition (VFAT). If you know that you want to install a Network File System (NFS) or a shareable Windows file system (smb), you can add those to the kernel. From the misc category, you can select a sound card, joystick, and other modules needed for your machine. The net category contains a list of several network card modules. This category is important for those systems that will be connected to a network.

Table 2-1
Category selection and device drivers

Category	Description
Block	Block drives such as RAID, floppy drives and other special drive devices (this does not include standard IDE drives on most systems).
Cdrom	Drivers for special CD drives (not needed for IDE CD Drives).
Fs	Select the file system drivers for all types loaded on the system. Dual boot systems with Windows 9x or NT will want Vfat or ntfs (read-only). Vfat reads and writes FAT and FAT32. Binfmt_aout and binfmt_misc read older style binaries.

Category	Description
ipv4	Special modules for IP version 4.
ipv6	Load IP version 6 drivers.
Misc	A hodgepodge of drivers that did not fit anywhere else; sound, joystick, mouse, and other similar drives fall in this category.
Net	Choose the network card for your system.
Scsi	Small Computer System Interface (SCSI). Unless you use a Zip drive, you will need ide-scsi (for SCSI emulation) and imm or ppa (depending on the age of the Zip drive).
USB	You can locate the USB drivers for new computers with USB devices.
Video	Frame buffer type video devices.

You can choose modules by using the arrow keys to first select the category of the module. For instance, moving the highlight to the *net* selection, then press Enter. Then moving the highlight again to the 3c59x selection and pressing Enter begins the process to install the module for the 3C59x family of 3Com Ethernet cards. Some modules give you the option to add customized settings to the module. In most case, taking the default will work, but some devices like ISA cards require specific settings be made. Once the requested module gets installed, the modules menu returns so you can add more modules. If you have trouble finding all the modules for your system, some modules get built into the kernel thus alleviating the need to add the module.

After you have chosen the modules and added them to the kernel configuration, exit the driver selection section. The modules should have installed correctly when they were selected. If you had trouble with any of them, make a note of the module name and consult the manufacturer for any notes on configuring that device for use with Linux.

Configuring the network

The Configure the Network option should pop up only if you selected a network card module. This is where you configure the networking device to work with the local network. If you have any questions about the information used here, contact your system administrator. Press Enter on the highlighted Configure the Network text to begin the configuration.

Note

If you did not install a network module, then you skip on to setting the host name for the machine. The host name is a name for the machine. In larger networks, Ayatem Administrators will name the machines based on a theme, like planets in our solar system or characters in a play. See Chapter 5 for more on networking.

The first dialog box asks you to choose the host name. This is the name of the computer on the network. Typically, system administrators take the liberty to have some fun with these names. You may see computers named after an administrator's favorite cartoon characters, planets from the solar system, or any number of themes. Alternatively, you can always give the computer a host name of `server1` to keep the names simple.

For networks that use Bootstrap Protocol (BOOTP) or Dynamic Host Configuration Protocol (DHCP) to assign the information to the computer, you can use the default Yes to the question of automatic network configuration. If you are not sure and use Yes anyway, you will be notified if no such protocols were found. If you don't know what the terms *Bootp* or *DHCP* are, choose No. Choosing No will cause you to configure the network settings manually. You will then configure the setting, as described in the following steps.

Cross-Reference   Refer to Chapter 5 for details about networking, protocols, and available IP addresses.

1. First you need to choose an IP address for the system. Each computer on the network requires a unique address. By default, one is assigned (192.168.1.1), but it cannot exist on any other computer on the network. 192.168.x.x is a private class of IP addresses. This means that they can only be used on private networks, not on the Internet. The x can be any number from 1 to 254, giving you over 65,000 devices on a private network.

2. You then need to select a network mask. This limits the number of addresses assigned to this network. By default, the mask is set to 255.255.255.0, which limits the number of addresses to 254. For a private network, using the default is fine.

3. The next question relates to your IP gateway address. This is the address of the computer or device that leads to the Internet or to another network.

4. When you get to the Choose the Domain Name dialog box, it will be blank. Here you type your Internet domain name. Do not make something up to fill in this option. If you do not know what the domain name is or you do not have one, leave the field blank.

5. Finally, you need to add the address for the Domain Name Service (DNS). You can add up to three DNS addresses to the entry. If you don't know the address, contact the system administrator.

Note   The network configuration section will not appear if no network modules are selected. It assumes that you have no networking with this system.

Installing the base system

The next step is to install the base system, the software for the base operating system, such as the kernel, the modules, and the supporting configuration files. You are given the option to select the basic tasks that this system will perform. The supporting software will load based on those selections. Press Enter on the Install the Base Systems to begin this process.

The next dialog box shown in Figure 2-3 enables you to select the source from which you are installing. For the purpose of following these instructions, use the CD-ROM option. However, those of you with fast, direct connections to the Internet (such as with cable modems), you may want to use the network option. This enables you to access all the Debian packages through the Internet, not just the ones available on the CD. The remainder of the installation steps remain don't change much either way you choose.

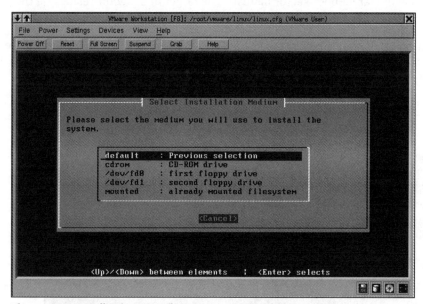

Figure 2-3: Install using CDs, floppies or mounted file systems.

After electing to install using the CD-ROM, you need to select the CD-ROM device. Normally, there will only be one option. After inserting the CD, you are then asked to choose the Debian archive path (/dist/stable). As earlier in the installation, if you press Enter twice, you accept the default path and then the default stable archive.

Configuring the base system

Time now to configure the base system. This primarily sets the time zone in which you live. Press Enter on the highlighted Install the Base System menu option to begin.

Select your location by first selecting the area where you live in the left column labeled Directories. Each time you select an area in the left column, the right column changes. Continue selecting until you find the appropriate city or time zone for your area of the globe.

Next, you are asked what time the clock is set to on your system. Most systems set the system clock to Greenwich Mean Time (GMT), and then adjust the time displayed based on the time zone. Many systems synchronize the time using GMT as a standard.

Booting Linux directly from the hard drive

This area of the configuration tells Linux where you want to boot. Under normal circumstances, you use the Master Boot Record (MBR) of the primary drive as the boot choice. This looks like /dev/hda. For those interested in dual booting, use this option unless you use a boot manager like BootMagic from PowerQuest. In that case, use the target boot sector instead. The target boot sector resides on the partition on which you specified to install Debian.

If you chose to boot from the target boot sector, you are given the option as seen in Figure 2-4 to use LILO as the boot manager. If you chose the MBR, this dialog box never appears.

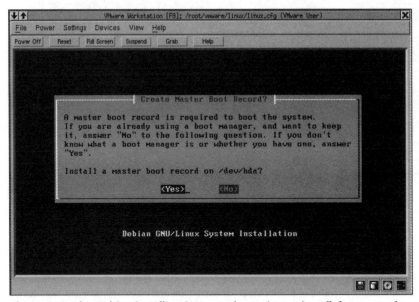

Figure 2-4: The Debian installer gives you the option to install the master boot record.

Making a boot floppy

It is always a good idea to have a backup boot disk. Especially when trying something different. This disk enables you to boot your system even when something went wrong while writing the boot record. Press Enter on the highlighted menu option labeled Make a Boot Floppy to begin making the boot disk.

To create the boot disk, insert a formatted floppy disk in the first floppy drive (or only floppy drive). Pressing Enter will make the installer begin writing the information to the disk. Once the procedure is finished, remove the disk from the floppy drive. Be sure to label the disk for later reference. This disk contains enough information about your system to boot successfully. This can be done other ways, but not was conveniently.

Rebooting the system

This is the last step before actually installing the program on the new system. Be sure to remove the CD from the drive before restarting the system.

Note If you are using a third-party boot manager, you will now need to add this operating system to the list of available operating systems before continuing. Each boot manager is a little different, so refer the boot manager's manual for details.

Configuring the Debian system

After restarting the system, you are ready to begin the configuration. This involves numerous questions regarding the base configuration of Debian GNU/Linux. As you go through these questions, keep in mind what the intent of this system is.

The first dialog box you see asks whether you want to enable md5 passwords. These passwords are discussed in more detail in Chapter 19. Essentially, this option enables longer, more secure passwords. Otherwise, passwords are limited to no more than eight characters. It is suggested that you *not* use this option if you intend to use Network Information Service (NIS).

The next dialog box asks whether you want to install shadow passwords. Shadow passwords are a method of encrypting the password so no one can directly read them. Systems not using shadow passwords can have the password file read straight from the file. Systems intended to be connected to the Internet should use shadow passwords. In fact, you should use shadow passwords regardless in my opinion for security reasons. See Chapter 19 for more information on security.

Now you are about to create the root account. This is the most important password of the system. If the password you select is too simple, it could compromise the security of the system. If it is too difficult, you could forget it and not have root access. This password can be changed later, so don't worry if you cannot think of a great password right away. The important thing is setting a password here that you will remember days later. Note that you will not see what you typed for the password. This is so that no one can look over your shoulder to discover the password.

Cross-Reference See Chapter 19 on security for more details and suggestions on creating good passwords.

Type the root password and press Enter. You will then be asked to confirm the password by retyping it. Retype the password and press Enter.

After creating the root password, you are asked to create a normal user account. This will be the user name that you log in with under normal circumstances. You will want to complete the user setup questions. Account names can be anything; however, corporations tend to observe more formal conventions, usually using a first initial combined with the last name. Thus, Joe Smith would have an account name of jsmith. First names, nicknames, and other names are all acceptable. At this point, you only have the option of creating one account name.

After creating the account name, a dialog box appears asking for the full name for the account. This is a descriptive name used as reference for the account. You then need to enter a password for the account. Be sure to make it different from the root password. Confirm the password by typing it again.

For most desktop systems, PCMCIA support is not needed. PCMCIA (Personal Computer Memory Card International Association) devices are normally found on laptops. Therefore, you can probably remove these services and related files as seen in Figure 2-5 as part of the installation. Laptop users, on the other hand, can keep these services for use on this specific hardware.

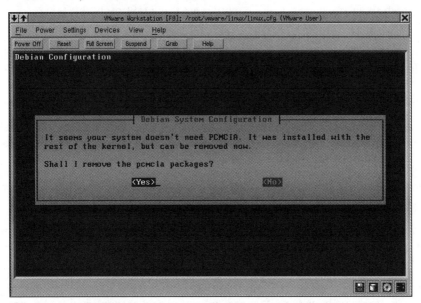

Figure 2-5: PCMCIA support is not needed for most desktop systems.

The next question may seem a bit odd, but it is merely asking if you intend to install any of the applications via a dial-up PPP connection. Because you are using a CD for the install, the default No is fine here. At this time, you don't want to install anything via a modem. Besides, the CD is much faster. Later, after you have the base systems installed, then updating and adding to your system can be done through an Internet connection. This is described in the "Changing the package archive source section" later in this chapter.

Apt configuration

Apt is the main component in the Debian package-management system. The apt tools enable packages to get installed from a variety of sources, manage the package archive sources, maintain a record of what you have installed and are used to install and remove packages for your systems. Apt is explained in more detail in the "Using the Debian Package-Management System" section. From here, you set the initial configuration for the system. Once initially set, you can always make changes later.

 Note   If you are using an Internet method of installation, select HTTP or FTP as an alternative source for packages.

After the CD is scanned for all the packages that it contains, you will be asked if you want to scan another CD. Because the book only includes one CD, you are ready to move on, so answer No.

The options shown in Figure 2-6 for configuring Apt are cdrom, http, ftp, filesystem, and edit sources list by hand. Unless you want to choose another installation location, insert the installation CD in the CD-ROM drive, and press Enter while cdrom is selected on the screen.

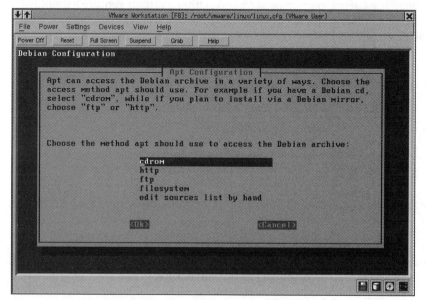

Figure 2-6: Choosing from several installation sources adds to the power of Debian installer.

Note   If you keep getting a message indicating that the system is unable to autodetect the CD device, make sure that the device name is correct. In some instances, the device /dev/cdrom may not exist. Try using /dev/hdd instead for the slave device on the second IDE chain.

As mentioned, you can configure Apt to use several means of installing packages — CDs, the Internet, or other file systems. You will learn more about Apt and the other Debian package tools later in the section "Using the Debian Package-Management System."

If you intend to install Debian over the network or Internet, you will need to select the network source at this time. The choices you have are shown in Figure 2-6. There are several mirrors to pick from all around the world. Finding one near you will not be difficult.

Once the information from the media is configured for Apt, the next dialog box asks you how you want to install the packages. You have two options: simple or advanced. I recommend using the simple option. The advanced option takes you directly into the package selection tool, where you pick exactly what packages you want installed. If you are not familiar with these packages, this can be overwhelming. The simple option opens a list of tasks. Each task includes those packages needed to operate the system appropriately.

You can navigate the list using the up and down arrows. To select a task, highlight it and press the spacebar, which marks the task with an asterisk (*). Systems that will use a modem to connect to the Internet should select the Dialup task. Laptop systems need the corresponding Laptop task. Other systems require a graphical interface. For beginning users, here is a list of tasks that are recommended for you to install:

✦ Dial-up — Dial-up utilities (for modem users only)

✦ Gnome apps — Applications and utilities

✦ Gnome desktop — The Gnome desktop environment

✦ Gnome Net — Network applications

✦ Laptop — Selection of tools for laptop users

✦ X Window system — Complete X Window system

After you have selected all the tasks that you want, tab to the Finish button and press Enter.

The next dialog box asks whether you want to attempt to autodetect your PCI video hardware. Some of the questions you might be asked can be answered using the inventory you did at the beginning of this adventure.

Tip   If the video detection fails, run xviddetect for more information about what was found. Once logged in, you can run /usr/bin/XF86Setup to configure the X environment. See Chapter 4 for more details.

To configure the video and monitor, follow these steps:

1. Options for choosing the X Window fonts appear first. The default 75 dpi is already selected and 100 dpi is still available for install. (100 dpi will offer larger fonts in applications that support 100 dpi)

2. Next choose what terminal emulators you want installed for use in the graphical interface. I'd recommend the xterm emulator at minimum.

3. After continuing from the terminal emulator, you now pick the window managers to install. You can add them now or later. Either way, you need to select at least one window manager. The choices on the CD are Enlightenment, Ice Window Manager (icewm and icewm-gnome), Sawmill, Tab Window Manager (twm), and Window Make (wmaker). I'd recommend Sawmill or IceWM-GNOME because they work well with the GNOME Desktop. (Chapter 4 covers the different window managers. Now might be a good time to look over that chapter.)

4. This next question asks whether you want to install the X Desktop Manager (xdm). This provides a graphical login screen and launches the system default graphical user interface after a successful login. For those who prefer to work with Linux via a command line, stay with the default and don't install xdm. You can always start X manually using the startx command or install xdm at a later time.

5. Now select the mouse you want to use. The PS/2 or Microsoft mouse will be the mouse of choice for most systems.

   The dialog box concerning three-button emulation lets you press both buttons on a two-button mouse to enable the third button. Many UNIX applications in a windowing environment use the third or center button on a mouse. This emulation takes advantage of those extra features.

6. Choose the device name for your mouse. This is the actual driver that controls the mouse. For example, PS/2 mice will use /dev/psaux. This may take a little experimentation if you're not sure what you are doing. You can change this setting later through either the configuration file or the configuration utility (XF86Setup).

7. Pick the keyboard you intend to use. This selection sets the keyboard for the X Window system. Normally this will be US/Standard.

8. Every monitor has a horizontal refresh rate. Check your monitor's specification for this value; if you try to guess, be conservative. Choosing too high a setting can damage the system.

9. Pick a vertical sync range the same way: Try to find the information from the specification sheet before making a guess. The actual values will prevent any damage to your system.

10. A monitor identifier is nothing more than a name for this monitor's particular settings. You can accept the default my monitor or change it to something else.

11. The video memory for your card can be found in your system's documentation or seen on the screen during a reboot. The numbers listed are in kilobytes (KB), so a video card with 1MB of memory would be represented as 1,024.

12. To name the video settings, enter a video card identifier name or use the default my video card.

13. Most newer video cards no longer use a clockchip. If you cannot find any information on a clockchip for your card, choose none. You are asked to probe for a clockchip again. This is not needed for modern hardware, so select No to continue.

14. Next, you pick the color depth for the system. This setting indicates how many colors the system has to choose from when displaying pictures, icons, and other graphics. The color depth ranges from 8 bpp (bits per pixel), which represents 256 colors, to 24 bpp, which represents 16 million colors. Higher end video cards can take advantage of using numerous colors, whereas the older cards with little memory should stick with 256 colors.

    When X window starts and brings up the graphical interface, the size of that interface is set with the default resolution. Once X windows has started, the resolution can be change. The supported resolutions indicate which ones are available.

    Just because you selected a default resolution, doesn't mean that you must stay with that choice later. You can add as many supported resolutions as you would like. I'd recommend choosing more than one.

Tip

If you have setup X to support more than one resolution, you can switch between the resolutions with keyboard commands. CTL+ALT+ increments the resolutions up and CTL+ALT- increments the resolution down.

15. Time now to save all these settings to a file. The default location to save the configuration file should be maintained. Other packages depend on settings from this file. Saving it to another location could cause another program to not work correctly if at all. The default path is /etc/X11/XF86Config. The default file is what X windows usually looks for when starting. Continue by accepting this filename. A dialog displays to confirm that the X configuration has completed and that the file was written.

Cross-Reference

Refer to Chapter 4 for more details on configuring, setting up, and using the graphical user interface.

You are now ready to install the packages onto your system. Be sure that the CD is in the drive before you begin. Shortly after the process begins, the CD will be scanned for packages. Another dialog box may appear asking if you have sound hardware installed. Answer appropriately to continue the installation. The installation time will vary depending the speed of your system (approximately 25 to 30 minutes).

After the packages are extracted to your system, the configuration process begins. Some applications require a little interaction to complete the configuration, such as exim, the mail tool. Refer to Chapter 25 for help configuring exim. As other dialog boxes appear (based on what task components are installed), continue to do your best to answer the questions based on the help text. The majority of the packages include help text to assist you to correctly answer the questions.

At the end, you will be asked whether you want to erase the .deb files. Because they are on the CD, they cannot be erased; therefore, it doesn't matter what you answer. You will then get a dialog box indicating that the installation is complete. Press Enter and you are ready to log in to a virtual terminal. If you install over an HTTP or FTP connection, the files get placed on your local drive before being installed. In that case, answering No could take up considerable drive space. (The local cache file for downloaded packages is at /var/cache/apt/archives.)

Use the root account to log in for the first time. Once you get a prompt, type dselect, and then press Enter. From the menu that appears, scroll to Select and press Enter. Press the spacebar to continue to the list of applications, and then press Enter once to return to the main menu. Make sure that Install is selected, and then press Enter. In some cases, not all of the applications will have been installed on the first pass. This process will pick up any stragglers and install them. Again, answer any questions during the configuration phase.

With all the files now installed, you are ready to start using your new Debian GNU/Linux system.

Using the Debian Package-Management System

Welcome to the last time you will ever have a need to install Debian from scratch. This may not seem like a rational statement, but you will agree once you understand the power in Debian's package management system. This system combines the power, flexibility, customization, and stability all into one system.

As you read through this section and begin to use some of the features available, you too will agree with me that the package-management system used in Debian makes this distribution stand out among others. This unique and handy approach to managing packages led the way for other package managers.

What are deb packages?

To help users install and manage their software, packages were developed to encapsulate each application. This encapsulation makes installations much easier. One package contains all the information that a specific application needs to operate properly. Some applications use shared resources, such as libraries that may be contained in a second package. The first package notifies the user that it depends on the second shared package, which must then be installed as well.

Each application must be assembled into a package for use with the Debian package management system. These packages are called *deb packages*. Their filenames end in .deb to indicate this. Over 4,000 packages are currently available from the Debian archives. When a package is installed, the package information is recorded to a database containing all the installed packages.

Adding deb packages

There are three tools that work together to install a deb package — dselect is used for a text-based user interface; apt get gets packages from a CD, the Internet, or other source; and dpkg actually installs the package. Each of these tools is discussed in the following sections.

dselect

The dselect user interface provides a pseudo-graphical interface from the command line. Issuing the command dselect brings up the initial menu, shown in Figure 2-7. To actually perform any management chores with this tool, it must first be executed using the root account. Once started, you have numerous options, including updating the database, selecting packages to install, installing the selected packages, and other options. The following list provides a short description of the most frequently used functions:

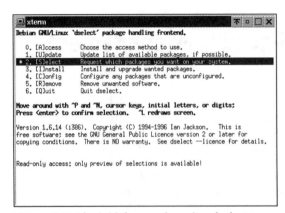

Figure 2-7: The initial menu for using dselect to manage packages

✦ **Update** — In this case, dselect looks at a configuration file to determine the source of the packages, and then compares the source against the local database for any changes.

✦ **Select** — Search the lists of packages and select those packages that you want to install. See Table 2-2 for a few of the key commands using dselect.

✦ **Install** — Queries the package database for any changes in install status. The appropriate actions then take place; for example, installing new packages, removing unwanted packages, or updating new versions. After the packages are expanded, any special post install configurations of the packages takes place before dselect asks whether it should delete the .deb packages.

Table 2-2
Key commands for dselect's select function

Command	Function
/name	The slash begins a search on filenames based on the pattern name.
+ or Insert	Selects a package for installation
- or Delete	Selects a package for removal
I	Changes the description area in the lower half of the display. There are three options for displaying the information.
Enter	Accepts the changes and returns to the main menu

The intelligent package manager — apt-get — is used in the background for dselect. This tool, when used from the command line, can retrieve a package from the Internet, along with any dependent packages (assuming the configuration specifies an Internet source). The following five commands are used with apt-get:

✦ update retrieves the available packages from the list of sources and updates the local database to reflect the available packages.

✦ install retrieves and installs all specified packages, plus any dependencies required for those packages.

✦ upgrade installs the most recent version of every package on your system, while doing its best not to make any changes to the system. This does not take into account dependencies.

✦ dist-upgrade works like upgrade, but changes the installation status of dependencies.

✦ dselect-upgrade works together with dselect. It reads the dselect status databases and makes changes based on the results.

In most cases, Apt tools have become the back end for other applications such as gnome-apt and dselect, making the true apt tools the core of the package management system.

dpkg

At the heart of the package management system is the package itself. This is where dpkg comes into play. One might even say that dpkg is at the heart of Debian as well. This is because each package is nearly a self-contained application, and dpkg performs the actual installation of the package.

To install a package, use the -i or --install option. The install option is how you would install a package named myapp.deb:

```
dpkg --install myapp.deb
```

You can install one or more packages using this tool by adding --recursive as an option. The --recursive option will search through any subdirectories specified and install any Debian packages found. If you have a directory (mydir) containing several packages to install, use:

```
dpkg -install --recursive ./mydir
```

To extract the files of a package only, use the --unpack option. This option unpacks the files from a package, saves the configuration for the current configuration, and does not configure the new installation. When finished, the package is installed, but not configured.

To configure the package later, use the --configure option. Adding the option -a or --pending configures all unconfigured packages on the system. Because dpkg does not take into account that there might be an order to configure packages, errors may occur. It exits after receiving 50 errors. Using -abort-after=500 tells dpkg to continue configuring until encountering 500 errors. Because dselect uses dpkg to configure the packages, it may error out before finishing configuring all packages, thus causing you to repeat the configuration a couple of times.

To remove packages with dpkg, use the -r or --remove option. This removes the packages, but leaves the configuration files behind. If you want to completely remove any trace of a package, use the --purge option.

Several other options work with dpkg; you can learn more about them by reading the man pages on dpkg.

Changing the package archive source

When you install Debian, the `apt` configuration file gets created, configured, and then used to install the packages. Later, if you want to make changes to the configuration, you can make those changes in one of two ways: using `apt-setup` or manual editing.

Using `apt-setup` (as the root account) lets you make all the same changes you were allowed to make when first installing Debian. It brings up a text-based display for you to navigate through, as seen in Figure 2-8. From this menu you can add another CD source, use an Internet archive site, or edit the source file by hand.

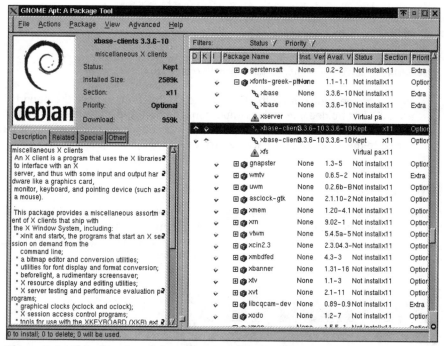

Figure 2-8: Changing the package source using apt-setup

 When editing the package source file, never add CD sources by hand. Each CD contains a label used to identify it, which gets recorded in the configuration file. Therefore, CD sources can be removed, but never added. Use `apt-cdrom` when you want to add a CD to the list of sources.

If you want to make changes by hand, use an editor to bring up
`/etc/apt/sources.list`. From here, you can change each entry by either adding
more sources or removing old ones. Lines starting with the pound sign (#) do not
get read as a package site. The following code shows the configuration file as it
would exist on your system after installing Debian for the first time:

```
# See sources.list(5) for more information, especialy
# Remember that you can only use http, ftp or file URIs
# CDROMs are managed through the apt-cdrom tool.
#deb http://http.us.debian.org/debian stable main contrib non-free
#deb http://non-us.debian.org/debian-non-US stable/non-US main contrib non-free
#deb http://security.debian.org stable/updates main contrib non-free

# Uncomment if you want the apt-get source function to work
#deb-src http://http.us.debian.org/debian stable main contrib non-free
#deb-src http://non-us.debian.org/debian-non-US stable non-US

deb cdrom:[Debian GNU/Linux 2.2 r0 _Potato_ - Official i386 Binary-1
 (20000814)]/ unstable contrib main non-US/contrib non-US/main
```

Note To change the source from the CD-ROM to the Internet, remove the pound sign
from the first bolded line in the sample configuration, and add a pound sign to the
second bolded line. Run Update from the `dselect` menu. You will then have
access to the entire Debian package archive.

Gnome-apt

A sister application to `dselect` is `gnome-apt`. It provides a graphical front end to
the package-management system. This tool lets you search through the available
packages, change how the packages appear grouped, and more — all with a click of
the mouse. Figure 2-9 shows the `gnome-apt` interface.

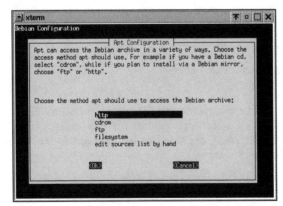

Figure 2-9: Using gnome-apt to install application
packages

The menus at the top give you control over the views in the right side of the window, the package status, and any actions to take. Using the mouse, you can toggle buttons on the packages listed to install, remove, and so on. The plus signs next to the names in the right panel let you expand groupings for easier navigation. You can also change the archive sources from gnome-apt.

Note   To install any packages, both dselect and gnome-apt must run from the root account. This is the only way the databases they rely on can be accessed.

This installation tool could virtually replace all the others, except that gnome-apt is only a graphical front end to the other applications. Gnome-apt still relies on the other Apt tools to complete the tasks.

Installing Non-Debian Software

Because the Debian system strives to maintain standardization, it can accommodate other types of packaged applications. Of course, source code for the programs can always be compiled, but you also can use pre-compiled packages such as RPM and tar.

RPM packages

The Red Hat Package Management (RPM) system was developed by Red Hat for their package. Since then, many other distributions have begun to use this package manager. The one thing RPM lacks is the customization scripts that are installed after a package is installed with the Debian system. Debian can, however, receive RPM packages.

To install an RPM package, you need to first install the rpm tool from the Debian archive. Once installed, you can install the RPM package.

RPM can operate in several modes, although the two important ones for most cases involve querying and maintaining. To query an RPM file, you list the content information about that file. This is similar to getting information about a Debian package using the -i option. Maintaining an RPM package includes installing, uninstalling, freshening, and verifying. The syntax listings for these modes are as follows:

```
Querying:
    rpm [--query] [queryoptions]
    rpm [--querytags]

Maintaining installed packages:
    rpm [--install] [installoptions] [package_file]+
    rpm [--freshen|-F] [installoptions] [package_file]+
    rpm [--uninstall|-e] [uninstalloptions] [package]+
    rpm [--verify|-V] [verifyoptions] [package]+
```

✦ Querying packages — To query a package using the `-q` option, you will see the package name, the version, and release information about any RPM installed package. Querying a package named `myrpm` would look like the following:

```
# rpm -q myrpm
myrpm-1.2.6
#
```

✦ Installing packages — This lets you actually install the package onto the file system. RPM packages generally end in `.rpm` and include a platform description for which they are built, such as an i386. Here is an example of installing an RPM package:

```
# rpm -ivh myrpm-1.2.6.i386.rpm
myrpm    ###################################
#
```

✦ Uninstalling packages — This is for removing unwanted packages. It requires only that you know the name of the package, and not the original package file name. The following command will uninstall `myrpm` from the system:

```
# rpm -e myrpm
#
```

✦ Freshening packages — Reinstalling a package using just the install options will generate an error that this package is already installed. You will need to replace the packages instead. This example shows installing a package using the `--replacepkgs` option:

```
# rpm -ivh --replacepkgs myrpm-1.2.6.i386.rpm
myrpm    ###################################
#
```

✦ Verifying packages — If you want to verify a package against the original RPM package file, use `-Vp`. This lets you know if any of the installed files have changed.

```
$ rpm -Vp myrmp-1.2.6.i386.rpm
```

There is much more you can do with the Red Hat Package Management System. The most important thing is installing applications found in the RPM format. The preceding list of commands should get you started installing packages you find along the way.

tar packages

Not all program creators take the time to create customized packages for different distributions. Some venders, on the other hand, have gone to great lengths to make their applications universal. `Tar` files are the universal packaging format for all UNIX systems. Often referred to as *tarballs,* these packages remain trusted and true.

A `tar` file contains the package, including any subdirectory structure. Tarballs are very easy to work with, which is why many people prefer to use them to distribute software. Here is an example of using `tar` to extract the files contained in a tarball:

```
tar xvf filename.tar
tar zxvf filename.tar.gz
```

The first example shows a straightforward `tar` file. The second example shows a `tar` file that was compressed after the file was created. The z option decompresses the file before the x option extracts the files. The v indicates verbose mode, for displaying all the files as they extract. The f option specifies that it uses the accompanying archive file.

After a package has been extracted, follow the instructions that accompany the `tar` package. Usually, those instructions reside in the first directory that the extraction created. From this point on, every application installation varies.

Cross-Reference You can find more uses for `tar` in Chapter 18.

Summary

Congratulations! Having completed an installation of Debian GNU/Linux, you have now joined the ranks of thousands of Debian users. This is only the first step on the road to using Linux in its many forms, such as Web servers, firewalls, and traditional workstations. The best thing about Linux is its ability to accommodate numerous environments, in addition to its stability — able to run for months without needing a reboot.

The instructions provided in this chapter set the groundwork for the rest of the book as you install other applications covered in the text. As noted earlier, you can change the `/etc/apt/source.list` file to point to one of many archive locations around the Internet. This is the only distribution I know of that can be fully installed with a floppy disk and an Internet connection — pretty amazing for a distribution built by volunteers.

In the next chapter, many of the basics are covered. These basics include logging on and off at the command prompt, stopping and restarting the system, and some of the essential commands you need to know to navigate the file system. This chapter also included a brief description of the file system layout. If you are a beginner, then you won't want to miss the contents of the next chapter.

✦　　✦　　✦

First Steps as a Linux User

After you install Debian GNU/Linux, the fun really begins. Now, you begin to use this operating system to explore the deep riches offered by Linux. But a question arises concerning what to do after you log in. I have been asked more times than I can remember, "Okay, I have Linux installed. Now what?" Linux is an untapped well of application opportunities. You have the privilege of discovering with me some of those opportunities as you get started using Linux.

This chapter begins laying the groundwork for Debian GNU/Linux by introducing commonly used essential commands. In this operating system, you cannot accomplish everything by clicking a mouse button. Therefore, knowing the commands and having the knowledge to navigate the file system becomes essential to maintaining your system.

Logging In and Out of Linux

Once you install and configure all of the packages, logging in for the first time isn't hard. You are always prompted to log in with a name and password, as shown in Figure 3-1. This prompt takes place through a terminal. A *terminal* is the text-based interface between the human and the machine with commands issued in text on a line.

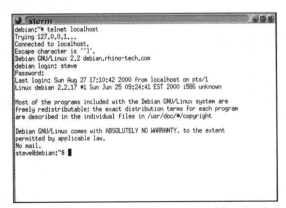

Figure 3-1: Logging in at the command line log in prompt

Note   If you are using a graphical interface like Gnome, WindowMaker, or one of the many others, you may get a graphical login. For details on using this type of interface, see Chapter.

Caution   Linux, UNIX, and other UNIX-like operating systems are case-sensitive. If a word, file name, or command should have one or more capitalized letters, then the operating system expects to see the capitalization in the commands that are issued. Mismatched case is one of the most common mistakes when first learning to use this operating system.

There are some simple rules to follow that can save you hours of grief in the long run. These common rules among the Linux/Unix community are meant only as guidelines — not steadfast rules.

✦ The logon account for common, everyday usage should not be root, but rather a separate account. As the root account, many vulnerable areas of the system are exposed to corruption and damage.

✦ Remember the root password. You can easily reset any account password by logging in as the root account. Resetting the root account becomes much more difficult to reset once forgotten.

✦ Use the tools provided when creating new accounts. You can create new accounts manually, but using tools such as adduser generates consistency among the accounts.

When you are all finished working on your Linux machine for the day, you can log out. Logging out of the operating system shuts down the environment you are working in without shutting down the entire computer. This is important because some of the functions of Linux run in the background.

You can use two different commands to log out: exit and logout. The logout command simply closes the current session, while exit does a little more. (I discuss exit's other property in Chapter 14). Both commands result in a closed session, so I tend to use `logout` because it *only* closes the session. These commands take you back out to a login prompt where you can log in again, someone else who has an account on this system can log in, or you can prevent anyone from accessing your files through the active session.

Cross-Reference See Chapter 12 for more details on accounts, permissions, and access. Also look at Chapter 19 for security-related information.

Basic Navigation with Linux

When I sat down to use Unix for the first time, I had an experienced friend sitting next to me to answer questions. He taught me a few commands that became the groundwork for learning more about Unix. You may not have that luxury, so I will be that experienced friend and give you the basics. All these basic commands operate from a command line. If you start your system in one of the graphical modes described in Chapter 4, then you can start one of the terminals installed on your system. There will be at least one. This will give you access to a command line from which you can use these commands.

The most important part of navigating your way around Linux is learning some of the basic terminal commands. Granted today's Microsoft Windows world provides easy graphical interfaces for every function. However, the truth about Linux is that these interfaces become crutches to the power of Linux.

Cross-Reference There are many more tools than what I describe in this chapter. To find a more complete list, see Appendix C.

Finding special file locations

The structure of the directories at certain locations make a defined layout for the files. This structure has a predetermined pattern. The first two layers of the file structure look like that in Figure3-2 when drawn out on paper.

```
/┬ etc
 │ usr
 │ bin
 │ sbin      ┌ jo
 │ home/ ─┤
 │ tmp       └ jane
 │ var
 │ root
 │ boot
 │ dev
 │ mnt
 │ cdrom
 └ floppy
```

Figure 3-2: The basic Linux filesystem structure

Using the figure as a reference, you can dissect the filesystem into its parts to discover the purpose of each of the parts. Table 3-1 shows the filesystem breakdown.

Table 3-1
The Linux filesystem

Path	Description
/	This is the beginning of the filesystem. It is known as root. The root of the filesystem is the starting point for the rest of the parts. If the filesystem were a tree, this would be the trunk from which all the branches (directories) attached.
/etc	Any system-wide configuration files are stored here. This includes configuration files for all the daemons such as Sendmail, Apache, and a host of others.
/usr	This is the source directory for all the user-accessible programs, program source code, and documents.
/bin	This is an application branch for commonly used system-wide programs (such as mkdir, cp, rm, and more applications I haven't talked about yet). Bin can be thought of as a short description of *bin*aries, which would be the programs themselves.
/sbin	This area contains server/administration programs like kernel and hardware-related programs, shutdown, reboot, and many more. You can also think of sbin as holding *system bin*aries.
/home	Anyone who has an account on this machine has a directory in /home.
/tmp	This branch stores files that need to be created as temporary files. This area should get purged from time to time and does when the system is restarted. You should not keep files here that you need to save.
/var	All the systems applications that log history, access, and errors record that information here. This is the system's storehouse of process information.
/root	The home directory for the *root* account. This is rarely used, except by the system administrator.
/boot	This area contains the *boot* critical information, such as the kernel and module information.
/dev	This is the location of the *dev*ices that the system uses. When you mount a device, for instance, it is located in this directory.
/mnt	Location for additional devices to be mounted (as subdirectories of /mnt)
/cdrom	Debian predetermines the mount point for the CD-ROM device.
/floppy	Debian predetermines the mount point for the floppy device.

This should give you an idea of the file structure of Linux. At least this is a good start for finding the files and file locations that you seek. It will also give you a reference as you read through the rest of this chapter.

Finding ready-reference documentation

If you are anything like me, you jump first and ask questions later. Whenever I get a new appliance, the first thing I do is set aside the READ ME FIRST piece of paper, the warranty card, and the owner's manual. Then when I get to a point when I have no other choice but to read the owner's manual I do.

Fortunately, Linux comes with nearly all the documentation you need readily available for your assistance. The key is to know what commands to use and how to look for them. You can look up commands for their syntax, definition, and related commands in a couple of different ways.

man

When you are looking for a ready-reference for available commands, use man (short for manual). Each program, utility, or function includes manual pages. Follow man with a command name to get the syntax, description, and list of options for that command. For example, man man produces:

```
# man man

man(1)                         Manual pager utils
man(1)

NAME
       man - an interface to the on-line reference manuals

SYNOPSIS
       man  [-c|-w|-tZT  device]  [-adhu7V] [-m system[,...]]
[-L locale] [-p string] [-M path] [-P pager] [-r prompt] [-S
list] [-e extension] [[section] page ...] ...
       man  -l  [-7]  [-tZT  device]  [-p  string] [-P pager]
[-r prompt] file ...
       man -k [apropos options] regexp ...
       man -f [whatis options] page ...

DESCRIPTION
       man is the system's manual pager. Each page argument
given to man is normally the name of a program, utility or
function.  The manual page associated with each of these
arguments is then found and displayed. A section, if provided,
will direct man to look only in that section of  the
manual.  The default action is to search in all of the avail_

Manual page man(1) line 1
```

This is the first page of the man manual. Press the Spacebar to view the next page. Notice that at the top you see man(1), which indicates the category or type of the manual page. You can see the section number and the associated type of pages in Table 3-2.

Table 3-2 Categories of manual pages	
Section	**Type of pages**
1	Executable programs or shell commands
2	System calls (functions provided by the kernel)
3	Library calls (functions within system libraries)
4	Special files (usually found in /dev)
5	File formats and conventions
6	Games
7	Macro packages and conventions
8	System administration commands (usually only for root)
9	Kernel routines (non standard)
n	New
l	Local
p	Public
o	Old

The manual pages consist of several parts labeled Name, Synopsis, Description, Options, Files, See Also, Bugs, and Author. Each part contains information particular to that part.

In addition, the following conventions apply to the Synopsis section. This section contains the command being looked up, any options for the command, and any required information. The following list can help you to interpret the Synopsis:

✦ bold text — Type exactly as shown

✦ italic text — Replace with appropriate argument

✦ [-abc] — Any combination of arguments within [ ] is optional.

✦ -a|-b — Options separated by | cannot be used together.

✦ argument ... — The argument is repeatable.

✦ [expression] ... — The entire expression within [ ] is repeatable.

apropos

When you don't know what manuals to look up, use `apropos` to find a list of the commands. The `apropos` command searches and displays installed command names based on keywords associated with the commands. This is useful when you are looking for a command but aren't quite sure what to use. For instance, issuing `apropos` with the keyword `security`:

```
$ apropos security
```

produces a list of installed applications, utilities, or functions that relate to the keyword as displayed here:

```
checkrhosts (8)   - program to check the users .rhosts files
for security problems
checksecurity (8) - check for changes to setuid programs
perlsec (1p)      - Perl security
perlsec (1p)      - Perl security
perlsec (1p)      - Perl security
Xsecurity (3x)    - X display access control
```

The results show the name of the command, which you can look up with the `man` command, along with a brief description to give you a better idea of the purpose of the listed command.

info

This program provides information about a specified command. It is a hypertext tool for reading documentation, which you can navigate using a regular keyboard. You can use this program with the following syntax:

```
info [option]... [menu-item...]
```

Here, `menu-item` is the name of the command you want to look up. It is hypertext-based, so you can navigate through the documents using the hypertext links. For a complete listing of the commands, type `info info` at the command prompt. Some screens show more menu options available. Pressing `m` and then typing the menu name takes you to another page called a node. *Nodes* are hyperlinks in the text that provide a somewhat interactive help system.

Pressing the `n` key takes you to the next node, and `p` brings you back to the previous screen. Using this navigation within the documentation not only helps you to find what you are looking for, but it also guides you to the most useful information.

Note Some documentation will be the same for both `man` pages and `info` pages. Other documentation will exist in detail as `info` and the `man` pages will reference the `info` documentation. In some cases you may find slightly different information from both sources because the authors of the documentation were not the same.

Maneuvering through the files

For most, the biggest struggle is maneuvering though all the files — remembering where you've been and knowing where you want to go. You can easily acquire this skill with a few simple commands. The following commands are not a complete set. However, mastering the basic set can help you with more advanced commands.

ls

The list command (ls) shows the contents of a directory. Issuing the ls command alone displays the contents of the current directory. Adding ls path reveals the contents of the path you specify. This is the syntax:

```
ls [option] [path]
```

Here's an example of ls:

```
$ ls
Mail        mail     misc        smb.conf     util.doc
util.txt
Xrootenv.0  mbox     public_html tmp          util.list
$
```

As you can see, these files are listed in order by columns. The priority starts with numbers, proceeds to capital letters, then follows with lowercase letters. This command also has several useful options to show the contents in various forms. Table 3-3 shows the most useful options.

Table 3-3
Commonly used ls options

Option	Description
-a, --all	Lists all the files in a given directory, including the hidden files
-l	Lists the file information in long format showing all the file's information
-F	Classifies each file by appending a character to the file name indicating the type
*	Regular executable files
/	Directories
@	Symbolic links (similar to shortcuts in MS Windows)
	Nothing for regular files
-R	Lists the contents of all directories recursively

These options play a crucial part in retrieving the most useful information about the files in the directories. In addition to using the options individually, you can employ the options in combination with one other to achieve the fullest listings. Here is one of the combinations (ls -al) that I use the most:

```
$ ls -al
total 284
drwxr-xr-x   8 steve    users       1024 Mar  6 10:47 .
drwxr-xr-x  23 root     root        1024 May  8 09:04 ..
-rw-r--r--   1 steve    users        383 Aug 31  1999 .FVWM2-errors
-rwxr-xr-x   1 steve    steve       1155 May 13  1999 .Xdefaults
-rwxr-xr-x   1 steve    users       3036 Jun  8 09:01 .bash_history
-rwxr-xr-x   1 steve    steve         24 May 13  1999 .bash_logout
-rwxr-xr-x   1 steve    steve        230 May 13  1999 .bash_profile
-rwxr-xr-x   1 steve    steve        163 Feb 21 06:29 .bashrc
drwx------   2 steve    users       1024 Feb 18 17:43 .elm
-rw-r--r--   1 steve    users         21 Feb 21 06:23 .forward
-rwxr-xr-x   1 steve    users      10327 Dec  1  1998 .pinerc
-rw-r--r--   1 steve    users          7 Aug 31  1999 .wm_style
drwx------   2 steve    users       1024 Feb 18 17:53 Mail
-rw-r--r--   1 steve    users        349 Aug 31  1999 Xrootenv.0
drwxr-xr-x   2 steve    users       1024 Dec  1  1998 mail
-rwxr-xr-x   1 steve    root         510 Jul 19  1999 mbox
drwxr-xr-x   2 steve    users       1024 Jun  1 12:15 misc
drwxr-xr-x   9 steve    users       1024 Feb 18 13:35 public_html
-rwxr-xr-x   1 steve    users        962 Sep  3  1998 smb.conf
drwxr-xr-x   2 steve    steve       1024 Jun  8 09:21 tmp
-rw-r--r--   1 steve    steve     208896 Aug  8  1999 util.doc
-rw-r--r--   1 steve    steve       1190 Aug  7  1999 util.list
-rw-r--r--   1 steve    steve      43439 Aug  7  1999 util.txt
```

You can see from using this command that there are more items listed for the same directory than when you simply use the ls command. The a option includes hidden files as well. As you look at this list of information, provided by the l option, let me help you decipher it into some useful information. Each column has special significance as follows:

✦ Column one shows the mode for the file or directory. *Mode* refers to the permission type for a file or directory (such as rwx, which means read/write/execute). I cover this information in detail in Chapter 12.

✦ The second column refers to the number of links to the file or directory. (A *link* is a shortcut or pointer to the real file or directory.) In the case of directories, a link refers to the number of subdirectories.

✦ The third column lists the owner of the file or directory by user ID.

✦ Column four lists the group that the file or directory belongs to by group ID.

✦ Column five shows the file size in bytes.

✦ Date and time appear in the next area.

✦ Finally, you see the names of the files or directories.

When you start using the `ls` command more, you may come across reasons to view lists of files meeting certain qualifications. In this case, wildcards become invaluable. In Table 3-4, you see the wildcards and their uses.

Note

A *wildcard* represents one or many characters, depending on the wildcard symbol used. Some wildcard symbols represent any length of characters and numbers, while other symbols reflect a single length. Wildcards are especially useful for doing searches when you only know part of a file name. You can also use them when you want to see a limited list—primarily when looking at files and directories. Using s* lists all files and directories that begin with the letter "s."

Table 3-4 Wildcards for the ls command	
Character	**Replaces**
*	Zero or more characters
[]	Any characters inside (includes ranges)
?	Any single character

Now, take a look at some examples using these wildcards to view, sort, or group lists of file. The first example shows all the files in a directory.

```
$ ls
Fig10-01.tif    Fig10-04.tif    Fig12-03.tif    Fig13-03.tif    Fig13-06.tif
Fig10-01a.tif   Fig10-05.tif    Fig13-01.tif    Fig13-04.tif    Fig13-07.tif
Fig10-02.tif    Fig12-01.tif    Fig13-01a.tif   Fig13-05.tif    Fig13-08.tif
Fig10-03.tif    Fig12-02.tif    Fig13-02.tif    Fig13-05a.tif
$
```

These files are very similar with the exception of a few minor changes. Now, let's see how you can create a list based on one character from the file name.

```
$ ls Fig1?-01.tif
Fig10-01.tif   Fig12-01.tif   Fig13-01.tif
$
```

This produces a subset of the full list, which includes only those files in which the fifth character is in question. Now, add an asterisk (*) before the period to include those files in the list that may have additional characters in the name after the fifth character.

```
$ ls Fig1?-01*.tif
Fig10-01.tif    Fig10-01a.tif   Fig12-01.tif    Fig13-01.tif
Fig13-01a.tif
$
```

This command sequence adds two more files to the list. Now, suppose you are looking for a series of files.

```
$ ls Fig13-0[2-5].tif
Fig13-02.tif   Fig13-03.tif   Fig13-04.tif   Fig13-05.tif
$
```

Again, this version produces a subset of the directory contents with a range of files fitting a certain category. As you begin to use these command options, I'm sure that you will find them as useful as I have.

cd

This change directory command (cd) allows navigation through the file system and enables you to change to a directory for up-close viewing. To get a better idea of the file structure, skip ahead to the section in this chapter on the filesystem. Here is the syntax for the command:

```
cd [directorypath]
```

Issuing the cd command without options takes you to the home account directory from anywhere.

directorypath is the directory path to which you wish to change. For instance, if your current path is /home/jo, issuing

```
$ cd /tmp
```

changes the current viewable directory to tmp directory.

To go someplace completely different, just specify the full path. For example,

```
$ cd /usr/bin
```

transports you from the current directory to another directory named bin under the usr directory. Again, if you get lost or want to quickly return to your home directory, use

```
$ cd
```

to take you from anywhere to the default account directory. The next command, pwd, will help you keep your barrings as you navigate the directory structure.

With some practice, changing directories will become second nature.

pwd

Once you start getting the hang of moving around through the directories, you may get lost. The question, "Where am I?" may cross your mind. A simple command shows you the current path — pwd. Use this command to help find out the directory path of your location. The results of using pwd look like this:

```
# pwd
/home/jo/tmp
```

mkdir

This make directory command (mkdir) creates a directory on the filesystem. This becomes important as you begin to organize a collection of files. Use mkdir *dirname* to create the directory called *dirname* at the current directory location. Here is the syntax:

```
mkdir [option] dirname
```

You can create a chain of directories at once by using the -p option. This option creates the destination directory plus all parent directories that don't exist. For example, suppose you want to create a directory called new inside the directory files. In this case, files is the parent directory for new. Neither directory exists currently. This is how you input it.

```
$ mkdir -p ./files/new
```

The results of this command are:

```
$ ls -Ral files
total 3
drwxr-xr-x   3 root      root           1024 Jun  8 15:16 .
drwxr-xr-x  10 steve     users          1024 Jun  8 15:16 ..
drwxr-xr-x   2 steve     users          1024 Jun  8 15:16 new

files/new:
total 2
drwxr-xr-x   2 steve     users          1024 Jun  8 15:16 .
drwxr-xr-x   3 steve     users          1024 Jun  8 15:16 ..
$
```

This shows the contents of the files directory, then shows the contents of the new directory. Of course they are both empty because we just created them.

rmdir

The remove directory command (rmdir) removes directories in the same way as they are created. The syntax for removing these directories is as follows:

```
rmdir [option] dirname
```

Using the same example you employ to make a chain of directories, you can remove those directories using the -p option. If you have a directory chain (/files/new) that you want to remove, issue this command:

```
$ rmdir -p ./files/new
```

Results:

```
$ ls -Ral files
ls: files: No such file or directory
$
```

This removes both new and files at the same time — but only if these directories are empty.

Caution   You cannot remove directories containing files using this command. Use the ls - a command to view the directory for hidden files that were not deleted previously. Use the ls -l command to make sure that you have permission to remove the directories. As the owner, you should have write permissions to the directory, which includes permission to remove it.

rm

The remove command (rm) deletes files and directories from the filesystem. rm is irreversible; you cannot access the deleted files. Use rm /filepath/filename to delete a file. The syntax looks like this:

```
rm [option] file1 [file2 .. filen]
```

This command has several options. Table 3-5 shows the common options available when using the remove command (rm).

Table 3-5	
rm command options	

Option	Description
-d, --directory	Removes a named directory. Example: rm -d /home/jo/test
-f, --force	Forces the removal of a file or directory. Example: rm -f ./ test
-r, -R, --recursive	Recursively removes the contents of all subdirectories. For example, rm -r /home/jo/tmp removes all files in /home/jo/ tmp plus any files contained in directories below this path.
-i, --interactive	Interactively removes a file by asking the user to confirm with a Yes or No the removal of each file. This is a good option to use as a confirmation before deleting files, for example, rm -i /home/jo/test

Caution   As a precaution, include the interactive (-i) option when removing files. Once you delete a file it's gone!

Tip If you are interested in removing massive amounts of data, try using `rm -Rf`. This command will *forcefully* remove all files and subdirectories contained in a directory you specify. It is useful if you want to get rid of directories in a hurry, but can be devastating if misused.

mv

The move command (`mv`) takes a file or the contents of a directory and moves them to a new location. You can also use this command to rename files. For instance, use `mv ./filename ./newfilename` to rename a file in a current directory and `mv ./ files /newdirectory` to move files into another directory. The syntax of the move command is:

```
mv [options] file1 file2
mv [options] directory1 directory2
```

Let's look at a couple of examples of using the `mv` command. First, suppose you want to rename the file `rpg45.txt`. This is how it looks:

```
$ mv rpg45.txt rpg45new.txt
```

Now, the file `rpg45.txt` no longer exists; it is renamed to `rpg45new.txt`. If the new file name existed, you would have been prompted with a Yes or No confirmation to make sure that you wanted to replace an existing file. This is the response you would have gotten:

```
$ mv rpg45.txt rpg45new.txt
mv: replace `rpg45new.txt'? y
$
```

Here, I just overwrote the file `rpg45new.txt` with `rpg45.txt`, but you can see that it required some intervention to complete the task.

In conjunction with the move command (`mv`), you can use the interactive option (`-i`) to confirm the moves that you make. This helps to prevent accidental moves that turn into headaches later because you moved the wrong files.

cp

The copy command (`cp`) does just that — it copies a file from one filename to another. Here is the syntax for the command:

```
cp [option] sourcefile destinationfile
```

The `cp` command is similar to the `mv` command, but it does not remove the source files. Let's see how it works. First, take a look at the files in the directory before you change anything.

```
$ ls -l
total 268
-rw-r--r--   1 steve      users          84649 Jun  8 09:55 Fig10-01.tif
-rw-r--r--   1 steve      users          36383 Jun  8 09:55 Fig10-02.tif
-rw-r--r--   1 steve      users          56636 Jun  8 09:56 Fig10-03.tif
-rw-r--r--   1 steve      users          52687 Jun  8 09:56 Fig10-04.tif
-rw-r--r--   1 steve      users          36367 Jun  8 09:56 Fig10-05.tif
$
```

Next, copy the last file (Fig10-05.tif) to also make it the sixth file
(Fig10-06.tif):

```
$ cp Fig10-05.tif Fig10-06.tif
```

Looking at the listing of the directory, you see:

```
$ ls -l
total 305
-rw-r--r--   1 steve      users          84649 Jun  8 09:55 Fig10-01.tif
-rw-r--r--   1 steve      users          36383 Jun  8 09:55 Fig10-02.tif
-rw-r--r--   1 steve      users          56636 Jun  8 09:56 Fig10-03.tif
-rw-r--r--   1 steve      users          52687 Jun  8 09:56 Fig10-04.tif
-rw-r--r--   1 steve      users          36367 Jun  8 09:56 Fig10-05.tif
-rw-r--r--   1 steve      users          36367 Jun  8 16:25 Fig10-06.tif
```

From this listing, you see that the file was indeed copied because the last two files
have the same size but a different time. You can see from this example how copying
files works. Table 3-6 shows some of the options available with the copy command.

Note   As good practice — whenever I consider making a change to any important, critical,
or essential file — I always copy the original file to a new filename. That way, if I
screw up the configuration file, I have a backup copy.

Table 3-6
Options for the cp command

Option	Command
-f, --force	Forces an overwrite of existing destination files without asking
-i, --interactive	Interactively asks you whether you want to overwrite existing destination files with a Yes or No
-p, --preserve	Preserves the original owner, group, permissions, and timestamps of the files copied
-r	Recursively copies directories and treats all nondirectories as if they were files

Note All files on a filesystem carry with then ownership and access permissions. When copying your own files, the ownership settings will remain the same, however, when copying someone else's files, the ownership changes to yours. As does the time stamp on the file. In some cases, you may want to preserve the ownership, permissions, and timestamp of the original file. You can use the -p option with cp to accomplish this.

Stopping the System

Stopping a Linux system takes a little more effort than turning the power switch to Off. In fact, doing so can cause the entire system to fail because of lost data still in memory. As a rule, you may find yourself in two different situations — shutting down the system or rebooting the system.

Using the reboot, halt, and poweroff commands

You can reboot or power down the computer using three different commands. You can find these commands in the /sbin directory, but they require the root administrator to invoke them. The syntax for these three commands is:

```
/sbin/halt [-w] [-f] [-i] [-p]
/sbin/reboot [-w] [-f] [-i]
/sbin/poweroff [-w] [-f] [-i]
```

Generally, you can issue these commands without options. However, you may find a few options quite handy. Table 3-7 shows the most valuable options for these commands. Notice that the halt command is the only one with the -p option. This is to enable the halt command with the power off feature.

Tip An alternate method for rebooting a Linux system is to use the three-fingered salute. When you press Ctrl+Alt+Del, the system interprets this command as a reboot.

Table 3-7
reboot, halt, and poweroff command options

Option	Description
-w	Don't reboot or halt the system; instead write the /var/log/wtmp record. This is the login record for your system. This makes a record of who has logged into the system.
-f	Forces a halt or reboot; don't call shutdown
-I	Shuts down all network interfaces just before a halt or reboot This option removes the computer from the network before shutting down. No more requests can come into the computer.

Option	Description
-p	When using halt, do a power off instead. This makes use of the auto-power-off features found in newer computer hardware.

Note   Not all computers have the capability to power off. This is partially a function of the hardware. Some computers have a power switch that you must flip manually in order to turn the power off. Power off is also a function of the Linux kernel. See Chapter 15 for further details regarding the kernel options.

Simply issuing any of these commands sends a warning that the system is about to shut down with a five-second delay before the rebooting sequence begins. A complete shutdown or restart of the system takes place without intervention, depending on the command you issue.

Using the shutdown command

Ultimately, using a different command to shut down the computer becomes slightly more involved. The shutdown command has several options (shown in Table 3-8), some of which are mandatory. These options give you the chance to customize the shutdown. You can set the delay before the process begins (default is five seconds) and the message that gets displayed. In addition, you can decide whether to halt or restart after the system is shut down. Here is the syntax for this command:

```
shutdown [-t sec] [options] time [warning-message]
```

To break down the syntax a little, the command appears first (obviously) followed by the delay between sending the signal to shutdown and changing the run level (described in Chapter 15). You then have your choice of a few options. I recommend either -h to halt or -r to reboot. Then you must insert a time given in minutes or use now to immediately shut down.

Table 3-8 shutdown command options	
Option	**Description**
-t sec	Waits sec seconds after sending processes the warning and kill signal and before changing to another run level
-k	Only sends the warning messages to those logged in. Doesn't really shut down the system
-r	Reboots the system after shutting down

Continued

Table 3-8 *(continued)*

Option	Description
-h	Halts the system after shutting down
-f	Skips the filesystem check on reboot for a faster system start time
-F	Forces the filesystem check on reboot
-c	Cancels an already running shutdown process. You cannot give the time argument with this option.
Time	Sets a time when to shut down the system The format can be either *hh:mm* or *+m*.
warning-message	Custom message to send to all users when the system begins to shut down

The minimum requirements to shut down a Linux system are the halt or reboot and a time. For the majority of situations, this command is all you need to halt the system:

```
$ shutdown -h now
```

This halts the computer when all processes are stopped. After that, you can turn off the computer.

Working with the Filesystem and Related Commands

To understand the filesystem, you need to lay some groundwork for how the filesystem falls into place. Somewhere, generally on the local computer, exists the hard drive or some other type of media that stores all the data. The significance here is in the way this information gets written to the drive. The more efficiently this occurs, the better the overall performance of the system.

A *hard drive* consists of multiple disks called platters. Each *platter* has running across it a tiny little device floating on a cushion of air as the disk spins. This little device, called a *head*, can read and write to the platter. The smallest usable unit on the disk is known as a *block*. The disk controller manages the information on the disk and instructs the disk on which blocks to read and write. The piece that fits the between the disk controller and the operating system is the *device driver*. This special piece of code takes the commands from the operating system and translates them into the language that the controller speaks and vice versa. The files for controlling the drives are usually located in the /dev directory on a Linux system.

The *filesystem* is the part of the Unix/Linux operating system that takes care of communicating with the drive system. Each operating system uses a preferred filesystem type. For instance, Linux systems can view the Microsoft world by using msdos, umbdos, and vfat filesystem types. The preferred Linux filesystem type is called ext2, and it has developed into a high performance filesystem offering the best in terms of speed and processor usage.

Mounting drives

For the operating system to work with the filesystem, you must first set it up to work with the devices. This process, called *mounting the filesystem*, normally happens automatically when the system first loads.

fstab

When the computer starts up in Linux, the filesystem information is read from the filesystem table file fstab. This table contains all the information about the devices that need to be mounted during the startup processes. Here is an example of what the contents of the /etc/fstab file look like:

```
# /etc/fstab: static file system information.
#
# <file system> <mount point> <type> <options>                <dump> <pass>
/dev/hdb1       /             ext2   defaults,errors=remount-ro 0      1
/dev/hdb2       none          swap   sw                          0      0
proc            /proc         proc   defaults                    0      0
# Uncomment the following entry if you use a 2.2.x or newer kernel for
# UNIX98-style pty handling
#none           /dev/pts      devpts gid=5,mode=620              0      0
/dev/fd0        /floppy       auto   defaults,user,noauto        0      0
/dev/cdrom      /cdrom        iso9660 defaults,ro,user,noauto    0      0
```

The information contained in the filesystem table matches the device with the mount point and the filesystem type. This becomes important when there are several drives, devices, and even drive partitions all contained on one system.

Not all drives are mounted automatically. You can see from the sample fstab file that the CD-ROM and the floppy have noauto listed as an option in the table. This just means that they are not mounted automatically at startup. Therefore, you need to mount them manually at some point in order to use them.

mount

When the computer starts, mount is issued to load the filesystem using the fstab file. Here is the syntax for the mount command:

```
mount [-fnrsvw] [-t vfstype] [-o options] device dir
```

When the time comes to use either the CD-ROM or the floppy, you need to mount these into the system. However, the fstab file already includes these devices, so the command to mount these is abbreviated to:

```
$ mount /dev/cdrom
$ mount /dev/fd0
```

The rest of the information comes from the fstab file. Use the mount command to mount new devices (for example, when you add another hard drive to your system). Table 3-9 shows the options for manually using mount load a filesystem.

	Table 3-9
	mount command options

Option	Description
-h	Prints a help message
-v	Verbose mode
-a	Mounts all filesystems mentioned in fstab
-r	Mounts the filesystem as read-only
-w	Mounts the filesystem as read/write. This is the default.
-t vfstype	Uses the filesystem type indicated by vfstype. Some of the available filesystem types are ext, ext2, hpfs, iso9660, msdos, smbfs, umsdos, and vfat.

These same options can be used in the fstab file to make changes to the parameters for mounting the drives.

umount

After a device is mounted, such as a CD-ROM, you must unmount it — especially in the case of a CD-ROM. If you do not unmount it, you cannot take the CD-ROM out of the drive. Here is the syntax for the command:

```
umount device | dir [...]
```

Therefore, to unmount the CD-ROM, issue this command:

```
$ umount /dev/cdrom
```

Now you can remove the CD-ROM from the drive. Notice that this command does not unmount the drive if someone is using the device — even if there is no activity. If someone changes directories to the device's mount point, the device is considered active.

Summary

Getting started with Linux requires a few tools. Once you begin working with these tools, you can branch out on your own. The most important tools help you log in and out of the virtual terminal, navigate around the Linux filesystem, and correctly stop and restart the computer.

Conquering the basics, you can move on to mounting and un-mounting the CD-ROM and floppy drives. You have many more features, functions, and commands to learn before you really become proficient at Linux, but this is an excellent start.

✦　　✦　　✦

Choosing a GUI

Although you can manipulate most aspects of the Linux system with only a command prompt through a terminal, most people prefer using some type of *graphical user interface.* As the operating systems have become more sophisticated, so has the interface. The point of the graphical user interface is to make the operating system more user-friendly, thus making navigation more intuitive and usable by novices. This isn't to say that only novices should use graphical user interfaces, but it does speed up the learning curve a bit.

The graphical user interface, sometimes called *GUI* (pronounced *goo-ee*), has advanced right along with the operating system. Today, you can choose from a number of interfaces in the Linux environment. This is not only because of Open Source applications, but also because of the way the graphical interface works on the GNU/Linux operating system.

Linux's Graphical User Interface

The graphical user interface on Linux systems is based on the X Window System. Today, X Windows System is currently at version 11 revision 6 and is properly known as X11R6, X11, or just X. X11R6 X servers are now developed and maintained by the XFree86 Project organization.

Note The following is quoted from the XFree86 FAQ found at /usr/share/doc/xfree86-common. This quote sums up the essence of the XFree86 project:

The XFree86 Project, Inc., is a not-for-profit group whose original, self-determined charter was to develop X servers that would work on the wide variety of video hardware available for Intel x86-based machines (hence the "86" in

"XFree86"). They also decided to release their X servers under licensing terms identical to that of the freely available X sources, hence the "Free" in the "XFree86." By keeping with the licensing terms of the original X source distribution, XFree86 has enjoyed immense popularity, and they no longer confine their activities to merely producing X servers for IBM PC-compatible video hardware.

The X environment is unique from the known Windows operating systems in that X is actually a server that provides graphical displays across platforms, even across networks. This makes the X environment very powerful because it has few restrictions pertaining to platform and network specifics. Using a client/server model allows for platform independence and network transportability. This client/server approach is a little different from the commonly known Windows environment; as such, you may need a little more time to understand it. Basically, the X server portion provides the necessary software to control the graphical and input hardware. The client application then tells the server what to display.

The X client does nothing to directly display the information, so a standard must be set. X defines that standard so that any X client can communicate with any X server by giving it certain display commands. The X server does the actual work of displaying the information. In this way, a client can display its information on any other platform. The only thing that other platform needs is an X server.

Using this client/server model lets the actual client application be *platform-independent*. This means that the client application can display itself on any platform architecture for which an X server is available. For instance, in a mixed environment where you have Linux running on Intel-based PC, Mac, and SPARC platforms, a client from the Intel-based PC can run on either the Mac or the SPARC workstation. The reverse is also true; the Intel-based platform can just as easily display applications from the other platforms.

In the previous scenario, a network links these different platforms together. As long as you have two or more computers connected to a network, they can share applications. Granted you have some security issues to consider, but the basic principle remains — the application runs as if it were local to the workstation.

All in all, this type of structure allows for an enormous amount of flexibility when creating applications. Although the X server sets the standard for displaying information, it does not specify a policy for interacting with the user; that is the job of other components that make up the GUI: the window manager and the desktop environment. Table 4-1 shows most of the window managers available in Debian, as well as the two most popular desktop environments.

Table 4-1
Listing of window managers and desktop environments

Window manager	Short name	Package name
AfterStep	AfterStep	afterstep
F?? Virtual Window Manager	FVWM	fvwm
F?? Virtual Window Manager2	FVWM2	fvwm2
Ice Window Manager	IceWM	icewm
OpenLook Virtual Window Manager	OLVWM	olvwm
Tab Window Manager	TWM	twm
Window Maker	Wmaker	wmaker
Enlightenment	Enlightenment	enlightenment
BlackBox	BlackBox	blackbox

Desktop environment		Package name
GNU Network Object Model Environment	GNOME	task-gnome
K Desktop Environment	KDE	task-kde

Note   You may have noticed that the F in FVWM did not stand for anything. The author of this window manager could not remember what he used the F for. As a result, the F stands for anything you want it to—fantastic and fabulous are just two examples of what you could use.

Deciding on a Graphical Interface

Picking a graphical user interface is more subjective than objective because of each person's individual preferences. Basically, the final decision is yours—although the following may help you make that final decision.

The first guideline involves the amount of resources you have available on your computer. The more resources you have—such as system memory, video memory, newer video card, and so on—the better your GUI performs. If you have a newer, faster computer, using a GUI can provide you with hours of fun.

If you have an older, slower system with limited resources, then you might want to consider not using a GUI because it can drastically slow down your performance. Also, if you use the system as a server, there is no real need to have a GUI installed.

Instead, you can leave more room for the other server applications. Granted, without a GUI on the system, you are limited to using only the command line to run programs, manipulate files, and generally maintain the system.

Your personal preference dictates the final interface. Some of the interfaces are more intuitive, providing more configurable options or whatever options you feel are important when you work. You may find that a simple interface is the best environment for your system to handle. The more buttons, icons, pictures and such, the more processing power it takes to keep it all updated.

Tip   To help determine the load of a window manager on your system, use a performance meter such as xload in the xcontrib package to gather resource information for comparing them. Most window managers include some type of performance meter. Because the meter itself consumes resources, you can't take it as gospel as to the resources used by the interface. However, it can give you a point of reference to compare different resources.

Installing and Configuring the X Environment

You need to install a few components on your system to make the X environment work. Among the required components, you must have an X server installed for your graphics card; and a window manager to give you control of the environment.

You can select from a number of available X servers. Most video cards work with the VGA X server; then, look for one that most closely fits your card. Table 4-2 lists all the X servers available with the Debian GNU/Linux system.

Table 4-2 Available X servers	
Server	**Supported adapter(s)**
xserver-3dlabs 3.3.6-10	3-DLabs GLINT and Permedia-based graphics cards
xserver-8514 3.3.6-10	ATI 8514/A-based graphics cards
xserver-agx 3.3.6-10	IBM XGA and IIT AGX-based graphics cards
xserver-common 3.3.6-10	Files and utilities common to all X servers
xserver-fbdev 3.3.6-10	Framebuffer-based graphics drivers
xserver-ggi 1.6.1-2.1	All LibGGI targets
xserver-i128 3.3.6-10	Number Nine Imagine 128 graphics cards
xserver-mach32 3.3.6-10	ATI Mach32-based graphics cards
xserver-mach64 3.3.6-10	ATI Mach64-based graphics cards

Server	Supported adapter(s)
xserver-mach8 3.3.6-10	ATI Mach8-based graphics cards
xserver-mono 3.3.6-10	Monochrome graphics cards and/or monitors
xserver-p9000 3.3.6-10	Weitek P9000-based graphics cards
xserver-s3 3.3.6-10	S3 chipset-based graphics cards
xserver-s3v 3.3.6-10	S3 ViRGE and ViRGE/VX-based graphics cards
xserver-svga 3.3.6-10	SVGA graphics cards
xserver-vga16 3.3.6-10	VGA graphics cards
xserver-w32 3.3.6-10	Tseng ET4000/W32 and ET6000-based graphics cards

If you don't have a window manager running with the X server, you can still run applications such as `xterm` but without any control of the window other than exiting the session and forcing an exit of the X environment. You can install more than one window manager on your system. Debian uses one of them as the default manager depending on what manager is installed.

Use the `dselect` application to install the X server, the window managers, and any dependencies (don't be surprised to find a few). This is the best way to install the applications to make sure that all other related applications, libraries, and supporting files get loaded.

Note

When you install the X servers, you are asked to set each server as default during the configuration portion of the install. You can only have *one* default X server. If you are unsure which one to select, say *no* to each one or say *yes* to the VGA16 server because it works with most video cards.

It is assumed that when your system installed, your video hardware was detected. If this was the case, then *anXious* installed the X servers that will work with your card and made the appropriate settings.

X system requirements

As with anything else that you install that utilizes your system resources, such as video hardware, you need to know what you have installed and whether you have adequate resources. X uses more system resources than most other applications. Therefore, knowing what resources you have is very important.

The bottom line is *know your hardware*. It never fails — as confident as you might be about knowing what you have, you'll get halfway through the install and need to know something that you don't have ready. Of course, I help you prevent that from happening. Make sure you write down pertinent manufacturer information about the hardware:

✦ The name of the video card

✦ The amount of onboard video memory

✦ The video chipset

✦ Type of mouse

✦ Type of keyboard

✦ Vertical monitor refresh rate range

✦ Horizontal monitor refresh rate range

Although the keyboard and mouse types are not critical components to the function of the X configuration, you still need to know them. The next thing you should know is if this version of Xfree86 supports your video card. Most popular video cards available on the market, including the integrated video chipsets found on some mainboards (also referred to as motherboards), have drivers available. (With so many different types, styles, and brands of video cards, maintaining an accurate list of compatible video cards is not feasible.)

When new technology becomes available to the computer world, new drivers are needed. This includes the 3-D graphics cards. Most of these 3-D accelerated video cards have drivers available in Linux. If not, visit the manufacturer's Web site to see if there is a compatible driver. Because of the migration of people using Linux, more manufacturers are accommodating the Linux community by providing drivers, configuration help, and more.

Note   Although the older versions of XFree86 work with a 3-D graphics card, they may not work optimally. XFree86 version 4 is optimized to work with these new cards to make full use of the hardware acceleration. You can find the latest version at www.xfree86.org.

Installing fonts

In order to display text, you must install fonts. These fonts come packaged separately and may be among the list of dependencies when you install the X server. You can also add them later. Assuming you have the space to spare, you can install them all—but at least install xfonts-base and xfonts-75dpi.

The Debian installation configures a *font server* as the default method for handling fonts packaged for the X environment; xfs is that server. The other method for handling fonts is internal to the X server. Debian uses the font server, so it also configures the server to start automatically using init at boot time. This is also configured at the time of installation.

A single configuration file in /etc/X11/xfs/config contains all the information about the system's fonts. Here are the default contents of the config file:

```
# /etc/X11/xfs/config
#
# X font server configuration file

# allow a maximum of 10 clients to connect to this font server
client-limit = 10
# when a font server reaches its limit, start up a new one
clone-self = on
# log errors using syslog
use-syslog = on
# turn off TCP port listening (Unix domain connections are still permitted)
no-listen = tcp
# paths to search for fonts
catalogue =
/usr/lib/X11/fonts/misc/:unscaled,/usr/lib/X11/fonts/cyrillic/:unscaled,
/usr/lib/X11/fonts/100dpi/:unscaled,/usr/lib/X11/fonts/75dpi/:unscaled,
/usr/lib/X11/fonts/Speedo/,/usr/lib/X11/fonts/Type1/,/usr/lib/X11/fonts/misc,
/usr/lib/X11/fonts/cyrillic,/usr/lib/X11/fonts/100dpi/,/usr/lib/X11/fonts/75dpi/
# in decipoints
default-point-size = 120
# x1,y1,x2,y2,...
default-resolutions = 75,75,100,100
# don't try to load huge fonts all at once
deferglyphs = 16
```

You can add more fonts to the system by adding their paths to the `catalogue` listing in the file. You must list each font directory as a separate entry.

Installing the Display Manager

Display managers fill in the gaps between the X environment, the window managers, and the applications. For the average person, the only difference is the graphical login screen that appears when the system first starts up. Using a desktop manager is very simple, and most newcomers to Linux prefer the graphical interface because it more closely resembles other graphically based operating systems such as Windows, Macintosh, or BeOS.

There are basically four desktop managers that you can use. `xdm` comes as part of the XFree86 packages. In most cases, it gets set to run at startup by `init`. The other three desktop shells are included with the GNOME Desktop Environment (`gdm`), the K Desktop Environment (`kdm`), and Wingz Display Manager (`wdm`). (Wingz Display Manager is the counterpart to the Window Maker window manager.) There is very little difference between the four desktop environments.

XF86Setup

After you install the base software, including the `xserver-vga` package, you need to configure the X environment for your system. You can run the `XF86Setup` configuration utility at any time from a command line as root. This configuration utility creates and modifies the /etc/X11/XF86Config file that contains all the necessary information about your system for X to function properly. First, I take you through the configuration utility, and then I talk about the resulting configuration file.

Start the X configuration utility any time by typing XF86Setup on a command line. This initiates the utility. If you already have a configuration file, you are asked if you want to use the existing file as the default. If you choose yes, then you can use the mouse from the previous configuration. The setup goes into graphics mode, from which you can use the mouse to interact with the interface.

Note   If your mouse doesn't work for some reason, use the Tab and arrow keys to maneuver to the mouse section. The Spacebar or Enter key activates the selected buttons. Once the correct mouse is set up and applied, you can start using the mouse immediately.

Setting up the mouse

Setting up the mouse can cause some confusion. If you use a standard PS/2 type mouse connected to the PS/2 mouse port of the computer, you can set up your configuration as shown in Figure 4-1. There are three sections of the mouse configuration you need to know: mouse protocol, mouse device, and 3-button emulation.

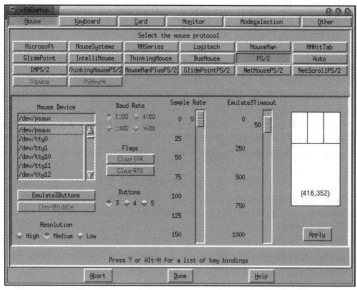

Figure 4-1: The mouse configuration section of XF86Setup

The *mouse protocol* defines the type of mouse you are using. This section shows a number of buttons to choose from to define the type of mouse you use. This covers a good many types of mice, but not all. Choose the one that most closely matches your mouse type.

The second section (the mouse device) is the most important. This section defines the driver used to control your mouse. Luckily, a USB mouse driver is included in the list. Again, this list is comprehensive, so pick the one that closely matches your mouse. Press the letter a to apply these settings and test your mouse. This representation of the mouse on the lower-right side displays mouse clicks by turning the button black, and the numbers on the mouse represent the x-y coordinates of the mouse pointer.

Note   If you install gpm and you have trouble controlling your mouse after you open an X session, check to see if gpm is running as a daemon. If so, stop the gpm service with

```
/etc/init.d/gpm stop
```

and then check to see if you are still having mouse control problems in an X session. If this does the trick, then remove the link from the run level:

```
rm /etc/rc3.d/S20gpm
```

The third consideration (3-button emulation) refers to the third button on the mouse. Your mouse may not physically have a third button; however, the software can emulate the third button. Many applications include capabilities only available through the third button. Simultaneously press both mouse buttons to activate the middle button.

Once you have mouse control, you can navigate the rest of the configuration using only the mouse.

Setting up the keyboard

Clicking the keyboard button takes you to the section where you can configure the keyboard. Normally, configuring the keyboard doesn't take any effort. Today, many computers come with additional keys on the keyboard for Microsoft Windows. The default keyboard (101) does not have these additional keys on either side of the Spacebar. The newer keyboards, which have the extra keys, are considered 104-keyboards. There is a provision in this area for those keyboards if you choose to configure it. The 101-keyboards work just fine with the newer keyboards and you do not need to change them. (If you want to use the Windows keys, choose the 104-keyboard.)

This image of the keyboard in Figure 4-2 gives you an idea of the style of the keyboard. If it matches yours, then you've likely selected the correct one. You can also specify the language of the keyboard.

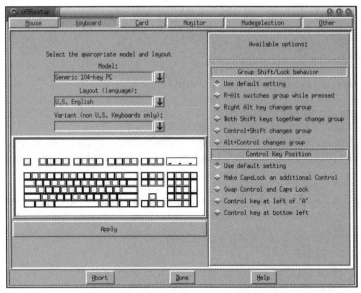

Figure 4-2: The keyboard configuration in XF86Setup

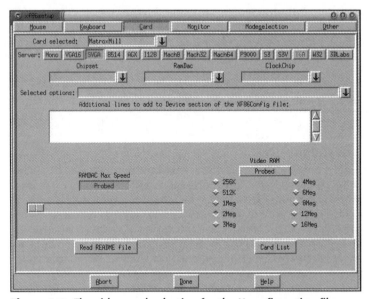

Figure 4-3: The video card selection for the X configuration file

Installing the video card

Video cards tend to cause the most trouble, yet are the most crucial of the components because you can't use X if you can't see it. It is imperative to select the correct card. You can go about this in one of two ways. Figure 4-3 shows the more difficult method — manually picking components. From here, you can select the card's video chipset, video memory, and even the X server. I suggest that only experienced individuals use the interface shown in Figure 4-3 to configure the video card.

The other option is to click the Card List button in the lower-right corner of the window. From there, you can select the specific video card you have by clicking it. The list contains hundreds of video cards, including some of the newer ones.

Again, if your card doesn't show up in the list, contact the manufacturer's Web site. Some video cards use the same video chips as other cards, making them compatible when it comes to configuring Linux.

When configuring X on laptops, the chipsets may be slightly different from the desktop models. Manufactures often use crippled or modified video components to accommodate size and power constraints. This slight difference can result in complications when configuring X on the laptop. You may need to fine-tune the card setting through the XF86Setup card details screen.

Setting up the monitor

The information on the monitor is important to the X server because it controls nearly every aspect of the display process. If the video card can display information to the monitor beyond what the monitor can display, you get streaked lines across the screen. Therefore, the closer to the monitor's true parameters you can make the settings the better.

Making guesses on the refresh frequencies can be hazardous to your monitor's health. Wrong settings can damage your monitor or video card. If you guess, it's better to choose one of the defaults such as VGA or SVGA, but you're on your own. Also, consult the manufacturer's Web site to see if it posts that information.

The most important information here is the refresh information. You can get that information from your monitor's manual. Figure 4-4 shows the preset options you have available. One of these settings should work; or if you have the specific horizontal and vertical frequencies, you can manually use those ranges by typing them in the appropriate spaces near the top. The bars on the top and left of the pictured monitor graphically show the frequency range that you set.

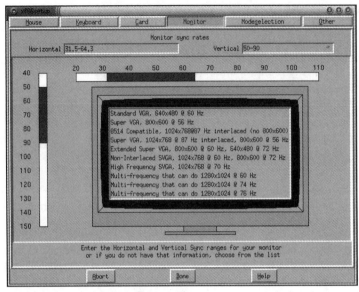

Figure 4-4: Configuring the monitor

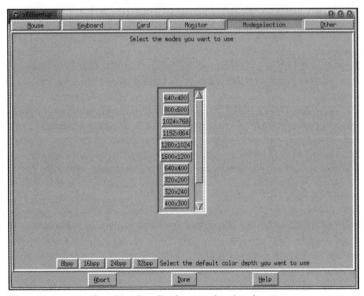

Figure 4-5: Configuring the display modes for the X server

Checking the default display modes

Using the X system, you have the ability to customize the screen size and color depth based on the capabilities of the video card. *Screen size* refers to the pixel dimension of the display. For instance, an 800 × 600 display shows a screen with 800 pixels across and 600 pixels high. The bigger the number, the more information fits on the screen. You can click as many of the screen size options (as seen in Figure 4-5) as you want to have available during your X session.

The color depth is another story. The numbers for the color depth represent the number of available colors. A color depth of 8 provides 256 colors. The larger the number, the more colors are available. Table 4-3 shows the relationship between the color depth and the number of colors. As you can see, choosing 32 gives you a lot of colors.

Table 4-3
Color depth

Color depth	Number of colors
8	256
16	65,536
24	16,777,216

Verifying the successful configuration

Once you completely configure all the different components, press the Done button. If you already have an XF86Config file, a dialog box appears to let you know that the old one is saved with a .bak extension. Then your system tests the configuration.

Assuming that the test is successful, you can then save, abort, or fine-tune the settings with xvidtune. Only those experienced with graphics hardware should try fine-tuning. Fine-tuning takes you into the inner workings of the video hardware. Making the wrong adjustments can potentially damage, if not destroy, your video card and/or monitor.

After you successfully save and finish configuring the X environment, you can find the configuration file in /etc/X11/XF86Config. This configuration file contains a section with something similar to the following:

```
Section "Screen"
    Driver          "SVGA"
    Device          "Generic VGA"
    Monitor         "My Monitor"
    BlankTime       0
    SuspendTime     0
    OffTime         0
```

```
SubSection "Display"
     Depth        8
     Modes        "800x600"
     Virtual      800 600
     ViewPort     0 0
  EndSubSection
EndSection
```

You can change this information manually if necessary. If you do make manual changes to the file, be sure to make a backup before starting. If the X server is working, making the wrong change can cause it to cease working. The most common changes are those affecting desktop size. Once you get comfortable changing the desktop size, you can consider making more serious manual changes.

Starting the X server

Now that you have the X server installed and configured, choosing the start method is the next step. There are basically two ways to start the X server. One way is to start the server after you log in through the terminal login prompt. The other way is to use the desktop manager, which starts automatically at boot up.

Manually starting the X server after you log in gives you the added control of deciding whether you want to use an X environment. If something fails in the X environment, you have the option of backing out to the shell and working from the command line. To start the X environment from the command line, simply type `startx`. X then launches using the system's default window manager.

You may find that having immediate access to the non-graphical command shell isn't that important to you. You can then use the desktop environment to log in through a graphical interface that takes you right into the window manager. As mentioned earlier in this chapter, you can use one of four desktop managers (although xdm is installed when you install X). There is a script that `init` uses located in `/etc/init.d/xdm`. You should make a symbolic link in the run level that normally functions at startup. See Chapter 15 for more details on run levels. If you installed xdm in the beginning, the post installer took care of adding a link to the run levels.

Starting X remotely

Because X was developed with the network in mind, some of the advanced functionality includes opening applications residing on remote computers. This type of functionality is not found natively on any other platform without the aid of additional software.

X accomplishes this through the network using some type of authentication. The appropriate method is through the `MIT-MAGIC-COOKIE-1` protocol. These cookies are essentially an identifier with a data encryption code. If the remote account does not have the cookie registered for the display, no connection can be established.

To begin, let's see what cookies are available on your system. From the command line, type the following:

```
xauth list
```

You should see a list of cookies, if any exist. This list may look something like the following:

```
newt/unix:0  MIT-MAGIC-COOKIE-1  bda676274e1c630e17b2575bd73f3ade
newt.mydomain.com:0  MIT-MAGIC-COOKIE-1  bda676274e1c630e17b2575bd73f3ade
```

Each console that authorizes a connection also specifies the encryption code. Both lines show the host (in this case, newt.mydomain.com) and display number (:0), followed by the protocol (MIT-MAGIC-COOKIE-1) and the encryption data. If you do not have any cookies, you can generate one with the following command:

```
xauth generate :0 .
```

This command generates the code for the :0 display using MIT-MAGIC-COOKIE-1 as the protocol. When a period is used, MIT-MAGIC-COOKIE-1 is assumed.

Now when I want to run an X application from the remote machine, I can. Here is the command syntax that starts the remote application:

```
ssh newt /path/application -display newt.mydomain.com:0
```

Here, the ssh establishes a secure connection to the host (newt) to execute the application. The full path is used because there are no default paths available. The -display option is used so the resulting graphics are displayed on your console. Finally, the cookie identifier (*newt.mydomain.com:0*) specifies the remote console to use. The application is actually running on the remote computer, with the display showing on your screen.

An excellent source for more information about remote access can be found in the X documentation. Look at /usr/share/doc/xfree86-common/FAQ.gz (use gless to open it).

Managing the X server

As with everything in life, some management is required (just as with your X Windows System). You need to know how to change the size of the screen area, select window managers, and close the X server without the graphical interface. After all, all software experiences glitches and sometimes locks; the same is true with the X Window System, too.

When you configure the X environment, you can choose to use more than one screen size. As soon as X starts, whether with xdm or startx, you can change the screen size with keystrokes. To make the screen size larger, press Ctrl+Alt++. Likewise, Ctrl+Alt+- makes the screen size smaller. Using these key sequences, you can scroll through the screen size options.

In some instances, you may need to temporarily change the screen size to see an entire window on one screen. Most window managers allow for *virtual desktops*. This means that the desktop area is actually larger than the resolution of the screen. Window managers can have from two to eight virtual desktops. This can be handy once you get used to it. Each desktop can have its own background and can hold on to any window you open in that area. You can also move windows from one desktop area to another by dragging them.

The virtual desktop really comes in handy when you have a low-resolution system. You can use one desktop for your clock and calendar, another for monitoring tools, and yet another as your workspace — all without having one desktop area cluttered with windows everywhere.

Occasionally, you may lose mouse control, open windows may lock up, corruption of the X environment may occur, or you may not be able to close the X environment (this doesn't happen very often). A keyboard command sequence closes all windows and shuts down the X system — Ctrl+Alt+Bksp. If you use `startx` to start X, then you return to a command prompt. If you use a desktop manager, then you return to the graphical login screen after X restarts through the desktop manager.

Another solution is to go to a different virtual terminal using the keyboard. The default Debian installation is configured with six virtual terminals. You can access them using CTL+ALT+F#, where # is a number from one to six. Debian has the X console set to F7, which means that when you are ready to return to the current X session, press CTL+ALT+F7.

Another maintenance issue is choosing your own window manager. No matter how you start your X session, you can customize which window manager gets started. This is true for each account on the system. Debian installs a default window manager, but you can override the default for your account. Create a file called `.xsession` in the home location of your account. The contents of the file are in text form and look something like the following:

```
xterm
exec fvwm
```

When the X session first opens, an `xterm` session also automatically opens and the FVWM window manager is used. You can insert the name of any applications you want to open at startup. This file is a script, so any valid scripting is executed.

 Cross-Reference To learn more about scripting, check out Chapter 14.

If you have problems with the X session, check in the `.xsession-errors` file of the account (in the home directory of the account) for clues to the problem. Or, if you happen to use `xdm`, then check out `/var/log/xdm.log` also. The desktop manager can have something to do with which window manager you use. If you employ the gdm desktop manager for GNOME and now want to use FVWM2 as your preferred window manager, you may need to stop the gdm window manager before switching so you don't end up back with GNOME.

Installing and Using Window Managers

In order for the graphical user interface to function, you must use a window manager. The window manager sits between the applications and the X server. It provides the control for the applications, interprets the graphical requests from the applications, and conveys them to the X server where the information is displayed for you to see.

Over the years, developers have created a number of window managers. Only a few are covered in this chapter, however. The window managers discussed here are the most commonly used.

FVWM

As one of the older, more traditional window managers found on UNIX systems, FVWM has evolved into several versions. Although each version is based on the same premise, the look and feel of each differs a little. Figure 4-6 shows FVWM, the original of the three. Notice the traditional look and feel of the UNIX window manager.

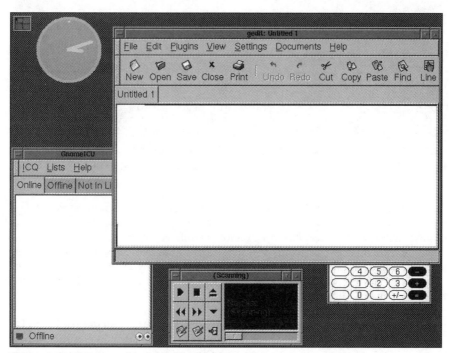

Figure 4-6: An example of the FVWM desktop

The second of the three window managers tries to model itself after the look and feel of the common PC operating system Windows 95. You can see from Figure 4-7 that FVWM95 includes a Start button and a task bar at the bottom of the screen. Each application that is opened also shows up on the task bar. The Start button produces the menu for the system in the same way that the Start button produces the menu for Windows.

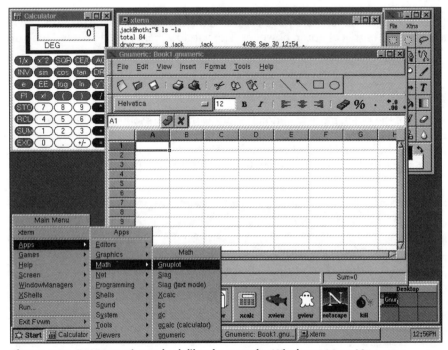

Figure 4-7: FVWM95 tries to look like the popular Windows 98 or Me.

The original version of FVWM has been around for a while, so updates have resulted in a spin off: FVWM2. This window manager combines the simplicity of the original window manager with up-to-date graphics controls. Like the other window managers, they allow for extensive customization of nearly every aspect. The default configuration file resides in /etc/X11/fvwm. If you copy system.fvwm2rc to your home directory with the name .fvwm2rc from your own directory, you can make as many modifications as you see fit.

Using the window manager environment without a mouse can get tricky, so I include some of the default keyboard controls in Table 4-4. You can reconfigure these controls to suit your preferences in the .fvwm2rc file. Other key commands appear in the configuration file itself.

Table 4-4
Keyboard commands for FVWM2

Command description	Keystroke
Display the list of windows	Alt+F2
Iconify the current window	Alt+F4
Move the current window	Alt+F5
Resize the current window	Alt+F6
Close the current window	Alt+F9
Jump to the next window	Alt+F11
Toggle maximize/normal window size	Shift+Alt+F3
Toggle sticky window in the desktop	Shift+Alt+F4
Next desktop down	Shift+Alt+Down_Arrow
Next desktop to the left	Shift+Alt+Left_Arrow
Next desktop to the right	Shift+Alt+Right_Arrow
Next desktop up	Shift+Alt+Up_Arrow
Move pointer down 5 pixels	Shift+Down_Arrow
Move pointer down 100 pixels	Shift+Ctrl+Down_Arrow
Move pointer left 5 pixels	Shift+Left_Arrow
Move pointer left 100 pixels	Shift+Ctrl+Left_Arrow
Move pointer right 5 pixels	Shift+Right_Arrow
Move pointer right 100 pixels	Shift+Ctrl+Right_Arrow
Move pointer up 5 pixels	Shift+Up_Arrow
Move pointer up 100 pixels	Shift+Ctrl+Up_Arrow

To use your keyboard with this or any X session, make sure that you have it configured correctly for your computer. XF86Setup, as described earlier in this chapter, can help you make any changes to your configuration.

Enlightenment

Enlightenment is one of the more advanced window managers. It offers many features not found on the traditional interfaces, such as desktop settings, themes, user menus, and more.

You can access many of the customizable features of this window manager by key-mouse button combinations. Leaving the mouse to hover over a certain area displays the key/mouse combinations called Tooltips, as seen in Figure 4-8. There is often more than one way to get to a particular menu. Once you get the hang of navigating through the menus, you can turn off Tooltips. To turn these tips off, right-click the background desktop and select Tooltips Settings from the menu.

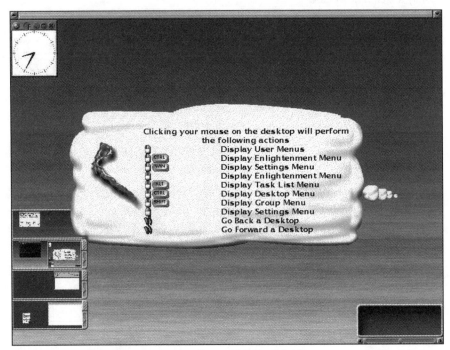

Figure 4-8: Enlightenment shows off one of its helpful features.

Another unique characteristic of this window manager is its use of themes. Most of the window managers don't make use of themes. The default installation only comes with the one theme, but you can download and install more through the Enlightenment Web site at www.enlightenment.org.

You can also see from Figure 4-8 that there are four small panels in the lower-left corner. These panels represent four virtual desktops, and each desktop has a size of two screen widths (a right and left screen). Each of these desktop panels floats freely for easy movement, and you can retract them to free desktop space. The panel in the lower right shows, in icon form, any applications that have been minimized from the display area.

Window Maker

Modeled after the NEXTStep user interface, Window Maker offers the same smooth, refined, elegant look. You can see from Figure 4-9 that a lot of work has gone into creating the look. Eye candy isn't the only thing you find with this interface, though. It is just as functional as any of the other interfaces.

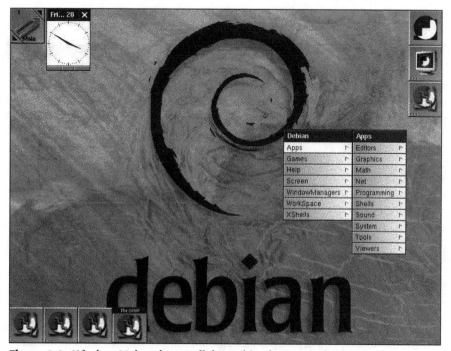

Figure 4-9: Window Maker shows off the Debian logo as its background.

The integrated configuration tool enables you to configure many aspects of the interface without having to edit a configuration file. You can configure things like window creation location, the workspace, animation, and so much more. Access the configuration menu by clicking the third button in the upper-right corner of the screen. Or access the menus by clicking the right mouse button anywhere on the background of the desktop.

This is not a single desktop interface. In the upper-left corner of the window is the control for the virtual desktop. To add a new workspace, right-click the desktop and select Workspace from the menu. Then select Workspaces from the second menu, and finally choose New from the last menu. You can add as many workspaces as you like. To access the newly created workspace, click the arrows in the corner of the workspace icon in the upper-left corner of the screen.

Installing and Using Desktop Environments

As the windowing applications have progressed, another layer has been added to the mix — the desktop environment. There are primarily two desktop environments used on Linux systems: GNOME and KDE. These environments use a window manager as the interface, which adds more function to the GUI. The desktop environment provides a degree of flexibility, which adds to the window manager's customization. Links to applications are represented as icons on the desktop. These icons on the desktop now link to drives that mount automatically when executed with a double click.

Because desktops traditionally provide the primary interface to the users, the applications handle the data, preferences, and such themselves. These desktop environments can instead handle some of this work for the applications. This frees the programmer to focus his or her efforts on the function of the application, resulting in better applications.

GNOME

Born out of the need for an entirely free desktop environment, *GNOME (GNU Network Object Model Environment)* leads on the cutting edge of desktops. However, some KDE enthusiasts may disagree. When it comes to the GNOME desktop, many of the features seem to have been copied from the early versions of KDE, although both were developed roughly around the same time. Using the object-oriented technology in the creation of the desktop environment, GNOME offers many great advantages to users, such as a file manager, application tool bar, and interface styles.

The GNOME desktop, seen in Figure 4-10, offers the same workspace as the other window managers. The desktop area can hold links to applications in the form of icons. As you can see from Figure 4-10, there is a menu bar at the bottom, which you can also customize to hold additional programs icons.

You can access files through the menu in two ways. The first is through the GNOME button. Clicking the GNOME foot in the lower-left corner produces a menu from which you can launch programs. Or, you can right-click the desktop, which produces the same menu.

Included with GNOME are applets that run on the bar at the bottom. To add GNOME applets, right-click the bar and select Add Applet from the menu. Follow the menus to locate the applet you wish to add.

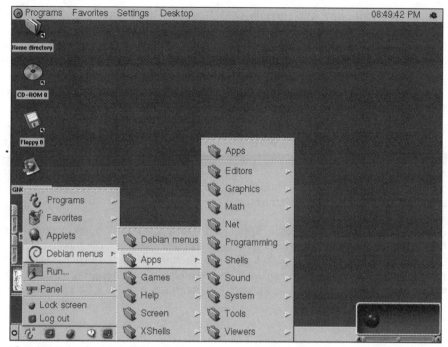

Figure 4-10: The GNOME desktop environment looks smooth with its fully functioning tool bar, menu, and desktop.

Installing GNOME

You can install GNOME through Debian's `dselect` application. To install GNOME, you must install `gnome-core`, `gnome-panel`, `gnome-session`, and `gnome-control-center`, plus any other dependent applications (there may be a number of them).

You can install as many of the GNOME-related applications as you want. Using `gnome` as a keyword, search in `dselect` for related applications. Some of these applications may not be official GNOME applications, but they may be worth installing anyway.

Once you have the main applications installed, you can run GNOME by executing `gnome-session`. GNOME still needs a window manager to run, so it uses the system default. You can also add whatever applications you want to start up automatically in the `.xsession` or `.xinitrc` file in your home directory.

When a GNOME user shuts down, GNOME saves the workspace (including open GNOME applications) and reopens them the next time the user starts GNOME. This process differs from that of the standard window managers, which only open what you configure them to open.

> **Note**   Some people are turning to Helix-GNOME for their installation of GNOME. They do
> have an easy installation for many distributions—even for Debian. You can reach
> the Helix-GNOME site at `www.helixcode.com/desktop/`. However, you may
> have trouble when you upgrade to the next version of Debian because HelixCode
> does not always hold to the Debian file system standards.

The GNOME control panel

The *GNOME control panel* enables you to customize the settings, themes, and features of the desktop without editing a file to make the change. The GNOME control
panel is more than a customizing tool for the GNOME interface; it also controls
aspects of other systems like MIME type, hardware, and more. (MIME stands for
Multipurpose Internet Mail Extensions, which lets e-mail, Web browsers, and other
applications send and receive messages containing predefined file types.)

Besides setting a desktop theme, appearance, and screen saver, you can also use
the GNOME control panel to set the default window manager. It even gives you the
capability to try it while you watch. To set any changes made to the GNOME settings, you must click the OK button. If you don't keep the changes or discard them
with a cancel, the control panel category turns to red to indicate a changed area.

KDE

The *K Desktop Environment (KDE)* has gained the attention of the Linux world along
with the GNOME desktop. KDE was designed to function similarly to the Windows
95/98/Me/NT/2000 operating systems interface, but it has superior features. You
have access to the desktop area, start/application bar (which includes the time),
links on the desktop as icons, and more.

As KDE develops, more applications are developed for it. There are literally hundreds
of KDE-specific applications ranging from databases to administrative tools. You can
find more information about KDE and its sundry applications at `www.kde.org`.

Installing KDE

KDE is available in the Debian distribution, which makes it easy to install. You can
find the installation package in the Debian archive as a task or install individual
packages. You may need to dig a little to find all the files if you install individual
packages. I recommend using the `task-kde` package for convenience.

Starting KDE

Every window environment needs to use a window manager. In KDE's case, it can
use its own window manager—the KDE window manager (`kwm`). Starting this window manager is a little different; you still need to edit the `.xsession` file, but
instead of naming the window manager to execute, just add `startkde` to the file.

If you prefer to have a graphical interface throughout, use kdm at startup instead of xdm, which gets loaded by default when X loads. You can find links to the file in /etc/init.d and on the run level directories. (See Chapter 15 for more information about setting up run levels.)

Setting up the desktop

As you can see from Figure 4-11, the KDE desktop is very similar to Windows 98/NT. As you will see after some use, KDE offers more flexibility than Windows 98/NT. There is a control bar at the bottom of the screen. The first button contains all the system's menus. They enable you to access the installed applications. Next, you have the menu of all the open applications followed by an icon that minimizes all opened windows to reveal the desktop. The next item on the bar initiates access to the KDE Control Center. To the right of that is the four-button area for the virtual desktops. Beyond the virtual desktop access buttons is the launch area for applications.

 Note   You can right-click any non-button area of the application bar and select Panel Menu: Configure from the menu to start making your own custom changes to the bar's behavior, menus, and many other features.

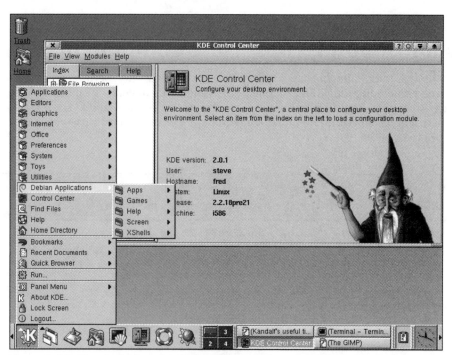

Figure 4-11: The desktop area of KDE offers a variety of configuration options.

The desktop area of KDE offers a variety of configuration options. Applications that are running appear as icons on the top bar. The application bar exists for all desktops, so accessing open applications is quick and easy. When an application is minimized, it becomes an icon on the bar and disappears when the application closes.

Another component of the KDE desktop is the use of themes. Anything goes when customizing the interface. Like GNOME and some of the other interfaces, you can use themes with the interface to convey a particular look. You can collect these themes from many sites, or you can create your own theme.

KDE Control Center

The *Control Center* is the configuration tool for KDE, which is accessible from the application bar or from the K menu. From the Control Center, you can customize the KDE interface graphically. Similar to the GNOME control panel, you can configure such things as the startup login display (kdm), the desktop environment, the hardware settings, and much more.

The Control Center enables you to configure areas you might not have considered before. The more you customize your interface, the more you'll find you like it.

Troubleshooting Your New Components

Although the Debian packages have extensive configuration scripts, you may still need help configuring XFree86, one of the window managers, or one of the desktop environments. Table 4-5 lists some Web sites where you can find FAQs, installation instructions, and other helpful documentation. For other hardware information, turn to Chapter 19.

Table 4-5 Important informational Web sites	
www.xfree86.org	The XFree86 Web site
www.fvwm.org	The FVWM window manager home page
www.enlightenment.org	The Enlightenment home page
www.windowmaker.org	The Window Maker home page
www.gnome.org	The GNOME Web site
www.kde.org	The KDE Web site

Another resource is the Debian user mailing list, found at `www.debian.org/support`. Here you can ask other users for their help. Or try one of the Usenet newsgroups, such as `muc.list.debian.user`.

For help with video cards, contact the manufacturer. Many of the manufacturers include support for Linux. Often, you can find the support on their Web sites. Because there are so many video cards out there, it is very difficult to give specific help. You can also seek help from one of the user groups. If you are having trouble, chances are someone else has gone through the same struggle.

Summary

Now that you understand that viewing a graphical interface to applications is a little more involved in Linux than in other operating systems, you can see the importance of the client/server model. It reduces the overhead of the applications, places the responsibility of the actual display on the server, and lets the application do its thing.

The window managers supply the connection between the application and the server, which does the work (in graphics terms). You can find links to other window managers at `www.plig.org/xwinman/`. Most window managers allow extensive customization through configuration files. Some are starting to use graphical interfaces to make them easier to change, such as in the case of Window Maker. You can find one that fits your tastes.

When you want more than a window manager — something that resembles the Windows 95/98 world — look to the desktop environments GNOME and KDE.

✦   ✦   ✦

Networking

If you always work on one computer as your workstation and the only time it gets connected to anything is when you use a modem to dial out, stick around to see what you are missing. Networks have been around nearly as long as computers have.

The best part about connecting the computers on a network is that it allows them to work together. These connected computers do not become supercomputers, but they communicate with each other and thereby enable you to share information among them. This, in turn, enables you to utilize their power more fully. This chapter takes you though networks, what they are, and how to get your Debian Linux computer connected to another machine.

Components of the Linux Network

There are two main aspects of a network—the hardware and the software. First, simple network hardware consists of a network interface card (NIC) in each computer, network cables, and a hub to connect them all. On the complex end of the network hardware scale, you have routers; switches; an array of file, print, mail, and Web servers; and so on. All of this hardware can be arranged in any number of ways to make up a network.

Demand and need determine the complexity of the network. A small office of 10 to 20 workstations may only need one server and a connection to that server from all the workstations.. On the other hand, a large multilocation corporation may require dedicated servers to provide specific tasks for a subset of the whole corporation (for example, a mail server servicing a single floor of a building). The network to those severs can include routers, bridges, and gateways to allow the workstations access to the servers. An enthusiast, on the other hand, may only have two computers at home that he or she wants to network together. As you can see, the potential is great and the opportunities abound to create your own network.

Figure 5-1 illustrates an example of two networks sharing a server between them. In this figure, you see 6 computers connected to network 1. (Each computer has its own IP address for its network. You can learn more about IP addresses chapter.) Network 2 only has three computers connected to it. However, one computer (Earth) is connected to both networks. This is just an example of one network layout.

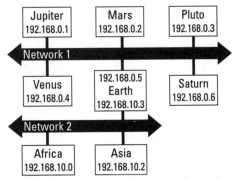

Figure 5-1: Two networks joined through one computer (Earth)

The software aspect of the network is much less romantic. All computers communicate using some form of protocol. These protocols are standardized and are generally determined by the preferred protocol of the servers on the network. For instance, UNIX/Linux prefers to use the TCP/IP protocol (the standard for the Internet), while Novell servers prefer IPX. Most everyone is moving to support TCP/IP because of the Internet. Let's start by exploring the software protocol, and then we'll move on to the physical side of the network.

TCP/IP Network Protocols

The default protocol for Linux is the *Transmission Control Protocol/Internet Protocol (TCP/IP)*. This protocol allows two computers to establish a connection and exchange data. Included with this apparent duo protocol is the *User Datagram Protocol (UDP)*, which is a connectionless protocol that makes TCP/IP an actual trio. Now, let's dig into the protocols themselves to gain an understanding of how they work.

All the transferred data eventually gets broken down into something called IP packets. These are very small pieces of data. Each piece of data gets wrapped with identifying information that includes where the packet originates, its destination, and other important information regarding the packet. This Internet Protocol is complex and would take quite a bit of time to explain in detail. Entire books are dedicated to explaining this protocol. The important thing to note here is that IP uses a set of numbers to identify each computer. You can see these numbers assigned to the computers shown in Figure 5-1.

TCP, the connection-based protocol, rides on top of the IP protocol in that it establishes the connection, splits the data into the IP packets to send as a stream of consecutive data, receives the packets of information, and finally reassembles the data from the sent packets. If a packet is missing or corrupt, TCP requests that it be transmitted again.

In contrast to TCP, UDP is a packet-oriented protocol, which has nothing to do with TCP/IP. This protocol is connectionless, does not have built-in missing packet checking, and does not check the order the packets' arrival. Because this protocol requires less overhead, it can be more efficient when used with small amounts of data on a fast connection such as a local Ethernet network.

On top of these protocols ride the network applications themselves. Any application that utilizes the network (such as Telnet, FTP, and others) must use TCP/IP to communicate with the other computers.

IP addresses

Now that you understand that each IP packet knows its source and destination, it's time to learn how these little packets are addressed. Every machine connected to a network must have an IP address associated with it. This address is usually bound to a network interface card and consists of four sets of numbers ranging from 0 to 255. Each of the four sets of numbers is separated by a period (.) to make the IP address look like 192.168.125.10 as an example. Each number (192) represents a series of 1s and 0s totaling eight (11000000). This is called *base-2* or *binary*, which is what computers understand. Humans better understand *base-10* or *decimal*. Regardless, the format of the decimals is most important.

These numbers are not arbitrary, but assigned so that no two devices share the same IP address. One organization, known as Internet Assigned Numbers Authority, ultimately assigns the numbers. You cannot go to this organization directly; you must get your numbers from your Internet Service Provider (ISP) who gets its numbers from its upstream registry. Networks that are not connected to the Internet still follow the same numbering conventions, but they may use private IP numbers that are set aside for the specific purpose of private networks.

Note   Currently, the IP standard (version 4) of numbers includes four sets of 8-bit numbers totaling 32 bits (in binary form). This standard was recently updated to IPv6 and approved to begin implementing by the regional registry organizations. The IPv6 standard uses eight sets of 16-bit numbers totaling 128 bits. This new standard includes the use of the current IPv4 numbers. The last 32 bits of the IPv6 address are the same as the IPv4 address. It will take some time for this implementation to filter down to user machines, but realize its coming.

Network classes

These IP numbers are broken down into two parts—the network and the host. The beginning of the network part determines to which of the three classes (A, B, or C) the address belongs. Table 5-1 shows the correlation between the class, the network portion of the address, and the host portion in which *a, b, c,* and *d* are all decimal numbers.

Table 5-1 IP class types			
Address Class	*Network*	*Host*	*Size*
A	*a*	*b, c, d*	16777216
B	*a, b*	*c, d*	65536
C	*a, b, c*	*D*	256

Classes basically define the number of available hosts (size column in Table 5-1) within each class. For instance, a network consisting of millions of computers needs a class A range of addresses. On the other hand, a small office of 30 computers can use part of a class C range.

Intermixed in these classes are sets of numbers reserved for use with private networks. These numbers are not recognized on the Internet as valid IP numbers, and therefore you should use them only with networks not intended to communicate directly with the Internet. Generally, networks that use private IP ranges never connect to the Internet or use a Firewall to connect to the Internet. (See Chapter 20 on setting up a Firewall.) Table 5-2 shows these sets of numbers.

Table 5-2 Private IP addresses		
Address Range From	*To*	*Network Class*
10.0.0.0	10.255.255.255	A
172.16.0.0	172.31.255.255	B
192.168.0.0	192.168.255.255	B

In addition to the private networks, a special series of IP addresses make up the *loopback network*. These addresses range from 127.0.0.0 to 127.255.255.255. Any number used in this range gets directed back to the host from where the packet comes. Typically, Linux sets this number to 127.0.0.1 and calls it `localhost`. This loopback address allows communication to take place within a system not connected to a network, as in the case with a standalone workstation.

Ports and services

Every TCP/IP address uses a list of ports; these ports are in numerical form and can be represented at the end of the IP address. For example, 192.168.0.16:80 uses port 80 of the IP address. The first 1,024 ports are reserved because they already have special functions. However, more ports are assigned all the time. Each port performs a specific service. For instance, port 80 is reserved for Web services. When you look up a Web page on the Internet, the request enters through port 80 of the destination computer. Table 5-3 shows a list of the common ports and their corresponding services.

Table 5-3 Common ports and services		
Port Number	*Service*	*Description*
21	FTP	File Transfer Protocol
23	Telnet	Remote Terminal Emulator
80	WWW	Web Server
110	POP3	Post Office Protocol version 3
443	https	Secure Web Server

You can find the list of these ports and matching services in the `/etc/services` file.

Netmasks

As you could imagine, a world full of computers all trying to talk to each other would be quite noisy. To limit the traffic throughout the world, each network uses a filter or network mask known as a *netmask*. This netmask is a number that gives the machine a better idea of the destination of the packet of information — local network or external.

Each section of the network portion of the IP address gets blocked, allowing the host part of the address to remain. For instance, a full class B address range has a netmask of 255.255.0.0, while a range of 32 class C addresses have a netmask of 255.255.255.224. You know that computers read the binary numbers, so convert a couple of IP addresses into their binary equivalents:

```
192.168.12.32 = 11000000 10101000 00001100 00100000
192.168.12.63 = 11000000 10101000 00001100 00111111
```

Not only is this a block of 32 IP addresses, but you can also see that only the last five binary digits have changes. The netmask for this address range is:

```
255.255.255.224 = 11111111 11111111 11111111 11100000
```

You can never use the first and last IP address of the range. The first number of the address range is the network address, and it identifies the network. The last address is the broadcast address, which all the computers on the network listen for. This leaves you with a total of 30 assignable addresses.

The *gateway* makes the decision to either send the packet out or direct the packet internally. If the IP address falls outside of the range of local addresses, then the gateway decides whether to allow the packet to pass to its destination. Your local machine considers the address assigned to its NIC its internal gateway to an external network. For some networks, a special computer with two NICs is the gateway between one network and another. With additional software, you can make that machine a firewall and a proxy server.

Cross-Reference   Chapter 20 discusses firewalls and proxy servers in detail.

Understanding Host Names

Each computer or host on a network that has an IP address assigned to it can be referred to by name instead of by address. Within a UNIX/Linux network, all hosts and their corresponding addresses traditionally are recorded in a host file: /etc/hosts. The computer translates these names into IP addresses in order to complete whatever commands you issue to the computer involving another computer like ping.

Note   The name you assign to your machine is called its *host name*. That name is stored in the /etc/hostname file on your machine. Change it and you change the name of your machine.

Referring to Figure 5-1, each of the computers on the networks has a host name assigned to it. This is the creative, fun part of the system administration where you get to set a theme for your network. The illustration shows that the hosts from one network are named after planets (Mars, Venus, and so on), while the others use names of continents (Africa, Asia, and so on). You can use your own ideas for naming the hosts in your network. You may have more systems than can fit a limited list of names (such as the planets), so you may decide that a name/number scheme is better (such as 166AE01, 166AE02, 166AE03, and so on).

The addresses and their corresponding names get entered in the `hosts` file. Here is an example of the file:

```
# Loopback address
127.0.0.1      localhost
# Our machine
192.168.0.2  Mars
# Other hosts
192.168.0.1  Jupiter
192.168.0.3  Pluto
192.168.0.4  Venus
192.168.0.5  Earth
192.168.0.6  Saturn
```

The loopback address entry in this example refers to the systems internal connector that allows network communication to occur within the computer itself. The other entries in the example identify the other computers on the network.

 Tip The code lines starting with the pound sign (#) are commented out (the computer does not read them). Therefore, you can use comments to group entries, which enables you to record a history for the file.

Understanding Domain Names and the DNS

Because humans cannot comprehend the binary language of computers nor distinguish very well among IP addresses, *domain names* were formed. With the onset of the World Wide Web, domain names have permeated the media. These names are important because they refer to an IP address pointing to some computer somewhere on the Internet. Much like the association in the /etc/hosts file, domain names refer to addresses all over the world through the Internet.

Domain names, like IP addresses, cannot be pulled out of a hat. You must register a domain name with a registering service such as Network Solutions, Register.com, or others. Therefore, you can only register a domain name that has not been registered before. These registering services update a global listing for all domains in the world to prevent duplication.

You can add the host name to the beginning of the domain name, assign an IP address to it, and include it the /etc/hosts file. Or you can use the *Domain Name Service (DNS)* to do the same thing. The DNS resolves domain names with their IP address for the entire Internet as well as for a small network. To do this, the DNS relies on the *bind* package to make the lookups between the name and the number. Bind is the application used in Linux to perform the Domain Name Services.

Note   Linux can utilize the native /etc/hosts file, as well as DNS services, to look up IP addresses. The hosts file works great for networks where systems rarely change. For large networks and the Internet, where changes occur all the time, DS works much better.

Every domain list in your DNS is called a *zone*. Each zone has two files for its database — one to match IP addresses to the host name, the other to match the host name to the IP address.

Assuming the you have bind installed, the file that contains the IP address to host name match for the local machine localhost is /etc/bind/db.local, and it looks like this:

```
; BIND data file for local loopback interface
;
$TTL    604800
@       IN      SOA     localhost. root.localhost. (
                            1           ; Serial
                        604800          ; Refresh
                         86400          ; Retry
                       2419200          ; Expire
                        604800 )        ; Negative Cache TTL
;
@       IN      NS      localhost.
@       IN      A       127.0.0.1
```

This file shows all the important DNS information for the localhost name. Lines beginning with the at sign (@) indicate a specific DNS entry. All text following a semi-colin (;) gets ignored and is considered a comment. The name of the file also comes into play, as it indicates the name of the domain. The counterpart to this file is /etc/bind/db.0, which contains:

```
; BIND reverse data file for broadcast zone
;
$TTL    604800
@       IN      SOA     localhost. root.localhost. (
                            1           ; Serial
                        604800          ; Refresh
                         86400          ; Retry
                       2419200          ; Expire
                        604800 )        ; Negative Cache TTL
;
@       IN      NS      localhost.
```

The same goes with this file. The main difference with these files are their names. The localhost zone may not do much for Internet lookups, but it does provide a starting point. Additionally, you can add more files to the DNS for the additional zones. As an example of adding a new domain, add the file, db.mydomain. This new file looks like this:

```
mydomain.net.   IN SOA host1.mydomain.net. root.mydomain.net. (
                         1                  ; Serial
                         604800             ; Refresh
                         86400              ; Retry
                         2419200            ; Expire
                         604800 )           ; Negative Cache TTL
;
;   Name Servers
;
mydomain.net.   IN NS   srv1.mydomain.net.
mydomain.net.   IN NS   srv2.mydomain.net.
;
;   Address for canonical names
;
localhost.mydomain.net.   IN A        127.0.0.1
www.mydomain.net.         IN A        192.168.0.2
ftp.mydomain.net.         IN A        192.168.0.3
srv1.mydomain.net.        IN A        192.168.0.4
srv2.mydomain.net.        IN A        192.168.0.5
;
;   Aliases
;
main.mydomain.net.        IN CNAME    srv1.mydomain.net.
jr.mydomain.net.          IN CANEM    srv2.mydomain.net.
```

The file for this zone includes information to associate IP addresses with names such as Web addresses, FTP hosts, and specific machine names. The file also includes alias information pointing one name to another real name. The corresponding file, db.0.168.192, looks like this:

```
0.168.192.in-addr.arpa.   IN SOA host1.mydomain.net.
root.mydomain.net. (
                         1                  ; Serial
                         604800             ; Refresh
                         86400              ; Retry
                         2419200            ; Expire
                         604800 )           ; Negative Cache TTL
;
;   Name Servers
;
0.168.192.in-addr.arpa.    IN NS   srv1.mydomain.net.
0.168.192.in-addr.arpa.    IN NS   srv2.mydomain.net.
;
;   Addresses that point to canonical name
;
2.0.168.192.in-addr.arpa.    IN PTR www.mydomain.net.
3.0.168.192.in-addr.arpa.    IN PTR ftp.mydomain.net.
4.0.168.192.in-addr.arpa.    IN PTR srv1.mydomain.net.
5.0.168.192.in-addr.arpa.    IN PTR srv2.mydomain.net.
```

You can see the similarities between these two files. The entries in each file look similar even though they are reversed. Notice that the IP address entries are in reverse order; the last number of the IP address gets entered first. This can be a little confusing at first glance. For more information, refer to the documentation for bind.

Each zone file gets listed in the `/etc/bind/named.conf` configuration file so the DNS server, `named`, knows the zone exists. For the *mydomain* example above, you add the following to the config file:

```
zone "mydomain" {
        type master;
        file "/etc/bind/db.mydomain";
};

zone "0.168.192.in-addr.arpa" {
        type master;
        file "/etc/bind/db.0.168.192";
};
```

This indicates that both files are primary entries for that zone, and it also tells you where to find the location of the files.

Hopefully, you now have a better understanding of name services and Internet hosting. Even though this is a brief description, it should be enough for you to get started. You can find more information online at `http://www.linuxdoc.org/HOWTO/DNS-HOWTO.html`.

Setting Up the Physical Network

The most common form of network uses the Ethernet. However, there are several other means by which two or more computers can communicate with one another, such as with a *parallel cable* (only two computers), *cross over cable* (again, only two computers), or *token ring* (another form of a network). Ethernet is so popular, so I only discuss Ethernet networks. The key components to the Ethernet network are:

✦ **Ethernet cards**—Each computer on the network must have an Ethernet card to communicate on the network.

✦ **Hubs and switches**—Every computer connects to a hub, which is a centralized location(s) where every computer can connect. (Newer technologies include switches).

✦ **Cables**—Special cables connect the computer's Ethernet card and the hub.

These are the basic components of the Ethernet network. Let's take a look at each of these in more depth.

Ethernet cards

The Ethernet card needs to be included in the kernel when it is compiled. The base install includes most, if not all, the driver modules available. Common compatible cards are:

✦ 3Com Vortex/Boomerang (3C59x/3C9x)

✦ 3Com 3C509

✦ Kingston KNE120TX

✦ DEC Tulip (21xxx)

✦ NE2000

These are just a few cards that work with the Debian kernel. Many manufacturers of Ethernet cards include instructions on making their cards work with Linux.

 See Chapter 15 for more details on the Linux kernel.

When you look for an Ethernet card, you begin to run across terms such as 10BaseT, 100BaseTX, and 10/100 Fast Ethernet. These terms indicate the speed of the network card. The 10, also known as 10BaseT, means that the network traffic is rated for 10Mbps (megabits per second). Likewise, 100 (also known as 100BaseTX) represents 100 Mbps.

Hubs and switches

The *hub* ties the network together and allows the computers to talk to one other. Hubs come in fixed speed ratings, generally 10Mbps and 100Mbps. However, the modern 10/100 hubs can adjust to either speed of the NIC connected to it. Hubs that are fixed at 10 Mbps or 100 Mbps are limited to only communicate with like speed NICs.

Switches are like hubs in that they also allow the computers to communicate. The difference is that each line coming into the switch can be connected directly to another port on the switch — the switch translates the information from one port to the other port. (A port on a hub or switch refers to a connection. If a hub has eight ports, it can connect up to eight devices.) This reduces the number of collisions of packets on the network, ultimately increasing the efficiency of the network. In contrast, a hub is like a room full of people trying to talk to each other from across the room all at once. A switch puts only the people together who are participating in the conversation.

Cables

The cables for your network are just as important as the other components. If you use the wrong cables, you may experience intermittent or erratic connections or no networking capabilities at all. Therefore, it is better to start out with as few problem areas as possible.

For most situations, buying cables is the preferred choice. Typically, the standard cable lengths work fine (within a couple of feet). Occasionally the need arises in which a standard length cable doesn't work and a special one must be made. Some computer stores make custom cables, so it never hurts to ask.

You can also make your own cables. Both 10BaseT and 100BaseTX use the same wiring for the cables. I suggest using Category 5 Ethernet cable because it is rated for the faster communication speeds. On either end of the cable is an RJ-45 connector (see Figure 5-2), which looks like a larger version of a telephone cable end. Table 5-4 lists the pin connections and the color wire. The color of the wire is not as important as making sure that the pairs of wire remain consistent. Also, four connections are listed as optional, which means that those connections are not needed for 10BaseT or for 100BaseTX networks but are included for 100Base networks.

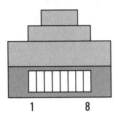

Figure 5-2: Front view of an RJ-45 connector showing the pin numbers

Table 5-4 Ethernet cable		
Connector 1 pins	**Wire color**	**Connector 2 pins**
1	Blue	1
2	Blue/White	2
3	Orange	3
4	Green	4 (Optional)
5	Green/White	5 (Optional)
6	Orange/White	6
7	Brown	7 (Optional)
8	Brown/White	8 (Optional)

Setting Up the Network

Setting up the network takes planning. You have to forecast the future of the network with projections and anticipate the current demands. For instance, a small office with three computers is very easy to deal with because the three computers can connect through one hub. Let's assume the projections for the business look good and a hiring spree is about to begin. It will result in 20 computers over the next five years. It is better to start the network with growth in mind. Large companies do this all the time as they plan for fluctuations in company size, usage loads, and resource demands.

After you plan the network, install the network cards into each computer, assemble the cables for all devices, and acquire a hub or switch, you're ready to start setting up the network. Figure 5-3 shows an example of how you set up a small, simple network of machines. The additional port of the hub provides the opportunity to expand the local five networked machines into a larger network, a bridge to a separate network, or a bridge to an Internet routing device. You may need to use a cross-over cable to connect hubs together unless the hub you use includes an uplink port. Most hubs and switches come in blocks of 8 (in other words 8, 16, and 24 port hubs).

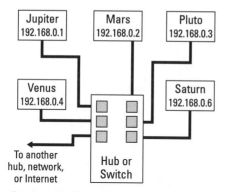

Figure 5-3: Five computers connected together through a hub or switch

Your network can be as complex or as simple as you need. Every environment is unique with unique requirements, so take the time to plan how to best set up your network.

For more information about other options to add to your network, see Chapter 20. It discusses firewalls and proxy servers that build a barrier of protection between your network and the Internet.

Making Changes to the Network

Occasionally, you might want to change your network settings on your Debian computer. You need to do so when changing ISPs or IP addresses, for example. Most of the computer settings are made when you first install Debian, so finding those settings can be difficult.

Making manual changes

Finding cool graphical interfaces to make changes to a network setting sometimes proves more difficult than just making the changes by hand. You should always know how to make changes by hand so that when things go wrong you know where look for the problems.

Earlier you learned about the /etc/hosts file. This file contains a reference between the IP address and the host name. What you now need to look at is the file that contains the information that associates the IP address with the Ethernet card. That file is called /etc/network/interfaces, and it contains all the network settings. Its contents normally look like this:

```
# /etc/network/interfaces
      # -- configuration file for ifup(8), ifdown(8)

# The loopback interface
iface lo inet loopback

# The first network card
      #- this entry was created during the Debian installation
# (network, broadcast and gateway are optional)
iface eth0 inet static
      address 192.168.0.26
      netmask 255.255.255.224
      network 192.168.0.0
      broadcast 192.168.0.31
      gateway 192.168.0.1
```

All the lines in this file starting with the pound sign (#) are comments. The two lines that start with iface define the network interfaces. Generally, the lo (localhost) interface gets set up regardless of whether you have any other NICs. The first NIC gets assigned the eth0, the next one would be eth1 and so on. The lines that follow the eth0 entry set the network parameters for the card.

Any changes to this file are reflected in the system. You don't have to restart the system for the changes to take effect. Instead, use the ifdown -a command string to take the interfaces offline and make the changes to the file. Then use the ifup -a command string to bring the modified interfaces back online.

Adding IP addresses to one Ethernet card

Under Linux, you can virtually reference more than one IP address with one Ethernet card. This is called *multihomed*, or *virtual, hosting*. This is a common practice when hosting Web sites for more than one domain. It's an easy process assuming that you know what to do.

Let's turn to the same file that you've been using — /etc/network/interfaces. You can manually add the required information to look like the following example:

```
# /etc/network/interfaces
    # -- configuration file for ifup(8), ifdown(8)

# The loopback interface
iface lo inet loopback

# The first network card
    # -- this entry was created during the Debian installation
# (network, broadcast and gateway are optional)
iface eth0 inet static
        address 192.168.0.26
        netmask 255.255.255.224
        network 192.168.0.0
        broadcast 192.168.0.31
        gateway 192.168.0.1

iface eth0:0 inet static
        address 192.168.0.23
        netmask 255.255.255.224
        network 192.168.0.0
        broadcast 192.168.0.31
        gateway 192.168.0.1
```

This is similar to how you would change the IP for a network card. The difference is that here you add a new interface by aliasing the real Ethernet card (eth0:0) with the new IP address. To change an address for a card, you just make changes to the existing file content. The rest of the information (netmask, network, broadcast, and gateway) is set to match the original, real network card. If you have more IP addresses to add, increase the alias number (such as eth0:1, eth0:2, and so on).

Troubleshooting the Network

The most frustrating part of administering a system can be tracking down problems. The key to solving those problems is knowing what tools you have at your disposal. Problems with a network can range from a bad physical connection to misconfigured software. The trick is learning the best methods of locating the problems.

Troubleshooting in general requires a series of logical steps or questions followed in a sequential order. You eliminate possibilities as you go along, much like a pilot's checklist to troubleshooting. Usually, you start with the physical (hardware) areas, and then you move to the software areas. Is the network card installed? Is the cable plugged in? Is it a working cable? Eventually you find the problem and can take the appropriate actions to solve it. Be sure to check these commons network areas when troubleshooting:

✦ Bad cable in which the cable does not work for whatever reason (broken internal wire, miswired homemade cable, and so on)

✦ Wrong device driver for the network interface card

✦ Missing or older module for the kernel version

✦ Misconfiguration of the interface (IP address, network, or gateway)

These are just a few of the common problem areas. There are a handful of tools — ifconfig, ping, traceroute, and route — that help you diagnose such problems. The next sections cover several of them.

Using dmesg to troubleshoot

The first line of defense — find out whether the modules loaded correctly.

```
$ dmesg | more
.
.
.
Adding Swap: 184736k swap-space (priority -1)
rtl8139.c:v1.07 5/6/99 Donald Becker http://cesdis.gsfc.nasa.gov/linux/drivers/r
tl8139.html
eth0: RealTek RTL8139 Fast Ethernet at 0x6900, IRQ 9, 00:c0:f0:46:0c:f2.
Serial driver version 4.27 with no serial options enabled
ttyS00 at 0x03f8 (irq = 4) is a 16550A
ttyS01 at 0x02f8 (irq = 3) is a 16550A
```

There is much more information displayed than shown here. Most of the information may not be of interest; however, other information can give incredible insight into problems. For instance, in this example, the NIC uses the RealTek RTL8193 driver module. If for some reason the driver could not communicate with the card, an error message would show up here. The same goes with other driver/hardware problems.

Using ifconfig to troubleshoot

This utility can actually make changes to the network settings in real time, but any changes must be redone after a restart of the system. However, this tool has its use in showing the current network settings. Note the configuration of my current network interfaces:

```
# ifconfig
eth0      Link encap:Ethernet  HWaddr 00:C0:F0:46:0C:F2
          inet addr:192.168.0.26  Bcast: 192.168.0.31  Mask:255.255.255.224
          UP BROADCAST RUNNING MULTICAST  MTU:1500  Metric:1
          RX packets:1788 errors:0 dropped:0 overruns:0 frame:0
          TX packets:525 errors:0 dropped:0 overruns:0 carrier:0
          collisions:0 txqueuelen:100
          Interrupt:9 Base address:0x6900

lo        Link encap:Local Loopback
          inet addr:127.0.0.1  Mask:255.0.0.0
          UP LOOPBACK RUNNING  MTU:3924  Metric:1
          RX packets:32 errors:0 dropped:0 overruns:0 frame:0
          TX packets:32 errors:0 dropped:0 overruns:0 carrier:0
          collisions:0 txqueuelen:0
```

Here you can see that eth0 and lo both show up. Were there a problem with the NIC for some reason, it would not show up at all. However, if it did show up and did not work, then you could glean information from the statistics like errors, dropped and such. This information may not be intuitive to look at but gives you clues when trying to track down problems.

By employing other options, you can use this tool to add, remove, and modify the properties of these interfaces without taking down the system. These changes take place in real time. Here is the syntax:

```
ifconfig [interface][options | address]
```

Table 5-5 explains the options.

Table 5-5
ifconfig options

Option	Description
interface	This refers to the identification of the network interface card or network adapter. Normally with Ethernet networks, the first network adapter is eth0, the second eth1, and so on. Other network adapters include ppp0 for point-to-point modem connections, sl0 for slip connections, and tr0 for token ring networks.
Up	When combined with an interface, this option activates that interface. If an address is given for the interface, up is implied.
Down	This option deactivates the specified interface immediately.
netmask addr	This option sets the netmask for the interface. A mask address must be provided.
broadcast addr	This option sets the broadcast address of the interface.
address	This is the IP address of the interface itself.

If the interface is added to the command, the status of that interface is displayed — active or not. When you use the command by itself, then all active interfaces are displayed. Including -a after the command means that all interfaces are displayed independent of active status. Ultimately, this command can show whether a device is working on a host, whether it's configured correctly, and whether it's active.

Using ping to troubleshoot

Whenever I have a question about a machine's capability to connect to other devices on the network, ping is my first choice. This small program essentially says to a remote computer, *"Hello, are you there?"* and waits for a response from that computer. If no response is given, then nothing gets returned and assumes that the two computers cannot talk for whatever reason. You start a ping by issuing the command and specifying the address or resolvable name of a remote machine. It continues until stopped with a CTRL+C command from the keyboard — unless the option -c num is given with the number num of tries. Here is an example of a bad connection:

```
# ping -c 10 192.168.0.10
PING 192.168.0.10 (192.168.0.10): 56 data bytes

--- 192.168.0.10 ping statistics ---
10 packets transmitted, 0 packets received, 100% packet loss
```

This example shows that 10 packets were sent to the remote IP address, but that none were received as confirmations. Only 10 packets were sent because of the count (–c) option. Without the count option, ping will continue until stopped with a CTL-C key sequence. Ping makes a good tool to make a quick check for network connectivity.

In this case, the IP address does not exist on my network. The last line reports on the ping activity with 100 percent loss on this try. Here's another example, but this time with a working domain name:

```
# ping -c 7 www.debian.org
PING www.debian.org (198.186.203.20): 56 data bytes
64 bytes from 198.186.203.20: icmp_seq=0 ttl=242 time=118.8 ms
64 bytes from 198.186.203.20: icmp_seq=1 ttl=242 time=108.7 ms
64 bytes from 198.186.203.20: icmp_seq=2 ttl=242 time=112.3 ms
64 bytes from 198.186.203.20: icmp_seq=3 ttl=242 time=111.3 ms
64 bytes from 198.186.203.20: icmp_seq=4 ttl=242 time=111.5 ms
64 bytes from 198.186.203.20: icmp_seq=5 ttl=242 time=115.9 ms
64 bytes from 198.186.203.20: icmp_seq=6 ttl=242 time=108.6 ms

--- www.debian.org ping statistics ---
7 packets transmitted, 7 packets received, 0% packet loss
round-trip min/avg/max = 108.6/112.4/118.8 ms
```

In this example, the ping completes with no losses, and the statistical results of the round trip times are displayed on the last line. Also, instead of using an IP address, I used a Web address that gets turned into an IP address before sending packets. I arbitrarily set the count to 7 for this test. As you can see, `ping` is an invaluable tool when diagnosing trouble on a network.

Using traceroute to troubleshoot

Nearly as important as `ping` is `traceroute`. This program maps the path the IP packets take to get to their destination. A packet of data may pass through many network devices (usually gateways) along the way. This is especially true with the Internet because it is made up of gateway upon gateway. You can think of the packet as an automobile driving across the country. As the car drives from New York to Chicago, it passes through several towns (think of them as gateways).

Here is an example of using `traceroute` on a Web site (www.debian.org):

```
# traceroute www.debian.org
traceroute to www.debian.org (198.186.203.20), 30 hops max, 38
byte packets
 1  10.156.83.31 (10.156.83.31)  1.944 ms  1.657 ms  1.638 ms
 2  10.146.169.142 (10.146.169.142)  20.040 ms  19.463 ms
    19.018 ms
 3  10.146.168.1 (10.146.168.1)  19.212 ms  20.197 ms
    19.076 ms
 4  207.251.151.89 (207.251.151.89)  26.763 ms  34.925 ms
    25.318 ms
 5  207.251.151.66 (207.251.151.66)  25.261 ms  51.066 ms
    55.571 ms
 6  seri3-1-0.chi-e100.gw.epoch.net (206.135.4.233)  53.008 ms
    113.708 ms  211.351 ms
 7  fast0-1-0.chi-c100.gw.epoch.net (155.229.126.161)
    27.000 ms  37.976 ms  37.071 ms
 8  seri9-0-0.dca-c100.gw.epoch.net (155.229.120.249)
    42.004 ms  41.741 ms  42.073 ms
 9  abovenet-eni.iad.above.net (216.200.254.117)  47.252 ms
    42.448 ms  48.701 ms
10  core1-core2-1.iad.above.net (209.249.0.21)  44.264 ms
    43.515 ms  45.584 ms
11  pao-iad-oc3.pao.above.net (207.126.96.145)  103.084 ms
    109.833 ms  104.334ms
12  via-abovenet.pao.via.net (216.200.254.178)  103.018 ms
    102.517 ms  102.829ms
13  209.81.23.54 (209.81.23.54)  200.284 ms  106.128 ms
    104.579 ms
14  va.debian.org (198.186.203.20)  104.597 ms  111.741 ms
    126.651 ms
```

In this example, the trace takes 13 hops with the destination as the fourteenth. Also notice that some of the hops record their host names as well as their IP addresses. Tracing the path of the packets can help to locate the trouble area of the network. If a trace fails at a specific location of your network, you know where to start looking into the problems further.

Using route to troubleshoot

The `route` command produces the *router table*. This table reports all the available networks, gateways, and hosts for this computer to access. Any computer, host, or domains (both real and virtual) are listed in the routing table. If this table produces incorrect data, the routes don't work. This problem shows up when you generate a report. Here is an example of the report that is generated when you execute `route`:

```
# route
Kernel IP routing table
Destination  Gateway       Genmask          Flags Metric Ref    Use Iface
localnet     *             255.255.255.224  U     0      0        0 eth0
localhost    *             255.0.0.0        U     0      0        0 lo
default      node-d8e9791.po 0.0.0.0        UG    0      0        0 eth0
```

In this example, you see a listing for the local network. It has no gateway defined, indicated by the asterisk (*). The flags indicate the status of the entry. For instance, the U flag indicates an up status and the G flag indicates this entry is the gateway for the interface eth0. Table 5-6 shows the possible flags and their meanings. The last line reads that it is the default gateway out of the localnet network showing the name of the associated IP address. This report comes from the routing table of a computer on a small network. Routing tables for large networks can take up many pages.

> **Note**
> Using the `route` command without any options produces a report with all IP addresses represented as their host names. You can use the option `-n` to display only IP addresses. This can help when you're trying to find specific addresses or making sure that an address falls in the range of the table.

Table 5-6 Routing flags	
Flag code	*Description*
U	The route is up.
H	The target is a host.
G	Use this as a gateway.
R	Reinstate this route for dynamic routing.
D	Dynamically installed by daemon or redirect
M	Modified from routing daemon or redirect
A	Installed by addrconf
C	Cache entry
!	Reject route

The `route` command also adds information to the table. Here are some examples of adding routes to the table:

✦ `route add isphost ppp0`—Adds the route to the isphost host via the PPP interface, assuming that isphost is the PPP host

✦ `route add -net 192.168.32.0 netmask 255.255.255.0 gw isphost`— This command line adds the network 192.168.32.x to be gatewayed using the route to the PPP interface (preceding).

✦ `route add -net 192.168.76.0 netmask 255.255.255.0 dev eth0`— This line adds a route to the network 192.168.76.x via the device `eth0`. You can find an entry similar to this one in most routing tables to let the local machine know its local network. The IP address and netmask will change base on the environmet.

✦ `route add default gw toad-gw`—Adds a default route (`toad-gw`) as a gateway. The device actually used for that route depends on how you can reach `toad-gw` (assuming the static route to `toad-gw` is set up already).

These examples show how to add routes to the table. There are other command options that enable you to remove routes, restrict routes, and more. Look at the online documentation for complete details. Typically, there are machines dedicated to routing for complex networks. In most cases with small networks, little routing is needed.

Summary

You should have an understanding of how data is transferred on a network, what constitutes a network, and the key components to setting up a network. This area alone is a career path for some individuals as they strive to master routers, gateways, and networks across the country.

If you are looking for your own domain name, try these services:

✦ Network Solutions at www.networksolutions.com

✦ Register.Com at `www.register.com`

The topics covered in this chapter may not be as in-depth as you need for your situation, or they may not cover the specific questions you might have. You can look into the following helpful Web pages. They are geared specifically to the topic, and they try to explain how to perform that task. Keep in mind though that these Web sites don't address any specific distribution of Linux.

✦ `www.linuxdoc.org/HOWTO/Chroot-BIND-HOWTO.html`

✦ `www.linuxdoc.org/HOWTO/DNS-HOWTO.html`

✦   ✦   ✦

Setting Up for the Internet

The biggest concern for the average user is applying Linux as a workstation. The workstation enables a person to perform normal functions such as writing letters, sending e-mail, reading news, and browsing the Internet. This is true for both office environments as well as for home use.

Those workstations in an office environment are generally less concerned with a connection to the Internet . This chapter covers the process of connecting to the Internet through a dial-up connection. There are other means of connecting, which typically involve the use of a network connection through a cable modem, ISDN router, or DSL router.

Once a connection is made to the Internet, a whole new world of applications awaits. This chapter also explores those applications associated with Internet use, some of which are specific to intermittent connections with a server as found with dial-up use. You can use the other applications I describe whether you have a full-time connection or an intermittent dial-up connection to the Internet.

Connecting to an ISP

For those just getting started with Linux, establishing an Internet connection is the most important part of the setup. The thought of getting it to work may intimidate you, so take a deep breath and relax.

There are two types of connection protocols: *Point-to-Point Protocol (PPP)* and *Serial Line IP (SLIP)*. SLIP is a much less efficient protocol and is rarely used. Conversely, PPP has become the standard protocol for modem communication. Both protocols allow the transmission of IP over a telephone line.

When connecting to the Internet, you need an Internet Service Provider (ISP) that also has modems into which you can dial. These modems have all the information necessary for dialing in.

Using wvdial to connect

The default, and probably the easiest dial-up client to use, is the `wvdial` utility. It lives up to its name as the intelligent PPP dial-up client by automatically negotiating the connection with the Internet whenever you issue the command.

When you install `wvdial` from the command, you are asked questions for configuring it. You need to know the phone number you dial to access the Internet Service Provider (ISP), the account name used for dialing in, and the password for the account. Follow these steps to configure `wvdial`:

1. When asked if you want to configure `wvdial`, answer Yes.

2. The next three questions ask for information about the dial-in account. The installation process assumes that you only have one account, and therefore asks the appropriate questions based on the one account.

   Add the telephone number. Don't include any special characters (such as parentheses, hyphens, or slashes) except those needed to dial the ISP. If you must add a pause to the number, use a comma for a 3-second pause. You can also add any number codes to disable features with the telephone as recommended by the ISP and/or the telephone company.

   Then add the account login name. This is the name of the account that the ISP assigns you when you sign up. Some ISPs include a special character, such as a dollar sign, to help keep their systems secure. The ISP can help with this information.

   Finally, enter the password that you were set up with for the account. As you type the password, notice that you cannot see what you are typing. However, you can clearly see this information if you look at the configuration file.

3. You are then asked to confirm that the information is correct. Answer Yes to this question to continue.

   As the configuration finishes, the script polls the serial devices for a modem. The found modem is added to the configuration file. You should turn on any external modems before the script queries for a modem.

You can find all the information you enter in the configuration file at `/etc/wvdial.conf`. Now that `wvdial` is configured, you just need to issue the command from a root shell. Then you should see something resembling the following dialog:

```
--> WvDial: Internet dialer version 1.41
--> Initializing modem.
--> Sending: ATZ
ATZ
```

```
OK
--> Sending: ATQO V1 E1 SO=0 &C1 &D2 S11=55 +FCLASS=0
ATQO V1 E1 SO=0 &C1 &D2 S11=55 +FCLASS=0
OK
--> Modem initialized.
--> Sending: ATDT 5551234
--> Waiting for carrier.
ATDT 5551234
CONNECT 115200
--> Carrier detected.  Waiting for prompt.
Welcome to the ISP DIGITAL Network
You are connected to:
iq-ind-as007 on slot:11/mod:17 at 10:47pm
ISP Login:
--> Looks like a login prompt.
--> Sending: myname
myname
Password:
--> Looks like a password prompt.
--> Sending: (password)
PPP session from  209.43.51.117 to  198.70.144.213 beginning...
[7f][03]@![01][01][1f][01][04][05]\[02][06][7f][7f][7f][7f][05]
[06]^[19][7f]0[07][02][08][02][11][04][05]\[13][03]~[7f]}#@!}!}
"}}?}!}$}%\}"}&[7f][7f][7f][7f]}%}&^}9[7f]0}'}"}(}"}1}$}%\}3}#}
;a~
--> PPP negotiation detected.
--> Starting pppd at Sun Oct 15 18:17:11 2000
```

If you press Ctrl+C, wvdial attempts to close the connection in a friendly fashion.

Using diald to connect

If you wish to connect to the Internet every time a request is made, then you want diald. Called *dial on demand*, diald functions in small offices and homes where a temporary dial-up connection is used without the need to manually connect.

diald monitors the traffic and determines if a connection needs to be made for requests going outside of the local network. Once the connection is established, diald monitors the connection to determine if it should shut down the link due to inactivity.

You need to change some settings for diald to work properly. The following script file, /etc/diald/connect, contains the settings that you need to change (specifically, the ones in boldface).

```
#!/bin/sh
# Copyright (c) 1996, Eric Schenk.
# Copyright (c) 1997, 1998 Philippe Troin <phil@fifi.org> for Debian GNU/Linux.
#
# $Id:$
#
```

```
# This script is intended to give an example of a connection script that
# uses the "message" facility of diald to communicate progress through
# the dialing process to a diald monitoring program such as dctrl or diald-top.
# It also reports progress to the system logs. This can be useful if you
# are seeing failed attempts to connect and you want to know when and why
# they are failing.
#
# This script requires the use of chat-1.9 or greater for full
# functionality. It should work with older versions of chat,
# but it will not be able to report the reason for a connection failure.

# Configuration parameters

# When debugging a connection, set DEBUG to -v to increase chat's
# verbosity and to report on this script's progress.
# WARNING: THIS MIGHT CAUSE YOUR PASSWORD TO SHOW UP IN THE SYSTEM LOGS
# DEBUG=-v

# The initialization string for your modem
MODEM_INIT="ATZ&C1&D2%CO"

# The phone number to dial
PHONE_NUMBER="5551212"

# If the remote system calls you back, set to 1; otherwise leave to 0.
CALLBACK=0

# If you authentify using PAP or CHAP (that is let pppd handle the
# authentification, set this to 0.
AUTHENTIFY=1

# The chat sequence to recognize that the remote system
# is asking for your user name.
USER_CHAT_SEQ="name:--name:--name:--name:--name:--name:--name:"

# The string to send in response to the request for your user name.
USER_NAME="USER"

# The chat sequence to recongnize that the remote system
# is asking for your password.
PASSWD_CHAT_SEQ="word:"

# The string to send in response to the request for your password.
PASSWORD="PASSWORD"

# The prompt the remote system will give once you are logged in
# If you do not define this then the script will assume that
# there is no command to be issued to start up the remote protocol.
PROMPT="annex:"

# The command to issue to start up the remote protocol
PROTOCOL_START="ppp"
```

```
# The string to wait for to see that the protocol on the remote
# end started OK. If this is empty then no check will be performed.
START_ACK="Switching to PPP."
```

The first bolded text in the file refers to the command sequence used to initialize your modem. Every modem can use a different sequence, so you should refer to your modem's manual for the specifics.

The next bolded text is the phone number. Here you type the phone number for your ISP. Only use numbers unless you need a pause — in which case, you use a comma for a 3-second pause.

The user chat sequence is the prompt you receive if a terminal is connected to the ISP. Often this is ogin:, but it may include other greeting information. The ISP should know this information.

Next is the account name — the name given when you sign up with the ISP. Note that some ISPs add a character, such as a dollar sign, to the account name to increase security.

The password chat sequence is like the user chat sequence. This appears at the prompt when ready for the password. Again, the ISP should know this information.

Next, you enter the password for the dial-in account. There are no special secrets with this one.

Finally, the prompt appears when you are logged in to the remote system. This confirms to diald that the attempt succeeded and there were no errors.

In addition to changing the etc/diald/connect file, you may need to look at and change other files including diald.conf and diald.options. You also need to perform the following steps to get diald up and working:

1. Make a symbolic link of /dev/modem to the /dev/ttySx that points to your modem. Here is an example of creating this link:

   ```
   ln -s /dev/modem /dev/ttyS1
   ```

   This creates a link to the modem on COM1 (represented by /dev/ttyS1) to the device called modem. diald uses this device name in its configuration files. Doing this also enables you to change modem devices without having to remember to make changes to other configuration files.

2. Remove lines mentioned in /etc/init.d/diald. When you edit this file, look for the following:

   ```
   #Remove the following lines after configuration
   echo Please read /usr/share/doc/diald/README.Debian for help
   setting up
   exit 0
   ```

Remove these lines for `diald` to work properly. As it is, the `exit 0` entry in the file assumes that you have not made the configuration changes needed to let `diald` connect to your ISP.

3. You can then start the `diald` service manually by inputting `/etc/init.d/ diald start` from a command line. When first installed, `diald` is added to the default run level so that it runs normally the next time you restart your system. However, it did not run normally the last time you started because the lines mentioned in Step 2 were still in the initialization script.

From here on out, when someone wants to connect to a system, Web site, or machine outside of your local machine or network, `diald` makes those connections for you. This machine is now your gateway to the Internet.

Web Browsers

One of the most common reasons to dial into the Internet is to access the World Wide Web. To do this, you need a Web browser. There are several Web browsers available to you for Linux:

✦ **Lynx** — A text-only Web page viewer. This works great on virtual terminals in which graphics is a problem. You can follow links by browsing page after page.

✦ **Netscape** — This is a Linux port of the commonly known Windows version. The latest version includes Java, JavaScript, and other plug-in support.

✦ **Mozilla** — An Open Source Web browser project using the code released by Netscape. It is now the basis for the next generation of Netscape version 6.

✦ **Opera** — A commercial Web browser offering commonly available features

✦ **Konqueror** — A Web browser built for the latest K Desktop environment

I cover these browsers in more detail in Chapter 7, although this should give you an idea of the types of browsers available.

E-Mail Clients

E-mail has become the most common form of written communication. Now, instead of sending out a paper memo to departments, a department head sends out the same memo in an electronic message. Likewise, pen-pals shoot notes back and forth at near light speed.

The tools people use range from crude command-line programs to completely graphical interfaces. This section lists some of these tools, which offer a broad range of flexibility.

Balsa

This mail client is included when you install the Gnome desktop environment. Balsa is Gnome's mail tool. It has all the features required of a mail tool, such as the capability to create, send, and read mail. If for some reason Balsa is not installed with Gnome, you can add it through the Debian package manager.

When you launch Balsa for the first time, a graphical wizard guides you through the configuration. It asks you for the account name, e-mail address, server, and local mail directory. Make any changes to this information to ensure it is correct before proceeding. The next screen of the configuration process shows the paths for the mailboxes. Accept the defaults unless you are sure where to create them. You are then finished with the configuration of Balsa.

A ~/balsarc file for each account contains the configuration information, but you can change it through the interface under the Settings menu option. Figure 6-1 shows what the interface looks like when reading a message. To access the mailboxes, double-click the desired mailbox from the left-hand column. A tab appears on the right with the name of the mailbox. Clicking a message in that box makes it appear in the lower-right window where you can read it.

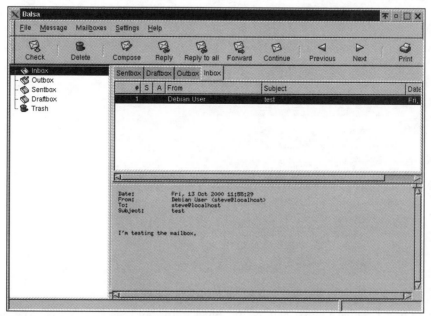

Figure 6-1: Reading a message with Balsa

You can create additional mailboxes from the Mailboxes menu option. Choosing Add from the menu initiates a wizard to acquire the needed information to create a mailbox. Once a new mailbox exists, you can organize your e-mail by highlighting it and then right-clicking the message for a menu to appear. From this menu, you can reply, forward, delete, and even transfer e-mail to another mailbox.

When creating a message to send, you can pick a name from the address book, which is extracted from the GnomeCard address book. GnomeCard is listed as the Address Book in the Applications section of the Gnome mail menu. You can add e-mail addresses to this address book for later retrieval in Balsa.

Note   Balsa is capable of using host names instead of domain names for sending mail. Most mail systems are connected to the Internet and therefore require fully quali-fied domain names. Private networks can send mail internally using a host name instead.

Netscape

Perhaps you first think of using Netscape as a browser. However, it also includes a fully functioning e-mail client. You have the advantage of using only one application for several functions. Another advantage is that when you browse a Web page and click a mailto link, a new message window appears for you to send an e-mail. Figure 6-2 shows the form used to create an e-mail message.

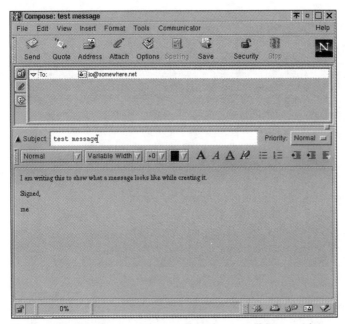

Figure 6-2: Creating a message using the e-mail form with Netscape Mail

You need to perform some customization for Netscape to work correctly. You can use the following instructions to set up Netscape for the first time or return to make changes at any time:

1. With the Netscape browser open, click the Edit menu item and select Preferences from the list of options.

2. From the left column of the dialog box, click the arrow next to Mail and Newsgroups. This expands a list of additional options.

3. Click the Identity item. From here, type the appropriate information about yourself in each field (name, e-mail address, and so on).

4. Click the Mail Servers. This displays the settings for the servers. The Add button enables you to add as many accounts as you need for picking up mail (as long as they are IMAP servers). You can have only one POP mail account. You can also set the outgoing mail server.

The details of the account — such as server names, type of server, and passwords — come from the ISP. You can change this information at any time using the preceding instructions.

Once the Netscape Mail is set up, you can access the mail, respond, and file the mail as you do with other mail tools.

mutt

You see a slightly different style of graphical interface with `mutt`. `mutt` is a text-based mail client that uses the full display. The top line shows available commands. The second-to-last line shows the status information, such as number of messages, number of old messages, and the total disk space used by the messages. The last line of the display shows any message from `mutt`-like commands, error messages, and other such messages.

`mutt` does not take any special configuration, and you can install it from the Debian package manager. Once installed, you can execute `mutt` from a command line or through the Debian Net menu under one of the desktops.

Once running, press the question mark (?) to receive help with the commands. Although the basic commands appear at the top of the screen, several more exist for simple, quick keystroke execution.

Tip   It is a good idea to become familiar with one of the text-based mail clients. When connecting to your systems remotely through a telnet session, you can still read your e-mail and respond to the messages. Some text-based clients may not work well under the virtual terminal session depending on the `telnet` client used on the remote system.

mail

On the basic virtual terminal, graphics cannot be displayed so the old standby is the text-based `mail`. This lists out, in a numbered fashion, the messages you have in your mailbox. This program is installed along with the basic system, and you execute it from the command line.

`mail`'s basic commands are a little less intuitive than those of `mutt` because its commands aren't displayed. Table 6-1 shows some of the more common commands you need to know.

Table 6-1
mail commands

Command	Description
R	Replies to the message
d	Deletes the message
u	Undeletes the message
h	Displays a one-line header of mailbox messages
n	Reads the *n* number message
l	Lists other commands
mail	Creates a new mail message
q	Quits the mail program

To create a message from within mail, issue `mail` *user* in which *user* is the e-mail address for the person you want to send the message. Press Enter; you are now prompted for the subject of the message. Type the subject you want to send. The next line begins the body of the message. When you are finished composing your message, press Ctrl+D at the beginning of a new line for the carbon copy prompt to send a copy of this message to anyone else.

Mail utilities

Some utilities are not a necessity, but rather a convenience. Tools such as new mail notification or utilities that grab the mail to be reviewed later are just a few types of mail utilities covered next. These niceties add to the power and automation available to you.

fetchmail

The first of the two mail utilities grabs e-mail off a remote system and then forwards it to your local system where you can read it at any time. `fetchmail`'s intended use is with dial on demand access.

Once you install the `fetchmail` and `fetchmailconf` packages using the Debian package manager system, run the `fetchmailconf` file from within an X Windows environment to configure `fetchmail`. Figure 6-3 shows the configuration introduction. There are two ways to configure `fetchmail`: using a novice or expert approach.

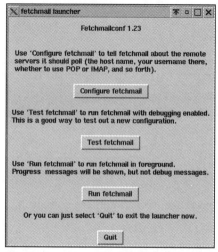

Figure 6-3: From fetchmailconf, you can configure, test, and run fetchmail.

Taking the novice approach allows for fewer controls than the expert option. Type a name where you see `New server` and then press Enter. This brings up a configuration dialog box for the intended server to which you want to attach. You can then fill in the information on the screen as appropriate.

The expert option gives you many more choices to fully customize aspects of the mail as it is captured and then forwarded (for example, rewriting the `To:`/`Cc:`/`Bcc:` fields).

You can use `fetchmail` to grab mail for as many accounts as you have access to on the remote system. Once you complete the configuration of `fetchmail`, a configuration file is created in your home directory called `fetchmailrc`. If this file does not exist, then `fetchmail` cannot run.

To retrieve mail using `fetchmail`, run it from the command line or start it up as a daemon using the `-d` option. You can then set it to check your remote mail every *n* seconds. Here is a command that runs `fetchmail` in the background and checks for new mail every 15 minutes:

```
$ fetchmail -d 900 &
```

You can get more information from one of the many resources on the Internet, such as `www.tuxedo.org/~esr/fetchmail`.

Tip   You can put the `fetchmail` background command in the `.bashrc`, `.login`, or `.profile` files (depending on the preferred shell or `.xsession` file for X users) so that `fetchmail` starts as a daemon after you log in.

biff

A standard program that is loaded with Debian is `biff`. This little program notifies you with a message that you have mail, but only in the virtual terminal. You can turn it on or off any time using:

```
$ biff y
```

or

```
$ biff n
```

When biff is turned on and you get a new message, you should see something like the following:

```
You have new mail in /var/spool/mail/jo
```

For those who use an X environment to work, `biff` has an X counterpart called `xbiff`. This shows a small picture of a mailbox, as seen in Figure 6-4. When new mail arrives, the flag goes up and beeps a notification. Clicking the mailbox lowers the flag.

Figure 6-4: The xbiff mailbox indicates that no new mail has arrived.

Those who need to know when new mail arrives may find one or both of these applications useful.

News Clients

News clients enable people to post messages to a type of message board based on a specific topic. There are over 20,000 different newsgroups to pick from, ranging from technical topics like programming, to sports, to jobs in a certain area of the world.

To read one of these newsgroups, you need to have a news client (also called a *newsreader*). There are several news clients to choose from, and each has its own characteristics.

PAN

An easy-to-use newsreader for X, PAN offers a straightforward configuration wizard for setting itself up. The configuration takes you through identifying who you are, the name of the news server to use, and e-mail information. The data for PAN is saved in ~/.pan/.

Once PAN starts, it downloads all the topics from the news server (which may take a while because of the large number of topics). You can then select a topic by double-clicking the left window. The list of current articles then appears in the upper-right window. Double-clicking one of those windows downloads the article so you can read it in the lower-right window (as seen in Figure 6-5).

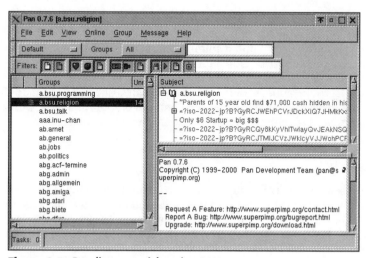

Figure 6-5: Reading an article using PAN

Threads, series of responses from a post, are viewed in a hierarchy. Click the plus sign to expand and the minus sign to contract. This helps to make sense of the seemingly endless messages.

PAN is a text reader with a graphical interface. Messages that include HTML- or MIME-encoded information show up in the raw form. With HTML messages, you see the code along with the message. With the encoded information, you also see the gibberish that makes up the file.

Netscape

With Netscape, the newsreader is mixed with the mail-reader portion. Netscape views messages containing HTML- and MIME-encoded files as they were originally meant to be viewed.

1. To configure the news portion of Netscape, click the Edit menu option and then Preferences. This brings up the Configuration dialog box.

2. Under the Mail and Newsgroups heading, click the arrow to expand the list of options. You should see an item labeled Newsgroup Servers. Click this item to display its configuration settings.

3. Click the Add button for the dialog box to enter the name of the news server. This information should be available through your ISP.

4. Click the appropriate buttons to accept the changes into place.

To subscribe to a newsgroup, right-click the server name you just configured. A dialog box appears to retrieve the list of topic names. You can either scroll through the list of names or type in the box to find a suitable newsgroup. Once you find a group to subscribe to, click the Subscribe button with the group highlighted.

All subscribed newsgroups appear under the server name. Click one of the topics. You should see the messages and the message contents on the right side. Unread messages appear in bold text; they appear in normal text after you read them.

tin newsreader

A text-based newsreader, tin gives you easy-to-use features that employ letters, numbers, and arrows to navigate and read messages. tin can read a message from either the local /var/spool/news directory or from a remote Network News Transport Protocol (NNTP) server. You can find the tin package among the non-free Debian packages.

When you first run the client, you can start it from the command line. If run as tin, the client looks locally for the news. Alternatively, if you use -g *server*, tin connects to the remote server for the news. The first time you run tin, it may take a few minutes as it downloads the topics. The subscribed newsgroups are saved in the

~/.newsrc file, and the server is specified in the ~/.tin/newsrctable file. Figure 6-6 shows what the interface looks like through the virtual terminal session.

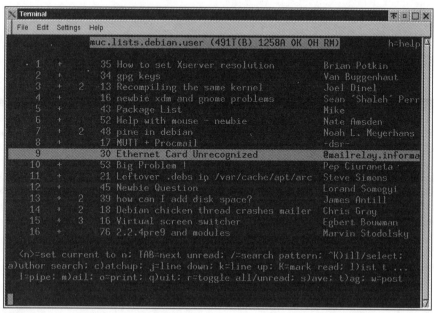

Figure 6-6: Reading news using tin

FTP Clients

Next to corresponding with e-mail and browsing the Internet, users want the ability to transfer files from machine to machine. Here, a special protocol called *File Transfer Protocol (FTP)* is used. It requires a special server and client to allow the transfer of these files over a network.

Chapter 22 discusses servers and clients in more detail. However, here is a list of some of the clients available with Debian:

   ✦ ftp — The standard command-line FTP client where you can retrieve and insert files on a remote computer

   ✦ ncftp — Offers pseudo-graphics for a terminal interface using the full-screen and single-key commands. This client offers the use of bookmarks for easier access to remote sites.

   ✦ xftp — Uses a graphical X window with buttons to click for transferring files

   ✦ gftp — A full functioning FTP client that enables you to see both the remote and local filesystems

In addition to the clients listed, you can also use Web browsers for transferring files using the File Transfer Protocol. However, browsers are limited in that they can only retrieve or download files. Browsers commonly function to retrieve files from anonymous FTP sites linked to Web pages.

Telnet

When working on a network with multiple computers, one essential tool stands out — Telnet. Telnet gives you command-line access to any computer on the network. You can do anything from checking e-mail to administering the server functions. Each computer you intend to connect to must have the `telnetd` daemon running. Easily installed from its Debian package, `telnetd` gets started through the inetd service.

The `telnet` daemon is activated whenever a request comes in to TCP port 23. A login prompt is sent to the requesting client. The client responds with an account name; then the server requests a password for the account. After the client replies with the password and the server verifies and authorizes the valid account, you can start using the session as you would if you were on the machine itself. As soon as you logoff, the session ends and the Telnet connection is terminated. The following shows a typical Telnet session:

```
$ telnet remotehost
Trying 192.168.0.12...
Connected to remotehost.
Escape character is '^]'.
Debian GNU/Linux 2.2 serv1.mydomain.com
hoth login: jo
Password:
Last login: Tue Oct 17 05:23:48 2000 from :0 on 0
Linux serv1  2.2.17 #1 Sun Jun 25 09:24:41 EST 2000 i686 unknown

Most of the programs included with the Debian GNU/Linux system are
freely redistributable; the exact distribution terms for each program
are described in the individual files in /usr/doc/*/copyright

Debian GNU/Linux comes with ABSOLUTELY NO WARRANTY, to the extent
permitted by applicable law.
You have mail.
jo@hoth:~$
```

Notice from this session that no password is displayed when you type it in. This is to secure the password from anyone looking over your shoulder.

A problem with using Telnet on an insecure network such as the Internet is that the information, including the password, is sent in clear form. This means that a packet sniffer can pick up the information to crack the server. You should always avoid using special accounts such as super user when connected via a mistrusted connection. This is not always possible, so just be aware of the potential danger to your system.

Dial-in PPP Server Setup

So far in this chapter, you have seen applications oriented for dialing out from your system. You can also accomplish the reverse — dialing in — by setting up a Linux system. This works for small offices in which few connections are needed. Larger environments and commercial dial-up services use modem pools, switching services, and routers.

As I'm sure you are aware, modems respond to incoming calls as well as outgoing calls. You need a program to capture the call when it comes in. Let's use `mgetty`, the smart `getty`. The `getty` program opens a terminal-like session using a serial port connection. This is reminiscent of the old teletypewriters (commonly called a TTY) used to communicate via written messages over a telephone line. Additional features to enhance its faxing capability accompany the `mgetty` Debian package.

Several configuration files that reside in `/etc/mgetty` control the connection. These configuration files are:

- ✦ `dialin.config` — Sets the rules for accepting calls. Using callerID, `dialin.config` compares the number coming in with each number in its file. Pound signs (#) are comments and are thereby ignored. Numbers starting with an exclamation mark (!) point out specific numbers to ignore when attempting to dial in.

- ✦ `login.config` — Contains the specific commands for logging in, starting the pppd service, and authenticating the account. The file is initially set up to automatically receive calls.

- ✦ `mgetty.config` — Sets the overall settings for `mgetty`, such as modem speed, ownership, tty settings, and more

Note Other configuration files involve faxing because `mgetty` accommodates receiving faxes. A separate program called `sendfax` helps you with faxing as well.

One of the first things to note is that you must set up your system to acknowledge an incoming call. You do this by setting `mgetty` to listen to the modem. Make sure that you modify the `/etc/inittab` file to include a line like the following:

```
S3:23:respawn:/sbin/mgetty -x0 -s 57600 ttyS3
```

When you install `mgetty`, the preceding line is added. This line specifies the short name for the modem device (S3), the run levels this service should make available (23), and whether to set the service active (`respawn`) or not (`off`). It also specifies the path and command to be used (/sbin/mgetty), followed by any options to employ with the command. In this case, the -x0 option indicates the debugging level to use. The higher the number (9), the more information is logged (a zero means no logging). The second option, -s 57600, indicates the speed to use with the modem. In this case, the speed is set for a 56K modem. Lastly, the line indicates where the modem is located (ttyS3 indicates COM4). Here is the general syntax for the inittab file:

```
<tt>:rlevel:<respawn|off>:/sbin/mgetty [options] <device>
```

The /etc/mgetty/login.config file should work as installed. However, you may need to make a few adjustments to it. All the files in /etc/mgetty include examples of the content. For more information on setting up the files, install the mgetty-docs package and read the files located at /usr/doc/mgetty/. These files can help if you run into trouble; however, the Debian packages are preconfigured to offer the fewest problems when setting up dial-up service.

For documentation, install the mgetty-docs package, use info mgetty from a command line, or visit alpha.greenie.net/mgetty/ for information on the installation, configuration, and use of mgetty.

If you want to use a Windows 9x machine to dial in, you need to install the pppd package. You also need to modify the /etc/ppp/options file to include an entry for the DNS. This file already contains examples, so you only need to modify the IP address to match a valid DNS that you use. In addition, you need to modify the /etc/ppp/pap-secrets file to enable incoming connections to use the /etc/passwd file for login authentication.

Summary

This chapter covered a wide variety of applications and tools used with the Internet. Now you know how to connect using a modem, send and receive e-mail, browse Web sites, catch up on newsgroup postings, and connect to a remote computer.

This chapter also described several clients available with each service and covered an overview of the application. You may need to install and try out the clients you find most interesting to see how they meet your personal preferences.

Also covered were three dial-up options: wvdial, diald, and mgetty. Each has its own niche where it works best. For instance, wvdial can get you connected quickly and easily with a single machine. diald works best in an office or network environment in which a connection is made automatically when someone wants to access the Internet. For those cases in which someone needs to dial in to your machine, mgetty works great.

✦   ✦   ✦

Working with Debian

Applications

◆ ◆ ◆ ◆

In This Chapter

Alternatives for running legacy DOS/Windows applications

Powerful graphics applications for Linux

Internet browsers for Linux

◆ ◆ ◆ ◆

There are thousands of applications already available for use with Linux in general — let alone Debian. Volunteer programmers are busily creating more applications every day. These applications range from small utilities for tracking network traffic to large applications with several developers (as with the Gnome desktop environment). Besides volunteers, businesses are beginning to join in the effort. Large companies, such as Sun Microsystems, contribute sophisticated application packages like StarOffice. Some of these programs cost money, and you only get the binaries. However, Open Source programs are available to anyone who can program.

The applications covered in this chapter fall into one of three categories — foreign operating system (OS) applications, graphical tools, and browsers. The foreign OS applications include running programs meant for another operating system such as Windows. Graphical tools include programs to create or manipulate graphical images and photos. Because of the Internet, browsers are important to all levels of the Linux community.

Installing Applications

Regardless of what application you use, you still need to install it on your system. Some applications are assembled into a single Debian package by some generous soul somewhere in the world. Other programs require a complete installation. Installing applications is generally a snap either way — especially with automated install scripts that are included with most applications.

As you learned in Chapter 2, you install Debian packages using the dpkg application or the dselect installation tool. These packages have all the compiled binaries, supporting libraries, and configuration files included in them. They also include the location information where the files should reside. Installing Debian packages is rarely a problem because the conflicting installed packages are identified through dselect before any damage occurs.

Installing non-Debian applications takes more effort on your part, but it is worth that effort. Generally, the applications come as a tarball (everything you need all wrapped into one file). Once you extract the files from the tarball, you can follow the included instructions for installing the application. The usual installation process is as follows:

1. Read the README file for installation tips, notes, and instructions.

2. Run the configuration script, which searches your machine to make sure that you have all the needed libraries and supporting files. It also asks any last-minute configuration questions.

3. Create the binaries using the last-minute configuration settings, and copy the working program and supporting files to the predetermined locations.

Now you're ready to run the newly installed program.

Note   More applications are including extensive scripting to help automate the install process and make the compile process of the source code simpler than ever.

Using the Windows Application with Linux

If you are a recent converter to Linux, live in both worlds, or haven't found replacement programs for those in Windows, then you're in luck. Using special programs — which emulate the Windows application, create special environments, or simply run the Windows application — gives you the best of both worlds. However, I caution you that you should not view this as a permanent solution to migrating application functions from another platform.

Using one of the following programs does not guarantee the success of launching your favorite Windows program. There are many unpredictable elements to consider, especially with x86 machines. The hardware for x86 machines was not designed to have more than one operating system running at a time. The hardware only allows one program that makes use of it; in the following program, an emulator must emulate the hardware as well as the operating system.

DOSEMU

When you have a legacy DOS program to run, you can use DOSEMU (www.dosemu.org) to run the application on your Linux system. This program creates a virtual machine for the DOS environment under Linux. You can see what the DOS environment looks like in Figure 7-1. You can even run Windows 3.1 in this environment. This is a self-contained environment for DOS. You can set it up in a couple of ways in order to access files.

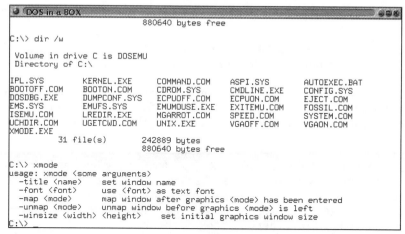

```
   DOS in a BOX
                        880640 bytes free

C:\> dir /w

 Volume in drive C is DOSEMU
 Directory of C:\

IPL.SYS         KERNEL.EXE     COMMAND.COM    ASPI.SYS       AUTOEXEC.BAT
BOOTOFF.COM     BOOTON.COM     CDROM.SYS      CMDLINE.EXE    CONFIG.SYS
DOSDBG.EXE      DUMPCONF.SYS   ECPUOFF.COM    ECPUON.COM     EJECT.COM
EMS.SYS         EMUFS.SYS      EMUMOUSE.EXE   EXITEMU.COM    FOSSIL.COM
ISEMU.COM       LREDIR.EXE     MGARROT.COM    SPEED.COM      SYSTEM.COM
UCHDIR.COM      UGETCWD.COM    UNIX.EXE       VGAOFF.COM     VGAON.COM
XMODE.EXE
           31 file(s)         242889 bytes
                              880640 bytes free

C:\> xmode
usage: xmode <some arguments>
  -title <name>      set window name
  -font <font>       use <font> as text font
  -map <mode>        map window after graphics <mode> has been entered
  -unmap <mode>      unmap window before graphics <mode> is left
  -winsize <width> <height>    set initial graphics window size
C:\>
```

Figure 7-1: DOSEMU works just like DOS run natively on a 386 machine.

One way to set up DOSEMU is to use a virtual DOS filesystem running on top of the Linux filesystem (the default). When you run DOS, it appears as if files are in their own drive space. The other option is to create a DOS partition and mount it under Linux. This can be a full drive or just a partition. You can change the parameters for specifying the drive and other configuration settings in the /etc/dosemu/conf file.

Note   Because DOSEMU is not an emulator, it requires a version of DOS to be installed. The Debian version of DOSEMU uses a free version of DOS called FreeDOS (www.freedos.org). FreeDOS works like any other version of DOS. There are a few drawbacks to it in that it is still under development. For instance, there is no SCSI support for DOS programs yet.

Through the configuration file, you can set the drives for the DOS system — hard drives, floppies, and CD-ROMs. You can also set the paths for the Windows files.

Installation

You can easily install DOSEMU using the dselect program for Debian. Search in the applications list for DOSEMU. There are no supporting packages; everything that it needs is installed. Once installed, DOSEMU is simple to use. Following are a few of the ways you can start a DOS session under Linux.

✦ dos — This starts the Linux DOS emulator known as DOSEMU.

✦ xtermdos — This brings up the DOS emulator in an xterm environment. It automatically detects the IBM VGA font and the best xterm to run and then runs the terminal with the proper parameters required to run DOSEMU.

✦ dosdebug — This controls or debugs an already running DOSEMU session.

✦ xdos — This starts DOSEMU in its own X window. You can also start it using dos -X.

✦ dosexec — This starts DOSEMU and then executes a DEXE file. You can also do load an executable DOS file using dos -L.

Now that you have a DOS session running on your Linux system, what do you do next? One thing you must know is how to close a DOS session. It takes a particular keystroke sequence to get out of the session. Press Ctrl+Alt+PgDn to close DOSEMU.

Caution

DOSEMU is not a finished product, so it produces many bugs and problems. However, improvements are made all the time. You can access the Web site to check for updates, report any bugs, and find out the latest news on the program. You can also check on the latest available Debian package at www.debian.org/Packages/unstable/otherosfs/dosemu.html.

Wine

Wine Is Not an Emulator, hence the name Wine. Similar to DOSEMU, Wine is more of a virtual machine where DOS loads an application into an emulated DOS environment. Wine is an environment in which Windows applications can run, but that environment is not emulated. Built using the Application Program Interface (API) for Windows, Wine reads the interaction that a program has in Windows and translates it to something that Linux can understand. You can find out more about Wine at www.winehq.com where advancements are made all the time.

Installation

When installing Wine through dselect, all the dependencies, required files, and conflicting applications are predetermined by the Wine package set of dependencies. Of course, that is true no matter which application you install using dselect. Search for the application using the forward slash (/), then type wine and press Enter. Use the backslash (\) to find the next instance of the string you are searching for. The only one you really need is wine; however, you may wish to install the wine-doc documentation package as well. There are a couple of library packages for Wine as well.

Configuration

The best way to use Wine is with a dual boot system — Windows and Linux. You can add the Windows partition to the filesystem to make it accessible to Linux. Add the following line to your /etc/fstab file:

```
/dev/hda1      /mnt/win      vfat      defaults,user      0      0
```

`/dev/hda1` is the Windows partition containing the Windows software. `/mnt/win` is the starting path that Linux uses to mount the Windows partition. Make sure that the path exists before mounting the partition. If not, you need to make a directory for it. If you choose to make the starting path the same as I have it here, you can create the path with this command:

```
mkdir /mnt/win
```

You can also change it to whatever you like. Just make sure that the path exists; otherwise, it cannot mount. The rest should remain the same for the filesystem table (`fstab`).

After the Windows partition has a mounting path, edit the Wine configuration file (`/etc/wine.conf`) to reflect the path. You can see from some of the settings in the configuration file shown next that the paths for the floppy, CD-ROM, and C drive all match the mounting path. By default, the C drive is set to `/c`, which I changed to match the actual path. The F drive in this configuration refers to the user's home directory. Finally, the WINE area sets the parameters that reflect the location of the Windows files and Windows system files.

```
[Drive A]
Path=/floppy
Type=floppy
Label=Floppy
Serial=87654321
Device=/dev/fd0

[Drive C]
Path=/mnt/win
Type=hd
Label=MS-DOS
Filesystem=win95

[Drive D]
Path=/cdrom
Type=cdrom
Label=CD-Rom
Filesystem=win95

[Drive E]
Path=/tmp
Type=hd
Label=Tmp Drive
Filesystem=win95

[Drive F]
Path=${HOME}
Type=network
Label=Home
Filesystem=win95
```

```
[wine]
Windows=c:\windows
System=c:\windows\system
Temp=e:\
Path=c:\windows;c:\windows\system;e:\;e:\test;f:\
SymbolTableFile=/usr/lib/wine.sym
```

The rest of the configuration file is safe to leave alone because it deals with the specifics of the programs. This is where you set some options — such as serial ports, parallel ports, and printer ports.

Running applications

Once the drives are mounted, the configuration file is set and you are ready to run your first application. Make sure that the partition with Windows is mounted and that you know the full path to the application you wish to run. Follow this syntax for loading programs:

```
wine [options] program1 [program2 ...]
```

You can load more than one program at a time by adding the path to the command line. Let's start with a simple example to test your setup. Launch the standard calculator using this command:

```
wine /mnt/win/windows/calc.exe
```

You should see the calculator as you would under Windows. Figure 7-2 shows the Windows calculator as viewed in scientific mode.

Figure 7-2: Running Windows programs, like calc, in a Linux world

Over the last few years, people have tried out Windows programs using Wine. When a person runs a program under Wine, they can have it added to a database and give it a 0-5 rating. Over 2,477 total programs were entered with a rating average of 2.4. Table 7-1 shows a few of the programs and the year they were tested. All the programs listed in the table have a rating of 5.0. There are 265 programs listed in the database with a rating of 5.0.

Table 7-1 **Programs tested under Wine**		
Manufacturer	*Product*	*Year Tested*
Adobe	Acrobat Distiller 3.01	1999
Blizzard	Starcraft	1998
Blizzard	Broadwars	1999
Blizzard	Diablo	2000
Corel	WordPerfect 9	1999
Corel	Corel Draw	1999
Metacreations	Bryce 4	2000
Microsoft	Solitaire	1998
Microsoft	WordPad	1998
Microsoft	Visual Basic 3	1998
Microsoft	Calc	1998
Microsoft	Freecell	1998
Microsoft	Excel 97	1998
Microsoft	Access 97	1998
Realnetworks	RealPlayer 7 (beta)	1999
Sierra	Half-Life	2000
Westwood	Red Alert	1998
Westwood	Tiberium Sun	1999

As you can see from this very short list, many of the tested programs are games. Some of the programs listed are mainline, while others are specialty programs. If you decide to use Wine with a program not listed, go ahead and submit it to the database with the rating you feel it deserves at www.winehq.com/Apps/edit.cgi.

VMware

Sometimes the demands of business, projects, and life demand that we use another operating system for whatever reason. One of those reasons might be in the area of software development. These programmers who want to test their software, but don't have the extra hardware to test on can use VMware. The solution is to load the appropriate operating system on your Linux machine in its own VMware virtual machine.

VMware, Inc. creates software that runs on Linux and Windows NT. The software emulates a machine — not an operating system. VMware can create as many of these virtual machines as you need. When you power on the virtual machine, it's like turning the power on for a real computer — only it all takes place from a window on the Linux desktop. The virtual machine doesn't care which operating system it loads. As far as it's concerned, there are no other operating systems. Its reality is defined by vmware. The virtual machine even thinks it's on a separate network.

Note   VMware is a completely commercial product. Prices range from $99 for the student/hobbyist to $399 for everyone else. You can get a 30-day evaluation of the software from its Web site. Debian does not include, support, nor promote this product in an official capacity.

The cost of running VMware on your system is performance. The virtual machine consumes disk space, RAM, and CPU resources. The processor is now doing the work of two systems, so it's bound to slow some. This division of resources makes the system requirements important. Here are the hardware and software requirements for VMware.

Hardware requirements for VMware:

✦ A standard x86-based PC running at 266MHz or faster

✦ A minimum of 96MB RAM; recommended: 128MB

✦ Enough free hard drive space to create the virtual drives for the other operating systems

Note   The latest version of VMware does currently support the recently released XFree86 version 4.0.

Software requirements for VMware:

✦ A standard Linux distribution with glibc version 2 or higher

✦ The kernel 2.0.32 or higher for single processors, or kernel 2.2.x for multiprocessors

✦ An X server for XFree86-3.3.3.1 or higher

If your system does not meet these requirements, then you have no guarantee that VMware will work on your system.

VMware installation

Although VMware is not a supported Debian product and does not have a Debian package to install, it does have an automated installation routine. It interactively installs the application in the appropriate locations. It also determines if the software works with the kernel version on your system and then recompiles it to match the kernel. You can answer most questions using the default response.

Upon visiting the VMware Web site (www.vmware.com), you can find out how to download an evaluation version of the software. The difference between the evaluation version and the full version of the software is the license code file that you receive. The demos have a 30-day expiration, while the purchased versions never expire. Download the tarball and complete the registration form so that VMware can e-mail the license to your account. Extract the tarball using the following command:

```
tar zxvf VMware-2.x.x-xxx.tar.gz
```

Change into the newly created vmware-distrib directory once the file extraction is complete. Then execute the vmware-install.pl Perl script to begin the installation process. Answer the questions concerning the installation locations by pressing Enter. Eventually, you are asked to read and respond to the licensing terms. Press the Spacebar as you read to reach the bottom where you must type yes to accept the licensing terms.

> **Note**
> To complete the installation of VMware, you may need to install the kernel headers so portions of VMware can compile to match your kernel version. You can use `apt-get install kernel-headers-2.2.xx` to install the headers for the kernel version you run. If you are unsure of your currently running kernel version, run dmesg | more and look at the first line of resulting text for the kernel version.

After you accept the license agreement, the script tries to match VMware's vmmon to your kernel. If the script fails to find a suitable one among the prebuilt modules, you need to compile one. In this case, you need the kernel's source and a C compiler installed on your system. Once the modules are compiled and installed and everything is configured, you're ready to run.

The first time you run vmware from your account, you get a notice that the license is not found. Place the license file in the .vmware directory and make sure that it starts with the word license. Now, you will no longer be troubled with the message. You also are introduced to the virtual machine setup wizard that sets the parameters to the virtual machine you create.

Figure 7-3: Install the entire operating system in a virtual machine.

Figure 7-3 shows Windows 98 being installed on a virtual machine. The environment looks and acts just like a machine to the operating system that is installed on it. If you click in the window, the mouse moves, clicks, and drags the components of that environment. When you press Ctrl+Alt+Esc, the mouse control returns to the Linux environment. The virtual machine has power on, cycle power, and suspend buttons to control the virtual machine. Even the network functions as if the virtual machine were a real machine networked to the real Linux machine.

Plex86

Does virtual machine software exist in the Open Source arena? The answer is an ambiguous yes and no. Yes, it exists in that a project is underway to create Open Source PC virtual machine software. This software will let the operating system and application software run natively as much as possible. What doesn't run natively will be emulated through the virtualization monitor.

The other side of that ambiguous answer is that the software is not very far along in development. The last word on the progress was that Plex86 could run DOS 6.22 and FreeDOS. Work continues all the time on the development of this software.

The hope of the Plex86 organization is that the software will be capable of allowing users to migrate to a Linux platform and still hang on to their legacy Windows applications a little longer. In some cases, a single application holds back the advancement to another operating system such as UNIX or Linux. You can keep up to date with the progress of the development at `www.plex86.org`.

Graphics Programs

For many years, the leaders in the graphics industry used graphical tools designed for the Macintosh platform (which are still used today). However, if your platform of choice is Linux, you can select from many excellent graphical tools. One of those tools is Gimp.

Gimp

Gimp is one of the more sophisticated graphics applications available for Linux. Some programs only view images, while others can make simple changes to a photo, image, or graphic. Gimp enables you to make all types of changes to an existing image — both simple changes and complex ones. Or if computer artistry runs through your veins, then you can compose your very own creation through the number of tools available with Gimp.

Installing and using Gimp

Gimp comes as a Debian package that you can easily install through the Debian package manager: `dselect`. After you install the package, the configuration takes place when you open Gimp for the first time (generating a `.gimp` directory in your home account). From there, you can completely customize Gimp to fit your needs. Any change made to the `gimprc` file takes precedence over the global file.

Figure 7-4 shows what the main Gimp control tool palette looks like. There are two menu options on the panel — File and Xtns. File gives you access to create new pictures, open existing ones, close the program, and more. Xtns gives you access to external programs such as Web browsers and scripts. Gimp also enables you to take snapshots of the screen in addition to creating/modifying pictures.

Figure 7-4: The core tool palette of Gimp

Table 7-2 lists all the functions of the additional button tools on the panel by row. Each row reads left to right.

Table 7-2 Features of Gimp's tool palette		
Row	**Column**	**Button description**
1	1	Selects rectangular regions
	2	Selects elliptical regions
	3	Selects hand-drawn regions
2	1	Selects contiguous regions
	2	Selects regions using Bezier curves
	3	Selects shapes from images
3	1	Moves layers and sections
	2	Zooms in and out
	3	Crops the image
4	1	Transforms the layer or selected area
	2	Flips the layer or selected area
	3	Adds text to the image
5	1	Picks colors from the image
	2	Fills area with a color or pattern
	3	Fills area with a color gradient
6	1	Draws sharp pencil strokes
	2	Paints fuzzy brush strokes
	3	Erases to background or transparency
7	1	Airbrushes with variable pressure
	2	Paints using patterns or image regions
	3	Blurs or sharpens
8		Selects foreground/background colors

Because of the way Gimp was built, custom plug-ins allow graphics artists to create the effects they look for in the creations they make. The Gimp Web page (www.gimp.org) references links to sample pages of plug-in effects. With a little programming skill, you can write your own plug-in. This book covers more than one application, so I leave programming for Gimp to another time.

Tip   For a good introduction to programming plug-ins, look at `www.oberlin.edu/ ~kturner/gimp/doc/`. This is a great site for beginning and advanced programmers to learn to create plug-ins for Gimp.

Other features that you can add to this program include custom palettes, fonts, patterns, brushes, gradients, and scripts. You can find some of these available to download from the Gimp Web site under the resources section. Use them to create new, amazing computer graphics.

Gimp is very useful if you want to touch up a photo, change the contrast, rotate the image, or apply some special effect. Figure 7-5 shows a photo about to be rotated to the correct orientation for viewing onscreen. To rotate an image, right-click the image to view the menu. Move the mouse to Image where another menu appears. Again, move the mouse to the Transforms menu item and then click Rotate from the third menu layer. A dialog box appears, and you can choose how many degrees to rotate. Once you select the rotation, click the OK button.

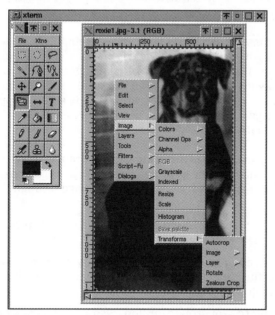

Figure 7-5: You can make changes to a photograph as simple as rotating an image or as complex as touching up image defects.

If you want to create graphics for Web pages, cover art, or just for personal enjoyment, then you can find everything you need in Gimp. Using special effects such as bevels, drop shadows, and chrome-it, you can create very unique art works. You can also take an existing photo of your family and turn it into an antique-looking photo. All these effects come as a result of the Script-Fu menu items, which come with the standard Debian install.

ImageMagick

Another powerful graphics manipulation program is ImageMagick. This program limits you to creating simple graphics as compared with Gimp. However, ImageMagick does enable you to make changes to existing graphics, which is its real power. If all you ever need to do is manipulate images by cropping, resizing, rotating, or other such procedures, then look no further.

To install ImageMagick, use `dselect` to find and select the program named `imagemagick` for installation. The package installs the suite of programs that make up ImageMagick. Once the program is installed, you can launch it through the window manager's application menu by looking under Viewers. Officially, the Debian install of ImageMagick considers itself a viewer instead of belonging to the graphics category and is found in the Debian menu tree.

Navigating ImageMagick's main menu is simple, as you can see from the left side of Figure 7-6. From this main menu, you can access all the different features this program has to offer. The main menu is broken down into functional groups. File, Edit, and View control the opening, saving, and viewing of the working image. Transform and Enhance control the overall changes to the image, while Effects and F/X apply special characteristics to the image. The following list details more explicitly what each of the main menu buttons enables you to do.

✦ **File** — From the File menu, you can open an existing file or grab an image on the screen. This comes in handy when capturing pictures to put in a book, like those shown in this chapter. You also save changes to an image through this menu button.

✦ **Edit** — You can undo the last change made to an image from here. You can also cut, copy, and paste images you want to manipulate.

✦ **View** — If the image is too small or too large for the screen, you can adjust the viewing area. Consider this the zoom function. You can also resize the image to give it a particular dimension for a Web page.

✦ **Transform** — When you want to crop, rotate, or flop (also known as mirror), here is where you do it. These features are easy to operate, and they control the orientation of the image.

✦ **Enhance** — Occasionally, you may wish to enhance an image by adjusting its brightness, hue, or saturation. These features adjust the tone of a picture; they can turn a dark image that is hard to make out into a clear photo.

✦ **Effects** — Sometimes you may want to make a few buttons for a Web page or labels for a presentation. From here, you can take a 2-dimensional image and turn it into a work of art by using one of these features. You can emboss, sharpen, or raise the edges of an image.

✦ **F/X** — You have five special effects available here. Each one is designed to take a normal photo and turn it into something unique. These five features are Solarize, Swirl, Implode, Wave, and Oil Painting. Give them a try to see how you like them.

✦ **Image Edit** — There are limited basic tools available to create, customize, or add to an image. Here you can draw simple shapes, add borders and frames, or change colors.

✦ **Miscellany** — Anything that doesn't fit in one of the other categories finds its way here. Mostly you find preview features, but preferences show up here as well. The preference settings control eight settings, including how much memory is used as cache.

✦ **Help** — Help is just that — access to an overview and online documentation.

ImageMagick may not be the best tool for creating images from scratch, but it does make an excellent tool for manipulating photos and existing graphics for Web use.

Note Some applications produce PostScript output that printers interpret to produce the desired graphics. This output can get routed to a file that PostScript viewers can read. The program, `ghostview`, reads these PostScript files and displays the information in the same way a PostScript printer prints the information.

Figure 7-6: ImageMagick showing a picture of a cute puppy.

Browsers

For some time, the only browser available on the Linux system was Lynx—a non-graphical HTML browser. This worked fine when the sites were mostly textual. However, with the advent of more sophisticated Web page designs, the need for a graphical based browser arose. Here entered Netscape, which joined in the Open Source community and offered a graphical browser to the graphical Linux desktop.

Outside of the text browser, Lynx, there are three main graphical browsers—but only one that isn't included in any Debian release. Opera is the only browser not included in the Debian distributions because it is not free software. Netscape and Mozilla are free and are therefore included in the Debian release.

Lynx

With today's Web pages becoming more graphical all the time, a text browser may not be very useful. So why bother mentioning it? I include it in this discussion for the simple reason that a graphical browser is useless when used through a terminal session. You'd be surprised the information you can glean from the text on a Web page. For instance, the Debian Web page contains numerous references, tidbits, and morsels buried in the page's text.

Tip   Lynx is a full-fledged browser, so you can also use it for FTP sites or for transferring files like any other browser. Even though the FTP client is text-based and usable through a terminal, Lynx gives you alternatives.

You can use Lynx from any command line, even through a remote connection. Here is the syntax for using this browser:

```
lynx [options] [path or URL]
```

There are a number of options available for use with Lynx. Table 7-3 shows only a few of those options. You can find a full listing when you look through the documentation.

When you install Lynx, part of the configuration asks for the default path for the browser. If you launch Lynx without a path or Uniform Resource Locator (URL), then the default path is used. Otherwise, Lynx points to any file or URL path you enter.

Table 7-3
Options for the Lynx browser

Option	Description
-anonymous	Applies restrictions for anonymous accounts; see also -restrictions
-auth=ID:PASSWD	Sets the authorization ID and password for protected documents at startup. Be sure to protect any script files that use this switch.
-blink	Forces high-intensity background colors for color mode, if available and supported by the terminal
-book	Uses the bookmark page as the startup file
-cache=NUMBER	Sets the NUMBER of documents cached in memory. The default cache is 10.
-case	Enables case-sensitive string searching
-cfg=FILENAME	Specifies a Lynx configuration file other than the default lynx.cfg
-color	Forces color mode on, if available. The default color control sequences are assumed if the terminal capability description does not specify how to handle color. (show_color=always setting found in a .lynxrc file at startup has the same effect)
-connect_timeout=N	Sets the connection timeout where N is given in seconds
-crawl -traversal	Outputs each page to a file
-crawl -dump	Formats the output the same as -crawl -traversal, but sends it to the terminal
-editor=EDITOR	Enables external editing using the specified EDITOR (vi, ed, emacs, and so on)
-emacskeys	Enables emacs-like key movement
-ftp	Disables FTP access
-help	Prints the Lynx command syntax usage message
-homepage=URL	Sets the home page separate from the start page
-image_links	Includes all the links for images within a document
-index=URL	Sets the default index file to the specified URL
-justify	Justifies the displayed text

Continued

Table 7-3 *(continued)*

Option	Description
-link=NUMBER	Starts the count for lnk#.dat files produced by the -crawl option
-localhost	Disables URLs that point to remote hosts
-nobrowse	Disables directory browsing
-noexec	Disables the execution of local programs (default)
-number_fields	Forces the numbering of links as well as form input fields in a document
-number_links	Forces the numbering of hypertext links in a document
-partial	Toggles the display of partial pages while loading
-print	Enables the print functions (default)
-source	Works the same as -crawl -dump, but outputs HTML source instead of formatted text
-startfile_ok	Allows a non-HTTP startup file or home page with -validate
-telnet	Disables the recognition of all telnet commands
-term=TERM	Tells Lynx which terminal type to assume it is using
-validate	Accepts only HTTP URLs (for validation). This implements complete security restrictions also.
-version	Prints Lynx version information
-vikeys	Enables vi-like movement using the keyboard

You can find the global settings for Lynx in the /etc/lynx.cfg file. This is a huge file to make sense of, but each item has comments explaining what it does. You should have no difficulty understanding this file.

If you need to customize any settings for yourself or tweak Lynx beyond the global settings, you can do this in one of two ways. The first, most common method is to use a .lynxrc file in your home directory that contains special customization. The other method is to copy and modify the global configuration file.

First, copy the global configuration file (/etc/lynx.cfg) to your home directory. Modify this copied file (~/lynx.cfg) to contain INCLUDE:/etc/lynx.cfg. You can then launch Lynx from the command line to use the new configuration by employing the argument (-cfg /where/is/lynx.cfg) or by adding an environment variable to .profile or .login. The environment variable looks like this:

```
LYNX_CFG=~/lynx.cfg; export LYNX_CFG    # in .profile for sh/ksh/bash/etc.
setenv LYNX_CFG ~/lynx.cfg              # in .login for [t]csh
```

Navigating this browser is a little more complicated because you can't use a mouse to click links, images, and such. Instead, you use keyboard commands to navigate from hypertext link to hypertext link. By default, Lynx is set to Novice, which provides some basic commands at the bottom of the screen. Here is a list of some of the basic commands you need to begin using this browser:

✦ Up arrow and down arrow scroll through the hypertext links. In color mode, the current link changes color while mono color mode becomes bright.

✦ Right arrow or Enter follows a highlighted hypertext link to the next page.

✦ Left arrow retreats backwards from the current page.

✦ Type **H** or **?** to access the online help and descriptions of the keys.

✦ Typing **K** gives a complete listing of the current key mappings for the commands.

✦ Type **O** to access the session options. This works like a form, so the navigation works the same.

✦ Typing **Q** quits Lynx altogether.

You may never need to use Lynx if you only work on one workstation. For those of us who use multiple workstations — or at least connect to multiple workstations — this program can come in handy.

Mozilla

Because Mozilla is Open Source, it is included in the Debian distribution. Mozilla is at the core, developed from the Open Source release of Netscape. Mozilla has been in various stages of development for some time. It may not be as integrated as some of the other browsers on other platforms, but it's only a matter of time.

The Mozilla interface, shown in Figure 7-7, incorporates many of the features that the popular browsers enjoy today. The left column incorporates a customizable sidebar. This sidebar enables the end user to view bookmarks, execute searches, look up related topics, and more. However, this may be more of an annoyance than a help to some users. If this is the case, never fear. You can disable it through the View menu options.

You can install Mozilla through the same method you employ for any other Debian package (using the dselect program). Once installed, you can run the browser from a command line (type mozilla) or from the Window manager menu. The first time you start Mozilla, you must set up a profile through a setup wizard. Profiles enable multiple people to use the same browser while maintaining their personalized information, such as bookmarks, My Sidebar, and more. This information is created in ~/.mozilla, but most of the contents of the directory are just links to the global files.

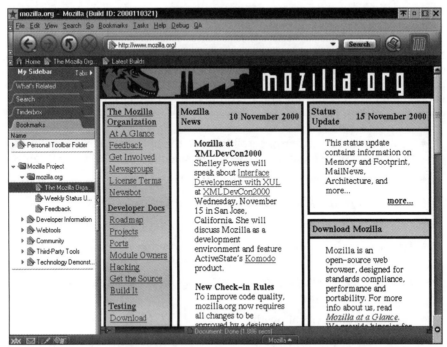

Figure 7-7: Mozilla provides a smooth, modern look to the browser interface.

Note   If you start Mozilla using a terminal command line, the debug information is output to the terminal display. This comes in handy when reporting problems to the development team.

Tip   When trying to download files through the Web page interface of the browser, right-click the link and select Save link as.... If there is a file at the other end of the link, the file is saved to the specified location. Otherwise, the file may be downloaded and viewed in raw form through the browser rather than being saved as a file. This solution works on all the browsers.

Because Mozilla is constantly undergoing development, you can stay on top of this development by looking at the official www.mozilla.org Web site for software-specific updates. You can also watch www.mozillazine.org for more general news on this browser.

Opera

For a commercial version of a Web browser, turn to Opera. Opera is a cross-platform Web browser with a fresh look. Figure 7-8 shows the style of this browser. You can see from the picture that the address link shows up at the bottom of the window. When it is connecting and downloading the page information, the address changes to a status bar showing the progress of the load.

Opera uses the Qt 2.1 libraries—the same libraries that KDE uses. This means that if you run the K Desktop on your Debian system, then you should have no problem running Opera on your system. Otherwise, you need to download the Qt 2.1 libraries and install them on your system before Opera can work. This is all explained on the Opera Web site at `www.opera.com/linux/index.html`.

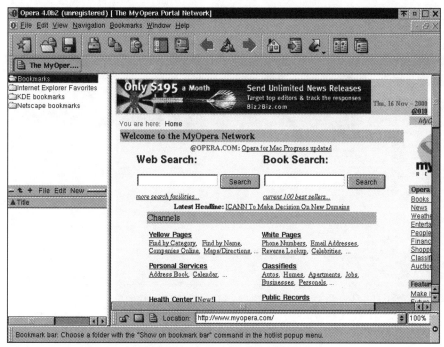

Figure 7-8: Opera gives a fresh new look to a browser.

Opera does provide its application in the Debian package format. You can easily download it from the Opera Web site. The price for a copy of Opera is $39 ($20 for educational use) with a discount scheme for quantity purchases. Obviously, you only get the binary version.

Netscape

For most of the popular distributions of Linux, Netscape is the regularly included browser. Originally, this was because it was the only stable, freely available browser for Linux. This is no longer true. Other browsers exist; however, in the minds of some people, Netscape is still the tried and true Internet browser of choice.

Figure 7-9 shows the Netscape browser as it is commonly known today. The beta version of Netscape, version 6, looks surprisingly like Mozilla (see Figure 7-6). In fact, it was taken from Mozilla, which explains why they look the same. I've heard many comments from peers regarding their frustration with the instability of the earlier versions of Netscape on the Linux platform. Perhaps the new version 6 will show some improvements in that area.

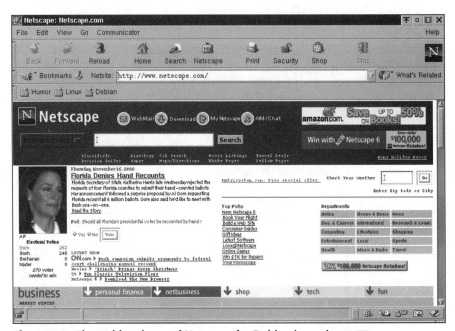

Figure 7-9: The stable release of Netscape for Debian is version 4.73.

You can install Netscape 4.73 through the Debian packages using `dselect`. You can find the package under `netscape-base` in the list of packages. You can also download the version of Netscape you wish to use through the anonymous FTP site (`ftp.netscape.com`). You have the choice of several languages, platforms, and versions. Each has its own easy installation routine. The UNIX versions come in compressed `tar` format; depending on the version you select, you may have the choice of a self-extracting archive (sea), an Internet installer, or an old-fashioned compile-the-source installation. Whichever version you choose, be sure to read the README file for detailed instructions on installing the program on your system.

If you choose to install a version through the Netscape site instead of through the Debian packaged version, you might end up returning to the classic Debian package because of the easy updates and upgrades.

When the Netscape program opens for the first time, you must create the preference files in the home directory. This happens the first time Netscape starts. After that, Netscape opens right up because the files exist.

Note Netscape by itself is only a browser. However, Communicator includes the Netscape browser and adds mail and news client tools as well. See Chapter 6 for more details on these other features.

Summary

Now that Linux is becoming more popular, many people are migrating to it from other operating systems. Of course, the masses are entrenched in Windows, so giving up the collection of software that has accumulated is difficult. Just remember that "you can have your cake and eat it, too".

Emulators and virtual machines create an environment in which all those programs that you thought were lost still have a chance to function while you look for replacements. That's not all; most of the programs that you would replace them with are free. The difference, again, between the emulator and a virtual machine is that the virtual machine actually emulates the hardware to install a legitimate operating system. Meanwhile, the emulator simply runs interference between the application and the foreign operating system.

Advancements are made every day it seems with Linux applications. In the graphics arena, Gimp is that shining beacon of light. Although there are other graphical manipulation tools available for Linux, Gimp actually resembles graphical creation programs on other platforms.

Let's not forget the milestones that browsers have made on Linux. They have come a long way from text browsers to graphical browsers. Even the graphical browsers have made their own improvements. Both Netscape and Mozilla are going in the same direction concerning the look of the browsers.

✦   ✦   ✦

Productivity Applications

As Linux finds its way into more homes, offices, and businesses, the need for productivity tools grows. With the market dominated by Microsoft's Office 95/98/2000 suite of word processor, spreadsheet, and presentation programs, a search ensued for equivalent tools on the Linux platform. Right now, two products stand out as having hope for a "what you see is what you get" (WYSIWYG) application for creating documents, spreadsheets, and presentations — StarOffice and Applixware.

StarOffice and Applixware both promise to provide many of the functions that are available in popular productivity packages. This may please the newcomers to Linux; but those who have grown up with UNIX and now use Linux can still take advantage of the power that document formatters can provide, such as TeX and Groff. This chapter covers both the WYSIWYG tools and the traditional forms of creating documents under Debian GNU/Linux.

StarOffice

Developed by Sun Microsystems, StarOffice offers a complete office suite of applications — word processor, spreadsheet, presentation, database, HTML editor, and more. Sun makes this suite of applications freely available from its Web site (www.sun.com/products/staroffice). The programs are in binary form, which requires no compiling. You only need to install them.

Sun Microsystems recently announced that they were making StarOffice Open Source and calling it OpenOffice. You can access more information about this Open Source project at www.openoffice.org. The source is written in C++, and it provides scriptable functionality including Java APIs. This and much more is planned for the new OpenOffice suite.

StarOffice currently offers 11 languages for each of its four compiled binary versions. The latest version, 5.2, is downloadable for Linux, Windows, and both Intel and Sparc versions of Solaris.

The main advantage of StarOffice is its near 100 percent compatibility with Microsoft Office. StarOffice can open and save Microsoft Word- and Excel-formatted files, thus allowing StarOffice to work effectively in an environment in which Microsoft is the standard. The drawback, however, is its compatibility with other suites such as Applixware.

Installation

You can install StarOffice in a couple of steps. First, you should download the files from the Internet. There are three files to retrieve; the main one is over 95MB. This can take a while, so I suggest picking a time to download that disrupts other activities the least (like at night). The other two files are roughly 15 to 16MB, and they only add to the function of the whole StarOffice package. A complete installation of StarOffice uses around 300MB of disk space. You should have at least 430MB of free disk space before attempting to download and install StarOffice.

You can obtain the files from Sun by going to `www.sun.com/products/staroffice/get.html`. Here you can pick the latest version available (5.2 at the time of this writing). Pick one of the four platforms and one of the 11 languages you wish to use. You must register with Sun to proceed. Remember what you use for the name and password so you can return without re-registering. After registering and accepting the license agreement, you have the choice to download one large file for StarOffice or 10 smaller files. Among the 10 smaller files are two optional files (the database and the player). All the downloadable files come in binary form, which means that they are executable, self-contained, and self-installing files.

To install StarOffice, you must log on as root and run a graphical window manager. Then you can follow one of two installation paths — single user or network. You should use the network install for multi-user or networked systems wishing to keep user files separate. Systems where only one person logs on, as with a standalone home system, can use StarOffice as a single user.

Tip

If you tend to have connection problems with the Internet or have trouble downloading the large file, you might have better success choosing the 10 smaller files.

✦ **Single-User Installation** — Once the files are downloaded to your system, you can begin the installation for a single user. This means that only the user that installs StarOffice can use it. With your system in graphical mode and an x-terminal running, use the main file that begins with `so-*` to start the installation this way:

```
cd /usr/src/download/staroffice
./so-5_2-ga-bin-linux-en.bin
```

Follow the directions from the dialog boxes as they appear requesting your intervention. By default, the installation path is directed to the home directory of the logged on account. For the single user, this is fine.

✦ **Network Installation** — Similar to the single-user install, the network install gives everyone access to use StarOffice from their own accounts. Again, while in graphical mode, use the main installation program to perform the network installation this way:

```
cd /usr/src/download/staroffice
./so-5_2-ga-bin-linux-en.bin -net
```

As before, follow the directions on the screen and answer the questions when asked. Again, a default location is given; you can accept this default or choose your own, although those using the suite still need to access the path. Each user must launch StarOffice from the installed location to copy and create individualized settings in his or her home directory. From that point on, the user can launch from the menu in KDE. Gnome users need will need to create a menu item manually.

Tip   StarOffice only creates a menu for KDE, so you can quickly add a link to Gnome by copying the link from `~/office52/soffice` to `~/.gnome-desktop/soffice`. Right-click the Gnome desktop and choose Rescan Desktop Directory from the menu.

Note   If you purchase the software on CD, the installation process is the generally the same for single user and network, except the filename of the file to start changes from `so-5_2-ga-bin-linux-en.bin` to `setup`. All other instructions remain the same.

As StarOffice installs, it inserts links into an appropriate place for launching if you happen to use the K Desktop Environment (KDE). If not, you need to launch StarOffice from a command line using the installation path chosen during the install. For instance, here's how to install StarOffice for the user logged in:

```
cd ~/office52
./soffice
```

When you launch StarOffice for the first time, a configuration wizard guides you in selecting the Internet settings needed for the browser, e-mail, and news. If not properly set in the beginning, you may change these settings by choosing Options from the Tools menu.

You install the two remaining install packages — database and player — in a similar fashion. Neither package is required for StarOffice to work. The database allows the StarOffice applications to integrate with its database component, while the player plays presentations created by the StarOffice Presentation application. It requires fewer resources to run and is available to those who don't use or have StarOffice installed.

The StarOffice desktop

StarOffice uses an integrated desktop environment from which the other components run. It attempts to be a complete desktop environment that provides all the necessary functions a user may need, such as browsing the Internet, reading and sending e-mail, and viewing news. Figure 8-1 shows the StarOffice desktop environment where you can click icons to create new documents.

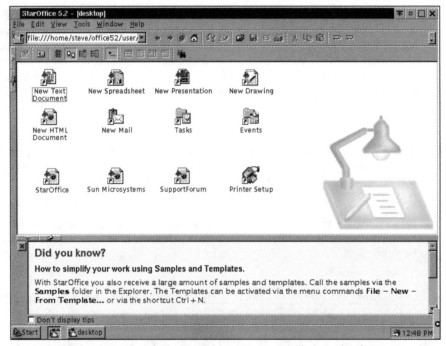

Figure 8-1: The StarOffice desktop enables you to quickly launch whatever tool you need.

In the upper-left corner is a text field that serves as a URL control where you enter a file path, Web site address, or anonymous FTP. The results display in the browser area. When viewing a file path, a tool bar is available to navigate the directory path and change the view of the directory contents. Each document opens in it own window within the desktop area.

With all applications, several pre-configured wizards can help you quickly create documents, spreadsheets, and so on.

StarOffice Writer

The *Writer* is the name for the word processor function in StarOffice. You have many of the commonly known tools in a left column tool bar on the side of the document window. Spell checking can be automatic or manual—you get to choose. It performs many automated tasks, such as auto-correcting text as you write or simply pointing out text that you need to correct.

Figure 8-2 shows a dialog box preparing to change the paragraph styles. You can access this and other configuration dialog boxes by right-clicking the document. You can use the same hot-key controls to perform many of the functions as you do from the Microsoft suite.

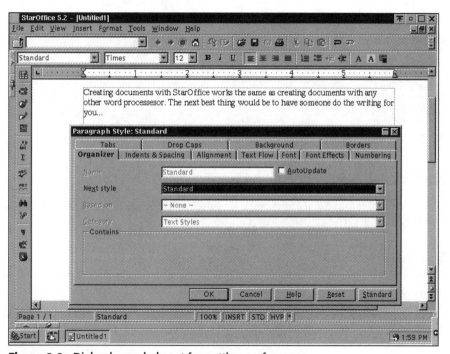

Figure 8-2: Dialog boxes help set formatting preferences.

StarOffice Calc

The name *Calc* gives away the function of this feature of StarOffice—the *spreadsheet*. It has many of the commonly used, favorite features people look for in a spreadsheet. Figure 8-3 shows the interface. In addition to creating its own files, Spreadsheet opens and works with most Excel spreadsheets.

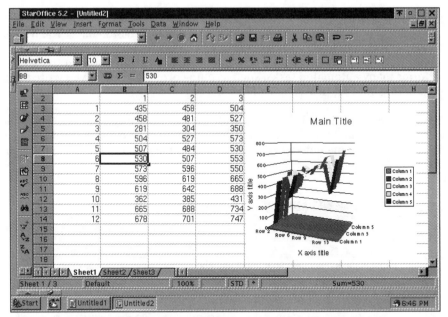

Figure 8-3: Spreadsheet showing a chart

Along with the standard row-column layout of cells typifying a spreadsheet, you can also create multiple worksheets. Each worksheet contains its own data. If all you need is to tabulate data, format cells, or run straightforward mathematical calculations on the data, then this feature can do the trick.

StartOffice Impress

When it comes time to present the annual report to the board of directors, you can make your slides using *Impress*. You can choose from one of the many pre-made templates, or you can make one yourself. To use one of the included templates, follow the instructions on the screen as the wizard takes you through the steps of picking the layout, the background, and so on.

Once the presentation is created, use the player to view your presentation on the screen in full view. The *player* is a smaller application that does not require you to load StarOffice in order to run. This enables you, for example, to create a presentation on a desktop machine and then load it on a laptop along with the player. This way, you can take them to another office, on the road, or to the conference room where you will make your presentation.

StarOffice Draw and Image

The *Draw and Image* components are both simple and advanced. They are simple because the controls are all graphically oriented. Click the tool, click the drawing area, and create the design you want. They are advanced because of the complex shapes you can create, such as three-dimensional blocks, spheres, and cones (all complete with color and shading).

The difference between Draw and Image is that Draw is a vector drawing program, whereas Image is a bitmap editor. Vector drawing programs like Draw enable you to create shapes and pictures, after which you can change the final size without losing the quality of the picture. Bitmap editors enable you to make changes to a picture, but may distort the picture quality if the size changes. Vector drawings produce great posters for presentations, while bitmap editor do a wonderful job touching up a scanned photo.

Another advanced feature this tool offers is the rotational control. Once you create an object in the drawing area, select the rotational control and drag one of the red dots to cause the object to rotate around a movable, rotational point.

Once you complete your masterpiece, you have the choice of saving the image as a StarOffice format or exporting it to one of many formats including common formats used on the Web.

Creating an HTML Document

After creating a masterful drawing using the Drawing tool, you can insert it into the graphically based Document creator, which lets you save this document as an HTML file. You can make Web pages using tables, text, and images — or you can use one of many types of objects. After inserting any objects on the page, you can move anchors, adjust dimensions, or add form fields.

I prefer to modify the code (instead of adjusting graphical images) and then switch to HTML Source from the View menu. There you can see the color-coded HTML source code, which you can add to, edit, and modify.

Tip Using the hot-key combination of Ctrl+Shift+J enables you to toggle between full screen view and normal desktop view. Both views leave the application bar of open files at the bottom of the screen.

Mail

The *Mail* tool works like most. The settings for this take place when you first start StarOffice.

In order to use the Mail function, you must first create an *outbox* as a storage location for sent mail. On the left side of the desktop is a tab that opens. Choose the Explorer item from the list. Right-click the white area, choose New from the menu, and then choose Outbox (as shown in Figure 8-4).

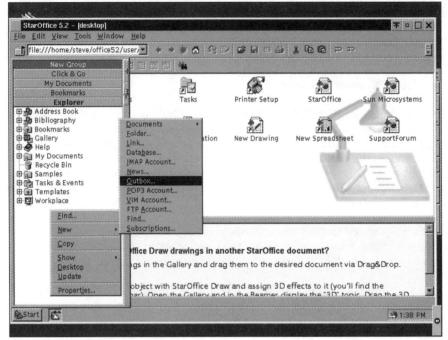

Figure 8-4: Creating an outbox in StarOffice

You also need to make sure that the information is correct for the main options. You can access these settings by clicking the Tools menu option and selecting Options. Two areas need to be completed: General – User and Internet – Mail/News.

Once all the information is available, the Mail interface appears. It enables you to create new mail messages, retrieve mail from the server, and read the mail. The Mail component supports POP, IMAP, and VIM mail protocols.

StarOffice Base

The Base database interface enables you to create front-end and back-end databases. You can connect to anything—from a text file to JDBC to ODBC to Adabas, the last of which you can also download and install. You can create your own interface for the database or use one of the many templates.

StarOffice Math

For scientific applications, documents, and such, you can create equations that require special symbols. Choosing File ➪ New ➪ Formulas takes you to the Math design area. From the special symbol window, you can pick the symbols to use. The tool then fills in the code used to create the symbols to produce the equation.

Task List

One of the features of a desktop application is the task manager. StarOffice offers a *Task List* as part of StarOffice Schedule, which enables you to create a to-do list complete with a start date and due date. Click the green and white notepad on the left end of the task to reveal an additional area for taking notes and cross-referencing tasks.

Calendar

The *Calendar* tool, also part of StarOffice Schedule, comes with the StarOffice program and integrates with the Task List and the Mail tool. Schedule a meeting with your staff, and then send them a notice of the meeting in e-mail. If the recipients use Netscape Calendar, you can format the meeting notice for them also.

The click-and-drag feature with this package enables you to create a task in the Task List displayed on the right side of the calendar and then drag it to the day and time you wish to perform that task. Figure 8-5 shows a sample of performing that duty.

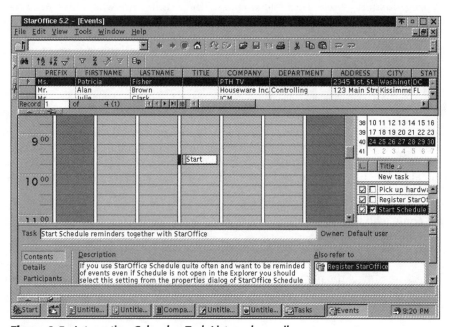

Figure 8-5: Integrating Calendar, Task List, and e-mail

Scheduling a meeting is as easy as setting the appointment in your calendar, double-clicking the event to view the details, selecting participants, opening your address book, and dragging those to attend the meeting in the participants list. The participants can be notified automatically of the meeting or notified only if the meeting changes.

Applixware

A commercial product owned by VistaSource, *Applixware* offers a complete outfit of tools and utilities needed to work in an office. It includes such common tools as word processor, spreadsheet, presentation creator, and so on. Applixware currently sells for around $99 retail. You can find more information about VistaSource and its products at www.vistasource.com.

This comprehensive office suite is built on the ELF language, which was made Open Source as SHELF (shelf.sourceforge.net). Because of the unique opportunity for programmers to use the same language that Applixware was built with. Programmers can then develop enhancements to Applixware ranging from integrating other applications to using Applixware as a back-end engine. Included with the suite is Builder, which enables you to make use of the ELF language for your own custom applications using object-oriented design tools.

Installation

Installation from the CD is straightforward. Before you install the Applixware suite, load the rpm Debian package. Applixware is distributed using RPM packages and complains if the installer cannot find rpm. You also need 250MB of free space for a typical install, but it can go up to 500MB with all the languages and dictionaries.

With a graphical interface running and logged on as root, follow the instructions that come with the CD on mounting. Mount the CD with the following command:

```
mount -r -t iso9660/dev/cdromdev /cdrom
```

Here, *cdromdev* is the name of the device you use, and *cdrom* is the mount point for your device. Once the CD-ROM is mounted, change to the CD directory and start the setup script:

```
cd /cdrom
./setup
```

The script initializes, makes sure it can install the files, and starts asking questions concerning language and so on. Answer these questions as they appear. You need to have the license number handy for one of the questions. At some point, you may be asked if you wish to update some Debian packages over the Internet. Doing this only upgrades any packages — nothing else is affected.

Once the installation completes, you are ready to start working. The installation routine places items in the menu for Gnome and KDE if you happen to use either of them. If not, then you can start the Icon bar using `applix` from the command line.

Note   It doesn't matter if one person or many intend to use Applixware. It only installs one way. Each machine you install Applixware on requires a purchased copy of the software according to the license agreement.

Navigating Applixware

Once Applixware finishes the installation, you need to restart Gnome and KDE in order to incorporate the additions into the menus. Using the menu system of Gnome and KDE, you have the option to open a specific component or launch the Icon bar. You can find these options under Applications on the main menu. Alternatively, you can open the Icon bar by issuing `applix` from the command line.

Applixware differs from StarOffice in that each function of its suite is independent of the rest. This means that there is no universal desktop for the suite. Another difference is that Applixware opens more formats than just Microsoft products.

Icon bar

The *Icon bar* opens when you choose Applixware from the menu. This reveals a bar, as shown in Figure 8-6, from which you can launch all the other applications. There are more components that what appears in the initial display. You can scroll back and forth to reveal the component you wish to use by employing the arrows on either end.

Figure 8-6: Using the Icon bar to access the office components

You need not open the Icon bar to open other applications. From each component there is a large, five-pointed star that enables you to open other components to the suite — most of which enable you to link data among them.

Applixware Words

The first component on the Icon bar is *Words*. This word processor component
enables you to create text documents. Figure 8-7 shows a letter composed in Words.
As you type, a red underline shows any misspellings; it disappears when you correct the item. Additional features include object insertion from other Applixware
files as well as a complete spell checker and thesaurus.

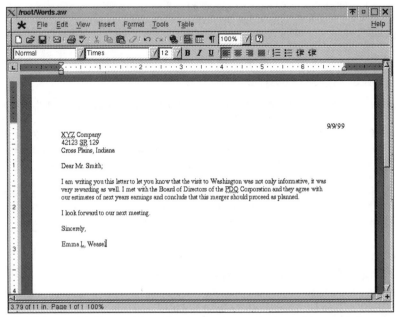

Figure 8-7: This letter, written in Words, shows the basic layout of the word
processor.

Words opens many forms of documents, including Microsoft Word and
WordPerfect. When you save documents in Words, you can choose to save them in
various formats as well — although most end up as Rich Text Format (RTF) for compatibility purposes.

Applixware Spreadsheets

When it comes time to keep your records, analyze last year's earnings, or just tabulate numbers, *Spreadsheets* is where you want to do it. As you can see from Figure
8-8, it comes with the regular row-column grid of cells and the multiple worksheets.
Like any spreadsheet, you can create formulas that reference the cells containing
the data used in the formula.

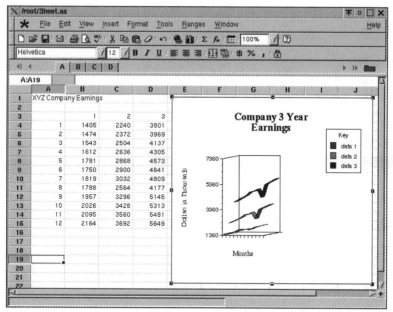

Figure 8-8: This spreadsheet shows how a chart displays the data in the cells.

The charting wizard enables you to choose which chart styles you wish to use, as well as make adjustments to the chart. When the data in the cells that produce the chart change, the chart itself updates to reflect the data changes.

Applixware Presents

After writing your letters and creating your charts, you now need to create a presentation to take to that important meeting. Employ *Presents* to create the slides used to impress those stockholders.

Presents can quickly take an object from another component and then use it in a slide. For instance, you can import the chart created in the spreadsheet shown in Figure 8-7 into a slide. Click the Insert menu option, choose Object from File, and then pick Applix Spreadsheet. Locate and select the file containing the chart for it to appear in the presentation slide.

Applixware Graphics

This graphics tool enables you to draw rough shapes and perform very simple tasks relating to the images. You can import images from files and other applications to incorporate in a new picture or to modify. This tool enables you to integrate imported images into documents. For instance, you can embed a picture created in Applixware Graphics into a Words document.

Applixware Data

The database is only a front end to some server. You must have a database server running in order to utilize this tool's complete functions. You can choose from the common database servers: Informix, ODBC, Oracle, Sybase, or ShelfSQL. You can configure ShelfSQL to use MySQL.

Applixware Mail

This tool provides a graphical interface to use as a mail tool. You can read, sort, and send new mail using this tool. It does provide a means for creating filters for the mail based on a set of criteria you specify. Depending on the results of the check, your incoming mail is processed as you dictate.

Use the *Send Applixware Mail* to create a new message to send. It brings up the appropriate interface where you can fill in the fields for the recipient, subject, and message and then send the message on its way.

Other features

Applixware offers several other features, which are described in the following list:

✦ Another graphical tool is the *Directory Displayer*, which enables you to see the directories and files in a graphical, clickable form. By default, it lists the Applixware files so you can click them to open the appropriate window.

✦ The *HTML Author* tool enables you to create simple, straightforward Web pages. You are limited to inserting only text and graphics on the page. Moving objects around on the design layout takes a little more effort than clicking and dragging to another area. There are provisions for using tables, but you must add the more advanced scripting features by hand.

✦ You can set global preferences for the Applixware suite of office components, such as macro location, filename preferences, and printer settings. These settings apply to all components in the Applixware suite.

Applixware BuilderUsing the *Macro Editor*, you can functionally add to the Applixware applications because the Applixware suite was created using Extended Language Facility (ELF). You can then use this language to create macros. The Macro Editor is the platform from which to create your enhancements.

Similar to the Macro Editor is the *Builder,* which graphically links several tools together. Figure 8-9 shows a form designed from Builder.

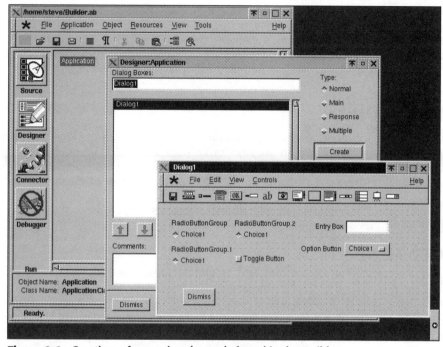

Figure 8-9: Creating a form using the tools found in the Builder

Reporting issues through SmartBeak

This is an automated method for submitting requests for help and reporting problems concerning Applixware or any of the other Open Source products built using ELF. You can also search a Web site for more help at www.smartbeak.com. You might want to search the site for any problem you have before submitting a report. Many people have already submitted reports that might address your problem. If you can't find an adequate description of your problem, then you can submit a report through the Web site or through the Applixware SmartBeak utility.

Caution

If you are running an older system that is low on resources — low memory, slow processor, little free disk space — you may want to choose an alternative. StarOffice (with its 300MB of disk space) and Applixware are voracious when it comes to resources. The features they offer are nice, but with a little effort you can replace them with smaller, lightweight applications.

Alternatives

You may want to use something simple for your office application. Perhaps you don't want to take the time to download over 100MB of installation files. Maybe you just don't have a system powerful enough to run StarOffice or Applixware. You have alternatives that still put a graphical interface into the essential office functions.

You may find that a graphical tool does not fit your situation. In this case, you may want to look at one of the layout languages — TeX, LaTeX, or Groff. These languages, when added to the text document, perform the formatting and layout adjustments when displayed or printed. This is something that can be produced as output from a program, manipulated using scripts, or produced automatically.

Gnome Office

This project combines several applications to create a complete office suite. Among the Gnome Office applications are AbiWord, Gnumeric, GIMP, Gnome-PIM, and Gnome-DB. Although Gnome has united them to create a complementary suite of tools, most of these are available as individual packages under Debian.

 Cross-Reference   Chapter 7 covers GIMP, a highly advanced graphics editor.

AbiWord

This word processor totes some heavy weight because it enables you to create letters, memos, and other written documents. This relatively small package includes such features as spell check notification, point and right-click spelling correction, and layout formatting. Figure 8-10 illustrates the right-click menu, which lists the correct word spelling. Click the correct word to automatically replace the misspelled word.

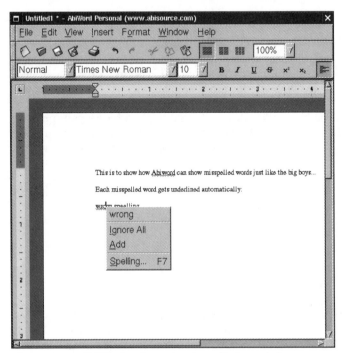

Figure 8-10: AbiWord points out misspelled words for easy correction.

When you're finished with the document and ready to save the file, you have a choice of formats to save as — AbiWord, Rich Text Format, HTML, or plain text. If you must share documents in a mixed environment, most word processors for other platforms accept the Rich Text Format.

Gnumeric

Unless you need to manipulate massive amounts of data, Gnumeric works well to tabulate, calculate, and evaluate numbers. Gnumeric is outfitted with the familiar rows and columns, so you can quickly enter the numbers, create a table, and calculate the sum. Figure 8-11 shows a simple 3-by-12 table with the sum created for the last column.

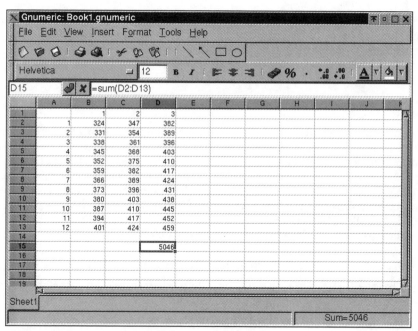

Figure 8-11: Use this spreadsheet to calculate data.

Even though a plotting mechanism is not integrated with this spreadsheet, there are tools to sort the data and perform analysis on the contents. When ready to save the data, you have several options from which to choose. You can save the data to anything from HTML to comma-delimited text or from TeX (explained next) to Excel 95 format.

Note On the horizon are plans to release a KDE set of office applications called KOffice. These tools include the standard word processor, spreadsheet, and presentation tools, but they also include image, chart, and database tools. You can learn more about the KOffice at `www.koffice.org`.

Publishing documents with text files

Traditionally, technical people tend to stay away from the WYSIWYG productivity tools. Because of their technical bent, these people use a publishing method that puts the formatting code into the text document. This is called *typesetting*. They can then employ other tools commonly used in Linux (such as `sed`) to manipulate the text document to add, remove, or change its contents.

There are two tools to format the documents. One is Groff, a document formatting system that can create different forms of output based on various macros. The other is LaTeX, which is an extensible language used to create formatting code within the document.

TeX

TeX is not actually an editor, but more of a layout language. While you create the document, certain commands are added to the text, which are converted into special formatting when the document is processed. The most common method for using TeX is to call macros to accomplish the formatting. There are several macros, but LaTeX is the highest functioning one and the one most commonly used. TeX interprets the LaTeX macros from the format file that is created when TeX is installed. This file is located at `/var/lib/texmf/web2c/`. One input file and three output files are produced when processing a document:

✦ `File.tex` — Input text file containing the formatting instructions

✦ `File.div` — Output file in a device-independent format for translation to various devices

✦ `File.log` — Output file containing diagnostic messages

✦ `File.aux` — Auxiliary output file used by LaTeX

When you create a document using a text editor, you include commands in that document having the syntax of:

`\string {option} [required]`

You replace *string* with the command you wish to use, and then add any options for that command. There is also a *required* field that you must fill in as well. Here is a simple LaTeX document:

```
\documentclass{class}
\begin{document}
Type your document text here.
\end{document}
```

Replace *class* with a valid class name, which includes book, letter, report, article, and slides. The contents of your document then go between the begin and end formatting commands. This is a basic layout for creating a LaTeX document.

There are tools to create LaTeX documents. A *converter* takes a document from another format and converts it into the LaTeX form. The last section of this chapter lists some of these converters. You can also use a graphical tool called *LyX* (package name lyx). This is a front-end text editor that can create LaTeX-formatted documents.

For more information about the LaTeX commands, read the information pages at:

```
info latex
```

Press the Tab key until the cursor appears on the line reading "Commands within a LaTeX document". Press the Enter key and start learning the commands.

Groff

Groff is the GNU front end to the nroff and troff text-formatting commands. These were the first set of commands that produced typeset quality documents on UNIX systems. The nroff commands produce formatted plain text; troff does everything nroff does, but also produces different kinds of fonts and spacing.

Because of its popularity with UNIX, Linux has adopted Groff for the creation of the man pages. Man pages are created with the typesetting language and then processed for viewing. The code in the document refers to macros initiated when Groff processes the document. Here are the most popular macros used to create documents:

✦ mdoc — The mdoc macros create the documents for the man pages.

✦ mm — The memorandum macros (mm) create memos, letters, and technical papers. They are capable of producing table of contents, figure lists, references, and other useful features.

✦ me — These macros create technical papers and memos (similar to mm).

There are more macros stored in /usr/share/groff/tmac. These macros can format the document for different types of output formats. Table 8-1 lists those formats.

	Table 8-1
	Groff output formats

Format	Description
ps	For the PostScript printers and viewers
dvi	For the TeX device-independent format (dvi)
X75	For a 75dpi X11 viewer
X100	For a 100dpi X11 viewer
ascii	For typewriter-like devices
latin1	For typewriter-like devices using the ISO Latin-1 character set
lj4	For a HP LaserJet4 compatible and other PCL5 compatible printers
html	To produce HTML output

For an example on formatting the output of a file using the eject man page, do the following:

```
cp /usr/man/man1/eject.1.gz /tmp/eject.1.gz
gunzip /tmp/eject.1.gz
groff -Tascii -man /tmp/eject.1 | more
```

These three command lines copy the file to a temporary directory so as not to damage the original file during a demonstration. The second command then decompresses the file to its raw form. Finally, Groff processes the file for viewing on the screen. Running man eject displays the same information. Now if you view the raw information, you see something entirely different. Running more /tmp/eject.1 displays the contents of the file, which you can see in Figure 8-12.

Figure 8-12: Viewing the document code for a file for processing by Groff

Now if you want to print the man pages, you can use Groff to format the document for the printer. Here is an example of formatting the output to a HP LaserJet 4 printer and sending it to the default printer:

```
groff -Tlj4 -man -l /tmp/eject.1
```

Table 8-2 shows some of the macros used when creating the manual pages. You can find more information about these commands by looking at the pages on the mdoc macro (man mdoc).

| | Table 8-2 | | |
| | **mdoc macros** | | |
Macro	**Description**	**Macro**	**Description**
.DD	Document data	.DT	Title
.SH	Section header	.SS	Subsection header
.LP	Begin paragraph	.PP	Paragraph break
.HP	Begin a hanging indent	.I	Italics
.B	Bold text	.DT	Set default tabs
.IP	Begin hanging tag	.TP	Begin hanging tag. Begins text on the next line
.TH	Title heading	.SM	Small text

You can find more information about Groff at www.gnu.org/software/groff/ groff.html. Here you can find out about the Groff project, catch up on the news, or ask questions on one of the mailing lists.

File Converters

On occasion, you may need to convert files from one format to another. Here is a list of programs and scripts you can use to convert a number of different file formats:

✦ info2www — Enables you to read info file through a Web browser

✦ man2html — Converts man pages to be viewed on a Web browser

✦ gif2png — Converts gif images to the png format

✦ div2ps — Converts device-independent files to PostScript

✦ latex2html — Replicates the structure of a LaTeX file to the HTML format

✦ `laytex2rtf` — Converts a LaTeX document to Microsoft's Rich Text Format (RTF)

✦ `a2ps` — Converts anything to PostScript

✦ `gnuhtml2latex` — Converts HTML files into the LaTeX format using a Perl script

✦ `html2ps` — Converts HTML documents to the PostScript format

✦ `word2x` — Transforms word files into text or LaTeX files

Summary

Although there does seem to be two separate camps when it comes to document creation, both have their place. For an average office worker, creating a document using TeX or Groff may not be as intuitive as a WYSIWYG program. For the administrator or programmer, the document formatting languages may work better because of their scripting potential. Fortunately, Linux can accommodate both types of needs.

On the horizon, as more people rely on GUI applications for home and office use, these tools will continue to develop and grow in popularity. While most may not care about creating documents with a formatting language, TeX/LaTeX's long history in the UNIX environment will not change soon.

✦   ✦   ✦

Essential Tools

Anyone using Linux for more than a platform to browse
the Internet needs to know how to administer their systems. To execute the administration successfully, they need to
know how to edit files — especially through a remote
connection.

This chapter covers two of the most popular text editors for
Linux — vi and Emacs. These editors are simple to use, and
you can employ them through a remote connection. This
chapter also covers a few of the more useful commands for
administrators (and everyday users).

Using Text Editors in Debian GNU

There is hardly a script, configuration, or text file that does
not require a change now and then within the Linux system.
These text files are generally easy to change, but you must
change them with a text editor. There are a number of text editors available for Linux systems, but choosing one usually
comes down to the person using the editor. These people fall
in one of two categories — graphical and nongraphical users.

The people who fall in the graphical category prefer to use a
graphical user interface style text editor. These people find
combining mouse clicks, menus, and typing more intuitive to
use. Working with these graphical interfaces can certainly
have its advantages. Graphical text editors enable you to use
the mouse to move the cursor, select text, and control menu
items. They also make available the control commands
through the menu so you don't need to remember special
commands to operate the editor. On the other hand, they
don't generally work through a remote connection.

Nongraphical text editors do have an advantage over graphical editors because they work over a remote Telnet connection. A Telnet connection is text-only, so nongraphical editors

work. This advantage weighs against the long list of commands used to maneuver through the document. People who are accustomed to using a nongraphical editor prefer using them in the long run. They feel that they have more control and power using a straight text editor than using a fancy graphical editor, even in the age of GUI desktops.

Learning to use vi

Some of you computer old timers may remember the line editor for DOS called edlin. This line editor enabled you to perform basic text editing in the DOS world. This editor was very simple to use, but it didn't offer much in the way of advanced text file editing. If you want a text editor that has many advanced editing features, then you can choose vi, which is easy to use while offering many of the advanced features of the more sophisticated editors.

The screen editor vi has its roots in the line editor ex. As a result, many of the commands used for ex also work with vi. vi enables you to view a text file in full screen; create, edit, and replace text within the file; and even execute shell commands outside of the editor.

The vi editor is a program that works within a terminal console. From a shell, simply execute the program from a prompt. When using vi while running in an X Window environment, you must open a terminal window to access the command line.

The vi editor opens any text file using one of three command syntax methods. The first syntax simply opens the specified file in the editor:

```
vi filename
```

Occasionally, when working with program files, an error may occur on a specific line. You can open that text file starting at that specific line using this syntax:

```
vi +n filename
```

Likewise, you may want to open a file to the first instance of a particular pattern, such as a variable name in a script or configuration file. You can do this by using this syntax:

```
vi +/pattern filename
```

In each of these three methods for opening a file using the vi editor, the filename reflects the name of the file you open. In the last two methods, *n* refers to the line number and *pattern* refers to the pattern you wish to find in the file.

In vi the entire screen fills with text. If the opened file only contains a few lines that don't fill a screen, the remaining (blank) lines display a tilde (~) in the line. The bottom of the screen displays information such as mode status. This is also where you enter commands when working in command mode.

vi commands

Once you have a file open in the editor, you then need to know how to maneuver, control, and edit the file. You can use this editor through a remote connection, so you can't employ a mouse to maneuver around the text window. However, with most modern vi implementations, you may use the keyboard arrow keys to move around your document. You must rely on the keyboard commands to maneuver the cursor through the document, change editing modes, and control the editor.

Insert mode

The first thing to discuss is inserting, appending, and editing a file. To do this, you must first enter insert mode. Table 9-1 shows a list of commands and descriptions for the various methods of adding text to a file.

Table 9-1
List of vi commands for adding text to a file

Command	Action
a	Append after cursor
A	Append at the end of the line
c	Begin change operation
C	Perform change from current cursor position to the end of the line
i	Insert before the cursor
I	Insert at the beginning of the line
o	Create a new line below the current line
0	Create a new line above the current line
R	Begin replacing or overwriting text
s	Substitute a character
S	Substitute the entire line

Pressing ESC terminates insert mode. Once out of the insert mode, you can perform other commands.

Line commands

Line commands provide methods of searching through a file to execute the line editor or shell commands. You can type these commands at any time. When a user presses the command character (/, ?, :, and so on), the cursor moves to the status line where the user can enter the rest of the command (see Table 9-2).

	Table 9-2
	Line commands

Command	Action
/pattern	Searches forward for a *pattern.* The pattern may be a simple word or string that you're searching for, or a regular expression.
?pattern	Searches backward for a *pattern*
:	Invokes an ex command.
!	Invokes a shell command that uses the buffer as the input and replaces it with the output from the command

Movement commands by character

Navigating through the screen (that is, moving the cursor to a specific position) requires that you not be in insert mode. Instead, you must be in command mode. Table 9-3 lists the commands used to move the cursor one character at a time when in command mode.

	Table 9-3
	Single-character movement commands

Command	Action
h	Left one character
j	Down one character
k	Up one character
1, SPACEBAR	Right one character

Movement commands by text

The commands listed in Table 9-4 enable you to move the cursor through the text more quickly by jumping to the next word, sentence, or paragraph.

Table 9-4 **Multi-character movement commands**	
Command	*Action*
w, W	Forward by one word
b, B	Backward by one word
), (	Beginning of the next or previous sentence from the current sentence
}, {	Beginning of the next or previous paragraph from the current paragraph
]], [[	Beginning of the next or previous section from the current section

Movement commands by lines

The commands listed in Table 9-5 enable you to maneuver through the screen line by line.

Table 9-5 **Line movement commands**	
Command	*Moves to*
0 (zero)	The first position of the current line
$	The last position of the current line
^	The first nonblank character of the current line
+, RETURN	The first nonblank character of the next line
- (dash)	The first nonblank character of the previous line
H	The top line on the screen
nH	n lines from the top line
M	The middle line on the screen
L	The last line on the screen
nL	n lines from the bottom line

Movement commands by screens

You may also move through your document quickly by moving an entire screen at a time. Table 9-6 summarizes these commands.

Table 9-6
Screen movement commands

Command	Action
CTRL+F	Scrolls forward one screen
CTRL+B	Scrolls backward one screen
CTRL+D	Scrolls down one-half screen
CTRL+U	Scrolls up one-half screen
CTRL+E	Scrolls down one line at the bottom
CTRL+Y	Scrolls up one line at the top of the screen
z, RETURN	Repositions with the cursor at the top of the screen
z.	Repositions with the cursor in the middle of the screen
z-	Repositions with the cursor at the bottom of the screen
CTRL+L, CTRL+R	Redraws the screen

Searching through files

Table 9-7 contains one of the most helpful groups of commands when working with large documents. You can search for text patterns found in the document to quickly display that section on the screen.

Table 9-7
Searching commands

Command	Action
/pattern	Searches forward in document for pattern
/	Repeats last forward search
/pattern/+n	Goes to line n after finding pattern
?pattern	Searches backward in document for pattern
?	Repeats last backward search
?pattern?-n	Goes to line n before finding pattern
n	Repeats previous search
N	Repeats previous search in the opposite direction
%	Finds the match of the current parenthesis, brace, or bracket

Saving your files and exiting the editor

There are different methods for saving documents and quitting the editor, as listed in Table 9-8. You may find that selecting a few methods serves you best.

Table 9-8
File commands

Command	Action
ZZ, :x	Writes the file to disk only if changes were made, then quits
:wq	Writes the file to disk and quits
:w	Writes the file to disk
:w *filename*	Writes a copy of the file to *filename*
:q	Quits only if no changes were made
:q!	Quits unconditionally, discarding any changes
:e *filename*	Edits *filename* without leaving vi

Options used by the :set command

On occasion, you need to set options used in the editor. You can set them from within the editor (see Table 9-9).

Table 9-9
Options for :set

Command	Action
:set all	Shows all available options
:set *option*	Enables *option*
:set no*option*	Disables *option*
:set *option=value*	Sets the *value* for *option*
:set *option*?	Shows the value of *option*

Alternatively, you can set options in the .exrc file you create in your home directory. If the file doesn't exist, then create it and add the settings you desire. You can put your :set commands in it, one per line.

Learning to use Emacs

Another popular editor is Emacs, which refers more to the family of editors rather than a specific editor. Most people think of GNU Emacs when you mention Emacs. GNU Emacs was developed by the Free Software Foundation and released under the General Public License (GPL) to the general public. You can install Emacs from the Debian package manager. Emacs is a large and versatile editor. This chapter gives you an overview. If you need more detailed information on a particular subject, you may access the Emacs Info documentation by pressing Ctrl+H and then i or the Emacs tutorial with Ctrl+H .

Emacs dates back to the days before graphical windows. By the time the graphical desktops were common, Emacs already incorporated many windowing features. In fact, Emacs was much more advanced than most applications. It incorporated text editing, shell command execution, and even e-mail access. The same Emacs works through a remote terminal connection or via an X server. Figure 9-1 shows Emacs running in an X Window environment.

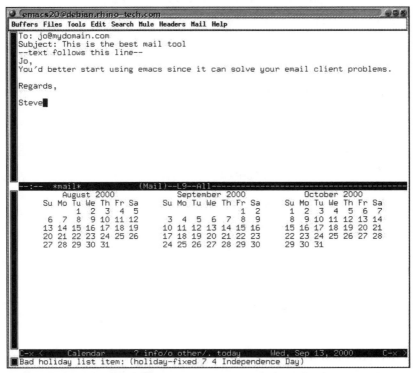

Figure 9-1: Emacs showing two windows: an e-mail message in one and a calendar in the other

Best used for creating, modifying, and compiling source code, the Debian GNU Emacs includes many useful features such as an interface to the Concurrent Version System (CVS), source code compiling, and debugging.

The Emacs menus

The Emacs' menus change, depending on which window buffer is active and the specific task that's running that window. You can click each window to make it active. You can then select the Buffers menu to select the buffer displayed in the active window.

Continuing on across the top menu, you come to the Files menu. Here you can open, save, or discard the buffers and manage the windows. You can split windows or combine them into one. You can also launch additional frames, which are essentially new instances of Emacs.

The Tools menu offers a number of advanced tools, mostly for programmers. From here, you can compare buffers, read news and e-mail, or compile and debug a program. You can also open a calendar showing the current, previous, and next months.

The Edit menu option contains the standard editing features (undo, cut, copy, and paste).

The Search menu also contains many of the searching features people like to use such as search, replace, and repeat search.

One of the interesting features that Emacs offers is multilingual support. To use this feature, you'll need to install one of the "mule" Emacs packages such as emacs20-mule. Then, you can access the multilingual support through the Mule menu option. You can use this option to change the language used while working in Emacs. Finally, there is the Help menu. This menu enables you to configure Emacs, set options, and get help for the program.

These are the basic menu options available in Emacs. When using one of the many special functions, you have access to even more options because the menus dynamically change to fit the environment.

Note   Other editors include vim, jed, and zed. **Look through the Debian packages under the category of editors for these and other editors you can install on your system.**

Using Commands and Programs

Besides the skill of using an editor, you, as an administrator or even as an end user, should know how to use a few commands and programs. Even though there are many more commands than what this chapter covers, this is a good start for your administrative tool belt.

alias

One of the complaints I've heard from novice users of UNIX and Linux is the use of cryptic command names. The alias program enables you to turn those cryptic commands into ones you can remember. It can also take frequently used, long strings of commands and shorten them to something easier to type. The syntax for alias is:

```
alias [-p] name='command'
```

This is actually a shell command, making it dependent on the shell you use. See Chapter 14 for more information on shells. Most common shells use the alias command because it is very useful. The -p option prints the list of aliases. Here's one example you might use:

```
alias longlist='ls -l'
```

After typing this command, in the future, you may use the longlist command to get a directory listing. The shell will actually run ls -l for you, but you don't have to remember that.

grep

Sometimes it is necessary to locate a pattern within a file. This is where grep is particularly useful. grep searches through a given file and, by default, prints the line that contains the matched pattern. The syntax for the grep command is:

```
grep [option] pattern [file] ...
```

The only required argument for grep is the pattern. It must have a pattern or it has nothing to find. Table 9-10 lists some of the options available for use with grep. As an example, if you want to scan for system errors in today's logs, you might use the command grep -i error /var/log/syslog. The -i option asks for a case-insensitive match. The result of this command will be each line that contains the word "error."

Table 9-10
Options for grep

Option	Description
-c, --count	Prints a count of matching lines for each input file instead of the normal output
-E, --extended-regexp	Interprets the pattern as an extended regular expression
-e *pattern*, --regexp=*pattern*	Uses *pattern*; this is useful to protect *patterns* beginning with a hyphen (-)
-F, --fixed-strings	Interprets the pattern as a list of fixed strings, separated by new lines, any of which is to be matched
-f *file*, --file=*file*	Obtains the search patterns from *file*, containing one pattern per line. An empty file contains no patterns and therefore matches nothing.
--help	Outputs a brief help message
-r, --recursive	Reads all files under each directory, recursively

There are two other commands related to grep—egrep and fgrep. Using egrep is the same as using grep with the -E option (from Table 9-10). Likewise, using fgrep is the same as using grep with the -F option. You can use the remainder of the options for any of these commands.

grep is very useful for programmers and coders. If you want to list all the lines of the source file that contain the variable *newfile*, you use the following command:

```
grep newfile mysource.c
```

grep then searches through mysource.c and displays each line that contains the text *newfile*. All other data in the file is ignored. In this example, the information is sent to the screen, but it can also be piped to another program or sent to a file.

find

Use find when you are looking for a file—whether you seek a file with a specific timestamp, a particular filename, or you are just looking for the location of a known file. Table 9-11 lists useful find expressions.

```
find [path] [expression]
```

Table 9-11
Useful find expressions

Expression	Description
-empty	The file is empty and is either a regular file or a directory.
-follow	Deference symbolic links. Implies -noleaf
-help, --help	Prints a summary of the command-line usage of find and exits
-user uname	The file that is owned by user uname (or the numeric user ID)
-group groupname	The file belongs to group groupname (the numeric group ID also allowed).
-fstype type	The file is on a filesystem of type type.
-name pattern	Searches base of the filename that matches pattern
-newer file	The file was modified more recently than file.
-iname pattern	Like -name, but the match is case-sensitive for pattern. For example, the patterns `mo*` and `M??` match the same filenames.
-version, --version	Prints the find version number and exits
-mount	Doesn't descend the directories on the other filesystems. An alternate name for -xdev, for compatibility with some other versions of find
-xdev	Doesn't descend directories on other filesystems

When faced with using the find command, you may wonder how it can specifically help you. Here are some applications in which find can come in handy:

✦ When searching for modified files to back up, use:

```
find /home/jo -newer /home/jo/lastbackup
```

✦ When looking for a file with a specific name, use:

```
find / -name picture
```

✦ When finding files belonging to a specific group, use:

```
find / -group users
```

This is only the beginning of what `find` can do when searching through the files on your system. You can link `find` with other programs, such as `tar`, to perform tasks on the found set of files.

locate

When all you want to do is track down a file, `locate` is very easy to use. `locate` lists the file paths of any file matching the given pattern. If no file exists, the prompt is returned. Otherwise, each file path is printed to the display. Here is the syntax for the `locate` command:

```
locate  [-d  path]  pattern...
```

The `-d path` option enables you to search a different path database instead of using the default database; however, the need for this is extremely rare. The `pattern` can be any pattern, and it can include wildcards. Here is an example of finding the filenames that contain `locate`:

```
# locate locate
/usr/bin/locate
/usr/lib/locate
/usr/lib/locate/bigram
/usr/lib/locate/code
/usr/lib/locate/frcode
/usr/share/emacs/20.7/lisp/locate.elc
/usr/share/man/man1/locate.1.gz
/usr/share/man/man5/locatedb.5.gz
/usr/X11R6/man/man3/XtAllocateGC.3x.gz
/var/lib/locate
/var/lib/locate/locatedb
/var/lib/locate/locatedb.n
```

cat

The `cat` command allows one or more files to be combined (or *concatenated*) and printed to the screen. This is a very simple program that has many uses. Here is the syntax:

```
cat [options] files ...
```

Table 9-12 lists the `cat` command options.

Table 9-12
Options for cat

Option	Description
-A, --show-all	Shows all characters, including all nonprinting characters (equivalent to -vET)
-b, --number-nonblank	Prints numbers at the beginning of each nonblank output line
-e	Shows nonprinting characters and tabs, but does not show end of line characters (equivalent to -vE)
-E, --show-ends	Shows the end of line characters
-n, --number	Prints numbers for all output lines
-s, --squeeze-blank	Never prints more than a single blank line from the output where more than one consecutive blank line occur
-t	Prints tabs and other nonprinting characters (equivalent to -vT)
-T, --show-tabs	Prints the tab characters as ^I
-v, --show-nonprinting	Uses ^ and M- notation for nonprinting characters, except for EOL (end of line) and TAB. This notation will show you control and meta characters as such and not print them directly to the terminal

Using the cat options helps you view a file, like the source code of a program, to check for the appropriate nonprinting characters. The main use for cat is to concatenate files together. You can use cat to take several small files and combine them into one large file. Here is how you do it:

```
cat file1 file2 file3 ... > newfile
```

top

A useful tool for administrators who need to watch the resources and activities for a system, top is a continuously running program that displays the processes and provides memory statistics and other useful information about the system. Figure 9-2 shows you what top looks like from the terminal console.

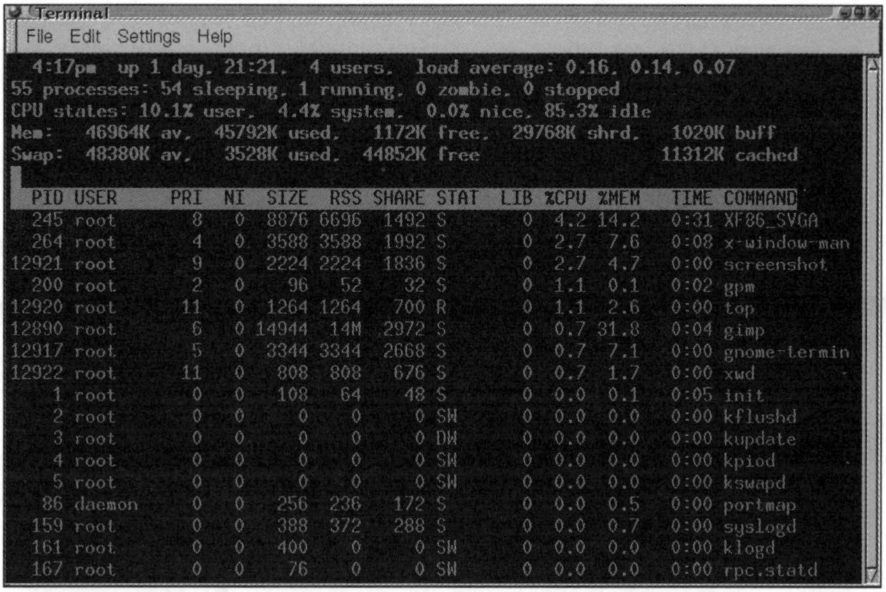

```
 Terminal
 File  Edit  Settings  Help
  4:17pm  up 1 day, 21:21,  4 users,  load average: 0.16, 0.14, 0.07
 55 processes: 54 sleeping, 1 running, 0 zombie, 0 stopped
 CPU states: 10.1% user,  4.4% system,  0.0% nice, 85.3% idle
 Mem:    46964K av,  45792K used,   1172K free,  29768K shrd,   1020K buff
 Swap:   48380K av,   3528K used,  44852K free                 11312K cached

   PID USER      PRI  NI  SIZE  RSS SHARE STAT  LIB %CPU %MEM   TIME COMMAND
   245 root        8   0  8876 6696  1492 S       0  4.2 14.2   0:31 XF86_SVGA
   264 root        4   0  3588 3588  1992 S       0  2.7  7.6   0:08 x-window-man
 12921 root        9   0  2224 2224  1836 S       0  2.7  4.7   0:00 screenshot
   200 root        2   0    96   52    32 S       0  1.1  0.1   0:02 gpm
 12920 root       11   0  1264 1264   700 R       0  1.1  2.6   0:00 top
 12890 root        6   0 14944  14M  2972 S       0  0.7 31.8   0:04 gimp
 12917 root        5   0  3344 3344  2668 S       0  0.7  7.1   0:00 gnome-termin
 12922 root       11   0   808  808   676 S       0  0.7  1.7   0:00 xwd
     1 root        0   0   108   64    48 S       0  0.0  0.1   0:05 init
     2 root        0   0     0    0     0 SW      0  0.0  0.0   0:00 kflushd
     3 root        0   0     0    0     0 DW      0  0.0  0.0   0:00 kupdate
     4 root        0   0     0    0     0 SW      0  0.0  0.0   0:00 kpiod
     5 root        0   0     0    0     0 SW      0  0.0  0.0   0:00 kswapd
    86 daemon      0   0   256  236   172 S       0  0.0  0.5   0:00 portmap
   159 root        0   0   388  372   288 S       0  0.0  0.7   0:00 syslogd
   161 root        0   0   400    0     0 SW      0  0.0  0.0   0:00 klogd
   167 root        0   0    76    0     0 SW      0  0.0  0.0   0:00 rpc.statd
```

Figure 9-2: From a terminal, you can only see the highly active processes.

While `top` is running, you can use a few interactive tools to control it. Table 9-13 lists a few of those commands. You can find more commands by using the help options. The most important interactive command is `quit`. It enables you to exit the program.

Table 9-13
Commands for top

Options	Descriptions
SPACEBAR	Immediately updates the display screen
^L	Erases and redraws the display screen
h or ?	Prints a help screen giving a brief description of the commands You can find information on the entire set of options supported by your version of top in that screen.
k	Kills a running process. You then are prompted for the PID of the process and the kill signal to send to it. A normal kill uses the signal of 15; for a sure kill, use the signal of 9.
q	Quits the top program

Note

Zombie processes are those processes that are stopped but not completely gone. These processes are already dead, so you cannot kill them. In most cases, a zombie goes away eventually. If a zombie does not go away, this generally means that there is a bug in the device driver or in the program from which the zombie came.

As you can see from Figure 9-2, the terminal window limits the number of visible lines. This can be a problem if you are looking for a process that shows up at the bottom of the list. If you use one of the window managers, an alternative tool to perform the same task is `gtop`, the GNOME System Monitor (shown in Figure 9-3).

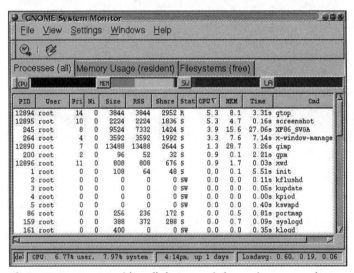

Figure 9-3: gtop provides all the same information as top, but in a graphical presentation.

`gtop` has three specific views — processes, memory, and filesystems. From the File menu, you can also add more views that enable you to watch certain groups of processes. Each view maintains its settings. Pressing any of the column headings sorts the list of processes by that column. There are also configuration controls that enable you to customize the settings for the program.

The more program

Granted you can use `cat` to view files. However, there are a couple of programs that will let you view a file in a much more convenient way. The first view program is `more`. Using `more` enables you to view the contents of a text file one screen at a time.

Once viewing the file, you can then interactively view the document. Table 9-14 shows some of the interactive commands. Most of the commands are based on the vi commands. If you are familiar with vi, working with more will be familiar.

Table 9-14	
Interactive control commands for more	
Command	**Description**
h or ?	Displays a summary of the commands
SPACEBAR	Displays the next screen of text
RETURN	Displays the next line of text. That line becomes the new starting point for the next screen.
q or Q	Exits
/pattern	Searches through the text for the occurrence of pattern.
CTRL+L	Redraws the current screen
. (period)	Repeats the previous command

You can use more to view one file or a series of files. Add each filename to the command line when executing the command to view it. For instance:

```
more text1 text2 text3
```

When text1 is finished viewing, text2 begins immediately, and so on.

The less program

The other text viewing tool, less, offers much more control while viewing the document. Whereas more only lets you scroll through the document in one direction, less lets you scroll in both directions. Table 9-15 shows only a few of the options available while viewing a document. Use less --help or view the man pages on less for more detailed descriptions of the available commands. The commands shown in Table 9-15 can get you comfortably started using less.

Table 9-15
Interactive control commands for less

Command	Description
SPACEBAR or f	Scrolls forward one window
RETURN or e or j	Scrolls forward one line
b or ESC+v	Scrolls backward one window
y or k	Scrolls backward one line
u or CTRL+U	Scrolls backward one half of the screen size
r or ^R or ^L	Repaints the screen
/pattern	Searches forward in the file for the line containing the pattern
n	Repeats the previous search from the last line containing the previous pattern
N	Repeats the previous search in the reverse direction
q or Q or ZZ	Exits less
! shellcommand	Invokes a shell to run the given shellcommand. A percent sign (%) in the command is replaced by the name of the current file. Two exclamation points (!!) repeats the last shell command. An exclamation point (!) with no shell command only invokes a shell.

less works much the same as does more. You can issue the command and then give the file to view as the argument:

```
less /usr/doc/README
```

When you start using the less command to view your documents and files, I'm sure you will find the up and down scrolling very useful.

Tip   When using commands that produce more than one screen of output, you can use the pipe (|) directive to view the output one screen at a time by using either more or less. Here is an example of the ls command using the pipe directive with less:

```
ls -l /etc | less
```

Automating Tasks

As the administrator of the system, you need to perform certain tasks on a regular basis. Each time you have to perform one of these repetitive tasks, it takes time away from performing other duties. Also, you cannot perform some of these tasks until later when the system is less busy. Doing this manually means either returning to the computer late at night or extremely early in the morning.

One way to solve the constant drain and demand of your time is to automate those routine activities. With the help of shell scripts (as found in Chapter 14) or by using a script language (like Perl, Python, or Tcl/Tk in Chapter 13), you can make the computer continue to work while you sleep. These scripts can then report back to you in the morning through e-mail.

Three primary automation tools initiate any programs, commands, or scripts. Each tool has its own unique method of execution.

The at command

The at command executes a specific command at a given time. at is limited to a one-time, automated execution of a given program. However, the specified time can be anytime in the future — from minutes to days. The syntax for the command comes in two forms. The first is as follows:

```
at [-q letter] [-f file] [-mlv] TIME
at -c job [job...]
```

Table 9-16 explains the various at options.

Table 9-16
at command options

Option	Description
-m	Sends mail to the user when the job (a running program) completes, regardless of the output. Normally, a message is only sent if the command generates output or has errors.
-f file	Reads the job to run from a file rather than the command line
-q letter	Places the program in the specified queue. The queue letter determines the priority at which a job runs. A queue letter designation consists of a single letter ranging from a to z and A to Z. Queues with higher letters run with lower priority. The a queue is the default for at, and the b queue is the default for batch.
-v	Displays the time the job executes. Times displayed are in the format "1997-02-20 14:50"
-l	Creates a listing of all the jobs scheduled to run for this user (the same as using the atq command)
-c	Concatenates the jobs listed on the command line with the standard output, usually the screen

Time is a mandatory component of the at command, with the exception of the -l option. Time can be in 12-hour time represented by hours:minutes (*hh:mm*) with the appropriate *am* or *pm* after the time. Or the time can display as a 24-hour designation of four digits (as in 1620, which is the same as 4:20 p.m.). You can also use one of the allowable keywords with the command—*midnight*, *noon*, *teatime*, or *now*. Use these keywords in place of the numerical time.

Specifying a date expands the at command functions even more. The text *month* and the numerical *day* comprise one of the allowable dates. Another option is stating the day of the week, or you can use *today* or *tomorrow*. If only a time value is given, then the command will be executed the first instance that your time is reached after the command is entered.

You can also add time. For example the time *now + 2 days* executes the job in two days at this time. You can also replace a *+1* with *next*. You then have *midnight next day* instead of *midnight +1 day*.

Here are some examples of times for the at command:

```
at 1620 pm Nov 12
at 4:20 pm November 12
at midnight next day
at midnight +1 day
at 2 am Monday
at now
```

Once jobs are queued to run, use at -l or atq to list them. You can also use atrm to remove a job by its job number.

The batch command

The batch command works much like the at command. The difference is that batch does not complain when you do not enter a time. In this case, the job runs when the system load falls below a 1.5. You can see from the following syntax that these options are similar to those of the at command:

```
batch [-q letter] [-f file] [-mv] [TIME]
```

The syntax for *time* is the same as with at except that *time* is optional. Refer to the at command's options to see what they do for the batch command.

The cron command

For systems that run all the time, as with servers, automatic tasks should run through cron. cron constantly runs once it gets started as a daemon when the system initializes, checking every minute to see if one of the listed jobs should run. The jobs that cron runs reside in /etc/crontab.

The jobs listed in /etc/crontab are generally for system tasks. You can see from the contents of the following file that there are only three jobs listed. Each of the jobs runs the contents of a directory containing scripts that need to run either daily, weekly, or monthly. You can still add more specific jobs falling outside of one of these times to the /etc/crontab file.

```
more /etc/crontab
# /etc/crontab: system-wide crontab
# Unlike any other crontab you don't have to run the `crontab'
# command to install the new version when you edit this file.
# This file also has a username field, that none of the other crontabs do.

SHELL=/bin/sh
PATH=/usr/local/sbin:/usr/local/bin:/sbin:/bin:/usr/sbin:/usr/bin

# m h dom mon dow user command
25 6 * * * root test -e /usr/sbin/anacron || run-parts --report /etc/cron.daily
47 6 * * 7 root test -e /usr/sbin/anacron || run-parts --report /etc/cron.weekly
52 6 1 * * root test -e /usr/sbin/anacron || run-parts --report
/etc/cron.monthly
#
```

The asterisk (*) represents a wildcard so that any day, week, or month works. After the first five fields, the user gets listed (as root is in the preceding example). The command then follows with all the information needed to run the command. When the time of the entry matches the current time, the job executes. Table 9-17 shows the syntax for adding a job.

Caution If the minute or hour is set to an asterisk (*), cron executes that command every minute or hour. This can cause the system to overload with job processes. I recommend that you only use the asterisk in the day of the month, month, or day of the week fields.

Table 9-17
Helpful crontab fields

Field Name	Allowed Value
Minute (m)	0-59
Hour (h)	0-23
day of month (dom)	1-31
Month (mon)	1-12
day of week (dow)	0-7 (0 or 7 refers to Sunday)

You can see by the contents of the `/etc/cron.daily` file that all the tasks run on a daily basis:

```
ls -l /etc/cron.daily
total 52
-rwxr-xr-x    1 root      root            311 May 25 14:13 0anacron
-rwxr-xr-x    1 root      root           3030 Apr 29 03:48 apache
-rwxr-xr-x    1 root      root            450 Jul 18 10:03 calendar
-rwxr-xr-x    1 root      root            427 Apr 29 19:07 exim
-rwxr-xr-x    1 root      root            277 Jul 28 17:46 find
-rwxr-xr-x    1 root      root             51 Sep 12  1999 logrotate
-rwxr-xr-x    1 root      root            238 Mar 15  1999 man-db
-rwxr-xr-x    1 root      root             41 Jul 28 17:46 modutils
-rwxr-xr-x    1 root      root            485 Jul 28 17:46 netbase
-rwxr-xr-x    1 root      root            383 Jun 20 21:07 samba
-rwxr-xr-x    1 root      root           2259 Mar 29 21:16 standard
-rwxr-xr-x    1 root      root            660 Jul 28 17:46 sysklogd
-rwxr-xr-x    1 root      root            157 May 19 04:26 tetex-bin
```

`cron` is not meant for only the root administrators to use; normal users can also take advantage of it. Each user can create his or her `crontab` file using the `crontab` *filename* command. Other options include `-l` (which lists the users' `crontab` files), `-e` (which edits the users' `crontab` files), and `-r` (which removes the users' `crontab` files). The contents of the files remain in the same format as found in the `/etc/crontab` file.

You can also restrict the users of `cron` because (by default) everyone on the system can use it. Create a `/etc/cron.allow` file and list each account name on a separate line to grant permission to the allowed users. You can also deny permission the same way by creating a file called `/etc/cron.deny` that contains a list of users to deny. You only need to create one of these files to enforce the restrictions.

The anacron command

In cases in which a computer does not run 24 hours a day and still needs to perform tasks, `cron` does not work. `anacron` does not depend on a computer running all the time to run an application. If the computer is off at the time the application is to run, `anacron` doesn't really care and can make sure that the job gets run anyway

`anacron` uses a configuration file to look up the jobs it should run. Each line in the file denotes an independent job to process. You can see from the following contents that the last three lines represent the commands needed to replace the `cron` command:

```
more /etc/anacrontab
# /etc/anacrontab: configuration file for anacron

# See anacron(8) and anacrontab(5) for details.
```

```
SHELL=/bin/sh
PATH=/usr/local/sbin:/usr/local/bin:/sbin:/bin:/usr/sbin:/usr/bin

# These replace cron's entries
1        5        cron.daily   nice run-parts --report /etc/cron.daily
7        10       cron.weekly  nice run-parts --report /etc/cron.weekly
30       15       cron.monthly nice run-parts --report /etc/cron.monthly
```

The first number of the job line denotes the period or number of days between runs. The second number indicates the delay before executing the command. Next comes the job identifier as indicated by cron.monthly in the last line. The job identifier can contain any nonblank character (except a slash). It identifies the job in anacron messages. The final option is the name of the command to run.

When the job runs, a timestamp is logged for that job so that anacron knows when the job was last run and knows when to run it again. The time between runs cannot be less than a day because anacron only compares the date, not the time. After a job finishes, a message is sent with the output of the job along with the job identifier.

Here is the syntax for the anacron command. Table 9-18 shows a list of options

```
anacron [-s] [-f] [-n] [-d] [-q] [job] ...
anacron -u [job] ...
```

Table 9-18
Helpful anacron options

Option	Description
-f	Forces the execution of the jobs and ignores the timestamps
-u	Updates the timestamps of the jobs to the current date only. Doesn't run any jobs
-s	Serializes the execution of the jobs. The next job does not start before the current one finishes.
-n	Runs the jobs now without waiting for the delay period of time specified in the /etc/anacrontab file. This implies the -s option.
-d	Doesn't send the job to the background. This option outputs messages to standard error, as well as to the syslog. The output of the jobs gets mailed as usual.
-q	Suppresses any messages to standard error. Only available with the -d option

These options add to the flexibility of this tool. However, anacron is a service and is therefore started through the initialization (or *run levels*) of the system. Any modifications to anacron need to be made to /etc/init.d/anacron and should be done by someone experienced with scripts.

Cross-Reference
Chapter 15 discusses run levels in more detail.

Summary

As you work along using Debian, you eventually will be required to edit a text file. Convenient graphical text editors may not be available. In this case, you should have a working knowledge of one or more text editors. Most likely, once you become comfortable with one text editor, you will stick with that editor for life.

In addition to using editors, some higher-end commands help to enhance the functionality of working with the system. These commands, especially when used with other commands, can perform remarkable tasks. The commands listed in this chapter, along with the automation tools, are designed to help make your life as an administrator easier.

✦   ✦   ✦

Multimedia

Computers are no longer just workhorses that process data, crunch numbers, or calculate the half-life of some atomic particle. Computers are also a great source for entertainment. You can use them to listen to music, watch movies, and so much more.

This chapter broadly covers these topics, showing you how you too can enjoy the pleasures of watching, listening, and experiencing multimedia on your system.

Listening to Audio Files

One of the greatest joys that a computer offers people is the ability to listen to music. Granted, a computer is an expensive radio or CD player if that were all it was used for. Many people listen to music while they work, like yours truly. This is a far cry from the muted sounds that emanated from the internal speakers of older computers.

The computer's capability to process sound has grown dramatically. Today, sound cards not only play back music, they can help to create music as well — through the Musical Instrument Digital Interface (MIDI) port. This is just one of the capabilities of the modern sound card.

The average sound card can record and play back sound by converting audio tones into digital data. The quality of a recording depends on the number of digital bits that are used when converting from sound to digital data — generally 8 or 16 bits. Another factor affecting quality is the rate at which the sound is sampled. The sample rate range is 5 kHz to 44.1 kHz, or 5,000 to 44,100 samples per second. The faster the sample rate, the better the quality of the recording, which also means the larger the size of the resulting data file.

Most sound cards can operate in *full duplex mode,* which means that sound can be recorded and played back simultaneously. This mode enables you to use a headset and talk live with others. Also included with the cards are various connections:

✦ Line-in — This port enables the use of external audio devices such as cassette decks, LP turntables (old-fashioned records), or any other device to connect to the computer for recording or playing back sound.

✦ Line-out — This allows the analog signal to output to an external device such as a tape recorder, stereo system, or some other device capable of receiving the audio signal.

✦ Speaker-out — Headphones and powered and nonpowered speakers connect here.

✦ Mic — This port accepts a microphone for recording audio input.

✦ Joystick/MIDI — This port connects to a joystick (usually for game play) or some type of MIDI device.

✦ Internal port — This provides an input port for audio devices internal to the computer. Normally, this is for the CD-ROM's audio output. Newer sound cards may have internal ports for a couple of CD devices, plus additional ones for auxiliary devices yet to be installed.

Sound cards require a driver to operate, which normally gets built into the kernel. The module that enables sound for Debian is called `soundcore.o` and should be added when first installed. It can also be added after initial installation by using `insmod /lib/modules/2.2.17/misc/soundcore.o` from the command line. Beyond that, the sound card may have a specific module driver. A variety of drivers are provided in the Open Sound System (OSS) module named `sound.o`. Other separate drivers available with the kernel include Ensonic, Creative Ensonic, ESS Maestro, Intel ICH, S3 Sonic Vibes, and Turtle Beach, just to name a few. A complete list can be found at `www.linux.org.uk/OSS`.

If you are installing a generic Sound Blast sound card, you will also need to load `soundlow.o` and set the parameters for the device. For the easiest method for installing and configuring the sound parameters, use the modconf interface. This is the same interface you used when you first installed Debian. Here is an example if the parameters you may need to add:

```
io=0x220 irq=5 dma=1 dma16=5 mpu_io=0x330
```

These parameters specify the hardware settings for the card. The `io=0x220` indicates the base IO address for the card. The `irq=5` specifies the card's interrupt. The `dma=1` and `dma16=5` indicate the direct memory access (dma) settings. The `mpu_io=0x330` refers to the IO address for the Musical Instrument Digital Interface (MIDI) connection on the card. You should refer to the manufacturers specifications and to the card's configuration for your sound card.

Note   For sound cards not found among the list of free drivers, go to `www.opensound.com`. This site offers downloadable sound drivers for evaluation. If you like them, you can buy them.

Several devices are used when accessing different features of the sound card, including the following:

✦ /dev/cdrom—This is a device used for listening to audio CDs.

✦ /dev/dsp—This stands for *digital signal processor,* which is used by many processes for handling sound.

✦ /dev/mixer—This is the sound mixing device.

✦ /dev/sequence—This provides the interface with MIDI, GUS, and FM devices at a low level.

✦ /dev/midi —This device provides the raw access to the MIDI port.

✦ /dev/sndstat—This device indicates the status of the sound card.

✦ /dev/audio—These are devices compatible with the Sun workstation audio implementation.

The dsp, mixer, midi, and audio device names have more than one device associated with them. This allows for multiple sound devices within the same machine. Regarding the /dev/dsp device, there also exists /dev/dsp1, /dev/dsp2, and /dev/dsp3 devices. Each of these devices can represent an additional piece of hardware.

You can determine the status of the sound card and the drivers loaded by using the following:

```
cat /dev/sndstat
```

The previous command results in the following output:

```
OSS/Free:3.8s2++-971130
Load type: Driver loaded as a module
Kernel: Linux hoth 2.2.17 #1 Sun Jun 25 09:24:41 EST 2000 i686
Config options: 0

Installed drivers:

Card config:

Audio devices:
0: Sound Blaster 16 (4.13) (DUPLEX)

Synth devices:

Midi devices:
0: Sound Blaster 16

Timers:
0: System clock

Mixers:
0: Sound Blaster
```

This code shows which drivers were installed for the sound card. In this case, Sound Blaster drivers (sb.o) are indicated for the audio, MIDI, and mixers. Remember that if no devices are listed, no drivers are loaded.

Note Most computers have, at minimum, a PC speaker. The kernel can be configured to use that speaker for audible beeps and dings. You can get the source to add speaker support as a patch to the kernel at `ftp.infradead.org/pub/pcsp`.

Audio file formats

Audio files come in several formats. Some applications work with a specific format, while other applications can play a variety of formats. For convenience, an application called SOund eXchanger (Sox) enables you to use over 20 types of sound files by converting them into a usable format (see Table 10-1).

Table 10-1
Sound formats used by Sox

Format extension	Description	Format extension	Description
aiff	File format used on Apple IIc/IIgs and SGI, which may require a separate archiver to work with these files.	au	Format used by Sun Microsystems.
cdr	Used to create audio master CDs	cvs	Continuously Variable Slope Delta modulation, which is used for speech compression such as voice mail
dat	This contains the text representation of the sound data.	vms	Used to compress audio speech
gsm	The Global Standard for Mobil tele-communications (GSM), which is used for some voice mail applications.	hcom	Macintosh HCOM files
maud	An AMIGA format that allows 8-bit linear, 16-bit linear, A-Law, and u-law in mono and stereo.	ossdsp	A pseudo-file for the OSS /dev/dsp device driver for playing and recording files
raw	Raw sound files containing no header information about the file	sf	Used by academic music software such as Csound
smp	Turtle Beach SampleVision files used to communicate with MIDI samplers	8svx	The Amiga 8SVX musical instrument description format

Format extension	Description	Format extension	Description
txw	Yamaha TX-16W sampler used for sampling keyboards	sb; sw; ub; ul; uw	Raw formats with characteristics. (sb signed byte; sw = signed word; ub = unsigned byte; uw = unsigned word; ul = ulaw)
voc	Sound file used for Sound Blaster	wav	The native Microsoft sound format
wve	Format used on the Psion palmtop portable computer		

Audio CDs

Music commonly comes on CDs. Audio CDs contain tracks whereby each song is equal to one track. A track is similar to a file. CD players use the information contained on the track to determine song length, which on some players can then be displayed. Songs can be pulled from a CD, but you need special software to do so.

Generally, you just want to listen to CDs. Several applications enable you to listen to CD music. The next sections cover some of the applications that work well.

GNOME CD player

The GNOME player is a rudimentary CD player specifically created to work in the GNOME environment. This application gets installed with the GNOME applications. As you can see in Figure 10-1, it contains the basic player functions, including play, rewind, fast forward, and even a button to eject the CD. The player shows the name of the group, the CD title, and the current track in the display.

Figure 10-1: Playing CDs with the GNOME CD player

To run the application from the command line, use `gtcd`. This application is loaded as part of the GNOME desktop.

XMMS

Another application that will play audio CDs is XMMS, formerly known as X11Amp. You can install this application using the xmms package found among the Debian package archives. This application has the look and feel of the popular WinAmp application found on the Windows platform.

When the application is running, place the CD into the CD drive, right-click the application panel, and select Play File or Playlist. Browse to the CD device, where you should see a list of the tracks on the CD.

With this program, not only can you listen to audio CDs, but you can also listen to your MP3 files (discussed later in this chapter). Figure 10-2 shows the additional features XMMS offers, such as an equalizer and a playlist. The highlighted song in the playlist is the one currently playing.

Figure 10-2: Listening to the MP3s with XMMS

If you have a directory with all the songs you wish to listen to, right-click the main display, select Add Location from the menu, and open the directory containing the song files. The rest of the controls follow the standard player conventions — play, rewind, fast forward, pause, and stop.

Grip

Another CD player of sorts is grip (also found among the Debian package archives). Launch grip from the command line and you will see a graphical interface like the one shown in Figure 10-3. In addition to playing CDs, this player enables you to copy the song tracks off the CD into a WAV file, which can be converted to MP3 format or left as a WAV. No MP3 encoder software comes as a Debian package. If you insist on creating MP3 files, you need to get one of the pre-configured converters or convert them separately.

Figure 10-3: Grip enables you to copy files from a CD into a WAV file.

One useful converter (also called an *encoder*) is `bladeenc`. This GPL application can be obtained from Tucows at `www.tucows.com` under Linux : Console : Multimedia/MP3 applications. It is a command-line application. Just remember to stay within the copyright guidelines and only make copies for personal use.

MP3 on Linux

A huge craze right now is the creation, sharing, and playing of MP3 song files. If you didn't know about it before, you probably learned about when the creators of Napster, a MP3 file-sharing program, were sued for copyright infringements. The appeal of MP3 is the small file size compared to the size of a CD track. The track for a five-minute song on a CD contains approximately 50MB of data. That same data can be compressed to 5MB with MP3.

You can see now how appealing the MP3 format is, if for no other reason than size. MP3 copies keep most of the original quality because of the way in which the data is converted. Studies have shown that there is virtually no perceivable difference between 1,000 kHz and 1,001 kHz audible tones. The original sound data may contain information about both frequencies, but this information gets dropped when converted to MP3. If you have ever tried to convert an MP3 file back to a larger format such as WAV, you may have noticed a reduction in quality because of the missing data.

Caution This is a disclaimer and warning to anyone wanting to share MP3 song files. Making copies of music for your own use is acceptable, but sharing or selling those files is considered a copyright violation. You should have the original media for all music copies.

Recording CDs

Recording CDs can be just as much fun as playing them. Compilations and "Best of" collections make great audio CDs. Use an application like grip to pull selected songs from other CDs, and then record them to a single CD with all your favorite songs.

Cross-Reference CDs can be used to store data files as well, a topic covered in Chapter 18.

Gramofile

If you grew up before the advent of CDs, you might remember listening to songs on long-playing (LP) records. If you still have any of those records hanging around, you may have considered copying them over to CD. Here is a little application to help you do that.

The gramofile package, found among the Debian archives, enables you to perform the complete process of recording an LP, processing the recorded sound file, and then recording the final file to CD. You can connect the output from your stereo (not the speaker output), which can play the LP to the input port of your sound card. Run the gramofile program from the command line of a virtual terminal. You will then get a menu to start your production process:

+ *Record audio to a sound file.* This option records the audio to create a sound file. The source can be a record, a tape, or any other source.

+ *Copy sound from an audio CD to a file.* This option is not yet implemented. You can use another program to record the contents of the CD onto the hard disk in a WAV format.

+ *Locate tracks.* LPs contain several songs separated by short periods of silence. This option locates the separation points and creates separate .track files for each song.

+ *Process the audio signal.* This option filters the song file to remove pops and cracks. Separate files get created for the filtered file.

+ *Write an audio CD.* This option is not yet implemented. You can use an application such as xcdroast to record the final song files to a CD.

Later versions should be fully functional, but at present, the version found in the Debian 2.2 release takes care of functions not found in many applications when recording from LP records, such as filtering and file separation.

xcdroast

There are several command-line applications for creating CDs. This CD creation process can be tedious. xcdroast uses a graphical interface to control the settings when recording CDs. You can doanload this package from one of the Debian mirror archives listed on the Debian Web site. Figure 10-4 shows what this interface looks like from the startup screen.

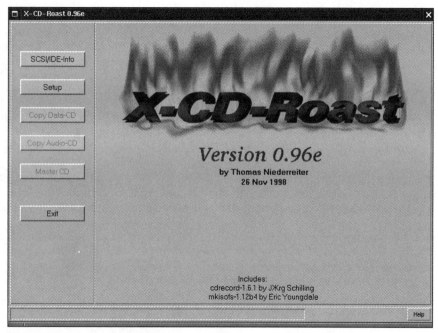

Figure 10-4: Introduction screen to xcdroast

The buttons along the left side take you to different control panels from which you can copy data, copy audio, create a master, or create an image to burn later.

This package depends on the existence of other packages in order to work properly. When you install the xcdroast package, make sure that you accept the other packages as well.

Streaming audio

Streaming audio has also soared in popularity, due in part to faster Internet connections and improved audio data compression. Streaming audio is similar to what you listen to on the car radio. A radio broadcast station transmits a signal that is picked up by your car radio antenna and processed by your local radio for you to hear.

Now, with access to the Internet, these same radio stations are broadcasting to your computer. If you would like to try your hand at becoming an online DJ, try Icecast, the subject of the next section.

Icecast client/server

Icecast is an open source project that was released to the public. The project enables anyone to set up an MP3 streaming broadcasting server. Icecast comes in two parts — a client and a server for installing in Debian. You can obtain these packages from one of the mirror sites found on Debian's home page. The server portion runs as a daemon and is controlled at /etc/init.d/icecast. The client feeds the MP3 stream to the server for others to pick up.

You can find a list of people broadcasting at icecast.linuxpower.org. The official Web site for Icecast is www.icecast.org. When you install the client and server portions on your Debian system, here is how it works:

The server gets started with /etc/init.d/icecast start. It then runs using the default settings, waiting for a device to stream audio to it for broadcasting. (Editing the /etc/default/icecast file will also allow icecast to start when system starts)

The client portion that streams the music to the Icecast server is called shout. Run shout from a command line to get the settings straight. Several options are available for use with the client. Later, you can create an executable with all the options fixed. Here is an example command using the shout client:

```
# shout localhost -P letmein -a -x -p ~/playlist -l -g techno
          -n "My techno server" -u "http://icecast.org"
```

Using the preceding line, shout would connect to localhost using the default password of letmein; stream the files listed in the file ~/playlist; and send directory server information indicating that the genre of music is techno, the name of the broadcast is My techno server, and the URL is http://icecast.org. You would then see the following when run:

```
cecast.org" /cdrom/technohe.mp3
Parsing arguments...
Base directory does not exist, trying to create
Adding /cdrom/technohe.mp3 without bitrate
Resolving hostname localhost...
Creating socket...
Connecting to server localhost on port 8001
```

```
Logging in...
Activating signal handlers..
Starting main source streaming loop..
Playing from /tmp/shout/shout.playlist, line 1
No bitrate or command specified, using autodetect
Checking mpeg headers...
Filename: /cdrom/technohe.mp3
Layer: III          Version: MPEG-1 Frequency: 44100
Bitrate: 128 kbit/s   Padding: 0    Mode: j-stereo
Ext: 0  Mode_Ext: 0   Copyright: 0   Original: 1
Error Protection: 1   Emphasis: 0    Stereo: 2
Playing /cdrom/technohe.mp3
[3:18] Size: 3180379 Bitrate: 128000 (40774 bytes/dot)
[                                                    ]
```

The sound begins to stream immediately. When the first song finishes, the next one starts broadcasting.

Once the Icecast server is set up, you can use one of three formats: mpg123, xmms, or freeamp. Because xmms was discussed in this chapter, here is how you would listen to streamed audio with the xmms client: Run xmms http://*host*:*port*, or press Ctrl+L and enter the URL. The *host* name and the *port* number (8000 by default for players) are defined by the Icecast server. In the case of the server you just set up, this is how you would start listening to your broadcast:

```
# xmms http://localhost:8000 | mpg123
```

RealPlayer

A popular player found in the commercial world is RealPlayer, which is in no way opensource. This player offers several advantages that most players don't, one of which is that it includes a plug-in for Netscape. Now, when you browse a Web site that includes playable links, you can listen as you would with streaming audio from radio stations.

If you want to use RealPlayer yourself or make it available for others to use on your system, here is how to you can download and install a free copy (you can also purchase a copy online if you would like):

1. Open a Web browser and connect to www.real.com/player.

2. Click the RealAudio Basic link in the lower left area of the Web page to get the free version of the player. This will take you to a form.

3. First click the OS version and select UNIX from the list. The form will change again.

4. Now you can fill in the fields with the appropriate information. When you get to the Select OS box again, select Linux 2.x (libc6 i386) from the list.

5. After the information is entered in the fields, click the download button. It will take you to the download location page.

6. Click a location, usually the one closest to you, to start the file downloading. It doesn't matter where you save the file locally, as the file you are downloading is a binary installer.

7. Once the file is local, make sure that it is executable. Launch the installer, and follow the directions presented during the installation.

```
# chmod u+x rp8_linux20_libc6_i386_cs1.bin
# ./rp8_linux20_libc6_i386_cs1.bin
```

The player is installed at /usr/local/RealPlayer7 when logged in at root, and the binary that starts the program is realplay. Otherwise, the program is installed in your home directory. When installed for the system, make a link from the executable program to /usr/bin so others can launch the player easily. Here is the command you use to create the link:

```
# ln /usr/local/RealPlayer7/realplay /usr/bin/realplay
```

Now, anyone with /usr/bin in their path (which is most anyone) can launch realplay from the command line.

Note   RealPlayer also displays a certain type of video media formatted for RealPlayer. These usually end with .rm to indicate that they are real media for the player. You can also use the player for streaming audio and video.

Watching Videos

Watching video is not unlike listening to audible media. Once you get the hardware configured correctly, you only need to make sure that you are trying to view a compatible file format.

A component built into the kernel these days goes by the name of video4linux. These are specific modules that enable the kernel to communicate and control video cards specifically designed to buffer captured video. These cards are referred to as *frame buffers* due to their capability to capture frames of video. Some of these cards, for example, are used in laboratory environments where they capture frames from a camera connected to a microscope. Normally, these cards are very expensive and not meant for the average desktop.

However, in most cases, as long as your video card can view X , it should be able to view video files.

Cross-Reference   For more information on setting up your video card to work in the X Window environment, see Chapter 4.

MPEG videos

Like audio, video also comes in several formats. The most common is the Moving Picture Experts Group (MPEG) format. This format can include sound as well as the video. To view an MPEG video, you need to install the `smpeg-plaympeg` package along with any other packages it depends on.

Once installed, you can start viewing a video file by typing the following:

```
plaympeg filename
```

The *filename* is the name of the MPEG video you intend to watch. The video will start playing in its own window. There are no controls for starting, stopping, or pausing the video once it starts.

Note You can find other players at one of the online repository sites, such as Tucows (`www.tucows.com`). Several Linux players work with X11, GNOME, and KDE. Many of them are freely available with the GNU public license, so feel free to share them with friends when you find one you like.

DVD videos

Playing Digital Video Disk (DVD) movies on your Linux workstation will take a bit more effort. First of all, there is the matter of obtaining the software. Since there has been some controversy over the DVD encryption — some contend that it has proprietary information, and law suits have cropped up to stop open source distribution. Clearing the legal hurdle is the first step. You can find out more about these issues at `www.opendvd.org/myths.php3`.

To get a DVD to work with your system, you must first have a DVD drive installed. You also need to add a patch to the 2.2.x kernel to enable the kernel to control the player. To get the patch, go to `www.linuxvideo.org/developer/dl.phtml`, where you will find other video-related applications as well. Contained in the compressed `tar` files is a README document that contains the instructions for compiling and installing the patch for the kernel. The 2.4 kernel includes the code for the DVD players and does not need the patch.

At the time of this writing, the DVD player software, called LiViD, is in alpha release. Some screen shots available on the Web site show remarkable clarity from the player. At present, the LiViD compressed `tar` package contains the DVD patch and other drivers. You can extract the contents of the packages using

```
tar zxvf filename
```

where *filename* is the name of the compressed `tar` file. Follow the instructions included in the compressed file to complete the installation.

Using Live Voice Chat

You can also use the sound card in your system for live two-way conversations via the Internet. All you need besides the sound card is a microphone, speakers, and software on each computer participating in the conversation.

One application that enables you to talk through the computer is called *SpeakFreely*, and it can be obtained from www.speakfreely.org as source code. Or, you can get an RPM package from a place such as Tucows' (www.tucows.com) Linux : X11 : Communications section. If you get the source, you need to compile it before running. Instructions for compiling can be found in the INSTALL file in the extracted directory.

This version of SpeakFreely, available at Tucows, is compatible with the Windows versions also available from the SpeakFreely Web site. In addition to SpeekFreely, another program, RogerWilco BaseStation (www.resounding.com/products/downloads), also allows verbal communication through the computer. The Web site offers the binaries for download as well as instruction for installation.

Summary

You can now turn your computer into a fully functioning multimedia station for listening and watching nearly any form of entertainment media that comes your way. You should now know how to convert audio formats to a form that you can use, and then listen to those files. With the convenient tools covered in this chapter, playing audio CDs should no longer be shrouded in mystery.

With the MP3 craze gaining steam, you now know how to listen to your own MP3 songs. You can even set up your own streaming audio server for a local network, as well as make a public station on the Internet.

MPEG-formatted video files can also be viewed on your local system. And watch for the open-source DVD players to soon become available in a stable version. All in all, there is no reason why a Debian GNU/Linux workstation cannot be used as a multimedia workstation using the tools discussed in this chapter.

✦   ✦   ✦

Games

Everyone needs time to play — what better way to take a break than with Linux? To some, gaming means taking a few minutes out of the day to play a little solitaire. To others, it means hours spent mastering a game to do battle with multiple players. Both can find satisfaction with Linux, as it offers something for everyone.

This chapter covers the games included as Debian packages, as well as commercially sold games suited for the abilities, interests, and skill levels of various users. The games range from simple text games to highly complex, beautifully designed games with intense action.

System Considerations for Gaming

Let's face it, the gaming industry drives the computer hardware industry. The demand for increasingly realistic games has produced sophisticated 3-D graphic cards and sound cards. Gone are the days when a game's graphics entailed images made up of a grid of ASCII characters on the screen. Today, smooth 3-D rendering of images through hardware graphic processors and software modeling produces some of the most outstanding game play.

The result of this sophistication is the prodigious hardware requirements you must meet in order to enjoy such works of art. That means you need 3-D graphic cards, compatible sound systems, more hard drive space and system memory, and even faster processors to get the most out of a game.

Graphical interfaces

Graphical interfaces are the heart of today's games. As developers include more graphical content with games, the attraction to those games increases. Linux has kept pace with this ever-changing technology. Currently, the Graphical Use Interface (GUI) environments consist of three primary areas: X Window System, SVGALIB, and GGI.

X Window

The X Window System, or X, is the normal graphical environment for most applications using graphical display. This environment consumes a majority of resources to manage the desktop environment, leaving less for the game itself. Game performance may suffer as a result.

The Super VGA Library

The Super VGA library interface (SVGALIB) for Linux enables games to run in their own environment. It controls both the graphics and mouse for the game application. This enables the game to run faster than in the X environment. Some games include the SVGA package, or it can be installed separately with the `svgalibg1` Debian package.

Tip   If you find that you don't have mouse control when using SVGA, edit the `/etc/vga/libvga.conf` file. This configures the mouse control for the SVGALIB interface.

Currently, support for this interface is lagging behind other technologies. Eventually, it may be replaced altogether by one of the newer technologies such as GGI. You can find out more about this interface at `www.svgalib.org`.

General Graphics Interface

The General Graphics Interface (GGI) provides an alternative to the older versions of the graphical interface—X and SVGALIB. It can actually run under the other interfaces and still provide the higher graphic performance. You can find out more about GGI at `www.ggi-project.org`.

You can install the `libggi2` package from the CD, but be aware that this package was made from a beta snapshot. If you are serious about using GGI, get the current version from their Web site.

One specific area where graphics has a large following is in the gamming arena.

Note   There is a GGI X server specially designed to take advantage of the performance that makes GGI enticing. This too comes as a Debian package. Look for the `xserver-ggi` package on the Debian archive.

Sound system requirements

What is a good graphical game without the sounds to go with it? For some games, such as the legendary *Doom,* the sound gives you hints for the games, such as where the next monster will come from. More recent examples of games providing sound along with the game would be *Quake, Quake II,* or *Quake Arena.*

As with graphic technology, sound systems are driven by the gaming industry, though to a lesser degree. Most games work with the Open Sound System (OSS), a set of drivers incorporated into the Linux kernel. A commercial version of the OSS drivers can be found at www.opensound.com. If you check the list of cards that are compatible with their drivers, you'll see that most are supported by Linux. For more specific information about sound in Linux, go to Chapter 10.

Other system demands

As games grow in complexity, so do the demands on your system. More intricate, detailed games take up more space on the hard drive and demand more memory to run. These demands encourage gamers to upgrade to new hardware, if not entirely new systems.

Because of the way in which Linux manages its resources, Linux games usually can operate with far fewer resources than some other operating systems. Moreover, the game hardware demands have not reached the levels you might see for other operating systems such as Windows. As more games are ported to the Linux platform from the Windows platform, you might start noticing the minimum systems requirements rising as well.

Playing Debian-Packaged Games

Games come in all varieties. Some are remakes of popular arcade-style games, others are played using only the text console with descriptions, and still others take advantage of the full graphical capabilities of Linux. Regardless of the type of game you want to play, there is something available for everyone.

Tip When you install a game, it is generally placed in the /usr/games directory. If you play games often, you may want to add the directory to your path. That way, you don't have to enter the full path each time you want to play.

A veritable smorgasbord of games awaits you, pre-packaged for Debian, and ready for you to install. The following sections classify the games as you would expect to find them in the Debian menu once the game is installed. Some of the listed games are text-based, while others are graphical.

Note Many of the games are packaged in the bsdgames package on the CD. This package includes games such as Adventure, Arithmetic, atc, Backgammon, Battlestar, bcd, Boggle, Caesar, Canfiled, Countmail, Cribbage, Fish, Gomoku, Hangman, Hunt, Mille, Monopoly, Morse, Number, Pig, Phantasia, Pom, ppt, Primes, Quiz, Random, Rain, Robots, Sail, Snake, Tetris, Trek, Wargames, Worm, Worms, Wump, and wtf.

Adventure games

Adventure games existed long before graphical games. Most of these were in the form of a textual adventure. A textual adventure works by describing the environment, objects, and possible directions you can go. For instance, the game Adventure starts with the following description of your location:

```
You are standing at the end of a road before a small brick
building. Around you is a forest. A small stream flows out of
the building and down a gully.
```

You then respond with the text of what action you would like to take:

```
goto building
```

The game then responds with:

```
You are inside a building, a well house for a large spring.

There are some keys on the ground here.

There is a shiny brass lamp nearby.

There is food here.

There is a bottle of water here.
```

You can then pick up an object, each of which provides help in completing the adventure. These textual adventure games respond to a number of text commands. Table 11-1 contains many of the adventure games packaged for Debian.

Table 11-1 Adventure games	
Game	*Description*
Adventure of Zork	Text-based adventure through caves. Similar to the first versions.
Battlestar	Text-based
GNOMEGNOME Hack	Graphical version of the Hack adventure game
Hunt the Wumpus	Text-based adventure in search of the Wumpus
Net Hack	Text-based multi-player Hack game
Phantasia	Hack-like text game
Rogue	Alternative Hack game
X NetHack	Graphical multi-player version of Hack

Arcade games

Many of the games that some of us grew up with in the arcade are now available for Linux, such as Space Invaders Galaga and Digger. These types of games generally consist of a 2-D graphical display, and are controlled by either the keyboard or the mouse. Table 11-2 describes some of the games packaged for Debian.

	Table 11-2 Arcade games
Game	**Description**
Amphetamine	A two-dimensional scrolling adventure
Galaga	Linux version of the arcade game Galaga
Gem DropX	Match three or more gems before they all fall on top of you.
GNOMEGNOME xbill	Play the role of administrator to save the computer systems before Bill changes them all to Windows computers.
Robots	Text-based game in which you move around the screen avoiding the robots.
Sabre	Flight simulator
Snake	Text-based game in which you move around the screen picking up dollar signs ($), but avoiding the snake
Space Invaders	Linux version of the arcade game Space Invaders
Star Trek	Star Trek adventure game
Xabuse	A side scrolling shoot'em up game.
Xbill	Play the role of administrator and save the computer systems before Bill changes them all to Windows computers.
XBlast	A multi-player game on the lines of Bomberman. Blast your opponent with a bomb before you get blasted your self.
XDigger	Linux version of the Digger arcade game. Dig through the dirt to gather the jewels, but don't get caught by the monster.
XEvil	A bloody two-dimensional adventure game
XKoules	Push the balls into the wall without hitting it yourself.
XPilot	A multi-player tactical maneuvering game where you blast the opponents to score points.
XScavenger	Old-style 2-D arcade game in which you pick up gems while avoiding capture

Continued

Table 11-2 *(continued)*	
Game	**Description**
XSoldier	2-D space shooter
XTux	Run the penguin around killing rabbits
Xbat	Scrolling Raptor-like game
Xboing	Advanced pong-like game
Xdemineur	Minesweeper-like game
Xjump	Jump to the next platform before the platform leaves the area.
Xkobo	2-D space shooting game
Xoids	Linux version of the Asteroids arcade game

A few of these arcade games are similar to some of the Windows arcade games, such as Minesweeper. Try a few out and see which ones you like.

Board games

In spite of today's sophisticated software, nothing can replace a classic board game like backgammon or chess. Many of the classic board games are available for Linux. Table 11-3 describes some of the board games packaged for Debian.

Table 11-3 **Board games**	
Game	**Description**
Backgammon	Text-based backgammon
GNOMEGNOME Gyahtzee	The game of dice
GNOMEGNOME Iagno	Othello-like game
GNOMEGNOME Mahjongg	Tile matching game
Go	The classic Japanese game
Monopoly	Text-based Monopoly
Penguine Taipei	Tile matching game with editor (same as Mahjongg)
Pente	Text-based Pente board
Xgnuchess	X Window Chess game
Xarchon	Chess-like board with different rules
Xboard	X Chess board (same as Xgnuchess)

Game	Description
Xgammon	X Window backgammon
Xbattle	A multi-player military game of conquest.
Xvier	A connecting game
Xchain	Chain reaction game in which squares react to one another

If you like the classic board games, something in this list will surely appeal to you.

Card games

If you enjoy card games, a slew of them are available for Linux. Some are text-based, while others are graphical. Whether you want to brush up on the rules for a game or improve your skill, these card games can be a nice diversion for a few minutes before returning to work. Table 11-4 describes some of the card games packaged for Debian.

Table 11-4
Debian card games

Game	Description
Canfield	Text-based Canfield
Cribbage	Text-based Cribbage
GNOME Freecell	Graphical Freecell solitaire
GNOME Solitaire Games	Includes 30 graphical solitaire games
Go Fish	Text-based game of Go Fish
Mille Bournes	Text-based version of the Mille Bournes card game
Penguin Freecell	Graphical Freecell solitaire
Penguin Golf	Graphical Golf solitaire
Penguin Solitaire	Graphical traditional Klondike solitaire
Spider	Graphical Spider solitaire
X Solitaire	Another graphical traditional solitaire
Xskat	A German card game defined by "Skatordnung."
Xmille	Graphical versions of the Mille Bourne card game
Xpatience	Two-deck version of solitaire
Xmahjongg	Tile matching game

The most popular card game is Klondike solitaire. Playing solitaire with a deck of cards just doesn't seem as much fun after you've played it on a computer.

Simulation games

The simulation games are a little different from the classic, arcade, or card games. These games let you control various environments, such as the growth of a city (see LinCity) or the control tower of a busy airport (see Air Traffic Controller). Table 11-5 describes some of the simulation games packaged for Debian.

Table 11-5 Simulation games	
Game	**Description**
Air Traffic Controller	Text-based game in which you are the air traffic controller
LinCity	Linux version of the SimCity game, in which you plan the expansion and growth of a city
Sail	Text-based sailing adventure
Xlife	A cellular-automation laboratory

LinCity

LinCity is a popular simulation game. It is similar to SimCity. Once installed, you can start this game from the menu or from the command line (with /usr/games/ xlincity). Either way, you end up with a screen interface that looks like the one shown in Figure 11-1.

When you start LinCity for the first time, it asks you to create a directory to save your games. You can then read up on how to play the game. You develop your city by adding roads, markets, ore mines, communes, and so on. These elements help the city grow. Following are some tips for playing the game:

   ✦ Right-click a button to read a description about it before selecting it.

   ✦ Use the Tips button on the left sidebar to create an area for trash.

   ✦ Food is important to the community. If you run out of food, people will either move out of the community or die. Have farms create the food or import it.

   ✦ Mills can create food, but the people running the mills also consume a lot of it.

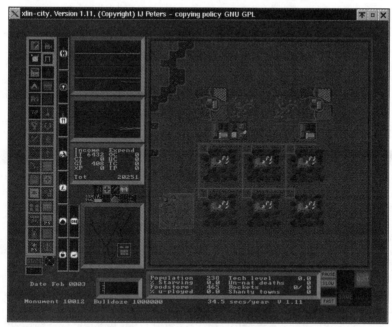

Figure 11-1: With LinCity, you can develop a virtual community.

Strategy games

If you need a real challenge, play a game of chess against the computer; and not on a single-layer board, but on a three-tiered board, as in 3-D chess. Other strategy games let you build a civilization or battle it out in space. Table 11-6 describes some of the strategy games packaged for Debian.

	Table 11-6
	Strategy games

Game	Description
3D Chess	Play chess on three levels at once.
Batalla Naval	Multi-player battleship-like game
Craft	A real-time strategy based on a version of WarCraft
Freeciv	A free client/server version of the Civilization game
XshipWars	Space battle game with *Star Trek* ships
Xconq	Civilization-like game
Xlaby	Complete the maze by tagging the colored squares with your mouse

Xlaby

If you like maze puzzles, then you'll like this fun little game. When you start this game from the Debian menu, a maze appears with your mouse "caught" in the maze. The cursor cannot cross the line of the maze, so you can't cheat. You must follow the maze to reach the colored dots in a particular order. When you get to the first dot that disappears, go on to the next dot that disappears. After you reach the last dot, the maze is completed and you can use it again.

Multi-player games

While playing games against the computer can be loads of fun, the fun may not last long as you master the game. However, when you play against other people of like skill, the challenge grows along with the game play.

This is where networked, multi-player games enter the picture. There is nothing like playing games with some friends on a network. Not only do you have the challenge of competing against a human, but there is the aspect of the friendly bantering.

Table 11-7 lists some of the games available that enable multiple players (some of which are commercial). Some of these have two separate components: a client and a server. Each runs independently, with the exception that in some cases, there must be a server running for the client to connect to. If one doesn't exist, you can't use the client to play.

Cross-Reference   Before playing games on a network, you need to have a network up and running. Turn to Chapter 5 to learn how to setup a networking chapter and get the network running.

Table 11-7 Multi-player games	
Game	**Description**
Lxdoom	First person shooter from the classic Doom game
Quake	First person shooter game
FreeCiv	Free variant of Civilization
XshipWars	Space battle using *Star Trek* ships
Batalla Naval	Battleship-like game played with up to eight players
Chess	Multi-player chess
Net Hack	Network version of the Hack adventure game

FreeCiv

In this popular game, you develop a civilization with the goal of conquering the world. FreeCiv is a client/server game, although you can play in the single-player mode. The client comes in two versions: Gtk and Xaw3d. Both client versions work in the X environment, but if I had to choose between them, I'd go with the Gtk version because of the interface. Figure 11-2 shows a game in progress using the Gtk client version.

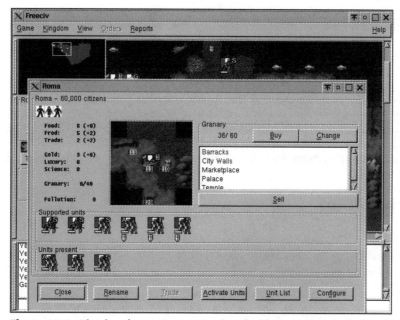

Figure 11-2: Viewing the resource associated with a community in FreeCiv

Once installed, the first step in playing FreeCiv is starting the server. The server appears in a text terminal. As people join the games, their names show up on the terminal and in each client's text box. Once everyone has joined the server, type start in the server console for the game to begin.

From the client console, the flashing character indicates which player is ready for instructions to move, build, or attack. Clicking on a city shows what the city is producing and lets you control what gets built in the queue.

Quake

This is one of the most popular first-person shooter games of all time. Two forms of this game are included among the Debian packages. One can be played as a single player fighting monsters. The other is the Quakeworld server with clients. The server gets used when playing against multiple people in Quakeworld. Once installed, both versions can be found in /usr/games—with the first listed starting with quake, and the second listed starting with qw.

> **Note**   There are external configuration files for the quake, quakeworld, **server and** quakeworld **client applications. If these files do not exist, the default settings apply. In order for the game to actually work, you need a commercial CD for the data files.**

Running the server for a multi-player session, first start the server (/etc/games/ qw-server) from a separate virtual terminal, and then run the quakeworld client for the video driver you wish to use—3dfx, ggi, or svga. When the screen opens for the client, press the keyboard button with the tilde (~) on it to enter the command shell for Quake. Type connect *hostname* at the console, where *hostname* is either localhost on the same machine as the server, the host name, or the IP address for the server. Pressing the tilde key again closes the command console. You should now be connected and able to play Quake in a multi-player session. Both versions only come with the first level, which is the shareware version. You can find more information about this game and other versions at www.linuxgames.com/quake.

GNOME games

Most, if not all, of the games listed in Table 11-8 are also included among the Debian packaged games. These games are both graphical and easy to control. When installed, they show up in main GNOME menu under Games. As with the other games, these are installed in /usr/games by default, and can alternatively be launched from the command line.

Table 11-8 GNOME games	
Game	**Description**
Freeciv	Free variant of the Civilization game (client only)
GNOME-Stone	A Digger-like game
Freecell	Freecell solitaire game
AisleRiot	Solitaire card game
GNOMEMines	Minesweeper game
Mahjongg	Tile matching game
Same GNOME	Match marbles of the same color

Game	Description
Gnibbles	Send the snake to get the diamond
GNOMEtris	Tetris-like game
Gnotravex	A puzzle of matching numbered squares
Gtali	Othello-like game
GnobotsII	Cause robots to collide as they follow you around the room
Iagno	Othello-like game of flipping chips
Gataxx	Conquer the board with your colored chip
GNOME xBill	Play the role of Administrator and save the computer system before Bill changes them all to Windows computers.
GNOME Batalla Naval	Multi-player battleship-like game
GNOMEhack	Graphical hack game

The special thing about GNOME games is that they all work well with the GNOME desktop environment specifically as opposed to KDE games. In addition, these games will show up in the GNOME games menu.

Playing Commercial Games

Most of the popular computer games you find in a game store are produced by independent software companies for the Windows platform. Some of these games are now being ported to the Linux platform by Loki Games (www.lokigames.com). Table 11-9 lists and describes these games.

Because of the commercial effort behind them and their popularity among the Windows gamers, these games are beginning to find their way into the Linux world. Now you can use the Linux platform, with all its stability, to play these high-quality games.

Even though you can find a number of excellent and quality games among the Debian package archives and for Linux in general, the commercial games tend to generate a larger following. In my opinion, the larger following of the commercial games is due to the quality of the graphics and the entertainment factor of the game. Many of the free open source games have a tremendous entertainment value; however, the interface may not have the same polished quality that the commercial competitor maintains.

Table 11-9
Loki games

Game	Description
Civilization: Call to Power	A turn-based game in which you build an empire through history
Myth II: Soulblighter	A 3-D strategy game in which you command an army to defeat the Soulblighter's hordes.
Railroad Tycoon II	Build a railroad empire across America, just as they did in the 1800s
Eric's Ultimate Solitaire	Play one of 23 stimulating solitaire card games
Heretic II	Using your magic, help save the world by finding the cure to the plague.
Heroes of Might and Magic III	Lead a battle against the common foe by organizing your legions of sorcerers, knights, and beasts.
Quake III Arena	The third generation of the greatest first-person shooter, where slaughter is the name of the game.
Heavy Gear II	Control a heavily armored robot-like machine as you infiltrate, recon, and defeat the enemy.
SimCity 3000 Unlimited	As the city official, your job is to plan the growth of a city over the years by developing zones, roads, and utilities.
Soldier of Fortune	As a soldier for hire, you battle for money and for keeps in this shooter game.
Sid Meier's Alpha Centari with the Alien Crossfire expansion	In this game, you are one of several civilizations that has crash-landed on an alien world. Dominate this world with your power or diplomacy in this turn-based game.
Descent 3	Fly your ship in this three-dimensional world, destroying the robot ships along the way.
MindRover	Build and design roving robots to seek out and destroy the others before yours get destroyed.
Unreal Tournament	Kill or be killed in this first-person action game. Designed for multi-player teams.
Kohan: Immortal Sovereigns	A real-time strategy game in which you lead great armies to fulfill your destiny.

Most of these games can be /played with other gamers over a network or on the Internet. This aspect of allowing multiple people to play in the games only adds to their appeal. With commercial versions of these games now available, you can play the same games against and with people using Windows.

Cross-Reference If you have a favorite game that only exists in the Windows world, look into using `wine` in order to play it on your Linux platform. You can find out more about `wine` in Chapter 7, or go to the Web site `www.winehq.com` for more information. One game that Linux users use `wine` to play is StarCraft.

Highlighted in the following sections are two of the more popular commercial games, including the system requirements necessary to play them. This will give you an idea of two very different commercial games. SimCity 3000 lets you act as a city planner, managing the city's resources as it grows. The other game is a fast action shoot'em up type of game. Both let you play with other people over the Internet.

SimCity 3000 Unlimited

SimCity 3000 is a simulator game in which you manage the development of a city as it grows. You have to be concerned with utilities such as power, water, and trash disposal. In addition to the infrastructure of the city, including roads, highways, subways and railways, you must also manage the economics by balancing residential, commercial, and industrial zoning.

In order to run the game successfully, you need to meet the following system requirements:

✦ Linux Kernel — 2.2.x and glibc-2.1 (both come with Debian 2.2)

✦ Processor — Pentium 233 MHz or faster (300 MHz Pentium II processor recommended)

✦ Video — 4MB graphics card, XFree86 3.3.5 or higher, and 16-bit color depth

✦ CD-ROM — 8x CD-ROM drive (600 KB/s sustained transfer rate)

✦ RAM — 32MB required; 64MB recommended

✦ Sound — 16-bit sound card and OSS-compatible (it works without sound, but isn't as much fun)

✦ Hard disk — 230MB free hard disk space plus space for saved games

The game comes compiled because the source code is not public. Follow the instructions that accompany the game to get it installed on your system and running. Figure 11-3 shows the game in action. The level of detail in the graphics can be adjusted to show animation. The right side enables control for adding zones, roads, utilities, and such.

Figure 11-3: Watching the neighborhood develop in SimCity 3000

If you want to try the game before purchasing it, you can download a demo version from the Web site at `www.lokigames.com/products/sc3k`.

Unreal Tournament

If unbelievable action combined with team play is what you have in mind, you need Unreal Tournament. This is one of the fastest action shoot-em-up games around. Enter rooms, pick up weapons, and blast anything that moves (except for teammates).

You'll need to meet the following minimum requirements in order to get the most out of the game:

✦ Linux Kernel — 2.2.x and glibc-2.1

✦ Processor — Pentium II with 3-D accelerator card

✦ Video — Video card capable of 640×480 resolution, XFree86 version 3.3.5 or newer at 16-bit color

✦ RAM — 64MB required; 128MB recommended

✦ Sound — OSS-compatible sound card

✦ Hard disk — Minimum 550MB free space

All the software requirements are met with Debian 2.2, so the only thing you need to worry about is your hardware. Follow the instructions that come with the software for installing the game and running it. Once you have it installed and running, the fun begins. Being a multi-player game, you can play online or via a network.

This game can be controlled by keyboard, keyboard and mouse, or joystick.

Summary

Everyone likes to have fun. Although Linux is tough enough to be used as a robust server, it can also be used for entertainment. Some of that entertainment can blow your socks off with its high-powered graphics.

If none of the games described in this chapter really appeal to you, you might check out some of the public software sites:

✦ Linux Games (`www.linuxgames.com`) — The site includes game news, how-to's, and all types of games.

✦ Download.com (`www.download.com`) — A public site for all platforms, including Linux. Contains more than just games.

✦ Tucows (`www.tucows.com`) — A general repository for publicly available programs, including games.

✦   ✦   ✦

Administering Linux

System Administration

Y ou work happily along as a client Linux/UNIX user on a network, oblivious to the hard work of the system administrator who's keeping the system working at peak performance. A large system may have several people working on different aspects of the administration — accounts, daemon services, network traffic, and more. If you have only one computer running Linux, then you are the system administrator as well as the end user.

The responsibilities of the system administrator cover many aspects of the Linux system, so this chapter describes the scope of these responsibilities. This chapter also offers instructions for some of the basic duties such as setting up accounts, file permissions, and portions of system monitoring. I reference other chapters in this book here in an effort to cover those duties in more depth.

The Roles of the System Administrator

The success of a stable, secure, and efficient computer system relies on the system administrator to maintain it. It's a tough job maintaining, tweaking, and updating the system daily to keep it in peak performance.

The occupation of system administrator can be a thankless job of managing the computer system while offering friendly support to the end user. This is a delicate task of diplomacy.

Following is a list of general duties that an administrator (admin) performs. Some of these are covered in this chapter; others are included in other chapters. This should give you an idea of the scope of the administrator's job — which encompasses a lot.

✦ Starting and shutting down (Chapter 3)

This is not a task you want available to just anyone who has an account on the system. For an individual machine or a single user, it can be more convenient. However, when you have processes and services that are expected to be running, limiting this responsibility is mandatory.

✦ User accounts (this chapter)

Creating accounts is another privileged activity. Many systems have special policies for the accounts; therefore, they need an administrator to dole them out appropriately. The wrong privileges in the right hands can turn into a hacker's paradise, thus spelling disaster for the administrator or even for the system.

✦ Security (Chapter 19)

The most secure system is one that only one person uses. That isn't practical, so limiting the numbers of accounts that have access to the more powerful functions is the next best solution.

✦ Monitoring the system resources (this chapter)

The system requires constant monitoring. Oftentimes, you can do this through scripts or programs, but occasions arise when someone must intervene. Disks fill with data, programs run away chewing up processor time, and properly running systems get overworked by overloaded use. It's the administrator's job to keep it all running.

✦ Automating tasks (Chapter 14)

This is a crucial duty. It involves creating scripts and programs to take over the mundane tasks in an effort to produce more reliability, repeatability, and regularity. These tasks can range from backing up files to searching through log files for anomalies — turning hours of work entering multiple commands and reviewing the results into minutes of issuing only a few simple commands that produce only the results you preprogrammed.

✦ System configuration (Chapters 5, 6, 9, 19, 23, 24, and 25)

Most all of the aspects of the daemons — such as printing, networking, e-mail, and so on — need some configuration for their environment and purpose. Most of these applications require special account privileges to run like those that come with root. These configuration files range in complexity from a simple test file with a dozen lines of information to text files that contain hundreds of lines.

✦ Filesystems and disk drives (Chapter 3)

The filesystem and, therefore, the disk drives are rudimentary to the whole operating system. Should something happen to the data on the drives, this can affect the performance (not to mention the function) of the system. Someone must watch the disk drives to make sure there remains room for the data. Set up quotas for accounts to prevent one person from using all the available space.

✦ Backups and restores (Chapter 18)

Nothing can take the place of a good backup when data is lost. Hundreds, thousands, and even millions of dollars have been saved because the administrator has faithfully backed up the valuable data. This duty, which can be automated fully, must be a priority for any administrator.

✦ Printing services (Chapter 17)

Any printing services that come through the network fall on the administrator's shoulders — from setting up the print spooling queues to configuring the printers to even changing the toner cartridges in the printers. I also have seen administrators taking charge of ordering, storing, and replenishing printer paper.

✦ Network management (Chapter 5)

When one or more computers are connected to communicate with one another, you have a network. Someone must monitor that network to keep it in peak performance. Included in this category are firewalls, routing, and Internet access. This is no small task for the administrator.

✦ Mail/Web/and other services (Chapters 20, 21, 22, 23, 24, and 25)

Each machine may function as a server, providing such services as hosting Web pages, sending and receiving e-mail as a central post office, or acting as a repository for a database. The size, demand, and shear volume of usage determine the number of services on one machine. Again, the administrator must manage the load on the computers.

From this list, you can begin to get some idea of the scope of an administrator's responsibilities. Yes, in an environment of hundreds of people working on workstations accessing servers of all types, the administrator's job may be spread over a few people. However, when there is only one machine — yours — then these duties fall to you. You get to make all the decisions concerning your machine.

The System Administrator and the Root Account

When you install Linux on your computer, you are forced to enter a password for the root account. All Linux systems have a root account, which has full rights to all services, functions, and controls. From that account, you can do anything you want — or don't want. Along with this power comes the accompanying danger — of accidentally replacing a crucial configuration file, deleting needed files, misconfiguring systems, and so on. You can see that giving everyone the root password is not the best thing to do for the system. Because of this power, root access should always be limited to the local machine console.

Using the su command

As the administrator, working along as a normal user of a system, you need the same privileges as root from time to time. One approach is to log out from the normal account, and then log back in as the root account. This takes time and disturbs any processes you may have running at the time. Or, you can change identities from the normal user into a *superuser* with the su command. This enables you to work along in your own account. When you need to perform a task at a higher level, you just issue the su command. This program still uses the root password and offers the same power as the root account, but there is no need to log out of your current terminal and then log back in as root.

Tip

I strongly suggest that you get in the habit of using the full path of /bin/su for the superuser privileges. It prevents the implementation of any unauthorized versions of this program, which can compromise the security of the system. You can find more on security in Chapter 19.

You can use this application in several ways. Employing the command without any options logs the person in as the superuser (assuming they know the password). All attempts to use the su command are logged into the /var/log/auth.log file as are all other logon attempts. Here is the syntax for the su command:

```
su [OPTS] [-] [username [ARGS]]
```

The su command has more uses than just logging in as the superuser. Adding an account name to the end enables you to log in as that user. This finds its usefulness when a new account is added because you can employ the new name to verify that the account is working. Adding the hyphen (-) between the command and the username requests that the shell assigned to the account be used instead of the current shell.

Using the -c option enables you to temporarily log in as the other account, execute the indicated command, and then return to your original account. Suppose you are logged in as yourself—a regular, unprivileged user. You need to briefly check on the status of the network card in the computer. You can use the su command to log in as root long enough to execute the one command, or you can log in as another user to list the contents of his or her directories. Here are the two examples and the corresponding results:

```
$ su -c ifconfig
Password:
lo        Link encap:Local Loopback
          inet addr:127.0.0.1  Mask:255.0.0.0
          UP LOOPBACK RUNNING  MTU:3924  Metric:1
          RX packets:534 errors:0 dropped:0 overruns:0 frame:0
          TX packets:534 errors:0 dropped:0 overruns:0
carrier:0
          collisions:0 txqueuelen:0
$
```

and

```
$ su -c 'ls -l /home/jo' jo
Password:
docs  pics  newfiles  programs
$
```

These examples show logging in as the other person long enough to execute the command and returning to the original account. Notice that the passwords don't get echoed back to the screen. To better prove this, I use the whoami command to display the different account identifications:

```
$ whoami
steve
$ su -c whoami
Password:
root
$ su -c whoami jo
Password:
jo
$ whoiami
steve
$
```

You can see from this listing that each time the su command runs the whoami command to identify the user, it returns a different name based on who is logging in.

Using the sudo command

If you want some people to only have access to certain programs, then implement the sudo command. (It can be installed using apt-get install sudo.) Some of the administrative duties can be delegated to other privileged users. Give those people access to run only those programs necessary to perform their duties. The syntax looks like this:

```
sudo -V | -h | -L | -l | -v | -H | [-b] [-p prompt]
     [-u username/#uid] -s | <command>
```

This may look a little confusing, but once you set it up it's really easy to use. Basically, sudo restricts only one command option at a time. Table 12-1 lists some of the available options.

Table 12-1
Options used with Sudo

Command	Description
-l	Lists the commands allowed and forbidden to the user
-L	Lists the commands and a short description of the allowed and forbidden commands
-h	Prints a help message and exits
-H	Sets the HOME environment variable to the home directory of the user logging in
-v	Validates the timestamp associated with the user. The *timestamp* enables the user to perform commands without needing a password (for a given period of time). This option does not execute any commands, but it does prompt for the password (if required) to extend the timestamp period.
-V	Prints the version and exits
-u *user*	Specifies that the command should be run by another *user* account, other than root

You can find a complete list of the options through the online documentation. You must edit the configuration file, located in /etc/sudoers, using visudo. This file contains all the users and the respective applications, commands, and features that they are allowed to access.

Administering and Setting up Accounts

Accounts give users access to use the system, so everyone needs one. If you have a large company, this can take quite a bit of time monitoring, setting up new accounts, and removing old ones. On the other hand, just one machine can demand a little account management from time to time. The following sections cover what you need to know to administer accounts.

The passwd file

The passwd file contains all the account information—well most of it, but I'll get to that in a minute. This file is referenced at the time of login; it verifies the account name, the account password, the home directory path, and the default shell for the account. It can also contain personal information about the account, such as the user's full name, address, and other information for identification purposes by the administrator. Here is an example of the contents of the passwd file.

```
root:x:0:0:root:/root:/bin/bash
daemon:x:1:1:daemon:/usr/sbin:/bin/sh
bin:x:2:2:bin:/bin:/bin/sh
sys:x:3:3:sys:/dev:/bin/sh
.
.
.
jake:x:1003:1003:jake,101,555-1234,555-4321,waterboy:/home/jake:/bin/bas
```

...and so on. Colons separate the information. To interpret a line, use this format:

```
Username:EncriptedPassword:UserIDnumber:GroupIDnumber:PersonalData,Comments,
and/or Descriptions:DefaultAccountPath:DefaultShell
```

You can edit this file manually with your favorite text editor. When you do so, leave the password area blank and assign a password to the account after you finish editing the file. The command to set the password is passwd followed by the new account name.

> **Note**   Sometimes you may need to create an account for a process that no one will ever log into. That account belongs only to that process. To keep anyone from accessing the system, use /bin/false for the shell (instead of /bin/sh or /bin/bash). This prevents a shell from activating at log in, thus preventing a live connection by any person.

The purpose of shadow passwords

You may have noticed that the passwords do not appear in the password file. This is so that no one can simply view the passwd file and have access to everyone's actual passwords. The passwords are actually kept in a separate file called shadow, with the password encrypted (assuming shadow passwords were enabled during the install process).

The group file

The /etc/group file contains group information. This information can apply to one user or many. Generally, each user account will belong to at least one group—often using the same name in the passwd and group files. Here is a sample of the group file contents:

```
root:x:0:
daemon:x:1:
bin:x:2:
sys:x:3:
adm:x:4:
tty:x:5:
disk:x:6:
```

Continued

```
  .
  .
  .
users:x:100:user1,user2
jake:x:1003:jake
```

As with the `passwd` file, the pertinent information uses colons to separate the values. Here is the syntax of the lines:

```
GroupName:Password:GroupIDNumber:User1,User2,...
```

Yes, groups can have passwords, too. Use the `-g` option with the `passwd` command to set group passwords. When a person becomes a member of a group, he or she gains access to the group's files along with his or her own files. Every account should belong to a group, even if the user accounts all belong to one group account.

Note The Debian distribution creates a separate group account for each user account created when using the `adduser` command. This helps to lock down the user's file access. See Chapter 19 for more information about access security.

You can add someone to a group by adding his or her account name to the end of the group name line. Each name assigned to a group must be separated by a comma (,). Again, your favorite editor can edit this text file.

As the administrator, adding a group for each user account can result in management problems. However, lumping all users into one group can also have the same result. If you expect to maintain a large number of accounts, you might consider creating functional groups. For instance, all users working in the engineering department would belong to the *engr* group, while all users working in the sales department would belong to the *sales* group. Smaller environments with few users may not need to create such a group, but can follow the one-user-one-group system used with the `adduser` command.

Employing adduser to add a user account

You now know how to set up accounts the hard way. Let me introduce you to the easy method of adding users to a system. Debian comes with several handy utilities. The `adduser` tool is no exception. This command takes care of all the responsibilities when creating a new account. Here is the syntax:

```
adduser [options] user [group]
```

You can use this tool with just a user name. You can also add the options to modify some of the default information. This information comes from the `/etc/adduser.conf` file. You can modify the configuration file for your environment, especially if this system will host many accounts. You may find some settings to adjust for your environment. Let's take a look at what happens when you add a user:

```
$ adduser john
Adding user john...
Adding new group john (1004).
Adding new user john (1004) with group john.
Creating home directory /home/john.
Copying files from /etc/skel
Enter new UNIX password:
Retype new UNIX password:
passwd: password updated successfully
Changing the user information for john
Enter the new value, or press return for the default
        Full Name []: john both
        Room Number []: 403
        Work Phone []: 555-1234
        Home Phone []: 555-4321
        Other []: 555-9867
Is the information correct? [y/n] y
$
```

This tool takes the user name and searches for the next available user ID to assign to the name. adduser takes the same name and uses it as a group name if you do not provide one. Then, it creates a home directory using the user name as the directory name. adduser then copies the essential files from the template directory and requests to set a password. Lastly, adduser requests reference information. This information is optional, but you can use it with other applications such as fingerd.

Note   While adding a new user, you are asked for a password for the account. You then are asked to confirm the password by retyping it. If the passwords do not match, then all the files and directories that were created for the new account are removed.

The new user template – skel

To make life even easier when adding a user to the system, a template directory was created called /etc/skel. There may be special settings, startup applications, or customizations that need to reside in the template directory as the skeleton for each new account. The default skel files included with the Debian distribution are shown here:

```
$ ls -la
total 28
drwxr-xr-x    2 root     root         4096 Jun  2 00:48 .
drwxr-xr-x   58 root     root         4096 Jun 15 01:53 ..
-rw-r--r--    1 root     root          266 Mar  7 18:18 .alias
-rw-r--r--    1 root     root          174 Feb 20 14:46 .bash_logout
-rw-r--r--    1 root     root          373 Feb 20 14:46 .bash_profile
-rw-r--r--    1 root     root          504 Feb 20 14:46 .bashrc
-rw-r--r--    1 root     root          375 Mar  7 18:18 .cshrc
$
```

You can make changes to these files, add new ones, or leave them as is. Be aware, however, that what resides in this directory is given to every new account set up with the `adduser` program.

Using userdel to remove a user

As employees come and go, oftentimes the hardest part of administering a system is keeping the accounts up to date. By that I mean removing "dead" accounts from people who have left or no longer need access to the system. To assist with the maintenance comes this nifty utility called `userdel`. This is the syntax for the `userdel` command:

```
userdel [-r] username
```

The `-r` option removes all traces of the account, including the user's directory and mailbox. If you omit this option, the directory remains to be dealt with later. In addition, the user must be logged out of the system and all processes owned by the user must be killed before you can successfully remove the account. As a precaution, you may want to back up `/home` before completely removing the user's account and directory. Better safe than sorry.

Restricting access to the root account

In some situations, such as when a machine works as a server, no one needs to access the machine by local or remote means except to make a few adjustments from time to time. In this case, you can limit access to the machine to only the root account. Adding a text file called `nologin` to the `/etc` directory allows only the root account to log in. If anyone tries to log in to the machine, the contents of the `nologin` file are displayed and the connection is closed.

One caveat to using this method is that you are now required to be at the machine to log in as root. For security reasons, root is not accepted as an account name through a Telnet session. Therefore, think carefully before implementing this level of restriction.

 Caution   By default, root does not have remote access to a system. This restriction can be lifted; however, doing so would be risky from a security standpoint. See Chapter 19 for more information about security.

Setting File and Directory Permissions

Now that you have accounts set up, take a look at the access these accounts have and what this all means. *Permissions* essentially define who has access to what files and directories. There are three levels of permission access modes for each file and directory on the filesystem: user level, group level, and other level.

User-level access gives permission to the account user for accessing files and directories. Users are defined in the /etc/passwd file. Group access allows all members of a group access to files and directories. Group members are defined in the /etc/group. Other access means anyone who can log onto that machine who does not currently belong in user or group categories will have access.

Access with chmod

At times, you may need to modify the degree to which a file or directory can be accessed. You accomplish this by changing the rights or permissions for a file or directory. Here is the syntax for the chmod command:

```
chmod [OPTION] MODE[,MODE] FILE...
```

To understand how to use this command, you need to have an understanding of the anatomy of the file information. When you list a directory to get a detailed view of the contents (as shown next), the beginning shows a cryptic series of letters and dashes. Take a closer look at the contents of Jo's directory.

```
$ ls -l
total 20
drwxr-sr-x    2 jo        jo            4096 Jun 14 16:00 docs
drwxr-sr-x    2 jo        jo            4096 Jun 14 16:01 misc
drwxr-sr-x    2 jo        jo            4096 Jun 14 16:01 newfiles
drwxr-sr-x    2 jo        jo            4096 Jun 14 16:00 pics
drwxr-sr-x    2 jo        jo            4096 Jun 14 16:01 programs
-rw-r--r--    1 jo        jo               0 Jun 15 03:26 test
$
```

The first column contains the permission levels. In detail, reading the first line for the docs file, you have drwxr-sr-x. The d stands for directory and refers to the type of entry. The next three, rwx, refer to the user mode. From here, you can tell that the user can read (r), write (w), and execute (x) these files and directories. The second set of three characters (r-s) refers to the group's mode, which has access to read (r), and no write access (indicated by the dash). All files created inside the directories inherit the directories' group identity. The last set of three characters refers to the rights other users have to the files. Here, others can read (r), cannot write (w), and can execute (x). Table 12-2 lists some of the available options for the access modes.

	Table 12-2
	Identifiers, operators, and permissions modes

Identifier	Description
u	User
g	Group
o	Other (those not part of the user or group)
a	All (includes user, group, and other)

Operator	Description
+	Adds
-	Removes
=	Assigns

Mode	Description
r	Reads
w	Writes
x	Executes or accesses directories
s	Sets user or group ID upon execution

There are other modes, but they are not commonly used. These modes set absolute control for the files. You can also use plus (+), minus (-), and equal (=) signs to modify the different levels. To get an idea of how this works, change a couple of modes for a directory. You just saw the modes for Jo's directory. Here is the current listing for the program directory:

```
drwxrws---   2 jo      jo          4096 Jun 14 16:01 programs
```

To change the modes for the program directory, you can add the ability to write for the group and remove all rights for the world. Here is the command string to accomplish this:

```
$ chmod g+w,o-rx programs
$
```

This command string says that you want to add write capability to the group access and remove read and execute from the other access. This produces the following:

```
$ ls -l
total 20
drwxr-sr-x    2 jo        jo        4096 Jun 14 16:00 docs
drwxr-sr-x    2 jo        jo        4096 Jun 14 16:01 misc
drwxr-sr-x    2 jo        jo        4096 Jun 14 16:01 newfiles
drwxr-sr-x    2 jo        jo        4096 Jun 14 16:00 pics
drwxrws---    2 jo        jo        4096 Jun 14 16:01 programs
-rw-r--r--    1 jo        jo           0 Jun 15 03:26 test
```

This looks relatively easy. When changing several things at once, as you just did, be sure not to add a space after the comma (which separates group changes from other changes). You can also make changes throughout an entire directory by using the recursive option (-R). Using the -R option immediately after the chmod command changes all files and directories below the specified directory to the same settings.

Changing user ownership with chown

From time to time, it is important to change the ownership of files and directories. If a file belongs to a certain individual and then gets transferred to another, the ownership of that file needs to change as well. This is the syntax for the chown command:

```
chown [OPTION] OWNER FILE...
```

To determine the ownership of a file, you can look at the long listing of a directory for the details. Here you can see that all the items listed belong to user jo. The specified user appears in the third column (in bold).

```
$ ls -l
total 20
drwxr-sr-x    2 jo        jo        4096 Jun 14 16:00 docs
drwxr-sr-x    2 jo        jo        4096 Jun 14 16:01 misc
drwxr-sr-x    2 jo        jo        4096 Jun 14 16:01 newfiles
drwxr-sr-x    2 jo        jo        4096 Jun 14 16:00 pics
drwxr-sr-x    2 jo        jo        4096 Jun 14 16:01 programs
-rw-r--r--    1 jo        jo           0 Jun 15 03:26 test
$
```

Suppose that Jo leaves the company and her coworker, Jane, takes over Jo's responsibilities. You can transfer the ownership of all the files and directories to Jane. This is the command that you use as root or superuser:

```
$ chown -R jane *
```

The command string changes ownership recursively (indicated with the -R option) to Jane, thus affecting all contents of the current directory (indicated by the wildcard asterisk); however, the group remains assigned to Jo. This results in the following changes:

```
$ ls -l
total 20
drwxr-sr-x    2 jane      jo            4096 Jun 14 16:00 docs
drwxr-sr-x    2 jane      jo            4096 Jun 14 16:01 misc
drwxr-sr-x    2 jane      jo            4096 Jun 14 16:01 newfiles
drwxr-sr-x    2 jane      jo            4096 Jun 14 16:00 pics
drwxr-sr-x    2 jane      jo            4096 Jun 14 16:01 programs
-rw-r--r--    1 jane      jo               0 Jun 15 03:26 test
```

You can see that only the user identifier for the files and directories changes. Everything else stays the same. Again, as indicated by the example, the recursive option (-R) changes the contents of all affected directories.

Changing group membership with chgrp

Likewise with groups as with owners, the group association changes from time to time. Changing the group association affects which group members have access to which files and directories. If only one person belongs to a group, only one person is affected. If a group has several members, you need to apply the correct group association. Here is the syntax for the chgrp command:

```
chgrp [OPTION] OWNER FILE...
```

Looking back at the previous chown example, user Jo left the responsibilities of the files and directories to user Jane. Jane now has ownership of these, but Jo still has group ownership. To completely remove Jo from having any control of the files and directories, the group identifier must change as well. The fourth column of the following listing indicates the group membership. Change the group membership for these as well.

```
$ ls -l
total 20
drwxr-sr-x    2 jane      jo            4096 Jun 14 16:00 docs
drwxr-sr-x    2 jane      jo            4096 Jun 14 16:01 misc
drwxr-sr-x    2 jane      jo            4096 Jun 14 16:01 newfiles
drwxr-sr-x    2 jane      jo            4096 Jun 14 16:00 pics
drwxr-sr-x    2 jane      jo            4096 Jun 14 16:01 programs
-rw-r--r--    1 jane      jo               0 Jun 15 03:26 test
$
```

To transfer the group ownership from Jo to Jane, you issue the following command:

```
$ chgrp -R jane *
```

Again, you changed the group recursively (indicated with the -R option) to Jane through all files and directories. Getting a long listing of the current directory now, you see that the group has changed over to Jane.

```
total 20
drwxr-sr-x    2 jane     jane         4096 Jun 14 16:00 docs
drwxr-sr-x    2 jane     jane         4096 Jun 14 16:01 misc
drwxr-sr-x    2 jane     jane         4096 Jun 14 16:01 newfiles
drwxr-sr-x    2 jane     jane         4096 Jun 14 16:00 pics
drwxr-sr-x    2 jane     jane         4096 Jun 14 16:01 programs
-rw-r--r--    1 jane     jane            0 Jun 15 03:26 test
```

The recursive option (-R) is very useful in situations where you change many files. This option is non-discriminating and affects all files in subdirectories where the conditions match. In situations where few files require changes, add the individual files to the end of the command string, with a space between each file.

Using Quotas for Accounts

A *quota* is a maximum limit setting for drive space. When only a few people are working on a system, drive space may not be a concern. As the number of users increases, so does the amount of "stuff" stored on the disk drive. Adding more drives is an option for the long term, but it is not always the better solution overall because more file creation, Web use, and mail use will continue to increase. Some individuals will utilize as much space as they have. Therefore, establishing quotas on the amount of allowable space for users of the system prevents the gluttony of disk storage.

Quotas can also prevent the accidental mishap of a runaway program as it continues to eat up more and more space on a drive. Limiting the amount of space for a user enables the other users on the system to continue to work while the unfortunate owner of the runaway program tries to recover from the accident.

Installing quotas

Installing quotas on a system involves only four steps: kernel configuration, program installation, quota configuration, and activation. The first is making sure that the kernel has quota support turned on. Generally, the Debian builds of the kernel include quotas by default; in the event they are omitted, you need to recompile the kernel with quota support enabled. Next, you need to install the application on the system by using the Debian packages (apt-get install quota). This is an easy process, so I don't expect you will have any difficulties with this step.

Configuring the system to use quotas takes only a couple of seconds. Using a text editor, modify the /etc/fstab file to include either usrquota or grpquota in the options area for each filesystem you want monitored. These options are ignored when the filesystem is mounted anyway, so you don't need to restart the filesystem. Here is an example of adding usrquota to the /etc/fstab file.

```
# <file       <mount
# system>     point>   <type> <options>                              <dump> <pass>
/dev/hdb1   /          ext2   defaults,errors=remount-ro,usrquota    0      1
```

Lastly, activate disk quota monitoring by starting the daemon with the following command:

```
$ /etc/init.d/quota start
```

Now you have quotas monitoring the drive space of all users on your system. When users reach the limit of their quota, they are notified. If users are curious about their current status, they can issue the `quota` command to find this information.

Likewise, quotas can be stopped by issuing the following command:

```
$ /etc/init.d/quota stop
```

Using edquota

A little utility that comes with `quota` when you install it is `edquota`. This program sets and edits the limitations to each person's account. This is the syntax for the command:

```
edquota [ -ug ] name..
```

The options `u` and `g` specify whether the quota values should apply the `name` as a user or as a group, because you can apply quotas to either. When you execute the `edquota` command for a user or group, an editor opens (`vi` by default unless you change the `EDITOR` environment variable) to create a temporary file that displays the current setting for the account, as shown here:

```
/dev/hdb1: blocks in use: 44, limits (soft = 1000, hard = 1500)
           inodes in use: 12, limits (soft = 500, hard = 550)
```

This shows that a user has a quota set on the hdb1 device setting both user and group limits. This user has a limitation on the number of blocks he or she can use. Each block consists of 1,024 bytes. The *soft setting* indicates when the user begins to be notified with warnings that he or she has reached the quota (giving this user around 1MB before warning start). The *hard limitation* (1.5MB in this example) is the absolute setting. Once reached, you cannot store any more data. At this time, the user must delete data or have the administrator increase the quota. To change these hard and soft limit settings, just edit the file directly at this time.

The second line indicates the number of inodes, or objects (such as files and directories), available to the user. Each inode is an object; therefore, every file, directory, and such counts against this setting. This limits the number of objects an account can create. You can change, add to, or set new quotas for other devices with these settings.

Once the user reaches the soft quota setting, he or she has a time limit to comply with the limit or it is treated as a hard limit. This is considered a grace period, which is seven days by default. You can change this time frame using `edquota -t` (similarly to changing user quotas).

Note

When you use quotas to control the amount of drive space an individual consumes, set up the quota amount when you create the account. You can set it up by modifying the `/etc/adduser.conf` file. At the end of the configuration file is a line resembling `QUOTAUSER=""`. Add a value for the quota amount variable between the double quotes ("") to enable setting up quotas when you create the accounts. By default, this is left empty.

Quota reporting

To be a good administrator, it's important that you know what's going on with the system. Therefore, checking on the status of your system quotas is crucial. There are two ways to get report information from the system. The first is by using the `quota` command.

```
quota [ -gv | q ] [name]
```

This command gives you instant information about anyone. By default, `quota` (when used without anything after it) shows the current user's quota information. Alternatively, employing one of the options shown in Table 12-3 produces the same results.

Table 12-3
Reporting options for quota

Option	Description
-g	Displays the quota for the group of which the user is a member
-v	Displays a report for those users who are not currently using the system
-q	Displays a concise message showing only the information on filesystems where usage is over quota

Both users and administrators can employ this command. However, some of the features — such as checking on users' account information — are only available to the administrator.

The second way to get information from the system is through the `repquota` command. This command provides a more thorough listing of all accounts. Administrators use this command to get complete accounting information. Here is the syntax for this command:

```
repquota [ -vug ] -a|filesystem...
```

The options listed in Table 12-4 explain the choices for the repquota command. These options give you the ability to report on combinations of filesystems, users, and groups.

Table 12-4
Reporting options for repquota

Option	Description
-a	Reports on all filesystems indicated in /etc/fstab that use quotas
-v	Reports on all quotas, regardless of usage
-g	Reports on quotas for all groups
-u	Reports on quotas for all users

The following example shows a report on all (-a) users on the root filesystem. A comprehensive report is generated. This particular report shows only one account with user quotas set for this filesystem. You can generate more individualized reports by using combinations of options.

```
$ repquota -a
                        Block limits              File limits
User              used  soft   hard  grace   used  soft  hard grace
root         --  548440    0      0          54337    0     0
daemon       --       8    0      0              3    0     0
man          --     768    0      0             50    0     0
lp           --      12    0      0              3    0     0
mail         --      80    0      0             19    0     0
news         --       4    0      0              1    0     0
www-data     --      24    0      0             11    0     0
identd       --       4    0      0              1    0     0
gdm          --       4    0      0              1    0     0
jo           --      28    0      0              7    0     0
jane         --      44    0      0             12  500   550
jake         --      24    0      0              6    0     0
```

Using this type of reporting can also help track suspicious activity — both from abusers among legitimate users and would-be hackers attempting to crack your system. One indication of potential abuse is when the limits for one user are set higher than all others. The user may have a legitimate use for all the space or not. At minimum, the discrepancy merits further investigation. (See Chapter 19 for more information about preventing hackers.)

Using System Monitoring Tools

One of the most important duties of the administrator is to monitor the system. This can be one of the most mundane of tasks; but when done properly, it reveals weaknesses with the system, areas where resources are running low, and areas where possible abuse has taken place. Monitoring the system becomes a skill over time as you become familiar with the system. Several aspects of the Linux system need monitoring. The first and foremost are the log files.

Monitoring system log files

Log files keep track of the system's activities. Consider them bank transactions. Each time money enters or leaves an account at a bank, a record is made of the transaction. The same goes for the Linux system. Each time a process starts, a person logs in, e-mail gets sent, or any number of other activities, a transaction is written to a file recording the activity.

There are a couple of processes that take care of this record keeping. These processes run as daemons, monitoring the activity of other daemons while recording various activities to text files.

System logging with syslogd

The `syslogd` daemon collects log information from the applications and functions specified in the `/etc/syslog.conf` file that is read at startup. Included in this configuration file are reports on login information, mail, news, and so on. The type of information that is put in the log files includes time of the event, hostname, and program name.

Kernel logging with klogd

The `klogd` daemon records information from the kernel. These Linux kernel messages report on the kernel's interaction with the hardware in the system — from the processor to the hard drives to the serial ports. All this information is placed in the `/var/log/kern.log` file.

Both the `syslogd` and `klogd` daemons start with the system when you first initialize it. These daemons must start first to capture the information from the other applications as they start.

Watching the system with top

When you want to know what processes are consuming the most resources, turn to the `top` program to view a text display of this information. This program lists the top processes and shows a variety of information about them. Each process is listed on a separate line. The display lists the process ID, the user, the status, the percentage of CPU usage, the percentage of memory usage, and other information. The following shows an example of how the `top` program displays the information:

```
8:24pm  up 21:46,  4 users,  load average: 0.07, 0.02, 0.00
57 processes: 56 sleeping, 1 running, 0 zombie, 0 stopped
CPU states:  0.3% user,  0.9% system,  0.0% nice, 98.6% idle
Mem:   46984K av,  46156K used,    828K free,   4368K shrd,  24012K buff
Swap:  48380K av,  10248K used,  38132K free                  4680K cached

  PID USER     PRI  NI  SIZE  RSS SHARE STAT   LIB %CPU %MEM   TIME COMMAND
 1771 jo        15   0  1264 1264   700 R        0  1.3  2.6   0:00 top
    1 root       0   0   108   64    48 S        0  0.0  0.1   0:05 init
    2 root       0   0     0    0     0 SW       0  0.0  0.0   0:00 kflushd
    3 root       0   0     0    0     0 SW       0  0.0  0.0   0:00 kupdate
    4 root       0   0     0    0     0 SW       0  0.0  0.0   0:00 kpiod
    5 root       0   0     0    0     0 SW       0  0.0  0.0   0:00 kswapd
   81 daemon     0   0    80    0     0 SW       0  0.0  0.0   0:00 portmap
  163 root       0   0   264  216   164 S        0  0.0  0.4   0:00 syslogd
  167 root       0   0   396    0     0 SW       0  0.0  0.0   0:00 klogd
  173 root       0   0    76    0     0 SW       0  0.0  0.0   0:00 rpc.statd
  175 root       0   0     0    0     0 SW       0  0.0  0.0   0:00 lockd
  176 root       0   0     0    0     0 SW       0  0.0  0.0   0:00 rpciod
  183 root       0   0    72    0     0 SW       0  0.0  0.0   0:00 inetd
  191 root       0   0    84    0     0 SW       0  0.0  0.0   0:00 lpd
  201 daemon     0   0   116   52    44 S        0  0.0  0.1   0:00 atd
  204 root       0   0   224  176   120 S        0  0.0  0.3   0:00 cron
  209 root       0   0   752   56    40 S        0  0.0  0.1   0:00 apache
```

The header information (the first five lines) lists the current time, how long the system has been running, the number of users connected to the system, and statistics on the system CPU, memory, and swap memory. Quickly perusing this information can help you to evaluate the status of your system and locate any trouble spots. In this case, the information in the columns list in descending order the processes using the CPU. As only one process is using the %CPU, all other processes are listed according to their process ID (PID). top only shows the processes that can fit on the screen. Table 12-5 shows the available commands for top.

Table 12-5
Commands for top

Command	Description
space	Updates the display
^L	Redraws the screen
f or F	Adds and removes fields
o or O	Changes the order of displayed fields
h or ?	Prints this list
S	Toggles cumulative mode
i	Toggles display of idle processes

Command	Description
c	Toggle display of command name/line
l	Toggles display of load average
m	Toggles display of memory information
t	Toggles display of summary information
k	Kills a task (with any signal)
N	Sorts by PID (numerically)
A	Sorts by age
P	Sorts by CPU usage
M	Sorts by resident memory usage
T	Sorts by time/cumulative time
U	Shows only a specific user
n or #	Sets the number of processes to show
s	Sets the delay in seconds between updates
W	Writes configuration file ~/.toprc
Q	Quits

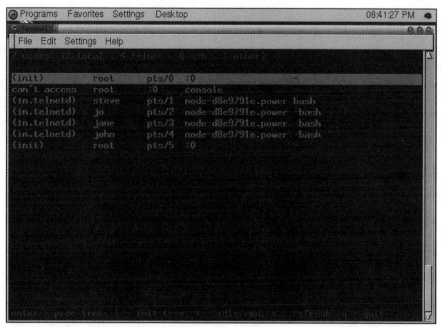

Figure 12-1: You can graphically monitor your system resources with gtop.

Watching the system with gtop

If you are interested in viewing the system information of top, but in a graphical interface, use gtop. This interface enables you to view, at a glance, how your system is currently performing. You get graphical representations of the CPU usage, memory usage, and swap space usage. Furthermore, the Memory tab contains a graphical representation of the used memory, the proportion used by each process, and the corresponding name of each of the processes. Figure 12-1 shows the gtop application launched from a command line.

The only advantage of gtop is the point-and-click interface and menu features. top only uses keyboard interaction. gtop is more limited; for instance, you cannot kill a command from within gtop, whereas you can using top. These more advanced features have not yet been developed for gtop.

Disk monitoring

Another aspect of monitoring involves looking at the consumable space on the hard drives. The first Linux system I built used a 120MB hard drive. Granted not much was installed on it, but I was very concerned about the usable space on the drive.

Users are not the only ones that consume disk space. Quotas can help to control user consumption, but the system itself can eat up a drive if you do not take some care. To track down these problem areas on the disk, you have to use disk utilities to monitor them. A couple of common disk utilities are du and df. They provide the useful information on the disks and filesystem, respectively.

Displaying used space with du

The du utility displays the space currently used by a file or directory. Here is the syntax for the du command:

```
du [OPTION]... [FILE]...
```

By default, the results are displayed in units of 1,024 bytes. Therefore, by issuing the du command of your home directory, you should get something that looks like this:

```
$ du
36       ./docs
5640     ./pics
48       ./misc
4        ./newfiles
2912     ./programs
8668     .
```

Each directory is listed separately, but the accumulation shows up as a period (.), which represents the current directory. As you can see from the example, the `pics` directory contains nearly 5.5MB of data while the `newfiles` directory contains only 4KB of data.

You may be interested in some of the options, which help to make the results more readable. You can combine these options to get the results in the form you most prefer (see Table 12-6).

Table 12-6
Disk usage options

Option	Description
-a, --all	Prints the size of all files and directories
-c, --total	Prints the total of all listed directories. (This is useful when listing more than one directory location.)
-h, --human-readable	Prints sizes in human readable format for easier reading, such as 10K, 256MB, or 3GB
-S, --separate-dirs	Excludes the size of subdirectories in the listing
-s, --summarize	Prints only a total for each specified file or directory

Checking used space on the filesystem with df

When a filesystem is spread across different drives or partitions, it is important that you monitor each filesystem to make sure that enough space remains for files to be written properly. When a filesystem reaches 100 percent capacity, you must create more room in order for more information to be written again. The `df` command shows the vital information you need to quickly check on the filesystem. Here is the syntax for the command:

```
df [OPTION]... [FILE]...
```

Here is an example of a system with its filesystem spread over several partitions of the same drive. This is not always necessary, but it illustrates how you can use the `df` command to get an immediate sense of a system's capacity.

```
$ df
Filesystem          1k-blocks     Used    Available Use% Mounted on
/dev/hdb1            992088      550464   391228     58%   /

Filesystem          1k-blocks     Used    Available Use% Mounted on
/dev/hda8            257598       24038   220256     10%   /
/dev/hda1            19485          593    17886      3%   /boot
```

Continued

```
/dev/hda6          909178   268815   593392   31%   /home
/dev/hda5          909178   515082   347125   60%   /usr
/dev/hda7          257598    51210   193084   21%   /var
```

Table 12-7 lists some of the options for this command. Use these options to get a listing in the format that makes the most sense to you.

<table>
<tr><td colspan="2">Table 12-7
Display filesystem options</td></tr>
<tr><td>Option</td><td>Description</td></tr>
<tr><td>-a, --all</td><td>Includes all filesystems, even those having 0 blocks</td></tr>
<tr><td>-h, --human-readable</td><td>Prints filesystem sizes in human readable format for easy reading, such as 10K, 256MB, or 3GB</td></tr>
<tr><td>-i, --inodes</td><td>Lists the inode information instead of block usage</td></tr>
<tr><td>-l, --local</td><td>Limits the listing to only local filesystems</td></tr>
<tr><td>--no-sync</td><td>Does not invoke sync before getting usage information</td></tr>
<tr><td>--sync</td><td>Invokes sync before getting usage information</td></tr>
</table>

sync forces any blocks stored in cache to be written to the disk. Depending on the system, this can accumulate to a significant amount of stored data in cache. Some administrators invoke the `sync` command as a ritual step to assure that the disk cache gets flushed.

User monitoring

A third form of monitoring involves monitoring the users. This is not a Big-Brother approach, but rather a means of tracking who uses the system. Tracking users as they log in helps you track login information (who is using the system, when, and for how long). This information helps you to manage the resources.

Each time anyone logs into the system, an entry is made in the /var/log/wtmp file. This includes only those who are currently logged directly into the system from the console or through a remote connection.

The last command

The `last` command filters through the /var/log/wtmp file and prints all users who have logged into the machine since the file was created (which can be a long list). It also searches based on certain criteria such as user and tty number (the tty stands for teletype and refers to the virtual terminal connection someone is using). Here is the syntax for the `last` command:

```
last [option] [name...] [tty...]
```

If at some point you feel the need to keep a record of the wtmp file for later review, make a copy of the file. If wtmp gets moved or deleted, nothing will be logged. For this reason, it is best to make a copy of the file. Some of the options for the last command are found in Table 12-8.

Table 12-8
Options used with last

Option	Description
-num or -n num	A count indicating last how many lines to show
-R	Suppresses the display of the hostname field
-a	Displays the hostname in the last column. Useful in combination with the next flag.
-d	For remote logins, the host name of the remote host and its IP number get stored. This option translates the IP number back into a hostname.
-i	This option is like -d in that it displays the IP number of the remote host, but it displays the IP number in numbers-and-dots notation.
-o	Reads an old-type wtmp file
-x	Displays the system shutdown entries and run level changes

Note

/var/log/wtmp keeps a log of all successful login attempts, so what happens when a bad attempt is made? Adding a /var/log/btmp file to the system starts recording all failed login attempts to the system. It makes sure that the mode, user, and group match the wtmp file—which is usually read/write for user and group only, root as user, and utmp for group. You can then use the lastb command to view a report on the bad attempts to login to the system. This command works the same as the last command, only it defaults to the btmp file. If either file doesn't exist, then the system makes no attempts to record any login information. Debian normally installs the wtmp file only.

When you reboot the system, a pseudo-user named reboot logs in. You can search on reboot to see all the times the system has been rebooted. The system logs remote hosts during log in, so it records the host IP address. Using the -d option prints a remote host as the hostname, while using the -i option displays the host as an IP address.

Tools from the acct package

The accounting package (`acct`) can help with monitoring users. When you install this package, three programs are included: `ac`, `sa`, and `lastcomm`. Table 12-9 explains these three tools.

Table 12-9
Accounting tools

Command	Description
ac	Prints the status of the user connection time in hours. Using option `-d`, you can get the daily total connection times for everyone on the system. You can use this information to determine load usage. You can also add user account names to determine individual accounting information.
lastcomm	Prints commands that have been executed on this system. You can list by command, user name, or tty connection. When you combine the search criteria, every instance of each criterion prints out. To restrict the output to match all conditions, use the `--strict-match` option.
sa	Prints a summary of processes that have run on the system. This is a strict account application. It shows such information as the CPU time to run an application, memory used, and so on. All the accounting information comes from the file `/var/account/pacct`.

The accounting application may not be useful for everyone, but it provides good information for your toolbelt in case the need arises. If you think you may need this information, it is better to install the package to begin tracking the information — even if you never use it.

Using who

The `who` command lists everyone presently logged on to a system. This command shows who is logged on, what time they logged on, and from where (local port or remote hostname). The syntax is:

```
who [OPTION][am i]
```

The `-m` option works the same as the `am i` argument at the end. These result in displaying who you are currently logged in as. This helps me after I log in as other accounts and forget whom I originally logged in as.

Another useful option shows the idle time. There are three choices that do the same thing: `-i`, `-u`, and `--idle`. The results show the time that use is idle. If a period (`.`) is displayed, the user has been active within the last minute. If "old" shows up instead of a time, then the user has been idle for more than 24 hours.

Using whowatch

When it comes to keeping track of individuals as they come and go on a system, having to use who all the time gets old. A handy little utility called whowatch runs in a terminal window (as seen in Figure 12-2). This program continuously updates itself to show any changes in the attached accounts.

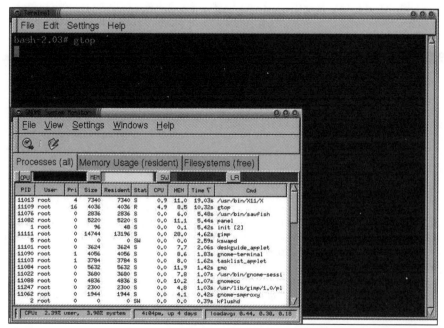

Figure 12-2: You can dynamically monitor who logs in and out of your system with whowatch.

This program goes further than the who application. Using the arrow keys, you can select a specific user and view his or her process tree. You can essentially see what this user is doing. As an administrator, this can be very important as you monitor the system.

Automated monitoring

Manually typing in commands, perusing through the screens of data, and remembering to perform those routine tasks is mundane after a while. However, you still need to do those things. The question is, can any of these tasks be automated to make the poor administrator's life easier? They certainly can be automated. Here I briefly touch on the subject of scripting, although I fully cover it in Chapter 13.

I was once told, "If you find yourself repeating a task over and over, then there has to be a shortcut to make doing the task faster." This has haunted me ever since.

Whenever you find that you are repeatedly typing the same command strings, enter that sequence into a text file. You can then change the mode of the file to executable. This is how you go about creating an automated task. Let's say that your daily task is to perform this command:

```
df -ah | grep -e [8-9][0-9]% -h
```

This command prints any filesystems that are in the range of 80 to 99 percent capacity. Now, type this line into a text file and name it dcheck. I use the chmod command to make the file executable for myself and my group by issuing this command line:

```
$ chmod u+x,g+x dcheck
$
```

which results in a listing of:

```
$ ls -l
-rwxr-xr--    1 root      steve        22 Jun 19 22:28 dcheck
$
```

All you have to do now is execute the new command of dcheck to perform the same task you normally type manually. This saves time and prevents you from making typos in the command line. You can follow this procedure to start making your own commands customized for your own special needs.

Cross-Reference   You can learn more about automating tasks from Chapter 9. Likewise, Chapter 14 describes how to use shell commands to make little, but powerful programs.

Summary

Through the course of this chapter, you read about the basics of the administrator's duties. I stress *basic* because there is more information and more to keep on top of all the time. Many of the commands listed in this chapter have more options than those highlighted; you can always look up additional ones yourself.

Of the duties, the most important are knowing how to set up and manage accounts; controlling permissions on accounts, groups and files; and monitoring the system resources. Also, keep guard of the superuser (root) account. Once the password for that account gets out, regaining security control is difficult.

✦   ✦   ✦

Scripting

The development environment of an operating system is one of the most powerful assets you have. With a programming language, you can do anything from automating repetitive tasks to writing entire applications. In this chapter, you learn about the different development environments on your Debian system.

Debian provides you with many different scripting languages. You can install each of them with the standard Debian package management tools. Each also features a number of plug-in modules or libraries for the different languages, which you can install separately. In addition to the four scripting languages covered, this chapter also discusses the C/C++ development environment in Debian.

Working with Perl

Perl is one of the largest and most complex scripting systems on Linux. Perl has its roots in several other scripting systems, such as the shell and awk. Debian ships with the Perl interpreter and a large collection of additional Perl modules.

To begin with Perl, you should install the `perl-5.005` and `perl-5.005-doc` packages. These packages provide you with a Perl environment and its documentation. After you do this, you are ready to begin writing Perl programs. There are, however, many extra add-ons that you can use with Perl; for details on these, see the "Using Modules" section later in this chapter.

Finding documentation for Perl

Documentation for Perl, its applications, and its modules are provided in two main ways: man pages and POD (Plain Old Documentation). While man pages for Perl and Perl libraries operate in the same way as man pages on the rest of the system, you do not see POD anywhere else.

man pages

Perl man pages are available at the discretion of each software author. Some packages may not provide information in man page form, or they may not provide all information in man page form. Sometimes, however, you can find information about Perl systems in the man pages.

Start out by running man perl. This man page describes the documentation that comes with the Perl system and refers you to other man pages for Perl. The other Perl man pages describe things such as the command line for invoking the Perl interpreter, syntax of the language, internal functions, the module system, and more.

Tip   You can get a list of man pages for any Debian package (including the Perl packages) by running dpkg -L package | grep /usr/share/man. For instance, if you use perl-5.005 for the package, you get output such as /usr/share/man/man3/IO::Select.3pm.gz. Then, you can run man IO::Select to get that particular man page.

Plain Old Documentation

POD (Plain Old Documentation) is a way for authors of Perl software to embed documentation for a Perl script right inside the source code for the program. This is convenient in several ways. First, it is nice for developers to be able to document the program right next to the code. Secondly, all users of the program automatically get the current documentation alongside it. Finally, some utilities display documentation for a Perl program given just a module or program name; you don't have to worry about finding the proper man page.

To bring up documentation for a particular Perl module, you can use the perldoc command, which takes the module name as an argument. For example, if you want to find documentation for the Net::Ping module, you type perldoc Net::Ping. The perldoc program finds the documentation for that module and displays it for you. This technique works with most of the modules that you find in Perl or Debian.

For Perl internal functions, you can use the perlfunc man page. However, this is a very large man page and it can be hard to find exactly what you seek. For instance, if you are looking for information on the join function, you have to spend some time searching through the perlfunc page because that word occurs many times. You can jump right to it by using perldoc, though; just run perldoc -tf join.

Tip   The output from perldoc -tf can be long. You can keep it from scrolling off the terminal by piping it through a pager such as perldoc -tf function | less.

The perldoc program also can give you documentation from individual files. You can use perldoc -F filename to obtain information about a specific file. This can be useful if you have a Perl program that does not come with Debian or is not installed in a system-wide location. It's also helpful for testing the POD documentation in your own programs.

Finally, `perldoc` looks up information in the Perl FAQ (Frequently Asked Questions) document. To do that, run `perldoc -tq` *keyword*. For instance, if you want to look up information about opening files, you can type `perldoc -tq open`. `perldoc` returns answers to frequently asked questions about the opening files.

Using modules

Perl is an extensible language with many available modules. Modules provide additional features for use in your Perl programs. Examples of these features include modules for communicating with Web servers, talking to databases, parsing data in various formats, or managing files.

Perl comes with some internal modules. There are also two other resources for finding Perl modules: Debian and CPAN. *CPAN* is the *Comprehensive Perl Archive Network;* one of its primary functions is to serve as a repository of Perl modules. The CPAN site, `www.cpan.org`, has hundreds of modules available for download — more than are present in Debian. However, the packages that you can find in Debian are generally easier to install than those on CPAN. You can install Debian packages with standard tools such as `apt-get` and `dpkg`. If you use CPAN packages, you must compile them, satisfy all their dependencies, and then put them in place. Table 13-1 lists some of the most popular Perl modules, along with their CPAN and Debian names where available.

Table 13-1
Popular Perl modules

CPAN module name	Debian package	Description
Net::IPv4Addr	libnetwork-ipv4addr-perl	Performs calculations on IP addresses
	libfcgi-perl	Provides a faster CGI interface for Web sites
Gtk	libgtk-perl	Interface to the Graphics Toolkit (GTK) widget set
Device::SerialPort	libdevice-serialport-perl	An interface to serial ports for Linux systems
String::ShellQuote	libstring-shellquote-perl	Quotes strings properly for passing through to a shell
GD	libgd-perl	Interface to the Gd library, which allows the run-time generation of graphics files (JPEG, and so on) from inside Perl programs

Continued

Table 13-1 *(continued)*

CPAN module name	Debian package	Description
Term::ReadLine	libterm-readline-perl	An interface to the readline library, which provides things such as command history and buffer editing for terminal applications
XML::Generator	libxml-generator-perl	Generates XML output from Perl programs
	libmail-imapclient-perl	Routines for communicating with an IMAP server
Authen::PAM	libauthen-pam-perl	Supports PAM (Pluggable Authentication Modules) functions from Perl. You need this if you intend to access the user name/password system on Debian.
IO::Pty	libio-pty-perl	Routines to support the use of pseudo-terminals in Perl
File::Sync	libfile-sync-perl	Interfaces to sync() and fsync() from the system
XML::Stream	libxml-stream-perl	Supports streaming XML over a socket
XML::Writer	libxml-writer-perl	Writes XML documents from Perl, including some well-formed checks
Compress::Zlib	libcompress-zlib-perl	Perl interface for compression and gzip file manipulation
XML::Dumper	libxml-dumper-perl	Dumps Perl data structures to XML format and reads this format back
Logfile::Rotate	liblogfile-rotate-perl	Rotates and saves versions of files
Net::FTP	libnet-perl	Perl interface to the Internet File Transfer Protocol for writing clients
Net::SMTP	libnet-perl	Routines for communicating with mail servers using SMTP (Simple Mail Transfer Protocol)

CPAN module name	Debian package	Description
`Net::Time`	`libnet-perl`	**Functions for reading the time from other computers**
`Net::NNTP`	`libnet-perl`	**Communicates with Usenet news servers**
`Net::POP3`	`libnet-perl`	**Allows access to remote mail folders via POP3**
`Net::SNPP`	`libnet-perl`	**Functions for communicating with SNPP servers**
`Mail::Sendmail`	`libmail-sendmail-perl`	**A client library for sending e-mail**
`Locale::gettext`	`liblocale-gettext-perl`	**A Perl interface to GNU** `gettext`—**a library for internationalization of programs**
	`pilot-link-perl`	**Functions for communicating with Palm Computing devices from Perl scripts**
`Pod::Parser,` `Pod::Select,` `Pod::Usage,` `Pod::PlainText,` `Pod::InputObject,` `Pod::Checker,` `Pod::ParseUtils`	`libpod-parser-perl`	**POD documentation**
`Net::SSleay`	`libnet-ssleay-perl`	**Secure Socket Layer (SSL) library for use in Perl programs**
	`libcorba-orbit-perl`	**Perl interface to CORBA systems**
	`libterm-slang-perl`	**S-Lang (console manipulation) library**
`Net::SNMP`	`libnet-snmp-perl`	**SNMP interface for Perl programs**
	`libpgperl`	**Perl interface to PostgreSQL database servers**
	`ipchains-perl`	**Provides an interface to the Linux firewall rule system:** `ipchains`
`Curses::Widgets`	`libcurses-widgets-perl`	**Library of functions for Perl programs to draw text on the terminal**

Continued

Table 13-1 *(continued)*

CPAN module name	Debian package	Description
	`dpkg-perl`	A Perl interface to Debian's `dpkg` package-management system
`Net::DNS`	`libnet-dns-perl`	Routines for performing DNS lookups
`Text::Format`	`libtext-format-perl`	Tools for formatting text with Perl
	`libtimedate-perl`	Time and date manipulation routines
`Net::LDAP`	`libnet-ldap-perl`	An interface to the Lightweight Directory Access Protocol (LDAP)
	`libcgi-pm-perl`	One of several different CGI interfaces for Perl
`GnuPG::Interface`	`libgnupg-interface-perl`	An interface to GnuPG, the GNU Privacy Guard for Perl
`DBI`	`libdbi-perl`	DBI, the Perl database interface. With DBI, you can write a single program that is capable of communicating with many different SQL servers.
	`libpalm-perl`	Provides support for generating and modifying Palm PDB and PRC files
`Tk`	`perl-tk`	An interface from Perl to the Tk widget toolkit, originally from Tcl.
`Language::Basic`		A BASIC interpreter written in Perl
`Language::Prolog`		An implementation of Prolog entirely in Perl
`File::Rsync`		Perl interface to `rsync`, a system for remotely synchronizing files

Installing Debian modules

To install Perl modules that are Debian packages, you simply install them like any other Debian package using the package manager of your choice. For instance, if you want to install perl-tk, run a command like this:

```
# apt-get install perl-tk
Reading Package Lists... Done
Building Dependency Tree... Done
The following NEW packages will be installed:
  perl-tk
0 packages upgraded, 1 newly installed, 0 to remove and 135 not
upgraded.
Need to get 0B/1997kB of archives. After unpacking 7139kB will
be used.
Selecting previously deselected package perl-tk.
(Reading database ... 59414 files and directories currently
installed.)
Unpacking perl-tk (from .../perl-tk_800.022-1.deb) ...
Setting up perl-tk (800.022-1) ...
```

So, with one command, you can install a Debian-packaged Perl module. This command installs the module system-wide, so all users and all accounts on the system can see it. Because you are using the Debian package manager to install it, this module also is upgraded automatically when Debian is.

Installing modules from CPAN

Installing modules from CPAN is more complicated. There are a couple of reasons that you might opt to install modules from CPAN rather than from Debian. First, if CPAN has a newer version of a module than Debian and you need features from it, you might choose to install the CPAN version. Secondly, Debian's collection of Perl modules is not as extensive as CPAN's; if Debian doesn't have a particular module, CPAN might be your only option.

You can install CPAN modules in one of two ways. First, you can download the tar.gz file directly from CPAN's Web or FTP site and install that. Secondly, you can use the Perl CPAN program to make the download and installation process a bit easier.

If you choose the first method, you have to complete an 8-step process:

1. Download the tar.gz file for the package you want to install.

2. Untar the package by running tar -zxvf filename.tar.gz.

3. Use the cd *packagename* command to change into the directory containing the package.

4. Run the command perl Makefile.PL to generate the Makefile.

5. Run the command make to build the package.

6. Become root (you can use the `su` command to do this).

7. Run `make install`.

8. Type `exit` to return to your normal account.

If you elect to use the CPAN program, your procedure looks like this

1. Become root with su.

2. Start the CPAN program by running `perl -MCPAN -e shell`. If this is the first time you run the CPAN program, you are asked a few setup questions. You can generally just hit Enter to accept the defaults.

3. Type install module. For instance, if you wish to install the GNU Privacy Guard interface module, you will type `install GnuPG::Interface`.

4. Type `exit` to return to the prompt.

Using Java

Java has stirred up intense interest in recent years, partly because of its promise of cross-platform execution of programs. Your Debian system contains several programs that support Java, each with their own particular advantages and disadvantages. Here are the various Java compilers and interpreters available for use on Debian systems:

✦ `kaffe` is a JVM (Java Virtual Machine — a bytecode interpreter) that is included with Debian. It can also function as a development environment, but it does not implement the entire Java specification from SunSoft yet. Unlike Sun JDK, `kaffe` is portable and runs on many Debian platforms.

✦ `gcj` is the GNU Compiler for Java. This program can compile Java sources and bytecode to native, machine-specific object (binary) code, which Sun's JDK cannot. You can also use `gcj` to compile Java source code into Java bytecode. The `gcj` system does not contain any interpreter, and it supports only Java 1.0.

✦ The `jdk1.1`, `jdk1.1-dev`, `jdk1.1-native`, and `jdk1.1-native-dev` packages are Linux versions of Sun's official JDK (Java Development Kit) version 1.1. However, Sun licensed these products under a license that is not compatible with the Debian Free Software Guidelines, so you will not find these as Debian packages. You can find them under the `devel` directory in the non-free section of `ftp.debian.org` or with your favorite package management tool.

✦ You can find implementations of **Java 2 version 1.2** and newer for Linux on the Internet at `java.blackdown.org`. Again, for licensing reasons, these are not packaged by Debian developers, so I advise you to use Debian packages (unless you have a specific need for a feature in Java 2).

Because of this fractured nature of Java support, getting Java libraries to work can sometimes depend on which specific Java interpreter or compiler you use. As a general hint, if you experience odd errors with one of the programs (particularly if your Java code contains a graphical interface), use another one of the interpreters or compilers just listed.

Using Kaffe and the Sun JDK

Because Kaffe and the Sun JDK behave almost identically, I talk about them together. The first thing you need to do is install the appropriate packages. If you are using Kaffe, all you need is the `kaffe` package. For the Sun JDK, I recommend the `jdk-1.1-native` package. If you plan to do development work, you also want the `jdk-1.1-native-dev` package. Kaffe has no development package.

For running Java programs, you need one of two programs: the `java` program and the `appletviewer`. The `java` command runs regular Java applications, which may have either a textual or a graphical interface. The `appletviewer` is designed for graphical programs intended for embedding inside a Web page and viewing by a Web browser. Running any sort of graphical Java application will require the X Window System.

To run a Java application, you have a `.class` file to invoke. You can do so by running `java filename.class`. Your application then runs.

If you want to view an applet, you invoke the applet viewer on the piece of HTML that contains the reference to the applet. To do so, run `appletviewer filename.html`. You should get a window onscreen with the applet inside; the remainder of the HTML in the file is not displayed.

If you develop your own Java programs, `javac` (the Java compiler) may be of interest to you. You can use `javac` to compile your `.java` sources into `.class` bytecode. Note that Kaffe does not come with an implementation of `javac`; you might, however, consider using `gcj` for your Java compilation needs if you use the Kaffe environment.

Using gcj

The `gcj` program is unique among the Java tools in Debian for two reasons. First, `gcj` is part of the GNU compiler toolchain; as such, it works more like a traditional C compiler than like the Java tools in the Sun tradition. Secondly, `gcj` is actually capable of generating a native executable for your system—that is, it does not require a Java interpreter to run. `gcj` has no man page or info documentation; however, documentation in `/usr/share/doc/gcj/README.java.gz` explains a bit about `gcj` and its command-line parameters. You may find it in the `gcj` package.

Before I show you the commands to use for compiling Java code with `gcj`, I want to point out some differences between `gcj` and other Java environments. First of all, unlike Sun's `javac`, `gcj` does not pull in all the classes that your main object requires necessarily. Like `gcc`, you need to manually specify all of them on the command line to `gcj`; otherwise, your program may fail to link. Also, `gcj` does not link your program unless you also specify (using `--main=class`) which object should be treated as your program's entry point.

For the following example, assume that you want to compile a program consisting of one class, `Test.java`, into a binary for your machine. You use this `gcj` command:

```
gcj --main=Test Test.java -o Test
```

The `-o` option tells `gcj` where to put the resulting executable. Assuming all goes well, you now have a file named `Test` that you can run just as you do any native executable (for instance, by running `./Test`). If your program uses other classes, you can just specify them on the command line like this:

```
gcj --main=Test -o Test Test.java AnotherClass.java AThirdClass.java
```

In this way, you can specify all the classes that comprise your application for `gcj` to link. If you don't do this, you usually receive an error message from `gcj` about undefined classes or subroutines. Also, if you get an error message about main being undefined, chances are you forgot the `--main` option.

Finding documentation for Java

Documentation for Java can be difficult to find. Unlike Perl, the various Java interpreters and compilers do not come with documentation on the language itself. You can find some man pages for things like the `kaffe` command on your system. However, in general, you have to look elsewhere for Java documentation.

You can find documentation for the Java language from many different third parties. One good starting point is `java.sun.com`, which provides detailed documentation for the standard Java API.

For individual Java applications or libraries, you have to consult the information that comes with the package. On a Debian system, you can often find this information in `/usr/share/doc/package`.

Using Java libraries

Like many other languages on a Debian system, Java has a number of libraries available for use with it. Unlike Perl, there is no central repository for Java, and Java applications and libraries obtained from third parties don't follow a rigid standard installation mechanism like Perl modules do. Therefore, in this section, I discuss only those Java libraries that come with Debian. If you want to install one of the many third-party Java libraries, please consult the documentation that accompanies the library for installation instructions. Table 13-2 highlights some of the most popular and useful Java libraries in Debian.

| | Table 13-2 Java libraries | |

Debian package name	Description
libservlet2.2-java	An implementation of Java servlets — applications for integration into a Web server
lib-openxml-java	*OpenXML* is a full-fledged suite of XML processing routines for Java. You can also install the lib-openxml-java-doc package for documentation on this library. Note that both packages might be in the "contrib" area of ftp.debian.org instead of on your CD.
lib-gnu.regexp-java	This package provides regular expression support for Java. With it, you can get some of the pattern matching features that you are accustomed to in languages such as Perl and awk.
lib-gnu.getopt-java	An implementation of the GNU getopt command line parsing library for Java
libpgjava	A JDBC driver for the PostgreSQL database. *JDBC (Java Database Classes)* is a portable, multidatabase set of libraries for communicating with database servers.
libldap-java	A Java interface for LDAP (Lightweight Directory Access Protocol)

To install any of these libraries, you can simply use your favorite package manager along with a package name from the left column. For instance, if you wish to use apt-get to install the JDBC driver for PostgreSQL, run apt-get install libpgjava.

Troubleshooting

While everything will work fine for you most of the time, you should know a few tips for dealing with some common problems. One of the most common problems when trying to run or compile Java programs involves the location of the classes and libraries that the program uses.

With a Java program, each class that makes up the application is generally stored in a separate file. Therefore, a single application can have dozens or even hundreds of required files to make it run properly. If the application cannot find its components, it may not start — or it may crash in the middle of execution.

The solution to this problem is to specify the location of the application's data in the CLASSPATH environment variable. CLASSPATH is a Java-specific search path used by the interpreter and compiler to locate components of your program.

Normally, it is automatically set to the correct value, but sometimes CLASSPATH cannot automatically determine the proper settings. In these situations, you have to give it some help.

CLASSPATH is a colon-separated list of directories or JAR files to search for program components. Some programs may come with one file, a Java Archive, containing all the individual classes. In this case, you can simply add the full path of that file to your CLASSPATH. Otherwise, you still need to specify a directory. You can set your CLASSPATH by using a command such as the following:

```
export CLASSPATH=/home/username/java:/usr/share/java/postgresql.jar
```

Tip

Some Debian packages might require an entry in your CLASSPATH so that the Java interpreter can see them. You can find a list of the locations of all files in a Debian package by using dpkg -L *packagename*. Also, you can search through the index of all Debian packages for a specific file by using dpkg -S *filename*.

Another common problem occurs when you try to run a Java application under a Java interpreter that is too old to support it. This can occur, for instance, if you have an application that uses features of Java 2 but you're running it under JDK 1.1 or Kaffe. This problem can display some of the same symptoms as the CLASSPATH one: complaints about missing components and classes. To solve this problem, determine which version of the JDK your program requires, and install the appropriate software on your machine.

Using Tcl/Tk

Originally written as a language for controlling hardware devices, *Tcl (Tool Command Language*, pronounced "tickle") has found increasingly wide usage for a variety of different tasks. Like Perl, Tcl is an interpreted language. It has a syntax that, in some ways, is vaguely reminiscent of C.

When people discuss Tcl these days, they often mention Tk in the same breath. *Tk* is a toolkit and widget set used for adding a graphical interface to Tcl applications. Tk was originally developed specifically for use in Tcl programs; however, there is also a Perl interface to Tk.

The base Tcl/Tk system contains two packages: one for Tcl and one for Tk. Debian includes several different versions of Tcl/Tk, so you have options. I suggest installing the task-tcltk and task-tcltk-dev packages, which always bring along the latest versions of the Tcl/Tk base and development packages (tcl8.2, tcl8.2-dev, tk8.2, and tk8.2-dev at this time.) You can install the task-tcltk package with either your favorite package-management tool or the tasksel application.

Once installed, the Tcl/Tk system comes with two main applications: `tclsh`, the Tcl shell; and `wish`, the windowing shell. The former is used strictly for Tcl programs; the latter is used for Tcl/Tk programs. If invoked without any arguments, both `tclsh` and `wish` are set to read program code interactively from the terminal. The difference you can see is that `wish` also pops up an empty X window on startup. Normally, however, your application is passed as a command-line argument to `tclsh` or `wish`, and you never see the Tcl command line.

Finding documentation for Tcl/Tk

The Tcl/Tk system comes with extensive documentation—all provided in the form of man pages. To access the documentation for the Tcl/Tk system, install the `tcl8.2-doc` and `tk8.2-doc` packages. These two packages together contain nearly 1,000 man pages! To get a list of the available man pages, try this command:

```
dpkg -L tcl8.2-doc tk8.2-doc | less
```

You get a listing of all the man page files installed on the system by either of these packages. To view them, use a command like `man AppInit` or `man Tcl_Concat`. The man pages whose names begin with `Tcl_` or `Tk_` are actually man pages for C programs that use the C interface to Tcl or Tk; thus, these man pages are of no interest to you unless you are writing C programs to interface to Tcl/Tk.

Adding Tcl/Tk libraries

Like the other languages covered in this chapter, Tcl/Tk also has a selection of add-on libraries available. Tcl/Tk libraries come in three flavors: binary libraries written in C, add-on libraries written in Tcl, and replacement shells along the lines of `tclsh` and `wish`. The `library(3tcl)` and `source(3tcl)` man pages discuss how to use these with your own Tcl/Tk programs. If you install Debian-supplied Tcl/Tk programs that require Tcl/Tk libraries, the Debian package-management system should resolve all the dependencies automatically and set up the libraries for your use.

Some operating systems don't have support for all three library styles like Debian does, so some libraries (especially older ones) are shipped as replacements for `tclsh`. Scripts that use them can simply call the modified `tclsh` to access the features within the library. This approach, though, is not employed much anymore because it limits programmers to using only one add-on library at a time.

Table 13-3 lists many of the Tcl/Tk libraries included in Debian. You can install them with standard Debian package tools such as apt.

Table 13-3
Popular Tcl/Tk libraries

Package name	Description
itcl3.1, itcl3.1-dev	This is a package of [incr Tcl], a version of Tcl that adds object-oriented programming to the language.
libtcl-ldap	Provides an interface to LDAP for Tcl programs
visual-tcl	Not really a library, this is a GUI builder for Tcl programs.
tcl-sql	A generic interface to SQL databases for Tcl programs
Tclreadline	A Tcl version of GNU readline, which provides command history and in-place editing for Tcl programs that support a command line
Gdtclft	Provides a Tcl interface to the GD graphics library, which enables you to create images such as PNG and JPEG at run time
Libpgtcl	An interface from Tcl to the PostgreSQL database server
newt-tcl	*Newt* is a pseudo-windowing toolkit for text-based terminals. newt-tcl provides a Tcl binding for this toolkit.
Tcllib	A collection of many Tcl modules for things such as parsing command- line parameters, basic file operations, e-mail support, and some advanced data structures

Programming With Python

Python is a language that has recently gained popularity with Linux developers. It is based on objected-oriented programming principles; but unlike Java, Python functions in a more traditional manner that is in some ways more like Perl. Debian, of course, features a full Python development environment.

The easiest way to get started with Python in Debian is to install the task-python package. If you wish to develop with Python, you should also install the task-python-dev package. Together, these packages bring in a full suite of Python tools including the interpreter, its documentation, and a number of Python libraries.

Finding documentation for Python

Documentation for Python is provided primarily in two formats: HTML and GNU info. You can view the HTML documentation with a standard Web browser such as Netscape from /usr/share/doc/python/html. These documents also appear in GNU info format and in the python-doc package. The documents included are:

python-api, the C API documentation; python-ext, a manual for extended Python; python-lib, the Python Library Reference; python-mac, documentation for using Python on Macintosh machines; python-ref, the Python Reference Manual; and python-tut, the Python Tutorial. To view the info documentation, you can use your favorite info browser: the info command, M-x info RET from within Emacs or XEmacs, or info2www. If you use the command-line version, you can type a command such as info python-tut to skip directly to the Python Tutorial document.

Documentation for add-on modules for Python is more haphazard; there is no particular standard for Python module documentation. You should check the usual areas for documentation for any particular module: man pages, /usr/share/doc/packagename, info pages, and the Internet.

| **Tip** | Remember, the dpkg -L packagename command can be useful. It gives you a list of all files provided by a package and helps you find the documentation. |

Installing Python libraries

Installing a Python library on a Debian system is as simple as using your favorite package manager to install the Debian package. You might be interested in the task-python-dev package, which installs many of the Python libraries for you. Table 13-4 summarizes many of the Python libraries available in Debian, including all of the libraries in task-python-dev.

Table 13-4
Common Python libraries

Package name	In task-python-dev?	Description
gadfly	Yes	An implementation of a simple SQL database engine written in Python. This is not a client library; it is a simple server.
htmlgen	Yes	A library for the generation of HTML documents from Python applications
idle	Yes	Not strictly a library, idle is an IDE (integrated development environment) for Python programs.
pydb	Yes	A debugger for Python
pyrite	Yes	A library for interacting with Palm devices
saml	Yes	Simple Algebraic Math Library provides functions for C and Python for some common algebraic functions.

Continued

Table 13-4 *(continued)*

Package name	In task-python-dev?	Description
`sulfur`	Yes	Generic routines for Python applications such as plug-in support and command-line parsing
`swig`	Yes	`swig` is actually not a library; it is designed to facilitate the integration of Python and C/C++ code.
`python-zlib`	Yes	An interface from Python to the `zlib` data compression library used by `gzip`
`zope-pythonmethod`	No	A Python library for the Python-based Zope application that makes it easier to use arbitrary Python code in your Zope environment
`python-mxdatetime`	Yes	Date and time manipulation routines
`python-pygresql`	Yes	A library for accessing a PostgreSQL database from Python
`python-gdk-imlib`	Yes	A Python binding for the imaging library `imlib`
`python-gnuplot`	No	Support for creating charts, graphs, and plots using `gnuplot`
`python-mxstack`	Yes	A stack data structure for use in your Python applications
`python-scientific`, `python-scientific-doc`	No	Modules of particular interest to scientific computing
`python-examples`	Yes	Python examples from the authors of the language
`python-bobopos`	Yes	The Bobo Persistent Object System, a way of saving Python objects to disk or other storage
`python-tk`	Yes	A binding of the Tk graphical widget toolkit for Python
`python-imaging-tk`	Yes	Tk support for the Python imaging library

Package name	In task-python-dev?	Description
`python-pmw`	Yes	Python MegaWidgets, a system for building Python widgets
`python-mxtools`	Yes	Some basic tools for Python. They add some LISP-ish features to Python.
`gimp-python`	Yes	This Gimp module supports Python-based plug-ins for the Gimp.
`python-kjbuckets`	Yes	Supports some additional data types in Python
`dpkg-python`	Yes	Preliminary (not finished) library for accessing the Debian package database from Python scripts
`python-imaging-sane`	Yes	Python interface to the SANE scanner library
`python-pcgi`	No	Python library that implements the Persistent CGI interface
`python-numeric`, `python-numeric-tutorial`	Yes	The Numeric Extensions to Python (NumPy) with some new object types and routines. The `python-scientific` package requires this one as well.
`python-glade`	Yes	A Python interface for the Glade designer
`python-rng`	Yes	Random Number Generator library
`python-ldap`	Yes	A Python interface for the Lightweight Directory Access Protocol
`python-gnome`	Yes	Support for using the Gnome graphical interface from within Python applications
`python-dev`	Yes	Not really a library, but contains various files that are useful for Python development
`python-newt`	Yes	Support for the Newt console/terminal windowing library for Python
`python-graphics`	No	Support for the Gist scientific graphics environment
`python-mxtexttools`	Yes	Tools for searching and processing text
`python-imaging`, `python-imaging-doc`	Yes (base package only)	*PIL*, the *Python Imaging Library*, enables you to generate and read photos and other images.

Continued

	Table 13-4 *(continued)*	
Package name	**In task-python-dev?**	**Description**
python-gtk	Yes	A Python binding for the Gtk graphical widget set
pythondoc	No	Library for generating documentation from Python objects
python-pam	Yes	Library for authentication with Pluggable Authentication Modules and Python
python-extclass	Yes	ExtensionClass, a system for integrating Python and C++ code
python-xml	Yes	Support for XML in Python
python-pdb	Yes	Python routines for PACT/PDB files
python-wpy	Yes	Class system for Tk on Python
python-mpz	Yes	A version of the GNU multiprecision library for Python
python-bobo	Yes	A library for interfacing Python code to Web servers
python-history	Yes	A library for historical data collection

Using C/C++

This final section of this chapter represents the largest, most complex, and most popular development environment in Debian: that of C and C++. Virtually every application on your Debian system can be traced back to C in some fashion.

Debian contains the entire GNU compiler *toolchain*; that is, the collection of C and C++ compilers plus all of the supporting programs necessary to make them work. Table 13-5 includes a list of the programs that make up toolchain and its related utilities.

Table 13-5
C and C++ toolchain programs

Program	Description
gcc	The GNU C compiler and the starting point for most of your programming
cpp	The GNU C PreProcessor; this program parses preprocessor directives such as #include and #ifdef.
ld	The linker, which combines all of your object code together with a loader to generate a finished executable
ldd	A utility to display which shared objects a dynamically linked executable requires
ld.so	The dynamic library loader
make	The automatic project building facility
autoconf and automake	Programs to help add portability to your C projects
gperf	The GNU performance analyzer, a profiler designed to find performance bottlenecks in your code
strace	The system call trace utility, a debugging aid that displays calls made by your program to the system
ltrace	The library call trace utility (not supported on all platforms)
gdb	The GNU debugger, a full-featured debugger for various compiled languages including C and C++
as/gas	The GNU assembler, used for generating machine language code
gasp	The GNU assembler preprocessor
ar	The archive creator and extractor. Used primarily for creating static libraries.
ranlib	Generates a symbol table for a static library

If this all looks daunting, don't worry! You only need to concern yourself with one or two of these programs for general-purpose applications. However, GNU does have a full-featured C toolchain, so the rest of the commands are necessary if you want to do more complex things such as writing C libraries, integrating with assembler, or developing kernels.

Cross-Reference

In addition to the tools used for C and C++, the GNU toolchain also includes compilers or translators for Ada, Java, Pascal, and Fortran. I discuss the Java compiler in the "Using Java" section earlier in this chapter.

You should install several packages for C development. For a basic development environment, you can get by with installing only `task-c-dev`. However, for a more complete system, you should install more packages. Here's an `apt-get` command line that you can use:

```
apt-get install task-c-dev task-c++-dev gcc-doc glibc-doc manpages-dev task-debug
```

Type that all on one line (not pressing Enter until the end). When you press Enter, `apt` automatically installs all of the dozens of components that make up the full C/C++ development environment.

Finding C/C++ documentation

Now that you have the C/C++ development environment installed, you need to know how to use it. Because the environment is so expansive, documentation comes in several different forms.

You can always rely on man pages for C/C++ information. In fact, sections 2 and 3 of the man page system are filled mostly with C/C++ information. In section 2, you find information on system calls such as `socket()` and `dup()`. Section 3 contains library functions such as `strcmp()` and `printf()`. Virtually every standard C function exists in the man page system, and you can jump right to the documentation for it with a command such as `man printf`. This ease of access makes man pages a favorite resource of many C developers.

For more detailed and up-to-date information on the C library functions (those in section 3 of the man pages), you need to refer to the GNU C library info documentation. It is not very fast at pulling up information on a specific function, but it tends to have the information you need.

 Tip   You can jump to a specific entry in the C library documentation with a little bit of typing. Here's the command: `info libc "Function Index"` *function*. Just replace "function" with the name of the function you want information about (such as `printf`). If all goes well, you should have the information you need. Note the required quotes in the command.

Many C/C++ libraries and add-ons provide documentation in man page or info format as well. Sometimes this documentation is quite extensive, and it is split off into a separate "-doc" package. If you can't find much documentation for a library you're using, you might check to see if there is a package in Debian named *package*-doc. If so, chances are it contains the documentation you seek.

Documentation for the C++ standard library is more difficult to find. As of this writing, the Debian distribution does not include C++ standard library documentation. However, you may find some C++ documentation in `.deb` form at `ftp.debian.org/debian/project/experimental`. Look for a file beginning with `"libstdc++-doc-ss"`. This package provides documentation in HTML format. Note that it's not 100 percent compatible with the version installed on your system.

For both C and C++, the documentation you can find for Debian covers only the function calls. The language syntax, structure, and so on is not covered in the online documentation, which is geared for people who already know C. If you need to learn C, you can find many good books on the subject.

Each program that makes up the toolchain also has its own man page detailing command-line options, interactions, and the like. If you're ever searching for obscure `gcc` options, the man pages are a good place to start.

Using C/C++ tools

To compile a simple C program, all you need is `gcc`. Create your program and save it, making sure it has a `.c` extension. Then, run the compiler:

```
gcc -o test test.c
```

Assuming all goes well, you have a new file named `test` (specified by the `-o` option) that contains the compiled version of your program. You can run `./test` to run the new executable. You can also name more files like this:

```
gcc -o test test.c module1.c module2.c
```

With the preceding command, `gcc` compiles all three source code files, links them together, and generates the executable named `test`. If you need to use libraries, you can do so with `-l`. Here's an example:

```
gcc -o test test.c -lncurses
```

The preceding command generates the executable named `test` and links it with the `ncurses` library. You can specify as many `-l` options as you need to link in all of your libraries.

In some cases, you may need to access library or header files from nonstandard locations. Most Debian libraries install their libraries and headers into the system standard location (`/usr/include` and directories beneath.) Some packages, most notably the X Window System, install to other locations. With `-I` and `-L`, you can specify additional directories to search for header files and libraries, respectively. Remember that all of the UNIX tools are case-sensitive; `-L` is not the same as `-l`. Here's an example:

```
gcc -I/usr/X11R6/include -L/usr/X11R6/lib -o test test.c -lX11
```

The preceding command specifies additional search paths for both the include files and the library files. Without it, the linker cannot find the X11 library and the compiler cannot find the include files that test.c presumably requires.

For compiling C++ code, the commands look exactly the same with two exceptions — the compiler is named g++ instead of gcc, and all programs should have a .cc or .C extension instead of .c. Here's an example:

```
g++ -o test test.cc
```

The compiler uses the extension to determine the type of code contained in a file. It is very important that you use .c for C code only and .cc or .C for C++ code. Otherwise, the compiler might get confused about what kind of code it is compiling.

Using C/C++ libraries

Your Debian system comes with literally hundreds of libraries for C and C++. Most of them function for various applications on your Debian system, so don't be surprised if some of them are already installed. C/C++ libraries come in two flavors: static and dynamic (or shared). Static libraries are rarely used on a modern Debian system. They are linked directly into the application binary when it is built.

Dynamic libraries, on the other hand, are not linked at compile time. Rather, they are linked by ld.so each time the program loads. This provides many benefits. First, for libraries used by lots of programs, the library needs to reside in memory only once rather than once for each program that uses it. Secondly, if you update the library, there is no need to rebuild all the programs that use it.

On a Debian system, most shared libraries are located in /usr/lib or /usr/lib/X11 and they have a .so (shared object) extension. When you use the library with the -l option to gcc, you strip off the leading "lib" and trailing ".so" before passing the name on to gcc. Packages with shared libraries usually — but not always — have a name that starts with "lib". In many cases, there is also a "-dev" package that contains things such as include files, which are useful when building software that uses the library.

Table 13-6 lists some of the most popular libraries for a Debian system. If you want to use one of these libraries, also check for *package*-dev and *package*-doc packages, which may have additional development and documentation files.

Table 13-6
Popular C and C++ libraries

Package	Description
libc6	The standard C library. This is used by almost every C program, and it provides such standard functions as printf(), strcat(), and the like.
libstdc++, libstdc++2.10, libstdc++2.9, and so on.	The standard C++ library, used by almost every C++ program, implements things such as streams and standard C++ classes.
libgii0	The General Input Interface, part of the General Graphics Interface system. It provides a framework for handling input in different environments.
libwrap0	The TCP wrappers library, which provides basic security services for network daemons
libpaperg	A library for obtaining information about the system's paper. It is primarily of use to programs that care about printed output.
libgd1g	The GD graphics library. With this library, you can generate images in various formats (for instance, PNG and JPEG) at run time.
libpng2	A library for manipulating PNG files
libungif4g, libungif3g	A library for manipulating the reading of all GIFs and the writing of uncompressed GIFs
libjs0	The NGS JavaScript interpreter as an embeddable library
libmagick++0	A C++ binding for the ImageMagick image manipulation system
libpanel-applet0	A Gnome component; applications that reside on the Gnome control panel use this library.
libgtk1.2	The Gimp Toolkit, a graphical widget set for X. Gnome applications are layered on top of Gtk.
libpcre2, libpcre3	The Perl-Compatible Regular Expressions library, which implements Perl-style regular expressions in C
libgnomeprint6	Support for printing under Gnome
libwww0	Routines for communicating with HTTP (Web) servers
librx1g	GNU implementation of POSIX standard regular expressions
libape1.2	Support for portable threading in a C++ environment

Continued

Table 13-6 *(continued)*

Package	Description
libawe0.4	Support for wavetable synthesis on the AWE32 and AWE64 sound boards
libkonq3	Shared functions used by Konqueror — KDE's file manager and Web browser
libgconf10, libgconf11	The Gnome configuration system library
lib-bdb2	Berkeley database library. Used for creating a binary tree database on disk
libmagick4g	C interface to the ImageMagick manipulation system
libqt2	Support for Qt format movies
libpgsql	Client library for connecting to a PostgreSQL database server
libbonobo1	The Gnome Bonobo library, which implements CORBA interfaces for various widgets
librxp1	XML parser library
libgtkmm	A binding in C++ for Gtk
libssl095a	Secure Socket Layer (SSL) library for use in establishing secure network communications in C programs
libsndfile0	A library for reading and writing to various types of audio files
libbz2-1.0	A library that implements the bzip2 block-sorting compression algorithm and routines for handling .bz2 files
libgnome-vfs0	The Gnome Virtual File System layer, used by the Gnome file manager
libpcap0	Packet capture library for C programs
libcapplet0	The Gnome control center application library
liblockfile1	A library that implements file locking. This library has support for dot locking, which is sometimes the closest you can come to safe file locking in NFS environments.
libcdparanoia0	Library for writing programs to read data from audio CDs
libmysqlclient10, libmysqlclient6	Client library for connecting to the MySQL database
libunicode0	Unicode support from Gnome
libident	A client library for talking to a remote RFC1413 ident server. Used to determine which user is on the other end of a socket connection

Package	Description
`libparted0`	The embeddable part of the GNU partition editor. This library supports partition creation, deletion, resizing, and moving for both FAT and `ext2` partition types.
`libosp2`	Library for the OpenJade SP suite with many functions relating to XML and SGML documents
`libglade0`	Library to dynamically load Glade interface files
`libgmp2, libgmp3`	The GNU MultiPrecision library, which is specifically designed to perform calculations on numbers larger than can fit in conventional C/C++ data types
`libgsl0`	The GNU Scientific Library, designed for numerical analysis
`libmhash1, libmhash2`	Routines for MD5 and SHA1 hashes
`libgnomesupport0`	The "grab bag" of miscellaneous Gnome libraries
`libmikmod1, libmikmod2`	A library for playing Amiga-format MOD sound files
`libmad0`	A C library — the MPEG Audio Decoder. You can use this to play MP3 files.
`librplay3`	Libraries that implement playing sound over a network
`libgsm1`	Library for using GSM speech compression in your programs
`liboaf0`	The Gnome Object Activation Framework library for C
`libmime1`	Libraries from KDE that implement MIME support in C++
`libgnomemm`	C++ binding for working with Gnome applications
`libsensors0, libsensors1`	Library to read information from I2C sensors common in many modern computers
`libglib1.2`	Implementation of data storage structures in C
`libdetect0`	Implementation of hardware autodetection as a library
`libcdaudio0`	Library to control a device that is playing an audio CD
`libcdk4`	The Curses Development Kit, which contains widgets to use in terminal interface programs
`libwine`	An alpha-quality release of the Windows emulation software in Debian
`libbz2g`	Implementation of the bzip2 block-sorting compression system with support for `.bz2` files
`libpisock3`	Palm Pilot communication library. You can use this to hotsync your application with a Palm device.
`librpm1`	Support for Red Hat-style RPM distribution files

Continued

Table 13-6 *(continued)*

Package	Description
librep5, librep9	A library implementing a LISP interpreter in the style of Emacs with a bytecode interpreter and a virtual machine
libgimp1	Implementation of various Gimp functions in a shared library
libwmf0	Support for reading and writing Microsoft WMF files
libctk0	The Console Toolkit, a widget set for writing interfaces for a terminal
libdb2++	C++ support for the DB2 database routines
libxml++0	A C++ binding of the XML library from Gnome
libpam0g	The Pluggable Authentication Modules library. If you intend to write programs that authenticate users against the system password or group databases, you need to use this library in your programs.
libgc4, libgc5	A garbage collection library for C and C++ programs
libusb0	USB support for C programs
libmcrypt4	A library that implements over a dozen different encryption algorithms
libxdelta2	Library for handling deltas (similar to diffs) to files
libzephyr2	Support for the MIT Zephyr messaging system
libquicktime4linux0	Support for reading and writing QuickTime movie files
libadns0	Asynchronous DNS resolver for C and C++
libgnome32	Standard libraries for Gnome applications and Gnome itself
libtcp4u3	Libraries implementing Telnet, HTTP, and SMTP for your C applications
libasound0.4	The Advanced Linux Sound Architecture libraries
libjsw1	A library to access a joystick or similar device from within X
libuulib5	Support for uuencode and uudecode commands from KDE
libgtkxmhtml1	Support for displaying HTML documents using Gtk
libldap2	The OpenLDAP library, version 2. You can use this library to access LDAP from your C programs.
libgnome-pilot0	Libraries for interacting with a Palm Pilot from within Gnome
libjpeg62	Support for reading and writing JPEG files from C

Package	Description
libmpeg1	Support for MPEG files from C
libzvt2	Implementation of an embeddable terminal widget for X programs. From Gnome
libtiff3g	Support for reading and writing TIFF graphics files
libxaw6	Interface to the X Athena Widget toolkit for writing X applications
libncurses5	Interface for terminal manipulation—colors, cursor movement, and so on

If you have trouble installing any of these libraries, you can check a few things. First, many C libraries have a part of their version number embedded in their package name. Check to see if there are libraries available with a different version. Secondly, for historical reasons, some libraries have a trailing "g" in their names and others do not. You can try adding or removing one as appropriate.

Summary

As you can see from this chapter, Debian GNU/Linux offers a wide variety of programming environments. If you already are a programmer, then you now have information on where to find the necessary compilers and associated tools to begin creating the programs in the language of your choice.

If you just dabble with programming, then you, too, have the needed information on where to find help when you get stuck as well as the needed tools. For those of you who are just starting out, this chapter is a great reference as you develop your programming skills.

✦   ✦   ✦

Shells

The true power and flexibility of the Linux operating system is perhaps best realized in the shell. With the shell, you have at your fingertips the means to accomplish almost any computing task. At its simplest, the shell provides an interface between the user and the operating system. The user enters commands into the shell, and the shell arranges for them to be carried out. But the shell's greatest strength is that it serves as a high-level programming language. This means that you can arrange the shell commands into programs called scripts.

This chapter explains what the shell is and what it does. It also explains important shell concepts that you need to understand in order to use commands most effectively. You will also learn the most common shells and the differences among the various shell "flavors." Understanding the shell is essential to getting the most out of the Debian GNU/Linux operating system.

What Is a Shell?

Previous chapters introduced the concept of the virtual terminal, as well as several important commands. Now it is time to put what you learned into the larger context of the command-line interface — the shell.

Upon entering one or more commands into the shell, the shell reads the input, interprets the commands, arranges for them to be carried out, and (if necessary) displays the results to the screen. Thus, the shell is a *command interpreter* that provides the interface between you and the operating system.

Many people may be familiar with graphical user interfaces (GUIs), as discussed in Chapter 4. A graphical user interface provides a simple and easy-to-learn method of carrying out computing tasks. This is certainly very important. However, you eventually will need to perform tasks that are not provided by the GUI, or that the GUI does not perform in the manner that you prefer. You need not worry; the shell provides a powerful solution to this problem.

The shell is like a toolbox; each command is a simple tool that expertly performs a single task. These tools can function together in an almost endless variety of ways to carry out any specialized task you desire. Learning how to use this toolbox requires an investment of time and effort on your part, but you reap the rewards of discovering the true power and flexibility of the Linux operating system.

Using the shell

When a shell session first begins, a prompt is displayed indicating that the shell is ready to receive input. This prompt may be a dollar sign ($), a percent sign (%), or a pound sign (#, also known as hash). You learn more about the different shells later in this chapter. The prompt indicates that the shell is ready to accept input from the user. To use the shell, enter one or more commands at the prompt and press Enter to tell the shell you are ready to run the commands. When the commands are finished running, the shell displays a prompt indicating that it is again ready to accept input.

The Command Line

A *command* is actually a program, and a *command line* is what someone types at a prompt to request that a program run in the shell. For example, if you enter the command line `ls  -al` at the prompt, you are requesting to run a program called `ls`. You also are providing the program with options that direct how it carries out its task.

Note Commands generally have two forms of syntax for specifying options on the command line. The form you are likely to use most is a single dash, followed by a single letter or number for each option. As seen in the previous example, the option `-al` directs `ls` to list all files in long format. The other form is a longer method of providing options, but it may make your commands clearer and more understandable to others. The syntax for the long option is a double dash followed by the name of the option. The previous example given in long form looks like this: `ls  --all  --format=long`. A notable exception to this rule is the command `chmod`, which also accepts + to specify options.

Many commands also accept *arguments*. Arguments are words or filenames that the program uses. For example, `grep sugar grocery_list` displays all lines containing the word "sugar" found in a file called `grocery_list`. The `grep` command uses the first argument as a pattern, or a series of characters to look for, and it uses the remaining arguments as files in which to search for the pattern.

Cross-Reference See Chapter 9 for a more detailed look at `grep` and other important commands. Refer to Appendix C for a listing of many other commands.

Standard input and output

Up until now, you have entered commands one at a time. In other words, you have performed one simple task at a time. As mentioned earlier, the shell enables you to combine many commands to perform specialized tasks. To understand how to do this, you must understand the concept of *standard input* and *standard output*, or *standard I/O*.

✦ **standard input** — a "channel" through which a command receives input. By default, standard input is attached to the keyboard.

✦ **standard output** — a "channel" through which the output of a command is delivered. By default, standard output is attached to the screen.

You have employed standard I/O all along with the commands you have used, but you have done so unknowingly because the standard output was already directed to the screen. Thus, when you entered `ls -al`, for example, the output of the command was displayed on the screen. Although you have not seen it yet, each command is also capable of receiving input through its standard input; by default, this input comes from the keyboard.

However, instead of the screen, a command may send its output to a file or to another command. Instead of the keyboard, a command may also receive its input from a file or from another command. Specifying where a command receives its input or where it sends its output is called *redirection*.

Redirection

You can accomplish redirection of the standard I/O on the command line by using special operators called *redirection operators*.

The > operator redirects the output of a command to a file. For example, if you want to record a listing of all the users currently logged in, enter the following command:

```
$ who > user_list
```

If the file called `user_list` already exists, it is overwritten.

Suppose tomorrow you want to add a list of users to the file called `user_list` without destroying today's list of users. Use the >> operator to append the output of the command to the end of the file:

```
$ who >> user_list
```

If `user_list` does not exist, >> acts just like > and creates a new file.

The < operator indicates that a command's input should come from a file instead of from the keyboard. For example, you can e-mail the contents of the user_list file to another user on the system by entering the following command:

```
$ mail steve < user_list
```

Here, the program called mail reads from the file and e-mails the contents to steve.

You can combine the redirection operators on the same command line. For example, here you read in the contents of a file called task_list and output the sorted lines to a file called todo_list:

```
$ sort < task_list > todo_list
```

Note   The order in which input and output redirection appear on the command line is not important. The command always reads its input first. This means that

```
$ sort > outfile < infile
```

is identical to

```
$ sort < infile > outfile
```

In both cases, sort gets its input from infile and sends the sorted output to outfile.

Tip   You can redirect output to a special file called /dev/null. Redirecting to /dev/null is like sending your output to nowhere. That is to say, the output is permanently discarded. Some commands perform some processing and frequently send messages to standard output indicating the status of the processing. If you are only interested in performing the task and do not want to be bothered with step-by-step status updates, redirect standard output to /dev/null. /dev/null is also useful in shell scripts where the script does not care about the contents of the output. It can also used to redirect output away from the standard output to keep the general public from getting distracted.

Pipes

Now, let's get back to this notion of combining many commands. This is one of the most powerful features of the shell. Using a type of output redirection called a *pipe* (|), you can connect individual commands. The pipe operator, |, tells the shell to take the standard output of the command on the left-hand side of the pipe and redirect it to the standard input of the command on the right-hand side of the pipe. In this way, you can join many commands in a pipeline: The input into the first command in the pipeline is processed in sequence by each command until the final result is output by the last command in the pipeline.

Earlier, you created a file containing a list of users on the system and then e-mailed that file to a user. Using a pipe, you can accomplish this in a single step. In this example, the output of who is the input of mail. The output is then sent via e-mail to jo:

```
$ who | mail jo
```

Sometimes, the output of a command takes up more lines than are available on the screen thus causing it to scroll by too quickly to read. You can solve this problem very easily with a pipe, which you probably will use often. In the following example, all files on the system are listed recursively starting at the root of the filesystem. Normally, this sends thousands of lines of text scrolling up the screen too fast to be of any use; however, by piping the output to less, you can scroll through the output one page at a time:

```
$ ls -R / | less
```

Now let's look at a more sophisticated example, one consisting of several commands connected in a pipeline:

```
$ tail -500 bigfile | grep the | wc -l
```

The last 500 lines of a long file called bigfile are read (tail -500 bigfile) and filtered for all lines containing the word "the" (grep the). Finally, the number of lines containing "the" are counted (wc -l). This is a silly example, of course, but it demonstrates the potential usefulness of pipes for processing data in highly versatile ways. Managing standard I/O is one of the most important jobs of the shell, and, as you can see, it provides you with extraordinary flexibility for accomplishing tasks in unique and various ways. Table 14-1 summarizes the redirection operators.

Tip   You can use a technique called *tab completion* to avoid typing long filenames on the command line. If you enter part of the filename on the command line and press Tab, the shell attempts to find a file whose name matches the part of the name you have entered so far. If it finds a matching file, the shell enters the remainder of the filename on the command line for you. If there is more than one matching file, the shell enters the matching part of the filenames. For example, suppose you have two files: this_is_a_really_long_name_for_a_file and this_is_not_so_long. Enter the following command line and press Tab:

```
$ less this<TAB>
```

The shell responds by adding what it could match:

```
$ less this_is_
```

The shell extends the filename as far as it can. You need to add at least one more letter to specify to the shell which file you want. Entering one more letter and pressing Tab yields the following:

```
$ less this_is_a<TAB>
```

Again, the shell responds by adding what it could match:

```
$ less this_is_a_really_long_name_for_a_file
```

You can now press Enter, and the command runs on the file specified. You save a lot of keystrokes this way!

	Table 14-1 **Redirection operators**	
Operator	**Usage**	**Result**
>	ls > *myfile*	Redirects the output of a command to a file. If the file already exists, it is overwritten.
>>	ls >> *myfile*	Redirects the output of the command to a file. If the file already exists, the output is appended to the end of the file.
<	sort < *myfile*	Redirects the input to come from a file
|	ls | less	Redirects the output of the first command to the input of the second command

Note   In addition to standard input and standard output, commands also have *standard error*. Commands use this channel to alert the user that the command did not succeed, to display help messages, or to prompt the user for more input. Standard error is sent to the screen by default so that the user can see and respond to messages and prompts — even when standard output is redirected. However, sometimes you may want to redirect standard error to a file (perhaps for diagnostic purposes) or redirect to /dev/null to discard the messages. You can accomplish this by preceding one of the output redirection operators with a 2. For example,

$ mv none myfile 2> err

attempts to move a file called none to a file called myfile. If none does not exist, the error message sent by mv is written to the file err.

Command substitution

Pipes are not the only method of using multiple commands together in a command line. *Command substitution,* another useful tool in your box, enables you to use commands together in versatile ways. It enables you to insert, or substitute, the output of a command into the command line. You must enclose the command you want to substitute in backquotes. Suppose you want to remove all files of a certain type, but there are many of these files and they are scattered throughout the filesystem. You might look for them one by one with find. In this example, I want to find all files called core under /usr:

```
$ find /usr -name "core"
/usr/bin/core
/usr/local/bin/core
/usr/share/public_beta/core
$
```

and then remove each of them one by one with rm. However, that is tedious and time-consuming. With command substitution, you can insert the output of find directly into the command line with rm, as in this example:

```
$ rm -v `find /usr -name "core"`
removing /usr/bin/core
removing /usr/local/bin/core
removing /usr/share/public_beta/core
$
```

The rm command requires one or more filenames as its arguments. The find command delivers filenames in its output. So, in the preceding example, the output of find becomes the arguments to rm and each file is removed in turn. It is the same as though you entered

```
$ rm -v /usr/bin/core /usr/local/bin/core /usr/share/public_beta/core
```

but you did not have to know the locations of the files ahead of time and it required much less typing!

Caution   Do not confuse the backquote (`` ` ``) with the single quote, or apostrophe ('), because these have very different meanings to the shell. On most keyboard layouts, the backquote key is located in the upper left near the Esc key.

Tip   You can group multiple commands on one line to run one at a time by separating them with semicolons (;). The important thing to remember is that the commands run in order, one after the other. The second command runs only after the first finishes, the third command runs only after the second finishes, and so on. This process works the same as when you enter the commands on separate lines. For example:

```
$ ls; rm -v *old; ls
```

Here, when the first ls command is finished listing the files, all files ending in "old" are removed. Following that, the files are listed again (perhaps to confirm that rm succeeded). Grouping is useful when you want to run a series of commands unattended.

Jobs and job control

When you enter a command at the shell prompt, the shell arranges for the command to be carried out then prompts you when the command finishes. A command or group of commands entered in the shell is called a *job*. While a job is in progress, you cannot run any new commands because the shell is not ready to accept more input yet. This behavior may be undesirable when a command is taking a long time to process. For example, when you copy a group (denoted by the -R option) of files contained under the work/ directory to the floppy disk:

```
$ cp -R work/ /floppy
```

You can expect this to take some time — especially if there are several files in the work/ directory. If you decide you want to enter another command before the previous command finishes, you can always cancel the job by typing Ctrl+C. This takes you back to the prompt, where you can enter other commands. Later, when you have time to wait, you can enter the command again to copy the files to floppy. This is a rather inefficient method — it requires you to start the processing all over again. It can also interfere, depending on the command you are restarting.

Job suspend and resume

A better solution is to pause the job so you can enter some more commands at the prompt and then resume the job right where it left off. You can do this very simply by typing Ctrl+Z. The result looks like this:

```
$ cp -R work/ /mnt/floppy
<CTRL-Z>
[1]+  Stopped                  cp -R work/ /mnt/floppy
$
```

The number in brackets tells you that the shell has assigned a *job ID* of "1" to this job, and the job has been stopped. The prompt reappears, indicating that the shell is now ready to accept more input. When you are ready to copy the files to the floppy, you can resume the stopped job by entering fg at the prompt. For example:

```
$ fg
cp -R work/ /mnt/floppy
```

The job resumes in the foreground, and you are again left waiting for the work/ directory and its contents to be copied to the floppy disk. But why wait at all? Linux is a multitasking operating system, which means that it can perform more than one computing task at a time. So shouldn't you be able to run more than one command at a time? The answer is yes. If you guessed earlier that running a job in the foreground implies that you can also run it in the background, you were right.

Background jobs

Let's go back to the point at which you stopped the job with Ctrl+Z. Instead of waiting until later to resume copying your files to the floppy disk, you can run the job in the background by entering bg at the prompt:

```
$ cp -R work/ /mnt/floppy
  <CTRL-Z>
[1]+  Stopped                     cp -R work/ /mnt/floppy
$ bg
[1]+ cp -R work/ /mnt/floppy &
$
```

The job resumes in the background, and you are immediately returned to the prompt. Any commands entered now run at the same time the files are copied to the floppy disk in the background. The shell appends an & (ampersand) to the command line, indicating that the job should run in the background.

If you know a job is going to take a long time, you can start it as a background job directly by simply adding the & to the end of the command line. For example:

```
$ find / -name "*.sh" -print> script_list &
[2] 22201
$
```

The shell is assigned a job ID of "2" (remember job "1" is currently copying your files to a floppy disk). The number "22201" is the *process ID*, which identifies the job's process among all processes on the system.

> **Tip**
> When a command runs in the background, its standard input is disconnected from the keyboard. However, the command's standard output and standard error remain attached to the screen. This means that even while a command is in the background, its results and its error messages may be displayed on your screen periodically while you are working. To run a background job "quietly", use redirection in addition to the &:
>
> ```
> $ find / -name "work*" -print> work_files 2>/dev/null &
> ```
>
> You are not bothered by any output from this command. When you are ready to see the results of the command, you can access them in the file called work_files.

By running commands in the background, it is possible to do many tasks at the same time. To get a listing of all of the jobs currently running in the background and their statuses, enter the jobs command at the prompt as follows:

```
$ jobs
[1]   Running                 cp -R work/ /mnt/floppy &
[2]-  Running                 find / -name "*.sh" -print> script_list &
[3]+  Running                 tar zxvf data.tar.gz &
$
```

The + (plus) next to the job ID indicates that this is the current job, or the job most recently started. The - (minus) designates the job started before the current job. When you enter fg with no arguments, the current job is brought to the foreground. To specify one of the other jobs, follow fg with an argument consisting of a percent sign and the job ID. This example brings job "2" to the foreground:

```
$ fg %2
find / -name "*.sh" -print> script_list
```

Instead of a % and a job ID, you can also use % and the name of the command. If there is more than one job running the same command, the most recent one is referred to.

You can end a background job with the `kill` command:

```
$ kill %find
$ jobs
[1]    Running              cp -R work/ /mnt/floppy &
[2]-   Terminated           find / -name "*.sh" -print> script_list
[3]+   Running              tar zxvf data.tar.gz &
```

After entering `jobs` again, you see that job "2" was terminated. The next time you enter the `jobs` command, job "2" will no longer be in the list.

Normally, after a background job finishes, the shell automatically displays a message like this:

```
$
[1]+   Exit 1               cp -R work/ /mnt/floppy
$
```

Table 14-2 summarizes the job control commands.

Table 14-2
Job control commands

Command	Result
Ctrl+C	Cancels the current job and returns to the prompt
Ctrl+Z	Suspends the current job and returns to the prompt
fg [n] [name]	Runs the current or specified job in the foreground. If the job was suspended, it is resumed. Here, n refers to the job number; and name refers to the job name.
bg [n] [name]	Runs the current or specified job in the foreground. If the job was suspended, it is resumed. Here, n refers to the job number; and name refers to the job name
&	Directs the shell to run the command in the background
Jobs	Displays the status of all background jobs
kill [n] [name]	Terminates the current or specified job. Here, n refers to the job number; and name refers to the job name.

Escaping — special characters

As you have seen, the shell interprets many characters to have special meanings. For example, ⟨ and ⟩ are special characters that redirect the standard input and output of a command. Sometimes, you may want to use such characters without their special meanings. For example, you might want to display a simple math problem. In this problem, the student must decide if 1 is less than 2, so you want to use ⟨ to mean "less than" and not to indicate redirection:

```
$ echo 1 < 2 = ?
bash: 2: No such file or directory
```

As you can see, the shell displays an error because it thinks you want to redirect the output of command 2 into a file named 1. This fails because 1 does not exist. You can turn off the meaning of, or *escape*, special characters with the *backslash*, \. You can make the previous example succeed like this:

```
$ echo 1 \< 2 \= \?
1 < 2 = ?
```

Here, the special meanings of the ⟨, =, and ? characters are turned off, and the characters are treated as a normal string.

Alternatively, you can enclose the characters in *single quotes*, ' ... ', as follows:

```
$ echo '1 < 2 = ?'
1 < 2 = ?
```

The shell does not interpret the meaning of any special characters inside the single quotes, but instead treats them as ordinary text. See Table 14-4 in the section, "Special shell characters" later in this chapter for a listing of most of the characters that have special meaning to the shell.

Shell variables

The shell provides a means for storing information for use by you or programs running in the shell. These information stores are called *variables*. Shell variables can store the location of certain files, the results of a command, personal information such as login name, or any other piece of information that you might need to retrieve later. For example, many programs use variables to store the location of files that the program requires, such as configuration files or shared library files. The system sets some of these automatically. Variables may be temporary information stores that are only available in the current shell, or they may be *environment variables* that store information that is globally available in all shell sessions.

There are many standard variables that are already a part of your shell's environment. Table 14-3 lists some of the most common of these.

Table 14-3
Common environment variables

Variable	Description
$?	The return value of the last command that was run in the shell. (Commands that are completed successfully return a 0.)
HOME	Path name of your home directory (for example, /home/jo)
MAIL	Name of the file to check for incoming e-mail
MAILCHECK	The time, in seconds, between attempts to check for new e-mail
LOGNAME	Your login name
SHELL	Path name of your shell
TERM	Your terminal type (for example, vt100)
PWD	Your current working directory
OLDPWD	Path name of working directory before previous cd command
PATH	The list of directories the shell searches for commands

Any word preceded by a $ symbol is interpreted as a variable. A simple way to see the value of a variable is to use the echo command, as in this example:

```
$ echo $TERM
vt100
$
```

Caution   You may remember that commands and filenames in Linux (and in UNIX) are case-sensitive. The names myfile and MyFile designate two different files. Similarly, shell variables are also case-sensitive. Thus, $TERM and $term do not refer to the same variables. Remember to employ the correct case when using variables on the command line or you may not get the behavior you expect. For example, chances are $term does not exist; thus, the command echo $term returns nothing. By convention, variable names typically are in all uppercase, so it is a safe bet that all of the variables you use are uppercase. It is also a good idea, when defining your own variables (you learn how to do this later in the chapter), to follow this convention.

When variables are used on the command line, the value of the variable is substituted in the command. For example, if the environment variable HOME contains /home/jo, then the command

```
$ mv somefile $HOME
```

produces the same result as the command

```
$ mv somefile /home/jo
```

and the file somefile is moved to /home/jo.

Tip

A useful shortcut for accessing files in your home directory is to use a tilde (~). It is an abbreviation for the path to your home directory. The command ls ~ produces the same result as ls /home/jo or ls $HOME. You can also access another user's home directory by combining the tilde with his or her user name. For example, cd ~jack/work changes your current directory to work/ in user jack's home directory.

The set command can list all variables currently available to the shell. The output looks something like this:

```
$ set
BASH=/bin/bash
BASH_VERSION='2.03.0(1)-release'
COLUMNS=80
EUID=1003
GROUPS=()
HISTFILESIZE=500
HISTSIZE=500
HOME=/home/steve
HOSTNAME=localhost
HOSTTYPE=i386
HUSHLOGIN=FALSE
LESS=-M
LESSOPEN='|lesspipe.sh %s'
LINES=24
LOGNAME=steve
LS_COLORS=
LS_OPTIONS=' --color=auto -F -b -T 0'
MAIL=/var/spool/mail/steve
MAILCHECK=60
MANPATH=/usr/local/man:/usr/man/preformat:/usr/man:/usr/X11R6/man:/usr/openwin/m
an
MINICOM='-c on'
MOZILLA_HOME=/usr/lib/netscape
OPENWINHOME=/usr/openwin
OPTERR=1
OPTIND=1
OSTYPE=linux-gnu
PATH=/usr/local/bin:/usr/bin:/bin:/usr/X11R6/bin:/usr/openwin/bin:/usr/games:.
PS1='\h:\w\$ '
PS2='> '
PS4='+ '
PWD=/home/steve
```

```
SHELL=/bin/bash
SHELLOPTS=braceexpand:hashall:histexpand:monitor:history:interactive-comments:em
acs
SHLVL=1
TERM=vt100
UID=1003
USER=steve
$
```

Now that you know how to get the values of shell variables, you may be wondering how you define the variables. The method for setting the values of variables differs somewhat in different types of shells, so the next section revisits the concept of shell variables and describes the major shell types and their differences.

The Shell Variants

Up until now, the concepts explained here have been common to most of the shells available in Debian GNU/Linux. However, other features not discussed yet differ among the shells. Before continuing, take some time to acquaint yourself with the various types of shells.

The different shells come in three major types:

✦ The Bourne shell: Includes `sh`, `bash`, and `ash`

✦ The C shell: Includes `csh` and `tcsh`

✦ The Korn shell: Includes `ksh`, `pdksh`, and `zsh`

When you first login to Linux, a shell is automatically started. This is the *login shell*. The login shell might be any one of the types of shells discussed in this section (which one depends on your configuration). You can also start additional shells, or *subshells*, by typing the name of the shell as a command.

The `exit` command instructs your current shell to terminate. If you start a subshell within a shell, typing `exit` terminates the subshell and returns you to the "outer" shell. Typing `exit` or `logout` in the login shell logs you off the system.

Entering the Ctrl+D key sequence at the shell prompt is the same as typing `logout`. In general, this key sequence terminates any active process.

Bourne shell

The *Bourne shell*, known simply as `sh`, is the standard command interpreter for UNIX. Stephen R. Bourne developed it at Bell Laboratories in 1978. The original `sh` is not included with the Debian software distribution; however, two clones are included in its place.

✦ The *Bourne Again shell*, or bash, is GNU's command interpreter (/bin/sh is linked to /bin/bash). Fully compatible with the Bourne shell, bash incorporates features from the Korn and C shells as well as other enhancements. This is the shell most commonly used by Linux users.

✦ Intended for use where space is at a premium, ash is the default shell on the Debian installation root floppy disk. Because it's lightweight, and because it runs commands somewhat faster than bash, it is useful in certain situations. However, it lacks some of the features of bash, and bash is a better choice for most users.

Bourne shell variable definition

In the Bourne-type shells (including bash and ash), you define variables by typing the name of the variable followed by the assignment operator (=) and the value to be assigned. There must be no space between the variable name, =, and the value. In this example, a shell variable is assigned the path to a directory:

```
$ WORKDIR=/home/steve/work
$ echo $WORKDIR
/home/steve/work
```

A variable is only available within the shell in which it is defined. To make a shell variable available to all shells — to make it part of the environment — you must export it. You can make the $WORKDIR variable available to other shells using the following command line:

```
$ export WORKDIR
```

You can then define and export the variable on the same command line, as in

```
$ WORKDIR=/home/steve/work export WORKDIR
```

or, even simpler

```
$ export WORKDIR=/home/steve/work
```

Bourne shell startup

When your login shell first starts up, it looks for certain files in your home directory that contain commands to customize the shell environment by defining environment variables or aliases. These are scripts, or collections of commands, which are executed in a batch, rather than entered in the command line one by one.

In the original Bourne shell, sh, .profile is the file used by the shell at startup. This simple shell script is where you enter any commands or customizations for sh.

However, bash has two special files that it reads at startup: .bash_profile and .bashrc. The .bash_profile script is executed at login time and is responsible for setting up the shell environment. The following is an example of a very rudimentary `.bash_profile`:

```
# $HOME/.bash_profile
export OPENWINHOME=/usr/openwin
export MINICOM="-c on"
export MANPATH=/usr/local/man:/usr/man/preformat:/usr/man:/usr/X11R6/man:/usr/
  op
enwin/man
export HOSTNAME="`cat /etc/HOSTNAME`"
export LESSOPEN="|lesspipe.sh %s"
export LESS="-M"
export MOZILLA_HOME=/usr/lib/netscape

# Set the default system $PATH:
PATH="/usr/local/bin:/usr/local/sbin:/usr/bin:/usr/sbin/:/bin:/sbin"
```

Unlike `.bash_profile`, the `.bashrc` script is executed whenever a shell is started. It contains customizations and commands local to that shell. This is an example `.bashrc` script:

```
PATH=$PATH:./bin
export PATH
umask 002
alias l='ls'
alias ll='ls -l'
alias la='ls -a'
alias ls='ls -F --color'
echo Welcome to Debian
```

C shell

Bill Joy developed the original *C shell*, called `csh`, as part of Berkeley UNIX. Intended to overcome many of the limitations of the Bourne shell, `csh` was the first enhanced shell. One of its most notable features (and source of its name) is a syntax similar to that of the C programming language. Debian includes `csh`, as well as `tcsh` (an enhanced version of the C shell).

C shell variable definition

In the C shell, variables are defined somewhat differently. The `set` command defines them, as in the following:

```
% set workdir = /home/steve/work
```

They can likewise be unset:

```
% unset workdir
```

Unlike in the Bourne shell, spaces are allowed, and (by convention) C shell variables are typically in lowercase.

To make a variable an environment variable that is available to all shells, use the `setenv` command as shown here:

```
% setenv workdir /home/steve/work
```

C shell startup

The startup scripts in the C shell resemble those of `bash`. Similar to `.profile`, a script called `.login` is executed at login time. A script called `.cshrc` is executed whenever a `csh` session is started, and `.tcshrc` is executed whenever `tcsh` is started.

Korn shell

David Korn of Bell Laboratories originally developed the *Korn shell*, or `ksh`, in 1982. It provides similar enhancements to those found in the C shell, but it maintains the syntax and features of `sh`. Although the original Korn shell is not included in the Debian distribution, the distribution does include two shells that are very similar to `ksh`.

   ✦ The *Public Domain Korn shell*, or `pdksh`, is intended to provide a `ksh`-like shell that is free of the license restrictions of the proprietary `ksh`.

   ✦ The *Z shell*, or `zsh`, is similar to `ksh` — although not completely compatible. It includes many unique enhancements, as well as features borrowed from `bash`, `csh`, and `tcsh`.

You define and export variables in the Korn shell using the same method as in the Bourne shell.

Like the C shell, the Korn shell reads your `.profile` script at login time to set up the shell's environment. It also reads a second file whenever a shell is started; but unlike the shells you've seen so far, the second file does not have a specific name or location. Instead, you define the name and location of the startup script by the variable `ENV`, which is defined in `.profile`. For example, if the value of `ENV` is `$HOME/.kshenv`, then the Korn shell executes `.kshenv` in the home directory every time a Korn shell session starts.

Tip   If you want a startup script to take effect immediately in the current shell, you can use the . (dot) command. For example, if you add an environment variable to your `.profile` and you want it to take effect immediately without logging in again, enter the following at the command line:

```
$ . .profile
```

The script is interpreted and the newly added environment variable is part of the shell environment.

Special shell characters

Table 14-4 presents a listing of the most comment characters that have special meaning when working with shells.

Table 14-4 Special characters	
Character	**Description**
<	Retrieves input for a command from a file
>	Writes output from a command to a file
>>	Appends output from a command to the end of a file
2>	Writes standard error from a command to a file
2>>	Appends standard error from a command to the end of a file
|	Sends the output of one command to another command
$	A word preceded by this character is interpreted as a variable.
#	Denotes a comment. The shell ignores everything to the right of #.
=	Assigns a value to a shell variable
*	Matches any string zero or more characters
?	Matches any single character
[...]	Matches any specified characters in a set
` ... `	Substitutes the output of the command in backquotes into the command line
&	Runs the command line in the background
-, --, +	A word following any of these characters is interpreted as a command option.
;	Allows multiple commands separated by this character to run in sequence
' ... '	Prevents the shell from interpreting any special characters inside single quotes
" ... "	Prevents the shell from interpreting any special characters inside quotes — except $, \, and double and single quotes
\	Turns off the meaning of the next character
.	The current directory
..	The parent directory
/	The root directory
~	The path of the home directory

Shell Scripts

As you saw with the startup scripts, you can group commands into a file and execute the commands in sequence by entering the name of the file on the command line. The file itself is a command that carries out all the commands that it contains. In fact, the shell provides a versatile and powerful programming language. It contains many of the constructs you might expect in a programming language, such as loops and conditional processing. By combining such programming constructs with shell commands in a file, and making the file executable with chmod, you are empowered by the shell to write programs for almost any purpose. Such an advanced topic is beyond the scope of this book, but I encourage you to explore shell programming further through the many books and Web sites available on the subject.

To make a shell script, create a text file with all the commands, just as if you were typing them at the command prompt. As an example, I've created a file that will search through the Apache Web server error logs and report the number of errors for each error type. Here is the code that I used:

```
#!/bin/sh
# The first line indicates the type of shell for the script.
#
# This shell script searches though apache error log files
# for the errors. It then generates a report of the errors.
#
# Prints a message to standard out to inform the public
# what the command is doing
echo "Looking at Apache error log file..."
echo ""

# Use the grep command to count (-c) the lines containing the
# search word, then save the results in the variable.
notice=`grep -c notice /var/log/apache/error.log`
warning=`grep -c warning /var/log/apache/error.log`
error=`grep -c error /var/log/apache/error.log`

# Print out results to the screen
echo "Number of notices  "$notice
echo "Number of warnings "$warning
echo "Number of errors   "$error
```

After creating this in a file, the next step is to make it executable. To accomplish this, use the chmod command to make the text file executable.

```
chmod u+x filename
```

This will make the script file run only for the user. To everyone else, it looks and acts like a text file. If you want to confirm that the script file is executable, view the file with ls -l to get the full details of the file:

```
# ls -l logchk.sh
-rwxr--r--   1  jo      jo          651 Jan 20 14:41 logchk.sh
```

You can see that the permissions now contain an x for the user. I use an extension of .sh to remind me that this is a shell command script. Now, when you run the new script from the command line, you get the following:

```
# ./logchk.sh
Looking at Apache error log file...

Number of notices  12
Number of warnings 2
Number of errors   1
#
```

Using this pattern for creating scripts, you too can start making scripts. Even though this example was simple in terms of programming, scripts can be extremely sophisticated and perform a myriad of tasks.

Summary

The shell provides the interface between you and the operating system. You enter commands into the shell, and the shell arranges to carry them out. You can accomplish simple tasks by entering commands at the shell prompt. Additionally, you can perform elaborate and specialized tasks by combining commands in various ways through redirection, pipes, and command substitution. The shell also serves as a high-level programming language; you can arrange the shell commands into programs called scripts.

The true power and versatility of Linux is revealed in the shell. Understanding the shell is essential to getting the most out of the Debian GNU/Linux operating system.

✦　　✦　　✦

Linux Kernel

The root of the Debian GNU/Linux system is the kernel.
From time to time, you may need to change it to fit your
needs and the needs of your system. This chapter covers various aspects of the kernel and how you can modify them to
meet your specific needs. For some, the thought of compiling
a new kernel is daunting and overwhelming. This need not be
the case. Compiling a kernel takes a few steps and does not
lead to irrevocable devastation if an error occurs, as you will
see in the chapter.

You will also find an explanation of the boot loader LILO, as it
affects the loading of the kernel. The kernel also affects the
starting of some of the system daemons. These, too, are discussed in this chapter. First, however, you need to understand
the kernel, as the system revolves around it.

Configuring the Linux Kernel

The kernel is the lowest denominator of the Debian
GNU/Linux system. The kernel sets up the environment in
which programs run, sets the parameters that communicate
with the hardware, and determines the efficiency of the
system. The kernel is really the key to the whole Debian
GNU/Linux operating system.

Linus Torvalds developed the Linux kernel using the Minix
operating system as a model. (Minix is a clone knock-off of the
popular UNIX operating system developed by AT&T.) Torvalds
created only the core component for GNU/Linux the operating
system — the kernel, which he called Linux. Although the kernel is the foundation of the GNU/Linux operating system, it
doesn't reflect the whole operating system. To be accurate,
the operating system name is GNU/Linux. (Although I refer to
it as Linux throughout this book, I really mean GNU/Linux; like
most people, however, I abbreviate it to just Linux).

Let's first look at what happens in the kernel as the system starts operation. When you first turn your computer on, the following processes take place:

✦ When the system first gets powered on, the boot loader hands control over to the kernel.

✦ With the kernel now in control, based on the configuration, it identifies the available hardware for the system. This includes memory, disk drives (both IDE and SCSI), the video system, serial and parallel ports, and so on.

✦ The kernel then starts any boot scripts, network services, or daemons. This includes connectivity with other servers for transferring files, mail, and news.

When you watch the screen as the operating system starts, you see the boot loader start and initialize the kernel. Then a stream of text (that is only occasionally recognizable) goes flying across the screen. At any time after the system has successfully started, you can read this text by issuing the command dmesg | more at the command prompt. This displays the text one page at a time. The following example only shows a few lines of the entire display, but it gives you an idea of what you should see on your system:

```
Linux version 2.2.17 (herbert@arnor) (gcc version 2.95.2 20000313 (Debian
GNU/Linux)) #1 Sun Jun 25 09:24:41 EST 2000
Detected 233029 kHz processor.
Console: colour VGA+ 80x25
Calibrating delay loop... 465.31 BogoMIPS
Memory: 45936k/49152k available (1732k kernel code, 416k reserved, 928k data,
140k init)
Dentry hash table entries: 8192 (order 4, 64k)
Buffer cache hash table entries: 65536 (order 6, 256k)
Page cache hash table entries: 16384 (order 4, 64k)
VFS: Diskquotas version dquot_6.4.0 initialized
CPU: L1 I Cache: 32K  L1 D Cache: 32K
CPU: AMD-K6tm w/ multimedia extensions stepping 02
Checking 386/387 coupling... OK, FPU using exception 16 error reporting.
Checking 'hlt' instruction... OK.
Checking for popad bug... OK.
POSIX conformance testing by UNIFIX
PCI: PCI BIOS revision 2.10 entry at 0xf04e0
PCI: Using configuration type 1
PCI: Probing PCI hardware
  .
  .
  .
```

As you can see from the first line, this display indicates the kernel version, the compiler version used to create it, and a timestamp indicating when it was created. This is useful information when building a new kernel.

Continuing on down through the code, you see how the kernel begins to detect the processor speed, the console, the memory, and available cache. It then tests the CPU and probes the hardware on the system. This continues until the entire system has been checked. If any part fails, it is listed in this data.

Kernel code and versions

The code that makes up the kernel is written in the C programming language, which makes the kernel portable to other platforms. The kernel may need tweaking to accommodate the various architectures, hardware parameters, and external devices on other systems, but mostly remains the same. Each platform has a kernel that has been compiled specifically for that architecture. The original kernel was developed for the Intel platform, but has since been compiled or ported to the other platforms. A kernel coded for one platform won't work on another. However, a program coded for one platform and recompiled on another platform will generally work because the program works with the kernel, not the platform. This is the power of the C language and the Linux operating systems.

Each time changes are made to the kernel, whether fixing bugs or making improvements, the version number changes. These numbers enable you to track changes and identify versions of the kernel. To determine the version number of the working kernel, type uname -a from any command line. The results of such a query are shown here:

```
$ uname -a
Linux debian 2.2.17 #1 Sun Jun 25 09:24:41 EST 2000 i586 unknown
```

This code shows the name of the operating system, the host name for the machine, the kernel release number, and the kernel version. At the end of the line, you see the machine type and the processor. The release number is 2.2.17, which breaks down as follows:

✦ The major number (2), which only changes rarely. When it changes, it indicates significant updates to the kernel.

✦ The minor number (2), which indicates new versions of the kernel.

✦ The current revision (17), which indicates new patches, minor bug fixes, and small feature enhancements to the current kernel.

The Linux kernel had many major changes made to it by the time it reached the 2.2.0 release. Even-numbered minor revisions denote official releases. Odd-numbered ones are considered experimental and should be used with caution. Even-numbered releases of the kernel are usually followed by updates to many of the Linux distributions, but it isn't necessary to upgrade a distribution version in order to upgrade the kernel.

Caution   If you have decided to install and use an experimental version of the kernel, there are a few guidelines to follow. You should first check any modifications made to the latest releases. You can keep an eye on the Linux-kernel mailing list, which you can find out more about at `www.tux.org/lkml`. Although the development group tries to release stable code, some changes to the kernel can cause unwanted effects on some people's systems. These problems can generally be traced to missing or specific libraries, modules, and other such dependencies. As a rule, only use experimental versions that have been released for a few days. Let the experts work out the bugs first.

Kernel modules

If you want or need to add anything for the kernel to identify, such as new hardware or a file system that currently isn't being recognized, it will need to be added to the kernel. You can accomplish this in two ways. One way is to incorporate it directly into the kernel. Making a generic kernel that would accommodate everyone's computer would make the kernel huge. Therefore, this is not done for every component. The other way is to add the service for the device as a module. Many devices that are not required to boot, such as sound cards, are typically added as modules. Because modules are so handy, you can set up your kernel to use all the modules you want, and the kernel will decide if they are required when the time comes. In this way, the kernel can mount the service using the module and then discard the service from memory after it has finished with it. This may be handy, but it is not very efficient to include all available modules. However, for devices that only get used once in awhile, such as with PPP connections, this works out well.

You can locate the existing modules for the current kernel at `/lib/modules/version/`, where "version" is the version number of your current kernel. A quick look will reveal that the Debian installation includes many modules. Table 15-1 briefly describes the Debian module categories and the various areas that they cover.

Table 15-1 Module kernel categories	
Category	**Components involved**
block	Block devices such as RAID controllers
cdrom	Older versions of CD-ROMs that require specific drivers
fs	The various file systems with which Linux communicates, such as vfat, hpfs, coda, and others
ipv4	Standard IP masquerading
ipv6	Adds the new IP version 6 standards to the kernel

Category	Components involved
misc	Contains modules for devices that don't fit in another category, such as serial, parallel, and PS/2 ports
net	Adds network cards to the system
scsi	Adds supported SCSI cards
video	Adds specialized video devices, such as high-end video capture cards

Adding modules on the fly

As discussed earlier, modules can be added and removed from the kernel as needed. You can load a module to the kernel dynamically by using /sbin/insmod, and you can remove one using /sbin/rmmod. Other tools that work with modules include /sbin/modprobe, which probes a module; and /sbin/depmod, which determines a module's dependencies.

It isn't unusual to run into difficulties when working with new kernels and modules. Some of the problems that occur when upgrading or changing kernels include, in no particular order, the following:

✦ A conflict with module dependencies

✦ Incompatibility with module utilities

✦ Mismatch of version numbers

Conflicts usually occur when devices loaded as modules are required to be active before a dependent program gets loaded. For instance, if the network support is required for a daemon, as in the case of bind DNS services, but the networking gets loaded as a module after the DNS services, the DNS will fail to load. In the short term, it seems like a great idea to load the networking services as a module, but in reality, it's best left as part of the kernel.

Although the likelihood of using old module utilities that are incompatible with your current kernel version is slim, the possibility remains. The chances of this happening increase when upgrading from an earlier kernel version. You can determine the currently compatible version of the utilities by looking in the /usr/src/kernel-source-version/Documentation/Changes file. This file shows not only the compatible version for the module utilities, but also the compatible versions of other supporting programs, libraries, and such.

When you try to install a module that doesn't exactly match the version of the kernel, you may receive a message that the module mismatches the kernel version. Watch the versions and you should be fine.

Caution   To prevent headaches when upgrading kernels, or to recover more easily from failed attempts to upgrade, be sure to back up the original working module files and kernel. That way, you can always get back to where you started.

Upgrading and updating the kernel

There are a few ways to approach updating your kernel. The most effective method of updating is through the Debian package manager. This method lets you rest reasonably assured that you will have the least number of problems. The packages are tested before being released to ensure that they are compatible with the standard Debian installation.

To update the kernel though the package manager, start `dselect`, update the package version database, and then install any updated packages immediately over the Internet. In fact, the preferred method is through the packages. Debian developers add changes, patches, and updates to a kernel of a Debian release, among other packages, ending up with a version that doesn't always match the version number.

For instance, at the time of the Debian 2.2 release, the current kernel version available at `ftp.kernel.org` was 2.2.16; however, the version released with Debian was version 2.2.17. The reason for this was to create a build of the kernel from the latest source. You can obtain the source for this version from the Debian package `kernel-source-2.2.17` found among the development files. Several dependencies may be required to go with it. Install all non-conflicting dependencies.

Note   You must install the kernel headers if you plan to compile software on your Debian system. This does not get done automatically when you load Debian. You can install the headers from the packages. They should read `kernel-header-2.x.x.deb`, **based on the kernel version (2.x.x) installed.**

Alternately, you can create your own build of the kernel from scratch. The details or building your own kernel follow in this section, but first you must have the source from which to build your kernel. You can obtain the source code from Debian in the kernel-source packages as described above, or from `ftp.kernel.org/pub/linux/kernel/v2.x` where *x* is the minor version number. (Remember that odd minor numbers are still considered experimental.)

Download the version you wish to compile to your `/usr/src` directory. From here, you will need to extract the compressed files. To do this, issue the following command from a command line:

```
tar zxvf kernel-filename.tar.gz
```

In this case, *kernel-filename* is the name of the file you just downloaded. It will extract the contents of the compressed file into a subdirectory of the same name. This subdirectory contains all the source files, documentation, and scripts you need to complete a successful kernel upgrade.

You can also update the kernel using patch files, which are also available on the kernel FTP sites. Be sure to download all patch files with release numbers larger than the kernel release number for which you currently have source. Once these kernel patches are on your machine, decompress the files and run the patch script for each of the patch files, starting with the lowest numbered patch:

```
gzip -cd patch-2.x.x.gz | patch -p0
```

This will update any source files changed since the kernel source available on your system. Alternately, you can use the `patch-kernel` script to automate this process. The default location for the kernel source is `/usr/src/linux` and the current directory for the patch files. You can modify the defaults using the desired kernel's source path as the first argument and the path for the patches as the second argument. Make sure that there are no failed patch files (indicated by *xxx#* or *xxx*.rej). If there are, try downloading and applying the patches again.

Making changes to the kernel

Now that you have the source files located on the machine, enter the newly created subdirectory. This will be the launching point for configuring, compiling, and installing your new kernel.

Caution Configure the kernel specifically for the machine on which it will be used. Adding features that will rarely or never be used results in sub-optimal performance of the kernel and may cause it to become unstable.

This first step is to configure the kernel to include all the devices on your machine. Table 15-2 describes the kernel areas you can configure. Clearly, much of the kernel can be customized.

Table 15-2 Kernel customization areas	
Area	**Description**
Code maturity level options	Enables or disables the usage of experimental drivers and code
Processor type and features	Set the processor class for the kernel (a kernel set for a 386 cannot run on higher processors)
Loadable modules support	Enable module support and associated options
General setup	Specify general types of support (enable networking support, PCI support, and so on)
Parallel port support	Enable parallel port support and associated devices

Continued

Table 15-2 (continued)

Area	Description
Plug and Play configuration	Enable plug-and-play support for PCI and/or ISA
Block devices	Determine block devices being used
Networking options	Set the networking options for the system
Telephony support	Enable telephony support
ATA/IDE support	Enable disk controller types
SCSI support	Enable SCSI devices
I2O Device support	Enable the use of Intelligent Input/Output (I2O) architecture
Network Device support	Set the drivers for the specific networking cards
Amateur Radio support	Enable amateur radio support and associated devices
Infrared support	Enable infrared support and associated hardware drivers
ISDN subsystem	Enable the ISDN subsystem and hardware
Old CD-ROM drivers	Set drivers for CD-ROM hardware (non-SCSI, non-IDE)
Character devices	Virtual terminal settings (includes mice, joysticks, special video adapters, floppy tapes, and so on)
File Systems	Set compatible file systems with this kernel
Console drivers	Set VGA text mode
Sound	Enable sound and set drivers for the sound card
USB Support	Enable USB support and set drivers for the USB devices
Kernel hacking	Enable the kernel to find bugs

To begin configuring the kernel for your machine, you need to run one of three configuration routines. These routines will take you step by step through the specific settings available for the kernel. The three available commands are as follows:

- ✦ `make config`
- ✦ `make menuconfig`
- ✦ `make xconfig`

The first one, `make config`, is a command-line style configuration script that asks you questions regarding what you want to enable. It does this somewhat intelligently by starting with the major categories, and then working down to the specific devices. If you answer yes to a major category, such as enabling networking support, you can later choose the network adapters to use with the kernel. This method of configuration can be tedious because if you make a mistake near the end, you must start all over again.

The next option for configuration, make menuconfig, uses ncurces to navigate through a menu-like screen from which you can navigate, select, and modify features using arrow keys. Using this tool to configure the kernel is much less overwhelming when adjusting and tweaking the configuration. Following the menus (see Figure 15-1), you can confidently set the configuration you want to use, indicating what you want to use as a module and what you want built into the kernel.

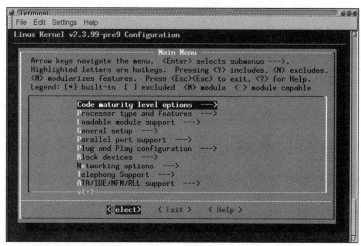

Figure 15-1: A graphical kernel configuration tool using ncurses on a text display

If you prefer to work from a complete graphical interface, use make xconfig to build the configuration file. This tool uses Tcl/Tk to interpret the configuration options, and then displays the categories as shown in Figure 15-2. You can use the mouse to click category buttons and select radio button options. You have the option to return each time to the main menu or progress through the entire configuration one window at a time.

Lastly, if you have configured your kernel before and would like to use the old configuration with a new kernel version, you can use make oldconfig to minimize your efforts. This is not commonly used for first-time kernel updates. You will only be asked questions for new features with this method of configuration.

After you have completed one of the configuration methods, you will have a .config file that the next process uses to compile the kernel.

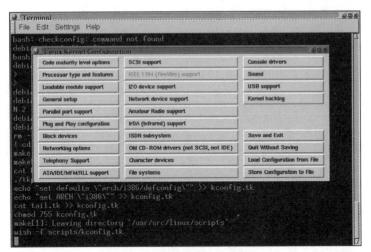

Figure 15-2: Using the convenient kernel configuration tool in an X environment

Compiling and installing a new kernel

After you have the configuration file created, you're ready to move on to compiling the kernel. This takes several steps and can take some time depending on your computer's speed and available resources. Moreover, certain programs and libraries must be up-to-date for a successful creation of binaries. A complete list can be found in `/usr/src/kernel-source-version/Documentation/Changes`. Use the following steps to create the binary of the kernel:

1. Set up all the dependencies correctly. From the command line, issue `make dep` to begin setting up and confirming the dependencies. Once finished, everything is set up to compile the kernel.

2. Issue `make zImage` to create a compressed kernel image. If everything goes as planned, the image (your new kernel) will be created, compressed, and then saved to the `./arch/i386/boot` directory. Alternately, if you wish to make a boot floppy from this kernel, insert a disk into the A: drive and run `make zdisk`. However, if the image was too large for the `zImage`, it will likely fail here also.

If no errors were generated, you can move on to Step 4. However, if you receive an error indicating that the image was too big (such as the one shown here), go to Step 3 instead:

```
tools/build bootsect setup compressed/vmlinux.out CURRENT > zImage2
Root device is (3, 65)
Boot sector 512 bytes.
Setup is 2316 bytes.
System is 818 kB
```

```
System is too big. Try using bzImage or modules.
make[1]: *** [zImage] Error 1
make[1]: Leaving directory `/usr/src/linux-2.3.99/arch/i386/boot'
make: *** [zImage] Error 2
```

3. Because the kernel image was too big in Step 2, you now need to use a different compression method. Run `make bzImage` to create the image using the alternative compression method. The file will be created in the same location as the `zImage` would have been, but under the name of `bzImage` instead.

4. If during the kernel's configuration you chose to make any portion a module instead of part of the kernel, you must compile these as modules. Run `make modules` at this time.

5. If you are compiling a kernel of the same version as you have installed, make sure that you have copied the old modules to a new location. One way to do this is by renaming the directory:

```
mv    /lib/modules/2.x.x    /lib/modules/2.x.x-old
```

6. After the modules have compiled, you can install them using `make modules_install`. This will copy the modules to the appropriate location on the file system. Because portions of the kernel have been compiled as modules, you are now responsible for loading them for the kernel.

Note In the unfortunate event that something goes horribly awry while upgrading your kernel, fear not, as you still can gain access to your system. You should have, if nothing else, the installation CD that comes with this book. Use the installation CD (or other rescue boot disks) to boot to the prompt. From there, you can `fsck` the drive, `mount` it, restore the working kernel image (that you made a copy of), and rerun `lilo`.

Reformatting and starting over is becoming far too prevalent for some operating systems these days. Starting over from scratch with Linux is rarely a thought that even crosses the mind of the experienced administrator. Only when all else fails, such as in the event of hardware failure, would one consider such a task; and even then, the experienced administrator has a catastrophic backup plan.

7. Now that you have a compiled, compressed kernel to install, you're ready to set up the kernel to run your system at the next reboot. To start, copy the new kernel, located at `/usr/src/Linux/arch/i386/boot/zImage`, to `/boot/vmlinuz-2.x.x` (depending on the version you compiled from) using a new name. Make sure you don't overwrite any of the existing images.

Copying the kernel image to the boot directory using a new name enables you to change the kernel with which you boot. If you experience a problem booting, you can easily switch to another kernel image.

That completes the creation and installation of the kernel. Finally, you need to configure the boot loader, LILO, to recognize the new kernel. You must edit the `/etc/lilo.conf` file and add the new kernel to the configuration. Then, to accept your changes, you re-install LILO by running `lilo` from the prompt. For more details about modifying the LILO configuration file, see the next section.

Tip   Debian includes a package of scripts to create a Debian kernel package using `make-kpkg kernel-image`. This script was born out of a desire to help automate the routine creation of building, updating, and loading a new kernel. You can read more on this script and how to use it by loading the `kernel-package.deb` package and reading the man pages on `make-kpkg`.

Using the Linux Boot Loader

The boot loader — in this case, LILO, is initiated when the hardware reads the starting sectors of the disk. Under normal circumstances, LILO is installed and linked to the Master Boot Record (MBR). LILO then starts when the system starts to boot.

When a system running LILO starts, it normally pauses to enable the user to enter the boot option, whether to configure an addition to a Linux driver, start a different kernel, or run a completely different operating system. LILO then passes control over to the selected operating system. If no input is added during the delay period, LILO passes control to whatever option happens to be the default. Table 15-3 describes some different command-line uses for LILO. As the administrator, you can use these commands to set the default boot kernel, to identify current kernel versions, or to set a specific option the next time the kernel boots.

	Table 15-3
	Uses for LILO

Command	LILO's main function
/sbin/lilo	Performs the basic install of the boot loader

Command	Auxiliary uses
/sbin/lilo -q	Runs a query of the boot map and displays the labels
/sbin/lilo -R *command*	Sets the default boot parameters for the next reboot. This is a once-only *command*.
/sbin/lilo -I *label*	Determines the path name of the current kernel identified by *label*
/sbin/lilo -u *devicename*	Uninstalls LILO by copying the boot sector back for *devicename*

There is a limit to the number of cylinders to which LILO can point. Anything you wish to boot using LILO as the boot loader must be within the first 1,024 cylinders of your hard drive. Images and operating systems beyond the first 1,024 cylinders cannot be started using LILO. If your drive has more than 1,024 cylinders, turn on Logical Block Addressing (LBA) on your system's BIOS. This may reduce the number of cylinders and put the operating system back within reach of LILO. Otherwise, you may need to use a boot floppy to access the other operating systems and images.

Configuring LILO

LILO is a highly configurable boot loader; it's able to load several versions of kernel images or operating systems. The configuration file for LILO is located at /etc/ lilo.conf and is easily modified using any text editor. This file contains all the options for starting your system. The following code shows an example of a LILO configuration file:

```
boot=/dev/hda5
map=/boot/map
install=/boot/boot.b
vga=normal
lba32
prompt
timeout=40
default=linux
message=/boot/bootmessage.txt
single-key
delay=100
image=/vmlinuz
        label=linux
        root=/dev/hda5
        read-only
        alias=1
image=/boot/vmlinuz-2.2.17
        label=failsafe
        root=/dev/hda5
        append="failsafe"
        read-only
        alias=0
other=/dev/hda1
        label=windows
        table=/dev/had
        alias=2
other=/dev/fd0
        label=floppy
        unsafe
```

The first three lines set the global parameters for LILO and the system LILO is on. This includes the boot partition, the location of the map file, and the path to the boot file. Next, the default VGA mode is set (in this case, `normal`). This can be changed to `ask`, which prompts you to enter the mode by which you want to start each time. `LBA` is then enabled for use with new systems with large hard drives. The configuration file then enables LILO to accept input at the prompt, enabling you to choose another option at boot time. If nothing is entered at the prompt, a `timeout` in seconds is then set. The configuration file then sets the default image or operating system so that LILO knows what to load with no user intervention.

The `message` option specifies a text file (with complete path) that is printed to the display when LILO first starts. This text file can include instructions, boot options, warning messages, or anything that you, as administrator, want. The `single-key` option enables you to select a single key from which LILO will boot. (The key can be included in the text message.) The length of time (in tenths of seconds) that LILO waits before continuing to load the image is set by the `delay` option.

The `per-image` section is where each image and operating system is identified, and individual options are specified for each image. The image options are identifiable in the file from the indented text. Each part gets its own customization, but is first identified as `image` or `other`, including the path to the device or image. Secondly, the image is labeled, which is nothing more than a name that can get used at boot time from the prompt. You can also specify the location of the root partition. This information is also kept in the kernel image, but specifying the root partition here keeps the root paths in one location for easy identification. This is useful when creating kernel images on other platforms and systems.

The `read-only` option instructs the kernel to start in read-only mode to perform the file system check (`fsck`), and then change to read-write mode afterward. The `append` option adds whatever is quoted to the image as an option for the image to load. This enables you to set up certain customizations here, rather than forcing the customization in the kernel. The `alias` option corresponds to the single key option mentioned previously, enabling the boot process with a single key instead of the label name.

If you have any questions regarding more options not shown here, check the online documentation (`man lilo.conf`).

Adding the new kernel to LILO

When you compile and add a new kernel to your system, you need to change the boot loader to recognize it. Because LILO only loads what is configured, any new configurations just need to be added to the system. Edit the LILO configuration file and add a section identifying the new kernel. The following example makes available an old kernel image at boot time:

```
image=/boot/vmlinuz-2.2.17-old
      label=OldLinux
      read-only
```

This identifies the image to use, including the complete path for the image and the image's complete name. As a suggestion, if you often make changes to a kernel, modify `lilo.conf` to use a symbolic link name. Then, when you want to test a new kernel, create a link to that new kernel using the link name you used in the configuration file.

Also identified here is the label (used at the boot prompt) for the image, and that the image should be started in read-only mode first. Once all the settings for the new kernel image are made to the file, reload this new configuration to the boot sector and you're ready to use it.

Booting to other operating systems

It is possible to have multiple operating systems loaded on the same machine. Choosing which operating system then becomes the responsibility of the boot loader. You need to configure LILO properly to access another operating system at boot time. To accomplish this, edit the `/etc/lilo.conf` file. At the bottom of the file, add the appropriate parameters for the drive partition on which the other operating system is loaded, the label, and any other settings that are needed. Here is an example for you to follow:

```
other=/dev/hda1
        label=Win95
```

The first line identifies the drive partition and the second line gives it a label. Once this change is implemented, the new operating system will be accessible via the LILO prompt when the system starts. Complete the modifications by installing the new LILO configuration into the boot sector.

This is the minimum you need to add to activate another operating system. More options can be found in the first example or by looking through the documentation (manpage) on `lilo.conf`.

Testing and installing a new LILO configuration

When all the necessary changes have been made to the LILO configuration file, you can test it using the `-t` option. This option does a dry run by creating the boot sector on the disk without changing the boot sector. Running `lilo -v -t` produces the following:

```
LILO version 21.5-1 beta (test mode), Copyright (C) 1992-1998 Werner Almesberger
'lba32' extensions Copyright (C) 1999,2000 John Coffman

Reading boot sector from /dev/hda
Merging with /boot/boot.b
Boot image: /vmlinuz
Added Linux *
```

```
Boot image: /boot/vmlinuz-2.2.17-idepci
Added LinuxOLD
The boot sector and the map file have *NOT* been altered.
```

After testing the configuration, it needs to be installed in order to create the boot sector using the setting from the configuration file. This *must* be done whenever changes are made to the configuration file or boot message file, or whenever a new kernel is loaded. To create the boot sector on the drive, simply run lilo again without the test option, as shown here (text in bold is entered by the user):

```
lilo -v
LILO version 21.5-1 beta, Copyright (C) 1992-1998 Werner Almesberger
'lba32' extensions Copyright (C) 1999,2000 John Coffman

Reading boot sector from /dev/hda
Merging with /boot/boot.b
Boot image: /vmlinuz
Added Linux *
Boot image: /boot/vmlinuz-2.2.17-idepci
Added LinuxOLD
/boot/boot.0300 exists - no backup copy made.
Writing boot sector.
```

Now the boot sector has been written and you're ready to restart the system to implement the changes.

System Initialization

When the Debian GNU/Linux system starts, any service specified to run continuously in the background is started as part of the system initialization. This includes file and printer processes, DNS processes, Web processes, and others. This initialization process is one of the advantages of using such a powerful operating system.

To accomplish this initialization, a program called init starts everything that needs to run. This "parent of all processes" uses a collection of scripts to start and stop the processes. Based on the event that occurs, init needs to start a process (such as at boot time) or stop it (such as when shutting the system down). The system defines various collections of programs to run at each state of booting. Each state is called a run level.

A series of directories contain links to the script. A configuration file (/etc/-inittab) contains the instructions for what run level to use at what time. When a system is shutting down, a program called telinit instructs init to change the run level, which in turn begins the process of following the instructions for the scripts. Run level 0 is used for halting the system.

The following code shows the configuration file for init:

```
# /etc/inittab: init(8) configuration.
# $Id: inittab,v 1.8 1998/05/10 10:37:50 miquels Exp $
```

```
# The default runlevel.
id:2:initdefault:

# Boot-time system configuration/initialization script.
# This is run first except when booting in emergency (-b) mode.
si::sysinit:/etc/init.d/rcS

# What to do in single-user mode.
~~:S:wait:/sbin/sulogin

# /etc/init.d executes the S and K scripts upon change
# of runlevel.
#
# Runlevel 0 is halt.
# Runlevel 1 is single-user.
# Runlevels 2-5 are multi-user.
# Runlevel 6 is reboot.

l0:0:wait:/etc/init.d/rc 0
l1:1:wait:/etc/init.d/rc 1
l2:2:wait:/etc/init.d/rc 2
l3:3:wait:/etc/init.d/rc 3
l4:4:wait:/etc/init.d/rc 4
l5:5:wait:/etc/init.d/rc 5
l6:6:wait:/etc/init.d/rc 6
# Normally not reached, but fallthrough in case of emergency.
z6:6:respawn:/sbin/sulogin

# What to do when CTRL-ALT-DEL is pressed.
ca:12345:ctrlaltdel:/sbin/shutdown -t1 -a -r now

# Action on special keypress (ALT-UpArrow).
kb::kbrequest:/bin/echo "Keyboard Request--edit /etc/inittab to let this work."

# What to do when the power fails/returns.
pf::powerwait:/etc/init.d/powerfail start
pn::powerfailnow:/etc/init.d/powerfail now
po::powerokwait:/etc/init.d/powerfail stop

# /sbin/getty invocations for the runlevels.
#
# The "id" field MUST be the same as the last
# characters of the device (after "tty").
#
# Format:
#  <id>:<runlevels>:<action>:<process>
1:2345:respawn:/sbin/getty 38400 tty1
2:23:respawn:/sbin/getty 38400 tty2
3:23:respawn:/sbin/getty 38400 tty3
4:23:respawn:/sbin/getty 38400 tty4
5:23:respawn:/sbin/getty 38400 tty5
6:23:respawn:/sbin/getty 38400 tty6
```

```
# Example how to put a getty on a serial line (for a terminal)
#
#T0:23:respawn:/sbin/getty -L ttyS0 9600 vt100
#T1:23:respawn:/sbin/getty -L ttyS1 9600 vt100

# Example how to put a getty on a modem line.
#
#T3:23:respawn:/sbin/mgetty -x0 -s 57600 ttyS3
```

The first bold text indicates the line where you can change the run level, which you can see is set to level 2. As you look through the configuration file code, you will also notice that a few other items are set in this file. For instance, the CTRL+ALT+DEL soft reboot command is interpreted here, and the corresponding command is issued. Another keyboard sequence is also included here, but at this point is not associated with any commands. CTRL+ALT+DEL only works when you are sitting at the system's console and not through a remote login.

Tip   Once a system is running, `init` doesn't read the configuration file until it's notified by `telinit` that the run level changed. You can force `init` to reread the configuration file without changing the run level with the `-q` option — `telinit -q`.

Run levels

Every run level has a specific purpose. Some can be changed, whereas others should not be touched. Table 15-4 lists the available run levels, their location on the file system, and the general purpose of each. As you can see, run levels 0, 1, and 6 are reserved for specific purposes; the others, run levels 2 through 5, are customizable. By default, Debian 2.2 uses run level 2 for the normal multi-user start routine. Most distributions use either 2 or 3, but primarily they use 3. Run levels 7 through 9 are also valid for use with `init`, although traditionally they are not used on UNIX variants.

Table 15-4 Available run levels		
Run level	**Location**	**Typical use**
0	/etc/rc0.d	Normal shutdown
1	/etc/rc1.d	Used to start in single-user mode
2	/etc/rc2.d	Multi-user customizable (used as the Debian default)
3	/etc/rc3.d	Multi-user customizable (used as default on other systems)
4	/etc/rc4.d	Multi-user customizable

Run level	Location	Typical use
5	/etc/rc5.d	Multi-user customizable
6	/etc/rc6.d	Used for system reboot
S	/etc/rcS.d	Prepares the system for single-user mode

When the Linux system starts, init reads the inittab file to determine what to do; in this case, init uses the default run level 2. It then reads the directory /etc/rc2.d for the scripts to run. All the files located in /etc/rc2.d are links to the actual scripts located in /etc/init.d. All linked run level files begin with either a K for kill or an S for start. These links use a numbering scheme to establish the start order. Links starting with low numbers (such as S20gpm) are started before links with high numbers (such as S99xdm). Links starting with the same letter and number are started in alphabetical order. This method of ordering the files enables some processes to start before others due to the dependency between the two processes.

In the same fashion, when the system gets shut down, a different run level is selected; and the links in that directory determine the order in which the scripts get stopped — typically, in the reverse order that they were started.

Run level S represents scripts that need to run before entering single-user mode. These are run in preparation for executing the scripts in run level 1.

Note You can determine the current run level by using the command /sbin/runlevel. It will return the mode of operation, where N indicates normal operation and S indicates single-user mode. The number that follows indicates the current run level.

Initialization scripts

The process initialization scripts enable init as well as administrators to start and stop the processes. Therefore, every daemon that must begin at start up has an init script file to control the processes.

The following script monitors the daemon that watches the TCP/IP ports for incoming requests:

```
#!/bin/sh
#
# start/stop inetd super server.

if ! [ -x /usr/sbin/inetd ]; then
    exit 0
fi

checkportmap () {
```

```
        if grep -v "^ *#" /etc/inetd.conf | grep 'rpc/' >/dev/null; then
            if ! /usr/bin/rpcinfo -u localhost portmapper >/dev/null 2>/dev/null
            then
                echo
                echo "WARNING: portmapper inactive - RPC services unavailable!"
                echo "        (Commenting out the rpc services in inetd.conf will"
                echo "         disable this message)"
                echo
            fi
        fi
    }

    case "$1" in
        start)
            checkportmap
            echo -n "Starting internet superserver:"
            echo -n " inetd" ; start-stop-daemon --start --quiet --pidfile \
                /var/run/inetd.pid --exec /usr/sbin/inetd
            echo "."
            ;;
        stop)
            echo -n "Stopping internet superserver:"
            echo -n " inetd" ; start-stop-daemon --stop --quiet --oknodo --pidfile \
                /var/run/inetd.pid --exec /usr/sbin/inetd
            echo "."
            ;;
        reload)
            echo -n "Reloading internet superserver:"
            echo -n " inetd"
            start-stop-daemon --stop --quiet --oknodo --pidfile /var/run/inetd.pid \
                --signal 1 --exec /usr/sbin/inetd
            echo "."
            ;;
        force-reload)
            $0 reload
            ;;
        restart)
            echo -n "Restarting internet superserver:"
            echo -n " inetd"
            start-stop-daemon --stop --quiet --oknodo --pidfile /var/run/inetd.pid \
                --exec /usr/sbin/inetd
            checkportmap
            start-stop-daemon --start --quiet --pidfile /var/run/inetd.pid --exec \
                /usr/sbin/inetd
            echo "."
            ;;
        *)
            echo "Usage: /etc/init.d/inetd {start|stop|reload|restart}"
            exit 1
            ;;
    esac

    exit 0
```

These scripts can be a little confusing to read at times, although most of them have a similar pattern. The scripts perform several checks on the files, their status, and the status of any supporting programs. Each of the script files can be broken down into two or three parts:

✦ Verification that the daemon file exists.

✦ A diagnostic or routine (this part varies among the scripts)

✦ A run condition for the daemon

The first part of the preceding code begins with the first if statement. This short section ensures that the daemon that it is supposed to run actually exists. If it doesn't exist, the script stops here and nothing happens.

The second part, in this case, checks to see if the portmapper is active. Other scripts check for their specific programs and the conditions under which they are able to run successfully. In the case of this script, a warning message is printed to the console if any program was found to have stopped running. In other cases, failure of this portion may lead to failure of the script.

The last part of the script is the conditional part. Depending on the option submitted at the time the script ran, any number of actions could take place. This is known as a *case statement,* conditions that provide various outcomes depending on each case. Table 15-5 lists the options accepted by the init script.

Table 15-5
Options accepted by the init script

Condition	Description
start	This is a request to start the process. This is used when the system starts or when inetd is started manually.
stop	This stops the process once it is running. When the system shuts down, stop is used. This is also used when you want to stop the process manually.
reload	This option stops and then restarts the process without performing any tests.
restart	This option stops the daemon completely, performs the standard checks, and then restarts the daemon.
*	This prints to the console all the available commands because an unrecognized command option was used. Note that all the options are lowercase.

Although these processes are started and stopped with `init`, you will occasionally need to stop, start, and restart these processes whenever a change to the process' configuration files is made. The change isn't implemented until that daemon is restarted.

Adding and removing daemon programs

From time to time, you may need to prevent a process from starting at boot up. For instance, you may wish to prevent your mail server from starting while you perform maintenance on local mailboxes. You can accomplish this in several ways, but some aren't very forgiving when you want to add it later. The best technique for preventing a process from starting is to rename the link in the run level that you use. This doesn't affect the other run levels and lets you disable the script without deleting it.

For example, if you always work in a window manager, then using a mouse in terminal mode doesn't provide any useful feature for you. The script that starts the mouse in terminal mode is `gpm`. Therefore, renaming the link in run level 2 will prevent `gpm` from loading at boot time. To rename the link, issue the following command:

```
mv /etc/rc2.d/S20gpm /etc/rc2.d/_S20gpm
```

Years from now, not only will you be able to re-engage the script at boot time, but you'll also remember what number to start it as.

Similarly, adding a process to a run level is just as easy. Add a link to the pertinent script process at the run level from which you want to start it. The script should be located in the `/etc/init.d` directory and should include instructions, as shown in the previous example.

Summary

It is hoped that after reading through this chapter, you now have a better understanding of kernels, including how to configure and compile your own, and how to use the newly compiled kernel in your system.

You should also now understand how to configure LILO. Even with its 1,024-cylinder limitation, it is a flexible boot loader. The sample configuration file included in this chapter has been highly modified from the default file that comes with the Debian installation. This should give you an idea of how to modify your own to fit your needs.

Adjusting which daemons are started through the run levels can have a huge effect on performance, security, and maintainability. Processes that aren't used can be left out of the startup run levels. This allocates more resources to the rest of the system and lowers the potential security risks that old forgotten processes might introduce.

✦   ✦   ✦

Maintenance and Upgrade

Finding Updated Files

Some users may work for years using the same programs
and never update the software or upgrade to a newer
version. Those people casually go about working, oblivious to
the inner workings of the software. This includes most users
today. I only have a vague idea of how much of the software
works because it really isn't important to know how it works
in order to use the software.

There are a few people who work very intensely with a piece
of software. These people not only know how it works, but
they have an understanding of the software's weaknesses. To
this group of people, software must be as free from problems
as possible. If the software does have problems, they know
about them right away. In the Open Source community, these
are the men and women who develop and test the software
you use.

This chapter begins by defining problems in software called
bugs. It goes on to explain the various aspects, concerns, and
issues surrounding these bugs. The chapter concludes by
showing you how to keep your system as bug free as possible.

Defining System Bugs

The first thing that comes to mind when you read about bugs
may be an infestation of insects. This is not farther from the
truth. Originally, insects would get inside the circuitry of large
mainframe computers, causing failures. However, the term
bug, in the software arena today, indicates a problem with a
software or hardware program. These problems vary from
something minor that occasionally is noticeable to server
bugs, which cause software to cease working properly (or at
all). Most software contains bugs; but by the time these bugs
reach the end users, the known serious bugs are fixed.

Other bugs may never surface or cause a problem. Even so, somewhere out there in the digital world, someone is testing the software in an attempt to find any and all bugs. Generally, this is how those bugs are legitimately found. Someone must perform testing to find problems in order to fix them. Because most of the programs, tools, and utilities used with the Debian Distribution are developed and maintained by volunteers, these testers also are volunteers.

Software bugs can cause problems in these common areas if not hunted down and fixed:

✦ **Security**—The biggest problems with bugs lie in the security exploits they allow. This means that there is some flaw with the program that allows an unprivileged user to abuse it in such a way that the program gives the user access to either a root account or affects other programs as a security risk.

✦ **Conflicts**—Bugs can also cause a conflict with other programs. Conflicts occur with programs that cannot work together because the way the programs use hardware, other software, or other related system components. Sometimes, though, the evidence that a program conflicts with another unrelated program shows up as a security issue.

✦ **Functionality**—Finally, some bugs cause a functional problem within a program when the bug changes or disables a function that the program normally carries out, for example, a bug that disables a menu option or prevents the action of a program option. These functional bugs are generally fixed before the software is released—although some may slip through the cracks.

✦ **Harmless bugs**—Bugs can also come in a benign form in which nothing noticeable happens. A device driver, for example, can cause the process that used it to die and then become a zombie process. If it weren't for the zombie process hanging around, you'd never know of a problem because the originating program and device still work fine.

How can bugs affect your system? You can only answer that question by knowing how your system is used. If you have only one machine that sits on a desk, disconnected from the computer world and with only one user, then the only bugs that are a major concern for you are the bugs that affect the function of the program. However, if you use the system or systems as a server, supporting hundreds of accounts across a network or over the Internet, then the slightest security bug can jeopardize the integrity of the system security. For such systems, staying on top of bug fixes is a part of routine activity.

Bugless software

Is there really such a thing as bugless software? Yes. Mission-critical applications—such as those programs needed to run the space shuttle, control a backup generator for a hospital, or any other application in which failure cannot happen—do use bug-free software. Developing bug-free software takes a long time because of the extensive, thorough testing process to ensure that the software contains no bugs.

For the Linux environment, not all applications are mission-critical. For instance, a solitaire game does not have to be bug free. On the other hand, the entire system depends on the kernel so it should be as close to bug free as possible.. Bugs in mission-critical software such as the kernel are more serious, but you can be less concerned with bugs in non-mission critical software.

Here again, the advantage of having an Open Source community supporting the programs comes into play. There are programmers from around the world using, testing and fixing the software. When a bug is found, it gets terminated swiftly.

Stable versus secure

Let me take a moment to explain the difference between stable and secure software. Debian is an Open Source project, so great efforts are made to ensure that the packages included with it are stable. Stable software means that the program will run with an extremely low probability of failure or crashing. Secure software means that someone cannot break it to gain access to unauthorized areas of the computer. Granted, stable software may not be secure, but secure software is generally stable.

A program may have a couple of known bugs and yet remain stable. A stable program can run for hundreds of hours without the first hint of a problem and still not be secure. If a program has 99 out of 100 bugs fixed, it's not secure. The Pretty Good Privacy (PGP) program, which is most often used to encrypt messages, was available for a year before anyone found a rather substantial security bug. Yet, for that year, it was (and still is) completely stable.

 To learn more about securing your Debian system, go to Chapter 19.

Debian strives to be both secure and stable. That is why it is so important to keep your system up to date. Subscribe to the security announcement mailing list to receive notifications of bug fixes. You can find a complete list of Debian-related mailing lists at www.debian.org/MailingLists/subscribe.

Bugs versus features

Some people experience anomalies with a particular program such as a lag in performance, a noticeable delay while the program runs, or some other type of glitch. A program bug does not always cause these conditions. Users only perceive some of these problems. Some of these perceived problems can come from the program's interaction with other software. These symptoms often appear the same as those when a bug is present, but thorough testing validates that the program works correctly.

These perceived anomalies found while running a program are often called *glitches*. They may not be the intended outcome, but they affect the perceived performance of the product. These features in no way affect the actual workings of the program, which is proven by thorough testing.

I hope that you now see that not every glitch means that a program has a bug in it. On the other hand, for mission-critical applications, you first should test a glitch (perceived, real, or otherwise). You can check the frequently asked questions and then query the developer of the application. The next section discusses this topic in more detail.

Getting help and reporting bugs

If you come across something you think is a problem, you should follow the preferred procedure. Much of this procedure involves making sure that the software isn't having this problem because of configuration issues.

1. First, check the online documentation and change notices. For the online documentation, use either `man` or `info`. The end of the documentation always includes any information on known bugs.

2. Every program that you install should have a change log of some sort. Debian packaged applications also have a separate change log file. You can find these files in the `/usr/doc` directory under the name of the application. The documents are in compressed `gzip` form. For instance, the directory `/usr/doc/gnome-bin` contains `changelog.Debian.gz`, `changelog.gz`, and `copyright` files. Other application directories may have more or fewer files in them. These change log files contain information about any modifications of configuration settings specific to the application. If you suspect a problem with the program, you can look through these log files to see if any changes have been made to the feature in question.

3. Most of the major applications have a Web site. You can check the application's Web site for any release notes, known bugs, or any other helpful information. For example, check `www.sendmail.org` for Sendmail information.

4. Check any Frequently Asked Questions (FAQ) listings from the Web site, FAQ document, or any other source for FAQs. Frequently asked questions are just that — a list of questions that other users and developers have already asked.

5. Ask around on a news or mailing list. Most applications have mailing lists you can subscribe to. When asking a question to the mailing list or news group community, make sure to include as much information as possible.

Finally, when you are ready to report a Debian bug, create an e-mail as described on the Debian bug-reporting Web page. This site, `www.debian.org/Bugs/Reporting`, includes step-by-step instructions for reporting bugs.

Basically, you need to send a specially formatted e-mail to a bug registration e-mail address. This e-mail must contain all the details pertaining to the bug, such as the name of the package in question, the version, what is happening, any error messages, and any other information that can help the developers recreate the problem. The Debian Web site for reporting bugs includes the full details on how to format the message.

Patches that fix bugs

The great selling point with Linux is the community of programmers that fix those bugs. When a problem is found, a new version of the software with the bug fix is released just hours later. Many commercial software companies take months to fix a bug; and even then, the fix may introduce other problems.

When a program has a bug fix, that fixed software is labeled as a new release version or a *patch*. As the administrator of your system, you should know the version of your software and know when new versions get released. Then you can make the decision to either install the patch or wait. You may need to test the patch on a duplicate system setup to make sure that all the functions still work for your particular environment.

Caution

When applying a patch to a program, you may be tempted to install the latest and greatest version available. Resist that urge and only install stable patches. Installing software that is still under development can introduce other problems – if not now, then later down the road. The disappointment of a corrupted system can quickly overshadow the excitement of using a bleeding-edge software version. If you do choose to install the latest version, know you are doing it at your own risk. The old adage "If it ain't broke, don't fix it" can be a good rule to administer by.

For software outside of the standard Debian packages, those programs generally have Web sites where you can obtain support in the form of bug notices and available release updates. Those companies and organizations often have a mailing list for special announcements, news, and notifications. I recommend subscribing to such a list.

Debian, on the other hand, is a different story.

Updating Debian Files with the Package-Management System

Getting updates on fixed packages could not be easier with the Debian package manager. Debian's uniquely advanced package-management system keeps a running database of all the programs installed on your system. When an application included with the Debian distribution is updated, the revision number changes to indicate that the package has also changed in some way.

The Debian package-management system uses the Internet to compare the version numbers on your computer with the version number in the selected remote location. It then updates only the installed packages requiring updating. Here is how to update your system (assuming that `dselect` is configured to get files over the Internet; see Chapter 2 if in doubt):

1. From a terminal window, type `dselect` at the prompt. This brings up the package-management interface.

2. Select the Update option from the menu by pressing the number 1. Press Enter. The appropriate commands issue a request to compile the latest list of packages with the version numbers. Figure 16-1 shows a terminal completing an update operation.

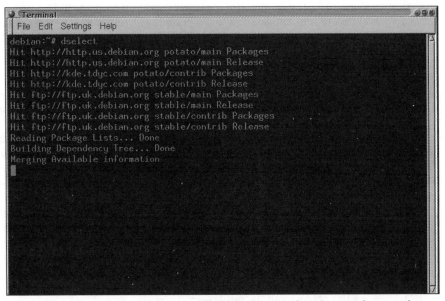

Figure 16-1: The list of packages is pulled from remote locations and a complete list is compiled locally.

3. Press the Select option (number 2) and move the up and down arrows through the list, pressing the Insert key on each updated package. These will have an *n*, for new, in the second column.

4. Once you select all the packages you want to update, install those packages by pressing number 3 and then pressing Enter. If there were any package updates, then these also install.

You now have some assurance that the list of available packages is up to date.

Note   Alternately, you can run `apt-get` to implement an update. First, use `apt-get update`; then run `apt-get upgrade`. All files that need upgrading will get installed.

Upgrading from an older Debian version

If you currently run an older Debian system, migrating to the latest version is extremely easy with the automated tools in the Debian package-management system. The Debian package-management system enables you to upgrade to the next version though an FTP or HTTP connection to the Internet.

Caution   Avoid upgrading from a different distribution of Linux like RedHat. There are slight differences from one distribution to the next, and changing midstream can cause the current distribution to stop working. If you currently are running something other than Debian, it is best to install from scratch.

Upgrading over the Internet

If you installed Debian over the Internet, there is not much you need to do to migrate to the latest version. The main point of concern on installing over the Internet is the speed of the access. Installing over a 56Kbps modem works fine, but it is extremely slower than installing over a cable modem. For the reason of speed, I'd avoid installing over a 56Kbps modem connection. Follow these steps to update versions:

1. Identify one or more remote mirrors from which to download. These locations use either `http` or `ftp` path names. For a complete list of mirror sites, go to `www.debian.org/misc/README.mirrors`. The most common US site is `http.us.debian.org`. As a rule, you should use the site closest to your location.

2. Next, you need to modify the `/etc/apt/sources.list` file. This file, shown next, contains the path for each site to which you will download the updated files. Look through the file paths for any reference to the previous version and change it to the version you wish to update to (or change it to stable). The following code shows the changed name in the bold text:

```
vi /etc/apt/sources.list
# See sources.list(5) for more information, especially
# Remember that you can only use http, ftp or file URIs
# CDROMs are managed through the apt-cdrom tool.
deb ftp://ftp.uk.debian.org/debian stable main contrib
#deb http://non-us.debian.org/debian-non-US stable/non-US
main contrib non-free
#deb http://security.debian.org stable/updates main contrib
non-free

# Uncomment if you want the apt-get source function to work
#deb-src http://http.us.debian.org/debian stable main contrib
non-free
#deb-src http://non-us.debian.org/debian-non-US stable non-US

deb http://http.us.debian.org/debian/ stable main
#deb-src http://http.us.debian.org/debian/ stable main
```

Note   You can add locations to the sources.list file manually, but make sure that the syntax is correct. The syntax should be deb *uri distribution* [*component1*] [*componenent2*] [...]. Here, *uri* refers to the source path, *distribution* refers to stable or unstable version of the release, and [*componentx*] refers to the groups of packages (main, contrib., or non-free). If you have more questions about the Debian package-management system, take a look at Chapter 2.

3. Start the dselect application, and execute the Update option by pressing the number 1 and then Enter. (See Figure 16-2.) dselect goes through the selected sources and updates the record of packages and current version numbers.

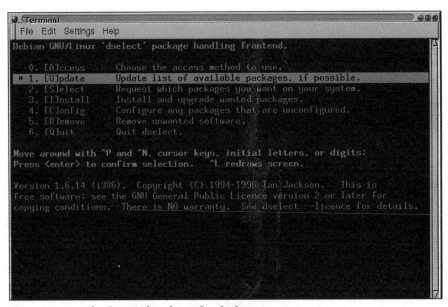

Figure 16-2: Selecting Update from the dselect menu

4. When dselect is finished updating the available packages, execute the Install option by pressing number 3. Then press Enter. dselect compares the record of the currently installed package versions with the newly updated database. If there are any updates, those packages are selected for installation.

5. When all the packages are installed, you return to the main menu. Quit dselect by pressing the number 6 and pressing Enter. The update is complete.

Upgrading from installation CD-ROMs

On the other hand, you may want to upgrade using a new CD-ROM set because access to the internet is slow or non-existent. If so, there are different steps you need to follow — even though the result remains the same. Use the following steps to upgrade with installation CD-ROMs:

1. Have available the new installation CD-ROMs.

2. Add the new CD-ROMs using the `apt-cdrom` tool. This tool is required when using installation CD-ROMs. It does more than just add the CD-ROM to the list of sources found in the `/etc/apt/sources.list` file. It also verifies the contents of the CD-ROM and adjusts for any problems with the CD. To add a CD-ROM, type `apt-cdrom add`. You then are prompted for the CD-ROM. Insert the CD-ROM into the drive and press Enter. The CD-ROM is scanned before being added to the sources file. Here is what the sources file should look like after you add the new CD-ROMs:

```
cat /etc/apt/sources.list
# See sources.list(5) for more information, especially
# Remember that you can only use http, ftp or file URIs
# CDROMs are managed through the apt-cdrom tool.
#deb ftp://ftp.uk.debian.org/debian stable main contrib
#deb http://non-us.debian.org/debian-non-US stable/non-US
 main contrib non-free
#deb http://security.debian.org stable/updates main contrib
 non-free


deb cdrom:[Debian GNU/Linux2.2r2_Potato_-Official i386
Binary-3]/ main
deb cdrom:[Debian GNU/Linux2.2r2_Potato_-Official i386
Binary-2]/ main
deb cdrom:[Debian GNU/Linux2.2r2_Potato_-Official i386
Binary-1]/ main
```

If you have more questions about the `apt-cdrom` program, take a look at Chapter 2.

3. Start the `dselect` application and execute the Update option by pressing the number 1 and then Enter. `dselect` goes through the selected sources and updates the record of packages and current version numbers.

4. When `dselect` is finished updating the available packages database, execute the Install option by pressing number 3 and pressing Enter. `dselect` compares the record of the currently installed package versions with the newly updated database. If there are any updates, those packages are selected for installation.

5. When all the packages are installed, you return to the main menu. Quit `dselect` by pressing the number 6 and pressing Enter. The update is complete.

The way the Debian package manager works to update and upgrade the installed applications has won it high praises from anyone who has used it — especially when those administrators have had to upgrade any other distributions. The people who maintain the Debian distribution work very hard to preserve compatibility across revisions. Keep using Debian and you, too, will be won over.

Summary

I'm sure that you have discovered what a software bug is and how it can affect your system. Bugs can be no more serious than having a few ants on your driveway — barely noticeable. They can also be as serious as a bad case of termites, which can damage the frame of your house. The degree of seriousness depends on the importance of the program and its influence on your system.

The end result of the bug discussion comes down to whether or not your system needs mission-critical, highly secure programs. If so, you need to stay on top of upgrades and patches. Debian offers a tremendous tool for doing so, but you still need to frequently check for updates and patches.

✦　　✦　　✦

Hardware

Hardware changes quickly in today's computer industry. A computer system considered top-of-the-line a couple of years ago now sits in the closet collecting dust. The versatility of Linux gives that older hardware a chance to be useful right alongside cutting-edge hardware.

One of the problems with cutting-edge hardware is finding drivers to make it work with Linux. Because Windows has an overwhelming influence in the computer industry, some hardware is specifically designed to work with that one operating system. This chapter attempts to help distinguish the hardware that works best with Linux. In the end, you may find that buying the cheapest Windows-related hardware may cost you in frustration when setting up Linux your system.

Finding Linux-Compatible Hardware

In order for Linux of any variety to work properly on a system, it must be capable of using the hardware and software installed on the machine. A kernel compiled for the PowerPC processor will never work on a system with an Alpha processor or any other processor. Of course, this is an obvious example, but it helps to illustrate how your hardware determines what software is used.

In order for specific piece of hardware to work, it may need a special driver. A *driver* is a small piece of software code that translates instructions from the kernel (the heart of Linux) to the hardware device. The driver or module is loaded into the kernel before accessing a device. Some modules are compiled directly into the kernel so you never notice them. You need drives for the following hardware:

✦ **Mainboards, processors, and chipsets** — These relate to the core of the computer. *Mainboards,* also called *motherboards,* contain components that must communicate together as well as with additional daughter cards such as network cards, sound cards, and such. Daughter cards are those extra cards that connect to the motherboard inside the computer's case.

Of these components, the processor takes care of all tasks and must work correctly. Generally, the installation of Debian GNU/Linux found in this book works with today's processors.

✦ **Graphics adapters, video cards, and monitors** — The graphics portion of the system is very important to many that rely on it to see what the system is doing. That may be an obvious statement, but an important one nonetheless. In general, most any video card can function as a text virtual terminal; however, some may not work with the X server to run a graphical interface. As newer cards are released, finding drivers for the new cards that work with Linux becomes difficult. The monitor is more immune to driver issues, but it must be compatible with the graphics card. For instance, an old VGA monitor does not work well with newer graphics cards.

✦ **Sound cards** — For a server system, listening to music, songs, or other sound files may not be important. Workstations are another story. Many people now listen to audio files, songs, and system messages on their computers. Check out the sound card manufacturer's Web site for hints on installing drivers.

✦ **Hard disks, SCSI, and RAID controllers** — Generally, most hard drives and controllers for the run-of-the-mill PCs available on the open market work with Linux. Compatible modules are available for a smaller group of SCSI (Small Computer System Interface) controllers and an even smaller group of RAID (Redundant Array of Independent Disks) controllers.

✦ **CD writers, CD-ROM drives, and changeable media** — This is somewhat of an extension of the hard disk's compatibility. Most CD-ROM drives and CD writers use the IDE controller, which is supported by the current kernel version. Other changeable media, such as Zip drives, take a little more work.

Note   CD writers need an IDE to SCSI bridge loaded at boot time for the software (`cdrecord`) to work with the IDE drives. You can load this module at boot time with `hdx=ide-scsi` or the `ide-scsi` module can be loaded into the kernel. (See Chapter 15 for details about kernels and modules.)

✦ **Input devices, keyboards, and mice** — These are not usually areas in which compatibility problems occur, although there are exceptions. Some unusual keyboards, International keyboards, and mice with special buttons could be among the devices with exceptions. With the introduction of Universal Serial Bus (USB) devices, compatibility has become a messier issue. The kernel 2.4 release includes rudimentary USB support.

✦ **Modems, ISDN adapters, and network adapters** — There are numerous versions and varieties of these types of adapters and cards. Problems come into play when using modems from systems with Windows installed. A variety of modems called *Winmodems* use software emulation to replace some of the modem hardware; this makes for a cheaper modem. These modems do not work with other operating systems without the emulation. ISDN adapters are a more sophisticated breed of modem, but few are supported (unless by the manufacturer).

There are numerous network adapters, many of which have a module available or use an available chipset. For instance, the inexpensive Kingston 120TX 10/100 card uses the Real Tech chipset module (rtl8139.o).

✦ **HAM radio** — A small, but loyal, group of hobbyists has latched onto the Open Source aspect of Linux and has developed a niche of HAM radio devices, which Linux supports.

✦ **Printers, scanners, tape drives, and UPS** — External devices also need support. The driver for the computer port that the external device connects to may work. However, the external device still needs information that goes through the port; therefore, not all external devices work with Linux.

If you ever have a question about any device's compatibility with Linux, check the manufacturer's Web site for information that can help the whole system to function. If you do have trouble with a device, post a question to a related newsgroup or mailing list. With the thousands of people using Linux in the world, someone else is bound to have had the same problem. For starters, try www.debian.org/MailingLists.

For most modern systems, compatibility is not an issue. A few exceptions include video, network, and SCSI cards. Table 17-1 lists the video cards compatible with the included version of X Windows. The next version of X Windows is touted as supporting the latest 3-D video technologies. If you don't see your card listed here, check the manufacturer's Web site for compatibility and/or drivers.

Table 17-1
Compatible video cards

Manufacturer/model	Manufacturer/model	Manufacturer/model
3DLabs Oxygen GMX	3DVision-i740 AGP	928Movie
ABIT G740	AGP 2D/3D	AGP-740D
AGX (generic)	ALG-5434(E)	AOpen 3D Navigator
AOpen PA50V	ARISTO i740 AGP	ASUS 3Dexplorer
ASUS AGP-V2740	ASUS PCI	ASUS Video Magic
AT25	AT3D	ATI 3D Pro Turbo
ATI 3D Pro Turbo PC2TV	ATI 3D Xpression	ATI 8514 Ultra (no VGA)
ATI All-in-Wonder	ATI Graphics Pro Turbo	ATI Graphics Ultra

Continued

Table 17-1 *(continued)*

Manufacturer/model	Manufacturer/model	Manufacturer/model
ATI Graphics Ultra Pro	ATI Graphics Xpression	ATI Mach32
ATI Mach64	ATI Rage	ATI Ultra Plus
ATI Video Boost	ATI Video Charger	ATI Video Xpression
ATI WinBoost	ATI WinCharger	ATI WinTurbo
ATI Wonder SVGA	ATI Xpert	ATI integrated on Intel Maui MU440EX motherboard
ATrend ATC-2165A	AccelStar Permedia II AGP	Acorp AGP i740
Actix GE32	Actix GE64	Actix ProStar
Actix ProStar 64	Actix Ultra	Acumos AVGA3
Alliance ProMotion 6422	Aristo ART-390-G S3 Savage3D	Ark Logic ARK
Atrend 3DIO740 AGP	Avance Logic	Binar Graphics AnyView
Boca Vortex (Sierra RAMDAC)	Canopus Power Window 3DV	Canopus SPECTRA
Canopus Total-3D	Cardex Challenger (Pro)	Cardex Cobra
Cardex Trio64	Chaintech AGP-740D	Chaintech Desperado
Chaintech Tornado	Chips & Technologies	Cirrus Logic GD54xx
Cirrus Logic GD62xx (laptop)	Cirrus Logic GD64xx (laptop)	Cirrus Logic GD754x (laptop)
Colorgraphic Dual Lightning	Compaq Armada 7400	Compaq Armada 7800
Creative Blaster Exxtreme	Creative Labs 3D Blaster PCI (Verite 1000)	Creative Labs Graphics Blaster 3D
Creative Labs Graphics Blaster Eclipse	Creative Labs Graphics Blaster	Creative Labs Savage 4 3D Blaster
DFI-WG1000	DFI-WG5000	DFI-WG6000
DSV3325	DSV3326	DataExpert
Dell S3 805	Dell onboard ET4000	Diamond Edge 3D
Diamond Fire GL	Diamond Monster Fusion	Diamond Multimedia Stealth 3D 2000
Diamond Multimedia Stealth 3D 2000 PRO	Diamond SpeedStar	Diamond Stealth
Diamond Stealth II	Diamond Stealth III	Diamond Stealth64
Diamond Viper	Digital 24-plane	Digital 8-plane TGA

Manufacturer/model	Manufacturer/model	Manufacturer/model
EIZO (VRAM)	ELSA ERAZOR II	ELSA ERAZOR III
ELSA Gloria	ELSA Synergy II	ELSA VICTORY ERAZOR
ELSA Victory 3D	ELSA Winner	EONtronics Picasso 740
EONtronics Van Gogh (CardPC)	EPSON CardPC (onboard)	EPSON SPC8110
ET3000 (generic)	ET4000 (generic)	ET6000 (generic)
EliteGroup(ECS) 3DVision-i740 AGP	Everex MVGA i740/AG	ExpertColor DSV3325
ExpertColor DSV3365	Flagpoint Shocker i740	Gainward CardExpert 740
Generic VGA compatible	Genoa	Gigabyte Predator i740
HOT-158 (Shuttle)	Hercules Dynamite	Hercules Graphite
Hercules Stingray	Hercules Terminator	Hercules Thriller3D
Integral FlashPoint	Intel 5430	Intel 740 (generic)
Intel Express 3D AGP	Interay PMC Viper	JAX 8241
Jaton Video	Jazz Multimedia G-Force	Jetway 740-3D
Joymedia Apollo 7400	LeadTek WinFast	MAXI Gamer AGP 8 MB
MELCO WGA AGP 4600	MSI MS-4417	Machspeed Raptor i740
Magic-Pro MP-740DVD	Matrox Comet	Matrox Marvel II
Matrox Millennium	Matrox Millennium G200	Matrox Millennium G400
Matrox Millennium II	Matrox Mystique	Matrox Mystique G200
Matrox Productiva G100	MediaGX	MediaVision Proaxcel 128
Mirage Z-128	Miro CRYSTAL VRX	Miro Crystal
Miro MiroMedia 3D	Miro MiroVideo 20TD	Miro Video 20SV
NVIDIA GeForce	NVIDIA Riva 128 (generic)	NVIDIA Riva TNT
NVIDIA Riva TNT2	NeoMagic (laptop)	Number Nine FX Motion
Number Nine FX Reality	Number Nine FX Vision 330	Number Nine GXE
Number Nine Imagine I-128	Number Nine Revolution 3D AGP	Number Nine Visual 9FX Reality 332
Oak 87	Ocean VL-VGA-1000	Octek AVGA
Octek Combo	Octek VL-VGA	Orchid Celsius
Orchid Fahrenheit	Orchid Kelvin 64	Orchid P9000 VLB
PC-Chips M567 Mainboard	Palit Daytona AGP740	Paradise Accelerator Value

Continued

Table 17-1 *(continued)*

Manufacturer/model	Manufacturer/model	Manufacturer/model
Paradise/WD 90CXX	PixelView Combo TV 3D	PixelView Combo TV Pro
PowerColor C740 AGP	QDI Amazing I	Quantum 3D MGXplus
Real3D Starfighter	Rendition Verite	Revolution 3D (T2R)
S3 Aurora64V+ (generic)	S3 Savage	S3 Trio32 (generic)
S3 Trio3D	S3 Trio3D/2X	S3 Trio64
S3 ViRGE	S3 Vision864 (generic)	S3 Vision868 (generic)
S3 Vision964 (generic)	S3 Vision968 (generic)	SHARP 9080
SHARP 9090	SMI Lynx	SMI LynxE
SNI PC5H W32	SNI Scenic W32	SPEA Mercury 64
SPEA Mirage	SPEA/V7 Mercury	SPEA/V7 Mirage P64
SPEA/V7 ShowTime Plus	STB Horizon Video	STB LightSpeed
STB MVP	STB Nitro	STB Pegasus
STB Powergraph 64	STB Systems Powergraph	STB Systems Velocity 3D
STB Velocity	STB nvidia 128	SiS 3D PRO AGP
Sierra Screaming 3D	Sigma Concorde	Sigma Legend
Soyo AGP (SY-740 AGP)	Spacewalker Hot-158	Spider Black Widow
Spider Tarantula 64	Spider VLB Plus	TechWorks Thunderbolt
TechWorks Ultimate 3D	Toshiba Satellite	Toshiba Tecra
Trident 3Dimage	Trident 8900/9000 (generic)	Trident 8900D (generic)
Trident Blade3D (generic)	Trident Cyber	Trident CyberBlade
Trident TGUI	Trident TVGA	Unsupported VGA compatible
VidTech FastMax P20	VideoExcel AGP 740	VideoLogic GrafixStar
ViewTop PCI	ViewTop ZeusL 8MB	Voodoo Banshee (generic)
Voodoo3 (generic)	WD 90C24 (laptop)	WD 90C24A or 90C24A2 (laptop)
Weitek P9100 (generic)	WinFast	XGA-1 (ISA bus)
XGA-2 (ISA bus)		

As you can see, there are several supported video cards (although I believe this to be just a short list). Many of these cards are very old — such as the Trident 8900, which supports only the most basic video settings. Others, such as the Diamond Stealth III, are newer and employ 3-D technology used primarily in games and 3-D modeling applications.

Network card manufacturers have picked up on the fact that many people are now using Linux and are therefore beginning to support the operating system with drivers. Many of the generic cards use the NE2000 compatible chipset, which may work with Linux. The more popular generic manufacturers, such as D-Link, now support Linux with their own drivers found at their Web sites. Most of the name-brand cards are supported (including 3Com, SMC, Intel, and others).

SCSI cards comprise a breed of their own, with fewer people using SCSI because of the overall expense of the drives and devices. I have always found the Adaptec line of cards worth the expense for compatibility. If you are considering the purchase of a SCSI device and card, check with the manufacturer for any accompanying support. Many of the RAID controllers are SCSI, although a few IDE versions are starting to emerge.

Finding Linux-Compatible Laptops

One comment that echoes from Linux users of all distributions is the difficulty of configuring the hardware on a laptop. Laptops are an unusual beast in that most of their hardware is integrated together — video, sound, and modems. Other devices include infrared (IR) port; PCMCIA devices like network adapters; SCSI; and modems. In some cases, these components may be slightly different from the desktop models. For example the video card on a laptop may use a different clock circuit or have limited capabilities specifically to work with the laptop.

Additionally, laptops use features such as power management, battery life monitors, and other functions specifically geared toward laptops. Debian offers many tools for laptop use, which you can include when you install the system. These applications are intermixed with the rest of the Debian packages.

Several resources are available specifically oriented for laptop use. Table 17-2 shows some of the laptop models used with Linux. Not all of these have worked with the Debian distribution specifically, but they have used Linux nonetheless. This list of laptop models comes from people who have installed some version of Linux on to them. Basically, if Linux could be loaded on the laptop, then Debian will likely work too. These models range from older 486 laptops to newer Pentium III laptops. Because there are so many laptops and each one has its own configuration, this section can only provide basic road signs to help guide you to a more helpful resource. Very new laptops may not be included in this list, but that does not mean that Debian will not work on the laptop.

Table 17-2
Linux-installable laptops

Manufacturer	Line	Models
Acer	Extensa	355, 367T, 368T, 390, 500T, 503T, 506T, 710TE, 711TE
Acer	TravelMate	312T, 330T, 340T, 502T, 510T, 511T, 512DX, 512T, 513T, 516TE, 518TX, 521TE, 524TXV, 600TER, 602TER, 721TX, 722TX, 732TE, 734TX
Acernote	Light	350PCX, 370PC, 372, 373
Compaq	Armada	1130, 1500C, 1520D, 1530D, 1540D, 1570, 1592, 1650, 1700, 1750, 1800T, 4120, 4131T, 6500, 7400, 7750MT, 7790DMT, 7800, E500, E700, M300, M700, V300
Compaq	Concerto	
Compaq	Contura	400c, 4/25c, Aero
Compaq	LTE Lite	4/25
Compaq	LTE Elite	4/40CX, 4/75
Compaq	LTE	5000, 5100, 5200, 5300
Compaq	Presario	305, 1000-Series, 1200-Series, 1600-Series, 1700T, 1800-Series, 1900-Series, XL-161
Compaq	Prosignia	162, 170
Dell	Inspiron	3000-Series, 5000, 7000, 7500
Dell	Latitude	433MC CP, M166ST, M233XT CPi, A366XT CPt, C333GT, C400GT CPi, D266XT CPt, V466GT Cpi, D266XT CPi, D300XT CPt, S500GT CS, CSx, LM, P-100 LM, P-133 LS, LT, LX4100, XP
Fujitsu	Lifebook	280Dx, 420D, 420D, 435DX, 500, 55T, 635T, 655TX, 690Tx, 731Tx, 735Dx, 755Tx, 765Dx, 790Tx, B110, B110, B110, B110, B112, B2130, C325, C350, C4110, C6320, C6330, C6535, E340, E342, E350, E6150, E6530, E, Series, L440, S4542
Fujitsu	LiteLine	C400DVD
Fujitsu		Milan
Fujitsu	FM-V	
Gateway 2000		Colorbook, Handbook 486 Liberty, Nomad 425DXL

Manufacturer	Line	Models
Gateway 2000		Colorbook, Handbook 486 Liberty, Nomad 425DXL
Gateway 2000	Solo	2100, 2150, 2200, 2200, 2300, 2500SE, 2500XL, 3100 Fireant, 3150 Fireant, 5100 LS, 5150, 5150SE, 5300, 9100, 9100, 9150, 9150, 9150, 9300, 9300, 9300E, 9300XL
Hitachi		C100T
Hitachi	Visionbook	Plus, 5280 Pro, 6930 Pro, 7000 Pro, 7560 Pro, 7580 Traveler
HP	Omnibook	XE, XE2, 600, 800, 800CT, 900, 900B, 3000 CTX, 3100, 4000C, 4000CT, 4100, 4150, 5500, 5500CT, 5700, 5700 CT, 6000, 7100
HP	Pavillion	3100, 3100, 3150, 3190, 3250, 3270, 3330, 3390
IBM	Thinkpad	230CS, 240, 310ED, 350, 360CX, 365XD, 380D, 380ED, 385CD, 385XD, 390, 500, 560, 570, 570E, 600, 700, 701, 750, 755C, 760, 765L, 770, A20m, A20m, A20p
IBM	Thinkpad i	1200, 1300, 1400, 1411, 1412, 1420, 1422, 1441, 1450, 1451, 1452, 1460, 1472, 1480, 1560, 1720, 1721, T20, X20
Micron		GoBook, Transport, TREK2
NEC	Ready	120LT, 330T, 340T
NEC	Versa	LX, LXi, FX, 2430CD, 2635CD, 2650CDT, 4200, 6030X, 6050MMX, 6200MMX, SX/440
Panasonic	Let's Note	CF-L1S, CF-Mini
Panasonic		CF-35, CF-41, CF-63, CF-71
Sharp	Actius	A100, A150, A250, A280, A800
Sharp	Mebius	5600
Sharp		PC-8650II, PC-8660, PC-8800, PC-9020
Sony	Vaio	PCG-505, 505F, 505TR, 505TX, 550, 705C, 707C, 737, 745, 747, 747, 748, 808, 838, C1F, C1X, C1XD, C1XG/BP, C1XS, F, series, F707, N505VE, N505X, SR1K, XG-18, XG-19, XG-28, XG-9, Z505FA, Z505HE, Z505JS, Z505R, Z505RX, Z505S, Z505SX, Z600NE, Z600RE, Z600TEK

Continued

Table 17-2 (continued)

Manufacturer	Line	Models
Texas Instruments	Extensa	355, 390, 560CD, 570CD, 570CDT, 575CD, 670CDT
Texas Instruments	TravelMate	4000M, 6030
Toshiba		T1900S, T1910CS, T2000SXe, T2100CS, T2105CDS, T2105CDS, T3300SL, T4500, T4600, T4700, T4800CT, T4850
Toshiba	Libretto	30, 50CT, 50CT, 50CT, 50CT, 50CT, 60, 70, 70CT, 100CT, 100CT, 110CT, SS1000
Toshiba	Portege	3010CT, 3010CT, 3015CT, 3015CT, 3110CT, 320CT, 3400, 3440, 3600CT, 7000CT, 7010CDT, 7020CT, 7140CT, 7200CT
Toshiba	Satellite	100CS, 100CS, 110CS, 1605, 1620CDS, 1640CDT, 1670CDS, 200CDS, 205CDS, 230CX, 2000-Series, 300CDT, 310CDT, 315CDS, 320CDS, 320CDT, 330CDS, 335CDS, 330CDS, 400CS, 410CS, 415CS, 425CDS, 430CDT, 440CDX, 460CDT, 480CDT, 490CDT, 490CDT, 4000-Series, 700CT, 7020CT
Toshiba	Tecra	500CDT, 530CDT, 550CDT, 660CDT, 710CDT, 750CDT, 8000, 8100
UMAX	Actionbook	318T, 333T, 333T, 520T, 530T
Winbook		FX, XL, XLi, XL2, XP, XP5

Check out www.cs.utexas.edu/users/kharker/linux-laptop for links to Web pages that describe the specifics for setting up some of these laptops. Hopefully, you can get the help you need for your specific laptop model.

You can also find help at www.linuxdoc.org/HOWTO/Laptop-HOWTO.html.

Adding Hardware to Your Linux System

With the onset of hands-free installation tools, automatic hardware detection, and other conveniences in operating systems, the knowledge of manually setting up and configuring hardware is slipping with this new generation of Linux users. Despite these conveniences, an administrator must know how to work with the hardware. The three most common areas in which you may need to replace or add hardware are storage media, video cards, and network cards.

Hard drives and CD-ROM drives

Because hard drives, CD-ROMs, and other drives consist of moving parts, they are more prone to failure and thus need replacing more often. Drives using removable media, such as CD-ROMs and floppies, don't pose a problem when replaced with an equivalent device. However, when it comes to hard drives in which live data is stored, this process is a little more difficult.

To add one or more drives to your current system, follow these steps:

1. Physically add the hardware to your system per the manufacturer's instructions.

2. Once you add the hardware, boot in as root to make the core changes. The file that you will change is /etc/fstab, which mounts the devices automatically at startup. If you wish, you can still add the device to the file but mount it into the filesystem on demand later.

3. Open the /etc/fstab file with a text editor and add a new line for each drive device you need to add. The line consists of the following:

```
filesystem  mountpoint  type options dump pass
```

   - The *filesystem* component refers to the device. IDE hard drives start with hd followed by the drive (a, b, c, or d), and then the partition number on the drive. The second partition for the slave drive on the primary controller is represented as /dev/hdb2. SCSI drives are similar; but their designation is sd, with each controller having a letter, and the device on the chain having a number. Therefore, the SCSI device four on the first controller is /dev/sda4.

   - The *mountpoint* represents the point in the filesystem where you can find the contents of the device. If this is a directory under root (/), be sure to create it using mkdir before trying to mount it.

   - The *type* indicates the format of the device. Linux uses ext2, while Windows uses vfat.

   - For *option*, use options available with the mount command. You can find more information about mount in Chapter 3.

   - *dump* indicates whether the filesystem gets backed up with the dump command.

   - *pass* indicates the number of passes the filesystem gets checked for errors at startup.

Here is a sample of the filesystem table:

```
# /etc/fstab: static filesystem information.
#
```

```
# <filesystem> <mount point>    <type>  <options>                       <dump> <pass>
/dev/hda4       /               ext2    defaults,errors=remount-ro         0      1
/dev/hda6       none            swap    sw                                 0      0
proc            /proc           proc    defaults                           0      0
/dev/fd0        /floppy         auto    defaults,user,noauto               0      0
/dev/cdrom      /cdrom          iso9660 defaults,ro,user,noauto            0      0
```

You can see that the first device (/dev/hda) is the main drive and that it mounts to become the root (/dev/hda4) of the filesystem. The second device uses the same drive but a different partition (/dev/hda6) to become the swap partition. The last two devices are the floppy and CD-ROM. Notice that these devices use removable media, yet are still listed in the filesystem table file.

The last line of the /etc/fstab file, shown above, uses /dev/cdrom instead of /dev/hdd. /dev/cdrom is not an actual device, instead, /dev/cdrom is a symbolic link to /dev/hdd as seen here:

```
$ ls -l /dev/cdrom
lrwxrwxrwx    1 root      root            3 Oct 15 08:41 /dev/cdrom -> hdd
```

You can add as many drives as your system can physically handle.

Replacing failed devices such as hard drives takes a little more effort. You can approach this from a couple of different directions. First, you can replace the failed drive and then restore the entire filesystem from a full backup. You can also install the new drive, reload the operating system from scratch, and then restore the configuration and data files from a backup copy. You can also install the new drive as the second drive, copy the content of the first to the second, and then replace the first drive with the second.

Tip   Because loading Debian GNU/Linux takes little effort, I only back up critical files like specific configuration files, personal data, and customized scripts and programs. You need to do backups routinely, and then save them onto a tape, another hard drive, or some other form of media storage. See Chapter 18 for more details on backing up a system.

Changing video cards

You may never need to change a video card on your system. However, you can do it if you want to upgrade or change video cards. Aside from the obvious physical installation per the manufacturer's instructions, you need to change the configuration for the X Windows system. You can either run the X configuration utility or manually change the configuration file.

First you must install the X server package for the new card. To make sure the X server is available when you configure the card, install all the X servers if you have room. Multiple X servers can be installed, but only one will run at a time. Then, to change the configuration using the utility, run the program from a command line:

```
# /usr/X11R6/bin/XF86Setup
```

You can then go through the graphical interface and select the new card from the list. After you finish the configuration, save the settings. Now you're ready to use a graphical interface again.

The manual process is much more difficult and can get you in trouble if you're not careful. You can learn more about the installing and configuring the X environment in Chapter 4.

Adding and changing network cards

You may never need to replace a network card because of failure, but you may want to upgrade an older 10BaseT card to a 100BaseTx card. There are two aspects to adding or replacing a network card. The first is getting the card to work with the kernel. The other is configuring the card for the network.

Making the card work with the kernel means that you need to add the appropriate module (driver) to the kernel. If you are replacing or adding an identical card that previously worked with the system, there is little to do because the kernel already has the module loaded. If you need to install a new module, follow these steps:

1. Identify the module that works with the network card. Using the Kingston 120Tx network adapter as an example, it needs the RealTech module rtl8139.o. The Kingston Web site specifies this module for Linux.

2. Install the card into the computer per the manufacturer's instructions.

3. Change to the /lib/modules/*kernelversion*/net directory, and load the module into the kernel with the isnmod command:

   ```
   # cd /lib/modules/kernelversion/net
   # insmod ./rtl8139.o
   ```

   Replace rtl8139.o for the name of your module. You can then confirm that the module is loaded using lsmod. You should see something like this:

   ```
   # lsmod
   Module            Size  Used by
   rtl8139          11496    0  (unused)
   ip_masq_vdolive   1368    0  (unused)
   ip_masq_user      2536    0  (unused)
   ip_masq_quake     1352    0  (unused)
   ip_masq_irc       1592    0  (unused)
   ip_masq_raudio    2936    0  (unused)
   ip_masq_ftp       2456    0
   serial           19564    0  (autoclean)
   3c59x            18656    1
   unix             10212    8  (autoclean)
   ```

4. After the module is loaded, add the module to the /etc/modules file so it gets loaded at boot time. Here is an example of what the modules file looks like:

```
# /etc/modules: kernel module to load at boot time.
#
# This file should contain the names of kernel modules that
are
# to be loaded at boot time, one per line. Comments begin
with
# a #, and everything on the line after them are ignored.
rtl8139
autofs
vfat
usb
```

If you don't receive any error while installing the module, then you likely have working device. This concludes the portion of the installation in which you have to get the device to work with the kernel. Next, you need the device to communicate on the network:

1. To get the network device to work on the network, you need to configure the device. Edit the /etc/network/interfaces file by adding something like this:

```
iface eth1 inet static
        address 192.168.0.10
        netmask 255.255.255.224
        network 192.168.0.0
```

This example shows that the Kingston card is a second card (as noted by eth1) that uses a static IP address. The other information about the card follows the first line. Values for gateway and broadcast are not needed for any additional cards.

2. After the information about the card is added to the file, restart the networking services like so:

```
# /etc/init.d/networking restart
Reconfiguring network interfaces: done.
```

3. Test to make sure that the interface is loaded by using ifconfig. You should see all the networking devices:

```
# ifconfig
eth0      Link encap:Ethernet  HWaddr 00:60:97:C2:DD:AF
          inet addr:192.168.120.27  Bcast: 192.168.120.31  Mask:255.255.255.224
          UP BROADCAST RUNNING MULTICAST  MTU:1500  Metric:1
          RX packets:47484 errors:0 dropped:0 overruns:0 frame:0
          TX packets:2179 errors:0 dropped:0 overruns:0 carrier:0
          collisions:0 txqueuelen:100
          Interrupt:5 Base address:0xb800
```

```
eth1      Link encap:Ethernet  HWaddr 00:C0:F0:68:95:1E
          inet addr:192.168.0.10  Bcast:192.168.0.255  Mask:255.255.255.224
          UP BROADCAST RUNNING MULTICAST  MTU:1500  Metric:1
          RX packets:0 errors:0 dropped:0 overruns:0 frame:0
          TX packets:0 errors:0 dropped:0 overruns:0 carrier:0
          collisions:0 txqueuelen:100
          Interrupt:11 Base address:0xb000

lo        Link encap:Local Loopback
          inet addr:127.0.0.1  Mask:255.0.0.0
          UP LOOPBACK RUNNING  MTU:3924  Metric:1
          RX packets:17484 errors:0 dropped:0 overruns:0 frame:0
          TX packets:17484 errors:0 dropped:0 overruns:0 carrier:0
          collisions:0 txqueuelen:0
```

You can perform other tests — such as pinging a device on the network — to verify that everything is working. You can find more information about network trouble-shooting in Chapter 5.

Adding Peripheral Devices

Some devices do not readily fall into a familiar category, such as IDE hard drives. I must address these extra devices separately. When I first started computing, a *peripheral device* meant a printer. Now it includes anything from that printer to tape drives to a digital camera. There are far more devices than can adequately be covered in this book. Therefore, the following sections describe two of the more popular devices: Iomega drives and scanners.

Iomega drives (Zip, Jaz, and so on)

When the Zip disk was introduced some years ago, many people started using it because of its larger storage capacity. As more people migrated to the Zip disk, it became a standard piece of hardware. The majority of individuals who use Windows also use the Windows drivers that Iomega provides. This left those in the Linux world out in the cold. Iomega still does not support drivers for the Linux operating system. However, third-party drivers are available on the Iomega Web site. The drivers, source, and instructions for installation are available at www.iomega.com/support/documents/10408.html.

Iomega devices come in three basic forms: parallel, ATAPI, and SCSI. As of version 2.2.14 of the Linux kernel, modules are available for these devices because they are included with Debian 2.2. The parallel devices need the parport.o, parport_pc.o, and vfat.o modules in addition to the module for the Zip drives. There are two modules for the Zip drive based on the age of the drive. ppa.o is for older Zip drives (VPI0), and imm.o is for the newer models (VPI1). This change took place some time around 1998.

The ATAPI (also known as IDE) and SCSI devices should work immediately because you should have hard drives using the same modules these devices use. To get a clue as to the devices, look through the kernel boot logs for the identification of the devices. The following example shows a portion of the dmesg text. You can see that the SCSI Jaz drive is detected, and its device and the partition information are listed.

```
scsi0 : Adaptec AHA274x/284x/294x (EISA/VLB/PCI-Fast SCSI) 5.1.31/3.2.4
       <Adaptec AHA-294X Ultra SCSI host adapter>
scsi : 1 host.
(scsi0:0:4:0) Synchronous at 8.0 Mbyte/sec, offset 15.
  Vendor: YAMAHA    Model: CRW4416S         Rev: 1.0g
  Type:   CD-ROM                            ANSI SCSI revision: 02
Detected scsi CD-ROM sr0 at scsi0, channel 0, id 4, lun 0
(scsi0:0:5:0) Synchronous at 10.0 Mbyte/sec, offset 15.
  Vendor: iomega    Model: jaz 1GB          Rev: H$70
  Type:   Direct-Access                     ANSI SCSI revision: 02
Detected scsi removable disk sda at scsi0, channel 0, id 5, lun 0
scsi : detected 1 SCSI cdrom 1 SCSI disk total.
sr0: scsi3-mmc drive: 16x/16x writer cd/rw xa/form2 cdda tray
SCSI device sda: hdwr sector= 512 bytes. Sectors= 2091050 [1021 MB] [1.0 GB]
sda: Write Protect is off
Partition check:
 sda: sda1
 hda: hda1 hda2
```

Cross-Reference For more information about installing modules, compiling modules, or compiling the kernel, turn to Chapter 15.

Scanners

Scanners are a different breed of external peripheral device. These devices no longer pose a problem because of the converter tool called *SANE (Scanner Access Now Easy)*. Installing SANE (the package name is sane) onto your system provides a number of configuration files for the more popular scanning devices located in /etc/sane.d/ (ranging from HP to Umax scanners). It also includes the QuickCam devices as scanner input.

You can also find instructions in the /etc/sane.d/saned.conf file for setting up remote network scanning, which gives the entire network access to a single device.

Printing

Printers are just as susceptible to compatibility issues as are other devices. Traditionally, UNIX (and therefore Linux) used PostScript as output intended for a laser printer. Printers that support PostScript are more costly than the inexpensive varieties available to the average consumer. For these printers, an Open Source interpreter called *GhostScript* comes into play. It converts the PostScript into something more palatable for lower-end printers. Table 17-3 shows both inkjet and laser printers supported by GhostScript.

Table 17-3
Linux-compatible printers

Inkjet printers

Manufacturer	Models
Canon	BJC-70, BJC-210, BJC-250*, BJC-600, BJC-610, BJC-620, BJC-800, BJC-4000, BJC-4100, BJC-4200, BJC-4300*, BJC-4400*
Citizen	ProJet IIc
Digital	DECwriter 520ic*
Epson	Stylus Color, Stylus Color 400, Stylus Color 440, Stylus Color 460, Stylus Color 500, Stylus Color 600, Stylus Color 640, Stylus Color 660, Stylus Color 670*, Stylus Color 740, Stylus Color 760*, Stylus Color 800, Stylus Color 850, Stylus Color 860, Stylus Color 900, Stylus Color 1160, Stylus Color 1500, Stylus Color 1520, Stylus Color 3000, Stylus Color I, Stylus Color PRO, Stylus Photo, Stylus Photo 700, Stylus Photo 720*, Stylus Photo 750, Stylus Photo 870, Stylus Photo 1200, Stylus Photo 1270, Stylus Photo EX
Hewlett Packard	710c*, 2000C, 2500C, DesignJet 3500CP, DeskJet 400, DeskJet 420C, DeskJet 500C, DeskJet 540, DeskJet 550C, DeskJet 560C, DeskJet 600, DeskJet 648C*, DeskJet 840C*, DeskJet 895Cse*, DeskJet 1200C, DeskJet 1600C, DeskJet 1600CM, PaintJet*, PaintJet XL*, PaintJet XL300*
Lexmark	Optra Color 40, Optra Color 45
Olivetti	JP350S*, JP450*, JP470*
Samsung	SI-630A*
Tektronix	4696*, 4697*
Xerox	DocuPrint C20

Laser printers

Manufacturer	Models
Apple	12/640ps, LaserWriter 16/600*, LaserWriter IINTX*, LaserWriter IIg, LaserWriter Select 360*
Brother	HL-4Ve, HL-8, HL-10V, HL-10h, HL-630, HL-660, HL-720, HL-730, HL-760, HL-820, HL-1020, HL-1040, HL-1070*, HL-1250, HL-1260, HL-1270N, HL-1660e, HL-2060

Continued

Table 17-3 *(continued)*

Laser printers

Manufacturer	Models
Canon	GP 335, GP 405, LBP-4+, LBP-4U, LBP-8A1, LBP-430, LBP-1260, LBP-1760, LIPS-III
Digital	LN03*, LN07*
Epson	Action Laser II, Action Laser 1100*, EPL-5200*, LP 8000
Fujitsu	PrintPartner 10V*, PrintPartner 16DV*, PrintPartner 20W*, PrintPartner 8000*
Heidelberg	Digimaster 9110*
Hewlett Packard	LaserJet 2 w/PS*, LaserJet 2D, LaserJet 2P, LaserJet 2P Plus, LaserJet 3, LaserJet 3D, LaserJet 3P w/PS, LaserJet 4 Plus, LaserJet 4L, LaserJet 4M, LaserJet 4ML*, LaserJet 4P, LaserJet 4Si, LaserJet 4V, LaserJet 5, LaserJet 5L*, LaserJet 5M*, LaserJet 5MP*, LaserJet 5P*, LaserJet 6, LaserJet 6L*, LaserJet 6MP*, LaserJet 1100*, LaserJet 2100, LaserJet 2100M, LaserJet 4050*, LaserJet 5000, LaserJet 8000, LaserJet 8100, LaserJet Plus*, LaserJet Series II*, Mopier 240*, Mopier 320*
Hitachi	DDP 70 (with MicroPress)*
IBM/Lexmark	4019*, 4029 10P*, Page Printer 3112*
Imagen (now QMS/Minolta)	ImPress*
Infotec	Infotec 4651 MF*
Kodak	DigiSource 9110*
Kyocera	F-3300, FS-600*, FS-600 (KPDL-2)*, FS-680*, FS-800*, FS-1200*, FS-1700+*, FS-1750*, FS-3750*, P-2000*
Lexmark	4039 10plus, Optra E*, Optra E+*, Optra E310, Optra E312, Optra Ep*, Optra K 1220, Optra M410, Optra M412, Optra R+*, Optra S 1250*, Optra S 1855*, Optra Se 3455*, Optra T610, Optra T612, Optra T614, Optra T616, Optra W810, Valuewriter 300*
Minolta	PagePro 6*, PagePro 6e*, PagePro 6ex*, PagePro 8*
NEC	SilentWriter LC 890*, SilentWriter2 S60P*, SilentWriter2 model 290*, SuperScript 660i*, SuperScript 1800
Oce	3165*
Okidata	OL 410e, OL 600e*, OL 610e/PS, OL 800, OL 810e/PS, OL400ex, OL810ex, OL820*, OL830Plus, Okipage 6e, Okipage 6ex*, Okipage 8p, Okipage 10e, Okipage 10ex, Okipage 12i, Okipage 20DXn

Laser printers

Manufacturer	Models
Olivetti	PG 306*
Panasonic	KX-P4410*, KX-P4450*, KX-P5400*, KX-PS600*
Personal Computer Products, Inc.	1030*
QMS	2425 Turbo EX*, LPK-100*
Ricoh	4081*, 4801*, 6000*, Aficio 220*, Aficio AP2000
Samsung	ML-85*, ML-4600*, ML-5000a*, ML-6000/6100*, ML-7000/7000P/7000N*, ML-7050*, QL-5100A*, QL-6050*
Sharp	AR-161*
Star Micronics	LS-04
Tally	MT908*
Xerox	4045 XES*, DocuPrint 4508, DocuPrint N17, DocuPrint N32*, Document Centre 400*

* Some information for marked printers has not been verified.

If you don't see your printer in this table, go to www.linuxprinting.org/printer_list.cgi and look up the printer you use. It should tell you if you have a compatible printer and what driver to use. It also indicates whether you have a Windows-type printer, in which case you may need to go to www.sourceforge.net/projects/pnm2ppa/. The pnm2ppa GhostScript print filter enables HP DeskJet 710C, 712C, 720C, 722C, 820Cse, 820Cxi, 1000Cse, or 1000Cxi printers to print PostScript Level 2.

Offline printing

Occasionally, you may need to print when a printer is not available. This is called *offline printing*. When you first install the Debian system, basic printing services (lpr) also get installed. Running as a service in the background, the lpd line printer spooler daemon constantly waits for a program to print. It then sends the print job to a queue where the print job waits for the availability of a printer. Three main programs manage the printer queues:

✦ lpq — The lpq program checks the queue for a listing of the print jobs waiting to print. When you use lpq by itself, it shows all waiting jobs. On larger systems with several people and printers, this list can be rather large. To help filter out some of the jobs, use options such as -Pprinter to list those jobs for a specific *printer* name. You can also filter by user name (for example, use lpq jo to see all of Jo's print jobs). The –l option displays a very verbose description of the print jobs.

✦ lprm—On occasion, you may need to remove a job from a queue. You can do this with the lprm command for all jobs sent to a printer or for a specific print job. The following example removes a specific job. First, the print job number is identified by listing the current print jobs; then it is removed by specifying the specific job number.

```
% lpq -l

1st:jo                                  [job #013]
          (standard input)              100 bytes
% lprm 13
```

✦ lpc—An administrative tool, lpc controls the queues and the jobs in each queue. With this command, you can enable or disable specific printers and queues or rearrange the order in a queue. Used without any parameters, the program responds with an interactive prompt in which the first option is interpreted as the command and the following options are interpreted as parameters to the command. Here is what you see:

```
# lpc
lpc> ?
Commands may be abbreviated.  Commands are:

abort    enable  disable help    restart status  topq     ?
clean    exit    down    quit    start   stop    up
lpc>
```

The next generation of the lpr group of print tools is lprng, which offers enhanced versions of the same commands and features. You still use the same three command tools to control and manage the print queues, but with more features for each command. You can go to www.lprng.org to find out more about lprng.

Some of the enhanced features in the lpc administrative tool include redirecting printing to other printers, restarting printing, and reprinting a job. The other tools, lpr and lprm, have additional options for more flexibility as well. Read the man pages on these commands to learn more about them.

For those looking for a graphical way to view and manage print queues, use printop. This interface employs the scripting language called tk, and requires lprng. You can find it among the list of Debian packages. As you can see from Figure 17-1, this tool offers all the basic functions you need.

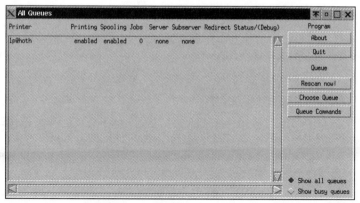

Figure 17-1: A graphical means of managing printers using printop

Setting up printer queues

When using a printer, you need to set up queues for each printer. Associated with each queue is specific information, such as which device the printer is connected to, the spool location that holds the jobs, where to write the log files, and so on. The file containing the information about the print queues is /etc/printcap, which looks like this:

```
# /etc/printcap: printer capability database. See printcap(5).
# You can use the filter entries df, tf, cf, gf etc. for
# your own filters. See /etc/filter.ps, /etc/filter.pcl and
# the printcap(5) manual page for further details.

lp|Generic dot-matrix printer entry:\
        :lp=/dev/lp0:\
        :sd=/var/spool/lpd/lp:\
        :af=/var/log/lp-acct:\
        :lf=/var/log/lp-errs:\
        :pl#66:\
        :pw#80:\
        :pc#150:\
        :mx#0:\
        :sh:

# rlp|Remote printer entry:\
#        :lp=:\
#        :rm=remotehost:\
#        :rp=remoteprinter:\
#        :sd=/var/spool/lpd/remote:\
#        :mx#0:\
#        :sh:
```

Notice that commented out at the bottom is a sample for configuring a remote printer. Remote printers are set up on other Linux systems (or other server operating systems) for network printing, thus allowing multiple machines to access one or more printers scattered across a network.

Apsfilter configuration tool

Reading through the `printcap` file just shown can be confusing. A tool to help automatically configure the `printcap` file is `apsfilter`. This tool identifies the converters and filters installed on your system, walks you through selecting the driver, identifies the location of the local printer, and modifies the `/etc/printcap` file with the settings.

`apsfilter` comes in a Debian package and runs the configuration script `apsfilterconfig` after `dselect` installs the package. Answering the questions for each of the screens, you eventually end up at the main menu seen in Figure 17-2. This main menu enables you to select the GhostScript-compatible printer (listed in Table 17-3) and the local device to which the printer is connected. You can then test the configuration to make sure you've selected the right drivers and devices by trying to print a page.

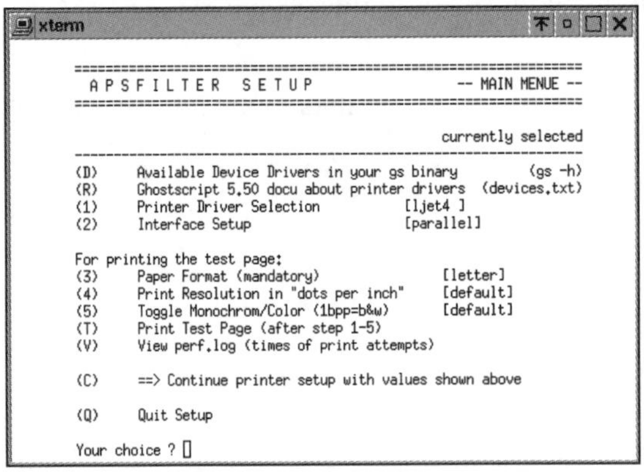

Figure 17-2: apsfilterconfig's main setup menu enables you to configure and test printer settings.

When you are satisfied that the settings are correct, you can continue the printer setup. The script asks more questions and adds the configuration settings to the selected printer's `/etc/printcap` file. The script comments out default settings in the `printcap` file and adds the new settings. You can then rerun the `apsfilter` configuration file later to add more printers.

Note The drawback to `apsfilter` is that no provision is made for remote printers. An alternative utility for configuring printers is Red Hat's graphical interface `printtool`. This tool not only enables you to configure local printers, but it also allows configuration of remote printers (including those hosted through Samba and NetWare). You can find this RPM package at `rpmfind.net/linux/RPM`, where you can also search for the `printtool` package. Depending on the version you choose, the selected package may depend on other packages. The main packages are GhostScript (`gs`), `tcl`, `tk`, `lpr`, `lprng`, and `/usr/bin/wish` (which comes with `tk`). You need to install the Debian packaged `rpm` program to `printtool`.

Summary

This chapter covered a lot of ground where hardware is concerned. There are so many variables to consider for each device. Add to that the plethora of hardware devices and you have an infinite list of possibilities. Unless a device falls under a known standard, as in the case of IDE hard drives, you need a special driver to make the device work with the Linux system. If some programmer does not create a drive and the manufacturer does not support the product with Linux, then there is little for you to do.

Some products, known as Win-products, only work with Windows. You should avoid these if you ever plan to use them with Linux. Little is being done to enable these devices to work with the Linux operating system.

Adding and replacing hardware in Linux is a snap as long as you have the appropriate module (driver) for the device. Once the module is in place, you need to do very little to get it to work.

Printers, like any other piece of hardware, depend on compatibility. Printers don't need module drivers, but they need a printer driver in order to interpret the information coming from Linux applications — much of which is converted through GhostScript to the particular printer device.

✦   ✦   ✦

Backups

Debian GNU/Linux has proven itself to be one of the more stable, secure Linux systems available. With a reputation like this, users can easily develop a false sense that this system is invincible. One day, this false sense of security can come back to bite you.

Unfortunately for some, it takes a devastating event to wake them to the reality that proper precautions can let them rest easy at night knowing that they can recover from the worst events. We rely heavily on computer systems and the supporting infrastructure to perform our daily tasks without even realizing the impact that the failure of those systems would have on us.

This chapter goes into the detail you need to prevent the catastrophic loss or corruption of your system data — or even an important file. It covers methods, strategies, and software used to back up and recover your data.

Planning for Failure

Once you have your system set up with Debian GNU/Linux, you undoubtedly have spent more than a couple of hours getting it just the way you want it. Regardless of the implementation of Debian, the environment, hardware used, and access to the system by others, you can still lose data. This loss can come not only from hardware failure, but also from viruses, accidental file deletion, or a compromised (cracked) system.

To avoid data loss, you must first take some steps to plan for failure. Larger companies have disaster recovery policies because loss of data can cost these companies millions in time and resources. Companies regulated by the government, such as pharmaceutical companies are required by law to have a backup and recovery policy in place. Some institutions even require the archival of data for months and years. The point is to have a plan.

✦ ✦ ✦ ✦

In This Chapter

Planning for system failure

Picking the appropriate backup model

Selecting the tools for backing up

Recovering from boot problems

✦ ✦ ✦ ✦

The strategy of your plan can be straightforward. Here is an example:

✦ **Document your system** — This includes the hardware configuration, hardware components, filesystem layout, and so on. I keep a three-ring binder with this information on each system. This binder acts as an operator's manual, revision log, and history keeper all rolled into one.

✦ **Have a recovery disk available** — When your system is down, it is very difficult to create a recovery disk. You can even use the installation CD-ROM to recover a system. Keep a recovery or boot disk with your system. I keep a recovery disk in my binder, along with the documentation.

✦ **Perform regular backups of your system** — Whether a large corporation, a small business, or just a single personal computer, regular backups are critical. You cannot recover wanted data unless you first back it up.

✦ **Maintain off-site media storage** — An important part of a backup and recovery policy is keeping a recent copy of backed up media at an off-site location in the event of a natural disaster such as fire, earthquake, or flood.

As you can see, planning for disaster can be straightforward. As you continue through this chapter, you learn in more detail how to perform the necessary steps to back up your system.

Choosing a Backup Technique

Now that you know that backups are essential, how should you perform them? Although making a backup copy of every file on your system is a safe backup strategy, not every file changes every day. Some never change. There are four backup techniques to consider: full, incremental, mirroring, and through a network.

✦ **The full backup** — A *full backup* is a complete copy of all the files on a disk or partition. From a full backup, you can restore to a new disk the entire operating system and all its files. You can use this technique regularly or periodically, depending on the frequency of changes to the system and the volume of data to store.

✦ **The incremental backup** — An *incremental backup* copies only those files that have changed or been added since the last backup. Generally, you employ this technique more often as an interim between full backups because it takes less time to complete and uses less backup storage.

✦ **Mirroring a disk** — *Disk mirroring,* as its name implies, takes the contents of one disk and copies it to another disk. This is an excellent technique for backing up data when you don't have time for your system to be out of commission. You can do this through software as well as through the appropriate hardware. See the following Note on Redundant Array of Independent Disks (RAID).

✦ **Backing up over a network** — When machines are part of a network, you can share resources from one computer through that network. Networked computers can utilize each of the listed backup techniques. Mirroring disks over a network reduces down time. When one system fails, you simply bring the mirror online. Full and incremental backups allow the use of fewer tape drives for a site by sharing those resources.

Note

You can mirror disks in one of two ways: either through software that runs periodically or through hardware known as Redundant Array of Independent Disks (RAID). There are several levels of RAID, although the two pertinent to this chapter are RAID 1 and RAID 5.

RAID 1 uses the hardware controller to write the same information to two identical disks at once. If one fails, then the other disk responds immediately. The system must be shut down for you to replace the failed drive, but you can do it at a non-critical time.

RAID 5 writes the data to at least three disks. If any one of the disks fails, the other two contain the information of the lost disk. You can replace the failed disk; the data originally on the disk is replicated to the new disk from the other two. This produces no down time.

Note that, in most cases, a combination of backup techniques is generally your best strategy.

Knowing what to back up

In the case of a full backup, the issue of what to back up is obvious — everything. However, this may not be possible every time because of limited storage space on the backup device, like with a floppy disk. You should back up only those files that you cannot replace by reinstalling the software. You also should regularly back up files that are original creations or modifications of the originals, such as modified configuration files, letters, graphical creations, and so on.

You can look at key directories to help determine the importance of what to back up. Be sure to check the following directories, from which you are likely to back up the majority of your critical data:

✦ /home — The home directory holds the data for each of the user accounts configured on your system. It holds users' personal data, their customized settings, and anything else each person may deem important.

✦ /etc — Any software installed on the system has configuration files saved in this directory. This also includes the account information for the user accounts. Losing this information can result in a lot of work for an administrator when recreating all the accounts for the users of the system, let alone when reconfiguring all the software. You can reload the software itself, but the configuration takes time.

✦ /var—Most of the core software uses this directory as a data repository. This includes the database of installed applications for Debian. Many mail servers use this directory to store mail. In addition, the log history for the system activity is stored here.

✦ /(custom)—Some system administrators prefer to customize the directory structure based on the purpose for the server. For instance, administrators of Web servers commonly create /www to store Web pages and related data. Therefore, you cannot easily reproduce this. You should add any directories created outside of the default directories to your list of data to back up.

Knowing what to back up with caution

Granted, a full backup includes all directories, but you should approach some directories with caution. Certain directories are acceptable to include for a full backup, but restoring them can have serious side effects. So, if you choose to make a backup of an entire filesystem, here are some points to consider before you proceed.

✦ /proc—This directory contains the core information used by the kernel. It is dynamic data that the kernel changes constantly. A full backup takes a snapshot of the system at a given point in time, so restoring this data to a new drive works great when recovering from a failed hard drive or making a duplicate system. The problem comes about when trying to restore a partial file that includes the /proc directory path.

✦ /tmp—When the system runs, non-critical data and files occasionally need to be stored temporarily in this directory. Therefore, backing up this directory eats up valuable backup storage space. If storage is abundant, then there is no harm in including this data.

✦ CD-ROMs, floppy drives and remote filesystems—When performing a complete backup of your system, this involves all mounted drives including CD-ROMs. You cannot change the data on a CD-ROM; therefore, there is no need to back it up. You should unmount these devices before executing a full backup. The same is true for floppy drives and any other mounted media. Also, backing up remote files that are backed up on a remote machine is another example of redundant data on storage. Unmounting these remote files also frees potential space for critical data.

✦ Devices and documentation—The documentation doesn't change after you install the software, so this is probably safe to skip when looking to save storage space. The documentation generally is stored in /usr/doc, and you can reload it with the software. Another example that doesn't change between installations is the device information found in /dev. This standard information is available when you reinstall the system.

✦ Duplicated data—With a network of a number of systems, you may choose to archive or mirror data from one system to another. Therefore, there may not be any reason to back up that data.

In most cases, the bottom line when selecting which data to back up is whether or not the data fits on the chosen medium.

Choosing adequate media

Every system and every environment requires different considerations when choosing a medium on which to back up its data. A person with a single computer has different needs than a company with several machines containing mission-critical data. Therefore, choosing how to back up these systems involves considering your needs.

Several forms of backup media are commonly used. Table 18-1 lists and compares the more commons forms of backup media. Following the table, I explain each medium type in more detail.

Table 18-1
Comparison of backup media

Medium	Capacity	Speed	Hardware cost	Medium cost
Tape	4-280GB	Medium to fast	$300–$9000	$30–$70
CD-R	640MB	Slow	$150	$1
CD-RW	640MB	Slow	$250	$4
Hard drive	2–180GB	Fast	$50–$1400	N/A
Floppy	1.44MB	Slow	$20	$0.25
Jaz	2GB	Fast	$340	$120
Zip	100–250MB	Slow	$100	$10–$20

Tape

The magnetic data storage tape is one of the computer industry's leading forms of backup media. The drives used for the tape backups may be a little more expensive than other devices, but the media used with the drive more than makes up for that expense. Tape drives and the corresponding media come in all styles, forms, and sizes. Most SCSI tape drives work with Linux, and many of the IDE versions are compatible as well with "SCSI emulation" turned on for the kernel.

Another attractive quality of tapes is their data-holding capacity. In a very small space, they can hold many gigabytes of data. For small systems, this may not be a concern; but for large sites, it can make all the difference in the world.

Tapes are also very well accepted as a backup medium with software supporting the devices. Much of the early software supports tape drives, so finding appropriate software to fit your needs is easy.

The tape media lends itself to making complete backups, backing up and restoring large chunks of data quickly. Each time you add data to a tape, it is added to the end of what you wrote last. Recovering files, on the other hand, is a long, arduous process that takes a lot of time when you do one file at a time. Because files are placed on the tape in sequential order, recovering random files can be a major drawback. The more frequently you perform a single file restore, the less desirable this medium looks.

CD-ROM

CD-ROMs are very affordable forms of backup media. The disks are cheap, and they hold enough data for most systems. The two forms of CDs are *writeable* and *rewriteable*. Both are limited to the amount of data they hold; however, the rewritable CD-ROM is reusable, which extends its life tremendously.

For smaller systems and individuals that wish to save only their vital data, CD-ROMs are an excellent choice. The media isn't very expensive as long as you don't have to make frequent backups. Software is also available specifically for doing backups on CD.

Restoring files from a CD-ROM is much quicker than tape because of its capability to randomly access files. In this case, a CD makes a great medium to back up frequently changing data such as document drafts, log histories from manufacturing equipment, and source code from programming projects in which making fast restores is important.

The major downfall with this medium is its low capacity. CD-ROMs only hold approximately 650MB. This, compared with some of the other options such as a hard drive, is very small.

Hard drive

As long as your equipment can hold an extra hard drive or two, invest in hard drives because they are fast and relatively inexpensive and they hold several gigabytes of data. This is the best choice when working with a mission-critical system. Hard drives are good when you can't afford to wait hours for a repair, restore, or rebuild of a system. Minutes of down time can cost you tons of money in lost sales revenue or data.

Hard drives can be removable in some manner, which enables you to replace the drives. Therefore, using hard drives increases the number of historical backup revisions. Non-removable drives fixed inside the case of a computer run the risk of losing all the data if something destroys the entire computer, as with a fire.

For data that you need to back up frequently throughout the day, the hard drive can serve you well. Using a hard drive increases the chances of the most recent data recovery. For very critical and not so critical environments where frequent backups and fast recovery are important, use RAID.

Tip As you look through the various forms of media, remember that you can also use a combination of backup media. For instance, use a hard drive mirror to provide the immediate recovery, and use tapes to provide the historical archive of backups. Combination methods can give you the best of both worlds.

Other media

There are several other forms of media to use as backup: high-density floppies, Iomega Zip and Jaz, and so on. You can use anything that holds data as backup media; the only hindrance is the hardware's capability to work with Linux. As long as the hardware can work with Linux, you can use its media.

Choosing a backup method

Generally speaking, the easiest method for backing up the data is to do it all. This is considered a full backup. However, full backups can take a long time and use resources that need to be available for other functions. Therefore, I recommend you perform the full backups on days or at times that the system isn't used as much (such as weekends or at night).

Your particular needs may not allow you to wait until a period of low system activity to make your backup. Therefore, you can use a combination of full and incremental techniques to accomplish the desired effect of more frequent backups.

Another twist to this method is the use of backup levels. *Levels* set priorities *(weights)* on the data that you back up. For instance, a full backup uses a level of zero (0). Every Sunday, a full backup is implemented. All other days of the week, an incremental backup with a level of one (1) is issued. Level 1 means that any data that you added or modified since the last level zero (0) backup is backed up. Therefore, a file that changes on Monday is backed up repeatedly the rest of the week.

To avoid backing up data that hasn't changed from one incremental backup to the next, you can increase the backup level each day. Table 18-2 shows an example schedule. This method lets data modified after Sunday's backup to be backed up on Monday. Then on Tuesday, any data that changed after Sunday's backup also is saved. On Wednesday, the data from Sunday through Tuesday is saved, and so on. This method enables you to back up essentially two sets of data—a full backup of the entire drive and data that changed or is new since the full backup. This method saves time, yet you don't lose any changes made through the week until the next full backup.

	Table 18-2 Example backup schedule		
Day	**Technique**	**Method**
Sunday	Full	Level 0
Monday	Incremental	Level 9
Tuesday	Incremental	Level 8
Wednesday	Incremental	Level 7
Thursday	Incremental	Level 6
Friday	Incremental	Level 5
Saturday	Incremental	Level 4

In addition to the one-week backup schedule, some larger sites also have a two-week cycle and a monthly backup cycle. These companies might archive backups for up to a year or more, depending on the value of their data.

Tip
Common practice as part of the disaster recovery plan includes securing a copy of the full system backup somewhere else. Usually this means taking the media off-site. Companies with large computer systems have a fireproof media vault where they store the archived data. Catastrophic disaster includes natural events as well (such as earthquakes, fires, floods, and tornadoes).

Selecting Your Backup and Restore Tools

After you choose the medium and method that best works for your environment, the next step is to pick software that goes along with the rest of your choices to complete the package. The available software varies from command-line-based tools with numerous options to highly graphical interfaces.

There are number of software choices to consider. Table 18-3 shows the programs included in this chapter, lists the media the programs work with, and describes the basic functions of the programs. This helps you select the best program for your needs. I then describe each program in detail later in the chapter.

Table 18-3
Backup tools and features

Program	Preferred medium	Description and feature
amanda	Tape	Client/server network backup system making use of dump or tar. Used for mass volumes of data sent to a single, high-capacity networked tape drive.
dump/restore	Any media except CD-ROM	Traditional command-line UNIX backup application. Works with any media, but designed to work with tapes.
KBackup	Any media except CD-ROM	This graphical (terminal) package is highly configurable.
mirrordir	Hard drive or remote system	Used to mirror drivers and directories. This is a very fast means of making a backup.
Taper	Any media except CD-ROM	This graphical (terminal) package reads backup tapes, regardless of format.
tar	Any media except CD-ROM	Commonly used command-line backup tool. Implemented with cron to make an automated backup process.

If you have a small system, you may even decide that performing manual backups of your data is all that you require. Administrators of larger systems want to automate as much of this process as possible. You can turn command-line applications into a script and include it with cron to set the frequency with which the automation takes place.

Cross-Reference For more information on cron and other automation techniques, see Chapter 9.

amanda

amanda, short for Advanced Maryland Automatic Network Disk Archiver, uses a network to back up the data to one tape drive. This is an excellent tool for large, networked environments. amanda comes in client/server portions and requires that one system, the server, contain a large storage disk. The clients simultaneously create backups and send them to the storage disk on the server. The server then sends each file one by one to the tape for backup.

amanda does some simple tape management to prevent writing over the wrong tape. When it recovers a file, amanda tells you what tape is needed and locates the file in the archive. It also supports tape changers through a generic interface. However, Amanda uses only one tape drive, making it a less desirable backup solution for systems with more than one tape drive.

amanda performs a pre-run error check on the server and the clients, and then sends an e-mail in the event that the check finds errors. It also reports backup results in full detail to administrators through e-mail.

Amanda requires three packages for proper functioning. amanda-comman should be installed on each machine you intend to backup. amanda-server should be installed on the machine with the tape drive. Finally, amanda-client should be installed on any machine for which you want a backup that does not have a tape drive. After the packages are installed, you are ready to use amanda. Table 18-4 shows the amanda command syntax and a description of each command.

Table 18-4
amanda commands

Command	Description
amdump config	Performs the actual dump to tape and sends an e-mail of the results. In the event that a tape cannot be written to, the backups are sent to a holding disk. config is the main directory in /etc/amanda where the configuration files are kept. These files are on the server only.
amflush [-f] config	In the event that amdump cannot write to a tape, fix the tape problem and then run amflush to send the contents of the holding disk to tape.
amcleanup config	This cleans up problems after amdump fails for some reason, possibly because the server crashed.
amrecover [[-C] config] [options]	When recovering or restoring a file, this tool provides an interactive interface to help browse the index directories of the backed up data.
amrestore [options] tapedevice [hostname [diskname]]	This searches a tape for a requested backup of anything—from a single file to a complete restore of all partitions.

Command	Description
amlabel *config label* [*slot slot*]	All tapes used by amanda must be labeled with amlabel. Unlabeled tapes are not recognized. This is part of the amanda tape management system.
amcheck [*options*]	This program verifies that the correct tape is in the tape *config* drive. You can automate to send an e-mail to someone who can correct any problems before running amdump.
amadmin *config command* [*options*]	Used by administrators of the system backups, this program enables someone to look up tapes needed for a restore, force hosts to do a full backup, and perform other administrative functions.
amtape *config command* [*options*]	This program controls the functions of the tape hardware, such as ejecting tapes, changing tapes, and scanning a tape rack.
amverify *config*	Verifies the contents of an amanda backup tape for errors. You can only use this with tapes containing tar backup formats.
amrmtape [*options*] *config label*amanda	This removes a tape from a tape list and from a tape database.
amstatus *config* [*options*]	Shows the status of a running dump to tape.

Each of the previous commands has a man page describing the options and how to use them. In addition to these commands, amanda uses three editable configuration files:

✦ Main configuration file (/etc/amanda/DailySet1/amanda.conf)

This file contains the server configuration, like who to mail backup reports to, how often to perform a backup, what to backup locally, and so on.

✦ A list of disks and hosts to back up (/etc/amanda/DailySet1/disklist)

✦ A list of active tapes on which the data is placed (/etc/amanda/DailySet1/tapelist)

You can find these files in /etc/amanda. If you plan to use a method in which one day a week you do a full backup and the other days you perform incremental backups, I suggest you create a separate subdirectory for each type—full and daily. Copy the configuration files into each of the directories (daily and full), and modify them according to the duties of each.

You can also find a sample file of which commands to add to `cron` in order to automate the backup process on the `amanda` server only (look in `/etc/amanda` for `crontab.amanda`). Here are what the commands look like:

```
0 16 * * 1-5    /usr/sbin/amcheck -m DailySet1
45 0 * * 2-6    /usr/sbin/amdump DailySet1
```

From these two lines, amanda first makes sure that the correct tape is in the drive at 4:00 p.m. (denoted by sixteen hundred hours in military time) every weekday afternoon. If not, then amcheck sends the administrator/operator an e-mail stating so (indicated by the `-m` option). The config file specifies where to send the mail. Then, each night at 12:45 a.m. (denoted as 45 in military time), the system is backed up based on the configuration files.

dump/restore

The most common tool used on UNIX systems for doing backups is `dump`. dump backs up the Ext2 filesystem to most any type of medium. As with many of the favored UNIX applications, it is available for Linux as well.

Use `dselect` to find the `dump` package and install it. `restore` comes along with it during the install. Once configured, dump reveals that the dump field in `/etc/fstab` indicates the dump frequencies for those drives. Leaving the default set to zero tells dump that you don't want to back up that drive. The configuration process also creates `/var/lib/dumpdates` to record the dates of the dumps and other information about the dump.

To use dump, you must employ options to control what, where, and how backups are performed. These optional parameters control such things as backup level, destination, or device. Table 18-5 lists these options and gives you some idea of what they do.

<table>
<tr><th colspan="2">Table 18-5
dump options and descriptions</th></tr>
<tr><th>Option</th><th>Description</th></tr>
<tr><td>-0 through 9</td><td>Dump levels indicate the priority for backing up the files. A level 0 indicates a full backup, guaranteeing that the entire filesystem is saved. A level number above 0 indicates an incremental backup, telling dump to copy all newer files or modified files since the last dump of a lower level. The default level is 9, which is the lowest level (the least amount of data is backed up).</td></tr>
<tr><td>-B records</td><td>This option supersedes the calculation of the tape size based on the length and density. For the records placeholder, you substitute a numerical argument for the number of dump records per volume.</td></tr>
</table>

Option	Description
-a	This bypasses all tape length considerations and enforces writing to the tape until an end-of-media indication is returned. This option works best with most modern tape drives and is recommended when appending to an existing tape or when using a tape drive with hardware compression.
-b *blocksize*	The number of kilobytes per dump record. A dump record is a block of backup data. Therefore, dump constrains writes to a maximum of MAXBSIZE (typically 64KB) to prevent restore problems.
-c	Changes the defaults for use with a cartridge tape drive, with a density of 8,000 bpi (bits per inch) and a length of 1,700 feet
-e *inode*	Excludes *inode* from this dump (You can use stat to find the *inode* number for a file or directory.)
-h *level*	Files marked with a nodump flag are backed up only for dumps at or above the given *level*. The default honor level is 1; therefore, incremental backups omit such files, but full backups retain them.
-d *density*	Sets the tape density to *density*. The default is 1,600 bpi.
-f *file*	Writes the backup to a file, device, or remote host named *file*. For a single argument, you may list multiple filenames separated by commas.
-L *label*	The user-supplied text string *label* is placed into the dump header, where tools like restore and file can access it. Note that *label* is limited to LBLSIZE (currently 16 characters), which must include the terminating \0.
-M	This option enables the multi-volume aspect for dump. It uses the name specified with -f as a *prefix*, then dump writes in sequence to *prefix*001, *prefix*002, and so on. Use this option when dumping to files on an Ext2 partition in order to bypass the 2GB file size limitation.
-n	Whenever dump requires attention, a notification is sent to all people in the operators group (/etc/group).
-s *feet*	Attempts to calculate the amount of tape needed, in feet, at a particular density. This option depends on the density (-d) and dump record options (-B and -b). The default tape length is 2,300 feet.
-S	Determines the amount of space needed to perform the dump (without actually performing the dump). Then this option displays the estimated size in bytes. This is useful with full or incremental dumps in determining how many volumes of media are needed.

Continued

Table 18-5 *(continued)*

Option	Description
-T date	This option uses the particular *date* as the starting time for the dump (instead of the time determined by looking in /var/lib/dumpdates). This option is useful for automated dump scripts that wish to dump over a specific period of time.
-u	Updates the file /var/lib/dumpdates after a successful dump. This is a suggested option when performing incremental backups.
-W	Tells the specified operator what filesystems need to be dumped. This information is gathered from /var/lib/dumpdates and /etc/fstab. Using the -W option ignores all other options and exits immediately after displaying the information.
-w	This option is like -W, but it prints only those files that you need to back up.

Note   On occasion, dump requires administrative intervention on certain conditions. These conditions include end of tape, end of dump, tape write error, tape open error, and disk read error. Use the -n option mentioned in Table 18-5.

A typical application of this utility looks something like this:

```
dump 0ufL /dev/ftape MyHome /dev/hdax
```

Here, a full backup is performed on the branch of the directory tree /home, and is sent to the device /dev/ftape because of option f. Then, the backup updates the dump file indicated by the u option. You can exchange the directory path for a partition, such as /dev/hdax. The results of this command are as follows:

```
DUMP: Date of this level 0 dump: Thu Sep  7 16:33:25 2000
DUMP: Date of last level 0 dump: the epoch
DUMP: Dumping /dev/hdax (/ (dir home)) to /dev/ftape
DUMP: Label: MyHome
DUMP: mapping (Pass I) [regular files]
DUMP: mapping (Pass II) [directories]
DUMP: estimated 27900 tape blocks on 0.72 tape(s).
DUMP: Volume 1 started at: Thu Sep  7 16:33:26 2000
DUMP: dumping (Pass III) [directories]
DUMP: dumping (Pass IV) [regular files]
DUMP: Closing /dev/ftape
DUMP: Volume 1 completed at: Thu Sep  7 16:34:12 2000
DUMP: Volume 1 took 0:00:46
DUMP: Volume 1 transfer rate: 609 KB/s
DUMP: 28015 tape blocks (27.36MB) on 1 volume(s)
DUMP: finished in 44 seconds, throughput 636 KBytes/sec
```

```
DUMP: level 0 dump on Thu Sep  7 16:33:25 2000
DUMP: Date of this level 0 dump: Thu Sep  7 16:33:25 2000
DUMP: Date this dump completed:  Thu Sep  7 16:34:12 2000
DUMP: Average transfer rate: 609 KB/s
DUMP: DUMP IS DONE
```

You can schedule backup dumps using `cron`, or you can perform them manually. When backing up your system, use the backup method described in Table 18-2. This enables you to use a combination of full and incremental backups.

If something happens, such as a disk failure requiring you to restore the filesystem, you can use the `restore` application to restore your "dumped" data. To restore an entire filesystem, mount the partition you wish to restore using this command:

```
mount /dev/hdax /restored
```

With the correct tape in the tape drive, you can restore the saved, full backup to the drive mounted at /restore. You need to change to the destination directory. Then you use the `restore` program:

```
cd /restore
restore rf /dev/ftape
```

This restores the entire dump archive to the current directory, which is /restore from the tape /dev/ftape. You need to make sure that /etc/fstab reflects any drive mountings in the filesystem changes.

Alternatively, if you only need to restore a few files or a directory, you can enter the interactive mode of the `restore` program. From here, you have commands such as `add`, `ls`, and `help`. To enter the interactive mode, use the following command:

```
restore if /dev/ftape
```

This mode enables you to read and move through the archive on the tape to select the files you need to restore. If you only need to restore a specific file, use the `-x filename` option to indicate the name of the file. You will need to specify the full path of the file and not just the name. If no `filename` argument is given to `-x`, the entire root filesystem will be restored.

KBackup

For you more graphical types, `KBackup` employs a graphical-like interface using a menu system. You can see from Figure 18-1 that its main menu screen includes the general topics needed for a complete package.

`KBackup` is packaged as a Debian package, so installing it is simple with `dselect`. Once installed, you're ready to run it. Make sure that your backup device is available to the system. This program backs up files using `afio` or `tar` to any writable device. `KBackup` also includes other features, such as compression and encryption.

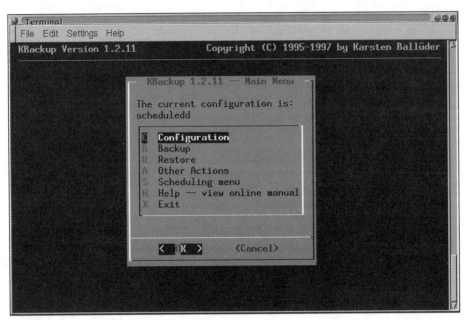

Figure 18-1: The main menu of KBackup

One special aspect of KBackup is its capability to schedule backups and restores (see Figure 18-2). This built-in configurable automation is unique to KBackup. Many other utilities need to use cron for their automation.

Figure 18-2: Use the menus to schedule the backups and restores.

mirrordir

When you want to mirror drives, you want a utility like mirrordir. This application enables you to make mirrored copies of directories and drives. The advantage to a mirrored drive is that it lets you speed the restoration of a failed drive on the system. In a matter of minutes, you can have everything back up and running with minimal data loss.

mirrordir comes with a collection of other applications that perform different functions when installed. Using dselect, search on mirrordir to find and install the package. Once you have it installed, you're ready to begin implementing mirrordir.

The following list explains the supporting applications that come with mirrordir:

✦ pslogin is a secure, remote TCP login alternative to ssh (secure shell).

✦ forward-socket performs arbitrary TCP socket forwarding over a secure channel.

✦ copydir and mirrordir copy or mirror a directory tree and its contents by updating only the changes locally, by FTP, or over a secure TCP connection.

✦ recursdir moves through a local or remote directory to find files, execute a command, or create a tar file out of the files it finds.

To use mirrordir to make a clone of a drive or directory requires a destination. Let's say that you have a second drive or additional partition in your computer. The first step to making a mirror is creating an area where the drive or partition can be mounted. As root, use the following commands:

```
mkdir -p /mirror
mount /dev/hdx /mirror
```

Tip   You can also use mirrordir to mirror over a network. Any device or host that can be mounted into the source's filesystem can mirror to the remote host.

Here, a mount point directory is created to mount the destination (/dev/hdb1) for the mirrored data. Then the drive is mounted to that directory. The filesystem now has access to the other drive, and you are ready to perform the mirroring. Enter the following to start mirroring the entire system:

```
mirrordir / /mirror
```

This makes a mirror image of all the files in the filesystem, and is equivalent to a full backup. Because your intention of creating a mirror may not be to create a duplicate of the original drive, you may want to modify these instructions a bit. Instead of making a copy of the entire drive, you may want to only include critical data, such as data created in the /home directory. You can then create a script to perform the step needed to make the mirror. This is how you can create your script.

```
>#  vi /usr/local/sbin/mirror.sh
#!/bin/sh
#
#   Creates a mirror image of the /home directory
#
/bin/mount /dev/hdb1 /mirror/home
/usr/bin/mirrordir /home /mirror/home
/bin/umount /mirror/home
```

This script mounts the drive into the filesystem, makes the mirror, and then removes the drive from the filesystem. Note that you must create /mirror/home before mounting for the first time. From here on, you can run this script to make the mirror or include it with cron's jobs.

You may have critical data on one system that needs to be backed up hourly to ensure that minimal data is lost. Performing this task manually is not feasible. For cron to run this script automatically every hour, you need to add a line such as the following to /etc/crontab:

```
0 * * * * /usr/sbin/mirror.sh
```

Every hour, cron runs this script to make a mirror of the /home directory. If you find that you need other directories mirrored, just add the commands to the script and cron does the rest.

Tip Using mirrordir to quickly make a copy of vital data and then using dump to make a backup of that data is a great combination for a backup plan.

Taper

Another backup utility that uses a graphical menu is Taper. This application does not have all the scheduling traits that KBackup has, but it still offers an extensible menu (as seen in Figure 18-3). This menu enables you to perform backups and restores as well as to verify the contents of a tape.

Another characteristic available in this tool is the utilities for testing tapes. You can make, erase, and reindex tapes, as well as recover modules. The scripts that Taper uses make the backups behind the scenes.

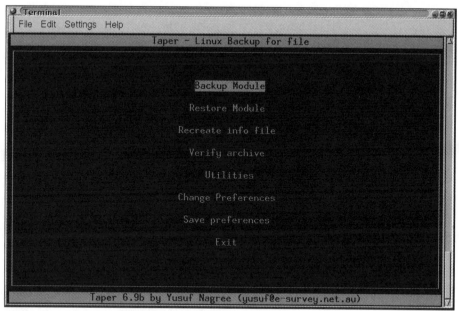

Figure 18-3: Taper's extensively configurable interface

tar

One of the most commonly used applications to create simple backups is `tar`. This program does more than just backups; you may be familiar with it because many programs are packaged using this tool. Using `tar` to create a backup is no different than using it to package a program. Using it to create full backups is very simple.

> **Note**   When `tar` receives a directory name to archive, it archives the total contents for that directory.

To perform a full backup of the filesystem (/) and save it to /dev/*device*, issue:

```
tar cvf /dev/device /
```

Performing an incremental backup is a little more involved. You must distinguish the modified files before backing them up. Here is an example command for accomplishing an incremental backup:

```
tar cvf - 'find / -mtime -1 ! -type d' > /dev/device
```

find sorts out the filenames based on the modification date as indicated by -mtime -1 (changed in the last hour) and excludes all directory names; tar then takes the modified files and archives them to the specified *device*.

tar has a number of additional options. It is a highly flexible and useful tool to keep in your arsenal.

Restoring files and directories from tar backups is as easy as creating them. To restore the /home directory from a tape, insert the tape into the tape drive and execute a command like this:

```
tar xvf /dev/ftape /home
```

You restore individual files by specifying the name of the file in addition to the path the file resides in. If the contents of the tape are in question, you can list the contents of the backup using these options with tar:

```
tar tvf /dev/ftape
```

This gives you the contents of the tape and points out the path of any files that the tape contains. tar also includes other options to more closely control the tape device, compression, and many other attributes.

Creating a backup using a CD-ROM

CD-ROMs present an unusual dilemma. Most CD-ROMs can be written to only once, so you only have one shot at making it work. This means that you must prepare the data for the CD before writing it. To accomplish this task, you need space on a hard drive for the data (approximately 700MB). You'll also need to install two programs: mkisofs and cdrecord. Both are available through deselect. The first program makes images for placement on CD-ROMs. It takes all the data you want on the CD-ROM and turns it into a file using this command:

```
mkisofs -o /tmp/mydata.cd /home/jo/mydata
```

After mkisofs creates the image from the data files, you see the statistics from the file creation. Ultimately, it tells you the size of the file. This is the bottom line. Make sure that the last line of the output (bold in the following example) is less than 650MB because that is all a CD-ROM can hold.

```
Total extents actually written = 126318
Total translation table size: 0
Total rockridge attributes bytes: 0
Total directory bytes: 0
Path table size(bytes): 10
Max brk space used 9024
126318 extents written (246 Mb)
```

After you create the image to put on the CD-ROM, you need to send the image to the CD writer. You must know the exact location of the CD writer, which the cdrecord program can determine (as shown here using the -scanbus option):

```
# cdrecord -scanbus
Cdrecord 1.8.1 (i586-mandrake-linux-gnu) Copyright (C)
1995-2000 Jörg Schilling
Using libscg version 'schily-0.1'
scsibus0:
        0,0,0      0) *
        0,1,0      1) *
        0,2,0      2) *
        0,3,0      3) *
        0,4,0      4) 'YAMAHA ' 'CRW4416S ' '1.0g' Removable CD-ROM
        0,5,0      5) *
        0,6,0      6) *
        0,7,0      7) *
```

You see from the output that the desired device (YAMAHA) resides on 0,4,0. You can now send the created image to the CD writer in confidence. The following command sends the image to the desired device:

```
cdrecord -v speed=4 dev=0,4,0 -data /var/tmp/mydata.cd
```

The -v option indicates that the program should run in verbose mode. The verbose mode prints lots of information to the screen about what is happening with this burn session. This option then sets the record speed to 4. Here, you should specify the device number you discovered before. Finally, you indicate the location of the data to put on the CD.

Note When using CDRs or CDRWs, the cdrecord program will check the media for the fastest speed the media can use. If the media can only write at 2x, then cdrecord will reduce the speed option to match the speed of the media. This is especially important with today's burner speeds.

The following output resulting from the verbose mode gives an indication of what is going on during the writing process. Any problems during the process will show up in the verbose output to the screen.

```
cdrecord: fifo was 0 times empty and 7734 times full, min fill was 96%.
[root@drake win_d]# more /var/tmp/cdmessage.txt
Cdrecord 1.8.1 (i586-mandrake-linux-gnu) Copyright (C) 1995-2000 Jörg Schilling
TOC Type: 1 = CD-ROM
scsidev: '0,4,0'
scsibus: 0 target: 4 lun: 0
Using libscg version 'schily-0.1'
atapi: 0
Device type    : Removable CD-ROM
Version        : 2
Response Format: 2
Capabilities   : SYNC
```

```
Vendor_info    : 'YAMAHA '
Identifikation : 'CRW4416S          '
Revision       : '1.0g'
Device seems to be: Generic mmc CD-RW.
Using generic SCSI-3/mmc CD-R driver (mmc_cdr).
Driver flags   : SWABAUDIO
FIFO size      : 4194304 = 4096 KB
Track 01: data  246 MB
Total size:     283 MB (28:04.26) = 126320 sectors
Lout start:     283 MB (28:06/20) = 126320 sectors
Current Secsize: 2048
ATIP info from disk:
Current Secsize: 2048
ATIP info from disk:
  Indicated writing power: 5
  Is not unrestricted
  Is not erasable
  ATIP start of lead in:  -11689 (97:26/11)
  ATIP start of lead out: 336350 (74:46/50)
Disk type: Long strategy type (Cyanine, AZO or similar)
Manuf. index: 19
Manufacturer: POSTECH Corporation
Blocks total: 336350 Blocks current: 336350 Blocks remaining: 210030
Starting to write CD/DVD at speed 4 in write mode for single session.
Last chance to quit, starting real write in 1 seconds.
Waiting for reader process to fill input buffer ... input buffer ready.
Performing OPC...
Starting new track at sector: 0
Track 01: 246 of 246 MB written (fifo 100%).
Track 01: Total bytes read/written: 258699264/258699264 (126318 sectors).
Writing  time:  437.780s
Fixating...
Fixating time:   67.876s
cdrecord: fifo had 7895 puts and 7895 gets.
cdrecord: fifo was 0 times empty and 7734 times full, min fill was 96%.
```

After a successful creation of a CD-ROM, the prompt returns to the screen. You can test the CD by trying to read data from it. If you can read a couple of random files, the data is good. Now you can delete the image file you created for the CD to prevent anyone else from getting at the data.

 Cross-Reference To learn more about the CD writer hardware, turn to Chapter 17.

Recovering from a Crashed System

If your system ever crashes due to hardware failure, file corruption, or any other reason, you need to know how to recover your system. Often times, the only boost needed to get a system back up and running is having access to that system. Now is the time for that boot disk you saved for this system.

Tip
To create a boot disk using your kernel (if you made changes to your kernel), insert a blank, formatted disk in the floppy drive. Issue the following three commands as root:

```
dd if=/vmlinuz of=/dev/fd0
rdev /dev/fd0
rdev -R /dev/fd0 1
```

This is the same thing that happens when you first install Debian on your computer and you are asked to create a boot disk.

Slip the boot disk into the floppy drive and power on the computer. (Make sure that the BIOS is set to boot to the floppy first.) This disk bypasses the LILO boot information on the hard disk, but it still boots to your system. You can then fix any problems affecting LILO, the kernels, or any of the initial boot parameters.

Rescue disk boot options

When you boot your computer using either the installation CD-ROM that comes with this book or the rescue disk you create from the Debian floppy image, you have some options at the boot prompt.

Pressing F1 lists the help keys. Pressing F3 shows the different ways you can start up using linux, ramdisk, floppy, or rescue. Loading linux starts the installation process. If you already have your system loaded, use this as a last resort. First try to use rescue and point it to the root partition, as shown here:

```
boot: rescue root=/dev/hdxx
```

This starts the filesystem and establishes a shell where you can begin to repair any mistakes made. If this doesn't work, try booting using floppy instead. This should load a small Linux environment in which you have very limited, rudimentary access and control.

You can also start the system with a rescue disk and enter single. This takes you into single user mode. You have root access to the basic system to check the hardware, make basic tests on the system, and determine what changes you need to make to get your system back up and running.

Fixing disk problems

If something does happen to the disk filesystem, you can check out the filesystem for any errors. The e2fsck program performs this check on the disk. It scans the disk for physical errors, misplaced data, and any other problems. An equivalent program for DOS is chkdsk; for Windows, use scandisk. Here is the syntax for this command:

```
e2fsck [options] filesystem
```

You should always use this program on filesystems that are unmounted or mounted in read-only mode, as in the case with the root filesystem. If not, you could possibly corrupt data on the filesystem. You can use a boot floppy to start the system in single user mode, and then run this check on the filesystem disks.

Summary

Like any good Boy Scout or Girl Scout, you always want to be prepared. Being a good administrator is no different. Life can get hot in a hurry when the spotlight is on you to repair a failed disk, fix a defective system, or just find those lost fishing pictures for the boss. I hope that this chapter gives you every reason to create a backup plan for your system.

From this chapter's examples, you should have an idea of what software to use to meet your environment's needs. Whether you are mirroring a disk on the same machine or across the network, using a single tape drive for the entire system of machines, or making a periodic CD of just the important files, you now have a sound place to start.

Sometimes you may run into trouble starting a system because of a simple mistake, a corrupt boot loader, or something a little more serious. Save reformatting and reinstalling for later. Generally, you can recover a system before going to that extreme. At worst case, you have a backup of your system from which you can recover.

✦   ✦   ✦

Linux Server

Security

◆ ◆ ◆ ◆

In This Chapter

Understanding the
need for security

Using the tools of the
trade

Locking down a
system by limiting its
services

Considering viruses,
permissions, and
passwords

Fixing a
compromised system

◆ ◆ ◆ ◆

It has been said that the only truly secure computer is one that is not connected to anything. As more computers communicate with one another through local area networks, wide area networks, and the Internet, security becomes a requirement. Moreover, security is something that constantly needs to be improved; it's more of an ongoing project than a static state of being.

This chapter covers some of the most common areas in which system integrity is compromised, explains how to lock down a system, and describes pertinent tools for protecting your system. Time now to turn on the paranoia switch concerning security.

Understanding the Need for Security

System security ensures that a system, or the data on a system, cannot be accessed by anyone without authorization. This means that if users accessed a system only in the way intended, security would not be an issue. However, this isn't in reality the way it works.

Note   Two terms are frequently used when talking about security: hacker and cracker. A *hacker* originally referred to a computer enthusiast who lacked formal training. Of late, however, the term hacker has become associated with individuals who compromise a computer system. In truth, this person is a *cracker,* a term coined by hackers in the mid-80s to differentiate themselves. The cracker's mission is to maliciously break into a computer system, whereas the hacker's goal is to gain knowledge.

With the growth of the Internet, more systems have access to one another. For example, Internet access was originally only available using dial-up modems. Once cable modems became available, people started hooking up to small networks through the cable company, leaving publicly shared file systems vulnerable. The key to successfully securing your system is to acquire the same knowledge of the would-be attacker and to know your system.

You must protect your system from two enemies—those who have legitimate access and those who don't. Those who have legitimate access may not intend to damage a system, but without appropriate precautions in place, they can still wreak havoc on a system. This is where permissions, disk quotas, and password encryption come into play. If the permissions on a file or directory are properly set, unauthorized users will not be able to gain access. Disk quotas limit the amount of disk space a user can take up, thus freeing the rest for the system. Using encrypted passwords prevents users from viewing one another's passwords.

Protecting yourself against outside intrusion requires a little more effort at the system level. This includes keeping software updated so that crackers don't use known vulnerabilities to gain access, limiting the services that run on a system, limiting the hosts that have access, and other similar tactics covered in this chapter.

Avoiding crackers

The basic goal of crackers is to gain root access to your system, after which they have complete control over it. But if they gain access as a normal user, they can still cause trouble for others. A common practice is to crack one system, and then use that system as a launching point for attacking other systems.

> **Note** One attack method is to use a common service, such as e-mail, the Web, or a database. The cracker will launch a Denial of Service (DoS) attack on a system by bombarding a service like e-mail, with normal requests to the point where the service breaks or the system crashes. When something like this happens, the victim may not have any recourse other than waiting until the attack finishes or dropping requests from the offending host.
>
> A DoS attack might never happen to the casual user, small business, or low-profile corporation. After all, crackers are more interested in creating havoc with higher profile sites such as Yahoo, Amazon, or CNN.

The best way to avoid becoming a target for attacks is to make it difficult enough for would-be crackers that they go elsewhere for an easier target. To accomplish this, you need to fill your tool chest with the appropriate tools.

> **Note** The security of a system is only as good as its weakest point. Knowing where those weak points are comes from experience and familiarity with the system.

Tools of the Trade

There are numerous tools that, when applied properly, can keep your system secure, as well as provide an avenue for tracking down the offender. This section covers tools for several areas to best protect a system. In most cases, these tools are used together for the best results in ensuring system integrity.

Authentication tools

As a first line of defense, you need to run certain tools; namely, password protection and encryption. This prevents someone from easily accessing all of your data.

Shadow passwords

The first form of password protection is the shadow password. This removes passwords from the /etc/passwd file and stores them in an encrypted form in /etc/shadow. You are asked whether you want to use shadow passwords when setting up Debian—it's a good idea to do so. You can tell whether you are using shadow passwords by looking at the /etc/passwd file. If there is an x after the first colon (:) for each account listed, you are using shadow passwords.

Crack

This program uses a dictionary to try to deliberately crack the passwords for the accounts on the system. When this tool cracks a password, an e-mail message is sent to the account to notify the person. The Debian package is cracklib-run. You can set it up using cron to run regularly to notify users of their weak, crackable passwords.

You can get more information about crack by going to /usr/doc/cracklib-runtime/index.html. The utilities that come with the run-time install are as follows:

✦ crack_mkdict—This takes a plain text file(s) containing one word per line to create the dictionary for cracking passwords. The utility lowercases all the words, removes any control characters, and sorts the list before sending the results to standard output.

✦ crack_packer—This takes the standard input and creates three database files that the test utilities understand. These files end in .hwm, .pwd, and .pwi.

✦ crack_unpacker—This utility sends to standard output the words making up the database files.

✦ crack_testlib—This tests the input to see whether it is a valid password.

✦ `crack_testnum`—Based on the index number, this checks the corresponding word in the database.

✦ `crack_teststr`—This checks for the word in the database and returns the index number if the word exists.

The `ispell` and `wenglish` packages provide word lists that can be used to create a dictionary database of words found in a dictionary.

MD5

The newest form of data authentication is the MD5 program. It accepts a message of any length as input and produces a 128-bit fingerprint or checksum as output. The idea is that no two messages will have the same checksum. This tool is an excellent method of verifying the integrity of data. If even the smallest change is made, the checksum changes. You can get the source from `ftp.cerias.purdue.edu/pub/tools/unix/crypto/md5/MD5.tar.Z`. Decompress the file once downloaded, unpack the `tar` file, and compile the source using the following:

```
$ uncompress MD5.tar.Z
$ tar xvf MD5.tar
$ make
```

To see how a slight difference in a file will change the checksum, look at the following example. First, create a simple file and display its contents:

```
$ echo 'Hello, Reader!' > test1
$ cat test1
Hello, Reader!
```

Next, use the MD5 program to generate a unique checksum for the file:

```
$ md5 test1
MD5 (test1) = 0c8e6a79de8cf4aec0e938d672b30eff
```

Then, make a copy of the first file, using the `diff` command to check for content differences between the first file and the copy. You can then verify that there are no differences by comparing the MD5 checksums for the two files:

```
$ cp test1 test2
$ diff test1 test2
$ md5 test1 test2
MD5 (test1) = 0c8e6a79de8cf4aec0e938d672b30eff
MD5 (test2) = 0c8e6a79de8cf4aec0e938d672b30eff
```

Make a small change to the second file by adding a new line with a space in it. Notice that the MD5 checksum of the modified file changes considerably:

```
$ echo ' ' >> test2
$ md5 test1 test2
MD5 (test1) = 0c8e6a79de8cf4aec0e938d672b30eff
MD5 (test2) = 117506fd1c0222825dc5e93d657c5e80
```

This tool cleverly verifies the contents of all types of data.

Network monitoring tools

Because computers are accessible thru networks, this makes them vulnerable to remote attacks. Another set of tools monitors the network traffic for various types of information to help detect these attacks.

Argus

This network-monitoring tool uses a client-server approach to capture data. It provides network auditing and can be adapted for intrusion detection, protocol analysis, and other security-related needs. You can find this tool at `ftp.andrew.cmu.edu/pub/argus/`.

Tcpdump

This Debian-packaged tool listens to the network traffic and reports what it finds. Each TCP packet is read, and the header information is sent to the screen. If you are suspicious of the traffic on a specific interface, you can set `tcpdump` to listen to that interface with the `-l` option. The `listen` option prints to the screen all traffic that passes on the selected device.

Swatch

This simple program monitors the log files for specific patterns you specify. It will filter out unwanted data and take action based on what you define. You can obtain the source files from `ftp.cerias.purdue.edu/pub/tools/unix/logutils/swatch`. Follow the instructions packaged with the source.

Logcheck

Logcheck is an included Debian package that monitors the log files and notifies the user via e-mail of any security violations and problems. This script is installed as `/usr/sbin/logcheck.sh` and is added to `/etc/cron.d` for routine checks. The configuration file is stored in `/etc/logcheck` and is already very thoroughly configured.

Caution   When picking up software source code, be careful when using beta versions of the code, which can contain bugs that make the program perform differently than expected. For peace of mind, use the tried-and-true version until the beta test completes and a final release is available.

Service and integrity tools

Every service that uses a TCP port has the potential of becoming a target of attack. Because actual users still need to use these ports, you can't just turn them off. The TPC ports are prone to attack because an application listens to the port and responds to requests as with Web servers listening to port 80. However, you can monitor the ports for valid activity and log the traffic. Two tools help with this: TCP wrappers and a program called *Tripwire*.

TCP wrappers

A TCP wrapper is activated when the request comes into a port. It then checks to make sure that the source is valid, and logs the transaction. Debian installs TCP wrappers as standard procedure. You can tell this by looking at the /etc/inetd.conf file, where you will see /usr/sbin/tcpd entries for each service wrapped.

Tripwire

For monitoring critical system files, Tripwire is the tool to use. When first installed, it looks at the files on the system to determine a baseline. Assuming you are starting with a secure system, then only someone with administrative authority will change the systems file. The administrator can rescan the system at any time to identify any unauthorized changes to the files on the system. Changed files are identified (because they have a different file size or time/date stamp) and reported to the administrator.

You can pick up a copy of Tripwire from www.tripwire.org, where the commercial package has become open source. The commercial site still exists at www.tripwire.com.

Diagnostic tools

To help ensure that your system is locked down as tightly as it can be, you need to know where all the security holes are. Diagnostic tools help identify those holes. Several diagnostic tools are available, three of which are covered in the following sections.

SATAN

Security Analysis Tool for Auditing Networks (SATAN) collects information about networked hosts by examining certain services such as NFS, NIS, FTP, and others. The following list briefly describes twelve of the vulnerable areas that are checked:

✦ File access through Trivial File Transport Protocol

✦ A Network File System (NFS) export through the portmapper

✦ An unrestricted NFS export

✦ An NFS export to unprivileged programs

✦ Vulnerabilities in Sendmail

✦ Access to the Network Information Service (NIS) password file

✦ `wu-ftpd` vulnerabilities

✦ Writeable Anonymous FTP home directory. (If using Anonymous FTP, limit the writeable area.)

✦ Unrestricted X server access. (Filter X at your firewall.)

✦ Remote shell access. (Comment out `rshd` in the file `/etc/inetd.conf` or protect it with a TCP wrapper.)

✦ `rexecd` access. (Filter the `rexd` service at the firewall and comment out `rexd` in the file `/etc/inetd.conf`.)

✦ Unrestricted dial-out modem accessible by the use of TCP. (Place modems behind a firewall or require a dial-out password.)

If vulnerabilities are found, recommendations for those vulnerabilities are made. Nothing is changed on your system. You then can do your best to correct any holes in your system.

Note   Be careful using SATAN because it does have an exploratory mode that will scan beyond the local network through a live connection to the Internet. You could unknowingly scan someone else's machines, setting an alarm off on their end.

SATAN is found at ftp.`cerias.purdue.edu/pub/tools/unix/scanners/satan/ satan`, where you can download the source, reconfigure it for your system, and compile it. Follow the instructions provided with the code.

ISS

Similar to SATAN, Internet Security Scanner (ISS) also scans your system, but is limited to an IP range. It looks for known vulnerabilities left open by the administrator. The following list describes the services checked by this tool:

✦ `Decode alias` — This should not be available through the mail `/etc/aliases` file. If it does exist, remove it and run `newaliases`.

✦ `rexecd` — Because this service allows remote execution of programs, this service should be disabled. Comment it out of the `/etc/inetd.conf` file, and then restart the `inetd` service.

✦ Anonymous FTP — Improperly configured anonymous FTP servers are often attacked. The best option is to disallow anonymous FTP. This requires anyone accessing the system using FTP to have an account on the system.

✦ NIS — ISS attempts to guess the NIS domain and get the password file.

✦ NFS — This should be restricted to only those hosts within your network.

✦ Sendmail—Sendmail should have `wiz` and `debug` disabled. To manually verify this, telnet to mail *host* on port 25 (`telnet host 25`). When you try to use `wiz` or `debug` as commands to the connection, you should receive an error (`500 Command unrecognized`).

✦ Default accounts—Accounts such as `guest`, `bbs`, and `lp` should not exist on systems that do not use them. If they must exist, they should use nontrivial passwords.

You can download the source for ISS from the anonymous FTP site `ftp.cerias.purdue.edu/pub/tools/unix/scanners/iss`. Decompress the files and follow the instructions in the README documentation about how to compile and install the tools.

COPS

Computer Oracle and Password System (COPS) checks for security holes on a system. If any are found, a report is created and sent via e-mail or saved to a file. This collection of about a dozen utilities checks areas such as password files, anonymous FTP setup, and much more.

COPS is obtainable from a number of locations, one of which is `ftp.cerias.purdue.edu/pub/tools/unix/scanners/cops`, where you can find the source code to compile. Follow the README files to configure and create the executable program.

Caution

When searching for programs related to security and core Linux systems, use reliable sites. Remember: The security administrator is paranoid; therefore, do a little research on each site. If a reputable site such as `www.cert.org` refers you to another site, you can be reasonably sure the recommended site is trustworthy. Other sites to include are educational institutions such as colleges and universities, official sites such as `www.debian.org`, and corporate sites such as `www.sendmail.com`.

Other helpful tools

Sometime a simple tool is all you need to ease your mind about suspicious activity. Two tools come in handy for performing simple checks: `isof` and `ifstatus`. One (`isof`) reports on open files; the other (`ifstatus`) confirms the status of the network interfaces.

isof

This little tool lists the open files and what processes have them open. You can download the binary executable from `ftp.cerias.purdue.edu/pub/tools/unix/sysutils/lsof/binaries/linux/proc/ix86`, but when you do, verify the MD5 checksum against what is shown in the CHECKSUMS file.

Ifstatus

Use `ifstatus` to check all network interfaces. This tool reports on any interfaces that are in debug or promiscuous mode, which may be an indication of unauthorized access. It can be found at `ftp.cerias.purdue.edu/pub/tools/unix/sysutils/ifstatus`.

This list of tools only scratches the surface. The section "Sources for additional information" near the end of the chapter includes some sites you might want to check out. If you can imagine a useful tool and are thinking of creating it yourself, first check to see whether someone else created one before setting off to program your own (unless you just can't help yourself).

Limiting the Available Services

Because attackers can do the most damage by gaining root access to your system, you should logically spend most of your effort protecting this part of the system. Once your systems are set up, consider disabling any services that you may not need, as they can potentially give an attacker root access. For instance, if you have a server set up as a file server and have old `imap` services running, a cracker could use an `imap` exploit to gain root access to your system. There is no need to have mail services running on a file server. Disabling the `imap` service from that machine keeps that service from weakening your system's security.

By default, Debian leaves some services enabled when it is first installed — `talkd`, `fingerd`, and remote access services come to mind. All the active port services in `/etc/inetd.conf` that aren't preceded by a pound sign (#) are enabled services. The fewer enabled TCP services, the better.

The following code shows the contents of the `inetd.conf` file, with the available services indicated in bold text. Each of these services must be evaluated for usefulness on the server in question.

```
# /etc/inetd.conf:  see inetd(8) for further information.
#
# Internet server configuration database
#
#
# Lines starting with "#:LABEL:" or "#<off>#" should not
# be changed unless you know what you are doing!
#
# If you want to disable an entry so it isn't touched during
# package updates just comment it out with a single '#' character.
#
# Packages should modify this file by using update-inetd(8)
#
# <service_name> <sock_type> <proto> <flags> <user> <server_path> <args>
#
```

```
#:INTERNAL: Internal services
#echo       stream  tcp   nowait  root   internal
#echo       dgram   udp   wait    root   internal
#chargen    stream  tcp   nowait  root   internal
#chargen    dgram   udp   wait    root   internal
discard     stream  tcp   nowait  root   internal
discard     dgram   udp   wait    root   internal
daytime     stream  tcp   nowait  root   internal
#daytime    dgram   udp   wait    root   internal
time        stream  tcp   nowait  root   internal
#time       dgram   udp   wait    root   internal

#:STANDARD: These are standard services.
telnet   stream  tcp  nowait telnetd.telnetd /usr/sbin/tcpd /usr/sbin/in.telnetd

#:BSD: Shell, login, exec and talk are BSD protocols.
shell   stream   tcp   nowait   root    /usr/sbin/tcpd /usr/sbin/in.rshd
login   stream   tcp   nowait   root    /usr/sbin/tcpd /usr/sbin/in.rlogind
exec    stream   tcp   nowait   root    /usr/sbin/tcpd /usr/sbin/in.rexecd
talk    dgram    udp   wait     nobody.tty   /usr/sbin/tcpd /usr/sbin/in.talkd
ntalk   dgram    udp   wait     nobody.tty   /usr/sbin/tcpd /usr/sbin/in.ntalkd

#:MAIL: Mail, news and uucp services.
smtp    stream   tcp   nowait   mail   /usr/sbin/exim exim -bs
nntp    stream   tcp   nowait   news   /usr/sbin/tcpd /usr/sbin/leafnode

#:INFO: Info services
finger  stream   tcp   nowait   nobody /usr/sbin/tcpd    /usr/sbin/in.fingerd
ident   stream   tcp   wait     identd /usr/sbin/identd  identd

#:BOOT: Tftp service is provided primarily for booting.  Most sites
# run this only on machines acting as "boot servers."

#:RPC: RPC based services

#:HAM-RADIO: amateur-radio services

#:OTHER: Other services
```

Obviously, you may want to keep some of these services available because they
serve a purpose. For instance, you may want to keep the telnet service enabled
for remote connection and control. You can disable the ones you don't want by
editing the /etc/inetd.conf file and inserting a pound sign at the beginning of the
line.

Tip   In addition to locking down a system, you should isolate the network from the
Internet with a *firewall,* which filters packets by allowing only certain ones to pass.
To the outside world, you appear to have only one computer, the firewall.
Computers on the network can browse the Internet with peace of mind. See
Chapter 20 for information about setting up a firewall.

Viruses, worms, and other creepy things

In the computer world, there are three types of computer illnesses — viruses, worms, and Trojan horses. A virus is a tiny foreign program embedded in another legitimate program with the purpose of duplicating itself and causing mischief, if not destroying data. Linux is designed so that those programs most likely to become infected with a virus are locked down extremely tightly, making it very difficult for a human — or program — to gain access. The virus would need to have root access to make changes to the programs, which is why root access is generally the goal of a cracker. Thus, you will rarely, if ever, hear of a virus infecting a Linux system.

Worms, on the other hand, exploit known weaknesses in applications with the purpose of cracking a system, and then propagate like a virus. The first known worm used a hole in Sendmail to gain access to a system.

The Trojan horse, although not quite a virus, can also be problematic. It is generally a program that is disguised as another program by using the same name. It can have just as much of a devastating effect on the system, but does not replicate itself like a virus. For this reason, to execute a program not included in the system path, you must include either the full path to the file or partial path to specify the exact file to run. For instance, to run a setup program on a CD, you must include the path for the CD or the relative path:

```
$ /cdrom/setup
$ ./setup
```

This prevents the wrong program from starting unintentionally. Generally, the only files damaged are those of the account currently logged in — yours.

Overall, the number of Linux viruses, Trojan horses, and such is relatively insignificant compared to those found on unprotected operating systems such as Windows, DOS, and Apple OS.

Setting secure permissions

When working with files, directories, and such, there may be a temptation to set the permissions on a file to 777, which gives full access to everyone. Although it may be convenient at the time, it can come back to haunt you later if you grant access to someone who makes potentially devastating changes to a file.

The Bash shell enables the setting of a mask that creates a default permission when new files and directories are created. This helps to control access to files without the extra effort usually required to do so. By default, the umask is set to 022, which masks the permissions on new files to rwxr__r__, or read/write for the user, read only for group, and other levels of access.

You can restrict the permissions on new files even further by setting the umask to 026 (for no permission to the universe), or 066 (for no permissions to group or universe). You can change the umask at any time with

```
umask 0xx
```

where the 0xx represents a three-digit number as a mask. Make sure that the first number of the three remains a zero, or only the root account will be able to make changes to the file.

A word about passwords

The accounts and corresponding passwords define the legitimate users of your system. If any user were to share his or her password with a few close friends, that account could compromise the security of the system. If you keep particularly sensitive material on that computer, the more risk to compromising the material.

Another thing that users commonly do is write their password on a sticky note and put it under the keyboard or, worse yet, on the front of the monitor. Anyone with a view of that person's computer has access to that person's account, and possibly more.

Controlling who gets passwords

For obvious reasons, you want to control who has password access to your system. There again this is a paranoid frame of mind, but just handing out passwords to anyone can get you into trouble. The easiest way for an attacker to gain access is from the inside.

If you have a system at home, you can trust the users of the system. But when you're talking about a corporation of several hundred employees, you won't know whom to trust. All it takes is one person giving out a password (which happens more than you would think) to someone who can and does compromise the system.

 When incorrect passwords are entered for an account, a warning message appears on the screen, indicating the number of failed login attempts. This only occurs when logging into the virtual terminal. When using xdm or another desktop manager to log in, there is no indication.

Rules for choosing passwords

It is only human nature for people to take the path of least resistance. This is also true when choosing a password. For obvious reasons, people choose passwords based on how easy they are to remember. Therefore, they will often pick children's names, anniversary dates, and other familiar information. All the more reason to use a password-checking program such as crack, mentioned earlier in this chapter. For the best security, urge users not to use passwords matching the following criteria:

✦ Dates such as anniversaries, birth dates, and holidays

✦ Telephone and Social Security numbers

✦ Names of family members, pets, or any other proper names

✦ Variations on the initials of the user or family members

✦ Personal words or phrases

✦ Any words straight out of a dictionary

Now that you have a list of what not to pick for a password, here are some suggestions for picking a good password. First, try to include non-alphabetical characters. This can be anything from numbers to any of the special characters — such as the percent sign (%), dollar sign ($), or others. If you must use a password that you can remember, choose a quote, saying, or phrase, such as "The rain in Spain falls mainly on the plain," and then take the first letters of each word, producing trisfmotp. Better yet, alternate the capitalization of the letters to end up with tRiSfMoTp.

Of course, the best passwords are completely random. There are two tools described in this chapter that help to generate random passwords: pwgen and makepasswd. pwgen tries to create a random password that is somewhat readable with a string of characters, numbers, and symbols. You must set the length of the password. Here is a typical command sequence:

```
pwgen -s 9
```

The –s (which stands for secure) option used in this example sequence produces a secure password. These sequences are random and not easily cracked. Users generally don't like these secure passwords because they are hard to remember.

makepasswd focuses on creating a truly random password. There is no concern for readability. This makes for a better password, although remembering it is a little more difficult. To generate a password between six and eight characters in length with this command, simply issue makepasswd at the command line. You can change this with command-line options.

Most important, memorize the password and then destroy the paper on which it was written. A password provides no security if it's written down where someone can access it.

Tips for Securing Your System

You can do a number of things to make a system secure. Some of these things may just mean a change in procedure. The following list of tips can help you create a more secure system:

✦ **Create multiple root accounts.** If more than one person needs root access, create a root account for each person. In doing so, you can track who is doing what. For example, suppose Jane, Paul, and Mark are system administrators who need root access. Create three new accounts with root access for each of them. You will need to edit the /etc/passwd file to look like the following:

```
root-jn:x:0:0:root-Jane:/root:/bin/bash
root-pl:x:0:0:root-Paul:/root:/bin/bash
root-mk:x:0:0:root-Mark:/root:/bin/bash
```

You can see that each of the accounts has a user ID and group ID of zero (0), but each has a different account name. You can now keep track of the account name in log files.

✦ **Use the full path for superuser.** If you're working from a user account and you need to run a task with the superuser account (su), start it by using the full path (/bin/su). This prevents a Trojan horse with the same name as su from executing and wreaking havoc on your system. Especially when creating scripts, use the full path to an application.

✦ **Monitor the root.** Watch for root activity in log files, system processes, and when creating new files. Attackers try to get root access so they can run programs on your system. Once they have root access, they have free rein.

✦ **Encrypt passwords.** For obvious reasons, encrypt the passwords in the /etc/passwd file using shadow passwords. Also, if possible, encrypt passwords transmitted via e-mail when logging into services such as telnet and the like. Clear-text passwords are susceptible to being picked up by someone listening to the traffic on the network.

This can be a challenge to accomplish, especially on a network. Some common programs, such as telnet and FTP, don't concern themselves with transmitting encrypted passwords. Therefore, assume that any program you connect to over the network does *not* use encrypted passwords unless you know that it does.

✦ **Use the lowest level of rights to accomplish the task.** When you do this, you limit the risk posed to the systems and the task. For instance, in setting permissions when creating a private directory, it most likely needs to be accessed only by you and not the universe. Setting the permissions on that directory so that only you can read and write to it provides the most security. Conversely, a common directory needs greater access permissions in order for more people to gain access.

✦ **Run what you need.** As mentioned earlier in this chapter, don't run services that are not needed. If a machine is acting only as a Web server, disable DNS services from the machine. Likewise, if the system only performs DNS services, disable FTP, Talk, and other services not intended to run on the machine. The fewer services running on a system, the fewer holes that need to be watched.

✦ **Watch** faillog. This little program shows you the accounts logged in and any errors at login. Login failures are logged to /var/log/faillog, and the /usr/bin/faillog program helps to read the log file. This is what faillog reports:

```
Username Failures Maximum  Latest
jo               0       0  Sat Sep 30 19:11:56 -0500 2000 on pts/3
```

✦ **Remove from** rc*.d **all services you don't use.** The rc*.d directories contain links to the daemons that will run. You can learn more about these directories from Chapter 15. Any services not needed can be removed and prevented from starting automatically. The best way to prevent a service from starting automatically is to rename the link. All starting service names start with a capital S followed by a number indicating the starting order. If you rename the link by placing an underscore in front of the name, that service will not start automatically at boot time. This should be done with the unwanted links on /etc/rc2.d and /etc/rc3.d, depending on which one is used at boot time. Here is an example of renaming one of the links:

```
$ mv /etc/rc2.d/S20exim /etc/rc2.d/_S20exim
```

Now, whenever the system starts, the exim mail service will not start.

✦ **Lock and/or clear the screen.** For single stand-alone machines at home, this is not critical, but it can be dangerous to leave individual workstations within a corporation unattended. The easiest way to gain access to a system is from the inside, especially when the door is standing wide open. To prove a point to a colleague who had an unattended stand-alone test system on his desk running as root, I changed the root password and then locked the screen. When he returned to his desk, he found he could no longer access his test system. If I were an actual cracker, I could have easily accessed the system again later whenever I wanted.

Most of the window managers can lock the screen. The only way to regain access is with the account password. If you use a virtual console, you can use vlock or lockvc (included Debian packages) to prevent access while you are away.

✦ **Quarantine new binaries.** When downloading and testing new binaries, including source code you compile, initiate the program using a special test account. Running the binary from the special account restricts the rights to only that account. If the program includes malicious code, the test account is the only one affected. Sometimes a cracker will offer free binaries, hoping that the recipient runs the program as root. The program is designed to create a hole in the system, allowing the cracker to easily gain access later. In short, be careful what you run as root.

Tip   Set up a firewall to protect the rest of the network from the Internet. Leave only those systems that require direct access to the Internet on the exposed side of the firewall. See Chapter 20 for details about setting up a firewall and related services.

The compromised system

It is hoped that you will never experience a compromised system. Depending on the degree to which a system is compromised, it may take quite a lot of work to recover. If your system is affected, assume that every file on it has been altered and, therefore, cannot be trusted. In such circumstances, you must replace all files on the system, including user data, configuration files, and, obviously, the core files.

Following are the steps to take after you diagnose a compromised system. Be sure to document every step you take, down to the minutest detail, even noting the day and time of the step.

1. Consult the company's security policy. If one does not exist, contact the appropriate persons to advise them of the situation. You may need to contact legal counsel and/or law officials.

2. Disconnect the affected system from the network to prevent the attacker from further progress and any chance to gain control of the system. It is recommended that you run the system in single-user mode. This prevents users, attackers, and the attacker's processes from making further changes to the system while you try to recover it.

Note   You may want to make a complete image or copy of the system at the time the compromise was discovered for later reference. If legal action is taken, the image can be used for investigative purposes. To make the copy, either use a full backup of the system or remove the compromised hard drive and use a new one to rebuild your system.

3. Evaluate the system to determine the what, how, and who of the attack. The following items detail the suggested investigation of your system:

   - **Examine log files.** From the log files, you can try to identify the intruder.

   - **Check for** setuid **and** setgid **files.** These files control the IDs of a process and would enable an attacker to run a process using another ID.

   - **Verify system binaries.** In most cases, you may not be able to find a compromised binary; however, you can look for files modified after a certain date using the `find` command.

   - **Examine the system for packet sniffers.** A packet sniffer examines packets as they travel over the network, and they are very difficult to detect. The attacker may have set up the compromised system to look for other vulnerable systems.

   - **Study files run by** cron **and** at **for unrecognized instructions.** Additional entries may have been added to start automatically.

- **Check for unauthorized services running on the system.** A process left behind by the attacker may still be running.

- **Scrutinize the** /etc/passwd **file for changes.** If nothing exists between the first and second colon on a line, then no password is needed for that account. Also look for new accounts created as a back door for reentering later.

- **Check system and network configuration files for modifications.** Modifications to these files could create more holes for other attempts to access the system.

- **Check the entire system for unusual or hidden files.** Check areas not normally used, such as /tmp, /var, and /dev.

- **Inspect all machines on the local network for possible compromises.**

4. Look for programs left behind by the attacker. These tools can provide clues about the method the attacker used to gain access to your system.

5. If another site was involved in the attack, contact the administration at that site to let them know that the attack appeared to come from them and that they might want to investigate for possible intrusion on their end. Give them as much information as you can to help them locate any problems, such as time and data stamps, time zone, and method of intrusion.

    You might also want to contact CERT at cert@cert.org to report the incident, giving them as much detail about the attack as possible as well.

6. Recover the system to its pre-attacked state. To be sure that nothing is left behind, completely reformat any system partitions before restoring the system. Doing this ensures that all vulnerable data, files, and programs on the system no longer exist.

7. To prevent further attacks, follow the suggestions in this chapter for improving security on your system. When you have restored the system to a secure state again, reconnect it to the network and/or Internet.

Sources for additional information

There are several good sources for obtaining more information on security. Some of the sites are more official than others, but all have valuable information.

The official site for security issues is www.CERT.org (or try the Australian version at www.auscert.org.au). Both sites contain pertinent information about security, including alerts, tools, and tips. Join the mailing list for the latest news on security alerts.

You can also subscribe to the debian-security-announce mailing list. It includes the latest information about Debian-related issues, includes the Debian package names, and other security issues relating to Linux applications. You can find a complete list of these mailing lists at www.debian.org/MailingLists/subscribe.

Table 19-1 lists some other sites that include resources, articles, how-tos, and other security information.

Table 19-1 Debian security-related sites	
Site	**Features**
`SecurityFocus.ORG`	Includes articles focusing on security. This site covers Linux as well as other platforms.
`www.linuxdoc.org`	How-tos on security for Linux as a part of the Linux Documentation Project.
`www.ugu.com`	UNIX GURU Universe offers general information for UNIX administrators. Among the topics is security.
`ftp.cerias.purdue.edu`	A full archive of security tools of many types can be found at this site, located at `/pub/tools/unix`. Most of the tools here require compiling in order to use.

Summary

The boon to the would-be cracker is the large number of new systems popping up around the Internet. User inexperience has become the cracker's greatest ally. Don't wait until you become a victim to discover that your system is vulnerable. Granted, the odds of something devastating happening to your system are slim, but so is being struck by lightning. It does happen often. It is best to prevent an intrusion from happening in the first place.

Developing a little healthy paranoia helps when securing your system. If you operate a home system, the same consequences apply if you get cracked. You must rebuild your system just like a large corporation, taking the added steps to make it more secure. If operating several servers for a corporation, then you may want to do what you can to discourage anyone from compromising your system.

The best thing to do is to become a student of security. Learn what you can from as many sources as you find. You don't need to become the world's foremost expert on the subject, but vanquishing the innocence can do more for preventing an attack than anything else.

✦   ✦   ✦

Firewall

With more and more computers accessing the Internet from home and from work, what prevents anyone on the Internet from accessing your computer? The answer is a firewall and related services. The term *firewall* refers to a line or wall of protection, typically from fire. In computer terms though, it means protection from intrusion. This is your first line of defense.

Along with the firewall is the control of Internet access from within the protected network. This is the job of the proxy. The *proxy* receives requests for Internet access, retrieves the information, and then passes the information back to the requester. This chapter covers both firewalls and proxies.

Protecting a Network

From reading Chapter 19, you discovered that systems are just as susceptible to intrusion from the Internet as they are from inside the office. The difference between Internet intrusion and internal intrusion is that the intruder must be at your computer to infiltrate from the inside, which leaves intrusion via the Internet.

Besides the countermeasures listed in Chapter 19, the best way to protect a network is to disconnect it from the Internet. Practically speaking, this may not always be feasible; therefore, you can remove it virtually. A firewall does just that — it creates a barrier between the mass of machines on your network and the Internet but still allows selected traffic out (such as Web, FTP, and similar Internet-related requests).

A firewall is a dedicated system that stands in the gap between the Internet and the internal network. A firewall is configured in such a way that each IP port request is looked at; based on the preset criteria, the firewall determines if that request can proceed to its intended destination or the request should be dropped.

Figure 20-1 shows an illustration of what a network looks like with a firewall in place. Basically, the firewall stands between the network and the Internet. If you have any dial-up services to your company, those services are on a system behind the firewall. If you only have a single system at home and want to use dial-up services to access the Internet, then you can perform those services on the firewall system.

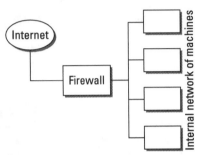

Figure 20-1: A firewall sitting between the Internet and the internal network

A similar device is a *router*. Though a firewall does route packets from one network to another, it discriminates the data contained in the packets. However, a router just routes packets from one network to another based on the destination. The router does not care what the packets contain, just where they're going. You can find routers installed between *subnets* (groups of IP address with different ranges), sometimes represented by physical location — as in between floors of a building or between the buildings themselves. The purpose of the router is to pass what is needed in the direction it needs to go.

Another aspect of using a firewall is disguising the originator of a request (called *masquerading the IP*). When a person behind the firewall makes a request for a Web page in the Internet, the page appears to come from the firewall instead of the real originator. In other words, the daily activity appears to come only from one machine for your entire site. This reduces the risk of someone exploiting your network.

Note   IP masquerading is the Linux version of *Network Address Translation (NAT)* found on commercial network routers and firewalls. You can get more information about IP masquerading at `ipmasq.cjb.net`.

Hardware Requirements and Preparations

You will need different hardware to meet minimum requirements for a firewall/router as compared to a proxy server. A firewall/router takes fewer resources than a proxy server does. Here are the minimum requirements for a system destined for a firewall only:

✦ A computer with at least a 486 running at 100MHz

✦ 32MB of RAM

✦ A 500MB hard drive to hold the operating system

✦ Two network cards compatible with Linux (I stick with name-brand PCI cards.)

Looking over the preceding specs, this might be a good time to make use of one of those old computers stored in the closet. The proxy server is another story. In order for a system to effectively run as a proxy server, the system needs the following:

✦ A computer running at least a Pentium II class processor

✦ 64MB of RAM

✦ A 2GB hard drive to hold the operating system and the proxy cache

✦ Two network cards compatible with Linux

As you can see, the requirements for the proxy server are a little higher than for the firewall. Most of the work for a firewall takes place at the kernel level, where packets are examined and either dropped or passed on. The proxy server needs a reserve of enough hard drive space to hold the information in servers.

Adding a Second Network Card

In general, the best means for protecting a network is to physically isolate it. The network card is the link from the computer to the network, so using a separate network card for each network a computer connects to helps to isolate it. Typically, a computer connects to two networks at a time (at the most).

 Cross-Reference For more tips on compatible hardware and adding a network card to your existing system, see Chapter 17.

Assuming that you configured at least one network card at the time of installation and it is working properly, you can power down the system to add the other network card. Once the second card is physically installed, then you need to load the driver if this card is different from the first card. Here is a scenario for adding a second network card:

1. Starting with a system with the first Ethernet card (3c905) already installed during the setup, add the second card (Kingston 120TX) by installing a new module for the new Ethernet card into the kernel. The first card is connected to the Internet, while the second card is connected to the Internet network. Initially, to install the module for the second card, use the following:

   ```
   # insmod /lib/modules/2.2.17/net/rtl8139.o
   ```

   Once the module is successfully added to the kernel, add the module name to /etc/modules so it gets loaded at boot time.

2. Then add the specifics about the new card to /etc/network/interfaces:

```
iface eth1 inet static
        address 192.168.0.10
        netmask 255.255.255.224
        network 192.168.0.0
        broadcast 192.168.0.31
```

This information identifies the second card as interface eth1; the IP address is static. The file also specifies the IP address for the card along with netmask, network, and broadcast numbers.

3. Restarting the networking service activates the card and assigns the information set up in the last step. To restart the networking services, issue the following command:

```
# /etc/init.d/networking restart
```

You should see some type of confirmation on the screen that networking was restarted.

4. To confirm that all the cards are now active and assigned the proper information, check them with the interface configure command (ifconfig). This command and its results are as follows:

```
$ /sbin/ifconfig
eth0      Link encap:Ethernet  HWaddr 00:60:97:C2:DD:AF
          inet addr:216.3.12.27  Bcast:216.3.12.31  Mask:255.255.255.224
          UP BROADCAST RUNNING MULTICAST  MTU:1500  Metric:1
          RX packets:84841 errors:1 dropped:0 overruns:0 frame:1
          TX packets:61296 errors:0 dropped:0 overruns:0 carrier:0
          collisions:0 txqueuelen:100
          Interrupt:5 Base address:0xb800

eth1      Link encap:Ethernet  HWaddr 00:C0:F0:68:95:1E
          inet addr:192.168.0.10  Bcast:192.168.0.31  Mask:255.255.255.224
          UP BROADCAST RUNNING MULTICAST  MTU:1500  Metric:1
          RX packets:391 errors:0 dropped:0 overruns:0 frame:0
          TX packets:221 errors:0 dropped:0 overruns:0 carrier:0
          collisions:0 txqueuelen:100
          Interrupt:11 Base address:0xb000

lo        Link encap:Local Loopback
          inet addr:127.0.0.1  Mask:255.0.0.0
          UP LOOPBACK RUNNING  MTU:3924  Metric:1
          RX packets:16 errors:0 dropped:0 overruns:0 frame:0
          TX packets:16 errors:0 dropped:0 overruns:0 carrier:0
          collisions:0 txqueuelen:0
```

This shows each adapter installed and running. From the information here, you can determine the configuration of the card, the IP addresses bound to the card, and other information unique to the network card.

5. Each card is connected to a different network — one to the Internet and the other to your internal network. You should be able to ping an address on each network from this machine. You also should be able to ping this machine from a remote computer on each network. If you try to ping a computer on the network attached to the eth0 card from a computer attached to the eth1 card, you should get a "request timed out" or no response at all.

Note In some cases, where the Internet provider is a cable modem service or other special access service, these instructions may need to be varied slightly. Some Internet services have requirements such as a pre-defined host name, a specific MAC address (a MAC address is the identifier for the Ethernet card), or some other criteria on your system. Because I can't account for all special conditions, you may need to seek additional help from your Internet service provider or other sources such as mailing lists.

6. In order to ping the other network, you must turn on ip_forward. Edit the /etc/network/options file, and change the *no* to a *yes* for ip_forward. Then, restart the networking services as in step 3.

7. At this point, IP forwarding should be active. Confirm that the service is enabled in the kernel by looking at the contents of the ip_forward placeholder, which should equal 1.

```
$ more /proc/sys/net/ipv4/ip_forward
1
```

Using ipchains

The kernel actually handles the packets once they arrive at the machine. The component in the kernel is called *ipchains*. This has been included in the kernel since version 2.1. Therefore, you need to compile the kernel to handle such things as forwarding, routing, and masquerading. When using the default kernel from the CD or Internet install, these functions are already available.

ipchains is essentially a series of rules for handling IP packets as they come into a machine (handled by the kernel). When the kernel looks at a packet, the packet is evaluated against the first rule in the chain. If the criteria don't match, the kernel tries the second rule, and so on down the line until a rule is found to apply to the packet.

There are three built-in chains — input, output, and forward. You can change the policy for each and add rules to refine their functions. Often, many more than just one or two rules are specified for a chain. Each rule can have a set of target values: ACCEPT, DENY, REJECT, MASQ, REDIRECT, or RETURN. The most commonly used targets are ACCEPT, DENY, and MASQ (short for masquerade).

Tip   For those who have never set up a firewall, have trouble understanding ipchains, or want to have it installed quickly, download and use the PMFirewall program described later in this chapter.

The ipchains utility applies, modifies, or deletes rules from a command line. The following is an example of how ipchains adds and changes rules. The first command changes the policy on the forward chain. The second adds a rule to forward to the ppp0 interface and MASQ the IP address. This is common practice with dial-up connections to the Internet.

```
# ipchains -P forward DENY
# ipchains -A forward -i ppp0 -j MASQ
```

To get a better handle on the options and parameters used while creating the rules, look over Table 20-1. You can use these options and parameters in any number of ways to create specific rules to control your firewall.

Table 20-1
ipchains options and parameters

Option	Description
-A	Appends to the end of the chain
-D	Deletes rules from the selected chain
-R	Replaces a rule in a chain
-I	Inserts a rule into a chain
-L	Lists all the rules of a chain
-F	Flushes, or removes, all the rules for a chain
-Z	Clears the accounting on the rules
-P	Changes the policy on a chain
-M	Views masqueraded connections
-S	Changes the masquerade timeout values

Parameter	Description
-p	The protocol of a rule (tcp, udp, icmp, or all)
-s	The source specification [!] address[/mask] [!] [port[:port]]
-d	The destination specification [!] address[/mask] [!] [port[:port]]
-j	Specifies the target of a rule
-i	The interface to be used

Notice that the source and destination parameters contain an exclamation point (!), which means the inverse of whatever follows it. This is referred to as *not*. So a rule that reads ! 192.168.10.120 means everything else but 192.168.10.120.

As you start getting the hang of adding rules, making rule changes, and removing rules, make sure that you save the finished state. Because you add them manually, those rule changes are out the window the next time the computer reboots.

Be sure to save the rule changes. It is a good idea to save as you go so you can return to any point along the way. There are two commands to help — ipchains-save and ipchains-restore. This command string saves the current rules for a later restore at boot time:

```
# ipchains-save > /etc/ipchains.rules
#
```

Use the -v option with the Save command to print all rules. You can then restore the rules from the created file using:

```
# ipchains-restore < /etc/ipchains.rules
#
```

You can create a script like the following to automatically add the rules at start time (this script is from IPCHAINS-HOWTO by Rusty Russell):

```
#! /bin/sh
# Script to control packet filtering.

# If no rules, do nothing.
[ -f /etc/ipchains.rules ] || exit 0

case "$1" in
    start)
        echo -n "Turning on packet filtering:"
        /sbin/ipchains-restore < /etc/ipchains.rules || exit 1
        echo 1 > /proc/sys/net/ipv4/ip_forward
        echo "."
        ;;
    stop)
        echo -n "Turning off packet filtering:"
        echo 0 > /proc/sys/net/ipv4/ip_forward
        /sbin/ipchains -F
        /sbin/ipchains -X
        /sbin/ipchains -P input ACCEPT
        /sbin/ipchains -P output ACCEPT
        /sbin/ipchains -P forward ACCEPT
        echo "."
        ;;
    *)
        echo "Usage: /etc/init.d/packetfilter {start|stop}"
        exit 1
        ;;
```

```
esac

exit 0
```

You can then create a symbolic link to this script in the `/etc/init.d` directory and add it to the rc2.d run level. The rules should run before networking in the run level. This script just adds and removes the rules kept in the `/etc/ipchains.rules` file created using the `ipchains-save` command.

You can find further examples in `IPCHAINS-HOWTO`, which is located at `www.linuxdoc.org`. `IPCHAINS-HOWTO` provides a lot of information, which can be confusing at first. The more you work with ipchains, the easier it becomes. However, once you set up ipchains, you may not need to change them again unless you feel that a configuration tool would work better.

Note   A special project has created all you need to make a router (software wise) and fit it on a 1.44 floppy disk. This may not be surprising; but by not using a hard disk, you can build a system that uses no moving parts to run. You can investigate the Linux Router Project (or LRP) at `www.linuxrouter.org`.

Masquerading a Private Network

In most cases, masquerading a private network is a great option. The purpose of the masquerade is to make numerous machines appear as one.

1. Install the `ipmasq` package using the Debian package-management system. There may be a recommended package that does not appear to be available. This second package is not needed for the firewall to work properly. `ipmasq` enables masquerading of your network for better protection.

2. Answer *no* to the question `Do you want to have ipmasq recompute the firewall rules when pppd rings up or takes down a link [Y/n]` if your system requires no dial-up services to connect to the Internet.

Note   Using a firewall with dial-up Internet is possible and also a good idea. Instead of using an Ethernet card for the Internet interface, use a `pppd` connection. When you install the `ipmasq` package, answer yes to the question about recomputing the firewall rules during the configuration portion of the install.

3. Ensure that both cards appear in the routing table, as shown here:

```
$ /sbin/route
Kernel IP routing table
Destination     Gateway        Genmask         Flags Metric Ref    Use Iface
localnet        *              255.255.255.224 U     0      0        0 eth0
192.168.0.0     *              255.255.255.224 U     0      0        0 eth1
default         node-d8e9791.po 0.0.0.0        UG     0      0        0 eth0
```

At this point, you should be able to ping across this machine from the internal network to the Internet. Anyone can get out to use the Internet; and as far as the Internet goes, all requests are coming from the firewall machine because of the masquerading. If you stop configuring at this point, you can run your systems with access to the Internet. However, for tighter control, set up rules for controlling what actually passes across the firewall. You can find the configuration files for doing so in /etc/ipmasq/rules.

Note   If you use real IP addresses for both sides of the network, then you should be able to ping in both directions. You must set up each remote machine to use this machine as the gateway, thus making the gateway address the same as the address assigned to the card connected to the same network. If you use a reserved set of addresses, as in 192.168.x.x, you cannot ping into that network.

Configuring a Firewall with PMFirewall

If you want to quickly and easily build a firewall, but don't understand the ipchains command strings, then use *PMFirewall*. Written in Perl script, it interactively configures the firewall on your system using ipchains. If you are interested in masquerading your internal network's IP addresses, you can configure that as well.

You can obtain a copy of the program at www.pmfirewall.com/PMFirewall. Once downloaded, move the file to /usr/src with:

    mv ./filename /usr/src

Then you can extract the contents of the tarball with

    tar zxvf filename.tar.gz

Change to the newly created directory and begin the installation (logged in as root) with

    /bin/sh ./install.sh

This installation process creates the program's new home at /usr/local/ pmfirewall. Here, all the configuration files are created. The script then confirms that you have ipchains installed and asks what you want to set as the external interface. Normally, the external interface is set to eth0. Figure 20-2 gives you an idea of what you might see during the installation.

If there are IP address ranges that require unrestricted access, then answer Yes and enter the address/netmask number in the next dialog box. If you are unsure, answer No to the first question.

If there are known IP addresses that should be blocked completely, then answer Yes to the question and enter those numbers. Again, if you are unsure, answer No to this question as well.

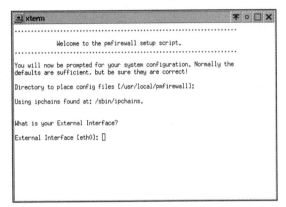

Figure 20-2: Answering configuration questions as PMFirewall installs

If your system receives its IP address via DHCP, then answer Yes to the next question. For the next few questions, you are asked about the specific services that you plan to run on this machine. These services are accessed from an external source. Typical firewall machines are used only as firewalls, which is the most secure practice. You should not use a firewall machine for any other Internet service, such as Web services, Domain Name Services (DNS), or File Transfer Protocol (FTP) services. For the purposes of security, I assume that you are installing a firewall-only server.

This is only a firewall machine, so answer No to all the services (such as FTP, Finger, Web, POP, and others). You should not allow some services, such as NetBIOS/Samba and NFS, on the firewall because of their tendency to allow file access.

You are then asked if you want to start PMFirewall when the system starts. Go ahead and answer Yes to this question, as automatically starting the firewall at system start won't require physical intervention by you later. When it does start, PMFirewall has the capability to detect the IP address for the machine. This is useful for systems that dial into an Internet Service Provider and get a different IP address each time.

If you don't care what address is used when someone from the inside makes an Internet request, then answer No to the question about masquerading. Then the configuration files are created and the firewall is ready to go.

If you do decide to set up masquerading of your internal network, there is no easier way to get it set up than with PMFirewall. Figure 20-3 shows where in the configuration you must make this decision.

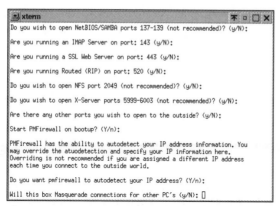

Figure 20-3: Masquerading is not configured by default.

There are just a couple of extra steps to perform if you want to set up masquerading. The first question asks you to specify the internal interface — the default is normally eth1 for the second card. The script then wants to autodetect the internal IP address. The script then asks if you use a DHCP server. Select the appropriate answer to continue. Several files are configured and then you are finished.

Note
If you use a group of private IP addresses for your internal network, then you need to employ masquerading, which you can easily set up using the PMFirewall script.

Locking Down the Firewall

When maximizing security, this is the most critical portion of the entire configuration. This is where you do your best to prevent people from cracking the firewall. If they get in here, then they have access to the entire network. With the proper setup on the firewall, you can still run some of the services for inside use only, such as OpenSSH, which provides a secure shell connection to a server.

The first step is to turn off all the ports on the firewall machine. An active port is an available door through which the attacker can enter. Normally these ports control daemons that start when a packet arrives. These ports include telnet, ftp, shell, and many others. To disable these ports, edit the /etc/inetd.conf file and place a pound sign (#) at the beginning of each line that does not have one (including discard, daytime, time, telnet, shell, login, exec, talk, ntalk, smtp, finger, and ident). Also, turn off any other ports not listed.

Once you comment out the services, restart the inetd daemon with the following:

```
# /etc/init.d/inetd restart
```

Test to make sure that the ports are no longer active by telneting to this machine. Try a couple of different ports.

```
$ telnet localhost
$ telnet localhost 25
```

The system should not respond to the telnet requests other than to inform you that the connection was refused.

If turning off the services is not an option for you and you want to add more security, here are a few simple additions and changes you can make:

✦ For added protection, create the file /etc/nologin. You can put a few lines of text in it such as, "This machine is off limits". When this file exists, the login does not allow any user to log on (except root from the console). These users only see the contents of this file and their refused logins.

✦ You can also edit the file /etc/securetty for a little more control of login locations. If the user is root, then the login must occur on a tty listed in /etc/securetty. The syslog facility logs all login failures.

With both of these controls in place, the only way to log in to the firewall is as root from the console. The server accepts no other attempts.

✦ If you need remote root access, use SSH (Secure Shell). I suggest that you turn off telnet. SSH provides a secure, encrypted data connection between two computers, whereas telnet transmits in clear text for anyone to see (including passwords).

✦ Add other countermeasures, such as Tripwire, to ensure that users do not tamper with anything.

As you might guess, if the software does not exist, then you cannot use it. Unfortunately, this is not always an option. Reducing the number of services, open ports, and number of actual accounts on a system is about all you can do in the end.

Squid Proxy Service

Because a firewall sets up a single point of access to the Internet for an organization, the traffic demands may be high at times. Many of those people may be looking at the same site. The point of a proxy, such as Squid, is to cache the Web pages for multiple requests at a location. For instance, if Joe visits www.fish-r-us.com, the page is loaded into cache on the proxy. Suppose a few seconds later Bob requests to visit the same site. This time, the proxy serves the page, rather than the request, to Bob.

Another service that a proxy can provide is controlling who gets access through the firewall; the network, IP address, or user name can do this. The proxy configuration file sets this and more.

The first step in setting up a proxy is making sure the software is in place. You need to install Squid from the archives. Once installed, you can begin to configure it for your system.

To configure Squid, you need to edit the `/etc/squid.conf` file. This file contains an example of nearly all settings available with this proxy server. By default, the server is set to not allow anyone to make requests through it. Setting up a Web browser to use the proxy server's default port of 3128 and attempting to access an external site produces the error message shown in Figure 20-4.

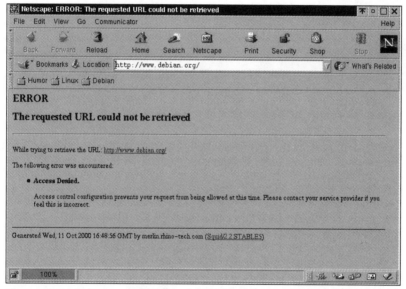

Figure 20-4: This error lets you know that the proxy is running but is not allowing you to grab the page.

You need to change a few settings in the configuration file. This is a large file to sift through using the text editor. The file is broken down into major categories:

- ✦ Network options
- ✦ Options affecting neighbor selection
- ✦ Options affecting the cache size
- ✦ Log file path names and cache directories
- ✦ Options for external support programs
- ✦ Options for tuning the cache
- ✦ Timeouts
- ✦ Access control

✦ Administration parameters

✦ Options for cache registration services

✦ HTTPD-Accelerator options

✦ Miscellaneous

The main change you need to make is in the Access control section. There is a line that reads as follows:

```
http_access deny all
```

Comment that line out and then add the following line:

```
http_access allow all
```

This enables anyone on your network to browse the Internet once you restart the Squid service. Restart the service using the following:

```
/etc/init.d/squid restart
```

You can continue to narrow the scope of who has access by creating an access group in that same section. The syntax at the beginning of the section reads as follows:

```
acl aclname src IPaddress/netmask
```

And a local group of IP addresses looks like this:

```
acl local src 192.168.10.1-192.168.10.30/255.255.255.224
```

This line sets the range of addresses as the source and gives it a name of `local`. You can then add that name to the `http_access` group:

```
http_access allow local
```

Likewise, you can also block a group of internal addresses. You can allow or deny access in several ways, whether you want to specify the source, the destination, or even a URL. Reading through the configuration file should give you some understanding of configuring the server. You can also look at `www.squid-cache.org` to get more information.

Accessing the Internet through a Firewall/Proxy

A firewall should act as a gatekeeper — letting requests go out from sources on the inside, but not letting requests come in. The outgoing requests are intercepted and redirected to the correct port on the remote server. The proxy only listens to one port and then interprets the request. If the server does not have the desired pages, then it goes out and gets them. You must set up your internal devices to make the requests to the correct internal proxy address and port number.

The most common device that needs configuration is the Web browser. To add the proxy information to Netscape, for instance, open the browser. Once the browser is open, click Edit and then Preferences. A dialog box appears. On the left side, click the triangle sign next to Advanced.

You should see two new items appear. Clicking Proxy changes the information in the right side of the dialog box. Select the Manual option, and press the button labeled View. For each service your server proxies, enter the IP address or the fully qualified domain name in the left box and the proxy port on the right. For the default HTTP proxy service, the port is 3128. Figure 20-5 shows the configuration screen in Netscape.

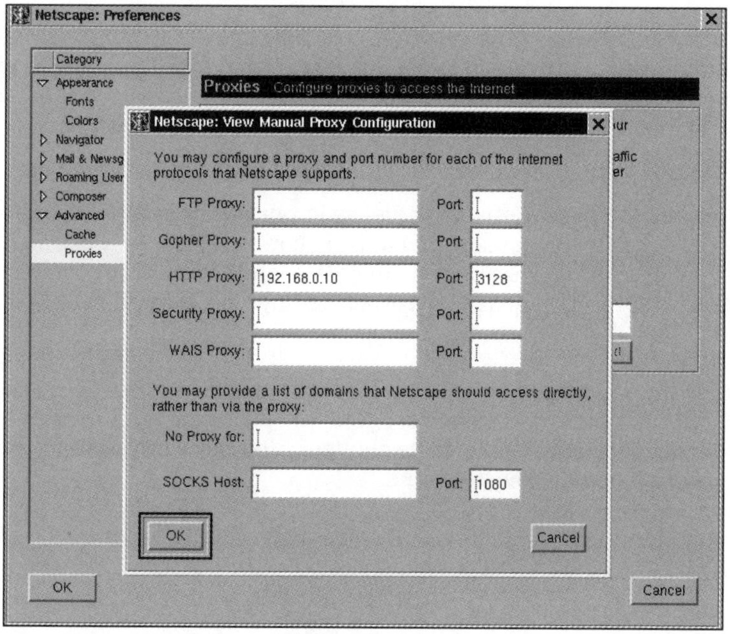

Figure 20-5: Configuring proxies in Netscape

For the lynx and Mosaic browsers, you can set an environment variable to define the proxy. The two shells, csh and tcsh, use the following commands to set the variable:

```
setenv http_proxy http://myhost:3128/
setenv gopher_proxy http://myhost:3128/
setenv ftp_proxy http://myhost:3128/
```

For the ksh and bash shells, you use:

```
export http_proxy=http://myhost:3128/
export gopher_proxy=http://myhost:3128/
export ftp_proxy=http://myhost:3128/
```

You can add any of these to the startup scripts for your preferred shell (for example, ~/.bashrc). You can also add them to /etc/profile to make them useful system wide.

The systems on the local network also need to point to the internal network IP of the firewall as the gateway. This tells traffic destined for the Internet where to go to reach its destination.

Summary

With an understanding of what a firewall does, you now know the importance of using a firewall to protect a private network. On top of that, masquerading the IP addresses lets your entire internal network of computers appear from the outside as if all requests come from the firewall. This adds to the degree of protection because those addresses are never transmitted over the Internet.

Setting up a firewall for a home network is just as important as setting up one for an office. Granted, configuring rules using ipchains by hand may not seem straightforward in the beginning, but it gives you the greatest control in choosing the restrictions. In addition, with tools such as PMFirewall, setting up a firewall keeps getting easier.

To control access from the inside, the proxy server controls what services are used, who can use them, and from what systems. Squid, the proxy server, provides an extensive list of configuration options in its configuration file. The possible configuration variations are too numerous to count.

You can find more information about firewalls, ipchains, and IP masquerading from the list of HOWTOs at www.linuxdoc.org.

✦   ✦   ✦

Web Server

Accessing Web pages on the Internet normally only takes a Web browser. However, somewhere in the world, those pages must be published. The Web server is the mechanism that publishes those pages for you to see. The content of those pages can vary from display, text-only information to graphics-only info, or it can be a combination of both graphics and text. Incidentally, you can also publish Web pages without accessing the Internet at all. They can be published for a private network or just for local use. This chapter covers the basics of the Apache Web server, how it is used, and a couple of the common variations to the straightforward Web server.

Introduction to Apache Web Server

All Web servers use a simple protocol known as *Hypertext Transfer Protocol (HTTP)* to standardize the way requests are received, processed, and sent out again. This allows various clients, called *browsers,* to interact with a variety of Web servers without dealing with compatibility issues. Having standards in a world where change takes place daily is crucial to the survival of any technology. Web servers are no exception.

As far as the Internet goes, Web servers have been around for some time. This particular "vision of a better mousetrap" developed into the Apache server, as it was born out of a need to repair or patch the Web server called NCSA Web server. Since that time, the Apache server has gone through several revisions to the fine product that it is today.

According to a May 2000 survey of over 15 million Web sites, Apache is the winner of Web servers. The number one (Apache) leads the number two (Microsoft-IIS) by almost three times as many servers. This is not surprising because Apache has been the leader since mid 1996. The source of the survey, Netcraft (www.netcraft.co.uk/survey), uses an automated process to evaluate Web servers all over the world. Table 21-1 shows the results of the survey.

Table 21-1
Survey of Web servers

Server name	Total Servers	Percentage of Market Share
Apache	9,095,140	60.44
Microsoft-IIS	3,168,831	21.06
Netscape-Enterprise	1,083,161	7.20
Zeus	301,073	2.00
Rapidsite	277,147	1.84
thttpd	204,187	1.36
WebSitePro	106,327	0.71
WebLogic	90,609	0.60
Stronghold	89,682	0.60
WebSTAR	81,901	0.54

One of the advantages to using the Apache server is the fact that it employs modules to provide various functions. This enables you to add new functions easily, while disabling functions that do not streamline the server. Part of the reason that Apache has taken such a lead in the Web server market is due to its effectiveness, efficiency, and power in processing HTTP requests. This is no small task considering that one server can receive hundreds, if not thousands, of requests per day.

Installing the Apache Server

The toughest part of getting this software to work is installing it — and that's really simple. Installing the Apache Web Server with `dselect` works the same as installing any of the other packages included on the CD-ROM. You simply start the `dselect` program from a command prompt, select the Apache server version from the CD for installation, and then install the Apache server and any required packages. You are then offered to make any configuration changes during installation to complete the setup. These configuration settings include the server administrator's e-mail address.

You can perform the configuration of the server using `apacheconfig` any time after the initial setup completes. This script configures the Web server for its most basic function — serving pages to a network or the Internet. The script automatically configures Apache for you.

Note This gets set to webmaster@hostname.mydoamin.com, which can be aliased or redirected to the mailbox of the actual person in charge. (See Chapter 25 for details on aliasing email)

Finally, you can save the configuration settings and restart the Apache server.

The other option (besides dselect) is to download the source files from the Apache Web site (www.apache.org) for a complete installation from scratch. You can find the latest files for downloading at www.apache.org. You have the choice of using binaries for all types of Linux flavors or getting the source code to compile yourself. Both methods include README instructions for installation. Follow those instructions for the smoothest installation.

The results of a successful installation are the same. You see a default Web page when looking through a Web browser at the machine. To accomplish this, open a Web browser and use http://localhost/ as the address for the Uniform Resource Locator (URL). This brings up the default Web page seen in Figure 21-1.

Figure 21-1: Hurray! A successful install

Note Apache comes in a *Secure Socket Layer (SSL)* version, which provides encrypted communication between the client and the server. This enables sites to pass data back and forth securely with little risk. The Apache-SSL version is available for install through the Debian installation files.

Installation and setup for Apache-SSL work the same as the regular Apache, but the SSL version includes additional security-related modules and directives. Search the www.apache-ssl.org Web site for more information about these features. Because of the encryption used, some areas of the world may not be permitted to use the SSL version.

Configuration files

Although the installation of Apache through the dselect program finishes with basic configuration settings, there is still much more that you can do with this Web server. Keeping in mind the use of the Web server, in most cases you can only use it for publishing HTML material. However, you can employ Apache for secure transactions, multihoming for hosting more than one domain on a machine, and providing secure, password-protected Web access.

Three files contain all the configuration data for Apache. You can find these configuration files (httpd.conf, access.conf, and srm.conf) at /etc/apache, and you can edit them with your favorite text editor. The following sections discuss each of the configuration files in detail. These files are accessed one at a time, starting with the httpd.conf file and ending with srm.conf. Any commands or instruction found in the first configuration file are not repeated in the others unless the order of execution is important.

The httpd.conf configuration file

The httpd.conf file contains the main configuration file for the server. This file houses the vital settings for type of server, locations of supporting log files, the account name the server runs as, and more. Also contained in this file are the settings to control the performance of the server itself.

You get to see the configuration file from the Debian Apache install. As you move through the file, I point out important parts of the configuration to help better explain those sections. This gives you a better understanding for configuring your own machine. The header of the configuration file contains the URL for Apache, the originator of the file, and a warning not to modify this file without understanding what you are changing. Any modifications can have a major impact on the performance, functionality, and (most of all) security of the Web server. The following code comes from the httpd.conf file, and sections of the file are scattered through the following pages.

```
# This is the main server configuration file.
# See URL http://www.apache.org/ for instructions.


# Do not simply read the instructions in here without
# understanding what they do. If you are unsure, consult
# the online docs. You have been warned.


# Originally by Rob McCool

# Shared Object Module Loading:
# To be able to use the functionality of a module which was
# built as a shared object, you have to place corresponding
# LoadModule lines at this location so the directives
# contained in it are available _before_
# they are used.
# Example:
```

Server type in httpd.conf

This option, better known as a *directive,* determines how the Web server runs on the system. As a standalone, you must start the server manually (or with a script) using the root account. The server continues to run until you stop it. Only the root, or superuser, can change user and group IDs; and only the root account can assign services to Internet ports lower than 1025. When Apache is packaged for Debian, it includes the apachectl script, which you use to start and stop the server.

Tip   A tool included with the Apache package is apachectl which easily starts, stops, and restarts the Apache server. You can also check the status of the server or test a new configuration. For a complete list of the options available with apachectl, check out the man pages

If you set the server type to inetd, then whenever a request comes to the port that the Web server is bound to, the server is started. Otherwise, the service stops until the next request is received. This option does not make for a responsive Web server. However, this works well when used in a software development environment in which the server must restart often to include configuration changes. The default server is standalone, and should remain as such unless you understand the implications of changing it.

```
# ServerType is either inetd or standalone.

ServerType standalone

# If you are running from inetd, go to "ServerAdmin".

# Port: The port the standalone listens to. For ports < 1023,
```

Continued

```
# you will need to run httpd as root initially.
Port 80

# HostnameLookups: Log the names of clients or just their IP
# numbers e.g. www.apache.org (on) or 204.62.129.132 (off)
# The default is off because it'd be overall better for the net
# if people had to knowingly turn this feature on.

HostnameLookups off
```

Ownership (user/group)

This directive is very important to the security of your system. The Web service must start as root, after which it changes to some user and group. This section specifies the name of the preferred user and group. By default, the Apache configuration of the Debian package creates a user and a group named www-data. This happens for security reasons in order to prevent anyone from hacking into the system through the Web server port. These accounts have very limited privileges.

When you start the Web server as root in the standalone mode and a request comes to the machine for a Web page, the server spawns a child process using the defined user and group to handle the request. (I discuss child processes later in this section.)

```
# If you wish httpd to run as a different user or group, you
# must run httpd as root initially and it will switch.

# User/Group: The name (or #number) of the user/group to
# run httpd as.
# On SCO (ODT 3) use User nouser and Group nogroup
# On HPUX you may not be able to use shared memory as nobody,
# and the suggested workaround is to create a user www and use # that user.

User www-data
Group www-data
```

Server admin and root

These sections may be self-explanatory, but they contain important references. The server admin manages the server in the event that something is wrong or needs changing. Normally, that person also is the root user. You can change this to anyone with a valid e-mail address. You must change the default address, root@your-domain.org, to your qualified root e-mail address. Most often, this gets changed to webmaster@mydomain.com, where mydoamin.com is the domain of the host server.

The server root indicates the default location where all related files for the server reside. As you can see, the Debian install uses /etc/apache as the root directory location. The server appends this path to the beginning of the references to configuration, error, and log files.

```
# ServerAdmin: Your address, where problems with the server
# should be e-mailed.
ServerAdmin root@your-domain.org

# ServerRoot: The directory in which the server's config, error, and log
# files reside.
# NOTE! If you intend to place this on an NFS (or other
# network) mounted filesystem, please read the LockFile
# documentation. You will save yourself a lot of trouble.

ServerRoot /etc/apache
```

The BindAddress

Apache has the capability of serving Web pages for more than one domain or IP address. This option sets the domains or IP addresses for which Apache serves the Web pages. This is similar to the virtual hosting covered at the end of this file. Using the asterisk (*), the server responds to all requests, domain names, and IP addresses associated with this machine. When using the asterisk, the Web server looks at all requests.

```
# BindAddress: You can support virtual hosts with this option.
# This option tells the server which IP address to
# listen to. It can either contain "*", an IP address, or a
# fully qualified Internet domain name.
# See also the VirtualHost directive.

BindAddress *
```

Modules loaded in httpd.conf

Part of the advantage of Apache is your ability to modify the overall function of the server by adding and removing features. These features are loaded into the server as modules. You can easily add new features simply by appending the appropriate module to this configuration file.

The following code lists all the modules available with the Debian install. Unused modules are commented out with the pound sign (#). This section shows all modules loaded by default. These modules cover server concerns such as security, access control, accounting, resource location, and more.

You can get the specifics about each module by going to the Apache Web site or looking it up on your machine at localhost/doc/apache.

```
# The Debian package of Apache loads every feature as shared
# modules. Please keep this LoadModule: line here, it is needed
# for installation.
# LoadModule env_module /usr/lib/apache/1.3/mod_env.so
LoadModule config_log_module /usr/lib/apache/1.3/mod_log_config.so
LoadModule rewrite_module /usr/lib/apache/1.3/mod_rewrite.so
```

Continued

```
# LoadModule mime_magic_module /usr/lib/apache/1.3/mod_mime_magic.so
LoadModule mime_module /usr/lib/apache/1.3/mod_mime.so
LoadModule negotiation_module /usr/lib/apache/1.3/mod_negotiation.so
# LoadModule status_module /usr/lib/apache/1.3/mod_status.so
# LoadModule info_module /usr/lib/apache/1.3/mod_info.so
# LoadModule includes_module /usr/lib/apache/1.3/mod_include.so
LoadModule autoindex_module /usr/lib/apache/1.3/mod_autoindex.so
LoadModule dir_module /usr/lib/apache/1.3/mod_dir.so
LoadModule cgi_module /usr/lib/apache/1.3/mod_cgi.so
# LoadModule asis_module /usr/lib/apache/1.3/mod_asis.so
# LoadModule imap_module /usr/lib/apache/1.3/mod_imap.so
# LoadModule action_module /usr/lib/apache/1.3/mod_actions.so
# LoadModule speling_module /usr/lib/apache/1.3/mod_speling.so
LoadModule userdir_module /usr/lib/apache/1.3/mod_userdir.so
# LoadModule proxy_module /usr/lib/apache/1.3/libproxy.so
LoadModule alias_module /usr/lib/apache/1.3/mod_alias.so
LoadModule access_module /usr/lib/apache/1.3/mod_access.so
LoadModule auth_module /usr/lib/apache/1.3/mod_auth.so
# LoadModule anon_auth_module /usr/lib/apache/1.3/mod_auth_anon.so
# LoadModule dbm_auth_module /usr/lib/apache/1.3/mod_auth_dbm.so
# LoadModule db_auth_module /usr/lib/apache/1.3/mod_auth_db.so
# LoadModule digest_module /usr/lib/apache/1.3/mod_digest.so
# LoadModule cern_meta_module /usr/lib/apache/1.3/mod_cern_meta.so
LoadModule expires_module /usr/lib/apache/1.3/mod_expires.so
# LoadModule headers_module /usr/lib/apache/1.3/mod_headers.so
# LoadModule usertrack_module /usr/lib/apache/1.3/mod_usertrack.so
LoadModule unique_id_module /usr/lib/apache/1.3/mod_unique_id.so
LoadModule setenvif_module /usr/lib/apache/1.3/mod_setenvif.so
# LoadModule throttle_module /usr/lib/apache/1.3/mod_throttle.so
# LoadModule php3_module /usr/lib/apache/1.3/libphp3.so
```

Logging events

Event logging is very important for a number of reasons, including troubleshooting, tracking misuse, and recording site activity. This section lists the location of these files. They normally reside in the /var/log/apache directory, but you can store them anywhere on the system you specify.

The type of information that is recorded in the files also is configured here. The LogFormat option associates a list of collectable information followed by an identifier. You can then use the CustomLog option to send the various LogFormat types to different log files. Likewise, you can include all the tracking information in one file.

```
# ErrorLog: The location of the error log file. If this does
# not start with /, ServerRoot is prepended to it.

ErrorLog /var/log/apache/error.log

# LogLevel: Control the number of messages logged to the
# error_log.
# Possible values include: debug, info, notice, warn, error,
```

```
# crit, alert, emerg.


LogLevel warn

# The following directives define some format nicknames for use
# with a CustomLog directive (see below).

LogFormat "%h %l %u %t \"%r\" %>s %b \"%{Referer}i\" \"%{User-Agent}i\" %T %v"
   full
LogFormat "%h %l %u %t \"%r\" %>s %b \"%{Referer}i\" \"%{User-Agent}i\""
   combined
LogFormat "%h %l %u %t \"%r\" %>s %b" common
LogFormat "%{Referer}i -> %U" referer
LogFormat "%{User-agent}i" agent
# The location of the access log file (Common Logfile Format).
# If this does not start with /, ServerRoot is prepended to it.

CustomLog /var/log/apache/access.log common

# If you would like to have an agent and referer log file,
# uncomment the following directives.

#CustomLog logs/referer_log referer
#CustomLog logs/agent_log agent

# If you prefer a single log file with access, agent, and referer
# information (Combined Logfile Format) you can use the
# following directive.

#CustomLog logs/access_log combined

# PidFile: The file the server should log its PID to
PidFile /var/run/apache.pid

# ScoreBoardFile: File used to store internal server process
# information. Not all architectures require this. But if yours # does
# (you'll know because this file is created
# when you run Apache), then you *must* ensure that
# no two invocations of Apache share the same scoreboard file.
# ScoreBoardFile logs/apache_runtime_status

# The LockFile directive sets the path to the lock file used
# when Apache is compiled with either
# USE_FCNTL_SERIALIZED_ACCEPT or
# USE_FLOCK_SERIALIZED_ACCEPT. This directive normally
# should be left at its default value. The main reason for changing
# it is if the logs directory is NFS mounted
# because the lock file MUST BE STORED ON A LOCAL
# DISK. The PID of the main server process is automatically
# appended to the filename.

#
LockFile /var/run/apache.lock
```

Server name in httpd.conf

This section describes how the Web server is known on the Internet. Generally, this is recognized as the host name. *Host names* are qualified, registered Internet domain names. As noted in the comments, you cannot use any name that comes to mind. The same goes for IP numbers. By default, this option isn't used; you must change it manually.

```
# ServerName enables you to set a host name which is sent back
# to clients for your server if it's different than the one
# the program would get (i.e. use
# "www" instead of the host's real name).
#
# Note: You cannot just invent host names and hope they work.
# The name you define here must be
# a valid DNS name for your host. If you don't understand
# this, ask your network administrator.

#ServerName new.host.name

# UseCanonicalName: (new for 1.3)  With this setting turned
# on, whenever Apache needs to construct a self-referencing
# URL (a URL that refers to the server
# the response is coming from) it will use ServerName and
# Port to form a "canonical" name.  With this setting off,
# Apache will use the hostname:port that the client supplied,
# when possible. This also affects SERVER_NAME and SERVER_PORT
# in CGIs.
UseCanonicalName on
```

Cache and KeepAlive settings

This section covers several related core directives. The first option, CacheNegotiatedDocs, refers to your server telling a requestor using a proxy server whether they are allowed to cache your pages. If left commented out (default), then each request is forced to return to your site for the pages. This helps with site statistics.

Occasionally, there are delays on the Internet due to high traffic, requestor disconnection, and system failures. The Timeout option sets, in seconds, the time between a request coming in (receives) and going out (sends). The server can stop requests if they exceed the timeout. You should set this at a high number to allow sufficient time for requests to be sent.

With KeepAlive turned on, the server allows multiple transactions over one connection. This greatly increases performance because each request doesn't need to establish a new connection. The next option sets the maximum requests from one client. This prevents one person from consuming all the server resources. Also, a request timeout is started as soon as the server receives the request.

```
# CacheNegotiatedDocs: By default, Apache sends Pragma:
# no-cache with each document that was negotiated
# on the basis of content. This asks proxy servers not
# to cache the document. Uncommenting the following line
# disables this behavior, and proxies will be allowed
# to cache the documents.

#CacheNegotiatedDocs

# Timeout: The number of seconds before receives and
# sends time out

Timeout 300

# KeepAlive: Whether or not to allow persistent connections
# (more than one request per connection). Set to "Off"
# to deactivate.

KeepAlive On

# MaxKeepAliveRequests: The maximum number of requests to allow
# during a persistent connection. Set to 0 to allow an
# unlimited amount.
# We reccomend you leave this number high, for maximum
# performance.

MaxKeepAliveRequests 100

# KeepAliveTimeout: Number of seconds to wait for the next
# request

KeepAliveTimeout 15
```

Server-pool

This area of the configuration file determines how the daemon maintains itself. MinSpareServers determines the minimum number of idle child servers allowed at any one time. An *idle child server* is any httpd server not responding to an HTTP request. If more requests come in, requiring more child servers to start, then at least five (set as default) idle ones remain alive after the requests die down. MaxSpareServers limits the total number of idle servers, meaning that no more than 10 (set by default) idle servers remain alive. If your Web server has an abnormally high number of requests, increasing the maximum number boosts the performance by keeping more child processes alive when the traffic slows for a few seconds. This makes the processes ready to respond when the traffic increases again.

The StartServers value determines the number of child servers that start when the daemon starts. This usually is set to the same number as the MinSpareServers value. `MaxClients` limits the number of connections that a server as a whole can handle at one time. Connection requests above that number are put in a wait state until a connection is available again.

The next directive, `MaxRequestsPerChild`, imposes a limit on the number of requests a child `httpd` server can respond to before its termination. Initially, this directive prevented a `httpd` process from degrading due to memory leaks. In most cases today, memory leaks from child processes are not a problem; however, this directive remains enabled as a matter of practice.

```
# Server-pool size regulation.  Rather than making you guess
# how many server processes you need, Apache dynamically
# adapts to the load it sees --- that is, it tries
# to maintain enough server processes to
# handle the current load, plus a few spare servers to handle
# transient load spikes (e.g., multiple simultaneous requests
# from a single Netscape browser).


# It does this by periodically checking how many servers are
# waiting for a request. If there are fewer than
# MinSpareServers, it creates a new spare. If there
# are more than MaxSpareServers, some of the spares die.
# These values are probably OK for most sites ---

MinSpareServers 5
MaxSpareServers 10

# Number of servers to start --- should be a reasonable
# ballpark figure.

StartServers 5

# Limit on total number of servers running, i.e.,
# limit on the number of clients who can simultaneously
# connect --- if this limit is ever reached, clients will
# be locked out, so it should not be set too low.
# It is intended mainly as a brake to keep a runaway server
# from taking UNIX with it as it spirals down.

MaxClients 150

# MaxRequestsPerChild: the number of requests each child
# process is allowed to process before the child dies.
# The child will exit so as to avoid problems after prolonged
# use when Apache (and maybe the libraries it uses) leak.
# On most systems, this isn't really needed, but
# a few (such as Solaris) do have notable leaks
# in the libraries.

MaxRequestsPerChild 30
```

Virtual hosting

The Listen directive allows a machine to assign the server to more than one IP address or port. This enables you to post Web pages for more than one IP address. The Listen directive is very similar to the BindAddress directive.

VirtualHost is common practice for Internet Web-hosting facilities. For each Internet domain, add the virtual host information to this section. The sample given here shows the basic information needed to host Web pages for several domains. You can find more specifics on setting up virtual hosting later in this chapter in the section "Enabling Virtual Hosting."

```
# Listen: Allows you to bind Apache to specific IP addresses
# and/or ports, in addition to the default. See also
# the VirtualHost command

#Listen 3000
#Listen 12.34.56.78:80

# VirtualHost: Allows the daemon to respond to requests for
# more than one server address, if your server machine
# is configured to accept IP packets for multiple addresses.
# This can be accomplished with the ifconfig
# alias flag, or through kernel patches like VIF.

# Any httpd.conf or srm.conf directive may go into a
# VirtualHost command. See also the BindAddress entry.

#<VirtualHost host.some_domain.com>
#ServerAdmin webmaster@host.some_domain.com
#DocumentRoot /var/www/host.some_domain.com
#ServerName host.some_domain.com
#ErrorLog /var/log/apache/host.some_domain.com-error.log
#TransferLog /var/log/apache/host.some_domain.com-access.log
#</VirtualHost>
```

Many of these directives are explained in varying degrees. You do not need to change most of these settings. The default settings provide the best performance in most cases.

For each new virtual domain, use the code between <VirtualHost domain> and </VirtualHost>, inclusive. For instance, suppose you were hosting three domains called fun.com, morefun.com, and extremefun.com. Each of these domains needs its own entry in the httpd.conf file.

```
<VirtualHost www.fun.com>
ServerAdmin webmaster@fun.com
DocumentRoot /var/www/fun.com
ServerName www.fun.com
ErrorLog /var/log/apache/www.fun.com-error.log
```

Continued

```
TransferLog /var/log/apache/www.fun.com-access.log
</VirtualHost>

<VirtualHost www.morefun.com>
ServerAdmin webmaster@morefun.com
DocumentRoot /var/www/morefun.com
ServerName www.morefun.com
ErrorLog /var/log/apache/www.morefun.com-error.log
TransferLog /var/log/apache/www.morefun.com-access.log
</VirtualHost>

<VirtualHost www.extremefun.com>
ServerAdmin webmaster@extremefun.com
DocumentRoot /var/www/extremefun.com
ServerName www.extremefun.com
ErrorLog /var/log/apache/www.extremefun.com-error.log
TransferLog /var/log/apache/www.extremefun.com-access.log
</VirtualHost>
```

Once these changes are made for these virtual domains, the Apache server restarts and the domain entries point to the hosting machine. Apache will now respond to requests for the new virtual domains.

The srm.conf configuration file

This is the resource configuration file for the Web server. It includes locations of various resources such as the Web pages, associations of files, and other such information. As this section proceeds through the file, I point out the different directives contained in it. Like the other files, be sure to understand the directive before making any changes to it.

```
# With this document, you define the name space that users see
# of your http server. This file also defines server settings
# which affect how requests are serviced, and how
# results should be formatted.

# See the tutorials at http://www.apache.org/ for
# more information.

# Originally by Rob McCool; Adapted for Apache
```

DocumentRoot

This is the default location where all Web pages reside for the Web server to dish out when requests come in for the default domain. When you first install Apache, this directory is created; and it includes the first page you see when pointing a browser to your new server.

```
# DocumentRoot: The directory out of which you will serve your
# documents. By default, all requests are taken from this
# directory, but symbolic links and aliases may be
```

```
# used to point to other locations.

DocumentRoot /var/www
```

UserDir

Individuals on the system can enjoy the use of personal Web pages. This enables users to create directories they can use to post Web pages for others to see. This path is set for *all* directories in the /home directory that contain the public_html directory. Those using this feature then employ the following as their URL:

```
http://localhost/~userID/
```

You can replace localhost with an IP address or domain name. The tilde (~) must remain; however, the userID changes to the name of the account.

```
# UserDir: The name of the directory which is appended onto
# a user's home
# directory if a ~user request is recieved.

UserDir /home/*/public_html
```

DirectoryIndex

This directive specifies the name of the default page the server looks at when the incoming request does not specify one. You may consider adding a few more to this list such as index.htm, index.shtml, and index.cgi. For recognition, a space must separate each new name. The order in which the names are placed also sets the priority determining which files are used.

```
# DirectoryIndex: Name of the file or files to use as
# a pre-written HTML directory index. Separate multiple
# entries with spaces.

DirectoryIndex index.html
```

FancyIndexing and icons

The FancyIndexing directive refers to the choice of using custom icons to reference files in a directory listing. A directory listing through the browser occurs when the DirectoryIndex file is missing. Often, you employ this feature when using anonymous access to public files and directories. Setting this to off displays standard, generic icons.

The icon directives — AddIcon, AddIconByEncoding, AddIconByType, and DefaultIcon — all associate specific file types with a descriptive icon image. Based on the file's extension, an image is displayed for the file when viewing the directory through a browser. These directive settings only function when you set FancyIndexing to on.

```
# FancyIndexing is whether you want fancy directory indexing
# or standard

FancyIndexing on

# AddIcon tells the server which icon to show for different
# files or filename extensions


AddIconByEncoding (CMP,/icons/compressed.gif) x-compress x-gzip

AddIconByType (TXT,/icons/text.gif) text/*
AddIconByType (IMG,/icons/image2.gif) image/*
AddIconByType (SND,/icons/sound2.gif) audio/*
AddIconByType (VID,/icons/movie.gif) video/*

AddIcon /icons/binary.gif .bin .exe
AddIcon /icons/binhex.gif .hqx
AddIcon /icons/tar.gif .tar
AddIcon /icons/world2.gif .wrl .wrl.gz .vrml .vrm .iv
AddIcon /icons/compressed.gif .Z .z .tgz .gz .zip
AddIcon /icons/a.gif .ps .ai .eps
AddIcon /icons/layout.gif .html .shtml .htm .pdf
AddIcon /icons/text.gif .txt
AddIcon /icons/c.gif .c
AddIcon /icons/p.gif .pl .py
AddIcon /icons/f.gif .for
AddIcon /icons/dvi.gif .dvi
AddIcon /icons/uuencoded.gif .uu
AddIcon /icons/script.gif .conf .sh .shar .csh .ksh .tcl
AddIcon /icons/tex.gif .tex
AddIcon /icons/bomb.gif core

AddIcon /icons/back.gif ..
AddIcon /icons/hand.right.gif README
AddIcon /icons/folder.gif ^^DIRECTORY^^
AddIcon /icons/blank.gif ^^BLANKICON^^

# DefaultIcon is which icon to show for files that do not
# have an icon explicitly set.


DefaultIcon /icons/unknown.gif
```

Description, Headers, and Readme files

You can add file description information to viewable directory indexes that contain information about the individual file types in the directory. As you can see, the AddDescription directive isn't used by default.

Headers and Readme files, however, are set here. The server first looks for HEADER.html and/or README.html files. If these don't exist, then the server looks for these filenames without the .html extension. If none of these options appear, then the server uses nothing. Oftentimes, these files contain general information about the site, legal disclaimers, and/or specific instructions regarding the site or files.

`IndexIgnore` specifies which files are ignored when the server displays the listing for the directory. You can add to this list, but remember that this global setting affects how these files are displayed throughout the entire server.

```
# AddDescription allows you to place a short description after
# a file in server-generated indexes.
# Format: AddDescription "description" filename

# ReadmeName is the name of the README file the server will
# look for by default. Format: ReadmeName name
#
# The server will first look for name.html, include it
# if found, and it will then look for name and
# include it as plaintext if found.
#
# HeaderName is the name of a file that should be prepended to
# directory indexes.

ReadmeName README
HeaderName HEADER

# IndexIgnore is a set of filenames that directory indexing
# should ignore. Format: IndexIgnore name1 name2...

IndexIgnore .??* *~ *# HEADER* README* RCS
```

Access, encoding, and language

These three main configuration files (`httpd.conf`, `asscess.conf`, and `srm.conf`) control the global response of the server, so a provision enables individual directories to set their own directives. Any directive that works in the main files works in the `.htaccess` file (which you can create in each directory served by the server). However, you have to make sure that the `access.conf` file allows overrides. The default setting doesn't enable this feature, so look for `AllowOverride` in the `access.conf` file to grant use of the `.htaccess` file. This file comes in handy when you want to individually control the server features that an individual has when publishing Web pages.

The Apache server uses the `mime.types` file to associate file extensions with the type of file. For instance, files ending with `.gif` are image files; files ending in `.wav` are audio files; and so on. When the file extension is not included in the `mime.types` file, then the `DefaultType` directive treats the file as a text file.

Using the `AddLanguage` directive enables the creator of the Web pages to add pages for multiple languages. When the client makes the request to the server, the content is delivered based on the client language. The `AddLanguage` directive also controls the language of a document after you remove any encoding. Then when a client neglects to set a language preference, LanguagePriority sets the order by which a language file is chosen for the client (assuming that multiple language versions of the document exist). In default case, the order of priority is English, French, and then German.

```
# AccessFileName: The name of the file to look for in each
# directory for access control information.

AccessFileName .htaccess

# DefaultType is the default MIME type for documents that the
# server cannot find the type of from filename extensions.

DefaultType text/plain

# AddEncoding allows you to have certain browsers
# (Mosaic/X 2.1+) uncompress information on the fly.
# Note: Not all browsers support this.

AddEncoding x-compress Z
AddEncoding x-gzip gz

# AddLanguage allows you to specify the language of a document.
# You can then use content negotiation to give a browser a
# file in a language it can understand.
# Note that the suffix does not have to be the same
# as the language keyword --- those with documents in
# Polish (whose net-standard language code is pl)
# may wish to use "AddLanguage pl .po" to avoid
# the ambiguity with the common suffix for perl scripts.

AddLanguage en .en
AddLanguage fr .fr
AddLanguage de .de
AddLanguage da .da
AddLanguage it .it
AddLanguage es .es
AddLanguage br .br
AddLanguage jp .jp
AddLanguage dk .dk
AddLanguage pl .pl
AddLanguage kr .kr

# LanguagePriority allows you to give precedence to some
# languages in case of a tie during content negotiation.
# Just list the languages in decreasing order of preference.

LanguagePriority en fr de
```

Redirection and aliasing

Redirect and Alias point Web pages and files to places other than where the clients specify them. Redirect takes an incoming page request and redirects it to another URL. Generally, Redirect functions for outside URLs. (For instance, requests coming in for /data1 can get redirected to http://www.somedomain. org/moredata.) Redirects come in handy when sites move from one host to another, or a domain's name changes. Old sites or domain names can redirect requests to the new location. To complement Redirect, Alias points to files and directories outside of the default server document root. You can tell from the following alias how this works. Whenever the directory /icons/ is referenced in a URL path, it points to /usr/share/apache/icons/ (which is where all the files are located). The Alias directive is used most frequently to substitute long path names (that actually exist) with shorter names.

ScriptAlias works similarly to Alias, but it specifies the real location of scripts for Web pages. Scripts improves the functionality of Web pages by processing results from a form, using data to dynamically update a Web page, or adding any number of other applications to enhance a Web page.

```
# Redirect allows you to tell clients about documents that
# used to exist in your server's namespace, but do not
# anymore. This allows you to tell the
# clients where to look for the relocated document.
# Format: Redirect fakename url


# Aliases: Add here as many aliases as you need (with no
# limit). The format is Alias fakename realname


# Note that if you include a trailing / on fakename then
# the server will require it to be present in the URL.
# So "/icons" isn't aliased in this example.


Alias /icons/ /usr/share/apache/icons/

# ScriptAlias: This controls which directories contain\
# server scripts.
# Format: ScriptAlias fakename realname

ScriptAlias /cgi-bin/ /usr/lib/cgi-bin/
```

File associations

The mime.types file is an extensive listing of associations between file extensions and their corresponding types. Occasionally, you may want to add a new file type association. One way to add it is by editing the mime.types file. The other option is to add the association with the AddType directive.

AddHandler tells the server what to do with certain file types. Table 21-2 lists the available handlers.

Table 21-2
Available AddHandler handlers

Handler	Purpose
cgi-script	CGI script files (programs)
send-as-is	Send the file as a normal HTTP file
server-info	Provides the server configuration
server-status	Provides the status of the server
server-parsed	Processed by the server (server-side includes)
imap-file	Processes image map files
type-map	Processes type maps for page content negotiation
action-name	Processes certain files using an action

Not all of these handlers will be useful for you to activate. The example of the PHP3 module may be one exception if you choose to use this script language.

```
# AddType allows you to tweak mime types without
# actually editing them, or to
# make certain files be certain types.
# Format: AddType type/subtype ext1

# For example, the PHP3 module (a separate Debian package)
# will typically use:
#AddType application/x-httpd-php3 .phtml
#AddType application/x-httpd-php3-source .phps

# AddHandler allows you to map certain file extensions to
# "handlers", which are actions unrelated to filetype.
# These can be either built into the server
# or added with the Action command (see below)
# Format: AddHandler action-name ext1

# To use CGI scripts:
# AddHandler cgi-script .cgi

# To use server-parsed HTML files
# AddType text/html .shtml
# AddHandler server-parsed .shtml

# Uncomment the following line to enable Apache's
# send-asis HTTP file
# feature
#AddHandler send-as-is asis

# If you wish to use server-parsed imagemap files, use
```

```
#AddHandler imap-file map

# To enable type maps, you might want to use
#AddHandler type-map var

# Action lets you define media types that will execute
# a script whenever
# a matching file is called. This eliminates the need for
# repeated URL pathnames for oft-used CGI file processors.
# Format: Action media/type /cgi-script/location
# Format: Action handler-name /cgi-script/location
```

Error responses

ErrorDocument responses are an important part of the Web server. Apache offers three types of customizable error messages. First, you can respond to the error using a text string with a double quote (") at the beginning of the string. Using %s in a message string, Apache can add information to the message based on the error if available. This approach works well for creating quick responses to the errors.

The second and third responses are similar in that they both redirect; one redirects to a local URL, while the other redirects to a remote URL. Both are Web pages that you can customize to present the appropriate message. You can match error messages with any of the available error codes. Table 21-3 shows some of the available Apache error codes.

Table 21-3
Apache error codes

Error code	Description
400	Server received a bad request
401	Requires authorization to access the page (must refer to a local document)
403	Forbidden to access document
404	Requested document not found
500	Internal server error

```
# Customizable error response (Apache style)
#   these come in three flavors
#
#   1) plain text
#ErrorDocument 500 "The server made a boo boo.
#   n.b.  the (") marks it as text, it does not get output
#
#   2) local redirects
```

Continued

```
#ErrorDocument 404 /missing.html
#  to redirect to local url /missing.html
#ErrorDocument 404 /cgi-bin/missing_handler.pl
#  n.b. can redirect to a script or a document using
# server-side-includes.
#
#    3) external redirects
# ErrorDocument 402
# http://some.other_server.com/subscription_info.html
#

# mod_mime_magic allows the server to use various hints
# from the file itself to determine its type.

#MimeMagicFile conf/magic
```

Customizing for the browser

Some browsers don't support all the available features that the Apache server can
provide. To accommodate those browsers, Apache disables unsupported features
for those specific browsers. BrowserMatch controls the environment variables
specifically for that browser client. The first variable defines the browser based on
the header the client sends on initial contact. The rest of the conditions are processed in the order they appear on the line.

```
# The following directives disable keepalives and HTTP
# header flushes. The first directive disables
# it for Netscape 2.x and browsers which
# spoof it. There are known problems with these.
# The second directive is for Microsoft Internet Explorer 4.0b2
# which has a broken HTTP/1.1 implementation and does
# not properly support keepalive when it is used
# on 301 or 302 (redirect) responses.

BrowserMatch "Mozilla/2" nokeepalive
BrowserMatch "MSIE 4\.0b2;" nokeepalive downgrade-1.0 force-response-1.0
# The following directive disables HTTP/1.1 responses
# to browsers which are in violation of the
# HTTP/1.0 spec by not being able to grok a
# basic 1.1 response.

BrowserMatch "RealPlayer 4\.0" force-response-1.0
BrowserMatch "Java/1\.0" force-response-1.0
BrowserMatch "JDK/1\.0" force-response-1.0

Alias /doc/ /usr/doc/
## The above line is for Debian webstandard 3.0,
## which specifies that /doc
## refers to /usr/doc. Some packages may not work otherwise.
## -- apacheconfig
```

The access.conf configuration file

Of the three Apache configuration files, this file controls the access to files and directories provided for outside requests. It defines the types of services that the server provides and under what circumstances. The file sets the global standard for the server, so be careful when making changes. Understand what you are doing before jumping in and changing something. Like before, this file starts with basic header information about the URL, description, and originator.

The options listed in each section of the file pertain to the specified document path, such as document root, so you should change the path (/var/www) to the same thing that DocumentRoot is set to. The directives allowed in each section apply to a given path — as with the document root, which can display indexes and follow symbolic links on files. You can add any combination of options as long as you don't mind someone taking full advantage of them.

Here is the listing of the access.conf file:

```
# access.conf: Global access configuration
# Online docs at http://www.apache.org/

# This file defines server settings that affect which
# types of services
# are allowed, and in what circumstances.

# Each directory to which Apache has access can be
# configured with respect to which services and features
# are allowed and/or disabled in that directory
# (and its subdirectories).
#

# Originally by Rob McCool

# This should be changed to whatever you set DocumentRoot to.
```

When setting up directives for a specific document path in this file, the directory is identified as shown here:

```
<Directory /var/www>
```

Options controls the features that a user has access to within the directory:

```
# This may also be "None", "All", or any combination
# of "Indexes",
# "Includes", "FollowSymLinks", "ExecCGI", or "MultiViews".

# Note that "MultiViews" must be named *explicitly*
# --- "Options All" doesn't give it to you
# (or at least, not yet).

Options Indexes FollowSymLinks
```

You can specify whether this directory path can make use of the `.htaccess` file with `AllowOverride`:

```
# This controls which options the .htaccess file
# in directories can override. Can also be
# "All", or any combination of "Options", "FileInfo",
# "AuthConfig", and "Limit"

AllowOverride None
```

`order` determines which option is looked at first — `allow` or `deny`. The first one is evaluated (`allow` in this case) and then implemented, and then the second one grants the exceptions to the first. This sets the order of the access control, first to allow access from all hosts, and then to deny access from none (which basically means let everyone in for the default example):

```
# Controls who can get stuff from this server.

order allow,deny
allow from all
```

This closes the access configuration for the directory path:

```
</Directory>
```

The continuation of this file contains the configurations of more directory paths. Each path is specified, defined, and closed.

```
# /usr/lib/cgi-bin should be changed to whatever
# your ScriptAliased
# CGI directory exists, if you have that configured.

<Directory /usr/lib/cgi-bin>
AllowOverride None
Options ExecCGI FollowSymLinks
</Directory>

# Allow server status reports, with the URL
# of http://servername/server-status
# Change the ".your_domain.com" to match your domain to enable.

# <Location /server-status>
# SetHandler server-status

# order deny,allow
# deny from all
# allow from .your_domain.com
# </Location>

# Allow server info reports, with the URL
# of http://servername/server-info
# Change the ".your_domain.com" to match your domain to enable.
```

```
# <Location /server-info>
# SetHandler server-info

# order deny,allow
# deny from all
# allow from .your_domain.com
# </Location>

# There have been reports of people trying to abuse an old bug
# from pre-1.1 days. This bug involved a CGI script distributed
# as a part of Apache.
# By uncommenting these lines you can redirect these attacks to
# a logging script on phf.apache.org. Or, you can record
# them yourself, using the script support/phf_abuse_log.cgi.


<Location /cgi-bin/phf*>
deny from all
ErrorDocument 403 http://phf.apache.org/phf_abuse_log.cgi
</Location>

# Debian Policy assumes /usr/doc is "/doc/", at
# least from the localhost.

<Directory /usr/doc>
Options Indexes FollowSymLinks
AllowOverride None
order allow,deny
allow from all
</Directory>

# This sets the viewable location of the mod_throttle
# status display.
#
# <location /throttle-info>
# SetHandler throttle-info
# </location>

# Do not allow users to browse foreign files using symlinks in
# their private webspace public_html.
# Note: This should be changed if you modify the
# UserDir-Option.
# We would really like to use LocationMatch but the Option
# we want is ignored with that directive.


<DirectoryMatch ^/home/.*/public_html>
Options SymLinksIfOwnerMatch Indexes
AllowOverride None
</DirectoryMatch>

# You may place any other directories or locations you
# wish to have access information for after this one.
```

Controlling the daemon

After making any changes to any of the configuration files, you have to restart the server. As with all Linux daemons, you can restart the server daemon without rebooting the computer. Also, for your convenience, a script comes included with the Debian distribution to assist with just this function in mind — apachectl. Run this script simply by issuing the commands to stop and start the server:

```
apachectl stop
```

and

```
apachectl start
```

Each time the server starts, the configuration files are read for implementation. An alternative method for the Apache daemon is through the startup script /etc/init.d/apache. Options with this command — such as start, stop, reload, and restart — give you choices for controlling the daemon.

```
/etc/init.d/apache restart
```

This restarts the Apache daemon after you make changes to one of the configuration files. If you do not restart Apache, those changes do not take effect.

Monitoring the Web server

Like any server service running on any computer, some monitoring must take place so you have warning signs when something isn't working correctly. This mostly occurs through the log files. All log files reside in the /var/log/apache directory. The logs give you signs of attack, help to diagnose improper configuration settings, and provide valuable information about site traffic.

For a quick look at the files, use the tail command. This command shows you the end of the file, which contains the last few lines of activity. The last few lines are important when tracking down problems or when looking for recent suspicious activity. Some of the log files can be huge and can take a while to print to the screen. tail displays only the end of the file. This is how you use tail to view the last few lines of the access.log file:

```
$ tail /var/log/apache/access.log
```

Several tools have been developed to create site statistics. One such application, Webalizer, graphically lists the server activity (as shown in Figure 21-2) on a Web site all compiled from the log files. You can install the Debian package of webalizer. It comes configured to match the Debian Apache install locations. If you need to make changes to Apache, double-check /etc/webalizer.conf to make sure that the default paths match.

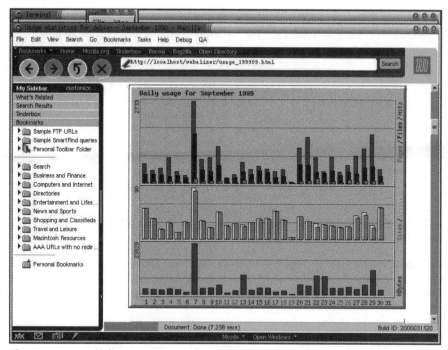

Figure 21-2: Webalizer creates graphical charts from the log file data, such as this one that shows usage for one month.

If you manage more than one domain or have more than one log file to analyze, you can set Webalizer to work off more than one configuration file. Using `-c conf.file.name` enables you to employ a customized configuration file for each log file. In fact, you can use the options to temporarily override the settings in the configuration file.

Setting Controls for Web Pages

From time to time, it is important to change the Web server functions for a specific directory. You might want to require a password to access a directory, page, or site. Depending on how you set this up, a password may be required to even access the site. This restricts access to the domain to only those who have a password for it. Restricting access for an entire domain may be a little extreme; restricting a directory is much more practical.

To do this, you must enable the `AccessFileName` directive in the `srm.conf` file by specifying a filename (`.htaccess` by default). Then in the `access.conf` file, add the `AllowOverride` directive for the specific directory to provide the restriction (or lack of it). All this is in preparation for adding the `.htaccess` file to the purposed directory.

Note Although the required module to allow authorization is loaded by default, it never hurts to double-check it. The module, `auth_module`, is loaded in the `httpd.conf` file.

Remember that whenever you make changes to any of the configuration files, you need to restart the Apache server. You can restart the server anytime using the `apachectl restart` command.

.htaccess

You can customize a directory by using nearly any directive within the `.htaccess` file. Simply create a file called `.htaccess` in the directory to which you wish to add directives. Then add those directives that aren't covered in the global files. This sets a per-directory configuration that customizes each directory to the individual needs of the server where the file exists.

You can use this file to adjust the `Options` for a directory or modify the `AllowOverride` directive or any number of directives. Here is an example of how you can use a file for a developer's site. Add the following to the `access.conf` file:

```
< Directory /home/userID/public_html>
AllowOverride Options FileInfo AuthConfig Limit
</Directory>
```

This enables the developer to add an `.htaccess` file to his or her public directory to override the options, document types, authorization, and access limitation directives.

One common use enables you to set passwords for the directory. Using passwords forces the client requesting to enter the pages to include a valid user ID and password. The ID and password are written to a text file with each ID, space, and password on a separate line. Here is a sample of the directives you find in the local `.htaccess` file.

```
AuthUserFile /etc/htusers
AuthGroupFile /dev/null
AuthName "ARC Members"
AuthType Basic
require valid-user
order deny,allow
allow from all
```

The preceding directives require that a password be given to match one of the users in the `/etc/htusers` file. This file contains the name and password for each user member. You may recognize some of the directives used in some of the other configuration files. When someone tries to access the Web page, the browser shows a logon window, as seen in Figure 21-3.

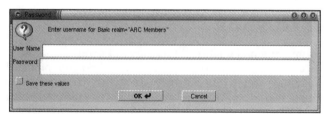

Figure 21-3: The basic logon dialog box, granting access to a Web site or files in a directory

If you enter an invalid password, the server sends a message informing you that authorization is required to access the document. It continues to explain that you either gave the wrong credentials or the browser doesn't know how to supply the credentials.

htpasswd

One of the features of the Apache Web server enables you to use passwords to access Web pages. Setting this up means that the document or directory must have authorization set up through an .htaccess or access.conf file. When you install Apache, the htpasswd file is installed along with it. This program enables you to create one or more files containing user IDs and encrypted passwords.

When setting up a password file for the first time, you use the create option. You also provide the filename and the first user name. When providing the filename, you can use the entire path. Following is the syntax you use:

```
htpasswd -c /etc/filename username
```

Caution

I suggest storing the password files in a secure area, like in the /etc or /etc/apache directories. Never use a publicly accessible directory to store these files. Although the passwords are encrypted, someone can copy, destroy, or decrypt the passwords. Preferably, the system administrator has control over the file to add, change, and remove IDs in order to ensure its security.

This creates a password file, /etc/filename, with the entry username as the initial ID. The Web browser then prompts you for the password for this user ID. You can continue to add IDs to this file through similar means, but without the create option. Otherwise, the existing file is overridden. To add any other user IDs, use the following syntax, where username2 is another ID:

```
htpasswd  /etc/filename username2
```

You can add as many IDs to a single file as you like. More than one .htaccess file can refer to this password file. The password file must contain any IDs for people needing to access the authorized documents.

Enabling Virtual Hosting

As a single server for a home or small business, you may not need to change a Web server much from the default for the one domain. However, when you look at the Internet, one machine publishes Web pages for many domains. This means that somewhere a machine hosts more than that for one domain. The term for this is *virtual hosting,* or *multihomed hosting.* In either case, you can configure the server to publish Web pages for more than one domain name. Domain names that are not associated with a real network or machine are considered virtual.

There are a couple of methods to make a virtual domain name available on a Web server. The first is to give each virtual domain an IP address in the domain name server (DNS) and assign the IP address to the Linux machine. (You can find more information about adding an IP address to a machine in Chapter 5.) For Internet use, these domain names and IP numbers must be registered and real. Making up names or IP numbers does not work. The other option is to assign the domains as conical names (CNAME) in the DNS.

In the case of real IP addresses, you need to add the information about the virtual server to the httpd.conf file. The following is an example of how to set the directives in the configuration file. These directives override the global directives set for the server when requests come in for this virtual domain.

```
<VirtualHost www.my_domain.com>
ServerAdmin webmaster@my_domain.com
DocumentRoot /var/www/my_domain.com
ServerName www.my_domain.com
ErrorLog /var/log/apache/my_domain.com-error.log
TransferLog /var/log/apache/my_domain.com-access.log
</VirtualHost>
```

However, when using one IP address for multiple domain names, you need to change one more line in the httpd.conf file. You must assign an IP address to the NameVirtualHost directive to identify the IP address to the Apache Web server. This line might look like this in your configuration file:

```
NameVirtualHost 192.168.0.32
```

The server then uses a variable name submitted to the server by the client browser that indicates the host name. The specific host name is added to the VirtualHost directive section in the httpd.conf file. I prefer to use separate IP addresses because it is easier to set up and making changes later is just as easy. You can see from this example that the VirtualHost remains the same for each host name. The differences are in the conical names.

```
<VirtualHost 192.168.0.32>
ServerAdmin webmaster@my_domain.com
DocumentRoot /var/www/my_domain/parts
ServerName parts.my_domain.com
```

```
ErrorLog /var/log/apache/parts.my_domain-error.log
TransferLog /var/log/apache/parts.my_domain-access.log
</VirtualHost>
<VirtualHost 192.168.0.32>
ServerAdmin webmaster@my_other_domain.com
DocumentRoot /var/www/my_other_domain/data
ServerName data.my_other_domain.com
ErrorLog /var/log/apache/data.my_other_domain-error.log
TransferLog /var/log/apache/data.my_other_domain-access.log
</VirtualHost>
```

Summary

Whether you use your Web server as a single workstation to display samples of Web pages you develop, as a main corporate Web server, or to host pages for multiple domains on the Internet, the Apache Web server can handle all your needs. It is hoped that after reading this chapter, you now have a better understanding of this server. You can customize it to meet the needs of your particular situation.

More than two-thirds of the servers on the Internet use Apache as their server, so there is a huge following. If you have questions beyond the scope of this chapter, I encourage you to investigate more about this wonderful server. You can look to the following Web sites for information:

✦ www.apache.org—Apache Software Foundation offers complete documentation on Apache.

✦ www.apache-ssl.org—Apache SSL provides documentation on the SSL version of Apache.

✦ modules.apache.org—Apache Module Repository provides additional modules for Apache.

✦ www.w3.org—World Wide Web Consortium strives to maintain universal standards and protocols for use on the Internet.

✦ www.apacheweek.com—Apache Week offers articles and news regarding Apache.

✦   ✦   ✦

FTP Server

The term *sneakernet* comes to mind when thinking of the antithesis of the convenience of transferring files on a network. When working with computers on a network, through a dial-up connection or over the Internet, transferring files from one computer to another takes on a whole new dimension. You no longer have to use your sneakers and run a file from one computer to another using a floppy disk. Instead, you can use the File Transfer Protocol (FTP).

This chapter attempts to alleviate the use of sneakernets and answers the questions of how to set up a FTP for your own use. The more you use FTP, the more you'll wonder what you ever did with out it. There are two components to FTP—the server and the client. This chapter describes examples of each.

All About FTP

FTP is the a popular way of transferring files from computer to computer, especially because most files no longer fit on a little floppy. It enables you to connect to a remote computer, whether it is five feet away or 5,000 miles away. Distance no longer matters with the Internet. The only requirement is the connection to some mutual network, such as through the Internet.

There are two ways in which you can configure FTP servers for use—privately and publicly (also known as *anonymous FTP*). Private FTP servers are the most secure and are highly recommended. These enable only those persons with valid accounts and passwords to have access to the FTP session. All others are rejected.

Anonymous FTP servers enable anyone to connect to them without having a specific account on the machine. This exposes the server to security vulnerabilities, especially if it is accessible through the Internet. I strongly suggest not using this aspect of the FTP server unless absolutely necessary— except if it is a dedicated and separate server with no vital data on it. Even though developers have gone to great lengths to eliminate security risks, security can be compromised. I'm not trying to make you paranoid, but you should have a healthy respect of the risks.

FTP works with the TCP/IP protocol and uses port 21 as the default port. You can change this, but any clients trying to attach to your server need to know this information. You can change the port number in the configuration files of most FTP servers, but this is not always as straightforward as entering a value in a file. You *must* be careful not to use a port that is used by some other service on your server.

The FTP service works as a standalone (always running) server or functions (when started by the `inetd` daemon) for each request coming into a designated port. The latter is the preferred choice because other services (such as `tripwire`) can monitor it for security concerns. The `inetd.conf` file contains the configuration information to launch the FTP services. You learn more about setting up the FTP server later in this chapter.

Anonymous FTP

Before continuing, I want to go more in-depth about anonymous FTP servers. You know that anonymous FTP servers are generic and very public, so accessing one eliminates the need to manage accounts and passwords. Your account is now *anonymous* and your password is, or should be, your e-mail address. This can be spoofed, so the password no longer matters except as a confirmation to the host that you want to connect.

If anyone and everyone can connect to your computer, how do you manage its security? That's a good question! The anonymous FTP servers have provisions to limit the number of connections made to the host, the time connected, and the area of the server that's accessed. First off, an anonymous connection normally does not allow access to the whole server. It only allows access to specific, predetermined directories where all contents are known. This does not eliminate the security risks involved. After all, the potential for hacking into the computer still exists due to the fact that anyone can now connect to your machine through an anonymous connection. However, the more limitations placed on the visitors, the less likely an attempt to break in will succeed.

 Caution Anonymous servers can pose security risks for other servers. Hackers sometimes use an anonymous server as a transfer point, uploading and downloading code for other hackers to use. A wise choice would be to have no upload (or incoming) directories on an anonymous server. If (for some reason) you need upload areas, then closely monitor the traffic and content.

Security on anonymous servers concerns everyone, so here are some hints that can help to reduce any risks:

✦ Limit the number of connections to the anonymous server to maintain its performance. The more connections allowed to your computer, the more resources are used.

✦ Eliminate upload areas. This prevents attackers from exploiting your site by taking up all your drive space, exchanging data, and such.

✦ Validate e-mail addresses for anonymous accesses. For some servers, this option is available. It requires a valid-looking e-mail address, regardless of whether the e-mail address works. This is no guarantee that the e-mail address is actually the one for the person logging in, but every bit helps.

✦ Logging, of course, gives you the ability to later trace the activities on your server. This record can enable you to backtrack to where an assailant accessed your machine.

✦ Isolate the anonymous FTP machine from all others. Using a separate machine from the machines that contain personal or business information prevents anyone from getting anything of value if a break-in does occur.

Installing and Configuring an FTP Server

You are about to embark on a journey that will make your file-transferring life much easier. This chapter covers the three Debian-packaged FTP servers, each with their own installation and configurations: `ftpd`, `wu-ftpd`, and `proftpd`.

I explain how to get each one running and how to make modifications to each as well as some of the pros/cons of each. You can install each of the servers simply by using the `dselect` program because all the servers listed are included as a Debian package.

Tip   Of the three FTP servers, I recommend the ProFTP server because of its security and ease of configuration — especially when setting up the anonymous FTP.

The ftpd server

Most distributions consider this FTP server to be the easiest to install — and they may be right. There is very little to this server involving installation and configurations. You can install the `ftpd` package, which installs basic configuration files. The two files placed on the system are `ftpusers` and `ftpchroot`. Let's take a look at each of these files more closely.

Caution   `ftpd` is also one of the weakest FTP servers that's available. If you work on a closed network, then feel free to use this server. However, if you are on the Internet, I suggest using a different FTP server.

The /etc/ftpusers file

This simple file contains the list of users that this machine does not allow to log on through an FTP connection. If a user's name appears in this file, that user cannot access the server. This is the opposite of what you might expect — don't confuse it with a list of allowed users:

```
# /etc/ftpusers: list of users disallowed ftp access.
# See ftpusers(5).

root
ftp
anonymous
```

Note the inclusion of the root user in this file. This is done to increase security on your system. By absolutely preventing root from being able to log in under any circumstances, you cut off one potential avenue for attack.

The /etc/ftpchroot file

Unless you are experienced, leave this file empty. This gives any listed user access to root. In the wrong hands, this is very dangerous. Therefore, I suggest only experienced users handle this file.

```
# /etc/ftpchroot: list of users who need to be chrooted.
# See ftpchroot(5).
bob
jane
```

The /etc/inetd.conf entry

In addition to the two configuration files for this server, the install script adds the below line to the inetd.conf file. This line responds to a request to the FTP port (normally port 21) by launching the ftpd service to handle the request. After the request is completed and the user logs off, the service shuts down and waits for the next request.

```
ftp stream tcp nowait  root  /usr/sbin/tcpd  /usr/sbin/in.ftpd
```

The log file

The logging information is sent to the /var/log/daemon.log file, which contains more information than what comes from FTP connections alone. As with any log file, you should look over this text file regularly for any signs of problems.

The wu-ftpd server

This is one of the most popular FTP servers available. It has several unique and highly configurable features. Because of its popularity, any security issues that arise are resolved quickly. Keep an eye out for any updates to make sure that you have the latest version.

When you install this package, you may notice two files with similar names: wu-ftpd and wu-ftpd-academ. Granted they appear the same; however, the latter one contains no files. It is designed to make sure that any existing versions of wu-ftpd are upgraded correctly. After the install, you can remove it with no consequences. The official site for `wu-ftpd` is located at `www.wu-ftpd.org`.

 Note No FTP server can run on a machine where you already have an FTP server installed. The installation scripts let you know that you must remove one before installing another one when you use the `dselect` installation application.

The `wu-ftpd` server allows a higher degree of configuration to the server. You can find these configuration files in the `/etc/wu-ftpd` directory. They include:

README	ftpconversions	ftpusers	msg.nodns	pathmsg
ftpaccess	ftpservers	msg.deny	msg.toomany	welcome.msg

Some of these files are canned messages that you can customize for your environment. I discuss some of these configuration files in more depth in the following sections. All of the `msg` files contain simple text messages that are sent to the clients under certain circumstances.

ftpusers

This file is nothing more than a symbolic link to `/etc/ftpusers` that other applications, such as `ftpd` and `tftpd`, utilize. You can find more information about `ftpusers` in the earlier section on the `ftpd` server.

ftpaccess

This file controls who has access, who doesn't, any restrictions to the access, and more. Most of the settings in this file are straightforward and fairly intuitive. You see the default as it is when first installed on your computer. In this section. I comment about some of the categories in this configuration file.

```
# Debian default wu-ftpd `ftpaccess' configuration file,
# derived from the `ftpaccess.heavy' example in wu-ftpd
# sources.
# For more options/commands see ftpaccess(5) and
# /usr/share/doc/wu-ftpd/*.

# Some of the example message files have been translated
# to Spanish and are available in
# /usr/share/doc/wu-ftpd/examples/.
# (thanks to Javier
# Fernandez-Sanguino Pen~a <jfs@dat.etsit.upm.es>
```

You need to set the e-mail for the administrator. This is not modified during the install. Use any qualified e-mail address.

```
# E-mail address of the FTP admin, can be accessed via
# the %E in messages.
email ftpadmin@misconfigured.host

# Which UIDs and GIDs may, and which may not, use
# the FTP service.
#deny-uid %-99
#deny-gid %-99
#allow-uid ftp ftpadmin
#allow-gid ftp ftpadmin

# Maximum number of retries after login failures,
# before disconnecting.
#loginfails 5

# Can users see anything else but their home directory
#restricted-uid lamer
#unrestricted-gid ftpadmin

# Allow use of private file for SITE GROUP and SITE GPASS?
#private   no

# What kind of greeting to give.
#greeting <full|brief|terse|text somemessage>

# Banner to show immediately on connect.
#banner /etc/wu-ftpd/welcome.msg

# Deny access to specified hosts, with message.
#deny  *.microsoft.com              /etc/wu-ftpd/msg.deny
#deny  /etc/wu-ftpd/denied.hosts    /etc/wu-ftpd/msg.deny
# !nameserved means hosts that can't be resolved.
#deny  !nameserved                  /etc/wu-ftpd/msg.nodns

# Various DNS-related options.
#dns refuse_mismatch <filename> [override]
#dns refuse_no_reverse <filename> [override]
#dns resolveroptions [options]
```

By default, the `class` sets who can access the server. In this case, anyone can access the FTP server. The other options are commented out and therefore not used. Enabling the local and remote classes enables you to control more closely whether someone is inside your domain (local) or outside your domain (remote).

```
# Class name typelist addresses
#class local real,guest,anonymous *.my.domain 192.168.0.0
#class remote real,guest,anonymous *
class all real,guest,anonymous *
```

The real type corresponds to users that have real accounts on the local system. Anonymous is for people that have logged in anonymously, and the guest type is for local accounts that are treated as anonymous.

This section sets the limit on how many people can connect to your machine at one time. By default, that number is set to 10 (as shown in the following code). The 11th person gets the `msg.toomany` message that too many people are connected and to try back later. You can change the limiting number for all or for the different classes independently.

```
# Limit  who     how many  date/time            message file
#limit   local   20        Any                  /etc/wu-ftpd/msg.toomany
#limit   remote  100       SaSu|Any1800-0600    /etc/wu-ftpd/msg.toomany
limit    all     10        Any                  /etc/wu-ftpd/msg.toomany
```

Next, you can set what messages are displayed when the client first logs into your server — as with the welcome message or any special directory message. When the hidden `.message` file appears in a directory, the contents of that file are displayed as a message to the visitors through their FTP client.

```
# The files that wu-ftpd will recognize as must-be-read,
# and display them.
message /welcome.msg          login
message .message              cwd=*

# The files that wu-ftpd will recognize as should-be-read,
# and warn about them.
readme  README*     login
readme  README*     cwd=*
```

This controls on-the-fly conversions. You can find more information in the `ftpconversions` configuration file later in this section. By default, conversions are allowed.

```
# Whether to use compression.
compress          yes          local remote all
tar               yes          local remote all
```

Here, you find the settings that determine what information is placed in the log files. By default, only files transferred by anyone logged in are recorded to a log file. These log files are stored in `/var/log/wu-ftpd`. Removing the pound sign (#) in front of the other three log lines starts the logging of commands that are issued regarding security and system information. This is a good thing to do if your system is connected to the Internet; however, make sure that the size of the log files doesn't eat up all your available drive space.

```
# Logging of actions.
#log commands  anonymous,guest,real
#log security
#log syslog
log transfers anonymous,guest,real inbound,outbound

# The file wu-ftpd will check to see if the server is going to
  be shut down.
# (use ftpshut to generate it)
shutdown /etc/wu-ftpd/shutmsg
```

If the /etc/wu-ftpd/shutmsg file exists, people will not be granted permission to login, and will instead receive that message.

This section identifies any files that you should not transfer. Normally, you never want to transfer the base system files, much less make them available to others to transfer. The files listed here are your most valued security files.

```
# These files are marked unretrievable
noretrieve /etc/passwd /etc/group
noretrieve core
```

This next section sets the default path for the anonymous connection. As seen here, the default is /home/ftp.

```
# The directory to which anonymous FTP user will chroot to.
# Note: if you change this {add,rm}ftpuser may stop
# functioning.
#anonymous-root /home/ftp
```

When someone logs in as an anonymous user, this section validates that login to make sure that the e-mail used as the password conforms to the rfc822 standard. This doesn't mean that the password is a valid, usable password.

```
# Password verification for the anonymous FTP user.
#       <none|trivial|rfc822> [<enforce|warn>]
passwd-check    rfc822  enforce
```

Limiting the length of time an anonymous connection can stay connected also helps to reduce attacks. Generally, this can be an annoyance to the legitimate users, so do not set it too short.

```
# Maximum connection time in minutes
#limit-time anonymous 30
```

This area sets the permissions that the anonymous connections have to the anony-mous FTP area. The fewer permissions, the better. I suggest you leave the default settings as shown here, unless you understand the ramifications of your changes.

```
# Some permissions for the anonymous FTP user.
# All the following default to "yes" for everybody
rename    no    anonymous    # rename permission?
delete    no    anonymous    # delete permission?
overwrite no    anonymous    # overwrite permission?
chmod     no    anonymous    # chmod permission?
umask     no    anonymous    # umask permission?
```

I recommend making some changes to the following section. This is where you set the upload area. You can leave this alone if you want to enable anonymous users to put files on your system; otherwise, change the yes to a no in the second upload line. This prevents anyone from uploading to this area.

```
# Anonymous FTP directories upload settings
# anon-ftp-root path allow? Owner group mode dirs?
Upload /home/ftp* no
Upload /home/ftp /pub/incoming yes ftp daemon 0666 nodirs

# What can a filename contain (this /etc is under the
anonymous-FTP root)
path-filter anonymous /etc/pathmsg  ^[-+A-Za-z0-9_.]*$  ^\.  ^-

# Shortcuts for anonymous FTP incoming (note: the ':' isn't
obligatory)
alias incoming: /pub/incoming
cdpath /pub
```

> **Note** By default, the `wu-ftpd` FTP server is not set up for use as an anonymous server.

ftpconversions

The configuration file `ftpconversions`, also a special feature of `wu-ftpd`, provides the client file-conversion capabilities on the server before transferring the file. This can be useful if the client does not have the available software to convert the file after the download. For instance, if the client is a Windows machine, it may not have the DOS `gzip` utility to uncompress the files after they are downloaded. Therefore, using this feature of `wu-ftpd`, you can uncompress the file on the server. Obviously, uncompressing binary UNIX executable files on a DOS machine is useless; but not all compressed files are binaries.

The configuration file that comes when you install `wu-ftpd` has most known UNIX compression schemes, so you may not need to make changes to this file. If you do need to make your own changes, remember to use a colon (`:`) to separate each field. The following code shows the format of a conversion line in the file, and Table 22-1 explains each field.

```
1 : 2 : 3 : 4 : 5 : 6 : 7 : 8
```

Table 22-1
ftpconversion field descriptions

Field	Description
1	Removes prefix at the beginning of a filename
2	Removes postfix at the end of a filename
3	Inserts add-on prefix string at the end of the file when the file is transferred
4	Inserts add-on postfix string at the beginning of the file when the file is transferred
5	External command that identifies the program that is executed on-the-fly during the transfer

Continued

Table 22-1 *(continued)*	
Field	**Description**
6	Types for files that can be acted on T_REG, T_ASCII and/or T_DIR. A pipe symbol (|) separates multiples.
7	Specifies the type of conversion used by O_COMPRESS, O_UNCOMPRESS, and/or O_TAR. A pipe symbol (|) separates multiples.
8	Describes the type of conversion taking place

You control the use of this feature in the main ftpaccess file. If the compress and tar options are not enabled there, this configuration file isn't used.

ftpservers

This configuration file allows for multiple configuration files. If you have a need for more than one configuration based on the machine connecting to your system, you can create separate configuration files for each IP address. These configuration files are based on all the files contained in the /etc/wu-ftpd directory. Each IP address listed in ftpservers has its own directory path to its configuration file specified in this directory.

This option is useful when setting up virtual domains. Each domain can have its own configuration without affecting the other domains. Suppose one domain wants to allow FTP use from anywhere, while another domain only wants allow local FTP usage. In this case, other domains don't have to be tied in, and you can handle each set of standards separately.

The /etc/inetd.conf entry

You can actually get this server to work by adding a command line to the inetd.conf file. This allows the FTP server to start when a request is made to the server on the FTP port (port 21). This line usually is inserted just after telnet. However, the important thing is that it gets inserted in the file.

```
ftp stream  tcp  nowait  root /usr/sbin/tcpd  /usr/sbin/wu-ftpd
```

The log file

You can find the log file(s) at /var/log/wu-ftp; unless you modify the configuration file, xferlog is the only log file you see. Any transfer activity is recorded in this file, so here is where you can find out what's going on with your system.

The proftpd server

The Professional FTP server, proftpd, is a robust, secure server and an excellent choice when used as the anonymous FTP server. You can set up this server as a standalone, or it can be invoked by `inetd` each time a request is made. This server is gaining popularity with heavy-duty FTP sites. You can find the source files at `www.proftpd.org`. This site contains more example configuration files. The configuration file shown in this chapter comes with the Debian installation.

The proftpd.conf file

The `proftpd` FTP server has only one configuration file. This file, located in the `/etc` directory, contains all the information to make `proftpd` work smoothly. The beginning of the file sets the name of the server, whether it is `standalone` or `inetd`. If `inetd` is set as the server type, then you must make an entry to the `inetd.conf` file as with `wu-ftpd` and `ftpd`.

```
# This is a basic ProFTPD configuration file (rename it to
# 'proftpd.conf' for actual use.  It establishes
#a single server
# and a single anonymous login.  It assumes that you
#have a user/group
# "nobody" and "ftp" for normal operation and anon.

ServerName        "ProFTPD"
ServerType        standalone
DeferWelcome      off

ShowSymlinks      on
MultilineRFC2228      on
DefaultServer     on
ShowSymlinks      on
AllowOverwrite       on
```

The timeout section identifies three circumstances that can time out a connection. The first is on an idle connection. This frees up the connection when the any of the three limits below (in seconds) are reached.

```
TimeoutNoTransfer    600
TimeoutStalled       600
TimeoutIdle          1200
```

The following message section sets the names of the message files. The first is displayed to users after they log in to the system. The second is displayed when a directory is entered, and the final option indicates that ls is given the -l option by default.

```
DisplayLogin                        welcome.msg
DisplayFirstChdir                   .message
LsDefaultOptions                    "-l"
# Port 21 is the standard FTP port.
Port                    21

# Umask 022 is a good standard umask to prevent new dirs and
# files from being group and world writable.
Umask                   022
```

This option sets the ownership of the server when it runs. You should leave these settings as they are in normal situations:

```
# Set the user and group that the server normally runs at.
User                    root
Group                   root
```

The anonymous section is, by default, commented out; therefore, it is unusable. To enable this section, edit the configuration file by removing the double pound signs (##) from this section. This section assumes that you have a user ftp and a group nogroup on your server. If you do not have these on your machine, then this section does not work.

After you enable the anonymous section of this configuration, uploading capabilities are not available because that section is also remarked out by default.

```
# A basic anonymous configuration, no upload directories.

## <Anonymous ~ftp>
##   User                ftp
##   Group               nogroup
##   # We want clients to be able to log in with "anonymous"
## as well as "ftp"
##   UserAlias           anonymous ftp
##
##   RequireValidShell   off
##
##   # Limit the maximum number of anonymous logins
##   MaxClients          10
##
##   # We want 'welcome.msg' displayed at login,
##   # and '.message' displayed
##   # in each newly chdired directory.
##   DisplayLogin        welcome.msg
##   DisplayFirstChdir   .message
##
##   # Limit WRITE everywhere in the anonymous chroot
##   <Directory *>
##     <Limit WRITE>
##       DenyAll
##     </Limit>
##   </Directory>
##
##   # <Directory incoming>
##   #           <Limit READ WRITE>
##   #           DenyAll
##   #           </Limit>
##   #           <Limit STOR>
##   #           AllowAll
##   #           </Limit>
##   # </Directory>
##
## </Anonymous>
```

Something not listed in this configuration file is the maximum number of instances of the server that can run simultaneously. Setting a maximum can help prevent any denial of service attacks. Look at the security chapter (Chapter 19) for more information about this kind of attack. To make this change, add this line to the configuration file:

```
MaxInstances      30
```

This limits the number of instances the server can start. You can adjust this value if you find that you need to have more instances running.

The log file

The log file for the `proftpd` server is placed in `/var/log/xferlog`. Again, look at your log files to help spot abuse, attacks, and any other problems. Log files are your friends — as I'm sure you are tired of me telling you.

Administering an FTP Server

As the administrator of an FTP server, you can benefit from having some tools assist you in administering the server. The tools available include an automated shutdown utility to shut the server down as pleasantly as possible, a monitoring tool that identifies the individual accounts currently connected and reports their activities, and an accounting of the number of current connections and from what class they are connected.

ftpshut

This tool automates the shutdown procedure and announces to any connected users that the FTP server will shut down at a certain time. You have options on this command as to the timing of the shutdown. You can set it for now, hours/minutes (HHMM), or a number using the 24-hour clock format (+number). Here is the syntax for these commands:

```
ftpshut [-d min] [-l min] now ["message"]
ftpshut [-d min] [-l min] +dd ["message"]
ftpshut [-d min] [-l min] HHMM ["message"]
```

The `-d` option indicates the time before the shutdown when all connections to the server will be disconnected. The `-l` option sets the time before the server shuts down when no more new connections are allowed. You can add a custom message to this procedure to inform the clients that the sever will shut down. One use for this might be to script it when the system is regularly shut down for maintenance or backups.

ftpwho

The `ftpwho` utility lists all users currently connected to your server. It also shows the current activities of each connected user.

ftpcount

When you are concerned about limitations on the different classes of your users, you can use this tool to help identify how many users are connected from each class — `local`, `remote`, and `any`. `ftpcount` also displays the limits as well as the current numbers.

Using FTP Clients

Even if you don't use an FTP server, you still need to use a client in order to take advantage of the services that FTP offers you. There are several clients, ranging from those that use the command line to those that are fully graphical. Having a working knowledge of each type of client — command line and graphical — helps when you use them in different interfaces and situations and for different reasons.

The ftp client

Most operating systems have a version of the command-line `ftp` client. They all use the same or similar commands; once you know how to use the FTP command line on one operating system, you can use it on other systems. I can't tell you how many times I've needed to transfer a file from one location to another. An FTP server on the remote computer saved the day.

Using the standard FTP client will become second nature after a while. To get started, you need to establish a connection to the remote computer. The syntax for the standard client is:

```
$ ftp [option] [remotehost] [port]
```

There are several options documented in the `man` page that you might occasionally use with the `ftp` program. You may also optionally specify a remote host name and port name on the command line, or you may use the `open` command once you're in `ftp`.

You can use IP addresses as well as host names or resolvable DNS names for the `remotehost`. Once the connection is established, the logon and password information is requested. Here is an example of connecting to an anonymous server:

```
ftp ftp.us.debian.org
Connected to ike.egr.msu.edu.
220 ike FTP server (Version wu-2.6.0(1) Fri Jun 23 08:07:11
CEST 2000) ready.
```

```
Name (ftp.us.debian.org:steve): anonymous
331 Guest login ok, send your complete e-mail address as
password.
Password:
```

The password information remains hidden for security reasons. After the password is approved, the connection is established and any textual greetings are displayed on your screen. You are now in FTP mode. To maneuver around in this interface, you need to use the commands for the FTP client shown in Table 22-2. These commands give you the control you need to transfer the files.

Table 22-2
Command-line ftp commands

Command Name	Description
ls	Displays a list of the files and directories on the remote computer
cd *path*	Changes directories to the specified *path* on the remote computer
lcd *path*	Changes directories on the local computer to the specified *path*
cdup	Changes the directory up one level on the remote computer
get *filename*	Retrieves the file *filename* from the remote computer
mget *filename(s)*	Retrieves multiple files *filename* from the remote computer. Uses wildcards such as * and ? or specifies each filename separated by spaces
put *filename*	Sends the file *filename* from the local computer to the remote one
mput *filename(s)*	Sends multiple files *filename* from the local computer to the remote one. Uses wildcards such as * and ? or specifies each filename separated by spaces
binary	Sets transfer mode to binary. All files are transferred in binary mode.
ascii	Sets the transfer mode to ASCII. All files are transferred in ASCII mode.
pwd	Shows the current path on the remote computer
open	Opens a connection to a remote computer. You should specify the remote hostname, and optionally, the remote port.
close	Closes the connection to the remote computer, but doesn't exit the FTP session
quit	Closes the connection to the remote computer and exits
bye	Closes the connection to the remote computer and exits

By looking at other FTP programs, you can see that these commands are universal. When transferring more than one file with mget or mput, you are asked to confirm each file unless the -i option suppresses the interactive mode.

To give you an idea of how to use the command-line ftp client application, I now show you how to change directories from the home directory to the docs directory, list the doc directory's contents, and then transfer a file from the remote computer. I have already connected to my account on the remote computer. These are the session results:

```
ftp> cd docs
250 CWD command successful.
ftp> ls
200 PORT command successful.
150 Opening ASCII mode data connection for '/bin/ls'.
total 32
-rw-r--r--    1 jo         jo              232 Jun 15 20:16
app1.doc
-rw-r--r--    1 jo         jo              199 Jun 15 20:16
app2.doc
-rw-r--r--    1 jo         jo            24277 Jun 15 20:16 rpm.doc
226 Transfer complete.
ftp> get app1.doc
local: app1.doc remote: app1.doc
200 PORT command successful.
150 Opening BINARY mode data connection for 'app1.doc' (232
bytes).
226 Transfer complete.
232 bytes received in 0.02 secs (12.0 kB/s)
ftp>
```

The binary transfer mode is what you would like to use most frequently. It will transfer a file unmodified from the remote machine to your local one. Occasionally, you may want to use the ASCII transfer mode. You'll only want to do this when transferring plain text files from a Microsoft or Macintosh environment; ftp will automatically take care of converting line endings for you in those cases. However, be careful! If you use the ASCII mode for anything other than plain text files, it will most likely corrupt your downloads!

You can see from this example that the client provides enough feedback to let you know what is going on during the transfer. This is typical for a session in which few transfers are needed. If you must connect to a site to transfer on a regular basis, you might consider using a different FTP client or scripting the connection for ease.

The ncftp client

The ncftp client is similar to the FTP command line. It still uses typed-out commands, but it adds features such as bookmarks, the display of the current remote path, and more. Table 22-3 shows the additional commands available with ncftp.

Table 22-3
Special ncftp commands

Command Name	Description
bookmark *name*	Saves the current connection into the `$HOME/.ncftp/bookmarks` file
bookmarks	Lists or edits the contents of the `$HOME/.ncftp/bookmarks` file (see Figure 22-1)
bgput	Queues a file for transfer to the remote computer in the background
bgget	Queues a file for transfer from the remote computer in the background
bgstart	Immediately processes all background transfer requests
jobs	Lists all active background file transfers
lls	Local listing that uses the same arguments as `ls`
lmkdir *directory*	Makes a local directory
lpwd	Displays the local path
lookup	Makes a request to the DNS and displays the corresponding IP address for any domain name(s) given as a parameter

Tip   You can use the arrow keys to scroll back through previous commands.

By default, ncftp assumes that most sites you want to visit are public; therefore, it tries to log on as anonymous. The client responds to nonpublic sites as a failure:

```
$ ncftp debian
NcFTP 3.0.0 beta 21 (October 04, 1999) by Mike Gleason
(ncftp@ncftp.com).

Copyright (c) 1992-1999 by Mike Gleason.
All rights reserved.

Resolving debian...
Connecting to 216.233.121.27...
debian.mydomain.com FTP server (Version 6.2/OpenBSD/Linux-0.10)
ready.
Logging in...
Login incorrect.
Sleeping 20 seconds...
```

You must use the `-u` *username* option to access a nonpublic or specific account on a host, as in this example:

```
ncftp -u jo debian
NcFTP 3.0.0 beta 21 (October 04, 1999) by Mike Gleason
(ncftp@ncftp.com).
Resolving ftp.us.debian.org...
Connecting to 35.9.37.225...
ike FTP server (Version wu-2.6.0(1) Fri Jun 23 08:07:11 CEST
2000) ready.
Logging in...
Password requested by 35.9.37.225 for user "jo".

    Password required for jo.

Password:
```

One of the added features of this client is that you can maintain a list of bookmarks. After launching ncftp, you can issue the command bookmarks to find your list of saved bookmarks (as shown in Figure 22-1). From here, you can add, edit, or remove bookmarks to manage them. Each entry includes information such as account ID, password, and destination directory. This feature usually accompanies graphical packages.

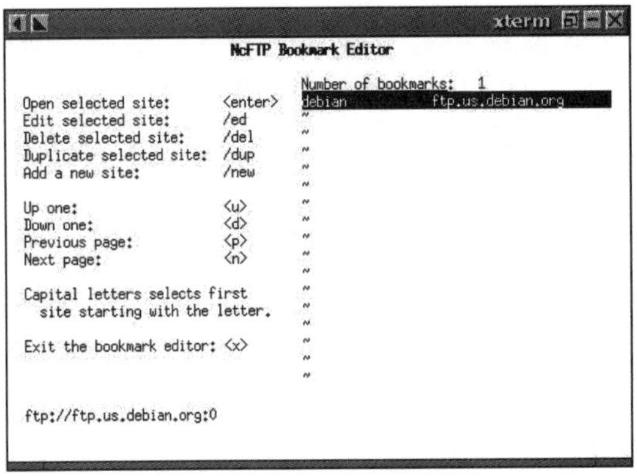

Figure 22-1: The bookmarks interface enables you to quickly select the connection you want to make.

Another unique feature of this FTP client is its capability to process jobs in the background. You can browse a site, specify the files you want to download with the bgget command, and then start the download later to get the files all at once with the bgstart command. You can even set up a time to get the files with the -@ *time* parameter. This parameter uses a full four-digit year and two-digit month, day, hour, minute, and second (*YYYYMMDDhhmmss*). This example shows a file downloaded at 2:30 a.m. on the first day of November, 2000.

```
bgget -@ 20001101023000 /pub/mystuff/somefiles/thisfile.zip
```

The specifics for the program are saved into a hidden directory within the home directory called .ncftp. Upon running ncftp the first time, three files are created in this directory: one to handle a firewall, one to let the program know that no further setup instructions are needed, and a history file of activity.

The xftp client

When you get accustomed to using a graphical interface for everything, you'll want one for an FTP client as well. xftp provides a rough interface with all the needed features for FTPing files across the wires.

The interface of xftp starts when you issue xftp from the command line (assuming that you are running some X-compatible window manager). Once the interface starts, you can see five main window components.

✦ The menus consist of Quit, Options, File Options, Multi File Options, and Help. Each menu provides control functions for the various commands where appropriate.

✦ The next component shows the status of the application, such as Connecting, Transferring, Connection Timed Out, and more. This single-line status window shows only a brief description.

✦ Next, you see a remote/local directory window. This shows the path of the currently displayed files.

✦ Control buttons. Use Login to initiate logging onto a remote host and toggling between local and remote directory displays. Also employ Command Shell to view and issue the FTP commands. Other buttons include Search, Next Search, Reconnect, and Archie. You may not use some of these features as often as you use others.

✦ Finally, you can see the directory display window where the file contents of the working, selected directory are displayed.

Figure 22-2 shows an anonymous login to a remote host. This is the screen you see after clicking the Login button. From here, you can make changes to any of the information in order to make a connection to a remote computer. Once you insert all the necessary information in the fields, you can click the Connect button to start the connection to the remote computer.

Most FTP servers have an inactivity timeout, so xftp provides a button to reattach to the foreign host without the trouble of reentering all the data. Also, the Login button changes function — it now displays Close in order to close your connection. The Remote button changes the displayed files from the remote machine to the local machine, which enables you to select from either display.

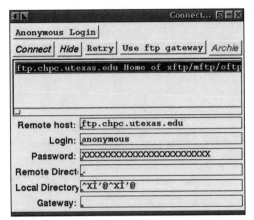

Figure 22-2: Connecting to a remote
computer through xftp

gftp clients

For a WS-FTP-like interface from the Windows world, try using gftp. This client
offers local and remote directory lists, single or group transfers, customizable
bookmark lists, and much more. If you are new to the Linux world, a convert, or you
happen to live in both worlds, you might find this client's layout most comfortable.

Figure 22-3 shows the interface for gftp. As you can see, near the top you have the
menu options as commonly found in windowed interfaces. Just below that is the
connection interface. Here you can enter the host, port, and user information.
Clicking the picture with the two computers starts the connection process. It also
acts as the Disconnect button after an established connection. The right and left
windows show the local (left) and the remote (right) directories and files. The sec-
ond-to-the-last box displays the transfer status of files, and the bottom box shows
the actual dialog between the computers.

You can select one file by clicking it; several files by holding the Ctrl key and clicking each file; or a list by clicking the first one, holding the Shift, and clicking the last
one. This may sound familiar because these are common techniques used in the
Windows world. To actually transfer the files, use the appropriate button in the center of the window.

Bookmarks add to the gftp application, as does the ability to edit sites already
bookmarked. As you develop a collection of anonymous site or create your own
FTP servers, bookmarks become even more important timesavers.

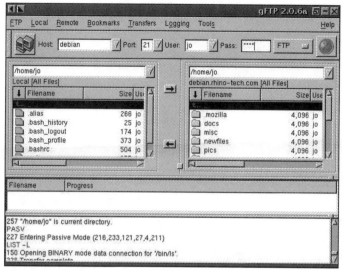

Figure 22-3: This self-contained FTP client shows everything in one window display.

Browsers

Internet Web browsers are also designed to handle file transfers. These can be a little more cumbersome because they generally function for anonymous FTP sites (because downloading one file at a time is slow). Each file is listed as a link on a page; clicking that link starts the download of that file. Figure 22-4 shows this process. This is a quick way to download a single file, but I discourage the use of this technique when downloading volumes.

Tip

Even though browsers commonly access anonymous Web sites, you can still access specific passworded accounts. Here's how it works. Where you normally type the URL, type:

```
ftp://user@server.domain.name
```

Here, *user* is a valid account ID and *server.domain.name* is a valid host name. You then are prompted for a password and can access your files for download.

Any browser can work to access FTP accounts. There is no special patch, plug-in, or setting you need to get it to work. Generally, employing a URL prefix of `ftp://` instead of the `http://` prefix (which is commonly used to access Web sites) enables you to access the FTP listings.

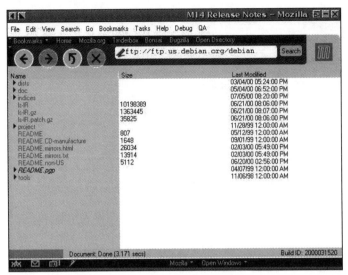

Figure 22-4: Browsers conveniently list and navigate anonymous FTP sites, such as the Debian site shown here.

Summary

The File Transfer Protocol (FTP) is one of the best tools on the Internet. It helps simplify the exchange of data from machine to machine through a network. It eliminates the need for using disks, tapes, or other media to transfer information. FTP also enables individuals from around the world to exchange information. As with the Debian project, you can download updates to programs almost as soon as a change is made. In the commercial world, it could take weeks to make and send out a CD-ROM.

Anonymous FTP servers are very vulnerable; avoid them when connecting to the Internet or other unreliable network sources. Granted, most holes are plugged in the servers, but that doesn't eliminate the discovery of a new one. So, my final words on this are to make sure you know what you are doing before using an anonymous FTP server.

You have many FTP client choices, ranging from text-only clients to complete graphical clients. I suggest you become skilled using both. The graphical interfaces are easy to use; but on those occasions when you don't have a graphics package loaded, or the platform can't handle such packages, the text-based FTP client may be all that stands between you and a completed download.

Network
Information
System

Managing one or two computers on a network is work-
able, but as that number grows, so do the headaches.
As the manager, you must make sure that group and password
information is distributed across each computer. When new
computers are added to the network, their host information
also needs to be distributed. You can see how managing a
growing network can get out of hand quickly. This is where
the Network Information System (NIS) comes in handy to help
administer a network.

The Network Information System

In the 1980s, Sun Microsystems released the first administrative database for managing a network of computers.
Originally, this system was called Yellow Pages, but was later
changed to Network Information System (NIS) due to copyright infringement. The NIS programs still reflect the original
name of the system, as they start with the letters yp.

In brief, NIS provides a single point of control for certain configuration files, which are distributed over the network to
other systems. This maintains better uniformity among all the
systems in the network. When a new user is added to the central NIS server, that user's information is propagated to the
other systems on that NIS domain by clients joining the NIS
host.

Don't confuse an NIS domain with an Internet domain,
although they both can use the same domain name. In fact,
many organizations do use the same domain name for both.

The NIS domain name identifies the group to which the servers and clients belong to, whereas the Internet domain name is used for DNS resolution. More than one NIS domain can exist on a network. The domain name is saved in /etc/defaultdomain. The master and the clients must all use the same domain name.

When you install the nis package using the deslect program, the configuration script will ask you for the name of your domain. By default, the Internet domain name is used. Otherwise, you can change the NIS domain name to any set of characters.

An overview of NIS

The NIS commands and the data files are stored in two areas on the Debian system. The commands are stored in /usr/lib/yp, and the data files are stored in /var/yp. The main or master NIS server creates a database that identifies the intended shared files, called *maps*. These are the files that you will be making available for access from more than one machine. Table 23-1 describes the mapped files. You use the make command in the NIS data directory—to create the databases for the domain. Each domain on the network has its own database.

Table 23-1
NIS mappable files

File Path	Description
/etc/aliases	Contains the redirection information of certain system accounts for redirecting mail
/etc/passwd	Lists the user account information
/etc/group	Lists the group level accounts
/etc/shadow	Contains the encrypted password information for user's accounts
/etc/hosts	Defines the hosts on a network
/etc/networks	Defines the networks to which a machine has accessto.
/etc/protocols	Lists the communication protocols available for a machine
/etc/services	Defines the TCP/IP services available to a machine
/etc/rpc	Stores information about remote procedure calls in programs, enabling remote access and remote communications
/etc/netgroup	Defines the groups of hosts, users, and domains for remote services such as remote login, remote mount, and remote shells

When a server is set up as a master, the following daemons will run: ypserv, yppasswdd, ypxfrd, and ypbind. The main NIS server, ypserv, registers with the portmapper when the daemon first starts to run, and then waits for calls from clients. ypbind, which also runs on the client machines, processes requests for information. A program needing information from one of the files listed in Table 23-1 is directed through ypbind. ypbind takes the request to the master server and gets the information from the appropriate map.

For instance, when someone logs into a client machine, /bin/login makes a request to ypbind on the client machine for information on account jo (the key) from the file passwd (the map). This request then goes to the master server, where the information is looked up and then sent back to the client.

To get a better idea of how NIS maps the file, look at the /var/yp/nicknames file. This file describes the maps. For example, by reading the following file, you can see that the map name *passwd* relates to the key *name*, while map *networks* relates to key *addr*. In the following file, you can see all the other relationships that NIS uses:

```
# cat /var/yp/nicknamespasswd          passwd.byname
group              group.byname
networks           networks.byaddr
hosts              hosts.byname
protocols          protocols.bynumber
services           services.byname
aliases            mail.aliases
ethers             ethers.byname
```

You can also get this information by using ypcat -x:

```
# ypcat -x
Use "ethers"     for map  "ethers.byname"
Use "aliases"    for map  "mail.aliases"
Use "services"   for map  "services.byname"
Use "protocols"  for map  "protocols.bynumber"
Use "hosts"      for map  "hosts.byname"
Use "networks"   for map  "networks.byaddr"
Use "group"      for map  "group.byname"
Use "passwd"     for map  "passwd.byname"
```

Configuring a Master NIS Server

To begin using the NIS services on a network, a master NIS server must be identified, established, and configured. The master server contains the source files for the network, and must be up to date and correctly configured. Use the following steps to configure the master NIS server:

1. The server must contain all the information for the whole network. All the server information is shared with the rest of the computers in the domain. Table 23-1 lists all the files that NIS will distribute. Make sure that all these files contain accurate information.

2. Edit the `/etc/init.d/nis` file to change the value for `NISSERVER` to `master`, as follows:

```
NISSERVER= master
```

3. For security reasons, limit the access to your master NIS server. Edit the `/etc/ypserv.securenets` file by changing the last line. The following code shows the default configuration file. If you do not properly configure this file, anyone will have access to the NIS server.

```
# cat ypserv.securenets
#
# securenets    This file defines the access rights to your
NIS server
#               for NIS clients. This file contains
netmask/network
#               pairs. A clients IP address needs to match
with at least
#               one of those.
#
#               One can use the word "host" instead of a
netmask of
#               255.255.255.255. Only IP addresses are
allowed in this
#               file, not hostnames.
#
# Always allow access for localhost
255.0.0.0       127.0.0.0

# This line gives access to everybody. PLEASE ADJUST!
0.0.0.0         0.0.0.0
```

Remove, replace, or comment out the last line of the file so that you no longer give access to the entire Internet, and then add in your network. The first set of numbers represents the net mask, while the second set of numbers represents the network address. For example, a network of 30 IP numbers has a net mask of 255.255.255.224, and the network address could be 192.168.10.0. This would enable access to all computers having an IP address from 192.168.10.1 to 192.168.10.30.

Cross-Reference

Refer to Chapter 5 for details about networks and netmasks.

4. NIS must use a master server database for all the files it shares. To create the database, run the following:

```
/usr/lib/yp/ypinit -m
```

The script creates a directory (named after your NIS domain in the /var/yp directory) to contain the maps. The script asks for the names of any other hosts. Add the name for each of the host servers. When you are done adding hosts, press Ctrl+D and the script will finish.

5. Restart the NIS server using the following command:

```
/etc/init.d/nis restart
```

After you have successfully configured and restarted the service, you'll need a NIS client to test the configuration. If you intend to use a slave NIS server on your network, the slave will first be configured as a client.

Note Slave NIS servers provide some redundancy in the system and help balance the network load. Without slave servers, your entire network could become unstable if your single master server goes down. Slave servers also work well in a multi-subnet network by having one slave in each of the subnets pointing to the single master, reducing network traffic.

Configuring a NIS Client

Setting up a client on NIS takes very little effort. You only need a machine that connects to the network with the nis package installed. When nis is installed, set the NIS domain to the same name as the master NIS server. Then follow these steps:

1. If you have already installed nis but are unsure what the domain was set to, edit the /etc/defaultdomain file to make any adjustments.

2. After the domain is set, confirm it by running domainname. The domain name you set will then be displayed on the screen before NIS returns to the prompt.

Note If the master server's domain name needs to be changed on a client for any reason, use the domainname command to reset it. The only other time this command is run is when the system starts.

3. Restart the local NIS service with the following command:

```
/etc/init.d/nis restart
```

4. You can now run ypwhich to test the NIS server. This will return the fully qualified name of the NIS server.

In the event that the NIS server resides in a different subnet, you need to edit the /etc/yp.conf file to point to the NIS server. Each NIS server on the network, whether the master or a slave, should be added to this file. The format to add a server is ypserver *server*, where *server* is either a qualified domain name or the IP address. Once you have added the names, restart the NIS server. You can then test the configuration with ypwhich.

If you run into problems, verify that the server's qualified domain names are included in the /etc/hosts file. Otherwise, the machine will definitely have trouble finding the servers.

Configuring a NIS Slave Server

Because NIS allows for some redundancy, you can set up one or more slaves for it. Each potential slave must be set up as a client before configuring it as a NIS slave. Follow these steps to configure your slaves:

1. The server must contain all the information for the whole NIS domain. All the slave's information is shared with the rest of the computers in the domain. Make copies from the master NIS server if you're unsure about the validity of your configuration files. Make sure that all these files contain accurate information.

2. Edit the /etc/init.d/nis file to change the value for NISSERVER to slave:

   NISSERVER= slave

3. For security reasons, limit the access to your master NIS server. Edit the /etc/ypserv.securenets file by changing the last line. If you do not do this, anyone will have access to the NIS server.

   Remove, replace, or comment out the last line of the file, and then add in your network. The first set of numbers represents the net mask, while the second set of numbers represents the network address. For example, a network of 30 IP numbers has a net mask of 255.255.255.224, and the network address could be 192.168.10.0. This enables access to all computers with an IP address from 192.168.10.1 to 192.168.10.30.

4. NIS must use a master server database for all the files it shares. To create the database, run the following:

   /usr/lib/yp/ypinit -s *masterserver*

   The script creates a directory named after your NIS domain in the /var/yp directory, which contains the maps from the master server (*masterserver*).

5. Restart the NIS server with the following command:

   /etc/init.d/nis restart

   Complete Steps 1 through 5 for each slave on the network. Each of those slaves must be added to the master, which you'll do in a later step.

6. Go to the master server to make a change there. Make the NOPUSH variable in the /var/yp/Makefile false:

   NOPUSH=false

7. Rebuild the NIS maps on the master server by running /usr/lib/yp/ypinit -m. Add all the slaves to the master's maps — this enables the master NIS server to keep the slaves up to date.

Using NIS Tools

Because NIS is supposed to take care of the common settings for a network, the end users of the network should see no difference between a machine using NIS and one that does not. They will be able to log on to any computer using the same account information. The differences between NIS and a standalone configuring come in to play when users try to change passwords remotely. Users will need to remember to use a different command: yppasswd, **ypchfn**, or ypchsh. These commands serve different purposes:

✦ yppasswd—Changes the uses password. Replaces passwd.

✦ ypchfn—Makes changes to the account's full name, the location, and other reference information about the user. Replaces chfn.

✦ ypchsh—Changes the default shell for the user's account. Replaces chsh.

Other useful commands that NIS provides include ypcat, ypwhich, and ypmatch. Their syntax is shown here:

```
ypcat mapname
ypcat -x
ypmatch key ... mapname
ypmatch -x
ypwhich
ypwhich -x
```

For each command, the -x option prints the mappings for the NIS server. ypcat prints the key information from a specified map. Running ypcat with the -x option lists the maps on the server. Running ypcat -x for a specific map produces the following results:

```
-# ypcat -x
Use "ethers"    for map "ethers.byname"
Use "aliases"   for map "mail.aliases"
Use "services"  for map "services.byname"
Use "protocols" for map "protocols.bynumber"
Use "hosts"     for map "hosts.byname"
Use "networks"  for map "networks.byaddr"
Use "group"     for map "group.byname"
Use "passwd"    for map "passwd.byname"
# ypcat passwd.byname
jo:x:1000:1000:Debian User,,,:/home/jo:/bin/bash
identd:x:100:65534::/var/run/identd:/bin/false
telnetd:x:101:101::/usr/lib/telnetd:/bin/false
```

The ypwhich command simply returns the name of the NIS server that supplies the NIS service. This command lists each master server and its slaves. ypmatch works similarly to ypcat, but returns the information for a specific key. For instance, the following command requests information about the key *jo* from the *passwd* map:

```
# ypmatch jo passwd
jo:x:1000:1000:Debian User,,,:/home/jo:/bin/bash
```

Administering NIS

As the administrator for the NIS server, you need to understand that when any of the NIS-managed files are changed, the map databases don't automatically change also. The databases must be manually updated using the /var/yp/Makefile script. This script looks for the files that have changed and re-creates the maps. The script then pushes those changes to any slave servers on the network.

If no changes are made to the master server's configuration files, NIS will keep working away, never needing any attention. The biggest problem with NIS is that the Makefile isn't run after changes are made. To prevent the master from forgetting to make the new maps, create an alias instead. Add the following line to your .bashrc file:

```
alias newuser='/usr/sbin/adduser;make -f /var/yp/Makefile'
```

Alternately, if so inclined, you can integrate the /var/yp/Makefile command into the adduser script so that each time a change is made while adding a new user, the NIS database is also changed. You can also do this with a script when changing any of the shared files on the master NIS server.

You can learn more about the various NIS commands and tools by looking at the documentation located at /usr/doc/nis/nis.debian.howto.gz or by viewing the man pages on any one of the following:

ypchsh(1)	ypcat(1)
yppasswd(1)	ypwhich(1)
ypmatch(1)	netgroup(5)
nicknames(5)	yp.conf(5)
ypserv.conf(5)	domainname(8)
mknetid(8)	makedbm(8)
nisdomainname(8)	pwupdate(8)
rpc.yppasswdd(8)	rpc.ypxfrd(8)
revnetgroup(8)	ypbind(8)

```
ypdomainname(8)          ypinit(8)
yppasswdd(8)             yppoll(8)
yppush(8)                ypserv(8)
ypset(8)                 ypwhich(8)
ypxfr(8)
```

Summary

When maintaining networks in which several servers operate as hosts for a number of clients, maintaining the same accounts and hosts can become a nightmare. To reduce your management headaches, run a Network Information System (NIS) on your network. That way, you'll only need to maintain the information on one system, instead of all systems. Because NIS runs in the background, very little will change from the end user's point of view. This leaves you free to work on other parts of the system, rather than maintaining all the files.

✦　　✦　　✦

File Server

Whether you work in a corporation, a small office, or at home with just two computers networked, sharing files across those computers is desirable. No longer must you use the sneaker-net to transfer a file from one computer to another via a floppy disk. Using a single server to store communal files, share printers, and enable remote connections is what a file server is all about.

Some of the most compelling reasons to use a file server in your environment include the following:

♦ Centralized files enable better backups. With everyone's import files saved on the file server, those files can be saved to tape for later recovery if needed.

♦ Shared files enable employees to collaborate on documents. In business environments where documents are created by one person, reviewed by another, and processed by still others, having a central location to store those files helps speed the process.

♦ Shared files enables remote and diskless workstations to use a common application. For some locations, managing applications becomes an overwhelming task. Setting up a common server where those applications can be accessed and used reduces the need to duplicate applications from machine to machine.

There are many applications for which sharing files, printers, and other resources makes good sense. This chapter covers the two main services used to share resources:

♦ Network File Systems, for file sharing in a mainly UNIX environment

♦ Samba, for incorporating Linux with Windows machines

Using the Network File System

The most commonly used method for sharing files among UNIX-like systems is the Network File System (NFS). NFS enables clients to connect to a remote server, and to mount part of that remote server's file system into the client's file system as if it were just another drive on the machine. Based on the client's permissions access, the client can then read and write files to the NFS server.

NFS, originating with UNIX systems, has now been ported to nearly every operating system, making it usable in a heterogeneous environment. This enables Windows machines (and others) exist in the same network and share files with other systems, which enables you to maintain a uniform interconnecting protocol.

NFS uses the User Datagram Protocol (UDP) to make connectionless transfers of information. This enables it to survive failures in the network. Once a server becomes available again, the transfer of data continues where it left off. With connected protocols like TCP, a failure in the network means the service also fails. Since its creation, though, NFS has been modified to use both UDP and TCP protocols.

Installing and running NFS

Three components must be installed to make an NFS server work properly:

✦ Portmap — This is installed by default as part of the base system and is included in the netbase package. The /usr/sbin/portmap script is started as a daemon when the system starts through the /etc/init.d/mountnfs.sh script, which runs at boot time to mount any remote file systems. The portmapper then translates between the service numbers and the available port numbers.

✦ rpc.mountd — This daemon, which is started by the /etc/init.d/ nfs-kernel-server script at boot time, only handles mounting requests. It verifies that the requesting client has access to the system and to the requested file system, and passes a file handle to the client for the requested file system.

✦ rpc.nfsd — This daemon is started by the /etc/init.d/nfs-kernel-server script at boot time as well. This daemon handles the transfer of information between the client and the server after the mount connection has been made.

At most, you need to have the netbase and nfs-common packages installed for NFS clients. Servers also need the nfs-kernel-server package. Once these packages are installed, they will set themselves up to run as daemons when the system starts.

Note   For more security, add portmap to the hosts.allow and hosts.deny files to limit access to it. The portmapper daemon uses these files to control access concerning its use. For more information about security, see Chapter 19.

With the `portmapper` running, you can query it using `rpcinfo` to list the registered programs. Using the `-p` option will output the results to the screen, as seen here:

```
rpcinfo -p debian
   program vers proto   port
    100000    2  tcp     111  portmapper
    100000    2  udp     111  portmapper
    100024    1  udp     757  status
    100024    1  tcp     759  status
    100021    1  udp    1025  nlockmgr
    100021    3  udp    1025  nlockmgr
    100007    2  udp     770  ypbind
    100007    1  udp     770  ypbind
    100007    2  tcp     773  ypbind
    100007    1  tcp     773  ypbind
    100003    2  udp    2049  nfs
    100005    1  udp    1040  mountd
    100005    1  tcp    1037  mountd
    100005    2  udp    1040  mountd
    100005    2  tcp    1037  mountd
    100005    3  udp    1040  mountd
    100005    3  tcp    1037  mountd
```

Note   NFS services must be built into the kernel or selected as a module when installed. Use the `insmod` command to load the `nfs.o` and `nfsd.o` modules into the kernel. See Chapter 15 for more details about kernel modules and how to load them.

Setting up the NFS shares in /etc/exports

In order to use NFS shares, each share must be specified in the `/etc/exports` file. Also specified in that file are clients that grant access to the share. The client can be represented in one of several ways:

✦ Single host — As the name implies, this identifies a single machine. You can use any resolvable name, such as a nickname, fully qualified name, or IP address.

✦ Netgroups — Any NIS netgroup given as *@groupname*. All hosts belonging to that group are then considered as if they had been listed individually as a single host.

✦ Wildcards — These include host names containing wildcard characters, such as * or ?. These characters do not include the dots in the domain names. For instance, `*.bar.com` accepts `foo.bar.com`, but not `a.foo.bar.com`.

✦ IP networks — Specifies an entire network by indicating the address/net mask combination. Also identifies a specific subnet on the network.

Table 24-1 contains a list of some of the more common options for setting client permissions. Even though some options are set by default, it is important to specify the permission option explicitly. This ensures that those options are set and eliminates potential confusion later. These permissions also set the level of security.

Table 24-1
NFS permission settings

Setting	Description
secure	Set by default, this option requires that requests originate on an Internet port less than 1,024.
insecure	This setting turns off the default secure setting.
rw	This enables clients to both read and write requests on this NFS volume. The default is to disallow any changes to the file system, as with the ro setting.
ro	Indicates that clients are to have read-only access to this share.
no_access	This specifies that no access be given to this share. This is useful when a parent directory gets shared, but a subdirectory is off-limits.
root_squash	This maps requests from *uid/gid 0* (root) to the anonymous *uid/gid*. This does not apply to any other IDs that might be equally sensitive, such as user *daemon*, *bin*, or *sys*.
no_root_squash	This turns off root squashing. This option is mainly useful for diskless clients.
anonuid and anongid	These options explicitly set the *uid* and *gid* of the anonymous account. Everyone accessing this volume will appear to use the same account.

Taking all this information into account, create a file in the /etc directory called exports. Using an editor, add a line to the file for each file system to export. The format is as follows:

```
/sharepath   client(option)
```

The *sharepath* must be a current file system on the NFS server. The *client* can take the form of anything mentioned earlier. Multiple *clients* can use the same share path, but must be separated with white space (a space). The options appear in parentheses following each client. Each option must be separated with a comma (,) and no white space. A line containing only the *sharepath* and *options* grants anyone access. The following code shows a sample of what an /etc/exports file looks like:

```
/              main(rw) trusted(rw,no_root_squash)
/code          dev*.my.domain(rw)
/usr           *.my.domain(ro) @trusted(rw)
/home/jo       192.168.10.31(rw,anonuid=150,anongid=100)
/pub           (ro,insecure,all_squash)
/pub/private   (no_access)
```

In this file, root access is given to two hosts. Both can read and write to the NFS server's entire file system, but only one gets full root privileges. The next line gives all hosts starting with `dev` and ending with `.my.domain` read/write access to the `/code` file system. The third line of the exports file gives everyone with the domain ending in `my.domain` read-only access; however, those hosts in the `@trusted` NIS netgroup have read/write access. The fourth line allows only one host matching a specific IP address read/write access. It also forces all accesses to occur as particular users, regardless of the actual user on the client. The last two lines in the file grant everyone read-only access to the `/pub` file system, but exclude everyone from access to the `/pub/private` subdirectory.

Mounting an NFS share automatically

In a corporate environment, many of the computers, if not all, will connect to a NFS share for storing common files, configurations, and data. To access those shares immediately without waiting for a console to mount them, the shares need to be set up for automatic mounting at boot time. As with the local file system, the shared NFS file systems need to be added to the `/etc/fstab` directory.

As with local file systems, remote NFS shares have certain options available for specifying the parameters of the connection. These options, listed in Table 24-2, are not mandatory, but provide greater flexibility and control over the shared volumes.

Table 24-2
Settings for mounting NFS shares in /etc/fstab

Setting	Description
`rsize=`*nnnn*	Specifies the number of bytes in *nnnn* to read over the network. The default is 1,024; however, throughput is improved when set to 8,192. Changing this setting to the incorrect number can adversely affect performance.
`wsize=`*nnnn*	Specifies the number of bytes in *nnnn* to write over the network. The default size is 1,024. See `rsize` for additional comments.
`Hard`	Sets a hard connection to the NFS server. If the server goes down or the connection is lost, any processes connected to it using this setting will hang until the server becomes available again, at which time the process will continue as if nothing happened.
`Soft`	Allows a process to time out if the NFS server has gone down or lost its connection. Use `timeo` to set the timeout duration.
`retrans=`*nn*	Sets the number of minor transmission timeouts, indicated by the *nn*, before the process is either aborted (in the case of a soft connection) or a message is posted to the console ("Server Not Responding").

Continued

Table 24-2 *(continued)*

Setting	Description
Intr	Enables a hard connection to be interrupted or killed while waiting for a response from the NFS server
timeo=*nn*	Sets the number of seconds, indicated by *nn*, to wait after an RPC timeout occurs before the next attempt is made. Used with the *soft* setting.
Bg	If mounting the filesystem fails on the first attempt, then retry mounting it in the background. This lets the mounting process for other filesystems to continue.
Fg	If mounting the file system fails on the first attempt, retry mounting it in the foreground. Use this for mounting file systems that must be mounted before proceeding, as with /usr.
Rw	Sets the file system as read-writeable.
Ro	Sets the file system as read only.

Initially, your /etc/fstab file may only contain the originally configured local file system. That file may look similar to the following:

```
more /etc/fstab
# /etc/fstab: static file system information.
#
# <file system> <mount point>   <type>  <options>                    <dump>  <pass>
/dev/hdb1        /         ext2   defaults,errors=remount-ro    1       1
/dev/hdb2        none             swap    sw                            0       0
/dev/hda1        /win_c vfat   defaults,user,ro              0       0
proc             /proc            proc    defaults                      0       0
/dev/fd0         /floppy          auto    defaults,user,noauto    0       0
/dev/cdrom       /cdrom           iso9660 defaults,ro,user,noauto 0       0
```

To add the NFS share, edit this file using a text editor such as vi. Then add a line to the file in the following format:

```
server:/share   /share      nfs      options      0      0
```

The *server* is the name of the host machine followed by the shared NFS volume on the remote host. This information comes from the /etc/exports file. Next is the local mount point, which you can set to be anything you want. *nfs* specifies that this file system uses an NFS connection. The options are found in Table 24-2. Each option used here must be separated by a comma (,), with no spaces. The last two zeros indicate not to dump the contents or to perform a file system check (fsck) at boot time.

Here is an example of the /etc/fstab file after adding NFS shares:

```
more /etc/fstab
# /etc/fstab: static file system information.
#
# <file system> <mount point>    <type>  <options>                      <dump>  <pass>
/dev/hdb1         /       ext2    defaults,errors=remount-ro    1       1
/dev/hdb2         none            swap    sw                             0       0
debian:/etc/remote    /etc    nfs     fg,ro,hard,intr               0       0
proj:/home/projects  /projects nfs    bg,rw,soft                     0       0
/dev/hda1         /win_c  vfat    defaults,user,ro               0       0
proc              /proc           proc    defaults                       0       0
/dev/fd0          /floppy         auto    defaults,user,noauto   0       0
/dev/cdrom        /cdrom          iso9660 defaults,ro,user,noauto 0      0
```

Now, at boot time, two new remote mounts will be established. The first one connects to host *debian* and must connect in order to allow the boot to proceed because of the *fg* option. The next one opens a command area for shared projects. The data from those projects is then stored on the host *proj*.

Note

In order for an NFS share to successfully mount, the directory it mounts to must exist. To create the mount point on the local file system, use mkdir as shown here:

```
mkdir /mnt/point
```

Change the path, /mnt/point, to wherever you would like the remote file system to mount.

Mounting an NFS file system manually

Mounting remote NFS file systems doesn't require having an entry in the /etc/fstab file. Those same file systems can be mounted from a command line:

```
mount server:/remote/share /usr/share
```

In this example, *server* refers to the remote computer that you want to share. The file system on the remote computer is then indicated by /remote/share, which the remote NFS server is sharing. This all gets followed by the mount point for the local file system, /usr/share.

You can also apply to a mounted file system the same options as those applied to file systems contained in the /etc/fstab file. You must add an -o to indicate the list of options for the mount. The following example shows options added to a mount:

```
mount -o rw,bg,hard,intr myserver:/shares/home /mnt/home
```

Unmounting an NFS filesystem

At some point while using mounted NFS file systems, you may need to remove the mount. If you have ever used `mount` to add local hard drives, CD-ROMs, or floppies, then you would have unmounted them when done. Unmounting an NFS mount works the same as unmounting one of your local devices. Here is an example:

```
umount /mnt
```

This will unmount any file system that you specify. However, if users are still utilizing the files of that file system, the file system cannot be unmounted. You can use `umount` with the `-f` option, which forces the selected file system to unmount, but this is far from the best choice. It leaves the programs using those files in a state of uncertainty, leaves the users of those programs confused, and any file data still in memory will be lost.

To determine what files are open in the file system that you want to shut down, use the list open files command (`lsof`). This command will list all the files in the given filesystem. The following example shows how you would list the open files for the `/home` directory, and the results:

```
$ /usr/sbin/lsof +d /home
COMMAND    PID  USER    FD    TYPE DEVICE SIZE   NODE NAME
bash     14839 steve    cwd    DIR   3,65 4096  47411 /home/steve
lsof     14878 steve    cwd    DIR   3,65 4096  47411 /home/steve
lsof     14879 steve    cwd    DIR   3,65 4096  47411 /home/steve
```

With this information, you can then request that the owner of the processes close them, wait for the processes to finish, or kill the processes. This is a better method, although unpleasant for the user.

Note   The methods indicated here for unmounting an NFS file system work for all file systems. The safest way to unmount a local file system, though, is to put the machine into single-user mode first. Unmounting at this point is by far the safest method.

Sharing Files Using Samba

Samba is a highly configurable communication tool that enables Linux boxes to communicate with machines using the NetBIOS networking protocol. NetBIOS is based on Server Message Blocks (SMB), which is the message format that DOS and Windows machines use to share files, directories, and devices. It is the common networking protocol among Windows environments.

Samba enables a full-fledged Linux server to exist in an entirely Windows environment, all the while speaking the Windows NetBIOS language. Because of the features that Samba offers, it could virtually replace much of the function that a Windows NT server provides — WINS resolution, primary domain controller, and password authentication.

A complete discussion of Samba is beyond the scope of this book, but you can find more information at the Web site, `www.samba.org`. Once installed, you can also obtain more information from the man pages (`man samba`). This chapter does, however, provide enough information to adequately get a file server up and running for a community of users.

Installing Samba

The primary package to install is the `samba` package, but I suggest also installing the `samba-doc` package as well, for documentation reference. Once selected and installed, the configuration script will ask you the following question:

```
Run Samba as daemons or from inetd?
Press 'D' to run as daemons or 'I' to run from inetd: [I]
```

Running Samba as a daemon forces it to run all the time, whereas using `inetd` causes Samba to run only when there is activity on the designated port. You can rerun this configuration script at any time with `/usr/sbin/sambaconfig`.

When initially installing Samba, you are also asked about creating a password file using the system's password file. The default answer to this question is no. If you choose to answer yes to this question, the Samba password file will include the names of all the services as well as the names of all the system's users. Choose no, so you can control the accounts for Samba. You don't want people getting access using default system accounts. You will create accounts later.

When Samba runs, two services will start: `nmbd`, the NetBIOS service; and `smbd`, the SMB (Samba)service. These services provide the backbone for sharing files with other Windows machines. The services must be restarted each time the Samba configuration file is changed. When running as a daemon, restart Samba as follows:

```
/etc/init.d/samba restart
```

The service reads the configuration file when it starts, applying any new changes.

Configuring Samba

The configuration file provided with the Debian package includes the most common settings. It has been very well commented to help explain many of the settings. The

following code is taken from the default install configuration file /etc/samba/
smb.conf. The text in bold is discussed following the code. Note that lines starting
with semicolons (;) and pound signs (#) are ignored when the file is read for configuration settings.

This file is included in the chapter to better explain portions of the configuration
process and to preserve it for you. Many of the configuration tools discussed later
in this chapter remove the commented text from the configuration file. Before making any changes to the file, manually or with a tool, make a backup copy first. Now
that you've been warned, let's take a look at the configuration file:

```
;
; /etc/smb.conf
;
; Sample configuration file for the Samba suite for Debian GNU/Linux
;
; Please see the manual page for smb.conf for detailed description of
;     every parameter.
;

[global]
    printing = bsd
    printcap name = /etc/printcap
    load printers = yes
    guest account = nobody
    invalid users = root

; "security = user" is always a good idea. This will require a Unix account
;     in this server for every user accessing the server.
    security = user

; Change this for the workgroup your Samba server will part of
    workgroup = WORKGROUP

    server string = %h server (Samba %v)

; If you want Samba to log though syslog only then set the following
;     parameter to 'yes'. Please note that logging through syslog in
;     Samba is still experimental.
    syslog only = no

; We want Samba to log a minimum amount of information to syslog. Everything
;     should go to /var/log/{smb,nmb} instead. If you want to log through
;     syslog you should set the following parameter to something higher.
    syslog = 0;

; This socket options really speed up Samba under Linux, according to my
;     own tests.
    socket options = IPTOS_LOWDELAY TCP_NODELAY SO_SNDBUF=4096 SO_RCVBUF=4096

; Passwords are encrypted by default. This way the latest Windows 95 and NT
;     clients can connect to the Samba server with no problems.
    encrypt passwords = yes
```

```
; It's always a good idea to use a WINS server. If you want this server
;    to be the WINS server for your network change the following parameter
;    to "yes". Otherwise leave it as "no" and specify your WINS server
;    below (note: only one Samba server can be the WINS server).
;    Read BROWSING.txt for more details.
  wins support = no

; If this server is not the WINS server then specify who is it and uncomment
;    next line.
;    wins server = 172.16.0.10

; Please read BROWSING.txt and set the next four parameters according
;    to your network setup. There is no valid default so they are commented
;    out.
;    os level = 0
;    domain master = no
;    local master = no
;    preferred master = no

; What naming service and in what order should we use to resolve host names
;    to IP addresses
  name resolve order = lmhosts host wins bcast

; This will prevent nmbd to search for NetBIOS names through DNS.
  dns proxy = no

; Name mangling options

  preserve case = yes
  short preserve case = yes

; This boolean parameter controls whether Samba attempts to sync. the Unix
;    password with the SMB password when the encrypted SMB password in the
;    /etc/samba/smbpasswd file is changed.
  unix password sync = false

; For Unix password sync. to work on a Debian GNU/Linux system, the following
;    parameters must be set (thanks to Augustin Luton
;    <aluton@hybrigenics.fr> for sending the correct chat script for
;    the passwd program in Debian Potato).
  passwd program = /usr/bin/passwd %u
  passwd chat = *Enter\snew\sUNIX\spassword:* %n\n
*Retype\snew\sUNIX\spassword:* %n\n .

; The following parameter is useful only if you have the linpopup package
;    installed. The samba maintainer and the linpopup maintainer are
;    working to ease installation and configuration of linpopup and samba.
;    message command = /bin/sh -c '/usr/bin/linpopup "%f" "%m" %s; rm %s' &

; The default maximum log file size is 5 MBytes. That's too big so this
;    next parameter sets it to 1 MByte. Currently, Samba rotates log
;    files (/var/log/{smb,nmb} in Debian) when these files reach 1000 KBytes.
;    A better solution would be to have Samba rotate the log file upon
```

```
;      reception of a signal, but for now on, we have to live with this.
   max log size = 1000


[homes]
   comment = Home Directories
   browseable = no

; By default, the home directories are exported read only. Change next
;     parameter to "no" if you want to be able to write to them.
   read only = yes

; File creation mask is set to 0700 for security reasons. If you want to
;     create files with group=rw permissions, set next parameter to 0775.
   create mask = 0700

; Directory creation mask is set to 0700 for security reasons. If you want to
;     create dirs. with group=rw permissions, set next parameter to 0775.
   directory mask = 0700

[printers]
   comment = All Printers
   browseable = no
   path = /tmp
   printable = yes
   public = no
   writable = no
   create mode = 0700

; A sample share for sharing your CD-ROM with others.
;[cdrom]
;   comment = Samba server's CD-ROM
;   writable = no
;   locking = no
;   path = /cdrom
;   public = yes
;
; The next two parameters show how to auto-mount a CD-ROM when the
;     cdrom share is accessed. For this to work /etc/fstab must contain
;     an entry like this:
;
;       /dev/scd0   /cdrom  iso9660 defaults,noauto,ro,user   0 0
;
; The CD-ROM gets unmounted automatically after the connection to the
;
; If you don't want to use auto-mounting/unmounting make sure the CD
;     is mounted on /cdrom
;
;   preexec = /bin/mount /cdrom
;   postexec = /bin/umount /cdrom
```

The Samba configuration file is initially broken down into three main sections: global, home, and printers. These sections are indicated by the brackets enclosing the word, as seen by the first bold text in the file ([global]). The global section sets the configuration for the overall function of the server. More than 160 parameters are available for the global environment. Before you feel overwhelmed, however, note that the ones most commonly used are already in the configuration file.

Jumping down the configuration file, you will see [home], which denotes the beginning of the home share configuration area. It too has a list of parameters. Samba refers to these as *service parameters*. This section enables users to connect to their own account on the Linux box and read their files. By default, this area is set as read-only. Users can only see their own area; they are prevented from viewing other account areas.

The printer share starts with [printers], and contains settings for the printers. By default, Samba is set up for all printers. As with the other shares, printers can be customized for your environment.

You can add more shares as needed. Commented out are the settings for sharing a CD-ROM from the Linux server. Removing the semicolons will quickly make a share for the CD-ROM.

The parameters for each section then take the following format:

```
parameter = value
```

Each parameter has a value such as *true* or *false*, *yes* or *no*, or a *string* or *path*, as in the case of the *comment* parameter, which looks like the following:

```
comment = "This is a comment!"
```

The first parameter I'd like to point out is invalid user (bold in the file listing earlier). This parameter is important because it limits those accounts that can compromise security. By default, only root is listed, but you can add any accounts you think should definitely not have access through Samba. Leave a space between each name added to this parameter.

Next is the workgroup. When Windows first sets up the NetBIOS network, it sets the workgroup to WORKGROUP. Many sites using this feature will change it to some other name. You need to change this parameter to match your environment.

Tip

To find the setting for the Windows 95/98 machine workgroup, right-click the Network Neighborhood icon on the desktop. Click the Identification tab after the dialog box opens. The box labeled Workgroup contains the name of your workgroup.

The encrypt passwords parameter enables the use of a separate password file for Samba. This is important because of the different way in which UNIX and Windows encrypt the passwords; therefore, the /etc/passwd file cannot be used to look up passwords at the time of login. Instead, a separate file, /etc/smbpasswd, is used to look up passwords. Use the smbpasswd utility to add users to the password file. Here is the syntax for adding the account tom:

```
smbpasswd -a tom
```

You will then receive a prompt for the new account's password. You will need to enter the password twice to confirm it.

In the [homes] section of the configuration file, the browseable parameter determines whether the clients can browse the share name. From a Windows machine, this means viewing the share names from the Network Neighborhood. By default, Debian configures this to no so that no one can see the home shares.

Debian also configures the home share to be read-only (set by the read only parameter). Changing this to yes enables users to write to the areas of access set by their login privileges.

In the [printers] section of the configuration file, the printable/writable combination enables users to create a spool file for printing purposes, but doesn't allow users to create or modify files. This is a typical configuration for printing. The public parameter is also set to allow only qualified users printing privileges. No guest printing is allowed on this server.

Table 24-3 lists Samba's parameters, including the default value and a short description of each. The default values listed in the table are those specified by Samba; the Debian values appear in the configuration file. All the active parameters in the configuration file are listed in this table.

Table 24-3
Samba's global parameters

Parameter	Default value	Description
browseable	Yes	Controls whether this share is viewable from a browse list when the server is queried
comment	none given	Descriptive text that appears next to the service when the client queries the server
copy	None	Allows cloning of services found earlier in the configuration file. Useful when creating multiple similar services.
create mask	0744	Used when converting DOS permissions to UNIX permissions during file creation
create mode	0744	Means the same as create mask

Parameter	Default value	Description
directory mask	755	Used when converting DOS permissions to UNIX permissions during directory creation
dns proxy	Yes	Determines whether unregistered NetBIOS names should be treated like a DNS name. Debian changes this setting to no, as WINS is disabled.
encrypt passwords	Yes	Specifies whether encrypted passwords are negotiated with the clients. Windows NT 4.0SP3 and Windows 98 expect encrypted passwords.
guest account	nobody	Specifies the user name to use for access to guest access
guest ok	no	A yes value allows access without requiring a password
guest only	no	Specifies that only guests can access the services
hide dot files	yes	Controls whether files beginning with a dot are treated as hidden files
invalid user	no valid users	A list of users who are not allowed to log in to this service
load printers	yes	Defines whether the printers listed in the printcap file are loaded for browsing
max log size	5000	Specifies the maximum size to which the log file can grow before renaming the file with a .old extension. The number represents kilobytes. A zero value means no limit.
name resolver order	lmhosts host wins bcast	Determines the order in which names are resolved
passwd program	/bin/ passwd	The local password program used for setting UNIX passwords
passwd chat	none given	Controls the conversation between smbd and the local password program to allow changing a user's password
preserve case	yes	Allows long filenames to remain as is, rather than being forced to a certain case
printable	no	Controls whether a client can write and submit spool files for the service
printcap name	/etc/ printcap	Holds the names and aliases of the available printers on the system

Continued

Table 24-3 *(continued)*

Parameter	Default value	Description
printing	bsd	Controls how the printer status information is interpreted. Currently, eight styles are supported: bsd, aix, lprng, plp, sysv, hpux, qnx, and softq.
public	no	Specifies the access privilege for the service
read only	no	Controls the ability to create or modify files
security	user	The most important setting in Samba, as it affects how clients negotiate a response
server string	Samba %v	A comment string that appears in browse lists for the server. Debian adds the server name as well.
short preserve case	yes	This option applies to 8.3 filenames common among DOS systems. It allows the 8.3 filenames to remain as is, rather than being forced to a certain case.
socket options	tcp_ nodelay	Lists the socket options that a server can use when talking with a client for better performance
syslog	1	Specifies the logging level. Zero maps to LOG_ERR, 1 maps to LOG_WARNING, 2 maps to LOG_NOTICE, 3 maps to LOG_INFO, and all higher levels map to LOG_DEBUG.
syslog only	no	When set to yes, sends debug messages to syslog only. Not recommended.
wins support	no	Controls whether the nmbd process will act as a WINS server
workgroup	WORKGROUP	Sets the workgroup environment that the server shows up in when checked by the clients
writable	no	Controls the ability to create or modify files
unix passwornd sync	false	Regulates whether the UNIX passwords are taken from the smbpasswd file when changed

Note   More information about Samba parameters can be found in the man pages on smb.conf. There are well over 160 available parameters for use in configuring Samba. If still more information is needed, read the frequently asked question (FAQ) area of the Samba Web site (www.samba.org).

Testing the Samba server

The best way to start using the Samba service is to make the configuration of Samba as simple as possible. With Samba running on the server, run

```
smbclient -L server
```

where *server* is your server name. This should result in a request for a password. Press Enter to display the listing, as shown here:

```
Password:
Anonymous login successful
Domain=[WORKGROUP] OS=[Unix] Server=[Samba 2.0.7]

        Sharename      Type       Comment
        ---------      ----       -------
        public         Disk
        IPC$           IPC        IPC Service (bath server (Samba 2.0.7))
        lp             Printer    Generic dot-matrix printer entry

        Server                    Comment
        ---------                 -------
        BATH                      bath server (Samba 2.0.7)

        Workgroup                 Master
        ---------                 -------
        WORKGROUP                 BATH
```

You can see from the output that the name of the server and the share names are correct. (Notice that the homes share does not appear here because it is dynamically created based on the user's ID.) Now try connecting as a user with the following:

```
smbclient '//host/homes' -U userid
```

Replace *host* with the resolvable name or IP address of the machine hosting the SMB service. Then replace *userid* with a valid account name.

The smbclient will communicate with the smbd service and negotiate a connection. You will then be asked for the password of the account name. Enter the password associated with the Samba account on the server. If all goes well, you will end up with a prompt like the following:

```
smb: \>
```

You can now view the files in your account on the server using the ls command. This proves the connection works. You can use q to quit the session.

If you receive a connection failure, make sure that Samba is running on the target machine. You should at least get a password request with the server running.

Tip   If you having trouble getting Samba to work, check out the Web site `us4.samba.org/samba/docs/DIAGNOSIS.html` for help in diagnosing your problem(s).

Configuring Samba with SWAT

The Samba Web Administration Tool (SWAT) provides a convenient means of administering Samba through a Web interface. This tool can be used from any operating system with a Web browser. SWAT uses port 901 for a connection request. To get this working on your system after the SWAT package is installed, you must make a few adjustments.

Modify the `/etc/inetd.conf` file to remove the # off # characters from the beginning of the configuration line. This line is added when SWAT is installed, but needs to be commented out. You then need to restart the `inetd` service with the following:

```
/etc/init.d/inetd restart
```

You can then configure Samba using SWAT via a browser. With the browser open, use the IP address or resolvable name for your server and add the 901 port number, as shown here:

```
192.168.22.126:901
```

You will then be prompted for a password. To make administrative changes, you need access to the root account. Enter `root` for the user name and the root password for the server. You will see the control interface, as shown in Figure 24-1. Clicking the various buttons will take you to different areas that you can configure.

Caution   Be advised that using SWAT in an open environment can pose a security risk. The passwords required to log in get sent in clear text format, meaning that someone could pick them up on the network. This tool should not be used for systems exposed to the Internet.

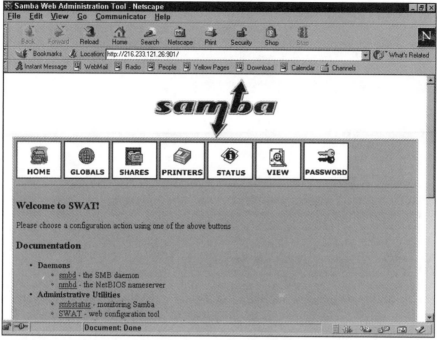

Figure 24-1: Configuring the Samba server from a Windows machine

Configuring Samba with gnosamba

A useful Gnome tool to configure Samba is gnosamba. This graphical interface, shown in Figure 24-2, enables you to open the configuration file, manipulate the settings, and then save the file. Before using this tool, be aware that all comments contained in the original configuration file are removed when saving. Therefore, if you have tweaked the configuration file before, make a copy to prevent any losses.

You can use this tool to add shares using a built-in wizard, to change permissions, or to create multiple configurations saved to different names for testing. Double-clicking a parameter brings up a selectable list of options for that parameter. This comes in handy if you are not familiar with all the available options for a parameters. Once you've made changes to the configuration, restart the Samba services from gnosamba.

The gnosamba package uses the Gnome environment to run; therefore, Gnome should be installed as well.

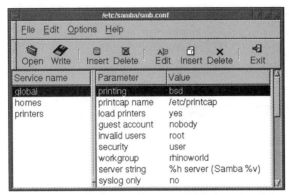

Figure 24-2: Samba configurations made easy with the use of gnosamba

Checking the network with smb-nat

This tool runs a simple security check on Samba. It runs through a series of checks to ensure that any known vulnerabilities are secure. A misconfiguration can expose a system quickly. You can set this tool to use custom files containing a user list or a password list, and even specify an output file. The smb-nat package includes default lists, which are used if none are specified. To use the default lists, run the program using nat localhost. Otherwise, use the following syntax:

```
nat [-o output] [-u userlist] [-p passlist] address
```

At minimum, I suggest using an output file (identified by *output*) to capture all the data produced, as it exceeds the viewable area of a terminal window. The address for the machine is required for this tool. It can be any resolvable name or an IP address.

Connecting to a Samba server from Linux

You can use the Samba client to connect to any machine hosting a share. The client will connect in text mode and enable you to access the files on the remote machine much in the same way the FTP client works. The following syntax is used:

```
smbclient //server/share [-U username] [-W workgroup] [-I Ipaddress]
```

The *server* refers to the name of the machine hosting the smbd service. Likewise, the *share* is the share name on that server you wish to connect. For logging in as a specific account, use the -U option with the *username*. If none is given, the account you are currently using is tried. Likewise, connecting to a specific *workgroup* or machine uses the corresponding workgroup name or machine's IP address. The IP address must be in the *a.b.c.d* format.

Once you are logged on, you can navigate using the common commands used for the FTP client: `ls`, `dir`, `cd`, `lcd`, `get`, `put`, and so on. Typing a question mark (?) at the prompt will give you a list of the commands. More specific descriptions are obtainable with ? `command`, where `command` is the command you have a question about.

Connecting to a Samba server from Windows

Because the NetBIOS protocol broadcasts the server name for the workgroup, finding and connecting to a server may only require you to browse the Network Neighborhood to establish a connection. This assumes, however, that your user ID and password are the same for both your Windows machine and the Samba account.

If the account IDs are not the same, you can connect another way. This means that you must know what share you intend to connect to. To establish a connection, right-click the desktop Network Neighborhood icon and select Map Network Drive from the menu. Enter the share path just as you would with the `smbclient` on a Linux box, as seen in Figure 24-3.

Figure 24-3: Mapping a drive from a Windows 98 machine to Debian using Samba

Once the drive is mapped, you can access the files through regular methods in Windows, such as the My Computer icon, Windows Explorer, and so on. The printers work the same as drives regarding mapping.

Sharing files between Linux and Windows machines

In the world of GUI tools, `TkSmb` provides a graphic interface to `smbclient`. You have all the convenience of a point-and-click GUI applied to the remote connection utility of `smbclient`. The `tksmb` package does depend on a couple of additional packages, noted when installed through `dselect`.

Figure 24-4 shows what the interface looks like. In the upper-right area, enter the user ID, the password, and the local path where files will be saved. The left pane lists the servers hosting shares on the network. After entering the correct information in the fields on the right, click the server name to which you want to connect.

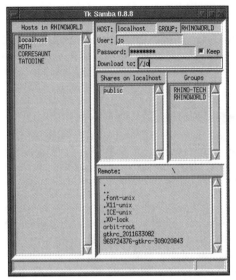

Figure 24-4: Using a graphical interface to browse the Windows network

A list of available shares will then appear in the center box. Clicking one of these share names will display the names of the files in the lower box. From there, you can navigate through the directories by clicking on the blue text. Right-clicking a filename gives you the option of downloading the file to the specified local directory.

The one drawback to using this tool is that there is no way to send files, only download them. Perhaps this will evolve later.

Summary

When it comes to Linux file servers, two stand out: NFS and Samba. NFS stands out because of its long history in the UNIX environment and because client utilities exist for nearly every platform. This enables mixed-platform environments to use NFS for file sharing.

In the predominantly Windows client networks, Samba stands out for its ability to enter those networks to become a Primary Domain Controller, in addition to becoming a file and print server. Samba definitely has its place among file servers.

✦　　✦　　✦

Mail

Of any application used on a computer system, e-mail ranks number. Even over the Internet, more traffic is taken up by e-mail than by other sources. The point of e-mail is to communicate with others — sending letters, notes, and more. The muscle behind this mass transfer of communications are *Mail Transfer Agents* (*MTAs*). The mail system can be divided into two main parts: Mail Transfer Agents and *Mail User Agents* (*MUAs*). MUAs are clients that communicate with the MTAs.

This chapter covers the basics of setting up an e-mail server on your system. From there, you can take it farther by setting it up to process mailing lists, to process mail for virtual domains, and even to relay mail to another mail server. In addition to handling incoming mail sent to your server, clients need to retrieve their mail from your machine. For more information on the available clients that communicate with the servers you set up in this chapter, see Chapter 6.

Understanding Internet E-Mail Protocols and Standards

In the early days of the Internet, many standards called *Requests for Comments* (*RFCs*) were created. Some of these standards are still used today. One such standard is the Mail Transfer Protocol, which developed in 1981 into the Simple Mail Transfer Protocol (SMTP). SMTP has been adopted primarily as the standard for transferring electronic mail over the Internet. Since its inception, SMTP has continued to develop to what it is today.

As SMTP continued to develop, other protocols emerged to work with mail servers servers, such as the Post Office Protocol (POP) and the Internet Mail Access Protocol (IMAP). These protocols developed as a means for clients to retrieve mail. Other protocols forced the development of `sendmail`, which was created by Eric Allman while at U. C. Berkeley. This program was a little different in that it could receive e-mail from various networks, fix the messages that would otherwise have been rejected, and pass the messages along to their final destination. To accomplish this feat, `sendmail` became extremely complex. Volumes have been written to explain how it works, with most barely scratching the surface.

The Post Office Protocol (POP) grew in popularity and has become the leading protocol for mail clients, primarily because this is the best way for users to dial into their ISP and download their mail. Having gone through several revisions, the most current being POP3, POP has flourished. Client software, which uses POP, can be found on nearly every platform. This protocol enables a client to connect to a remote mail server; log in using the user ID and password; and retrieve e-mail to a local machine for later viewing.

If a person needs to access e-mail from more than one location or machine, however, POP doesn't work very well. This is one of the drawbacks of using POP. Another limitation is that POP can only access one folder on the remote mail machine. Some clients enable users to create folders to sort and manage their e-mail, but the folders can only reside on the local machine. For example, if you use a Windows e-mail client such as Eudora, Pegasus Mail, or Outlook Express, you can access your e-mail from a Linux mail server using the POP3 protocol, but it only picks up mail from one folder (the inbox) from the mail server. If you went to another computer and tried to access the e-mail there, you would not be able to because the mail is now on the first machine, where you used the Windows mail client.

This brings our discussion to the client mail protocol, which is gaining popularity as users need to use more than one computer to access their mail. The IMAP protocol, now in its fourth version, avoids POP's limitations. More people are traveling with their laptops, while using desktops at home and at work. IMAP4 lets users connect to the mail server, create the folders on the server, access those folders, and get their mail from any machine with an IMAP client. IMAP clients exist for all the major platforms, and their numbers are growing.

IMAP also keeps track of the state of the mail — read, unread, and marked for deletion. This aspect of IMAP enables you to check your mail on one machine, read a few messages, shut down the first machine, and go to another machine to finish reading your mail. For those who travel, this can be a lifesaver. If you are in a hurry, you can read only those messages you deem critical. You can determine which are critical by checking the message headers, downloading only those messages you need immediately. Later, you can access the rest of the messages from any other computer.

For all this to work, the correct applications need to be loaded on the server. Table 25-1 lists some of the Debian-packaged applications for a mail server. The packages are sorted according to category: — SMTP, POP, IMAP, and Tools. The Tools category includes the programs that work with the mail servers, such as a mailing list server, or the tool that helps send mail through a firewall.

Table 25-1
Mail servers and tools

Type	Name	Description
SMTP		
	sendmail	The most popular e-mail server, and also the most versatile. However, configuration can be tricky.
	exim	An easy-to-configure mail server
	postfix	A high-performance mail server
POP		
	pop3d	A standard pop server for client access
	qpopper	An enhanced mail pop server for client access
IMAP		
	imap	A standard imap server for client access
Tools		
	smtpd	A mail proxy for firewalls
	berolist	An easy-to-use and install mailing list server
	biff	A mail notification utility

Tip   With biff installed, you can add biff y to your .bashrc file to get notifications when new mail arrives for you.

exim

The Debian choice of mail servers is exim. This is a replacement mail server for sendmail. It is the simplest, by far, to configure. Users must answer a series of questions at the time of install. Understanding these questions, and the terms used, will enable you to better configure a working server. The following sections will help get you started.

Because exim is simpler to configure than sendmail, it's less flexible sendmail in some respects. For instance, exim requires that every address be associated with a domain name. If one is missing, it will add it to the address.

Inversely, exim can limit the relaying of messages to only certain domains. This avoids the relaying of bulk spam e-mail, which, in my opinion, has reached epidemic proportions. You can find comprehensive data about the exim package in the /usr/doc/exim/spec.txt file.

Questions during installation

When you install `exim` using `dselect`, you will proceed through a series of questions or steps during the configuration stage of the installation. Reviewing each of the questions and steps here will save you some time and trouble before you have to answer the questions on your computer.

The first step simply lets you know that you are about to start configuring the `exim` package. Press Enter to begin the configuration.

1. Here you are given five options that specify how this mail server is to be used. These options are as follows:

   - **Internet Site** — Mail is sent and received directly using SMTP.

   - **Internet Site Using a Smart Host** — This is primarily used for dial-up systems. You can receive mail directly or by using a utility such as `fetchmail`. Sent mail goes to a smart host (such as an ISP mail server).

   - **Satellite System** — All mail is sent to another machine (smart host) for delivery, and no mail is received locally. Use this option for workstations on a network.

   - **Local Delivery Only** — This machine is not on a network. Only mail for local users is delivered. This option is for a stand-alone system.

   - **No Configuration** — Nothing will be configured and the mail system cannot be used. The configuration must be completed manually or rerun with the `/usr/sbin/eximconfig` script as root.

   In most cases, the first two options are used.

2. What is the visible name of your system? This will appear on outgoing messages. You can use the domain name (`domain.com`) of your system.

   Press Enter to accept the default name or retype the name you want to use.

3. Does the system have any other names that need to appear on incoming messages? Use this for systems with multiple domain names.

   Add each name separated by a space or comma. If no additional domain names are needed for this machine, enter `none`.

4. Name the domains that you are willing to relay. This means that you will accept mail for them, but they are not local domains. Enter any domain that specifies you as the MX (mail exchanger; their mail server).

   Use spaces and commas to separate each domain. You can also use wildcards. Enter `none` if no domains apply.

5. If you want to relay networks for local machines, use the standard address/length format (192.168.123.213/24) for each network. You can also use IPv6 standard addresses.

   Press Enter if there is no network to relay.

6. Do you wish to filter spam using the Realtime Blackhole List? You can filter (f), reject (r), or not use (n) this option.

   The default is not to use this option (n). If you choose to filter (f), you will be asked for the Internet address for the filter list. You can press Enter to accept the default address.

7. Who should the postmaster and root accounts be redirected to? This should be the administrator of the system.

   Enter the name of the account that exists on this machine. The configuration will create an alias file or replace an existing one. The default is y, to replace the existing one.

8. Lastly, you can review the settings you've made during the configuration. Press Enter to accept them.

This completes the configuration of exim for your system. It can now send and receive e-mail.

The exim configuration file

From time to time, you may need to reconfigure your mail system in order to accomplish the mailing activities you want to perform. This may require modifying the configuration file. The information for the exim application is kept in the /etc/exim.conf file, and is relatively easy to modify.

Most of the file can be read and understood by the variable names. A few parameters are a bit cryptic. I suggest leaving these alone until you have a clear understanding of them. The configuration file's major components are covered in the following sections.

Main settings

The main settings control the overall system parameters. The bulk of the necessary configuring is done at the beginning of this file. This file was modified when exim was initially installed by the dselect configuration script. Among the settings made here are the qualified, local, and relayed domain names. These are domain names that have been listed as the MX record in the DNS. You can also set usernames for which no mail will be accepted, and the names of trusted users.

```
qualify_domain = hoth.rhino-tech.com

# qualify_recipient =

local_domains = localhost:hoth.rhino-tech.com

local_domains_include_host = true
local_domains_include_host_literals = true
```

```
#relay_domains =
#relay_domains_include_local_mx = true
never_users = root

host_lookup = *

# headers_check_syntax
#rbl_domains = rbl.maps.vix.com
#rbl_reject_recipients = false
#rbl_warn_header = true

host_accept_relay = localhost

# percent_hack_domains=*

trusted_users = mail
smtp_verify = true
gecos_pattern = ^([^,:]*)
gecos_name = $1

smtp_accept_queue_per_connection = 100
freeze_tell_mailmaster = true

received_header_text = "Received: \
        ${if def:sender_rcvhost {from ${sender_rcvhost}\n\t}\
        {${if def:sender_ident {from ${sender_ident} }}\
        ${if def:sender_helo_name
{(helo=${sender_helo_name})\n\t}}}}\
        by ${primary_hostname} \
        ${if def:received_protocol {with
${received_protocol}}} \
        (Exim ${version_number} #${compile_number}
(Debian))\n\t\
        id ${message_id}\
        ${if def:received_for {\n\tfor <$received_for>}}"
end
```

Transport configuration

This section sets the transport that is used for local delivery to user mailboxes. On Debian systems, group mail is set to write to the /var/spool/mail directory. This section also sets how pipes are used when in alias and .forward files. Auto-replies also are handled in this section.

```
local_delivery:
  driver = appendfile
  group = mail
  mode = 0660
  mode_fail_narrower = false
  envelope_to_add = true
  file = /var/spool/mail/${local_part}
```

```
address_pipe:
  driver = pipe
  return_output

address_file:
  driver = appendfile

address_directory:
  driver = appendfile
  no_from_hack
  prefix = ""
  suffix = ""
# maildir_format

address_reply:
  driver = autoreply

procmail_pipe:
  driver = pipe
  command = "/usr/bin/procmail -d ${local_part}"
  return_path_add
  delivery_date_add
  envelope_to_add
  check_string = "From "
  escape_string = ">From "
  user = $local_part
  group = mail

remote_smtp:
  driver = smtp

end
```

Directors configuration

This section controls local mail delivery, aliasing, and forwarding. The drivers, location, and transports are all set here. Local mail gets matched with the local user's mailbox. The location of the alias file is set here, as is the file to which the user forwards his or her mail.

```
real_local:
  prefix = real-
  driver = localuser
  transport = local_delivery

system_aliases:
  driver = aliasfile
  file_transport = address_file
  pipe_transport = address_pipe
  file = /etc/aliases
  search_type = lsearch
# user = list
```

```
procmail:
  driver = localuser
  transport = procmail_pipe
  require_files =
${local_part}:+${home}:+${home}/.procmailrc:+/usr/bin/procmail
  no_verify

userforward:
  driver = forwardfile
  file_transport = address_file
  pipe_transport = address_pipe
  reply_transport = address_reply
  no_verify
  check_ancestor
  file = .forward
  modemask = 002
  filter

localuser:
  driver = localuser
  transport = local_delivery

end
```

Routers configuration

The setting in this section routes, through SMTP, mail addressed outside of the domains hosted by this server. The `lookuphost` option uses the default DNS to look up the domain, and the `literal` option uses the exact IP address.

```
lookuphost:
  driver = lookuphost
  transport = remote_smtp

literal:
  driver = ipliteral
  transport = remote_smtp

end
```

Retry configuration

This section sets the rules for retrying to send mail. The settings in the following example try to resend the message every 15 minutes for two hours. After two hours, retries are attempted every factor of 1.5, up to 16 hours. Then a try is made every eight hours for four days from the first failed attempt to deliver the message.

```
# Domain          Error      Retries
# ------          -----      -------

*                 *          F,2h,15m; G,16h,2h,1.5; F,4d,8h
end
```

Rewrite configuration

This section specifies where to look up the real mailing address for all local users, and rewrites it in the mail. This is useful for users without a domain of their own.

```
*@mail.mydomain.com        ${lookup{$1}lsearch{/etc/email-
addresses}\

                           {$value}fail} bcfrF
```

Using Sendmail

Sendmail set the standard for Internet mail and it remains the most widely used e-mail package on Internet systems. Sendmail is used by Linux systems and the various UNIX systems alike. If flexibility is what you are looking for in a mail system, you've come to the right place.

Note

Eric Allman, creator of `sendmail`, has gone on to create a company around the `sendmail` program. The core application of `sendmail` is still available as an open source program. The company makes its money by providing support to businesses, and offers enhanced versions of `sendmail`. These enhanced versions include a Web-based configuration utility for installing, configuring, and maintaining `sendmail` on the server. The company's site is located at `www.sendmail.com`, whereas information about the free versions of `sendmail` can be found at `www.sendmail.org`.

In spite of its popularity, it is also one of the more complex packages to install, configure, and keep running. To give you an idea of its complexity, the main configuration file contains hundreds of lines of customizable code. Granted, under normal circumstances, no one would need to touch them. The Debian package of `sendmail` includes a configuration script to assist in making the configuration of `sendmail` a little less painful. (You can rerun the configuration script later using `/usr/sbin/sendmailconfig`.)

Questions during installation

If you choose to install `sendmail` through the `dselect` installation program (which I recommend), you'll be asked a series of questions to help you configure it for use with your particular environment. It is critical that `sendmail` be configured correctly in order for it to function properly. The following questions are numbered, although the configuration script questions are not. This helps you keep track of where you are in the process and how much further you have to go.

1. **Introduction** — Here you are introduced to the `sendmail` configuration. You must answer the following questions to complete the installation and configuration of `sendmail`. Most of the questions have a default answer, which will work for most installations.

   Press Enter to continue.

2. **Mail Name** — This is the host name that is shown on outgoing messages. For Internet mail, it must be a Fully Qualified Domain Name (FQDN). This would look something like `domain.com`.

   To accept the default, press Enter or type in a new FQDN.

3. **Smart Host** — A smart host can deliver external mail to the Internet. With a smart host, you don't need a DNS or a dedicated connection. This option works well for dial-up users or people who sit behind a firewall. Generally, the smart host will be the ISP's mail server.

   Enter the name of the smart host or leave it blank. Press Enter.

4. **Address Canonification** — Enabled by default, you are asked if want to disable this. This feature resolves addresses to their host names. Under normal circumstances, you want to leave this enabled.

   Press Enter to accept the `No` default.

5. **SMTP Mailer** — This enables your computer to exchange mail with other mail servers. Communicating with other mail servers is very important when working on the Internet. If you work on an isolated network and have no need (nor ever will) to correspond with other networks, you could disable this feature. This should be enabled in most cases.

   Press Enter to accept the default.

6. **Masquerade Envelope** — This enables mail coming from your machine (`test.domain.com`) to appear as if it came from the server (`domain.com`). This is helpful when working with a smart host.

   Press Enter to accept this option.

7. **All Masquerade** — Enabled, this causes all mail being sent to have `@domain.com` added to the name. This may cause problems if you send mail to a mailing list called mail list, because `maillist@domain.com` does not exist. Leave this feature disabled unless you know what you are doing.

   Press Enter to accept the default.

8. **Always Add Domain** — This adds the domain name to the sender's name. Normally this doesn't get added. The sender usually uses a complete name when creating a message.

   Press Enter to accept the default.

9. **Mail Acceptance** — This tells `sendmail` to accept mail for your mail name (`domain.com`). You may want to disable this if mail for `domain.com` is directed in the DNS to another machine.

   It is safe to leave this as `Y`(es).

10. **Alternate Names** — You can add acceptable mail names other than `domain.com`. This options works for multi-domain machines. You can add as many names as you need. Separate each name with a space. This option is saved in the `sendmail.cw` file.

Type `NONE` to eliminate this option, or press Enter if you don't have any to add but want to keep the option.

11. **Trusted Users** — This enables a special group of users, such as list servers. Use the names of those system users (not real people) with this feature. This option is saved in the `sendmail.ct` file. The people listed here are allowed to do certain things that would ordinarily raise flags of suspicion inside sendmail, such as masquerade as other users.

Separate each name with a space or type `NONE` to disable this option. Press Enter to keep the option without using it.

12. **Redirect Feature** — This enables the system to send an error message to the sender of an e-mail message sent to a user's former e-mail address, and adds the user's new email address. Add an entry to the `/etc/mail/aliases` file the name with `<new-address>.REDIRECT` as the aliased name. The sender will receive the error message with the new address.

Press Enter to keep this option disabled unless your system is likely to have a high turnover of users.

13. **UUCP Addresses** — Answering Yes to this enables `sendmail` to be smart about UUCP addresses. If you use a smart host, answer `Yes` to this to prevent a mail loop, unless the smart host does not deal with UUCP addresses.

Answer N(o) to this only if you are sure that no UUCP addresses are used on the mail system.

14. **Sticky Host** — Enabling this option sets `domain.com` as a distinct namespace. Mail sent to `user@domain.com` is marked as sticky and is not compared against local addresses.

Leave this option disabled if in doubt.

15. **DNS** — Enable this option if you have access to a Domain Name Server and are connected to the Internet. This option includes systems connected to and used as an ISP for mail services.

Press Enter to accept Y(es).

16. **Best MX is Local** — This option generates additional DNS traffic, which is OK for low to medium traffic hosts. Enabling this option causes `sendmail` to accept mail from any host that lists this machine as best possible MX record, as though the mail were addressed locally. This feature cannot be used if you have a wildcard MX record that matches your domain.

Press Enter to accept the default.

17. **Mailertable** — This enables the use of mail routing rules found in the `/etc/mail/mailertable file`. Mailers like `ifmail` and fax programs should use this option. Otherwise, leave the option disabled.

The default disables this option.

18. **Sendmail Restricted Shell** — This feature causes `sendmail` to use the restricted shell program (`smarsh`) instead of `/bin/sh` for mailing to programs. Enabling this restricts programs that can be run via e-mail to only those programs that appear in a special directory for heightened security.

    The default is disabled.

19. **Mailer Name** — This is the name that is internally generated for outgoing messages. The default is `MAILER-DAEMON`, but it can be changed to something like `POSTMASTER` instead if desired.

    Press Enter to accept the default name, or enter a new name.

20. **Me Too** — Enabling this option includes the sender in a group expansion of e-mail names. This enables a sender's address to be included in a group mailing. It's OK to leave this disabled.

    Press Enter to keep this option disabled.

21. **Message Timeouts** — A warning message is sent to the sender if a message cannot be delivered in a reasonable amount of time. The default time is four hours for a warning message, and five days for a failure notice. Some people think that a four-hour warning is premature. If you agree, you can extend the time for the warning message. However, from the sender's point of view, four hours may be a very long time.

    Press Enter to accept the default times.

The script finishes at this point and completes the installation. You may find that a few errors occur as the script completes. One possible error is that some missing files were identified. This error is more a warning message than a critical error. Possible missing files are `/etc/mail/relay-domains` and `/etc/mail/users`. These files can be added manually if they are needed. The warning resulted from only accepting the defaults during the configuration, leaving no information to be created in these files. The missing files will not prevent `sendmail` from working.

Many of the files that were modified will end up in the `/etc/mail` directory. You can make changes to these files by hand at any time after the installation. Note, though, that incorrect file contents may result in the `sendmail` server not working.

Alternatively configuring sendmail

You can configure `sendmail` manually through a text editor. This should be done only if you have some understanding of the configuration file. This file uses a somewhat cryptic code in its configuration. The main file is located in `/etc/mail/sendmail.cf` and is divided into several sections. The purpose of some of the sections are obvious by their titles, while other sections seem more ambiguous, such as the section named `Ruleset 96 -- bottom half of ruleset 3`.

Tip   I recommend making a copy of the original configuration file before making any manual changes to it. You never know when something may go awry, causing havoc with the original setup. Having a backup of the working file gives you an out if you need to start at the beginning again.

To give you an idea of the substance of the file, here is a sample of its code:

```
##############################################################
###   Ruleset 96 -- bottom half of ruleset 3   ###
##############################################################

S96

# handle special cases for local names
R$* < @ localhost > $*      $: $1 < @ $j . > $2     no domain at
all
R$* < @ localhost . $m > $*  $: $1 < @ $j . > $2    local
domain
R$* < @ [ $+ ] > $*         $: $1 < @@ [ $2 ] > $3     mark
[a.b.c.d]
R$* < @@ $=w > $*  $: $1 < @ $j . > $3    self-literal
R$* < @@ $+ > $*  $@ $1 < @ $2 > $3    canon IP addr

# pass to name server to make hostname canonical
R$* < @ $* $~P > $*   $: $1 < @ $[ $2 $3 $] > $4

# local host aliases and pseudo-domains are always canonical
R$* < @ $=w > $*    $: $1 < @ $2 . > $3
R$* < @ $j > $*     $: $1 < @ $j . > $2
R$* < @ $=M > $*    $: $1 < @ $2 . > $3
R$* < @ $* $=P > $*   $: $1 < @ $2 $3 . > $4
R$* < @ $* . . > $*    $1 < @ $2 . > $3
```

You can see from this portion of the code that the sendmail configuration file takes some effort to understand. Each character in the line means something. Detailed coverage of each of these commands is beyond the scope of this book. However, the script that runs at the time of installation will take care of most situations.

Testing and using sendmail

You can test sendmail after you have it installed by sending mail through it. Create a text file using an editor such as vi. The contents of the text file can be something as simple as this is a test. Use thefollowing command line to send the file to yourself, assuming your username is jo:

```
& /usr/sbin/sendmail -v jo < letter
```

The results of the test should appear as follows:

```
jo... Connecting to local...
jo... Sent
```

The -v tells sendmail that you want to use it in verbose mode, which means it prints everything it does. The account the mail was sent to is jo, and the letter is what you created. Now jo should have some mail if everything worked. Log in as jo to get the mail. You can also include all the To:, From:, and Subject: information usually found in messages.

Normally, sendmail is used through some type of client. Some situations may call for sending mail through the command line, in which case the previous command will work. Some examples of situations in which you might want to use sendmail from the command line include during, after, or as a result of an automated task. In this way, sendmail can notify administrators of problems or the completion of tasks, or it can broadcast an e-mail message.

General Mail Considerations

Now that you have a mail server installed on your system, you need to understand a few topics. that tend to affect more than one specific mail system. As such, they are covered in the following sections under different categories.

E-mail aliases

Most e-mail servers make use of an alias file. Because it is not recommended that certain accounts log in to a console such as root, daemon, and several others, mail sent to these accounts can be rerouted to another account that does log in on a regular basis. Mail sent to these system accounts, usually error messages, typically get aliased to the root account. Then the root account can be aliased to the administrator of the system. This just means that when the server goes to send mail to one of these accounts, it will be redirected to whomever needs to see the mail. The alias information is kept in /etc/aliases (or alternately /etc/mail/aliases, depending on your choice of mail server), which can be edited so that the correct people receive the mail notices.

You can also add virtual accounts in this file. A virtual account is not a real account, but a name by which users can receive e-mail. For instance, "webmaster" may not be an account set up for log in, but the person who manages the Web pages may want to use that ID for e-mail. In cases where several people may rotate through a position, it's easier to change a name in a file to redirect mail, than to change an e-mail address on hundreds of Web pages.

After all changes have been made to the aliases file, a database must be created for the mail server to read. This is done easily with the `newaliases` command. You must be in the directory of the aliases file, and then issue the command. If all the alias names and formats are correct, a database will be created; otherwise, you may receive error statements that necessitate correcting the file.

Forwarding your mail

Today, many people have more than one e-mail account through the Internet. To avoid confusion, all the mail from one system's e-mail address can be redirected to an account on another system. This is known as *forwarding*. Forwarding e-mail is very useful.

You may work in an environment with several servers running. These servers can be set up to automatically generate a report, which can be e-mailed to the administrator of the mail server. The administrative account can then forward the mail to a central location, where the administrator can read the report. This enables the administrator to avoid logging on to each server to read the e-mail.

Similarly, an individual user can forward mail from one e-mail address to another, be it on the same machine or to another system. Suppose that an individual is expecting an important e-mail message, but is going to be away on vacation. With one of the many available free Internet e-mail accounts, which can be accessed anywhere, he or she can temporarily forward any messages.

 Caution   As with most text-based Internet tools, e-mail is also subject to security risks. Sending and receiving e-mail is not at all secure. There are some methods, however, that can help to increase the security of e-mail messages, such as encrypting the message and using encryption keys. See Chapter 19 for more information on security.

To forward your mail to another address, you must create a file in the home account location. Create the ~/.forward file and add a line with the e-mail address to which you would like the mail forwarded. For instance, if my e-mail address were jo@domain.com and I wanted to have my e-mail forwarded to jo@mydomain.com, I would do the following:

```
$ vi ~/.forward
```

In the file, I would add jo@mydomain.com, and then save and exit the editor. Now, whenever mail is sent to jo@domain.com, it will be forwarded to jo@mydomain.com instead. If you wish to cancel the forwarding, you can simply delete the ~/.forward file.

Virtual mail server

Virtual mail server is not a function that most individuals would want to use; however, for businesses that host Web pages, process e-mail, and provide other Internet-related services, it is an important one.

The virtual mail server receives mail for a domain that doesn't have a real machine. One method of working around this is to use the relay functions with the mail servers. This enables mail to be received on a mail server without the machine having the same domain name. The drawback to this method is that each address must have a unique name. Two domains with the same account ID will end up with mail going to the one account; for instance, jo@domain.com and jo@example.com will be treated as the same address.

Alternatively, virtual mail server can be set up to receive mail addressed to anything@mydomain.com, which is routed to only one account. For instance, suppose mail sent to sale@mydomain.com and mail sent to debianrules@mydomain.com is routed to the account jo on the mail.domain.com machine. This way, Jo can pick up her mail whenever she wants. In other words, she can have mail sent to any name as long as it ends in @mydomain.com.

In order to set up sendmail to route mail sent to anything for a domain, you must add a line to the /etc/mail/sendmail.cf file. Always make a back up copy of the configuration file before making any changes. Use an editor and locate section 98 (S98). If you are using vi as your editor, use the search command to find this section (/S98). After this section identifier, add a line that looks like the following:

```
R$* < $* domain.com. >        $#local $@ $:username
```

Replace domain.com with the name of the domain that will be virtually hosted. There must be a TAB between the two halves of the command. After R$* < $* domain.com. >, enter a TAB and then finish the line. Replace username with the account name to which the mail will be sent. If the TAB does not appear in the line, the virtual hosting will not work.

Once you have edited the configuration file, restart the sendmail service. Following are the commands to accomplish this:

```
# /etc/init.d/sendmail stop
# /etc/init.d/sendmail start
```

Sendmail will now be ready to receive mail from the new virtual domains. You can test mail sent to the new domains in the same way that you tested to see if sendmail worked initially. You should be able to send mail to any name as long as it is addressed to the virtually hosted domain.

DNS and Internet mail

On the Internet or within a local network, where a Domain Name Server (DNS) is used to match domain names with actual IP addresses, mail is not handled in the same way. The DNS just wants to know the names of the mail exchangers; that is, the identities of the mail servers that can receive mail for a domain or forward it along. Each domain's mail server, or mail exchanger, needs an MX (Mail Exchanger) record created for it. It also needs to be registered.

If there is more than one mail exchanger for a domain, each MX record is weighted for priority. Even on a domain that has only one mail exchanger, that mail exchanger is still weighted with a priority. The number representing the priority can be anything from 0 to 65,535 (that's a lot of mail servers). Lower numbers are taken to be a higher priority.

For example, assume you have a network with a DNS. You have the mail services running on `mail.domain.com`, with the name of that machine registered in the DNS. You want all the mail for the domain `domain.com` to use `mail.domain.com` as the mail exchanger. You add an MX record to the DNS that would look like the following:

```
domain.com      IN      MX      1      mail.domain.com.
```

For larger facilities that require more than one mail server, add more servers, and then enter them in the DNS:

```
domain.com      IN      MX      10      mail1.domain.com.
domain.com      IN      MX      20      mail2.domain.com.
domain.com      IN      MX      20      mail3.domain.com.
```

Mail sent to `domain.com` using the preceding example would read the DNS as follows:

1. Mail would try to use the server with the lowest priority first —
   `mail1.domain.com`.

2. If mail.domain.com is unreachable, disconnected, or busy, then
   `mail2.domain.com` or `mail3.domain.com` would be tried next (both have
   the same priority).

3. The remaining two servers (mail2 and mail3) would be tried last.

This scheme of MX records enables the use of secondary and backup mail servers. Because the names are registered in the DNS, these servers need not exist on the same network or location on the Internet.

 Cross-Reference   To learn more about the Domain Name Server, see Chapter 5.

Using mailing lists

Mailing list servers, commonly called *list servers,* automate the use of mailing lists, including distribution, subscriptions, and mailing requests — all without much human management. Computers can work much more efficiently than we can.

Think of the list server as a dedicated program that monitors a mailbox for new mail. It then determines if incoming mail has a command associated with it or if it should be sent back to the subscribers of the list. Typically, the commands appear in the form of *subscribe* or *unsubscribe* requests. This automatically enables users to add or remove their e-mail address from a list. Other commands might include requests for specific documentation.

Mailing lists are used everywhere as a common e-mail forum in which people to get help, share ideas, or, in some cases, just complain. And, yes, some mailing lists merely generate junk mail. Some e-mail claims to be from a mailing list when in fact it is just plain, old-fashioned spam (junk mail). The bottom of these messages gives a bogus e-mail address for you to unsubscribe, which only bounces back an error that no one exists at that address. Legitimate sites always respond to an unsubscribe request.

Debian uses many mailing lists. When you visit their Web site (www.debian.org/MailingLists), you will see several mailing lists, all designed to enable people to communicate with one another on a variety of topics. There are lists for end users, developers, and specialty groups.

Setting Up POP

You were already introduced to the Post Office Protocol (POP) earlier in the chapter, but let's review a few points. Because clients that use POP exist on nearly every platform, it has become the most popular protocol for picking up mail. The disadvantages of using POP are that you have to get all your mail at one time and can use only one computer to do so. This limits your flexibility and mobility because you can't read your downloaded mail on another machine. Moreover, POP reads only one folder on the mail server. Clients compensate for this by creating local folders in which you can read, sort, and manage your mail.

Installing and configuring POP

To begin, you must install a POP server on the mail server. Table 25-1, at the beginning of the chapter, lists the two POP servers that Debian provides in package form: ipopd and qpopper. By default, Debian installs the ipopd package, which works fine; however, qpopper has some enhanced features added.

The packages are easy to install with dselect. The configuration stage of the install modifies the inetd.conf file so that the 110 TCP/IP port gets monitored for mail requests. This is the official port for POP services. The configuration script adds the following line to the /etc/inetd.conf file (in this case, I installed qpopper instead of ipopd):

```
pop-3           stream  tcp     nowait  root
/usr/sbin/tcpd  /usr/sbin/in.qpopper
```

If you make changes in the inetd.conf file, be sure to restart the inet service to activate the changes. Use the following command string to restart the service:

```
# /etc/init.d/inetd stop
# /etc/init.d/inetd start
```

Testing POP

With the POP service installed and running, you can now test the connection. Because POP uses a TCP/IP port, you can use telnet to connect to that port:

```
# telnet localhost pop-3
```

Alternately, you can check the port from a remote computer; use the same command, but replace localhost with the fully qualified domain name. You can also specify the port number (110) instead of using the name (pop-3). Here are the results of a connection to a server running qpopper as the POP server:

```
$ telnet localhost pop-3
Trying 127.0.0.1...
Connected to localhost.
Escape character is '^]'.
+OK QPOP (version 2.53) at debian.mydomain.com starting.
<3008.965876676@debi
an.rhino-tech.com>
user jo
+OK Password required for jo.
pass foobar14
+OK jo has 0 messages (0 octets).
quit
+OK Pop server at debian.rhino-tech.com signing off.
Connection closed by foreign host.
$
```

The bold text in the preceding example shows the commands that you would need to use. I logged in using user jo. The account for jo had to be created before testing the POP server. The server then responded by asking for a confirmation in the form of a password. I then entered the password command (pass) and the password. Note that the password is not encrypted for this test, so don't use a critical account to do your testing (lest someone evil is watching in the background). Satisfied that the POP service was working properly, I issued the quit command to close the connection. The server then notified me that the connection was closed.

Cross-Reference   You can find out more about mail clients and retrieving mail in Chapter 6.

Setting Up IMAP

Although POP took off in the early days of computing, IMAP has found its niche as distributed computing has increased. IMAP users benefit from the capability to access more than one folder on the server, to mark mail as read or unread, and to leave mail on the server so that it is accessible from multiple machines.

Because an IMAP system leaves the mail on the server, the mail is available to you whether you are traveling with a laptop, working at the office with a desktop, or checking in at home with your personal system. This is the major advantage to using IMAP.

Installation and configuration

IMAP installation and configuration is as easy as they come. Using `dselect` to install the `imap` package, the configuration script that is executed at the end makes all the needed changes. IMAP also uses the `inetd` service to watch the TCP/IP port. Here is the line the script adds to the `/etc/inetd.conf` file:

```
imap2  stream  tcp     nowait           root
/usr/sbin/tcpd  /usr/sbin/imapd
```

You can make changes to this script, but I don't advise it. The script automatically restarts the `inet` service; but if you need to restart the service for any reason, implement the following commands:

```
# /etc/init.d/inetd stop
# /etc/init.d/inetd start
```

With the software installed and running, the IMAP service is activated anytime a request comes into the IMAP port.

Testing IMAP

Once installed, you'll want to test the service to make sure that it works. This can be done through a terminal connection to the machine, either locally or remotely. Initiate the connection to the IMAP port with the following command line:

```
telnet localhost imap2
```

This starts a connection to port 143 through TCP/IP, which is the IMAP port on your Debian machine. Alternatively, you can connect remotely by replacing `localhost` with the name or IP of the remote machine hosting the IMAP service.

```
# telnet localhost imap2
Trying 127.0.0.1...
Connected to localhost.
Escape character is '^]'.
* OK localhost IMAP4rev1 v12.264 server ready
A001 login jo foobar14
A001 OK LOGIN completed
A002 logout
* BYE debian.domain.com IMAP4rev1 server terminating connection
A002 OK LOGOUT completed
Connection closed by foreign host.
```

In the previous example, you can see the response of the IMAP server. The bold text shows what I entered. The A001 login told the IMAP server that someone wanted to log in. It then took the next entry as the user ID, followed by the password. These must be valid accounts and passwords or the server will respond with a login request. Once the server validates the login, it will respond with a confirmation that the login is complete. You can then log out of the IMAP server.

Caution

Always keep the versions of all your servers up-to-date. Security holes are fixed quickly, but it won't matter if you keep running the old buggy versions of software. See Chapter 19 for more details about security.

Getting Help

When you install mail serviceson your system, in most cases it *should* work. Of course, with no two machines alike, the potential for problems always exists.

The following guidelines will help you troubleshoot any problems with mail:

✦ Make sure that you have an MX record in the DNS for each domain receiving mail. This entry should point to the machine that runs the mail server.

✦ Make sure that the /etc/mail/sendmail.cw file is properly configured if you are using sendmail. It contains all domains for which this server is responsible for receiving mail.

✦ The alias file (/etc/aliases or /etc/mail/aliases) should contain an entry for the postmaster, the mailer-daemon, or whatever name was set to receive error messages from the mail server. This name should be aliased to an administrator for the system. This will help to track down other problems.

A good source for help is always other users, peers, and administrators. You can find great advice and helpful hints through Web sites, newsgroups, and mailing lists. If you visit www.debian.org/MailLists, you'll find tons of mailing lists of knowledgeable people to help answer your questions.

You might also find useful information at one of the Web sites focused on the various applications. Here are a few sites that might provide answers to your questions:

✦ www.exim.org — Site for the exim mail server

✦ www.sendmail.org — Site for the Open Source version of Sendmail

✦ www.imap.org — Site for the IMAP mail client server

No matter what the problem, it's likely that someone else has battled with it. Be sure to thoroughly explain your problem when posting to a mailing list or newsgroup, or enlisting online support through a Web site.

Summary

This chapter has been fairly comprehensive in covering topics regarding electronic mail. You have learned about several mail-related programs, some used for transferring mail, and some used for retrieving mail. You've also learned about several mail-related concepts:

✦ MTA — A Mail Transfer Agent is a program that routes mail from system to system. These are the programs that actually deliver the mail to its destination.

✦ SMTP — Simple Mail Transfer Protocol is the language the MTA programs use to communicate in order to transfer the mail. These programs don't have to be the same program; they just need to be able to speak SMTP.

✦ MUA — A Mail User Agent is a program that retrieves the mail. These are client applications, and are covered in Chapter 6.

✦ POP — Post Office Protocol is the protocol that the MUA applications use to retrieve the mail. This protocol enables users to get their mail and remove it from the server. POP limits users to one machine from which to read their mail.

✦ IMAP — Internet Mail Access Protocol enables users to access their mail on the server. Users can also leave their mail on the server, thus enabling them to access their mail from different machines and locations. This protocol also can mark the mail as read, unread, or deleted. It also can access more than one folder on the server, enabling users to manage their mail.

Also covered in this chapter was the installation and configuration of two mail servers. The Debian packages include configuration scripts to help configure these packages for most situations. You also learned about some common e-mail topics, including forwarding mail, setting up aliases, and virtual hosting e-mail. These topics can help you with most SMTP programs that you choose to install. You also learned how to install two protocols that are used to retrieve mail from the server: POP and IMAP. In addition, you were also introduced to mailing list servers.

You should now have the basic knowledge needed to set up and run your own mail server. Happy mailing.

✦   ✦   ✦

What's On the CD-ROM

Appendix A provides you with information on the contents of the CD-ROM that accompanies this book.

There are 1,194 programs and supporting packages included on this CD. Among them are:

✦ Gnome Desktop Environment

✦ GIMP graphic design tool

✦ Apache Web Server

Although Debian GNU/Linux offers its distribution for many platforms, the media that accompanies this book is only for the i386-based PC platform.

Using the CD with Linux

To install Debian GNU/Linux from the CD to your hard drive, follow the steps listed in Chapter 2 of this book. These instructions will thoroughly take you through the installation process.

What's On the CD

The contents of this CD contain the core files for installing Debian GNU/Linux on your system. All software on this CD is free to use and free to copy under the GNU General Public License. The following summary shows some of the contents of the CD-ROM arranged by category.

Applications

The following applications are on the CD-ROM:

Graphical interfaces

A graphical interface provides a "point and click" environment where you can operate programs.

✦ **Gnome** — A graphical desktop environment offering many customizable features.

For more information: www.gnome.org

✦ **WindowMaker** — A window manager used to control the window environments for other programs to run in.

For more information: www.windowmaker.org

Development environments

Linux makes a stable environment for developing applications.

✦ **Perl** — A popular scripting language used on several platforms.

✦ **Tc/Tkl** — An interpretive language used mainly for graphical interfaces.

✦ **g++** — The equivalent to c++ for Linux using the C language.

Server Applications

Linux offers the stability, security, and control to become the platform for running various server functions.

✦ **Apache** — The most popular Web server offering addition modules for specific customization.

For more information: www.apache.org

✦ **Samba** — Allows Windows machines on a network to share files and resources from the Debian server.

For more information: www.samba.org

In addition to these programs, you will find a complement of other server applications like FTP, News, and Domain Name Services.

Source code

All source code for the programs are available through a mail in coupon found in the back of this book. Fill out the information on the coupon and mail it in. A CD with the source code will then get mail to you.

Troubleshooting

If you have difficulty installing or using the CD-ROM programs, try the following solutions:

✦ **Enable CD booting from the system BIOS** — Some systems set the boot device order. Make sure that the CD-ROM device is chosen before the hard drive C. If you have an older system, this may not be an option in which case you will need to follow the instructions in Chapter 2 on creating a boot disk. (Consult your systems manual on accessing the BIOS)

✦ **Make sure the Rescue disk is in the floppy drive** — When booting the system using the floppies, the first floppy to use for booting is the `rescue` disk. You will then get asked for the `root` floppy once the system gets initialized.

If you still have trouble with the CD, please call the Hungry Minds Customer Service phone number: (800) 762-2974. Outside the United States, call (317) 572-3993. Hungry Minds will provide technical support only for installation and other general quality control items; for technical support on the applications themselves, consult the program's vendor or author.

✦   ✦   ✦

Linux Commands

There are programs and commands that are scattered across the Debian filesystem. Appendix B attempts to cover many of the commands found in the common areas on the filesystem. This is not a comprehensive list since some of the commands are included in the text of this book.

If you need more information than a general description for any of these applications, then look at the manpage for the specific application. Any of these applications that are installed on your system will have the corresponding documentation associated with it. You can access the documentation at any time from a virtual terminal by typing:

```
man command
```

For example, if you want the information about ae, you would type:

```
man ae
```

Each command listed includes the command path along with the name of the command. For instance, /bin/ is the path and ae is the command. Following the command is a short description of the command.

Linux Commands

Below each command is the syntax for the command. The syntax may contain brackets [ ], which indicate that these are optional for the command to perform. Any three dots (...) indicate that more than one of those options can be used. The pipe (|) indicates that one or the other can be used.

bin commands

/bin/ae—Tiny full-screen text editor

```
ae [-f config_file ] [ file ]
```

/bin/arch—Prints machine architecture

```
arch
```

/bin/cat—Concatenate files and print on the standard output

```
cat [OPTION] [file]...
```

/bin/cp—Copy files and directories

```
cp [OPTION]... source dest
```

/bin/date—Print or set the system date and time

```
date [OPTION] [MMDDhhmm[[CC]YY][.ss]]
```

/bin/dd—Convert and copy a file. Often used when sending a file to floppy

```
dd [OPTION]...
```

/bin/df—Report on filesystem disk space usage

```
df [OPTION]... [file]...
```

/bin/dir—List directory contents.

```
dir [OPTION]... [file]...
```

/bin/dmesg—Print or control the kernel ring buffer

```
dmesg [ -c ] [ -n level ] [ -s bufsize ]
```

/bin/ed—Text editor

```
ed [-] [-Gs] [-p string] [file]
```

/bin/kill—Kill a process based on the process ID

```
kill option PID
```

/bin/ls—List directory content

```
ls [OPTION]... [file]...
```

`/bin/more` — File perusal filter for terminal viewing

   `more [OPTION] [file ...]`

`/bin/mount` — Mount a file system

   `mount [OPTION] device`

`/bin/mt` — Control magnetic tape drive operation

   `mt [-f device] operation [count]`

`/bin/ping` — Send ICMP ECHO_REQUEST packets to network hosts

   `ping [-c count] [-i wait] [-s packetsize] destination`

`/bin/ps` — Report process status

   `ps [OPTION]`

`/bin/rm` — Remove files and directories

   `rm [OPTION]... file...`

`/bin/sh` — GNU Bourne-Again Shell

   `bash [OPTIONS] [file]`

`/bin/su` — Becomes super user

   `su [OPTION] [-] [username [ARGS]]`

`/bin/tar` — The GNU version of the tar archiving utility

   `tar [OPTION] file... | directory ...`

`/bin/umount` — Unmount file systems

   `umount [OPTION] device`

sbin commands

`/sbin/activate` — Read/write flags marking active boot partition

   `activate device partition`

`/sbin/cfdisk` — Cursor-based disk partition table manipulator for Linux

   `cfdisk [ OPTION ] [ device ]`

`/sbin/fdisk`—Partition table manipulator for Linux

> `fdisk [-u] [-b sectorsize] device`

`sfdisk`—Partition table manipulator for Linux

> `sfdisk [OPTION] device`

`/sbin/fsck`—A file system consistency checker for Linux

> `fsck [OPTION] [-t fstype] [--] [fsck-options] filesys [...]`

`/sbin/getty`—Alternative Linux getty

> `getty [OPTION] port baud_rate,... [term]`

`/sbin/hwclock`—Query and set the hardware clock (RTC)

> `hwclock OPTION`

`/sbin/init`—Process control initialization

> `init [ -a ] [ -s ] [ -b ] [ -z xxx ] [ 0123456Ss ]`

`/sbin/kbdrate`—Reset the keyboard repeat rate and delay time

> `kbdrate [ -s ] [ -r rate ] [ -d delay ]`

`/sbin/losetup`—Set up and control loop devices

> `losetup [ -d ] loop_device`

`/sbin/mkfs`—Build a Linux file system

> `mkfs [ -V ] [ -t fstype ] [ fs-options ] filesys [ blocks]`

`/sbin/mkswap`—Set up a Linux swap area

> `mkswap [-c] [-vN] [-f] [-p PSZ] device [size]`

`/sbin/sfdisk`—Partition table manipulator for Linux

> `sfdisk [options] device`

`/sbin/swapoff`—Enable/disable devices and files for paging and swapping

> `swapoff OPTION`

/sbin/swapon—**Enable/disable devices and files for paging and swapping**

    swapon *OPTION*

/sbin/update—**Periodically flush filesystem buffers**

    update [*OPTION*]

usr commands

/usr/bin/822-date—**Print date and time in RFC822 format**

    822-date

/usr/bin/Mail—**Send and receive mail**

    mail [-iInv] [-s *subject*] [-c *cc-addr*] [-b *bcc-addr*] *to-addr*...

/usr/bin/MakeTeXPK—**Create a PK file for a font**

    mktexpk [*OPTION*] *font* [*redirect*]

/usr/bin/a2p—**Awk to Perl translator**

    a2p [*OPTION*] *filename*

/usr/bin/access—**Determine whether a file can be accessed**

    access *-mode file*

/usr/bin/addftinfo—**Add information to troff font files for use with groff**

    addftinfo [*-param value...*] *res unitwidth font*

/usr/bin/ar—**Create, modify, and extract from archives**

    ar [-]{dmpqrtx}[*OPTION*] [*membername*] [*count*] *archive files*..

/usr/bin/as—**The portable GNU assembler**

    As [*OPTIONS*]

/usr/bin/at—**Queue, examine or delete jobs for later execution**

    at [-V] [-q *queue*] [-f *file*] [-mldbv] *TIME*

/usr/bin/awk—**Pattern scanning and text processing language**

    awk [-W option] [-F value] [-v var=value] [--] 'program text'
    [file ...]

`/usr/bin/bc`—An arbitrary precision calculator language

   `bc [ -lwsqv ] [`*`long-options`*`] [  `*`file`*` ... ]`

`/usr/bin/cal`—Displays a calendar

   `cal [-jy] [[`*`month`*`] `*`year`*`]`

`/usr/bin/cc`—GNU project C and C++ Compiler

   `cc [ `*`OPTION`*` | `*`filename`*` ]...`

`/usr/bin/chkdupexe`—Find duplicate executables

   `chkdupexe`

`/usr/bin/ci`—Check in RCS revision

   `ci [`*`OPTIONS`*`] `*`file`*` ...`

`/usr/bin/cmp`—Compare two files or byte ranges

   `cmp [ `*`OPTIONS`*` ] -I `*`file`*` ...`

`/usr/bin/co`—Check out RCS revision

   `co [`*`OPTIONS`*`] `*`file`*` ...`

`/usr/bin/col`—Filter reverse line feeds from input

   `col [-bfx] [-l `*`num`*`]`

`/usr/bin/comm`—Compare two sorted files line by line

   `comm [`*`OPTION`*`]... `*`LEFT_FILE RIGHT_FILE`*

`/usr/bin/cut`—Remove sections from each line of files

   `cut [`*`OPTION`*`]... [`*`file`*`]...`

`/usr/bin/dc`—An arbitrary precision calculator

   `dc [-V][-h][-e `*`scriptexpression`*`] [-f `*`scriptfile`*`] [`*`file`*` ...]`

`/usr/bin/ddate`—Converts Gregorian dates to Discordian dates

   `ddate [+`*`format`*`] [`*`date`*`]`

/usr/bin/dig—**Send domain name query packets to name servers**

   dig [@*server*] *domain* [*OPTIONS*] [*%comment*]

/usr/bin/du—**Estimate file space usage**

   du [*OPTION*]... [*file*]...

/usr/bin/edit—**Alias to execute edit function via entries in the mailcap file**

   edit <--opt=val> [...] [<mime-type>:[<encoding>:]]<file> [...]

/usr/bin/editor—**Text editors**

   editor [-eFRrSsv] [-c *cmd*] [-t *tag*] [-w *size*] [*file* ...]

/usr/bin/etex—**Extended TeX**

   etex [*OPTIONS*] [*commands*]

/usr/bin/ex—**Text editors**

   ex [-eFRrSsv] [-c *cmd*] [-t *tag*] [-w *size*] [*file* ...]

/usr/bin/file—**Determine file type**

   file [-bcnsvzL] [-f *namefile*] [-m *magicfiles*] *file*

/usr/bin/find—**Search for files in a directory hierarchy**

   find [*path*...] [*expression*]

/usr/bin/fmt—**Simple optimal text formatter**

   fmt [-*DIGITS*] [*OPTION*]... [*file*]...

/usr/bin/free—**Display amount of free and used memory in the system**

   free [-b | -k | -m] [-o] [-s *delay*] [-t] [-V]

/usr/bin/from—**Print names of those who have sent mail**

   from [-s *sender*] [-f *file*] [*user*]

/usr/bin/getopt—**Parse command options (enhanced)**

   getopt [*OPTIONS*] [--] *optstring parameter*

`/usr/bin/gettext` — GNU gettext utilities

   `gettext [OPTION] [[[TEXTDOMAIN] MSGID] | [-s [MSGID]...]]`

`/usr/bin/groff` — Front end for the groff document formatting system

   `groff [ OPTIONS][ files... ]`

`/usr/bin/host` — Query nameserver about domain names and zones

   `host [-v] [-a] [-t querytype] [OPTIONS]  name | zone [server]`

`/usr/bin/icat` — "cat" a mailbox from an IMAP source

   `icat [ OPTIONS ] mailbox`

`/usr/bin/id` — Print real and effective UIDs and GIDs

   `id [OPTION]... [USERNAME]`

`/usr/bin/info` — Read Info documents

   `info [OPTION]... [MENU-ITEM...]`

`/usr/bin/ipcrm` — Provide information on ipc facilities

   `ipcrm [ shm | msg | sem ] ID...`

`/usr/bin/ipcs` — Provide information on ipc facilities

   `ipcs [ -asmq ] [ -tclup ]`

`/usr/bin/ld` — The GNU linker

   `ld [-o output] objfile...`

`/usr/bin/locate` — List files in databases that match a pattern

   `locate  [-d path][-e ][--version] [--help] pattern...`

`/usr/bin/logger` — Make entries in the system log

   `logger [-is][-f file][-p pri][-t tag][-u socket][message ...]`

`/usr/bin/mag` — Computes fontsizes and magsteps

   `mag [-Rdpi] magstep . . . |  fontsize . . .`

`/usr/bin/mail` — Send and receive mail

    `mail [-iInv] [-s `*`subject`*`] [-c `*`cc-addr`*`] [-b `*`bcc-addr`*`] `*`to-addr`*`...`

`/usr/bin/mailx` — Send and receive mail

    `mail [-iInv] [-s `*`subject`*`] [-c `*`cc-addr`*`] [-b `*`bcc-addr`*`] `*`to-addr`*`...`

`/usr/bin/make` — GNU make utility to maintain groups of programs

    `make [ -f `*`makefile`*` ] [ `*`option`*` ] ...  `*`target`*` ...`

`/usr/bin/man` — An interface to the on-line reference manuals

    `man  -l [-7] [-tZT  `*`device`*`] [-p  `*`string`*`] [-P `*`pager`*`] [-r `*`prompt`*`]`
    `file` `...`

`/usr/bin/mcookie` — Generate magic cookies for xauth

    `mcookie [-v] [-f `*`filename`*` ]`

`/usr/bin/mesg` — Control write access to your terminal

    `mesg [y|n]`

`/usr/bin/namei` — Follow a pathname until a terminal point is found

    `namei [-mx] `*`pathname`*` [ `*`pathname`*` ... ]`

`/usr/bin/nice` — Run a program with modified scheduling priority

    `nice [`*`OPTION`*`]... [`*`COMMAND`*` [`*`ARG`*`]...]`

`/usr/bin/nl` — Number lines of files

    `nl [`*`OPTION`*`]... [`*`file`*`]...`

`/usr/bin/nm` — List symbols from object files

    `nm [`*`OPTIONS`*`]`

`/usr/bin/ns` — Query nameserver about domain names and zones

    `ns [-v] [-a] [-t `*`querytype`*`] [`*`options`*`]  `*`name`*`  [`*`server`*`]`

`/usr/bin/od` — Dump files in octal and other formats

    `od [`*`OPTION`*`]... [`*`file`*`]...`

/usr/bin/poff—Shuts down the log of PPP connections

```
poff [ -r ] [ -d ] [ -c ] [ -a ] [ -h ] isp-name
```

/usr/bin/pon—Starts up the log of PPP connections

```
pon [ isp-name ]
```

/usr/bin/pr—Convert text files for printing

```
pr [OPTION]... [file]...
```

/usr/bin/print—Alias to execute print function via entries in the mailcap file

```
print <--opt=val> [...] [<mime-type>:[<encoding>:]]<file> [...]
```

/usr/bin/refer—Preprocess bibliographic references for groff

```
refer [ OPTIONS ][ filename... ]
```

/usr/bin/renice—Alter priority of running processes

```
renice priority [[-p] pid ...] [[-g] pgrp ...] [[-u] user ...]
```

/usr/bin/reset—Terminal initialization

```
reset [-IQqrs][-][-e ch][-i ch][-k ch][-m  mapping][terminal]
```

/usr/bin/rev—Reverse lines of a file

```
rev [file]
```

/usr/bin/script—Make typescript of terminal session

```
script [-a] [file]
```

/usr/bin/see—Alias to execute the see function via entries in the mailcap file

```
see <--opt=val> [...] [<mime-type>:[<encoding>:]]<file> [...]
```

/usr/bin/setsid—Run a program in a new session

```
setsid program [ arg ... ]
```

/usr/bin/setterm—Set terminal attributes

```
setterm [OPTIONS]
```

/usr/bin/sg—Execute command as different group ID

  sg [-] [*group* [[-c] *command*]]

/usr/bin/size—List section sizes and total size

  size [*OPTIONS*] *objfile*...

/usr/bin/sort—Sort lines of text files

  sort [*OPTION*]... [*file*]...

/usr/bin/split—Split a file into pieces

  split [*OPTION*] [*INPUT* [*PREFIX*]]

/usr/bin/sum—Checksum and count the blocks in a file

  sum [*OPTION*]... [*file*]...

/usr/bin/tac—Concatenate and print files in reverse

  tac [*OPTION*]... [*file*]...

/usr/bin/tack—Terminfo action checker

  tack [-itV] [*term*]

/usr/bin/test—Check file types and compare values

  test *EXPRESSION*

/usr/bin/tic—The terminfo entry-description compiler

  tic [-1CINRTcfrsx] [-e *names*] [-o *dir*] [-v[*n*]] [-w[*n*]] *file*

/usr/bin/tie—Merge or apply WEB change files

  tie -c|-m *outputfile masterfile changefile* ...

/usr/bin/time—Run programs and summarize system resource usage

  time   [*OPTIONS*] *COMMAND* [*ARGS*]

/usr/bin/top—Display top CPU processes

  top [-] [d delay] [p pid] [q] [c] [S] [s] [i] [n iter] [b]

`/usr/bin/tput`—Initialize a terminal or query terminfo database

```
tput [-Ttype] OPTION [parms ... ]
```

`/usr/bin/tr`—Translate or delete characters

```
tr [OPTION]... SET1 [SET2]
```

`/usr/bin/troff`—Format documents

```
troff [ OPTIONS ] files...
```

`/usr/bin/tty`—Print the file name of the terminal connected to standard input

```
tty [OPTION]...
```

`/usr/bin/ul`—Do underlining

```
ul [-i] [-t terminal] [name ...]
```

`/usr/bin/users`—Print the user names of users currently logged into the current host

```
users [OPTION]... [ file ]
```

`/usr/bin/vi`—Screen text editor

```
vi [-eFlRrSv] [-c cmd] [-t tag] [-w size] [file ...]
```

`/usr/bin/view`—Screen text editor

```
view [-eFRrSv] [-c cmd] [-t tag] [-w size] [file ...]
```

`/usr/bin/w`—Show who is logged on and what they are doing

```
w - [husfV] [user]
```

`/usr/bin/wall`—Write a message to users

```
wall [file]
```

`/usr/bin/watch`—Execute a program periodically, showing output fullscreen

```
watch [-dhv] [-n <seconds>] [--interval=<seconds>] <command>
```

`/usr/bin/wc`—Print the number of bytes, words, and lines in files

```
wc [OPTION]... [file]...
```

/usr/bin/whereis—Locate the binary, source, and manual page files for a command

    whereis [-bmsu] [-BMS *directory*... -f] *filename* ...

/usr/bin/write—Send a message to another user

    write *user* [*ttyname*]

/usr/bin/zone—Query nameserver about domain names and zones

    host [-v] [-a] [-t *querytype*] [*options*] -l *zone* [*server*]

/usr/sbin/accessdb—Dumps the content of a man-db database in a human readable format.

    accessdb [*<index-file>*]

/usr/sbin/addgroup—Add a user or group to the system

    addgroup [*options*] [--gid *ID*] *group*

/usr/sbin/adduser—Add a user or group to the system

    adduser [*options*][--home *DIR*][--no-create-home][--uid *ID*][--gid *ID*] *user*

/usr/sbin/arp—Manipulate the system ARP cache

    arp [-vn] [-H type] [-i if] -a [hostname]

/usr/sbin/cytune—Tune Cyclades driver parameters

    cytune [-q [-i *interval*]] [-s *value*] [-g] [-t *timeout*] *tty* ...

/usr/sbin/pac—Printer/plotter accounting information

    pac [-P*printer*] [-c] [-m] [-p*price*] [-s] [-r] [*name* ...]

/usr/sbin/readprofile—A tool to read kernel profiling information

    readprofile [*options*]

/usr/sbin/tunelp—Set various parameters for the lp device

    tunelp *<device>* [*OPTION*]

✦   ✦   ✦

Debian Packages

Appendix C presents a list of commonly used Debian packages with a short description of each package. Not all packages are included since there are over 4,000 packages available. Categories or package areas covered include: Administrative Utilities, Base Utilities, Communication Programs, Editors, Graphics, Mail, Miscellaneous, Network, Newsgroups, Other OS's and file systems, Shells, Sound, Utilities, and Web Software.

You can find a complete list of packages for each of the categories at `packages.debian.org/stable`.

Administration utilities

Table C-1 shows common utilities for managing system resources, user accounts, and other system administration tasks and functions.

Table C-1 Administration utilities	
Package	**Description**
acct 6.3.5-17	The GNU Accounting utilities
adjtimex 1.10-1	Utility to display or set the kernel time variables
alien 6.54	Install Red Hat, Stampede, and Slackware Packages with `dpkg`
anacron 2.1-5.1	A cron-like program that doesn't go by time
apcd 0.6a.nr-7	APC Smart UPS daemon
apmd 3.0final-1	Utilities for Advanced Power Management (APM) on laptops

Continued

Table C-1 (continued)

Package	Description
apt-move 3.0-13	Move cache of Debian packages into a mirror hierarchy
apt-zip 0.9	Update a non-networked computer using apt and removable media
aptitude 0.0.4a-4.1	Console based apt front-end
arpwatch 2.1a4-3	Ethernet/FDDI station activity monitor
at 3.1.8-10	Delayed job execution and batch processing
autolog 0.35-3	Terminates connections for idle users
base-config 0.32	Debian base configuration package
boot-floppies 2.2.16	Scripts to create the Debian installation floppy set
bpowerd 2.2-1	Monitor UPS status for Best Patriot power supplies
calife 2.8.4-2	A lightweight alternative to Sudo
cfengine 1.5.3-4	Tool for configuring and maintaining network machines
chos 0.84-7	Easy Boot loader with a Boot-Menu
chrony 1.10-3	It sets your computer's clock from time servers on the Net
cron 3.0pl1-57	Management of regular background processing
cruft 0.9.6-0.1	Find any cruft built up on your system
debconf 0.2.80.16	Debian configuration management system
debconf-tiny 0.2.80.16	Tiny subset of debconf for the base system
debian-cd 2.2.2 [contrib]	Tools for building (Official) Debian CD set
debsums 1.2.6	Tools to handle md5sums for installed packages
defrag 0.73-1	`ext2`, `minix`, and `xiafs` file system defragmenter
dftp 4.8-3	Alternative Debian package manager
dialdcost 0.2-1	Cost estimation and X Control panel for DIALD
divine 0.7-2	Automatic IP configuration detection for laptops
dpkg-repack 1.2	Puts an unpacked `.deb` file back together
dqs 3.2.7-3 [non-free]	A Distributed Queuing System
eql 1.2-1	Load balancing tool for serial network connections
equivs 1.999.12	Circumventing Debian package dependencies
ext2resize 1.0.6-1	An `ext2` filesystem resizer
extipl 4.22-4	Yet another boot selector for IBM-PC compatibles
extipl-boot 4.22-4	ExtIPL, an enhanced boot code (IPL) for IBM-PC
fbgetty 0.1.4-1	A console getty with and without framebuffer capability

Package	Description
fbset 2.1-6	Framebuffer device maintenance program
file-rc 0.5.5	Alternative one-config file boot mechanism
genpower 1.0.1-11	Monitor UPS and handle line power failures
genromfs 0.3-5	This is the mkfs equivalent for the romfs filesystem
gnome-admin 1.0.3-2	Gnome Admin Utilities (`gulp` and `logview`)
gnome-apt 0.3.9	Gnome front-end to apt
gnome-print 0.10-5	The Gnome Print architecture
gnosamba 0.3.3-2	A graphical configuration utility for Samba
gpart 0.1f-1	Guess PC disk partition table, find lost partitions
gps 0.4.1-2	Graphical PS using GTK
gtop 1.0.5-1	Graphical TOP variant
hdparm 3.6-1	Tune hard disk parameters for high performance.
i18ndata 2.1.3-10	GNU C Library: National Language (locale) data [source]
idled 1.16-8.1 [non-free]	Idle Daemon. Removes idle users
ja-trans 0.7-3.1	Japanese gettext message files
jmon 0.3-2	Distributed resource monitor
lavaps 1.9-1	A lava lamp of currently running processes
lexmark7000linux 0.1999-03-28-1	A printer driver for Lexmark 7000 "GDI" printers
libgtop-daemon 1.0.6-1	`gtop` daemon for monitoring remote machines (part of Gnome)
libpam-ldap 43-2	Pluggable Authentication Module allowing LDAP interfaces
libpam-pwdfile 0.1-1	PAM module allowing /etc/passwd-like authentication
libpam-smb 1.1.5-2	Pluggable Authentication Module allowing Samba interface
librpm1 3.0.3-1	RPM shared library
librpm1-dev 3.0.3-1	RPM shared library, development kit
libsnmp4.1 4.1.1-2	UCD SNMP (Simple Network Management Protocol) Library.
linuxconf 1.17r5-2	A powerful Linux administration kit
linuxconf-i18n 1.17r5-2	International language files for Linuxconf
linuxconf-x 1.17r5-2	X11 GUI for Linuxconf
loadlin 1.6a-4	A loader (running under DOS) for LINUX kernel images
locale-ja 14	Locale definition files for Japanese

Continued

Table C-1 *(continued)*

Package	Description
locale-ko 4-3	Locale definition files for Korean
locale-vi 1-3	Locale definition files for Vietnamese
locale-zh 0.9+0.05-2	Locale definition files for Chinese zh_CN.GB2312 and zh_CN.GBK
locales 2.1.3-10	GNU C Library: National Language (locale) data [binary]
logcheck 1.1.1-4	Mails anomalies in the system logfiles to the administrator
logrotate 3.2-11	Log rotation utility
lshell 2.01-9	Enforce limits to protect system integrity
lvm 0.8i-1	The Logical Volume Manager for Linux
m68k-vme-tftplilo 1.1.2-1	Linux kernel TFTP boot loader for m68k VME processor boards
makepasswd 1.10-1	Generate and encrypt passwords
mdutils 0.35-27	Multiple Device driver utilities
members 19990831-2	Shows the members of a group; by default, all members
memstat 0.2	Identify what's using up virtual memory
menu 2.1.5-3	Provides update-menus functions for some applications
mingetty 0.9.4-7	Console-only getty
mkrboot 0.9	Make a kernel + root image bootable from one disk or from DOS
mon 0.38.15-1	Monitor hosts/services/whatever and alert about problems
moodss 9.0-2	Modular object-oriented dynamic spread-sheet
mtx 1.0-10	Controls tape autochangers
ncurses-term 5.0-6	Additional terminal type definitions
netenv 0.82-10	Configure your system for different network environments
nscd 2.1.3-10	GNU C Library: Name Service Cache Daemon
opie-client 2.32-1.1	OPIE programs for generating OTPs on client machines
pciutils 1:2.1.2-2	Linux PCI Utilities (for 2.[123].x kernels)
pcmcia-source 3.1.8-16	PCMCIA Card Services source
powstatd 1.4.1-4	Configurable UPS monitoring daemon
printop 1.12-4	Graphical interface to the LPRng print system
psmisc 19-2	Utilities that use the proc filesystem
pwgen 1-15	Automatic Password generation
quota 1.65-4	An implementation of the diskquota system
radiusclient1 0.3.1-7	`/bin/login` replacement which uses the RADIUS protocol for authentication

Package	Description
raidtools 0.42-21	Utilities to support "old-style" RAID disks
raidtools2 0.90.990824-5	Utilities to support "new-style" RAID disks
rpm 3.0.3-1	Red Hat Package Manager
sac 1.8b8-1	Login accounting
satan 1.1.1-18 [non-free]	Security Auditing Tool for Analysing Networks
shapetools 1.4pl6-4	Configuration and release management using AtFS
slay 1.2-6	Kills all of the user's processes
stow 1.3.2-11	Organiser for `/usr/local/` hierarchy
sudo 1.6.2p2-1	Provides limited super user privileges to specific users
suidmanager 0.43.2	Manage file permissions
super 3.12.2-2	Execute commands setuid root
svgatextmode 1.9-3	Run higher-resolution text modes
syslog-ng 1.4.0rc3-2	Next generation logging daemon
syslog-summary 1.8	Summarize the contents of a syslog log file
sysnews 0.9-4	Display system news
systune 0.5.3	Kernel tuning through the `/proc` filesystem
tcpquota 1.6.15-7.1	A dialout/masquerading monitoring package
timeoutd 1.5-2	Flexible user time-out daemon
tmpreaper 1.4.11	Cleans up files in directories based on their age
tripwire 1.2-16.1 [non-free]	A file and directory integrity checker
ttysnoop 0.12c-7	TTY Snoop — allows you to spy on telnet + serial connections
upsd 1.0-9	UPS Monitor Program
userlink-source 1:0.99a-1	BSD IP Tunneling Driver for Linux (source package)
userv 1.0.1.1potato	User Services — program call across trust boundaries
uutraf 1.1-7	An UUCP traffic analyzer and cost estimator
vrms 1.6	Virtual Richard M. Stallman
watchdog 5.1-0.3	A software watchdog
whowatch 1.3-1	Real-time user logins monitoring tool
xezmlm 1.0.3-6 [contrib]	A `ezmlm mailinglist` configuration tool for the X Window System
xlogmaster 1.6.0-5	A program to monitor logfiles
zh-trans 0.8.1-2	Chinese (zh_CN and zh_TW) message files and manpages

Base utilities

Base utilities, shown in Table C-2, includes the basic utilities needed of every Debian system. (You needn't install these utilities. Most are installed as parts of the base systms.)

Table C-2 Base utilities	
Package	**Description**
adduser 3.11.1	Add users and groups to the system
ae 962-26	Anthony's Editor — a tiny full-screen editor
apt 0.3.19	Advanced front-end for dpkg
base-files 2.2.0	Debian base system miscellaneous files
base-passwd 3.1.7	Debian Base System Password/Group Files
bash 2.03-6	The GNU Bourne Again SHell
bsdutils 1:2.10f-5.1	Basic utilities from 4.4BSD-Lite
console-tools 1:0.2.3-10.3	Linux console and font utilities
console-tools-libs 1:0.2.3-10.3	Shared libraries for Linux console and font manipulation
debianutils 1.13.3	Miscellaneous utilities specific to Debian
diff 2.7-21	File comparison utilities
dpkg 1.6.14	Package maintenance system for Debian
dpkg-ftp 1.6.7	Ftp method for `dselect`
dpkg-mountable 0.8	Enhanced access method for `dselect`
dpkg-multicd 0.16.1	Installation methods for multiple binary CDs
e2fsprogs 1.18-3	The EXT2 file system utilities and libraries
elvis-tiny 1.4-9	Tiny `vi` compatible editor for the base system
fdflush 1.0.1-5	A disk-flushing program
fileutils 4.0l-8	GNU file management utilities.
findutils 4.1-40	Utilities for finding files — `find`, `xargs`, and `locate`
gettext-base 0.10.35-13	GNU Internationalization utilities for the base system
grep 2.4.2-1	GNU `grep`, `egrep` and `fgrep`
grub 0.5.93.1	Grand Unified Bootloader

Package	Description
gzip 1.2.4-33	The GNU compression utility
hostname 2.07	A utility to set/show the host name or domain name
isapnptools 1.21-2	ISA Plug-And-Play configuration utilities
kernel-headers-2.0.38 2.0.38-3	Header files related to Linux kernel version 2.0.38
kernel-image-2.0.38 2.0.38-3	Linux kernel binary image for version 2.0.38
kernel-image-2.2.17 2.2.17pre6-1	Linux kernel binary image for version 2.2.17
kernel-image-2.2.17-compact 2.2.17pre6-1	Linux kernel binary image
kernel-image-2.2.17-ide 2.2.17pre6-1	Linux kernel binary image for version 2.2.17
kernel-image-2.2.17-idepci 2.2.17pre6-1	Linux kernel binary image
ldso 1.9.11-9	The Linux dynamic linker, library and utilities
libc6 2.1.3-10	GNU C Library: Shared libraries and time-zone data
libgdbmg1 1.7.3-26.2	GNU dbm database routines (runtime version) [libc6 version]
libncurses5 5.0-6	Shared libraries for terminal handling
libnet-perl 1.0703-3	Implementation of Internet protocols for Perl
libnewt0 0.50-7	Not Erik's Windowing Toolkit — text mode windowing with slang
libpam-modules 0.72-9	Pluggable Authentication Modules for PAM
libpam-runtime 0.72-9	Runtime support for the PAM library
libpam0g 0.72-9	Pluggable Authentication Modules library
libreadline4 4.1-1	GNU readline and history libraries, runtime libraries
libstdc++2.10 1:2.95.2-13	The GNU `stdc++` library
libwrap0 7.6-4	Wietse Venema's TCP wrappers library
lilo 1:21.4.3-2	LInux LOader — The Classic OS loader can load Linux and others
login 19990827-20	System login tools
makedev 2.3.1-44	Creates special device files in `/dev`
mawk 1.3.3-5	A pattern scanning and text processing language

Continued

Table C-2 *(continued)*

Package	Description
mbr 1.1.2-1	Master Boot Record for IBM-PC compatible computers
modconf 0.2.26.14	Device driver configuration
modutils 2.3.11-8	Linux module utilities
mount 2.10f-5.1	Tools for mounting and manipulating filesystems
ncurses-base 5.0-6	Descriptions of common terminal types
ncurses-bin 5.0-6	Terminal-related programs and man pages
netbase 3.18-4	Basic TCP/IP networking binaries
passwd 19990827-20	Change and administer password and group data
pcmcia-cs 3.1.8-16	PCMCIA Card Services for Linux.
pcmcia-modules-2.2.17 3.1.8-14+ 2.2.17pre6+1	PCMCIA Modules for Linux (kernel 2.2.17)
pcmcia-modules-2.2.17-compact 3.1.8-14+ 2.2.17pre6+1	PCMCIA Modules for Linux (kernel 2.2.17-compact)
pcmcia-modules-2.2.17-ide 3.1.8-14+ 2.2.17pre6+1	PCMCIA Modules for Linux (kernel 2.2.17-ide)
pcmcia-modules-2.2.17-idepci 3.1.8-14+2.2.17pre6+1	PCMCIA Modules for Linux (kernel 2.2.17-idepci)
perl-5.004-base 5.004.05-6	The Pathologically Eclectic Rubbish Lister
perl-5.005-base 5.005.03-7.1	The Pathologically Eclectic Rubbish Lister
perl-base 5.004.05-1.1	Fake package assuring that one of the -base packages is installed
ppp 2.3.11-1.4	Point-to-Point Protocol (PPP) daemon
pppconfig 2.0.5	A text menu based utility for configuring ppp
procps 1:2.0.6-5	The /proc filesystem utilities
sed 3.02-5	The GNU sed stream editor
setserial 2.17-16	Controls configuration of serial ports
shellutils 2.0-7	The GNU shell programming utilities
slang1 1.3.9-1	The S-Lang programming library — runtime version

Package	Description
sysklogd 1.3-33	Kernel and system logging daemons
syslinux 1.48-2	Bootloader for Linux/i386 using MS-DOS floppies
sysvinit 2.78-4	System-V like `init`
tar 1.13.17-2	GNU `tar`
tasksel 1.0-10	New task packages selector
tcpd 7.6-4	Wietse Venema's TCP wrapper utilities
textutils 2.0-2	The GNU text file–processing utilities
update 2.11-1	Daemon to periodically flush filesystem buffers
util-linux 2.10f-5.1	Miscellaneous system utilities
whiptail 0.50-7	Displays user-friendly dialog boxes from shell scripts

Communication programs

Software shown in Table C-3 is used with your modem in the traditional sense.

Table C-3 Communication programs	
Package	Description
adbbs 3.0-1.1	ad! BBS. A perl-based bbs or easy menu system
casio 2.2-5	Backup utility for the CASIO diary
efax 1:0.9-4	Programs to send and receive fax messages
gettyps 2.0.7j-8 [non-free]	Replacement for getty
hylafax-client 4.0.2-14	HylaFAX client software
hylafax-server 4.0.2-14	HylaFAX server software
ifcico 2.14tx8.10-11	Fidonet Technology transport package
ifgate 2.14tx8.10-11	Internet to Fidonet gateway
lrzsz 0.12.21-3	Tools for `zmodem` and `ymodem` file transfer
mgetty 1.1.21-2.1	Smart Modem `getty` replacement
mgetty-docs 1.1.21-2.1	Documentation Package for `mgetty`
mgetty-fax 1.1.21-2.1	Faxing tools for `mgetty`

Continued

Table C-3 *(continued)*	
Package	**Description**
mgetty-viewfax 1.1.21-2.1	Program for displaying Group-3 Fax files under X
mgetty-voice 1.1.21-2.1	Voice mail handler for mgetty
minicom 1.82.1-1	Clone of the MS-DOS "Telix" communications program
mserver 0.21-3	Network Modem Server
seyon 2.20c-1	Full-featured native X11 communications program
smsclient 2.0.8r-7	A program for sending short messages (SM / SMS)
speaker 1.0.1-3	Tcl/Tk speaker-phone application
tkhylafax 3.2-1	/Tk interface to hylafax
uqwk 1.8-4	Offline mail and news reader
uucp 1.06.1-11	UNIX to UNIX Copy Program
wvdial 1.41	PPP dialer with built-in intelligence
xringd 1.20-2	Extended Ring Daemon — Monitors phone rings and takes action
xtel 3.2.1-4	An X emulator of the french Minitel

Editors

Table C-4 lists software to edit files. Editors can be used to manipulate the text in a file or act as programming environments.

Table C-4 **Editors**	
Package	**Description**
abiword 0.7.7-1	WYSIWYG word processor based on GTK
ada-mode 3.4a-7	Ada mode for Emacs and XEmacs
addressbook 0.7-13	Tk personal address manager
apel 10.2+20000308cvs-4	A Portable Emacs Library
august 0.50-2	Tcl/Tk HTML editor
axe 6.1.2-6.4 [non-free]	An editor for X
beav 1:1.40-13	Binary editor And viewer

Package	Description
bitmap-mule 8.1-2	Package to use bitmaps in `MULE` or `Emacs/mule`
bvi 1.2.0-1.1	A binary file editor
cooledit 3.11.6-5	A portable, fast X Window text editor with beautiful 3D widgets
crypt++el 2.87-2	Emacs-Lisp Code for handling compressed and encrypted files
custom 1.9962-2	Tools for declaring and initializing options
custom-mule 1.9962-3	Tools for declaring and initializing options for Mule2
debview 1.7-4	Emacs mode for viewing Debian packages
dedit 0.5.9	Editor Tool with Japanese extension for beginners
ed 0.2-18	The classic UNIX line editor
ee 126.1.89-11	An "easy editor" for novices and compuphobics
elib 1.0-10	Library of commonly-used Emacs functions
elvis 2.1.4-1	A much improved `vi` editor with syntax highlighting
emacs-czech 3.8-7	Czech and Slovak support for Emacs
emacs-dl-canna 1.2+19991112cvs-7	Canna DL module for emacs20-dl
emacs-dl-wnn 0.4.1-9	Wnn DL module for emacs20-dl
emacs19 19.34-26.5	The GNU Emacs editor
emacs19-el 19.34-26.5	GNU Emacs LISP (`.el`) files
emacs20 20.7-2	The GNU Emacs editor
emacs20-dl 20.7-4	The GNU Emacs editor (dynamic Loading supported)
emacs20-dl-el 20.7-4	GNU Emacs LISP (`.el`) files (for emacs20-dl)
emacs20-el 20.7-2	GNU Emacs LISP (`.el`) files
emacsen-common 1.4.12	Common facilities for all `emacsen`
emacspeak 11.0-3	Speech output interface to Emacs
emacspeak-ss 1.5-2	Emacspeak speech server for several synthesizers
exuberant-ctags 1:3.2.4-0	Reincarnation of the classic ctags(1): facilitates source navigation
fonter 1.7-5	Interactive font editor for the console
fte 0.49.13-10	Text editor for X-Window with I18N support (for programmers)

Continued

Table C-4 *(continued)*

Package	Description
fte-console 0.49.13-10	Text editor for console (no I18N support) (for programmers)
fte-docs 0.49.13-10	HTML documentation and example of configuration
fte-terminal 0.49.13-10	Text editor for terminals (for programmers)
fte-xwindow 0.49.13-10	Text editor for X Window with I18N support (for programmers)
gaby 1.9.15-0.2	Small Gnome personal databases manager
gedit 0.5.4-1	Small, lightweight gnome-based editor for X11
gnotepad+ 1.2.1-1	GTK-based Notepad editor
gnotepad+-help 1.0-1	This is the help documentation for Gnotepad+
gnuserv 2.1alpha-5	Client/server addon for the emacs editor
gxedit 1.23-4	A graphical text editor using GTK
hexedit 1.1.0-2	View and edit files in hexadecimal or in ASCII
jed 0.99.9-14	Editor for programmers (textmode version)
jed-canna 0.98.7.j055-2	jed with canna support (textmode version)
jed-common 0.99.9-14	Byte compiled Slang runtime files for jed and s
jed-common-ja 0.98.7.j055-2	Byte compiled Slang runtime files for jed and xjed (Japanese)
jed-ja 0.98.7.j055-2	Editor for programmers for Japanese (textmode version)
jed-sl 0.99.9-14	Sources of Slang runtime files for jed and xjed
jed-sl-ja 0.98.7.j055-2	Sources of Slang runtime files for jed and xjed (Japanese)
jered 1.6.7-1	Simple full-screen text editor with colored C/C++ syntax
joe 2.8-15	Joe's Own Editor — A Free ASCII-Text Screen Editor for UN*X
jove 4.16-5	This is Jonathan's Own Version of Emacs (jove), a small and powerful editor
jvim-canna 3.0-2.0-2	Japanized VIM (canna version)
le 1.5.5-2	Text editor with block and binary operations
levee 0.6-1.1	A very small vi clone
mule-ucs 0.63-2	Character code translator system on Emacs
mule2-bin 2.3+19.34-7potato6	MULtilingual Enhancement to GNU Emacs — support binaries
mule2-canna 2.3+19.34-7potato6	MULtilingual Enhancement to GNU Emacs (Canna supported)

Package	Description
mule2-canna-wnn 2.3+19.34-7potato6	MULtilingual Enhancement to GNU Emacs (canna wnn supported)
mule2-plain 2.3+19.34-7potato6	MULtilingual Enhancement to GNU Emacs (plain binary)
mule2-support 2.3+19.34-7potato6	Mule — architecture independent support files
mule2-supportel 2.3+19.34-7potato6	Mule — non-required library files
mule2-wnn 2.3+19.34-7potato6	MULtilingual Enhancement to GNU Emacs (wnn supported)
nano 0.8.6-3	Free Pico clone with some new features
ncurses-hexedit 0.9.7-4	Edit files/disks in hex, ASCII and EBCDIC
nedit 5.02-7 [non-free]	NEdit is a powerful, customizable, Motif based text editor
nvi 1.79-15	4.4BSD re-implementation of vi
nvi-m17n 2:1.79+ 19991117-2.2	Multilingualized nvi
nvi-m17n-canna 2:1.79+19991117-2.2	Multilingualized nvi with canna
nvi-m17n-common 2:1.79+19991117-2.2	Multilingualized nvi's common files
records 1.4.3-3	Save and index notes in Emacs environment
sam 4.3-9	The plan9 text editor — ed with a GUI and multi-file editting
sex 0.18	Simple editor for X
smalledit 3.11.6-5	Stripped down version of Cooledit
sted 0.3.0-10	Small/Stupid Text Editor
ted 2.6-1	An easy rich-text editor
the 3.0-1	Full-screen character mode text editor
the-doc 3.0-1	THE Reference Manual
vche 1.7.2-3	Virtual Console Hex Editor
vile 9.0s-1	VI Like Emacs — vi work-alike
vile-common 9.0s-1	VI Like Emacs — support files for vile/xvile
vile-filters 9.0s-1	VI Like Emacs — highlighting filters for vile/xvile
vim 5.6.070-1	Vi IMproved — enhanced vi editor
vim-gtk 5.6.070-1	Vi IMproved — GTK version

Continued

Table C-4 *(continued)*

Package	Description
vim-perl 5.6.070-1	Vi IMproved — with perl support
vim-python 5.6.070-1	Vi IMproved — with python support
vim-rt 5.6.070-1	Vi IMproved — runtime support files
vim-tcl 5.6.070-1	Vi IMproved — with tcl support
vim-tiny 5.6.070-1	Vi IMproved — minimal build
wily 0.13.41-0.2	A work-alike of the Acme programming environment for Plan 9
x-symbol 3.3b-4	WYSIWYG TeX mode for XEmacs
xcoral 3.14-2	Extensible mouse-based text editor for X
xemacs21 21.1.10-4	Editor and kitchen sink
xemacs21-basesupport 1999.12.15-1	Editor and kitchen sink — elisp support files
xemacs21-bin 21.1.10-4	Editor and kitchen sink — support binaries
xemacs21-mule 21.1.10-4	Editor and kitchen sink — Mule binary
xemacs21-mule-canna-wnn 21.1.10-4	Editor and kitchen sink — Mule binary compiled with canna and wnn
xemacs21-mulesupport 1999.12.15-1	Editor and kitchen sink — Mule elisp support files
xemacs21-nomule 21.1.10-4	Editor and kitchen sink — Non-mule binary
xemacs21-support 21.1.10-4	Editor and kitchen sink — architecture independent support files
xemacs21-supportel 21.1.10-4	Editor and kitchen sink — non-required library files
xjed 0.99.9-14	Editor for programmers (x11 version)
xjed-canna 0.98.7.j055-2	xjed with canna (x11 version)
xjed-ja 0.98.7.j055-2	Editor for programmers for Japanese (x11 version)
xtrkcad 2.2.0-2 [non-free]	Sillub Technologies Model Train Track CAD Program
xvile-xaw 9.0s-1	VI Like Emacs — xvile (Xaw)
xvile-xm 9.0s-1	VI Like Emacs — xvile (Xm)
xvile-xt 9.0s-1	VI Like Emacs — xvile (Xt)
xwpe 1.5.22a-1	Programming environment and editor for console and X11
yc-el 0.0.19991014-3	Yet another canna client for Emacsen

Package	Description
yudit 1.5-2	Edit and convert Unicode text of different languages
zed 1.0.3-1	Powerful, multipurpose, configurable Text Editor
zile 1.0a5-4	"Zile is a lossy emacs" a very small emacs-like editor

Graphics

Editors, viewers, and converters that are graphics related are found in Table C-5 —
everything you need to become an artist.

Table C-5 Graphics programs	
Package	**Description**
acidwarp 1.0-4	This is a Linux port of the popular DOS program Acidwarp
aview 1.2-8.1	An high quality ASCII-art image (pgm) browser
barcode 0.94-1	Creates barcodes in `.ps` format
blender 1.71-2 [non-free]	Very fast and versatile 3D modeller/renderer
camediaplay 980118-1	Still Camera Digital Interface
cdlabelgen 1.5.0-2	Generates frontcards and traycards for CDs
chbg 0.8pl1-1	A tool for changing the desktop background image in X11
cqcam 0.89-0.90pre7-1	Color QuickCam (PC/Parallel) control program
cthugha 1.3-4 [non-free]	An oscilloscope on acid
device3dfx-source 2.3.4-2	Device driver source for 3Dfx boards for 2.x kernels
dia 0.83-2	Diagram editor
ean13 0.4-6	Create an EAN-13 or UPC barcode in .xbm format
eeyes 1:0.3.11-5	The Electric Eyes graphics viewer/editor
egon 3.1.22-5	The animator program from Siag Office
fbtv 3.06-3	Video4linux viewer using the kernel framebuffer
fnlib-data 0.4-3	Font files needed by Fnlib
fractxtra 6-5 [non-free]	Fractint Extras Collection
freewrl 0.20.a1-3	Vrml browser and netscape plugin

Continued

Table C-5 *(continued)*

Package	Description
gdk-imlib-dev 1.9.8-4	Header files needed for Gdk-Imlib development
gem 0.81-7	Graphics Environment for multimedia, OpenGL animation tools.
gfont 1.0.2-5 [non-free]	Create GIF image rendered with TeX-available font
gif2png 2.2.5-1	GIF → PNG conversions
giflib-bin 3.0-5.2 [non-free]	Programs to convert GIF images
giflib3g-dev 3.0-5.2 [non-free]	Shared library for GIF images (development files)
gifsicle 1.12-1 [non-free]	Powerful program for manipulationg GIF images
giftrans 1.12.2-5	Convert any GIF file into a GIF89a
gimp 1.0.4-3	The GNU Image Manipulation Program
gimp-data-extras 1:1.0.0-1	An extra set of brushes, palettes, and gradients for The GIMP
gimp-nonfree 1.0.4-3 [non-free]	GIF and TIFF support for the GNU Image Manipulation Program
gimp1.1 1.1.17-3	Developers' release of the GNU Image Manipulation Program
gimp1.1-nonfree 1.1.17-3 [non-free]	GIF and TIFF support for the GNU Image Manipulation Program
gimp1.1-perl 1.1.17-3	Perl support and plugins for The GIMP
glide2-base 2.60-6	Voodoo detection and texture utilities
glut-data 3.7-2	Data files for use with some of the examples in glut-doc
glut-doc 3.7-5	Example programs and support documentation for GLUT
gnome-gv 0.82-2	Gnome PostScript/PDF viewer
gphoto 0.3.5-6	Universal application for digital cameras
gqview 0.7.0e1-1	A simple image viewer using GTK+
gsumi 1.1.0-1	Pressure sensitive "ink" drawing
gtk-engines-gtkstep 2.0-2	N*XTStep theme for GTK+ 1.2
gtk-engines-metal 0.10-1	Metallic theme for GTK+
gtk-engines-notif 0.10-1	Motif-like theme for GTK+
gtk-engines-pixmap 0.10-1	Pixmap-based theme for GTK+
gtk-engines-redmond95 0.10-1	Windows-like theme for GTK+
gtk-engines-thinice 1.0.3-1	ThinIce theme for GTK+ 1.2

Package	Description
gtksee 0.3.0-1	A GTK-based clone of ACDSee, the image viewer
gxanim 0.50-1 [contrib]	GTK front-end to xanim
hp2xx 3.3.2-1	A HPGL converter into some vector and raster formats
hpscanpbm 0.3a-11	HP ScanJet scanning utility
imagemagick 4.2.8-9	Image manipulation programs
imgstar 1.1-4 [non-free]	IMG* Image Processing Toolset and C Library
imlib-base 1.9.8-4	Common files needed by the Imlib/Gdk-Imlib packages
imlib-dev 1.9.8-4	Header files needed for Imlib development
imlib-progs 1.9.8-4	Configuration program for Imlib and GDK-Imlib
imlib1 1.9.8-4	Imlib is an imaging library for X and X11
ivtools-bin 0.7.9-6	Drawing editors evolved from idraw
jpeg2ps 1.8-1 [non-free]	Convert JPEG compressed images to PostScript Level 2
jpeginfo 1.5a-1	Prints information and tests integrity of JPEG/JFIF files
libfnlib-dev 0.4-3	Header files needed for Fnlib development
libgd-gif-tools 1.3-2	GD command-line tools with gif support
libgd-perl 1.18-2.1 [non-free]	Perl gif-manipulation module module GD.pm
libgd1g-tools 1.7.3-0.1	GD command-line tools
libgifgraph-perl 1.10-2 [contrib]	`perl` GIFgraph — Graph Plotting Module for Perl 5
libgtkdatabox 0.1.12.3-1	GTK+ widget to display coordinate systems
libgtkdatabox-dev 0.1.12.3-1	GTK+ widget to display coordinate systems
libgtkimreg 0.1.0-2	GTK+ widget to select regions of GdkImages
libhdf4g-dev 4.1r3-6	The Hierarchical Data Format library — development package
libhdf4g-run 4.1r3-6	The Hierarchical Data Format library — runtime package
libjpeg-progs 6b-1.2	Programs for manipulating jpeg files
libjpeg62-dev 6b-1.2	Development files for the IJG JPEG library [libc6]
libmagick4-dev 4.2.8-9	Image manipulation library (free version) — development
libmagick4-lzw-dev 4.2.8-2 [non-free]	Image manipulation library (non-free version) — development
libmagick4g 4.2.8-9	Image manipulation library (free version)

Continued

Table C-5 *(continued)*

Package	Description
libmagick4g-lzw 4.2.8-2 [non-free]	Image manipulation library (non-free version)
libpng0g-dev 0.96-5	PNG library — development
libpng2-dev 1.0.5-1	PNG library — development
libsrgpg1 1.0-4 [non-free]	Simple Raster Graphics Package
libsrgpg1-dev 1.0-4 [non-free]	Simple Raster Graphics Package development files
libtiff-tools 3.5.4-5	TIFF manipulation and conversion tools
libtiff3g-dev 3.5.4-5	Tag Image File Format library, development files
libungif-bin 3.0-3	Programs to convert GIF images
libungif3g 3.0-3	Shared library for GIF images (runtime lib)
libungif3g-dev 3.0-3	Shared library for GIF images (development files)
libwmf-bin 0.1.16-2	WMF conversion programs
mentor 1.1.13-11	A collection of algorithm animations
mesademos 3.1-4	Example programs for Mesa
mesag3-glide2 3.1-17	A 3D graphics library which uses the OpenGL API [libc6]
mesag3-widgets 3.1-17	Widgets for use with Mesa
moonlight 0.5.3-6	Create and render 3D scenes
netpbm 1:19940301.2-13	Graphics conversion tools
netpbm-dev 1:19940301.2-13	Development libraries and header files
netpbm-nonfree 1:19940301.1-5 [non-free]	Graphics conversion tools (nonfree)
panorama 0.13.1-2	A framework for 3D graphics production
paul 0.1-1	Yet another image viewer (displays PNG, TIFF, GIF, JPG, and so on)
photopc 3.02-2	Interface to digital still cameras
phototk 0.9.9.0-2	GUI interface for digital cameras
picon-domains 1999.10.14-1 [non-free]	Picon (Personal Images) database of for Internet domain logos
picon-misc 1999.09.05-1 [non-free]	Picon (Personal Images) database of common accounts and misc

Package	Description
picon-news 1999.09.05-1 [non-free]	Picon (Personal Images) db of Usenet newsgroups and hierarchies
picon-unknown 1999.09.05-1 [non-free]	Picon (Personal Images) database for very high-level domains
picon-usenix 1995.04.13-5 [non-free]	Picon (Personal Images) database of Usenix conference attendees
picon-users 1999.10.28-1 [non-free]	Picon (Personal Images) database of individual Internet accounts
picon-weather 1999.09.05-1 [non-free]	Picon (Personal Images) database for displaying weather forecasts
pixmap 2.6pl4-8	A pixmap editor
pnmtopng 2.37.4-1	PNG ←→ netpbm (pnm, pbm, ppm, pgm) conversion
povray 3.0.20-10 [non-free]	Persistence of Vision raytracer
povray-doc 3.0.20-10 [non-free]	Persistence of Vision raytracer
povray-manual 3.0.20-1	Persistence of Vision Raytracer 3.0.20 manual in HTML
povray-misc 3.0.20-10 [non-free]	Persistence of Vision raytracer — include files
ppmtofb 0.27	Display netpbm graphics on framebuffer devices
propaganda-debian 13.5-2	A Propaganda background image volume for Debian
pstoedit 3.15-1	PostScript and PDF files to editable vector graphics converter
python-graphics 1.5-11.5.1	PyGraphics — Enables use of Gist and Narcisse from Python
python-imaging 1.0.1-3	The Python Imaging Library.
python-imaging-sane 1.0.1-3	The Python Imaging Library SANE interface
python-imaging-tk 1.0.1-3	The Python Imaging Library (Module with Tk support)
qcad 1.3.3-2	Professional CAD System
qcam 0.91-10	QuickCam image grabber
qiv 1.1-1	A quick image viewer for X
qvplay 0.10-1	Casio QV Camera Communications Tool
sane 1.0.1-1999-10-21-12	Scanner front-ends
sane-gimp1.1 1.0.1-1999-10-21-12	Scanner front-ends

Continued

Table C-5 *(continued)*

Package	Description
saoimage 1.26-2	A utility for displaying and processing astronomical images
scansort 1.81-1	A CSV-based image sorter and verifier
sketch 0.6.4-2	An interactive X11 drawing program
smpeg-gtv 0.3.3-1	SMPEG GTK+ MPEG audio/video player
smpeg-plaympeg 0.3.3-1	SMPEG command-line MPEG audio/video player
streamer 3.06-3	Video capture program for bt848 and video4linux
svgalib-bin 1:1.4.1-2	SVGA display utilities
svgalibg1-dev 1:1.4.1-2	Shared, non-x, graphics library used by Ghostscript et al
terraform 0.5.2-1	A height field manipulation program
tgif 1:4.1.34-2 [non-free]	Interactive 2-D drawing facility under X11
tkpaint 1.5.4-4	Versatile bitmap/pixmap editing tool
tkxanim 0.43-5 [contrib]	Tcl/Tk front-end to xanim
transfig 1:3.2.3-rel-0-3	Utilities for printing figures from xfig
ucbmpeg 1r2-6 [non-free]	MPEG video encoder and analysis tools
ucbmpeg-play 2.3p-9 [non-free]	Software-only MPEG video player
vstream 0.4.4-1	`bttv` video capture utility aimed at making MPEGs
wallp 0.64-0	GTK+ and Imlib based app for periodically updating root of X
whirlgif 3.04-1 [non-free]	Create animated GIFs
xanim 2.80.1-9 [non-free]	Plays multimedia files (animations, pictures, and sounds)
xanim-modules 2.80.1.7 [contrib]	Installer for xanim binary-only modules
xaos 3.0-18	Real-time interactive fractal zoomer
xawtv-tools 3.06-3	Miscelaenous tools distributed with `xawtv`
xbmbrowser 5.1-6	Browser for pixmaps and bitmaps
xfig 1:3.2.3.a-6	Facility for interactive generation of figures under X11
xfig-doc 1:3.2.3.a-6	XFig on-line documentation and examples
xfractint 3.04-6.1 [non-free]	UNIX-based fractal generator
xli 1.16-12	View images under X11
xloadimage 4.1-5	Graphics file viewer under X11

Package	Description
xmorph 1:17nov97-2	Digital image warper
xpaint 2.5.1-4	A reasonably versatile X-based bitmap/pixmap editing tool
xpcd 2.08-3	PhotoCD tool collection: Base
xpcd-gimp 2.08-3	PhotoCD tool collection: Gimp Support
xpcd-svga 2.08-3	PhotoCD tool collection: SVGA Viewer
xplanet 0.43-5	Render images of the earth
xsane 0.50-5	A gtk based X11 frontend for SANE (Scanner Access Now Easy)
xsane-gimp1.1 0.50-5	A gtk based X11 frontend for SANE (Scanner Access Now Easy)
xshodo 2.0-4 [non-free]	A virtual "SHODO — Japanese calligraphy" tool on X
xv 3.10a-25 [non-free]	An image viewer and manipulator for the X Window System
xv-doc 3.10a-25 [non-free]	XV documentation in PostScript and HTML formats
xwpick 2.20-5 [non-free]	Grab an X11-screen and store in files
zgv 3.3-2	SVGAlib graphics viewer

Mail

Mail programs to route, read, and compose e-mail messages are found in Table C-6.

Table C-6
Mail programs

Package	Description
af 2.0-5	An Emacs-like mail reader and composer
asmail 0.51-2	AfterStep mail monitor
auto-pgp 1.04-4 [contrib]	PGP tools for command-line and Emacs use
balsa 0.6.0-1.1	Gnome email client
bbdb 2.00-6	The Insidious Big Brother Database (e-mail Rolodex) for Emacs
bbmail 0.6.2-2	Mail Utility for X
biff 1:0.10-3	A mail notification tool

Continued

Table C-6 *(continued)*

Package	Description
binkd 0.9.3-3	FidoTech TCP/IP mailer
bsmtpd 2.3pl8b-6	Batched SMTP mailer for sendmail or postfix
bulkmail 1.11-1	Speed up delivery of e-mail to large numbers of recipients
c-sig 3.8-2	A signature tool for GNU Emacs
cmail 2.60+19991208-1	A mail user agent for GNU Emacs
cmail-icons 2.60+19991208-1	Icons for cmail on XEmacs
compface 1989.11.11-17.1	Compress/decompress images for mailheaders, user tools
coolmail 1.3-2	Mail notifier with 3D graphics
courier-imap 0.31-1	IMAP daemon with PAM and Maildir support
crashmail 0.60-1	JAM and *.MSG capable Fidonet tosser
cyrus-admin 1.5.19-2 [non-free]	Cyrus mail system (administration tool)
cyrus-common 1.5.19-2 [non-free]	Cyrus mail system (common files)
cyrus-imapd 1.5.19-2 [non-free]	Cyrus mail system (IMAP support)
cyrus-nntp 1.5.19-2 [non-free]	Cyrus mail system (NNTP support)
cyrus-pop3d 1.5.19-2 [non-free]	Cyrus mail system (POP3 support)
deliver 2.1.14-2	Local mail delivery agent
dot-forward-src 0.71-2 [non-free]	`.forward`-compatibility for qmail (source)
elm-me+ 2.4pl25ME+66-1	MIME & PGP-aware interactive mail reader (enhanced)
emil 2.1.0-beta9-9	Conversion filter for Internet messages
exim 3.12-10	Exim Mailer
exim-doc 3.10-1	Exim MTA info documentation
exim-doc-html 3.10-1	Exim MTA html documentation
eximon 3.12-10	X monitor for the exim mail transport agent
exmh 1:2.1.1-1	An X user interface for MH mail
ezmlm-src 0.53-3.1 [non-free]	Easy-to-use high-speed mailing list manager for qmail (source)

Package	Description
fastforward-src 0.51-3 [non-free]	Aliases-style mail forwarding for qmail (source)
fetchmail 5.3.3-1.1	POP2/3, APOP, IMAP mail gatherer/forwarder
fetchmailconf 5.3.3-1.1	`fetchmail` configurator
fidogate 4.2.8-5	Gateway Fido ←→ Internet
flim 1:1.12.7-14	Library to provide basic features about message for Emacsen
flim1.13 1.13.2. 19991021-4	Faithful Library about Internet Message for Emacsen
fml 3.0+beta.20000106-1	Mailing List Server Package
gbuffy 0.2.2-2	A GTK+-based, XBuffy-like multiple mailbox `biff` program
grepmail 4.1-1	Search mailboxes for mail matching an expression
ifmail 2.14tx8.10-11	Internet to Fidonet gateway
im 1:133-2	Internet Message
imap 4.7c-1	Remote mail folder access server for Pine and others
ipopd 4.7c-1	POP2 and POP3 servers from UW
junkfilter 19990331-1	A junk-e-mail filtering program for procmail
lbdb 0.18.5	The little brother's database for the mutt mail reader
libcompfaceg1-dev 1989.11.11-17.1	Compress/decompress images for mailheaders, libc6 devel
libmail-cclient-perl 0.6-4	Interface to UW c-client library
libmime-perl 4.121-2.1	Perl5 modules for MIME-compliant messages (MIME-tools)
listar 0.129a-2	Fast, flexible mailing list manager
listar-cgi 0.129a-2	CGI front-end for Listar
mailagent 3.68-9.potato.1	An automatic mail-processing tool
mailcheck 1.0	Check multiple mailboxes/maildirs for mail
mailcrypt 3.5.5-6 [contrib]	Emacs interface to GPG (and PGP) and anonymous remailers
maildrop 0.75-2	Mail delivery agent with filtering abilities
mailleds 0.93-5	It show new mails with the keyboard-leds
mailman 1.1-6	Powerful, Web-based list processor
mailtools 1.13-4	Manipulate e-mail in Perl programs
mailx 1:8.1.1-10.1.3	A simple mail user agent
masqmail 0.0.12-2	A mailer for hosts without permanent Internet connections
metamail 2.7-34	An implementation of MIME

Continued

Table C-6 (continued)

Package	Description
mew 1:1.94.1-2	Messaging in the Emacs World
mh 6.8.4-JP-3.03-32.4	Rand mail handling system
mh-papers 6.8.4-JP-3.03-32.4	Documentation for the Rand mail handling system
mhonarc 2.4.4-1	Mail to HTML converter
mime-construct 1.7	Construct/send MIME messages from the command line
mimedecode 1.8-8	Decodes transfer encoded text type mime messages
mlock 4.7c-1	Mailbox locking program from UW
mpack 1.5-5	Tools for encoding/decoding MIME messages.
mu-cite 8.0.0.19991019-1	Message Utilities for emacsen
multimail 0.32-2	Offline reader for Blue Wave, QWK, OMEN and SOUP
mush 7.2.5unoff2-8.1 [non-free]	Mush, the mail user shell
mutt 1.0.1-9	Text-based mail reader supporting MIME, GPG, PGP and threading
mutt-ja 0.95.4i.jp2-2.1	Text-based mail reader for Japanese
nmh 1.0.2-9	A set of electronic mail handling programs
pgp4pine 1.71b-5 [contrib]	A PGP/GPG Wrapper for Pine
pine-docs 1998-02-15-2 [non-free]	Pine user guide and getting started
pine396-diffs 5 [non-free]	Diffs to build a Debianized pine
pine396-src 3 [non-free]	The original source code for pine
pine4-diffs 2 [non-free]	Diffs to build a Debianized pine
pine4-src 1 [non-free]	The original source code for pine
pinepgp 3.7 [contrib]	Automates the pgp sign, encrypt, and decrypt functions within pine
poppassd 1.2-11	Password change server for Eudora and NUPOP
postfix 0.0.19991231pl05-2	A mail transport agent
postilion 0.9.2-3	An X Mail User Agent which handles MIME, PGP and Spelling
procmail 3.13.1-3	Versatile e-mail processor
procmail-lib 1:1995.08.28-4.1	A library of useful procmail recipes

Package	Description
qmail-src 1.03-14 [non-free]	Source only package for building qmail binary package
qmtpssh 0.1 [contrib]	Transfer mail over SSH tunnels
qpopper 2.53-5	Enhanced Post Office Protocol server (POP3)
rblsmtpd-src 0.70-5 [non-free]	Source only package for building `rblsmtpd` binary package
select-xface 0.14-1	Insert X-Face mail heaer with viewing and selecting a bitmap
semi 1.13.7+emiko. 1.13.9.20000105-3	Library to provide MIME feature for GNU Emacs
semi1.12 1.12.1-11	Library to provide MIME feature for GNU Emacs
sendmail 8.9.3-23	A powerful mail transport agent
sendmail-wide 8.9.3+3.2W-20	WIDE patch applied `/usr/sbin/sendmail`
serialmail-src 0.72-3 [non-free]	Tools for passing mail across serial links (source)
sharc 2.1-1	Sendmail H? Access and Relay Control
signify 1.06-1	Automatic, semi-random `.signature` rotator/generator
sigrot 1.1-2	Signature file rotation program
smartlist 3.13-2	Versatile and Intelligent List Processor
smtp-refuser 1.0.3	Simple spam-block with refusal message
smtpd 2.0-1	Mail proxy for firewalls with anti-spam and anti-relay features
smtpfeed 1.02-2	SMTP feed — SMTP Fast Exploding External Deliver for Sendmail
sortmail 19910421-5	A simple mail sorter
splitdigest 2.4-2	A program that splits mail-digests
spruce 0.5.9-3	GTK+ application for sending/receiving e-mail
ssmtp 2.33-1	Extremely simple MTA to get mail off the system to a Mailhub
sympa 2.6.1-3	Modern mailing-list manager
task-imap 1.0-1	IMAP Server
tkmail 4.0beta9-4	An X windows interface to mail
truc 1.0.7-3	Transfer big files through e-mail
turqstat 1.2-1	Fidonet message base statistics program
vchkpw 3.1.2-6 [contrib]	Virtual POP-domains and users for qmail

Continued

Table C-6 *(continued)*

Package	Description
vm 6.75-8	A mail user agent for Emacs
vrfy 990522-1	Verify electronic mail addresses
wemi 1.13.7-4	Branch of SEMI kernel package using widget
wemi1.12 1.12.1-8	Branch of SEMI kernel package using widget
wl 1.0.3-9	Wanderlust — Yet another message interface on Emacsen
x-pgp-sig-el 1.3.5.1-3 [contrib]	X-PGP-Sig mail and news header utility for Emacs
xbuffy 3.3.bl.3-9	Monitor mailboxes and/or newsgroups
xfaces 3.3-14	Displays an image for each piece of mail in your mailbox
xfmail 1.4.4-1 [non-free]	X Forms application for sending/receiving e-mail
xlbiff 3.0-3	X Literate Biff. Displays Froms and Subjects of your new mail
xmailbox 2.5-7	A version of `xbiff` with animation and sound effects
xmailtool 3.1.2b-1.3	The good old BSD style mail reader
xmh 3.3.6-10	X interface to MH mail system
xyoubin 2.13-12	The conventional mail arrival notification client for X
youbin 2.13-12	The conventional mail arrival notification server
youbin-client 2.13-12	The conventional mail arrival notification client
zmailer 2.99.51.52pre3-2	Mailer for extreme performance demands

Miscellaneous

Miscellaneous utilities for a variety of functions and tasks are found in Table C-7.

Table C-7
Miscellaneous utilities

Package	Description
appindex 0.5-1	Simple ncurses-based Freshmeat `appindex.txt` browser
barracuda 0.8-5	Web-based Task Tracking (and document directory) System
bb 1.2-9	The `aalib`-demo with sound support
biomode 1.002-2	[Biology] An Emacs mode to edit genetic data
bioperl 0.05.1-1	[Biology] Perl tools for computational molecular biology

Package	Description
birthday 1.1	Display information about pending events on login
bl 1.2-4	Blink Keyboard LEDs
blast2 6.0.2-1.1	[Biology] Basic Local Alignment Search Tool
cbb 1:0.8.1-2	The Check-Book Balancer — a Quicken clone
chasen 2.0-2	Japanese Morphological Analysis System
chasen-dic 2.0-2	Dictionaries for ChaSen
clustalw 1.7-7 [non-free]	[Biology] A multiple sequence alignment program
dbf 1.6-12 [non-free]	Xbase manipulation package
dbf2pg 2.0-7	Converting xBase files to PostgreSQL
dbview 1.0.3-4	View dBase III files
debbugs 2.3-1	The bug tracking system based on the active Debian BTS
debian-keyring 2000.01.3 [contrib]	GnuPG (and obsolete PGP) keys of Debian Developers
debroster 1.5	A package for use at expos
dgpsip 1.29-1	Correct GPS location with DGPS signal from internet
diskless 0.3.6	Generate NFS file structure for diskless boot
diskless-image-secure 0.3.6	Files required for secure NFS-Root image
diskless-image-simple 0.3.6	Files required for simple NFS-Root image
display-dhammapada 0.20-3	Displays verses from the Dhammapada
distributed-net 2.7106-7.1 [non-free]	Donate unused CPU cycles — client for distributed.net
distributed-net-pproxy 280-3 [non-free]	Personal proxy for distributed.net clients
dtaus 0.4-1	Paperless money transfer with German banks on floppies
dtlk 1.12-7	Linux device driver for the DoubleTalk PC
ecdl2k-108-client 1.1.0-1	Gpl Cpuburner
edb 1.21-9	A database program for GNU Emacs
eject 2.0.2-1	Ejects CDs and operates CD-changers under Linux
emwin 0.92-3	Weather data processing
fastdnaml 1.2.1-1	[Biology] A tool for construction of phylogenetic trees of DNA sequences
fastlink 4.1P-1	[Biology] A faster version of pedigree programs of Linkage

Continued

Table C-7 *(continued)*

Package	Description
file-kanji 1.1-10	`kanji` code checker
gatos 0.0.4-3	ATI All-in-Wonder TV capture software
gcpegg 5.1-4	Global Consciousness Project EGG Software
gmt 3.3.3-3	Generic Mapping Tools
gmt-coast-low 19991001-3	Low resolution coastlines for the Generic Mapping Tools
gmt-doc 3.3.3-1	HTML documentation for the Generic Mapping Tools
gmt-doc-ps 3.3.3-1	PostScript docs for the Generic Mapping Tools
gmt-examples 3.3.3-1	Example scripts illustrating the use of Generic Mapping Tools
gmt-manpages 3.3.3-1	Manpages for the Generic Mapping Tools
gmt-tutorial-ps 3.3.3-1	Tutorial for the Generic Mapping Tools (PostScript)
gnome-pm 0.8.0-1	Gnome stock portfolio manager
gperiodic 1.1.1-3	A periodic table application for Linux, using gtk
gpm 1.17.8-18	General Purpose Mouse Interface
gpstrans 0.34-6	Communicate with a Garmin Global Positioning System receiver
gstalker 1.2-9	Stock and commodity price charting utility
gtksql 0.3-2	GTK front end to the `postgresql` database
gtktalog 0.09-2	Disk catalog
ical 2.2-6	An X11/Tk Calendar application
iraf 2.11.3-1 [contrib]	Image Reduction/Analysis Facility (astronomy/imaging)
iraf-common 2.11.3-1 [contrib]	IRAF (Image Reduction/Analysis Facility) — Common files/sources
iraf-ibin 2.11.3-1 [contrib]	IRAF — Core i386 Linux binaries
iraf-noaobin 2.11.3-1 [contrib]	IRAF — NOAO i386 Linux binaries
irda-common 0.9.5-2	IrDA management utilities
irda-tools 0.9.5-2	IrDA handling tools
java-common 0.2	Base of all Java packages
java-compiler-dummy 0.2	Dummy Java compiler
java-virtual-machine-dummy 0.2	Dummy Java virtual machine
joystick 1.2.15-5	Testing and calibration tools

Package	Description
kernel-package 7.04.potato.3	Debian Linux kernel package build scripts
kernellab 0.2.2	Manage kernel configs for many machines easily
launcher 0.85-1	Selects which program to launch according to extension
linuxlogo 3.0.2-2	Color ANSI System Logo
lm-sensors 2.4.4-1	Utilities to read temperature, voltage, and fan sensors
lm-sensors-source 2.4.4-1	Kernel drivers to read temperature, voltage, and fan sensors (source)
lockfile-progs 0.1.7	Programs for locking and unlocking files and mailboxes
malaga-bin 4.3-1.1	A system for automatic language analysis
mdate 1.0.1-3	A utility to report Mayan dates
megahal 8.6-8	A conversation simulator that can learn as you talk to it
miscutils 999.0-4	Obsolete utilities package
mmorph 2.3.4-4	A two-level morphology tool for natural language processing
mpsql 2.1-2 [non-free]	A graphical front-end for PostgreSQL
mxmaps 1.0-6 [contrib]	Some raster and vector maps for Mayko xmap
mysql-client 3.22.32-3 [non-free]	`mysql` database client binaries
mysql-gpl-client 3.22.30-2	`mysql` database client binaries
mysql-server 3.22.32-3 [non-free]	`mysql` database server binaries
netplan 1.8.3-2	Network server for "plan"
otp 970425-3	Generator for One Time Passwords
pc532down 1.1-7	Downloader for pc532 monitor ROM
perspic 1.4-6	A text indexing and word search program
perspic-texts 1.4-6	Some pre-indexed texts for perspic
pgaccess 6.5.3-23	Tk/Tcl front-end for PostgreSQL database
phylip 3.573c-1 [non-free]	[Biology] A package of programs for inferring phylogenies
pkg-order 1.12	A package dependency checker and install ordering tool
plan 1.8.3-2	X/Motif day planner (dynamically compiled with LessTif)
popularity-contest 1.0-1	Vote for your favorite packages automatically
postgresql 6.5.3-23	Object-relational SQL database, descended from POSTGRES

Continued

Table C-7 *(continued)*

Package	Description
postgresql-client 6.5.3-23	Front-end programs for PostgreSQL
postgresql-contrib 6.5.3-23	Additional facilities for PostgreSQL
postgresql-slink 6.3.2	Package to ease upgrade of postgreSQL from Debian 2.1 to 2.2
postgresql-test 6.5.3-23	Regression test suite for PostgreSQL
prime-net 19.1-2 [non-free]	Donate unused CPU cycles - PrimeNet GIMPS client
puzzle 4.0.2-2	[Biology] Reconstruction of phylogenetic trees by maximum likelihood
readseq 0.0-2	[Biology] Conversion between sequence formats
screen 3.9.5-8	A screen manager with VT100/ANSI terminal emulation
seaview 0.0-4 [contrib]	[Biology] A multiple sequence alignment editor
setiathome 2.4-3 [contrib]	SETI@Home Client (install package)
siagoffice-common 3.1.22-5	Common files for Siag Office
siagoffice-plugins 3.1.22-5	Plugins for Siag Office
simh-rsts-images 1-1 [non-free]	RSTS/E V7.0-07 images for simh
simh-unix-images 1-1 [non-free]	UNIX V[567] images for simh emulator
smtm 0.9.0	Show Me The Money is a configurable Perl/Tk stock ticker program
solid-desktop 2.2-3 [non-free]	Solid SQL Server
solid-devel 2.2-2 [non-free]	Solid SQL Server Development
solid-doc 2.2-1 [non-free]	Solid Server Documentation
solid-tools 2.2-1 [non-free]	Solid Server Tools
stopafter 1.2.5-6	Kill commands after a given time
sysvbanner 1.0-9	System-V banner clone
task-chinese-s 0.6	Simplified Chinese environment
task-chinese-t 0.6	Traditional Chinese environment
task-database-pg 0.1	PostgreSQL database
task-german 0.5	German-speaking environment

Package	Description
task-japanese 0.7	Japanese-speaking environment
task-laptop 1.1	A selection of tools for laptop users
task-polish 0.1	Polish-speaking environment
task-spanish 0.2	Spanish environment
titrax 1.98.1-1	TimeTracker is an program to keep track of time
tkcdlayout 0.5-0.1	Simple X program to create labels for CD jewel-cases
tkpgp 1.11-2 [contrib]	Tcl/Tk script that serves as a GUI shell for PGP or GnuPG
tkseti 2.12-2 [contrib]	GUI front-end to the SETI@Home client for UNIX
tpctl 0.8.1-5	Console interface to ThinkPads' SMAPI BIOSes
tpctl-source 0.8.1-5	Source for device drivers to interface with ThinkPad's BIOSes
ud 0.7.1-5	Uptime Daemon
urlview 0.7-8	Extracts URLs from text
user-de 0.8	Settings for German-speaking users
user-es 0.5	Settings for Spanish-speaking users
user-ja 0.28.potato.1	Simple configuration tool for Japanese environment
webrt 1.0.1-4 [contrib]	Request Tracker, a GPL'd Trouble Ticket System
worklog 1.7-1.1	Keep track of time worked on projects
x-face-el 1.3.6.8-2	XFace utility for GNU Emacs
x11iraf 1.1-5 [contrib]	X utilities for IRAF (Image Reduction Analysis Facility)
xacc 1.0.18-4	A personal finance tracking program
xacc-smotif 1.0.17-1 [non-free]	A personal finance tracking program
xcal 4.1-8	A graphical calendar with reminder alarms
xephem 3.2.3-2 [non-free]	An interactive astronomical ephemeris for X
xmap-dmotif 1.0.2-2 [non-free]	Interactive map program, with gps hooks (dynamic motif version)
xmap-smotif 1.0.2-2 [non-free]	Interactive map program, with gps hooks (static motif version)

Network

Daemons and clients, listed in Table C-8, connect your Debian GNU/Linux system to the world.

	Table C-8 **Network programs**
Package	**Description**
3c5x9utils 1.1-2	Configuration and diagnostic utils for 3Com 5x9 cards
amcl 0.4.2-2	A Simple Mu{d,ck,sh,se} Client
amd upl102-33	The 4.4BSD automounter
archie 1.4.1-10 [non-free]	Command-line Archie client
arpd 1.0.2-7	A user-space ARP daemon
asp 1.7	Discovers present IP-address of dynamically connected hosts
bezerk 0.3.2-4	GTK-based IRC client
bind 1:8.2.2p5-11	Internet domain name server
bind-dev 1:8.2.2p5-11	Libraries used by BIND
bind-doc 1:8.2.2p5-11	Documentation for BIND
bing 1.0.4-5.3.1	Empirical stochastic bandwidth tester
bitchx 1:1.0-0c16-2	Advanced Internet Relay Chat client
bitchx-gtk 1:1.0-0c16-2	GTK interface for BitchX
bnetd 0.4.19-1	Battle.Net server for UNIX-like systems
bootp 2.4.3-3	`Bootp` and DHCP server
bootparamd 0.10-2	Boot parameter server
bootpc 0.64-1	bootp client
bridge 0.1-7	Control software and documentation for bridging in 2.0 kernels
bridgex 0.30	Bridge Control software and documentation
bwnfsd 2.3-3	RPC daemon for BWNFS
cfingerd 1.4.1-1	Configurable and secure finger daemon
cftp 0.9-10	A full-screen FTP client
circus 0.43-1 [non-free]	IRC client for X with many features
cricket 0.70-2	Program for collection and display of time-series data
cucipop 1.31-13 [non-free]	Cubic Circle's POP3 daemon

Package	Description
cupsys 1.0.4-7	Common UNIX Printing System™ - base
cupsys-bsd 1.0.4-7	Common UNIX Printing System™ - BSD commands
cvsup 16.1-3	A network file distribution system optimized for CVS (client)
cvsupd 16.1-3	A network file distribution system optimized for CVS (server)
dante-client 1.1.1-4	Provides a SOCKS wrapper for users behind a firewall
dante-server 1.1.1-4	SOCKS server
darxcmd 0.4-3	Darxite client that sends a raw command to the daemon
darxget 0.4-3	Darxite client to get a URL from the command line
darxite 0.4-3	Daemon that transfers files via FTP/HTTP in the background
darxite-applet 0.4-3	Darxite Gnome panel applet allowing DnD from Netscape
darxite-control 0.4-3	Gnome control for darxite
darxstat 0.4-3	Darxite client to display the current batch status
dhcp 2.0-3	DHCP server for automatic IP address assignment
dhcp-client 2.0-3	DHCP Client
dhcp-dns 0.50-3	Dynamic DNS updates for DHCP
dhcp-relay 2.0-3	DHCP Relay
dhcpcd 1:1.3.17pl2-8	DHCP client for automatically configuring IPv4 networking
diald 0.99.1-1	Dial on demand daemon for PPP and SLIP
dlint 1.3.3-2	Checks DNS zone information using nameserver lookups
dnrd 2.7-1	Proxy DNS daemon
dns-browse 1.6-4	Front-ends to DNS search
dnscvsutil 0.5	Maintain DNS zone files under CVS control
dnsutils 1:8.2.2p5-11	Utilities for Querying DNS Servers
dnswalk 2.0.2-2	Checks DNS zone information using nameserver lookups
donkey 0.5-11	One Time Password calculator
dsgtk 0.4-3	Display the Darxite transfer status in a GTK window
dxclip 0.4-3	GTK-based clipboard monitor for Darxite
dxftp 0.4-3	Darxite-based command-line FTP client
dxpref 0.4-3	GTK interface to modify preferences for Darxite
echoping 2.2.0-2	A small test tool for TCP servers

Continued

Table C-8 *(continued)*

Package	Description
efingerd 1.3	Another finger daemon for UNIX capable of fine-tuning your output
eggdrop 1.3.28-2	Advanced IRC robot
epan 1.3.1-1 [non-free]	Offline Ethernet protocol analyzer
epic 3.004-16	Modified IRCII client with additional functionality
epic4 pre2.508-2	Epic IRC client, version 4
epic4-help pre2.003-1	Help files for epic4
epic4-script-lice 1:4.1.4-1	Very functional script for epic
epic4-script-splitfire 1.6-4	The ONLY |<-lame IRC script!
epic4-script-thirdeye 1.7-1	Third Eye EPIC script
ethereal 0.8.0-1	Network traffic analyzer
eudc 1.28b-5	Emacs Unified Directory Client
fakebo 0.4.1-2	Program to detect Back Orifice and NetBus scans
ffingerd 1.25-2.1	A secure finger daemon
filerunner 2.5.1-1	X-Based FTP program and file manager
finger 0.10-3	User information lookup program
fingerd 0.10-3	Remote user information server
fmirror 1:0.8.4beta-2	Memory efficient FTP mirror program
fping 2.2b1-1	Send ICMP ECHO_REQUEST packets to network hosts
frad 0.20-4	Frame Relay Tools for DLCI/SDLA Drivers in 2.0/2.1 kernels
fsp 2.81.b3-2	Client utilities for File Service Protocol (FSP)
fspd 2.81.b3-2	A File Service Protocol (FSP) server
ftp 0.10-3.1	The FTP client
ftp-upload 1.0	Put files with FTP from a script
ftpd 0.11-8potato.1	FTP server
ftpgrab 0.1.1-1	File mirroring utility
ftpmirror 1.2l-5	Mirroring directory hierarchy with FTP
ftpwatch 1.8	Notifies you of changes on remote FTP servers
fwctl 0.25-6	Configure ipchains firewall using higher level abstraction
gdict 0.7-1	Small GTK app to retrieve definitions from MIT's dictionary server

Package	Description
gfcc 0.7.3-2	GTK firewall control center
gftp 2.0.6a-3	X/GTK+ FTP client
gmasqdialer 0.99.7-1	A masqdialer client for Gnome
gnomba 0.5.1-3.1	Gnome Samba browser
gnome-napster 0.4.1-0.2	Locator of MP3 files on the Internet
gnome-network 1.0.2-5	The Gnome network utilities
gnomeicu 0.90b-1	Small, fast, and functional clone of Mirabilis' ICQ
gpppon 0.2-1	A gnome applet that is a wrapper around pon and poff
gq 0.2.2-3	GTK-enabled LDAP client
gtm 0.4.4-3	Multiple files transfert
httptunnel 3.0-2	Tunnels a data stream in HTTP requests
hunt 1.4-1	Advanced packet sniffer and connection intrusion
hx 0.7.10-2	The UNIX client for Hotline
icmpinfo 1.11-1	Interpret ICMP messages
ifhp 3.3.10-3	Printer filter for HP LaserJet printers
ipac 1.05-3	IP accounting configuration and statistics tool
ipgrab 0.8.2-1	Tcpdump-like utility that prints detailed header information
ipip 1.1.4	IP over IP Encapsulation Daemon
iplogger 1.1-7	TCP and ICMP event logger
ipmasq 3.4.4	Securely initializes IP Masquerade forwarding/firewalling
ippl 1.4.10-1	IP protocols logger
iproute 991023-2	Professional tools to control the networking in 2.2.x kernels
iptraf 2.1.1-4	Interactive Colorful IP LAN Monitor
ipx 2.2.0.17-1	Utilities to configure the kernel `ipx` interface
ipxripd 0.7-7	IPX RIP/SAP daemon
ircd 2.10.07-1	IRC Server daemon
ircd-dalnet 4.6.7-3	DALnet IRCd (IRC server)
iroffer 0.1b32-2	IRC file distribution bot
irquery 0.4.7-4	Clients for ddns.org's service
irssi 0.7.21-5	A Gnome IRC client
isdnbutton 2.6-970413-6	Start and Stop ISDN connections and display status

Continued

Table C-8 *(continued)*

Package	Description
isdnutils 1:3.0-20	ISDN utilities
jail 1:1.5-2	Just Another ICMP Logger
jhcore 19981207-2	Jay's House Core, an enhanced core database for lambdamoo
jwhois 2.4.1-1	Improved caching Whois client
lambdacore 19990215-1	Core database for lambdamoo
lambdamoo 1.8.1-1	A server for an online multiuser virtual world
lambdamoo-docs 1.8.0p6-7	LambdaMOO user and programmer manuals
ldap-rfc 1:1.2.11-1	LDAP Related RFC's from OpenLDAP package
lftp 2.1.10-1	Sophisticated command-line FTP/HTTP client programs
libcupsys1 1.0.4-7	Common UNIX Printing System(tm) — libs
libcupsys1-dev 1.0.4-7	Common UNIX Printing System(tm) — development files
libnss-ldap 110-2	NSS module for using LDAP as a naming service
libwww-search-perl 2.07-1	Perl modules which provide an API to WWW search engines
licq 0.76-2.1	ICQ clone (base files)
licq-data 1.3-1	Data files for the Licq ICQ clone
licq-plugin-qt2 0.76-2.1	Graphical front-end for LICQ using the QT2 libraries
liece 1.4.1.0.20000107-2	IRC (Internet Relay Chat) client for Emacs
liece-dcc 1.4.1.0.20000107-2	DCC program for `liece`
links 0.84-1	Character mode WWW browser with ncurses
linpopup 1.1.1-2	Xwindow port of Winpopup, running over Samba
lpr 1:0.48-1	BSD `lpr`/`lpd` line printer spooling system
lprng 3.6.12-6	`lpr`/`lpd` printer spooling system
lsfcc 0.1	Linux Socket Filter Command Compiler
lukemftp 1.1-1	The enhanced FTP client
lurkftp 0.99-5	Monitor changes in FTP sites and opt. Mirror to a local directory
macgate 1.14-5	User-space programs for Appletalk-IP routing
madoka 4.1.15-1	IRC personal proxy, stationing, logger, and bot program (`pirc`)
mason 0.13.0.92-2	Interactively creates a Linux packet filtering firewall
masqdialer 0.5.5-2	Client-server daemon for controlling PPP links

Package	Description
mclient 2.8-1	Client for the MasqDialer PPP control system
micq 0.4.3-3	Text-based ICQ client with many features
mime-support 3.9-1	MIME files `mime.types` and `mailcap`, and support programs
mirror 2.9-15	Perl program for keeping FTP archives up-to-date
modemu 0.0.1-3	Telnet svcs. for comm progs
mrouted 3.9-beta3-1	Multicast routing daemon to connect MBone to your subnet
[non-free]mrtg 2.8.9-1	Multi-Router Traffic Grapher
mtr 0.41-5	Full screen ncurses or X11 traceroute tool
ncftp 1:3.0beta21-1	A user-friendly and full-featured FTP client
ncftp2 1:2.4.3-5	A user-friendly and full-featured FTP client
ncpfs 2.2.0.17-1	Utilities to use resources from NetWare servers
net-acct 0.7-2	Usermode IP accounting deamon
netatalk 1.4b2+asun2.1.3-6	Appletalk user binaries
netboot 0.8.1-4	Booting of a diskless computer
netcat 1.10-12.1	TCP/IP Swiss Army knife
netdiag 0.7-2	Net-Diagnostics (`trafshow`, `strobe`, `netwatch`, `statnet`, `tcpspray`, and `tcpblast`)
netleds-applet 0.9.1-1	Gnome network LEDs applet
netmask 2.3.3	Helps figure our network masks
netobjd 1.1.13-11	The Network Object agent daemon
netpipe-lam 2.3-1	A network performance tool using LAM MPI
netpipe-mpich 2.3-1	A network performance tool using MPICH MPI
netpipe-pvm 2.3-1	A network performance tool using PVM
netpipe-tcp 2.3-1	A network performance tool using the TCP protocol
netselect 0.2-5	Choose the fastest server automatically
netstd 3.07-17	Legacy package that you should remove
nfs-common 1:0.1.9.1-1	NFS support files common to client and server
nfs-kernel-server 1:0.1.9.1-1	Kernel NFS server support
nfs-server 2.2beta47-4potato.2	User space NFS server
ngrep 1.35-1	`grep` for network traffic

Continued

Table C-8 *(continued)*

Package	Description
nhfsstone 1:0.1.9.1-1	NFS benchmark program
nis 3.6-2	Clients and daemons for the Network Information Services (NIS)
nmap 2.12-5	The Network Mapper
noctftp 0.4-3	Graphical FTP client for the Darxite
npadmin 0.8-2	Query information from SNMP featured printer
nslint 2.0a5-1	Lint for DNS files, checks integrity
nsmon 2.3e-3	Intranet/Internet server checker
nstreams 1.0-2	Network streams — a tcpdump output analyzer
ntop 1.2a7-10	Display network usage in top-like format
ntp 1:4.0.99g-2	Daemon and utilities for full NTP v4 timekeeping participation
ntp-doc 1:4.0.99g-2	HTML documentation for the ntp and ntpdate packages
ntpdate 1:4.0.99g-2	The `ntpdate` client for setting system time from NTP servers
oidentd 1.6.4-2	Replacement `ident` daemon
omirr 0.3-6	Online Mirror daemon
openldap-gateways 1:1.2.11-1	OpenLDAP Gateways
openldap-utils 1:1.2.11-1	OpenLDAP utilities
openldapd 1:1.2.11-1	OpenLDAP server (`slapd`)
pcnfsd 2.0-4 [non-free]	PC NFS authentication and print request server
pftp 1.1.2-1	Fast file transfer program (no authentication!)
pidentd 3.0.7-3	TCP/IP IDENT protocol server
pkspxy 0.5-4	PGP Public Key Server Proxy Daemon
pkspxyc 0.5-4	PGP Public Key Server Proxy Client
plum 2.33.1-2.1	IRC proxy, stationing, logging, and bot program (`pirc`)
pppoe 1.0-1	PPP over Ethernet driver
pptpd 1.0.0-4	PoPToP Point to Point Tunneling server
ppxp 0.99120923-1	Yet another PPP program
ppxp-tcltk 0.99120923-1	Tk console of ppxp
ppxp-x11 0.99120923-1	X console of ppxp
proftpd 1.2.0pre10-2	Versatile, virtual-hosting FTP daemon

Package	Description
pump 0.7.3-2	Simple DHCP/BOOTP client for 2.2.x kernels
python-ldap 1.8-1	An LDAP module for Python
qpage 3.3final-1 [non-free]	SNPP client, or SNPP-to-TAP/IXO gateway
qtss 3-3	Streaming multimedia server
queso 0.980922b-1	Guess the operating system of a remote machine
radiusd-cistron 1.6.1-0.1	Cistron version of Radius
radiusd-livingston 1.16.1-0.1	Remote Authentication Dial-In User Service (RADIUS) server
rat 4.0.3-2 [non-free]	RAT — unicast and multicast audio conferencing tool
rbootd 2.0-5	Remote Boot Daemon
rdate 1.3-3	Set the system's date from a remote host
rdist 6.1.5-1	Remote file distribution client and server
realplayer 7.0.2.2 [contrib]	RealPlayer (installer)
redir 2.1-1	Redirect TCP connections
rexec 1.5-2	Remote execution client for an exec server
rinetd 0.52-2	Internet redirection server
rlinetd 0.5.1	Gruesomely over-featured inetd replacement
rlpr 2.02-3	A utility for lpd printing without using `/etc/printcap`
routed 0.12-3	Network routing daemon
rrlogind 1:2.35-2	Login daemon for the Road Runner Cable Modem Service
rsh-client 0.10-7	Rsh clients
rsh-server 0.10-7	Rsh servers
rstat-client 3.03-2	A client for rstatd
rstatd 3.03-2	Display uptime information for remote machines
rsync 2.3.2-1.2	Fast remote file copy program (like `rcp`)
ruptime 1.0-2	Show host status of local machines
rusers 0.11-1	Displays who is logged in to machines on local network
rusersd 0.11-1	Logged in users server
rwall 0.10-1	Send a message to users logged on a host
rwalld 0.10-1	Write messages to users currently logged in server
rwho 0.10-8	Who is logged in on local machines
rwhod 0.10-8	System status server

Continued

Table C-8 *(continued)*

Package	Description
samba 2.0.7-3	A LanManager-like file and printer server for UNIX
samba-common 2.0.7-3	Samba common files used by both the server and the client
samba-doc 2.0.7-3	Samba documentation
scotty 3:99-08-12-5	The Scotty and Tkined Network Management Tools
sdr 2.8-1.2	An Mbone Conference Scheduling and Booking System
sendfile 2.1-20.1	Simple Asynchronous File Transfer
shaper 0.15-2	Traffic Shaper for Linux
sirc 2.211-3	The full-featured Perl IRC client
sliplogin 2.0.2-3	Tool to attach a serial line network interface
slirp 1.0g-2	SLIP/PPP emulator using a dial-up shell account
smb-nat 10-2	SMB Network Analysis Tool
smb2www 980804-8	A Windows Network client that is accessible through a Web browser
smbclient 2.0.7-3	A LanManager like simple client for UNIX
snarf 2.0.8-1	A command-line URL grabber
sniffit 0.3.7.beta-6.1	Packet sniffer and monitoring tool
snmp 4.1.1-2	UCD SNMP (Simple Network Management Protocol) Applications
snmpd 4.1.1-2	UCD SNMP (Simple Network Management Protocol) Agent
snmptraplogd 1.0-6.1	A configurable snmp trap daemon
snort 1.5.1-11	Flexible packet sniffer/logger that detects attacks
socket 1.1-5	Multi purpose socket tool
socks4-clients 4.3.beta2-9	Socks4 enabled clients as rtelnet, rftp, and so forth
socks4-server 4.3.beta2-9	SOCKS4 server for proxying IP-based services over a firewall
stone 2.1-1	TCP/IP packet repeater in the application layer
swat 2.0.7-3	Samba Web Administration Tool
tac-plus F4.0.2.alpha-5	This is the daemon for the tacacs+ protocol
talk 0.10-7	Talk to another user
talkd 0.10-7	Remote user communication server
task-dialup 0.3	Dial-up utilities
task-dialup-isdn 0.4	Dial-up utilities (ISDN)
task-dns-server 1:8.2.2p5-11	DNS Server

Package	Description
task-gnome-net 1.0.4	Gnome network applications
task-samba 0.3	Samba SMB server
tcpdump 3.4a6-4.1	A powerful tool for network monitoring and data acquisition
tcpslice 1.1a3-1	Extract pieces of and/or glue together tcpdump files
tcputils 0.6.2-3	Utilities for TCP programming in shell-scripts
telnet 0.16-4	The `telnet` client
telnetd 0.16-4	The `telnet` server
tftp 0.10-1	Trivial file transfer program
tftpd 0.10-1	Internet trivial file transfer protocol server
tik 0.75-3	Tcl/Tk client for the AOL Instant Messenger service
tinyirc 1:1.1-4	A _Tiny_ IRC Client
tinyproxy 1.3.1-1	A lightweight, noncaching, optionally anonymizing http proxy
tirc 1.2-4	Token's IRC client
tkirc 1.202-7 [contrib]	Tcl/Tk based client to the Internet Relay Chat
tkmasqdialer 1.12-1	Tcl/Tk client for the MasqDialer modem connection daemon
tn5250 0.14.1-5	5250 Telnet emulator for accessing an IBM AS/400
traceroute 1.4a5-2	Traces the route taken by packets over a TCP/IP network
traceroute-nanog 6.0-1	NANOG traceroute
ucspi-tcp-src 0.84-1 [non-free]	Source only package for building ucspi-tcp binary package
ugidd 2.2beta47-4potato.2	NFS UID mapping daemon
umich-ldap-docs 3.3-3	Documentation for the LDAP server and utilities
umich-ldap-utils 3.3-3	LDAP utilities
umich-ldapd 3.3-3	LDAP server
utalk 1.0.1.beta-3	Talk-like program with additional features
vic 2.8ucl4-2	Video conferencing tool
wanpipe 2.1.1-2	Configuration utilities for Sangoma S508/S514 WAN cards
wbd 1.0ucl4-1	Multicast White Board
wdsetup 0.6b-2	Configuration utility for Western Digital and SMC Ethernet cards
webcam 3.06-3	Capture and automatically upload images to a Web server

Continued

Table C-8 *(continued)*

Package	Description
whois 4.4.14	Whois client
wmppp.app 1.3.0-1	A PPP and network load monitor with the NeXTStep look
wmppxp 0.51.0-2	PPxP console for Window Maker Dock
wu-ftpd 2.6.0-5.1	Powerful and widely used FTP server
wu-ftpd-academ 2.6.0-5.1	Wu-ftpd upgrade convenience package (removable)
wxftp-doc 0.4.4-2	Documentation for wxftp, needed for the help menu
wxftp-gtk 0.4.4-2	A graphical FTP program with GTK interface
xchat 1.4.2-1.1	IRC client for X similar to AmIRC
xchat-common 1.4.2-1.1	Common files for X-Chat
xchat-gnome 1.4.2-1.1	IRC client for Gnome similar to AmIRC
xchat-text 1.4.2-1.1	IRC client for console similar to AmIRC
xfingerd 0.6-2	BSD-like finger daemon with qmail support
xftp 2.2-13	Athena X interface to FTP
xinetd 1:2.1.8.8.p3-1	Replacement for inetd with many enhancements
xisp 2.6p1-2 [contrib]	A user-friendly X interface to pppd/chat
xnetload 1.7.2-1	An Xload for network interfaces packet rates/totals
xntp3 1:4.0.99g-2	Empty package to facilitate xntp3 →ntp, ntpdate name change
xtalk 1.3-4	BSD talk compatible X-Window client, written in Python
xtell 1.91	Simple messaging client and server, sort of networked write
xwhois 0.3.9-1	RFC954 Whois client
ytalk 3.1.1-1	Enhanced talk program with X support
zebra 0.84b-3	A GPL'd, BGP/OSPF/RIP capable routing daemon
zenirc 2.112-6	Major mode for wasting time
zephyr-clients 2.0.4-7	The original "Instant Message" system client programs
zephyr-server 2.0.4-7	The original "Instant Message" system server
zicq 0.2.9-3	Small ncurses based ICQ client
zircon 1.18.224-1	Powerful X Internet Relay Chat client
zone-file-check 1.01-2	Syntax-checker for BIND zone files

Newsgroups

Software listed in Table C-9 is used to access Usenet, set up news servers, and so forth.

Table C-9	
Newsgroup applications	
Package	**Description**
aub 2.0.5-3.1	Assembles binary files from USENET
c-nocem 3.5-1 [contrib]	Applies NoCeM actions on the local spool
chaos 1.13.0-4	Replacement of Gnus with gnus-mime for SEMI
cnews cr.g7-19.4	Simple News Server for Usenet news
diablo 1.29-1 [non-free]	News transport system without reader support
gnus 5.8.3-9	A versatile news and mailing list reader for Emacsen
gup 0.5.3	Lets a remote site change their newsgroups subscription
inews 2.1-11	A replacement for the C News inews program
inewsinn 1:1.7.2-16	NNTP client news injector, from InterNetNews (INN)
inn 1:1.7.2-16	News transport system InterNetNews by the ISC and Rich Salz
inn-dev 1:1.7.2-16	The libinn.a library and manpages
inn2 2.2.2.2000.01.31-4	News transport system InterNetNews by the ISC and Rich Salz
inn2-dev 2.2.2.2000.01.31-4	The libinn.a library and manpages
inn2-inews 2.2.2. 2000.01.31-4	NNTP client news injector, from InterNetNews (INN)
innfeed 0.10.1.7-6	This is the INN feeder program `innfeed`.
knews 1.0b.1-2	Graphical threaded news reader
leafnode 1.9.9-4	NNTP server for small leaf sites
linleech 2.2.1-2	A program to selectively download Usenet articles
newsflash 0.99-3	Get news with the newnews command from a server
newsgate 1.6-12 [non-free]	Mail to News and News to Mail Gateway
newsx 1.4-3	An NNTP client for posting and fetching news
ninpaths 1.5-1	Paths Survey reporting program
nn 6.5.1-7	Heavy-duty Usenet news reader (curses-based client)

Continued

Table C-9 *(continued)*	
Package	**Description**
nntp 1.5.12.1-8	A NNTP server for use with C News
nntpcache 1:2.3.3-3 [non-free]	News proxy cache
nntpcache-dev-doc 1:2.3.3-3 [non-free]	NNTPCACHE source code documentation
pan 0.7.6-1	Pimp A** Newsreader (Uses GTK, looks like Forte Agent)
peruser 4b33-6	Suite for offline reading and composing of Usenet articles
post-faq 0.10-4	Post periodic FAQs to Usenet newsgroups
postit 0.5-1	A program sending news
semi-gnus 1:6.10.12. 19990528cvs-9	Replacement of Gnus with gnus-mime for SEMI
slrn 0.9.6.2-7	Threaded news reader (fast for slow links)
slrn-ja 0.9.5.5-1	Threaded news reader (fast for slow links), Japanese version
slrnpull 0.9.6.2-7	Pulls a small newsfeed from an NNTP server
statnews 1.6	Extracts some useful statistics out of a newsgroup
strn 0.9.2-9 [non-free]	Scanning threaded Usenet news reader, based on trn and rn
suck 4.2.2-4	Small newsfeed from an NNTP server with standard NNTP commands
t-gnus 6.13.3.00-2	Latest branch of Semi-gnus with New Features
task-news-server 2.2.2.2000.01.31-4	Usenet news server
tin 1:1.4.1-1 [non-free]	Threaded Internet news reader
trn 3.6-13 [non-free]	Threaded Usenet news reader, based on rn
uucpsend 1.0-1	Additional front end for uucp batching

Other OS's and file systems

Software to run other operating system programs, and to use their filesystems are in Table C-10.

Table C-10
Other OS and filesystem utilities

Package	Description
apple2 0.7.3-5 [contrib]	Apple II Emulator
atari-fdisk-cross 0.7.1-3	Partition editor for Atari (running on non-Atari)
atari800 0.9.8a-2 [contrib]	Atari Emulator for `svgalib/X/curses`
cdrdao 1:1.1.3-3	Write audio- or mixed-mode CD-Rs in disk-at-once mode
cdrecord 3:1.8-3	A command-line CD/DVD writing tool
cdrtoaster 1.04p2-2	Tcl/Tk front-end for burning cdrom
cdwrite 2.0-2	CD writing tool for Orange Book CD-R drives
dosemu 0.98.8-2	The Linux DOS Emulator
dosfstools 2.5-1	Utilities to create and check MS-DOS FAT filesystems
gcombust 0.1.28-1	GTK+ based CD mastering and burning program
gpasm 0.0.7-5	GNU PIC assembler
gtoaster 0.19991130-1	Gnome Toaster, a GUI for creating CD's
hfsutils 3.2.6-1	Tools for reading and writing Macintosh volumes
hfsutils-tcltk 3.2.6-1	Tcl/Tk interfaces for reading and writing Macintosh volumes
ibcs-base 981105-1	Intel Binary Compatibility Specification Module
ibcs-source-2.0 981105-1	iBCS Emulator Modules for Linux (2.0.x kernel)
ibcs-source-2.2 981105-1	iBCS Emulator Modules for Linux (2.2.x kernel)
imgvtopgm 2.0-1	PalmPilot/III Image Conversion utility
jpilot 0.97-1	A GTK app to modify the contents of your pilots DB's
libwine 0.0.20000109-3	Windows Emulator (Library)
libwine-dev 0.0.20000109-3	Windows Emulator (Development files)
lpkg 19980629-2	Newton MessagePad PDA Package Loader
lx-gdb 1.03-4	Dump and load databases from the HP palmtop
lxtools 1.1-5	Allows file management on HP100/200LX palmtops
macutils 2.0b3-7	Set of tools to deal with specially encoded Macintosh files
mcvert 2.16-6 [non-free]	Tool to deal with specially encoded Macintosh files
mixal 1.08-5	A MIX Emulator and MIXAL interpreter
mkhybrid 1.12b5.4-4	CD-ROM authoring tool. Creates CD-ROM filesystem images
mkisofs 3:1.8-3	Creates ISO-9660 CD-ROM filesystem images

Continued

Table C-10 *(continued)*

Package	Description
mtools 3.9.6-3.1	Tools for manipulating MS-DOS files
p3nfs 5.4-3	Mount Psion series 3[ac], 5 drives
palm-doctoolkit 1.1.4	E-text tools for PalmPilot users
picasm 1.6-0.1 [non-free]	Assembler for the Microchip PIC-family Microcontrollers
pilot-link 0.9.3-3	Tools to communicate with a 3COM Pilot PDA over a serial port
pilot-manager 1.107-1.2	PalmPilot PIM, UI, and Conduit Manager
pilot-template 1.31-1	Code generator for PalmPilot programs
pilrc 2.4-2	PalmPilot/PalmIII resource compiler and editor
pose 3.0a3-3 [contrib]	PalmOS Emulator
prc-tools 0.5.0r-3.1	GCC, GDB, binutils, etc. for PalmPilot and Palm III
pyrite 0.9.3	Palm Computing(R) platform communication kit for Python
simh 2.3d-2 [non-free]	An emulator for various DEC computers
smbfs 2.0.7-3	`mount` and `umount` commands for the `smbfs` (for kernels version 2.0.x and greater)
stella 1.1-2 [non-free]	Atari 2600 Emulator for X windows
tkchooser 2.0651-1	Modular X windows network browser
tksmb 0.8.8-3	SMB (Samba and Windows) network browser
uae 0.7.6-4 [contrib]	The Ubiquitous Amiga Emulator: Base
uae-exotic 0.7.6-4 [contrib]	The Ubiquitous Amiga Emulator: Exotic binaries
uae-suid 0.7.6-4 [contrib]	The Ubiquitous Amiga Emulator: Suid root binaries
umsdos 0.9-14	This is the distribution of the UMS-DOS filesystem utilities
vice 1.0-3 [contrib]	The Versatile Commodore Emulator
wine 0.0.20000109-3	Windows Emulator (Binary Emulator)
wine-doc 0.0.20000109-3	Windows Emulator (Documentation)
xapple2 0.7.3-5 [contrib]	Apple II Emulator
xcdroast 0.96e-3	X-based CD-writer software
xcopilot 1:0.6.6 [contrib]	Pilot Emulator
xspectemu 0.94-1	Fast 48k ZX Spectrum Emulator for X11
xtrs 3.9a-1 [contrib]	Emulator for TRS-80 Model I/III/4/4P computers
xzx 2.9.0-1 [non-free]	X11 based ZX Spectrum Emulator

Shells

Table C-11 lists command shells. Friendly user interfaces for beginners.

Package	Description
Table C-11 **Shells**	
Package	*Description*
ash 0.3.5-11	NetBSD `/bin/sh`
csh 5.26-10	Shell with C-like syntax, standard login shell on BSD systems
es 0.90beta1-6	An extensible shell based on `rc`
esh 0.8-5	The easy shell
flin 0.5.1-8	Menuing system with `fvwm`-like syntax
kiss 0.21-1	Karel's Interactive Simple Shell
lsh 0.70-1	Baby Shell for Novices with DOS-compatible commands
osh 1.7-5	Operator's Shell
pdksh 5.2.14-1	A public domain version of the Korn shell
pdmenu 1.2.59	Simple full-screen menu program
rc 1.6-3	An implementation of the AT&T Plan 9 shell
sash 3.4-3	Standalone shell
tcsh 6.09.00-8	TENEX C Shell, an enhanced version of Berkeley `csh`
tcsh-i18n 6.09.00-8	TENEX C Shell message catalogs
tcsh-kanji 6.09.00-8	TENEX C Shell, an enhanced version of Berkeley `csh`
zsh 3.1.6.pws21-1	A shell with lots of features
zsh30 3.0.7-4	A shell with lots of features
zsh30-static 3.0.7-4	A shell with lots of features

Sound

Utilities listed in Table C-12 deal with sound: mixers, players, recorders, CD players, and so forth.

Table C-12
Sound utilities

Package	Description
abcde 1.0.1.1-1 [contrib]	A Better CD Encoder
abcmidi 1.7.3-1	A converter from abc to MIDI format and back
alsa-base 0.4.1i-5	ALSA driver common files
alsa-headers 0.4.1i-5	ALSA driver header files
alsa-source 0.4.1i-5	ALSA driver source
alsaconf 0.4.2-3	ALSA configurator
alsalib0.3.0 0.4.1e-2	`dummy` package to fix previous broken versions
alsaplayer 0.99.26-2.1	PCM player designed for ALSA
alsaplayer-alsa 0.99.26-2.1	PCM player designed for ALSA
alsaplayer-esd 0.99.26-2.1	PCM player designed for ALSA
alsaplayer-oss 0.99.26-2.1	PCM player designed for ALSA
alsautils 0.4.1-5	Advanced Linux Sound Architecture (`utils`)
amp 0.7.6-7 [non-free]	The Audio MPEG Player
ascd 0.13.1-2	CD player and mixer
ascdc 0.3-7	AfterStep CD changer
asmixer 0.5-4	AfterStep audio mixer
aumix 2-1	Simple text-based mixer control program
awe-drv 0.4.3.1-1	Linux AWE32 driver source and utilities
awe-midi 0.4.3.1-1	Linux AWE32 driver MIDI player
awe-netscape-libc5 0.4.3.1-1	Linux AWE32 MIDI player Netscape plug-in
awe-netscape-libc6 0.4.3.1-1	Linux AWE32 MIDI player Netscape plug-in (libc6/glibc2.0)
bplay 0.99-2	Buffered audio file player/recorder
cam 1.05-4	Cpu's Audio Mixer for Linux
cccd 0.3beta3-2	Small GTK CD player program
cd-discid 0.2-2	CDDB DiscID utility
cdcd 0.5.0-2	Command-line or console-based CD player
cdda2wav 3:1.8-3	Creates WAV files from audio CDs
cddb 2.5pl1-7	CD DataBase support tools
cdindex-client 1.0.0-1.1	`cdindex` is intended to be the Open Source replacement of cddb™

Package	Description
cdparanoia 3a9.7-2	An audio extraction tool for sampling CDs
cdtool 2.1.5-4	Some text-based commands for managing a CD
csound 1:3.53.0.1d-1 [non-free]	Computer Music language from Berry Vercoe
dcd 0.80-1	Command-line CD player
dtmfdial 0.2-1	A DTMF Tone Dialer
esound 0.2.17-7	Enlightened Sound daemon – Support binaries
esound-alsa 0.2.17-7	Enlightened Sound Daemon (ALSA) – Support binaries
esound-common 0.2.17-7	Enlightened Sound Daemon – Common files
extace 1.2.15-3	Waveform viewer
festival 1.4.1-1	Speech synthesis system
festival-dev 1.4.1-1	Development kit for the Festival speech synthesis system
festlex-cmu 1.4.0-1	CMU dictionary in Festival form
festlex-oald 1.4.0-1 [non-free]	Festival lexicon from *Oxford Advanced Learners' Dictionary*
festlex-poslex 1.4.0-1	Part of speech lexicons and `ngram` from English
festvox-don 1.4.0-1 [contrib]	Minimal British English male speaker for Festival
festvox-ellpc11k 1.4.0-1 [non-free]	Castilian Spanish male speaker for Festival
festvox-kallpc16k 1.4.0-1	American English male speaker for festival, 16 kHz sample rate
festvox-kallpc8k 1.4.0-1	American English male speaker for festival, 8 kHz sample rate
festvox-kdlpc16k 1.4.0-1	American English male speaker for festival, 16 kHz sample rate
festvox-kdlpc8k 1.4.0-1	American English male speaker for festival, 8 kHz sample rate
[non-free] festvox-rablpc16k 1.4.0-1 [contrib]	British English male speaker for festival, 16 kHz sample rate
festvox-rablpc8k 1.4.0-1 [contrib]	British English male speaker for festival, 8 kHz sample rate
fmtools 0.2.1-1	FM radio tuner
freeamp 2.0.6-2	A GPLed MPEG (MP2/MP3) audio player with a nice X front-end
freeamp-doc 2.0.6-2	FreeAmp documentation and help files
gamix 1.00b5-3	Graphical mixer for ALSA using gtk+

Continued

Table C-12 *(continued)*

Package	Description
gcd 2.91-1	A GTK-based CD player
gmod 3.1-7	Module player for Ultrasound and SB AWE soundcards
gmp3 0.080-3 [contrib]	A graphical front-end to mpg123 (plays MP3 audio files)
gnome-audio 1.0.0-3	Audio files for Gnome
gnome-media 1.0.51-2	Gnome Media Utilities (gmix, gtcd)
gom 0.29.103-6	A generic audio mixer (Base versions)
gom-x 0.29.103-6	A generic audio mixer (X version)
gqmpeg 0.6.3e1-1 [contrib]	A GTK front-end to the mpg123 mpeg audio player
gradio 1.0.0-2	GTK FM radio tuner
gramofile 1.5-3	Transfer sound from gramophone records to CD
grip 2.91-1	A GTK-based CD-player and CD-ripper
groovycd 0.51-5	A ncurse-based CD player
gtick 0.1.3-2	GTK-based metronome
icecast-client 1.0.0-1	Streaming Mpeg Layer III feeder
icecast-server 1.0.0-1	Streaming Mpeg Layer III server
id3 0.12-1	An ID3 Tag Editor
id3ed 1.9-2	Another ID3 Tag Editor
libcdparanoia0 3a9.7-2	Shared libraries for cdparanoia (runtime lib)
libcdparanoia0-dev 3a9.7-2	Development files needed to compile programs that use libcdparanoia.
libfreeamp-alsa 2.0.6-2	ALSA plug-ins for FreeAmp
libfreeamp-esound 2.0.6-2	EsounD plug-ins for FreeAmp
librplay3 3.3.2-2	Shared libraries for the rplay network audio system
librplay3-dev 3.3.2-2	Development libraries for the rplay network autio system
libwsound-dev 0.2.2-3	WSoundServer development files
maplay3 1.1-3	An MPEG Audio Player
mctools-lite 970129-9	A CD player and audio mixer for X
mikmod 3.1.6-2	Portable tracked music player
mixer.app 1.4.0-3	Another mixer application designed for WindowMaker
mixviews 1.20-11	Powerful soundfile editor
mp3asm 0.01-1 [non-free]	MP3 diagnostic tool

Package	Description
mp3blaster 2-0b16-1.1	Full-screen console mp3 player
mp3info 0.2.16-2	MPEG audio layer header info decoder
mpg123 0.59q-2 [non-free]	MPEG layer 1/2/3 audio player
nas 1.2p5-11	The Network Audio System (NAS) (local server)
nas-bin 1.2p5-11	The Network Audio System (NAS) (client binaries)
nas-doc 1.2p5-11	The Network Audio System (NAS) (extra documentation)
pd 0.28-5	Realtime Computer Music and Graphics System
playmidi 2.3-25	MIDI player
radio 3.06-3	Listen to the radio available on certain v4l cards
recite 1.0-2	English text speech synthesizer
rexima 1.0-1	A nice little ncurses mixer
rio 1.07-3	A command-line Diamond Rio MP3 player controller
rosegarden 2.1pl2-1	An integrated MIDI sequencer and musical notation editor
rplay 3.3.2-2	A fake transitional package
rplay-client 3.3.2-2	The basic `rplay` clients
rplay-contrib 3.3.2-2	Contributed binaries for the rplay network audio system
rplay-perl 3.3.2-2	Perl modules for the rplay network audio system
rplay-server 3.3.2-2	The rplay network audio system server
rsynth 2.0-5 [non-free]	Text to speech program
s3mod 1.09-11	Player for MOD and S3M music files
saytime 1.0-7	Speaks the current time through your sound card
sidplay 1.36.35-2	Music player for tunes from C64 and Amiga (console)
snack 1.6-3	Sound functionality extension to the Tcl/Tk language
snack-dev 1.6-3	Snack development files
snd 3.4-4	Soundfile editor
sound-recorder 0.05-6	Direct-to-disk recording and play-back programs
soundtracker 0.3.8-1	Sound module editor/player. Supports `.xm` modules, `.xi` instruments
sox 12.16-6	A universal sound sample translator
speech-tools-bin 1.4.1-1	Edinburgh Speech Tools Library – user binaries
speech-tools-dev 1.4.1-1	Edinburgh Speech Tools Library – developer's libraries and docs

Continued

Table C-12 *(continued)*

Package	Description
speech-tools1 1.4.1-1	Edinburgh Speech Tools Library
splay 0.8.2-10	Sound player for MPEG-1,2 layer 1,2,3
synaesthesia 2.0-1	A program for representing sounds visually
timidity 2.9.1-2	Software-only MIDI sequencer
timidity-patches 0.1-4	Instrument files for software-only MIDI sequencer
tkmixer 1.0-6	An audio mixer with Tk interface
tracker 4.3-8 [non-free]	Plays Amiga MOD files
transcriber 1.4-4	Transcribe speech data using an integrated editor
vkeybd 0.4.3.1-1	Virtual Keyboard program
wav2cdr 2.3.2-2	Converts wav files into CD-ROM audio file format
wavtools 1.3.2-3	WAV play, record, and compression
wmcdplay 1.0beta1-4	A CD player based on ascd designed for Window Maker
wmxmms-spectrum 0.1-1	XMMS spectrum analyzer plug-in for the Window Maker dock
workbone 2.40-2	A simple text-based CD player
workman 1.3.4-3	Graphical tool for playing audio CDs on a CD-ROM drive
wsoundprefs 1.1.0-2	Preferences editor for the Window Maker sound server
wsoundserver 0.2.2-3	Window Maker Sound Server from scratch reimplementation
xamixer 0.4.1-5	Graphical mixer for ALSA
xfreecd 0.7.8-3	A GTK-based CD Player
xgmod 3.1-7	GUI based module player for Ultrasound and SB AWE sound cards
xmcd 2.5pl1-7	X11-based CD player
xmix 2.1-3.1	An X11-based interface to the Linux sound driver mixer
xmms 1.0.1-2	Versatile X audio player that looks like Winamp
xmms-dev 1.0.1-2	XMMS development static library and header files
xmp 1.1.3-1	XMP, a module player supporting AWE32, GUS, and software-mixing
xsidplay 1.3.8-5	Music player for tunes from C64 and Amiga (X11; qt)

Utilities for I/O and storage

Table C-13 shows utilities for file and disk manipulation, backup and archive tools, system monitoring, input systems, and so on.

Table C-13	
Utilities for I/O and storage	
Package	**Description**
afbackup 3.1beta1-1.1	Client-Server Backup System (Server side)
afbackup-client 3.1beta1-1.1	Client-Server Backup System (Client side)
afio 2.4.6-1	Archive file manipulation program
aish 1.13-1	Ish/base64/uuencoded_file converter
amanda-client 1:2.4.1p1-12	Advanced Maryland Automatic Network Disk Archiver (Client)
amanda-common 1:2.4.1p1-12	Advanced Maryland Automatic Network Disk Archiver (Libs)
amanda-server 1:2.4.1p1-12	Advanced Maryland Automatic Network Disk Archiver (Server)
apcupsd 3.6.2-1	APC UPS Power Management
artist 1.1beta1-3	Emacs Lisp drawing package
ascii 2.6	Prints aliases and tables for ASCII character
authbind 1.1.5.1	Allows non-root programs to `bind()` to low ports
autofs 3.1.4-9	A kernel-based automounter for Linux
bash-builtins 2.03-6	Bash loadable built-ins — headers & examples
binstats 1.05-1	Statistics tool for installed programs
blinkd 0.3.4	Blinks keyboard LEDs for an answering machine or fax machine
bonnie 1-3	File System Performance Benchmark
bonnie++ 0.99e	This is Russell Coker's hard drive bottleneck testing program
bsdmainutils 4.7.1	More utilities from 4.4BSD-Lite
btoa 5.2.1-5 [non-free]	Convert binary to ASCII and vice versa
buffer 1.17-5	Buffering/reblocking program for tape backups, printing, and so on
bug 3.2.10	Bug Reporting Tool interfacing with the Bug Tracking System
bzip2 0.9.5d-2	A high-quality block-sorting file compressor — utilities

Continued

Table C-13 *(continued)*

Package	Description
calamaris 2.29-1	Perl script which produces nice statistics out of squid log files
canna 3.5b2-25	A Japanese input system (server and dictionary)
canna-utils 3.5b2-25	A Japanese input system (utility)
cce 0.36-1.1	Console Chinese Environment — display Chinese (GB) on console
chase 0.5-1	Follow a symlink and print out its target file
chdrv 1.0.13-0.1	Chinese terminal for the Linux console
chdrvfont 1.0-2	Kuo Chiao 16x16 font for CHDRV Chinese console terminal
console-data 1999.08.29-11.2	Keymaps, fonts, charset maps, fallback tables for console tools
cpbk 2.0-1	An advanced copy and directory mirror program
cpio 2.4.2-32	GNU cpio — a program to manage archives of files
cracklib-runtime 2.7-8	A pro-active password checker library
cracklib2 2.7-8	A pro-active password checker library
cracklib2-dev 2.7-8	A pro-active password checker library
dbskkd-cdb 1:1.01-6	The fastest dictionary server for SKK
dds2tar 2.4.21-3	Tools for using DDS features of DAT drives with GNU tar
ddskk 11.2.cvs.20000108-1	Simple Kana to Kanji conversion program
debget 1.0	Download/compile source and binary Debian packages
disc-cover 0.9.4-3	Generates CD-disc covers for jewel-cases
doschk 1.1-1	SYSV and DOS filename compatibility check
dotfile 1:2.4-1	Easy configuration of popular programs through Tcl/Tk interface
dotfile-bash 1.02-6	Dotfile Generator, module for `bash`
dotfile-elm 1.0b1-8	Dotfile Generator, module for `elm`
dotfile-fvwm1 1.3-5	Dotfile Generator, module for `fvwm1`
dotfile-fvwm2 1.1-3	Dotfile Generator, module for `fvwm2`
dotfile-ipfwadm 0.25b-3	Dotfile Generator, module for `ipfwadm`
dotfile-procmail 1.3-1	Dotfile Generator, module for `procmail`
dotfile-rtin 0.02-8	Dotfile Generator, module for `rtin`
dotfile-tcsh 1.4-3	Dotfile Generator, module for `tcsh`
dpkg-cross 1.10	Tools for cross-compiling Debian packages

Package	Description
dpkg-dev 1.6.14	Package building tools for Debian
dump 0.4b16-1	4.4bsd dump and restore for `ext2` filesystems
dynafont 1.0-8	Module for konwert package that loads UTF-8 fonts dynamically
eb-utils 2.3.6-1	EB (Electric Book) access library — utilities
estic 1.61-5	Administration program for ISDN PABX ISTEC 1003/1008
fakeroot 0.4.4-4.1	Gives a fake root environment
falselogin 0.2-1	False login shell
fdupes 1.1.1-3	Identifies duplicate files residing within given directories
fdutils 5.3-3	Linux floppy utilities
file 3.28-1	Determines file type using "magic" numbers
floppybackup 1.3-2	Floppy backup using a diversity of floppy formats
fonty 1.0-8	Fonts on Linux console
freecdb 0.61	A package for creating and reading constant databases
freetype-tools 1.3.1-1	Bundled tests, demos, and tools for FreeType
freewnn-common 1.1.0+1.1.1-a016-1	Files shared among freewnn packages
freewnn-cserver 1.1.0+1.1.1-a016-1	Chinese input system
freewnn-jserver 1.1.0+1.1.1-a016-1	Japanese input system
freewnn-kserver 1.1.0+1.1.1-a016-1	Korean input system
ftape-util 1:1.07.1999.03.17-2	Bleeding edge floppy tape driver (utilities)
fttools 1.2-4 [contrib]	FreeType font utilities
gaspell 0.29.1-1	Gnome front-end to the aspell spell checker
gcal 2.40-7	Prints calendars
gfloppy 0.9.2-8	GUI for formatting floppy
git 4.3.19-2	GNU Interactive Tools
gmc 4.5.42-11.potato.4	Midnight Commander — a powerful file manager — Gnome version
gmemusage 0.2-5	Displays a graph detailing memory usage of each process

Continued

Table C-13 *(continued)*

Package	Description
gnap 0.1.5-3	Gnome client for Napster
gnofin 0.6.1-4	Gnome financial manager
gnome-pim 1.0.55-4	Calendar and address book for Gnome
gnome-utils 1.0.50-5	Gnome Utilities (`gtt`, `ghex`, and more)
gnotes 1.74	Yellow sticky notes applet for Gnome
gnucash 1.3.4-3	A personal finance tracking program
grep-dctrl 1.3a	Grep Debian package information
grmonitor 0.81-1	Graphical Process Monitor
gtimer 1.1.2-1.2	GTK-based X11 task timer
guitar 0.1.4-7	A GTK+ archive extraction/viewing tool
gxset 0.2-2	GTK based graphical front-end to the X command-line tool `xset(1)`
hex 204-5	Hexadecimal dumping tool for Japanese
hextype 3.0-8	Hexdump according to the old DOS Debug output format
honyaku-el 1.02-2 [contrib]	Honyakudamashii client for emacsen
hwtools 0.5-0.2	Collection of tools for low-level hardware management
installwatch 0.5.5-2	Track installation of local software
iselect 1.2.0-3	An interactive line selection tool for ASCII files
jazip 0.32-2 [contrib]	Mount and unmount Iomega Zip and/or Jaz drives
jaztool 1.0-3	Utility for manipulating Iomega Jaz drives
jdresolve 0.5.2-3	Fast alternative to Apache `logresolve`
jfbterm 0.3.7-3	Japanized framebuffer terminal with Multilingual Enhancement
kbackup 1.2.11-3	KBackup is a single host backup solution for various media
kbackup-doc 1.2.11-3	The documentation for KBackup
kbackup-multibuf 1.2.11-3	Multibuf extends kbackup for multivolumes
kbd 0.99-9.2	Linux console font and keytable utilities
kbd-compat 1:0.2.3-10.3	Wrappers around console tools for backward compatibility with `kbd`
knl 1.0.1-2	Query/set kernel image parameters
kon2 0.3.9b-3	Kanji ON Console
konfont 0.1-4	Public domain Japanese fonts for KON2

Package	Description
ksymoops 2.3.4-1	Linux kernel oops and error message decoder
lam-runtime 6.3.2-3	Enables parallel processing across multiple processors
lcdproc 0.3.4-3	LCD display driver daemon
leave 1.8-2	Reminds you when you have to leave
lha 1.14e-0 [non-free]	`lzh` archiver
libv-bin 1.22-1	V - a C++ GUI Framework (binaries)
libxdelta2 1.1.1-3	`xdelta` runtime library
libxdelta2-dev 1.1.1-3	`xdelta` development environment
limo 0.2.1-1	Lists files in a custom way
linuxinfo 1.1.2-1	Displays extended system information
loadmeter 1.20-0.1	Attractive X11 load meter
loadwatch 1.0-2	Run a program using only idle cycles
lockvc 3.4-2	Program to lock your Linux console(s)
lsof-2.0.36 4.43-1	List open files
lsof-2.2 4.48-1	List open files
ltrace 0.3.10	Shows runtime library call information for dynamically linked executables
lzop 1.00-3	A real-time compressor
makepatch 2.00a-2	Generate/apply patch files with more functionality than plain diff
mc 4.5.42-11.potato.4	Midnight Commander—a powerful file manager—normal version
mc-common 4.5.42-11.potato.4	Common files for mc and gmc
mirrordir 0.10.48-2	Duplicate a directory by making a minimal set of changes
mmv 1.01b-8.1	Move, Copy, Append, and Link multiple files
multitee 3.0-1	Send multiple inputs to multiple outputs
ncdt 1.5-1	Display directory tree
ncompress 4.2.4-9 [non-free]	Original Compress / Uncompress for News Transfers, and so on
nosql 2.1.3-5	A Relational Database Management System for UNIX
nwrite 1.9.2-9	Enhanced replacement for the write command
parted 1.0.13-1	The GNU Parted disk partition resizing program

Continued

Table C-13 *(continued)*

Package	Description
patch 2.5-2.2	Apply a diff file to an original
pax 1:1.5-6	Portable Archive Interchange
pcal 4.7-3	Makes printable PostScript calendars without X
perforate 1.0-8	Utilities to save disk space
pgrep 2.08-1	Grep utility that uses Perl compatible regexes
pmtools 1.00-6	Perl module tools
postmark 1.11-0	File system benchmark from NetApp
powertweak 0.1.7-2	Tool to tune system for optimal performace
procmeter 2.5.1-3	X-based system status monitor, older version
procmeter3 3.2-1	X-based system status monitor
pydf 0.9	Colorized df(1)-clone
qps 1.9.3-3.1 [contrib]	Qt-based process status monitor
quickppp 1.0-1	PPP Config tool
rar 2.60-1 [non-free]	Archiver for .rar files
ras 1.03-1	Adds redundancy files to archives for data recovery
rel 1.3-3 [non-free]	Determines relevance of text documents to a set of keywords
remind 03.00.19-2 [non-free]	A sophisticated reminder service
reportbug 0.54	Reports bugs in the Debian distribution
rrdtool 1.0.7-5	Time-series data storage and display system (programs)
safecat 1.0-2	Safely copy stdin to a file
set6x86 1.5-4	Cyrix/IBM 5x86/6x86 CPU configuration tool
setcd 1.4-1	Control the behavior of your CD-ROM device
sformat 3.4-1	SCSI disk format and repair tool
sharutils 1:4.2.1-1	Shar, unshar, uuencode, uudecode
skk 10.57-2	Simple Kana to Kanji conversion program
skk-dictools 10.57-2	SKK Dictionary maintenance tools
skkdic 10.57-2	SKK Dictionary files
skkserv 10.57-2	SKK Dictionary server
slocate 2.2-0.0	A secure locate replacement
splitvt 1.6.3-7.1	Run two programs in a split screen
stat 2.2-1	Wrapper for stat() and statfs calls

Package	Description
statserial 1.1-18	Displays serial port modem status lines
strace 4.2-4	A system call tracer
symlinks 1.2-2	Scan/change symbolic links
synaptics 0.1.1-1	Configure a Synaptics TouchPad
sysutils 1.3.6.1	Miscellaneous small system utilities
t-code 1:2.0beta9-1	Yet another Japanese input method
tag-types 0.0.9-1	Utilities for handling tagged files
taper 6.9rb-2	Full-screen system backup utility
ticker 0.14	Configurable text scroller, with slashdot and freshmeat modules
time 1.7-9	The GNU time command
tkps 1.14	X-based process management tool similar to "top"
tleds 1.05beta10-7	Blinks keyboard LEDs indicating TX and RX network packets
tob 0.14-17	Small yet powerful program for tape-oriented backups
toshutils 1.9.9-1	Toshiba laptop utilities
tree 1.3-0.1	Displays directory tree, in color
ttylog 0.1.a-2	Serial port logger
type1inst 0.6-1	Install Adobe Type 1 fonts into X11 and GhostScript
unarj 2.41a-6 [non-free]	Arj unarchive utility
units 1.55-2	Converts between different systems of units
unzip 5.40-1 [non-free]	De-archiver for .zip files
uptimed 0.03-3	Utility to track your highest uptimes
uudeview 0.5.13-2.1	Smart multifile multipart decoder
vfu 1.51-3	A versatile text-based file manager
vje-delta 2.5glibc-4 [non-free]	VJE Delta version 2.5 for Linux/BSD installer
vlock 1.3-5	Virtual Console locking program
vold 1.1-9	Volume daemon for CD-ROM devices
w-bassman 1.0-10	An alternative w command
windows-el 2.26-3	Window manager for GNU Emacs
wipe 0.16-1	Secure file deletion

Continued

Table C-13 *(continued)*	
Package	*Description*
wmmon 1.0b2-2	Monitor CPU load and average system load
wmmount 1.0beta2-2	Mount utility and free space monitoring tool, NeXTStep-like
xcolmix 1.07-4 [contrib]	An RGB color mixer
xdelta 1.1.1-3	A version-control utility that works with binary files
xdu 3.0-3	Display the output of du in an X window
xmcpustate 3-9	Displays CPU/Swap/Memory/Network load
xosview 1.7.3-1	X-based system monitor
xsysinfo 1.6-10	Display some Linux kernel parameters in graphical form
xvmount 3.6-10	Small graphical utility for mounting devices by users
xwatch 2.11-4 [contrib]	Monitor log files and display new logs in an X window
yard 1.17.patch1-5	Perl scripts to build rescue disk(s) to revive a system
ytree 1.65-4	Is a file manager for terminals
zcav 0.06	Test the read throughput of a hard drive at different tracks
zip 2.30-1	Archiver for .zip files
zlib-bin 1:1.1.3-5	Compression library — sample programs
zoo 2.10-7 [non-free]	Manipulate archives of files in compressed form

Web software

Table C-14 lists all types of Web servers, browsers, proxies, and download tools.

Table C-14 **Web software**	
Package	*Description*
adacgi 1.4-1	Ada CGI interface
amaya 2.4-1	Graphical HTML Editor from w3.org
amaya-dict-de 2.4-1	German dictionary for Amaya
amaya-dict-en 2.4-1	English dictionary for Amaya
amaya-dict-es 2.4-1	Spanish dictionary for Amaya
amaya-dict-fr 2.4-1	French dictionary for Amaya

Package	Description
amaya-dict-it 2.4-1	Italian dictionary for Amaya
amaya-dict-ne 2.4-1	Dutch dictionary for Amaya
amaya-dict-se 2.4-1	Swedish dictionary for Amaya
analog 1:4.01-1	Analyzes log files from Web servers
aolserver 3.0rc2-4	AOL Web Server
aolserver-postgres 3.0rc2-4	PostgreSQL Driver for the AOL server
apache 1.3.9-13.1	Versatile, high-performance HTTP server
apache-common 1.3.9-13.1	Support files for all Apache Web servers
apache-dev 1.3.9-13.1	Apache Web server development kit
apache-perl 1.3.9-13.1-1.21.20000309-1	Versatile, high-performance HTTP server with added Perl support
arena 1:0.3.62-1	An HTML 3.0 compliant WWW browser for X
bk2site 1:0.9.7-4	Utility to turn bookmarks into Yahoo/Slashdot-like pages
bluefish 0.3.5-1	A Gtk+ HTML editor
boa 0.94.8.1-1	Lightweight and high-performance Web server
bookmarker 1.6-4	WWW-based bookmark management, retrieval and search tool
bookmarks 0.10	Just another bookmarks collection
browser-history 2.4-7	User daemon that tracks URL's looked at and logs them
c2html 0.7.2-1	Highlight C sources for WWW presentation
cern-httpd 3.0A-3	The CERN HTTP (World Wide Web) server
cgic-capture 1.06-4	CGI environment capture for debugging
cgiemail 1.6-1	CGI Form-to-Mail converter
cgilib 0.5-1	Simple CGI Library
cgiwrap 3.6.4-2	Allows ordinary users to run their own CGI scripts
checkbot 1.58-1	A WWW link verifier
chimera 1.70p1-1 [non-free]	X11 World Wide Web Client
chimera2 2.0a19-3	Web browser for X
cocoon 1.5-2.3 [contrib]	A XML/XSL publishing framework servlet
communicator 1:4.73-32 [contrib]	Meta package that depends on other packages

Continued

Table C-14 *(continued)*

Package	Description
communicator-base-47 4.7-14 [non-free]	Communicator base support for version 4.7
communicator-base-472 4.72-16 [non-free]	Communicator base support for version 4.72
communicator-base-473 4.73-19 [non-free]	Communicator base support for version 4.73
communicator-nethelp-47 4.7-14 [non-free]	Communicator online help for version 4.7
communicator-nethelp-472 4.72-16 [non-free]	Communicator online help for version 4.72
communicator-nethelp-473 4.73-19 [non-free]	Communicator online help for version 4.73
communicator-smotif-47 4.7-14 [non-free]	Netscape Communicator 4.7 (static Motif)
communicator-smotif-472 4.72-16 [non-free]	Netscape Communicator 4.72 (static Motif)
communicator-smotif-472-libc5 4.72-16 [non-free]	Netscape Communicator 4.72 (static Motif) (libc5 version)
communicator-smotif-473 4.73-19 [non-free]	Netscape Communicator 4.73 (static Motif)
communicator-smotif-473-libc5 4.73-19 [non-free]	Netscape Communicator 4.73 (static Motif) (libc5 version)
communicator-spellchk-47 4.7-14 [non-free]	Popular Web browser software (spelling dictionary)
communicator-spellchk-472 4.72-16 [non-free]	Popular World Wide Web browser software (spelling dictionary)
communicator-spellchk-473 4.73-19 [non-free]	Popular World Wide Web browser software (spelling dictionary)
cronolog 1.5b9-2	Log file rotator for Web servers
curl 6.0-1	Get a file from an FTP, GOPHER, or HTTP server (no ssl)
cvs2html 1.59-1	Create HTML versions of CVS logs
dejasearch 1.8.4-1	Front-end to Deja.com(tm)
dhttpd 1.02a-5	Minimal secure Web server. No cgi-bin support
express 0.0.7-2.1	GTK Web browser for Gnome
faqomatic 2.603-1.1	Online interactive FAQ CGI
freetable 0.5	A Perl script that facilitates the production of HTML tables

Package	Description
gnats2w 0.13.4	Yet another Web interface to GNATS
gnujsp 1.0.0-3 [contrib]	A free implementation of Sun's Java Server Pages (JSP 1.0)
gtml 3.5.2-1	An HTML pre-processor
gzilla 0.2.1-2	GTK-based Web browser
hns2 2.00.pl4-2	Hyper Nikki System (Perl version)
horde 2:1.2.0-6	Core elements for the Horde Web Application Suite
htdig 3.1.5-2	WWW search system for an intranet or small Internet
htget 0.93-1	A file grabber that will get files from HTTP servers
htmldoc 1.7-4	HTML processor that generates indexed HTML, PS, and PDF files
htmlgen 2.2.2-3	Generation of HTML documents with Python scripts
htp 1.10-3.1	An HTML pre-processor
http-analyze 1.9e-4.3 [non-free]	Fast WWW-log server analyzer
hypermail 2.0b25-1	Create HTML archives of mailing lists
imaptool 0.6.1-1	A tool for creating client-side image maps
imgsizer 1.6-1	Add WIDTH and HEIGHT attributes to IMG tags in HTML files
imp 2:2.2.0-6	Web-based IMAP Mail Program
java2html 0.7.2-1	Highlight Java and C++ sources for WWW presentation
jserv 1.1-3 [contrib]	Java Servlet 2.0 engine with an optional Apache module
junkbuster 2.0-7.1	The Internet Junkbuster!
latte 2.1-1	The Language for Transforming Text (currently to html)
libapache-filter-perl 1.005-1	Perl Apache::Filter — Alter the output of previous handlers
libapache-mod-auth-pam 0.8-5	Authenticate Web access using PAM
libapache-mod-dtcl 0.7.3-2	Allows the use of Tcl as a server parsed language, similar to PHP
libapache-mod-perl 1.21.20000309-1	Integration of Perl with the Apache Web server
libapache-mod-ruby 0.1.4-2.2	Embedding Ruby in the Apache Web server
libapache-ssi-perl 2.09-1	Perl Apache::SSI — Implement Server Side Includes in Perl
libcgi-perl 2.76-17	Modules for Perl5, for use in writing CGI scripts
libcgi-pm-perl 2.56-4	Perl CGI — Simple Common Gateway Interface Class

Continued

Table C-14 *(continued)*

Package	Description
libcgicg1-dev 1.06-4	C library for developing CGI applications
libhtml-clean-perl 0.7-3	Perl HTML::Clean — Cleans up HTML code for Web browsers, not humans
libhtml-embperl-perl 1.2.1-1	Library for embedding Perl in HTML
libhtml-ep-perl 0.2008-1	HTML::EP — a system for embedding Perl into HTML
linbot 1.0b9-1.1	WWW site link checker
lists-archives 20000212-1	Web archive for mailing lists
lynx 2.8.3-1	Text-mode WWW Browser
mailto 1.2.6-3	WWW Forms to Mail Gateway
mozilla M14-2	An Open Source WWW browser for X and GTK+
muffin 0.9-1 [contrib]	A personal and extensible Web proxy
navigator 1:4.73-32 [contrib]	Meta package that depends on other packages
navigator-base-47 4.7-14 [non-free]	Navigator base support for version 4.7
navigator-base-472 4.72-16 [non-free]	Navigator base support for version 4.72
navigator-base-473 4.73-19 [non-free]	Navigator base support for version 4.73
navigator-nethelp-47 4.7-14 [non-free]	Navigator online help for version 4.7
navigator-nethelp-472 4.72-16 [non-free]	Navigator online help for version 4.72
navigator-nethelp-473 4.73-19 [non-free]	Navigator online help for version 4.73
navigator-smotif-47 4.7-14 [non-free]	Netscape Navigator 4.7 (static Motif)
navigator-smotif-472 4.72-16 [non-free]	Netscape Navigator 4.72 (static Motif)
navigator-smotif-472-libc5 4.72-16 [non-free]	Netscape Navigator 4.72 (static Motif) (libc5 version)
navigator-smotif-473 4.73-19 [non-free]	Netscape Navigator 4.73 (static Motif)
navigator-smotif-473-libc5 4.73-19 [non-free]	Netscape Navigator 4.73 (static Motif) (libc5 version)

Package	Description
netscape 1:4.73-32 [contrib]	Meta package that depends on other packages
netscape-base-4 1:4.73-32 [contrib]	Popular World Wide Web browser software (base support)
netscape-base-4-libc5 1:4.73-32 [contrib]	Popular World Wide Web browser software (base support)
netscape-base-47 4.7-14 [non-free]	4.7 base support for Netscape
netscape-base-472 4.72-16 [non-free]	4.72 base support for Netscape
netscape-base-473 4.73-19 [non-free]	4.73 base support for Netscape
netscape-java-47 4.7-14 [non-free]	Netscape Java support for version 4.7
netscape-java-472 4.72-16 [non-free]	Netscape Java support for version 4.72
netscape-java-473 4.73-19 [non-free]	Netscape Java support for version 4.73
netscape-smotif-47 4.7-14 [non-free]	This is a pseudo package that installs a standard set of Netscape programs
netscape-smotif-472 4.72-16 [non-free]	This installs a standard set of Netscape programs
netscape-smotif-472-libc5 4.72-16 [non-free]	This installs a standard set of Netscape programs (libc5 version)
netscape-smotif-473 4.73-19 [non-free]	This installs a standard set of Netscape programs
netscape-smotif-473-libc5 4.73-19 [non-free]	This installs a standard set of Netscape programs (libc5 version)
netscape3 3.04-8 [contrib]	Popular World Wide Web browser software (installer)
newsclipper 1.17-3	Create HTML with dynamic information from the net
pas2html 0.6.2-2	Highlight Pascal and Modula sources for WWW presentation
pcd2html 0.2-3	Scripts to convert PCD images to commented HTML pages
perl2html 0.7.2-1	Highlight perl sources for WWW presentation
php3 3:3.0.16-2potato3	A server-side, HTML-embedded scripting language
php3-cgi 3:3.0.16-2potato3	A server-side, HTML-embedded scripting language

Continued

Table C-14 *(continued)*

Package	Description
php3-cgi-dbase 3:3.0.16-1 [non-free]	dbase module for PHP3 (cgi)
php3-cgi-gd 3:3.0.16-2potato3	GD (graphic creation) module for PHP3 (cgi)
php3-cgi-imap 3:3.0.16-2potato3	IMAP module for PHP3 (cgi)
php3-cgi-ldap 3:3.0.16-2potato3)	LDAP module for PHP3 (cgi
php3-cgi-magick 3:3.0.16-2potato3	ImageMagick module for PHP3 (cgi)
php3-cgi-mhash 3:3.0.16-2potato3	`mhash` module for PHP3 (cgi)
php3-cgi-mysql 3:3.0.16-2potato3	Mysql module for PHP3 (cgi)
php3-cgi-pgsql 3:3.0.16-2potato3	PostgreSQL module for PHP3 (cgi)
php3-cgi-snmp 3:3.0.16-2potato3	SNMP module for PHP3 (cgi)
php3-cgi-xml 3:3.0.16-2potato3	XML module for PHP3 (cgi)
php3-dbase 3:3.0.16-1 [non-free]	dbase module for PHP3 (apache)
php3-dev 3:3.0.16-2potato3	Header files for PHP3 module development
php3-doc 3:3.0.16-2potato3	Documentation for PHP3
php3-gd 3:3.0.16-2potato3	GD (graphic creation) module for PHP3 (Apache)
php3-imap 3:3.0.16-2potato3	IMAP module for PHP3 (Apache)
php3-ldap 3:3.0.16-2potato3	LDAP module for PHP3 (Apache)
php3-magick 3:3.0.16-2potato3	ImageMagick module for PHP3 (Apache)
php3-mhash 3:3.0.16-2potato3	`mhash` module for PHP3 (Apache)
php3-mysql 3:3.0.16-2potato3	Mysql module for PHP3 (Apache)

Package	Description
php3-pgsql 3:3.0.16-2potato3	PostgreSQL module for PHP3 (Apache)
php3-snmp 3:3.0.16-2potato3	SNMP module for PHP3 (Apache)
php3-xml 3:3.0.16-2potato3	XML module for PHP3 (Apache)
php4 4.0b3-6	A server-side, HTML-embedded scripting language
php4-gd 4.0b3-6	GD module for php4
php4-imap 4.0b3-6	IMAP module for php4
php4-ldap 4.0b3-6	LDAP module for php4
php4-mysql 4.0b3-6	MySQL module for php4
php4-pgsql 4.0b3-6	PostgreSQL module for php4
php4-snmp 4.0b3-6	SNMP module for php4
php4-xml 4.0b3-6	XML module for php4
phplib 1:7.3dev-3.1	Library for easy writing Web applications
plugger 3.2-3 [contrib]	Netscape Mime Plug-in
python-bobo 2.1.4-4	Python Object Publisher
python-bobodtml 2.2.1-3	Document templates with fill-in fields
python-bobopos 2.1-3	The Bobo Persistent Object system
python-pcgi 1.999a5-1	Persistent CGI for Python
roxen 1.3.122-13	The Roxen Challenger Web server
roxen-doc 1.3.122-13	The Roxen Challenger Web server HTML documents
roxen-ssl 1.3.122-13 [contrib]	SSL3 modules for the Roxen Challenger Web server
rpm2html 0.70p1-1.1	Generate HTML index from directories of RPMs
screem 0.2.1-1	A Web site development environment
sitecopy 1:0.8.4-1	A program for managing a WWW site via FTP
squid 2.2.5-3	Internet Object Cache (WWW proxy cache)
squid-cgi 2.2.5-3	Squid cache manager CGI program
squidclient 2.2.5-3	Command-line URL extractor that talks to (a) squid
squishdot 0.3.2-3	Web-based News/Discussion System
swish++ 3.0.3-3	Simple Web Indexing System for Humans ++
swish-e 1.1-1	Simple Web Indexing System for Humans
task-python-web 1.2	Python Web application development environment

Continued

Table C-14 *(continued)*

Package	Description
tidy 20000113-1	HTML syntax checker and reformatter
urlredir 2.01	Utility for squid to perform url redirection
vrwave 0.9-7 [non-free]	VRML 2.0 Java-based browser
vrweb 1.5-5	A VRML browser and editor
w3-el-doc 4.0pre.46-7	Documentation for w3-el
w3-el-e19 4.0pre.46-7	Web browser for GNU Emacs 19
w3-el-e20 4.0pre.46-7	Web browser for GNU Emacs 20
w3-el-lisp 4.0pre.46-7	Elisp source for w3-el Web browser
wdg-html-validator 1.0-6 [contrib]	WDG HTML Validator
webalizer 1.30.4-3	Web server log analysis program
weblint 1.93-1	A syntax and minimal style checker for HTML
webmagick 1.45-2	Create gallery thumbnails for Web site
websec 1.3.1-9	Web Secretary
wget 1.5.3-3	Utility to retrieve files from the WWW via HTTP and FTP
wmf 1.0.5-3	Web Mail Folder
wml 1.7.4-6	Web site META Language by Ralf Engelschall
www-mysql 0.5.7-4	A WWW interface for the TCX mySQL database
www-pgsql 0.5.7-4	A WWW interface for the PostgreSQL database
wwwcount 2.5-5 [non-free]	Web page access counter
wwwoffle 2.5c-10	World Wide Web OFFline Explorer
wwwtable 1.3-6 [non-free]	A Perl script that facilitates the production of HTML tables
xsitecopy 1:0.8.4-1	A program for managing a WWW site via FTP (Gnome version)
zope 2.1.6-5	The Z Object Publishing Environment
zope-mysqlda 1.1.3-1	A Zope Database Adapter for MySQL
zope-pygresqlda 0.3rjr2-1	A Zope Database Adapter for PostgreSQL
zope-siteaccess 1.0.1-1	Zope virtual hosting and folder access rules
zope-tinytable 0b2-2	Present tabular data in Zope

✦   ✦   ✦

Index

Symbols & Numbers

Continued

Continued

R

r command, 196
^R command, 196
R command, 181
R flag, 110
r mode, 248
-r option, 34, 189, 246
    cp command, 55
    grep command, 189
    mount command, 60
    removing packages, 34
    removing users, 246
    rm command, 53
    shutdown command, 57
-R option, 48, 53, 249–251, 261, 420
radios, HAM, 349
RAID. *See* Redundant Array of Independent
    Disks
RAID controllers, 348
Railroad Tycoon II, 230
ranlib program, 283
raw format, 206
Raymond, Eric, 8
rc*.d directories, 411
rcp.mountd daemon, 496
read only parameter, 510
read-only option, 326
reading, output from PostScript files, 147
Readme file, 446–447
RealPlayer, 213–214
reboot command, 56–57
recording CDs, 210–211
records, copying to CD, 210–211
recovering, data from crashes, 393–394
recovery disks, 372
recursdir application, 387
- - recursive option, 34, 53, 189, 249–251
Red Hat, 8–9
Red Hat Package Management (RPM) packages,
    installing, 37–38
Redirect directive, 448–449
redirection operators, 295–298
redundancy, Network Information System
    (NIS), 489
Redundant Array of Independent Disks
    (RAID), 373
refresh frequencies, monitors, 73
- - regexp=pattern option, 189
Register.com, 97
registering domain names, 97

reinstalling packages, 38
reload option, 333
Remote button, xftp client, 481
remote computers, connecting, 476
remote filesystems, backing up, 374
remote printers, 369
remotehost, 476–477
- - remove option, 34
removing
    daemons, 334
    directories, 52–54
    files, 53–54
    modules from kernels, 317
    mounts, filesystems, 502
    packages, 34
    print jobs, 366
    users from accounts, 246
renaming links, daemons, 334
replacing
    hard drives, 358
    network cards, 359–361
    video cards, 358–359
reporting, bugs, 340
reports, quotas, 253–254
repquota command, 253
Requests for Comments (RFC), 517
rescue command, 393
rescue disks, 16, 393, 541
resources, viewing, 192–194
restart option, 333
restore backup tool, 379, 382–385
restoring files and directories, 390
restricting access, 241–242, 246–251
resuming jobs, 300
retrans=nn option, 499
retrieving mail, fetchmail, 124
retry settings, exim configuration file, 524
RETURN command, 195–196
rewrite settings, exim configuration
    file, 524
rexecd service, 403
RFC. *See* Requests for Comments
Rich Text Format, 173
right arrow, 151
rm command, 53–54
rmdir command, 52–53
ro option, 498, 500
Robots, 221
RogerWilco BaseStation, 216
Rogue, 220

Continued

GNU General Public License

Version 2, June 1991
Copyright © 1989, 1991 Free Software Foundation, Inc.
59 Temple Place, Suite 330, Boston, MA 02111-1307, USA

Everyone is permitted to copy and distribute verbatim copies of this license document, but changing it is not allowed.

Preamble

The licenses for most software are designed to take away your freedom to share and change it. By contrast, the GNU General Public License is intended to guarantee your freedom to share and change free software—to make sure the software is free for all its users. This General Public License applies to most of the Free Software Foundation's software and to any other program whose authors commit to using it. (Some other Free Software Foundation software is covered by the GNU Library General Public License instead.) You can apply it to your programs, too.

When we speak of free software, we are referring to freedom, not price. Our General Public Licenses are designed to make sure that you have the freedom to distribute copies of free software (and charge for this service if you wish), that you receive source code or can get it if you want it, that you can change the software or use pieces of it in new free programs; and that you know you can do these things.

To protect your rights, we need to make restrictions that forbid anyone to deny you these rights or to ask you to surrender the rights. These restrictions translate to certain responsibilities for you if you distribute copies of the software, or if you modify it.

For example, if you distribute copies of such a program, whether gratis or for a fee, you must give the recipients all the rights that you have. You must make sure that they, too, receive or can get the source code. And you must show them these terms so they know their rights.

We protect your rights with two steps: (1) copyright the software, and (2) offer you this license which gives you legal permission to copy, distribute and/or modify the software.

Also, for each author's protection and ours, we want to make certain that everyone understands that there is no warranty for this free software. If the software is modified by someone else and passed on, we want its recipients to know that what they have is not the original, so that any problems introduced by others will not reflect on the original authors' reputations.

Finally, any free program is threatened constantly by software patents. We wish to avoid the danger that redistributors of a free program will individually obtain patent licenses, in effect making the program proprietary. To prevent this, we have made it clear that any patent must be licensed for everyone's free use or not licensed at all.

The precise terms and conditions for copying, distribution and modification follow.

Terms and Conditions for Copying, Distribution, and Modification

0. This License applies to any program or other work which contains a notice placed by the copyright holder saying it may be distributed under the terms of this General Public License. The "Program", below, refers to any such program or work, and a "work based on the Program" means either the Program or any derivative work under copyright law: that is to say, a work containing the Program or a portion of it, either verbatim or with modifications and/or translated into another language. (Hereinafter, translation is included without limitation in the term "modification".) Each licensee is addressed as "you".

   Activities other than copying, distribution and modification are not covered by this License; they are outside its scope. The act of running the Program is not restricted, and the output from the Program is covered only if its contents constitute a work based on the Program (independent of having been made by running the Program). Whether that is true depends on what the Program does.

1. You may copy and distribute verbatim copies of the Program's source code as you receive it, in any medium, provided that you conspicuously and appropriately publish on each copy an appropriate copyright notice and disclaimer of warranty; keep intact all the notices that refer to this License and to the absence of any warranty; and give any other recipients of the Program a copy of this License along with the Program.

   You may charge a fee for the physical act of transferring a copy, and you may at your option offer warranty protection in exchange for a fee.

2. You may modify your copy or copies of the Program or any portion of it, thus forming a work based on the Program, and copy and distribute such modifications or work under the terms of Section 1 above, provided that you also meet all of these conditions:

   a) You must cause the modified files to carry prominent notices stating that you changed the files and the date of any change.

   b) You must cause any work that you distribute or publish, that in whole or in part contains or is derived from the Program or any part thereof, to be licensed as a whole at no charge to all third parties under the terms of this License.

   c) If the modified program normally reads commands interactively when run, you must cause it, when started running for such interactive use in the most ordinary way, to print or display an announcement including an appropriate copyright notice and a notice that there is no warranty (or else, saying that you provide a warranty) and that users may redistribute the program under these conditions, and telling the user how to view a copy of this License. (Exception: if the Program itself is interactive but does not normally print such an announcement, your work based on the Program is not required to print an announcement.)

These requirements apply to the modified work as a whole. If identifiable sections of that work are not derived from the Program, and can be reasonably considered independent and separate works in themselves, then this License, and its terms, do not apply to those sections when you distribute them as separate works. But when you distribute the same sections as part of a whole which is a work based on the Program, the distribution of the whole must be on the terms of this License, whose permissions for other licensees extend to the entire whole, and thus to each and every part regardless of who wrote it.

Thus, it is not the intent of this section to claim rights or contest your rights to work written entirely by you; rather, the intent is to exercise the right to control the distribution of derivative or collective works based on the Program.

In addition, mere aggregation of another work not based on the Program with the Program (or with a work based on the Program) on a volume of a storage or distribution medium does not bring the other work under the scope of this License.

3. You may copy and distribute the Program (or a work based on it, under Section 2) in object code or executable form under the terms of Sections 1 and 2 above provided that you also do one of the following:

   a) Accompany it with the complete corresponding machine-readable source code, which must be distributed under the terms of Sections 1 and 2 above on a medium customarily used for software interchange; or,

   b) Accompany it with a written offer, valid for at least three years, to give any third party, for a charge no more than your cost of physically performing source distribution, a complete machine-readable copy of the corresponding source code, to be distributed under the terms of Sections 1 and 2 above on a medium customarily used for software interchange; or,

   c) Accompany it with the information you received as to the offer to distribute corresponding source code. (This alternative is allowed only for noncommercial distribution and only if you received the program in object code or executable form with such an offer, in accord with Subsection b above.)

The source code for a work means the preferred form of the work for making modifications to it. For an executable work, complete source code means all the source code for all modules it contains, plus any associated interface definition files, plus the scripts used to control compilation and installation of the executable. However, as a special exception, the source code distributed need not include anything that is normally distributed (in either source or binary form) with the major components (compiler, kernel, and so on) of the operating system on which the executable runs, unless that component itself accompanies the executable.

If distribution of executable or object code is made by offering access to copy from a designated place, then offering equivalent access to copy the source code from the same place counts as distribution of the source code, even though third parties are not compelled to copy the source along with the object code.

4. You may not copy, modify, sublicense, or distribute the Program except as expressly provided under this License. Any attempt otherwise to copy, modify, sublicense or distribute the Program is void, and will automatically terminate your rights under this License. However, parties who have received copies, or rights, from you under this License will not have their licenses terminated so long as such parties remain in full compliance.

5. You are not required to accept this License, since you have not signed it. However, nothing else grants you permission to modify or distribute the Program or its derivative works. These actions are prohibited by law if you do not accept this License. Therefore, by modifying or distributing the Program (or any work based on the Program), you indicate your acceptance of this License to do so, and all its terms and conditions for copying, distributing or modifying the Program or works based on it.

6. Each time you redistribute the Program (or any work based on the Program), the recipient automatically receives a license from the original licensor to copy, distribute or modify the Program subject to these terms and conditions. You may not impose any further restrictions on the recipients' exercise of the rights granted herein. You are not responsible for enforcing compliance by third parties to this License.

7. If, as a consequence of a court judgment or allegation of patent infringement or for any other reason (not limited to patent issues), conditions are imposed on you (whether by court order, agreement or otherwise) that contradict the conditions of this License, they do not excuse you from the conditions of this License. If you cannot distribute so as to satisfy simultaneously your obligations under this License and any other pertinent obligations, then as a consequence you may not distribute the Program at all. For example, if a patent license would not permit royalty-free redistribution of the Program by all those who receive copies directly or indirectly through you, then the only way you could satisfy both it and this License would be to refrain entirely from distribution of the Program.

If any portion of this section is held invalid or unenforceable under any particular circumstance, the balance of the section is intended to apply and the section as a whole is intended to apply in other circumstances.

It is not the purpose of this section to induce you to infringe any patents or other property right claims or to contest validity of any such claims; this section has the sole purpose of protecting the integrity of the free software distribution system, which is implemented by public license practices. Many people have made generous contributions to the wide range of software distributed through that system in reliance on consistent application of that system; it is up to the author/donor to decide if he or she is willing to distribute software through any other system and a licensee cannot impose that choice.

This section is intended to make thoroughly clear what is believed to be a consequence of the rest of this License.

8. If the distribution and/or use of the Program is restricted in certain countries either by patents or by copyrighted interfaces, the original copyright holder who places the Program under this License may add an explicit geographical distribution limitation excluding those countries, so that distribution is permitted only in or among countries not thus excluded. In such case, this License incorporates the limitation as if written in the body of this License.

9. The Free Software Foundation may publish revised and/or new versions of the General Public License from time to time. Such new versions will be similar in spirit to the present version, but may differ in detail to address new problems or concerns.

   Each version is given a distinguishing version number. If the Program specifies a version number of this License which applies to it and "any later version", you have the option of following the terms and conditions either of that version or of any later version published by the Free Software Foundation. If the Program does not specify a version number of this License, you may choose any version ever published by the Free Software Foundation.

10. If you wish to incorporate parts of the Program into other free programs whose distribution conditions are different, write to the author to ask for permission. For software which is copyrighted by the Free Software Foundation, write to the Free Software Foundation; we sometimes make exceptions for this. Our decision will be guided by the two goals of preserving the free status of all derivatives of our free software and of promoting the sharing and reuse of software generally.

No Warranty

11. BECAUSE THE PROGRAM IS LICENSED FREE OF CHARGE, THERE IS NO WARRANTY FOR THE PROGRAM, TO THE EXTENT PERMITTED BY APPLICABLE LAW. EXCEPT WHEN OTHERWISE STATED IN WRITING THE COPYRIGHT HOLDERS AND/OR OTHER PARTIES PROVIDE THE PROGRAM "AS IS" WITHOUT WARRANTY OF ANY KIND, EITHER EXPRESSED OR IMPLIED, INCLUDING, BUT NOT LIMITED TO, THE IMPLIED WARRANTIES OF MERCHANTABILITY AND FITNESS FOR A PARTICULAR PURPOSE. THE ENTIRE RISK AS TO THE QUALITY AND PERFORMANCE OF THE PROGRAM IS WITH YOU. SHOULD THE PROGRAM PROVE DEFECTIVE, YOU ASSUME THE COST OF ALL NECESSARY SERVICING, REPAIR OR CORRECTION.

12. IN NO EVENT UNLESS REQUIRED BY APPLICABLE LAW OR AGREED TO IN WRITING WILL ANY COPYRIGHT HOLDER, OR ANY OTHER PARTY WHO MAY MODIFY AND/OR REDISTRIBUTE THE PROGRAM AS PERMITTED ABOVE, BE LIABLE TO YOU FOR DAMAGES, INCLUDING ANY GENERAL, SPECIAL, INCIDENTAL OR CONSEQUENTIAL DAMAGES ARISING OUT OF THE USE OR INABILITY TO USE THE PROGRAM (INCLUDING BUT NOT LIMITED TO LOSS OF DATA OR DATA BEING RENDERED INACCURATE OR LOSSES SUSTAINED BY YOU OR THIRD PARTIES OR A FAILURE OF THE PROGRAM TO OPERATE WITH ANY OTHER PROGRAMS), EVEN IF SUCH HOLDER OR OTHER PARTY HAS BEEN ADVISED OF THE POSSIBILITY OF SUCH DAMAGES.

End Of Terms And Conditions

CD-ROM Installation Instructions

Installing Debian GNU/Linux can be a big job — too big to adequately describe in the space available here. For complete step-by-step instructions, see Chapter 2.

Installing the Debian GNU/Linux operating system on a computer is no different than installing any other operating system by following straightforward guidelines. Chapter 2 covers those guidelines and, if followed, will get Debian GNU/Linux installed on your system (barring any unforeseen troubles like hardware incompatibility).

Experienced Linux users can use Chapter 2 as a reference for things to watch for during the installation process. Those who are less familiar with Linux or installing operating systems can follow along step-by-step to accomplish the installation.

Chapter 2 covers the following general principles to install and configure Debian GNU/Linux:

+ Preparing your system for installation
+ Installing Debian
+ Using the Debian package-management system
+ Using non-Debian package tools

Although many of the applications covered are available on the book's CD, others are accessible from one of many archives found on the Internet. Chapter 2 also describes how to access those archives.